Key Determinants of National Development

The editors are admirably suited to meet the objectives of this compendium, combining experience of policy fieldwork in various nations with an insider's view of developing economies. The result is an excellent book that will appeal to a wide audience, yet meets professional standards.

H.E. John Agyekum Kufuor, President, Republic of Ghana, 2001–09

It is amazing to run through the topics of what have been well and eloquently treated in this book and relate the issues dealt with to our present situation in Ghana. The book offers practical advice based on facts and truths and it is a "must read" for business executives, public sector executives and for those in politics aspiring to rule our dear country, Ghana.

Elizabeth Joyce Villars, Founder and Chairperson, Camelot Ghana Limited

This book is exciting, engaging, and above all, very readable. The chapters are well researched and many of the epigrams are superb. Those inquiring seriously into national development issues cannot fail to consider its key determinants which are competently presented in this collection.

E.H. Amonoo-Neizer, Vice Chancellor Emeritus,
Kwame Nkrumah University of Science and Technology, Ghana

An undeniably well researched and practical compendium for all emerging market followers; especially for those committed to an Africa "rising" and the unique contribution of Ghana.

Ken Ofori-Atta, Chairman and Co-Founder of Databank Financial Services
(Ghana) Ltd and Databank Africa SME Agriculture Fund

With passion for learning and the determination to promote knowledge and wisdom, hence this book has come to fruition, bravo.

Captain (rtd) Prince Kofi Amoabeng, Executive Chairman, UT Group of Companies

For the sheer breadth and completeness of the topics covered on the subject of development; and for the diversity of voices represented – from Ghanaian academia, private sector and public sector – this book is worth reading by anyone who is truly interested in Ghana's path to a brighter future.

Patrick G. Awuah, Jr, Founder and President, Ashesi University College, Ghana

This remarkable book is the fruit of sustained painstaking research. Collectively the authors seamlessly elucidate the multiplicity of factors that significantly contribute to development – but they do so thankfully, using such a colourful style and language that the book comes to life and is a pleasure to read. I highly recommend it.

Francis K. Allotey, President, Ghana Academy of Arts and Sciences

Key Determinants of National Development

Historical Perspectives and Implications for Developing Economies

Edited by

KWAKU APPIAH-ADU
Central University, Ghana

and

MAHAMUDU BAWUMIA
Central University, Ghana

Routledge
Taylor & Francis Group

LONDON AND NEW YORK

First published 2015 by Gower Publishing

2 Park Square, Milton Park, Abingdon, Oxfordshire OX14 4RN
52 Vanderbilt Avenue, New York, NY 10017

Routledge is an imprint of the Taylor & Francis Group, an informa business

First issued in paperback 2020

Gower Applied Business Research
Our programme provides leaders, practitioners, scholars and researchers with thought provoking, cutting edge books that combine conceptual insights, interdisciplinary rigour and practical relevance in key areas of business and management.

British Library Cataloguing in Publication Data
A catalogue record for this book is available from the British Library

Library of Congress Cataloging-in-Publication Data
Appiah-Adu, Kwaku.
  Key determinants of national development : historical perspectives and implications for developing economies / by Kwaku Appiah-Adu and Mahamudu Bawumia.
     pages cm
  Includes bibliographical references and index.
  ISBN 978-1-4724-6283-1 (hardback)
1. Developing countries--Economic policy. 2. Developing countries--Economic conditions. 3. Economic development. I. Bawumia, Mahamudu. II. Title.
  HC59.7.A8218 2015
  338.9109172'4--dc23
                                                                    2015003942

ISBN: 978-1-4724-6283-1 (hbk)
ISBN: 978-0-367-60610-7 (pbk)

Contents

List of Figures

List of Tables

About the Editors

Kwaku Appiah-Adu is Professor of Strategy at Central University, Dean of the Business School and Principal Strategic Advisor to the Oxford Policy Management's Oil and Gas Programme, Ghana. Previously, he worked at the Office of the President, Ghana, where he was Head of Policy Coordination, Monitoring and Evaluation, Chairman of the Oil and Gas Technical Committee, Director of Ghana's Central Governance Project and member of the President's Investors' Advisory Council, as well as the Advisory Board for the UN Initiative on Continental Shelf Delineation. Prior to that, he worked as a consultant with PricewaterhouseCoopers and lectured at the Universities of Cardiff and Portsmouth. An author of several books, he has recently edited a book entitled *Governance of the Petroleum Sector in an Emerging Developing Economy*, published by Gower. With over 100 publications, he has facilitated workshops and presented papers at several international forums. He has been elected to the ANBAR Hall of Excellence for Outstanding Contribution to the Literature and Body of Knowledge. He has also served on various boards in the public and private sectors. Currently, he is Board Chairman of GLICO Pensions Trustee Company Ltd, Chairman of the Centre for Advanced Strategic Analysis, Advisory Board member of the Lupcon Centre for Business Research (Germany), Director of Traders International Africa (USA) and Independent Trustee of the Shell Pensions Fund. He has received many awards, including the President's Award for exceptional contribution to national development.

Mahamudu Bawumia is Visiting Professor of Economic Governance at the Central University, Ghana. He has extensive experience as a senior policy maker and policy advisor, and has worked with governments as well as international organizations. He was resident representative for the African Development Bank in Zimbabwe from 2011 to 2012. He served as Deputy Governor of the Central Bank of Ghana between 2006 and 2009. Between 2009 and 2010, he was a visiting professor at the University of British Columbia (Canada) and Senior Associate Member of St. Antony's College, University of Oxford. He also served as an Assistant Professor of Economics at Hankamer School of Business, Baylor University, Texas, US (1996–2000), where he received the Young Researcher Award in 1998. He has published several articles in refereed journals and has also published a book entitled *Monetary Policy and Financial Sector Reform in Africa*. He holds a BSc Economics (First Class Honours) degree from the University of Buckingham, UK, an MSc Development Economics from the University of Oxford and a PhD in Economics from Simon Fraser University (Canada). He holds a Chartered Institute of Bankers (UK) diploma (ACIB) and is a Fellow of the Chartered Institute of Bankers (FCIB), Ghana.

About the Contributors

Gheysika A. Agambila was born in Bolgatanga. He is a published writer of fiction for children and adults and has several manuscripts awaiting publication. He is currently a consultant and the Vice President of the Ghana Association of Writers. He is a member of Ghana's Constitution Review Implementation Committee. Previously, he served in Ghana's government as a Deputy Minister at the Ministries of Finance and Economic Planning, Harbours and Railways, and Environment and Science. He was also Senior Lecturer of Public Finance at the Ghana Institute of Management and Public Administration (GIMPA). He was educated at Navrongo and Achimota secondary schools. He has a PhD from New York University. His membership in professional associations includes the American Institute of Certified Public Accountants (AICPA) and the American National Association of Certified Fraud Examiners.

Ebenezer Ofori Agbettor is currently the Executive Director of Institute of Human Resource Management Practitioners, Ghana (HR Professional Body). Prior to this, he worked as General Manager/HR Business Partner for Vodafone Ghana. He also worked as Head/Human Resource Management, Head/Customer Service and Senior Overseas Operations Manager at different times for Ghana Airways Ltd and served as a Tutor & Learning Advisor on Henley Management College (UK)'s MBA distance learning programme, Senior Management Consultant for Lexcroft Consulting Ltd and Management Consultant (OD) for PricewaterhouseCoopers. He holds an MBA (Distinction) from London South Bank University (UK), a PG Diploma in Accounting & Finance from Thames Valley University (UK), a PG Diploma in Management Studies from Kingston University (UK), is a Fellow of the Ghana Institute of Management and a member of the Institute of Human Resource Management Practitioners, Ghana. He is the Chairman of the National ISO Committee on Human Resource Management in Ghana. He serves on a number of evaluation panels and committees for organizations such as the Mineral Commission, the National Petroleum Authority, the Ghana Statistical Service, the Public Service Commission and various government ministries. He has managed several consultancy projects and facilitated numerous management development programmes for various organizations, both in Ghana and abroad. He has 10 publications to his credit and is married with two children. He serves as the Head of the Counselling Department of Believer's Temple, ICGC-La-Accra.

Kwesi Amonoo-Neizer is an experienced investment manager and investor with several years of experience in creating, growing and managing capital for individuals and corporate organizations. He is currently the CEO of Mega African Capital Ltd, a listed company on the Ghana Stock Exchange, and a Partner of Oak Partners Ltd. He is a member of the Board of Directors of Omega Capital Ltd, Metropolitan Insurance Ltd and Haradari Capital Tanzania. He holds a Bachelor's degree in Electrical Engineering from Kwame Nkrumah University of Science and Technology (Kumasi, Ghana), an MSc from Strathclyde University (Glasgow) and an MBA from the Cranfield School of Management, UK.

Samuel Aning is currently Director of the African University College of Communications Pensions Academy and is also a part-time senior lecturer in contemporary issues at the Methodist University. In addition, he lectures in Media and Governance and Social Entrepreneurship, and was educated at Mfantsipim School and University of Science of Technology in Ghana, London School of Economics, UK and Galilee College, Israel. Prior to assuming his current position, he was a policy advisor in the Policy Coordination, Monitoring and Evaluation Unit of the Office of the President, Ghana, where he provided policy advice and evaluated a number of government programmes for six years. He has also served as a consultant on a number of projects. When Ghana discovered oil in 2007, he was appointed as a member of the Oil and Gas Technical Committee that developed the country's oil and gas masterplan and policy. He also served as a Board Member of the National Identification Authority, the President's Special Initiative on Distance Learning and the Review Committee on the upgrade of senior secondary schools. He serves on the NAGRAT Fund Board and the GAPOHA Pension Fund Board, the AUCC Pensions Academy Governing Council and the Board of the Centre for Advanced Strategic Analysis.

Nana Kegya Appiah-Adu (Mrs) is a lawyer by profession and a lecturer at the Ghana School of Law. She holds a Bachelor's degree in languages and also a Bachelor's degree in law. In addition, she holds a Master's degree in commercial and maritime law. After qualifying as a lawyer in Ghana, she worked at the Central Bank of Ghana for several years. Owing to her interest in education, she left the Central Bank and started a career as a lecturer at the Ghana School of Law, where she is a lecturer in banking law. She has published in the area of banking law as well as oil and gas management. In addition to being a law lecturer, she is a pastor and Director of Ace Educational Services.

Toni Aubynn is the Chief Executive Officer of the Minerals Commission. From 2011 to 2014, he was the Chief Executive Officer of the Ghana Chamber of Mines. He has served as Director of Corporate Affairs for Tullow Ghana Ltd, operator of the Jubilee Oil Fields in Ghana, Senior Manager of Gold Fields Ghana as well as Human Resource Manager/Head of Corporate Affairs and Sustainable Development of the Abosso Goldfields-Damang Mine. He also played a leading role in the brokering and implementation of Ghana's first major corporate sponsorship with an initial $6.4 million of the senior national team, the Black Stars. He is a member of various boards, including the Council of the University of Mines and Technology (UMaT) and chairs a number of them, including the Amenfiman Rural Bank and Junior Achievement Ghana. He undertook his undergraduate education at the University of Ghana and obtained various postgraduate degrees at the Universities of Oslo (in Norway), Tampare and Helsinki (in Finland). He was the first Ghanaian PhD Fellow at the United Nations University's Institute of Advanced Studies in Tokyo and was also a Fellow of the University of Tokyo. He has written over 40 academic papers (published and unpublished) and presented at various international conferences.

Charles Blankson is Associate Professor of Marketing at University of North Texas, Denton, Texas, USA. He received his PhD in Marketing from Kingston University, UK. He has many years of managerial experience in the retail and services industry in the UK and France. He has been a visiting scholar in marketing at Kingston University Business School, the University of Ghana Business School and the Ghana Institute of Management and Public Administration (GIMPA). In addition, he supervises doctoral theses at the University of Ghana Business School. His research interests include strategic marketing, industrial and services marketing in developing countries, bank services marketing, small business marketing and international marketing. His research articles have been published or are forthcoming in the *Journal of Advertising Research, Journal of Public Policy and Marketing, Journal of Business Research, European Journal of Marketing, Industrial Marketing Management, Psychology & Marketing, Journal of Marketing Management, Journal of Current Issues and Research in Advertising, International Journal of Advertising, Journal of Services*

Marketing, Journal of Business and Industrial Marketing, Journal of Product & Brand Management and *Journal of Strategic Marketing*, among others. He is also on the editorial review boards of *Industrial Marketing Management* and *Journal of International Marketing*.

Charles K. Boakye is the Chief Executive of Strategic Policy Associates, a consulting and development policy firm focusing on public policy, environmental and infrastructure matters. He is also Director of Institute for Infrastructure Development, a think-tank that helps policy makers formulate policy and infrastructure choices to deliver vital services. Formerly a Senior Municipal Engineer at the World Bank, he has many years of experience advising, formulating and overseeing the implementation of infrastructure and urban municipal engineering, water and waste management systems, roads and railways, and housing projects in Ghana, Nigeria, Sierra Leone and the Gambia. He has also consulted for the African Development Bank and other African countries. Prior to that period, he worked in the Design Office and as Resident Civil Engineer on many projects for a consulting engineering firm, ABP Consult Ltd. He is former Managing Director of Switchback Park Project, a large luxury mixed-use development on the Independence Avenue in Accra, owned by SSNIT and other private investors. As an infrastructure practitioner, his unique experiences encompass strategy and policy dialogue, design and implementation, monitoring and evaluation of various infrastructure and industrial installations. He has written on infrastructure development, urbanization and industrialization, and how African countries can progress in terms of economic development.

Kwabena G. Boakye is Assistant Professor of Quantitative Analysis at the College of Business Administration at Georgia Southern University. He received his doctorate in Management Science from University of North Texas (US), his MS in Statistics from the University of Idaho (US), and his Bachelor's degree from the Kwame Nkrumah University of Science and Technology (KNUST), Ghana. He is an American Society of Quality Certified Six Sigma Black Belt and Green Belt. He is also a visiting scholar in research methodology at the Ghana Institute of Management and Public Administration (GIMPA), where he teaches structural equation modelling, and also serves as an external examiner. His research interests include service operations management, quality management, service innovation and applied statistics. His research works have appeared in *Operations Management Research, Quality Management Journal, Journal of Retailing and Consumer Services, International Journal of Bank Marketing, International Journal of Information and Operations Management Education*, and *Proceedings of the Decision Science Institute Conference*.

Osei Boeh-Ocansey is currently Chairman of the Ghana Statistical Service Governing Board and a member of the Governing Council of the Ghana Institute of Management and Public Administration. He was formerly the Director-General and CEO of the Private Enterprise Foundation, Ghana and Managing Director of Pioneer Food Cannery, a subsidiary of J.H. Heinz & Co, and a member of the Governing Board of the Public Procurement Authority, Council for Scientific & Industrial Research and the Ghana Inter-Bank Payment & Settlement System, a subsidiary of the Bank of Ghana. He is a Fellow of the Institute of Directors, Ghana. He was educated at the University of Ghana, Legon and the Languedoc University of Science & Technology, Montpellier, France, where he obtained a doctorate degree in Process Engineering and Food Science. He also obtained a postdoctoral certificate from Massachusetts Institute of Technology (US). He is a practising certified consultant and a development professional. He has undertaken research with teams based at the University of Edinburgh, Institute of Education, University of London, England and taught in several universities, including the Universities of Nigeria, Nsukka, and Ghana, Legon. He has written numerous publications in international journals in food science, food technology, food engineering and food policy, and has contributed chapters to industry/higher education and related development titles.

Judy Cavanagh (Ms) has over 25 years of senior management experience working with the public sector in the areas of policy development and management, designing and implementing decision-making processes. In 2001, she established the Cavanagh Group, an international consulting practice offering expertise in governance, public sector reform and project management. She worked in Ghana from 2003 to 2009 in the Ghana Central Governance Project. Prior to 2001, she held a number of positions in the government of British Columbia, Canada, including Deputy Minister of Government Priorities, Deputy Minister of Women's Equality and senior positions in the Cabinet Office and inter- and intra-government relations. She is a firm believer that good policy development and management results in good public policy decisions.

Osei K. Darkwa is President of Ghana Technology University, Accra. Prior to this, he was at the University of Illinois, Chicago, where he taught courses in social work research, social welfare policies and services, and inter-group relations in a multi-cultural environment at the Jane Addams College of Social Work. He has participated and presented papers at numerous information technology conferences and at workshops in a number of countries, such as Botswana, Ghana, India, South Africa and the USA. He consults with international development agencies in exploring the establishment of community learning centres and multi-purpose community tele-centres in designated countries in Africa. He is the initiator of the Asante Akim Multipurpose Community Telecentre (AAMCT), a solar-powered centre that uses computers and information communications technologies to empower rural communities. He is the founder and President of the Ghana Computer Literacy and Distance Education, Incorporated (GhaCLAD). In 1998, he led an initiative to organize the first international conference on information technology in Ghana. He chaired the GhaCLAD International Program Committee, which planned the GhaCLAD 2000 conference in Accra. He was educated in Ghana and Norway, and earned his PhD at Washington University, St Louis, Missouri, USA.

Clifford D. Mpare is Chairman and CEO at Frontline Capital Advisors, Ltd (FCA), an investment banking firm that he founded in Ghana in 2008. He is also a co-founding member of the AUCC Pensions Academy, a trustees training institute in Ghana. Previously, he served as Senior Vice President and Director of Research at Piedmont Investment Advisors, and as Executive Vice President and Chief Investment Officer at NCM Capital Management Group, where he managed over $6 billion in institutional funds in the USA. He has served as portfolio manager for the Drefyus Third Century Fund and the Dreyfus Socially Responsible Growth Fund, and has been featured in a variety of publications, including *Fortune*, the *Wall Street Transcript*, *Black Enterprise*, *CFA Institute Conference Proceedings Quarterly* and *Emerging Markets Weekly*. He is on the Chartered Financial Analyst (CFA) speaking circuit, focusing on investment opportunities in Africa, and currently serves as Board Chairman of AFB Ghana and Scanbech Ltd, Ghana. He is a Certified Management Accountant (CMA) and holds a Bachelor of Commerce degree from St Mary's University and an MBA from Dalhousie University in Canada.

Nana Kumapremereh Nketiah is an experienced strategist, corporate revivalist and research consultant with particular expertise and experience in private equity/venture capital, hedge funds, real estate and investment management industries. He is currently the CEO of Omega Capital Ltd. He is a board member of Omega Equity Fund Ltd, Acorn Properties Ltd and Core Financial Service Ltd, Malawi. He holds a Bachelor's degree and an MBA from the University of Ghana Business School, Legon. He is also a member of the Institute of Directors, Ghana.

Samuel Nii Odai is Pro-Vice Chancellor of Kwame Nkrumah University of Science and Technology (KNUST). He studied at Koforidua Secondary Technical School and the Hohai University in China, where he graduated with BEng in Irrigation and Water Conservancy Engineering, and the Tokyo University of Agriculture and Technology, where he obtained his MSc and PhD degrees. In 1999, he was appointed as Lecturer in the Department of Civil Engineering, KNUST, and was then promoted to the position of Senior Lecturer in 2002 and Associate Professor in 2007. In the area of research, his niche is in computational hydraulics and water management. He developed Burgers' Equation Model. His research findings have been published in top journals like *ASCE Journal of Hydraulics* and *IAHR Journal of Hydraulic Engineering, Physics and Chemistry of the Earth*, among others. Currently he is Head of the KNUST Quality Assurance and Planning Unit and the Editor-in-Chief of the Journal of Science and Technology. He was awarded the best research scientist at the First Ghana Research Science Congress under the theme 'Water, Sanitation and Environment: Securing our Future through Science'.

Wordsworth Odame Larbi is a land policy specialist with over 25 years of expertise in land economics, administration, land policy formulation, implementation and analysis. He has considerable experience in land policy issues in the West African sub-region. He consulted for the Africa Union for the AU-UNECA-AfDB initiative on Land Policy in Africa. He led a team of consultants to prepare the West Africa Regional Study for the Land Policy Initiative and was involved in the development of the Framework and Guidelines on Land Policy in Africa. He also led a team to prepare a 'Framework on Formulation and Implementation of Harmonized Land Policies in the ECOWAS Region'. He is currently undertaking a study on 'Mainstreaming Land Issues in the Operations of the Regional Economic Communities' of West and Central Africa. He is the former Chief Executive of the integrated Ghana Lands Commission, former Executive Secretary of the previous Lands Commission and former Project Director of the Ghana Land Administration Project Phase 1 (LAP 1). He combines professional work with church administration and is currently the Circuit Steward of the Kaneshie North Circuit of the Methodist Church, Ghana.

Anthony E. Paul is the Managing Director of Association of Caribbean Energy Specialists (ACES) Ltd., a leading Caribbean oil, natural gas and power advisory firm, based in his native Trinidad and Tobago. He has spent over 35 years in the petroleum and mining industries, having several technical, commercial and leadership roles along the entire petroleum exploration and production value chain (licensing, exploration, appraisal, development and production), in government, state, private, local and multi-national companies. As a consultant, he provides strategy and industry/business development support through critical analysis of the inter-related industry facets of policy, regulatory and technical and commercial matters. He draws on the extensive experiences from Trinidad and Tobago's energy sector in transmitting to developing countries the integrated approach (known as the 'Trinidad and Tobago Model') for capacity development, local value addition, and retention and good governance in support of sustainable development from natural gas. He has developed and supported the implementation of policies, strategies, plans, training and tools for governments (including regulators and parliaments), multi-national companies, civil society and small- and medium-sized enterprises in East and West Africa, the Middle East, Asia, Latin America and the Caribbean that are interested in ensuring that more value from the full chain is retained in the countries and regions of resource extraction. He has worked with the Trinidad and Tobago Ministry of Energy (as Director of Geology & Geophysics), Petrotrin (the national integrated oil and gas company as Senior Geophysicist) and BP's Trinidad & Tobago subsidiary, bpTT (as Exploration and Appraisal Programme Manager, Resource Manager for bpTT's oil production assets and

Sustainable Developments Manager). He has also worked with Exxon in Houston (as Senior Geophysicist) and BP plc in London (as e-Business Strategy Consultant).

Atiba Phillips is the Founder and Principal Consultant at INFOCOMM Technologies (ICT) Ltd (www.ict.co.tt), an ICT for Development Strategy Consultancy based on Trinidad. Clients in this role have included the EU, UNECLAC, IDB and CARICOM, as well as other regional and domestic entities. He has also served in the post of Chairman and CEO of the National ICT Company Ltd for Trinidad and Tobago (dubbed iGovTT), where he was the state's ICT lead in prime ministerial missions to India, Brazil and the USA. During his time in this role (2011–12), Trinidad and Tobago jumped 19 places in the World Economic Forum's Networked Readiness rankings and won the Organization of American States' (OAS) award for e-Government in the LATAM Region. He also has energy industry experience, having worked with BP and MCT and Associates. He is a current member of the ICT Program Advisory Board of the University of Trinidad and Tobago and has lectured at the Master's level in Strategic IT in e-Business and e-Marketing through the University of Greenwich, UK. He holds an MBA from the University of California at Berkeley, US and is both a Fulbright and a Haas Merit Scholar. He is also the Founder and Chairman of the Community HUB Corporation (www.mycommunityhub.org).

Anne Richmond (Ms) is a former civil servant with a career in Canada, the UK and the UN. Holding an MA in Political Science from the University of Toronto, she has developed a more practical understanding of governance and development from working 'in the trenches' of the civil service and as an advisor and consultant. She entered the civil service in Canada as a policy analyst in women's equality and has worked on pay and employment equity, labour market training, economic development and public service development issues, among others. Her current consulting practice is global, ranging from work on civil service reform for the Federal Government of Nigeria to workplace safety for the garment industry in Bangladesh. She currently lives in rural British Columbia, Canada.

Vicky Wireko-Andoh (Mrs), a journalist and public relations professional, has worked with the *Daily Graphic*, the Institute of Chartered Accountants, UAC Ghana Ltd and Unilever Ghana Ltd in different communication roles. He was formerly Head of Corporate Relations at Unilever Ghana, where she was responsible for Unilever Ghana and its associated companies in Ghana. She is currently the Media Relations Adviser for the Coca-Cola Company in Ghana. She has provided PR consultancy services to Fidelity Bank and Unilever Ghana between 2010 and 2013. She currently serves on the Boards of the Coconut Grove Regency hotel chain, the Millennium Excellence Foundation, the Zawadi Africa Educational Fund, the Multimedia Educare Fund, the New Horizon Special School for Autism/Children with Learning Disabilities and the CSR Foundation. She is a Council Member of the African University College of Communications Pensions Academy. She is also a columnist for the *Daily Graphic* and has contributed over 400 published articles. She is the Editor of *CSR Watch*, a quarterly magazine of the CSR Foundation, and *Ridge Alive*, the newsletter of the Accra Ridge Church. She won the Ghana Journalists Association (GJA) Awards for Best Columnist in 2009 and 2010. She is also the immediate past President of the Institute of Public Relations, Ghana.

Acknowledgements

The editors wish to express their sincerest gratitude to the contributors who spent numerous valuable hours of their time writing the chapters of this book, thus making it possible for this project's dream to become a reality: Anthony E. Paul, Samuel Aning, Nana Kegya Appiah-Adu (Mrs), Vicky Wireko-Andoh (Mrs), Judy Cavanagh (Ms), Anne Richmond (Ms), Dr Gheysika Agambila, Ebenezer Ofori Agbettor, Dr Wordsworth Odame-Larbi, Dr Toni Aubynn, Professor Samuel Nii Odai, Dr Osei K. Darkwa, Charles K. Boakye, Dr Osei Boeh-Ocansey, Clifford D. Mpare, Kwesi Amonoo-Neizer, Nana Kumapremereh Nketiah, Atiba Philips, Professor Charles Blankson and Dr Kwabena G. Boakye.

To our wives Nana Kegya and Samira, and our children Afua, Kwaku and Akua, as well as Abdul Mumin, Nadia, Mahmoud and Aidan, who gave us the time and breathing space to complete the project on schedule, words cannot express our appreciation for your patience and encouragement which were more than adequate to propel us to higher levels of motivation when the going got tough.

On behalf of the whole team, we wish to thank the following eminent citizens who inspired the team by demonstrating their confidence in the project: Dr Mohamed Ibn Chambas, who wrote the Foreword, His Excellency John Agyekum Kufuor, Mrs Elizabeth Joyce Villars, Professor Francis Kofi Allotey, Professor E.H. Amonoo-Neizer, Captain (rtd.) Prince Kofi Amoabeng, Ken Ofori-Atta and Dr Patrick Gyimah Awuah, who provided compliments.

Our sincere gratitude also goes to Ama Kessewa Ampofo-Gyekye, our research assistant and Nana Akosua Ode Agyare, our indexing specialist on this project, for their meticulous approach to work and attention to detail. Finally, to all others that time and space would not permit us to list, we say a big thank you for the various roles you played in making this project see the light of day.

Foreword

The issue of national development has always been an important subject amongst economists, practitioners of development and business executives, as well as a wide range of professionals, scholars and society as a whole. Indeed, its significance has grown considerably over the last few decades, both in individual countries and globally. This has largely been driven by increasing globalization and the fact that the deregulation of industries, increased competition, variations in demand, the application of new information, communication technologies and persisting wealth and income disparities continue to present formidable challenges to nations. Consequently, countries, industries and organizations require new approaches to address these challenges. Moreover, the significance of national development as a source of comparative advantage amongst nations has grown immensely since the turn of the twenty-first century, particularly as we witness a new economic order with the emergence of new economic power blocs and nations.

Throughout roughly the same period, economists, development practitioners, business executives, the world of finance and investment, business schools, researchers and science and technology experts have been emphasizing how important it is for countries to focus on economic growth as a major contributor to national development. At first sight, this message would appear to have hit home, because today many countries claim to be putting in place policies and programmes that are aimed at achieving socio-economic advancement. However, more often than not, national leaders, particularly in developing countries, tend to only pay lip service to the concept and practice of national development. They confuse attending to short-term political exigencies with what true development is all about, and the result is that they merely succeed in creating a veneer and a vocabulary of national development when in fact no socio-economic transformational changes are realized. For economic growth to really take root and ultimately have a significant impact on national development, not only must a country learn new skills, but often new attitudes have to accompany them to ensure structured and sustainable re-alignments of the productive sectors of the economy and society.

Interestingly, this compendium of chapters encompasses investigations into the impact of various contributors to economic growth and national development. These studies have been systematically conducted across various facets of the national fabric, such as its leadership, governance, policy and strategy; culture, institutions and people; public and private sectors; science, technology and infrastructure; natural resources; financial markets; branding and service delivery. Given the increased turbulence in economies throughout the world and the changing dynamics of competition in the global environment in both industrialized and developing economies, I highly commend Professors Appiah-Adu and Bawumia for their insightful approach in compiling, analysing and focusing particularly on the key determinants of national development and their implications for developing economies. The clarity of thought on their part and of the other contributors throws much light on the issues taken up by the book.

Undeniably, these are works with which every individual with an interest in economic growth and national development should be familiar and to which they should have ready access. The book will be a valuable supplement to advanced undergraduate courses in science and economics, as well as business and management, and to postgraduate courses in these or related areas. I strongly believe that economists, practitioners of development, lecturers, academic researchers, business practitioners, management consultants, politicians and policy makers will also find it useful to have these critical works in their libraries.

Dr Mohamed Ibn Chambas
Head, United Nations Office for West Africa
Former Secretary General, African Caribbean and Pacific Group of States
First President of the ECOWAS Commission

Preface

What are the critical factors for a country to develop? Why are some countries successful while others fail? These are the major questions that the literature on economic development has been trying to answer. In many developing countries, the main thrust of national development is to transform the economy for enhanced growth and job creation in order to support the delivery of social services to the people of that country, regardless of their geographical location, or social and economic circumstances. Several countries achieve this *inter alia* through good governance, sound management of public finances, investment in infrastructure, accelerated human resource development, agricultural modernization, value-added processing of natural resource endowments, industrialization, regional integration and the promotion of trade, and the execution of a national development plan.

Some countries have facilitated economic development through a largely free economic system that promotes the allocation of factors of production through the interaction of private operators, while other economies have relied more on state intervention to drive the allocation of resources and the development process. Which path has proven to be most successful historically? Are the two paths mutually exclusive? What factors are necessary and/or sufficient to drive the development process?

In this book, we attempt not only to provide our audience with some instructive findings regarding national development, economic growth and their determinants, but also to provide historical perspectives on the subject and their implications for developing countries. The themes covered are as follows: leadership, governance, policy and strategy; public sector and public financial management; culture, institutions and people; natural resources; science, technology and infrastructure; private sector and financial markets; marketing, branding and service delivery; and their respective effects on national development. Generally, this thematic approach enables the authors to explore the impact of the constituents of each thematic area on national development within the context of a developing economy. The implications of the findings for the relevant stakeholders are consequently discussed. This book constitutes an invaluable insightful compendium traversing a spectrum of subjects that all those wishing to acquire knowledge about national development issues ought to be well acquainted with. It is recommended to decision makers in government, policy makers, development practitioners, business executives, scholars and students in the sciences, arts and business.

Acknowledgement

Please note that all websites referenced in this book were correct as of 31st December 2014.

Introduction

Kwaku Appiah-Adu and Mahamudu Bawumia

This book focuses on key determinants of national development, drawing on historical perspectives and examining the implications for developing economies. Against the background of global developments and experiences as well as those within the national setting, factors that are considered crucial to the achievement of national development in a developing country economy are explored. The book addresses a suite of critical themes regarded by development experts to be germane in considering the pertinence of policies and their effective execution. Seven general themes are explored.

Thematic Areas

- Leadership, governance, policy and strategy
- Public sector and public financial management
- Culture, institutions and people
- Natural resources
- Science, technology and infrastructure
- The private sector and financial markets
- Marketing, branding and service delivery

Underlying all of the above themes are the concepts of economic growth and national development. Economic growth is a multi-dimensional concept. It refers to the increase in a specific measure such as real national income, gross domestic product (GDP) or per capita income. National income or product is commonly expressed in terms of the aggregate value-added output of the domestic economy, which is called GDP. When the GDP of a nation rises, economists refer to it as economic growth. Economic growth also describes an increase in the productive capacity of an economy as a result of which the economy is capable of producing additional quantities of goods and services. National development is described by the World Bank as the transformation of an economy for enhanced growth and job creation in order to support the delivery of social services to the people of that country, regardless of their geographical location or social and economic circumstances.

Leadership, Governance, Policy and Strategy

CHAPTERS

2. Leadership, Governance and National Development
3. Strategic Thinking and Economic Development
4. Policy Management and National Development

Theme one provides the opportunity to consider the contribution of leadership, good governance, policies and strategies to national development based on strategies and experiences across the globe. Chapter 2 discusses the leadership challenge facing developing nations and the various styles of leadership. Next, the principles and features of good governance are explored. Also addressed are the concept of national development and the challenges faced by developing countries as they make concerted efforts to achieve growth and advancement in various areas of their economies. Chapter 3 examines the significance of strategic management for economic development in developing economies and provides an array of techniques for assisting executives to adapt organizations to the marketplace in order to achieve their key objectives. Chapter 4 explores government and public policy followed by policy management reform as a development strategy. In an effort to understand the policy management concept, the roles of different policy actors and, in particular, the executive and legislature arms of government are discussed. To appreciate the policy process in detail, an in-depth analysis of the steps involved in policy conceptualization, analysis, formulation, implementation, monitoring and evaluation as well as feedback on objective setting is undertaken. Furthermore, examples of the policy cycle are drawn from advanced countries, emerging economies and developing nations to illustrate how robust the system must be for a government to reap the full benefits of effective policy management processes.

The Public Sector and Public Financial Management

CHAPTERS

5. The Public Sector as an Enabler of National Development
6. The Impact of Sound Public Financial Management on National Development

The second theme concentrates on the public sector's contribution to national development. Chapter 5 examines the ways in which the public sector enables national development, in part by exploring the ways in which in developing countries it is failures or lack of capacity in the public sector that are seen as the main barriers to development. The public sector is generally understood as that part of the economy which is publicly owned – in practice, government and government-controlled entities – and which provide benefits and services (public goods) to all. These services, particularly those which create a fair and regulated environment for production and trade, are clearly necessary to the development and growth of the private sector: enterprises and industries which produce and trade in goods and services, employ citizens and generate revenue, some of which returns to the public sector in the form of taxes and fees. Hence, the public sector is inherently an enabler of development. Subsequently examined are: the role of the public sector as an enabler of development; what steps are taken to improve its functioning and remove barriers to development; and how a public sector may respond in practice to 'enable development', with the particular example of its role in labour markets. Chapter 6 provides an understanding of the concept of public financial management and establishes the significance of public financial management systems. Subsequently, an effort is made to relate national financial management and national economic development. Finally, the implications of sound public financial management for national development are espoused, drawing on examples from industrialized nations, emerging economies and developing countries. In this regard, selected public financial management policies and their individual effects or combined effects with other policies are examined with recommendations as to what the best permutations and combinations could be for developing countries.

Culture, Institutions and People

CHAPTERS

7. Institutional Building and National Development
8. National Culture and Economic Development
9. Human Capital and National Development

Theme three examines how culture, institutions and people contribute to national development. In this context, Chapter 7 examines the rationale for strong institutions in a country, followed by a discussion of national development strategy as a subject. Also investigated is how effective national institutions can contribute to national development and, in this regard, an effort is made to achieve a deeper understanding between strong institutions and national development. Furthermore, a detailed analysis of institutions that impact on growth and national development is undertaken, including a productive and proactive public sector, strong labour market institutions, rule of law and protection of property rights, integrity of governance and social inclusion that results in political stability. Chapter 8 examines the importance of national culture and whether certain cultures perform better economically. Within this context, the concepts of values and attitudes are discussed. Subsequently, there is a focus on how these issues are pertinent to the economies of the developing world, with an attempt to determine how national development can be propelled through culture. The focus of Chapter 9 is that the creation of an excellent human capital base that is skilled, knowledgeable, healthy, flexible and mobile is central to the vision of leapfrogging from a developing nation status to one that is fully developed. It examines how governments over the years have embarked on various initiatives that aim to transform the way in which human capital is developed to achieve national development. It uses the evaluation of the perspectives provided by various philosophers and economists on human capital as an excellent platform for lessons of invaluable resource to policy makers, administrators and educationists.

Natural Resources

CHAPTERS

10. Harnessing Land Resources for Economic Development
11. Management of Energy Resources for National Development
12. Mineral Resource Policy Dynamics and the Contribution of Mining to Ghana's Development

The fourth theme explores how best natural resources may be utilised for national development. In this context, Chapter 10 investigates how land resources may be harnessed for economic development. It is contended that land is the basic asset on which the wealth of most nations is built. Indeed, the concept of land is a complex phenomenon that is not regarded simply as an economic or environmental asset, but also as a social, cultural and ontological resource which defines the construction of social identity, the organization of traditional religious life, and the production and reproduction of culture. The contribution of land and its resources to economic development lies in the property rights that exist in the land. These rights define the ownership, control, use and management of land. In addition, the complex relationship between property rights, land administration, land governance and economic development is explored, and critical challenges that militate against unleashing the full potential of property rights for a country's social and economic development of the country are identified, alongside key recommendations to build a land administration infrastructure and improve upon the land governance system. The central concerns of Chapter 11 are: first, how developing economies with characteristic flagship primary export industries can enhance their sustainability and diversify their economies; and, second, how these countries/economies capture more of the value that they create in a manner that allows them to diversify and sustain their economies. This chapter illustrates that economic activity, including schemes of attracting foreign direct investment, must be orchestrated in a coordinated and targeted manner towards the goals of developing indigenous strategic and technological *human resource capability*, the engendering of *local ownership and control* of the nation's economic and productive assets, and the engendering of a *learning environment*. In this light, a framework of analysis is suggested that can guide developing nations towards the ideal of sustainable economic growth. Chapter 12 adds to the debate on whether the exploitation of natural resources, particularly, mineral resources, contributes to the development benefit of host countries and discusses a range of issues that have a bearing on how such countries can harness the benefits of their natural resource extraction for national development. Using Ghana as a case study, the chapter discusses why it is essential to ensure effective impact in the actual mining communities and underscores the imperative for managing the seemingly exaggerated expectations of how mineral exploitations can carry the burden of development. The chapter challenges both critics and supporters of the mining industry to improve their understanding of the mechanisms that allow for increased developmental benefits of mining and advocates for the deepening of integration of mining into the economy through local supply chain development.

Science, Technology and Infrastructure

CHAPTERS

13. The Role of Science, Technology and Innovative Industries in National Development
14. Information Technology and National Development
15. The Impact of Sound Infrastructure on National Development

Theme five investigates the contributions of science, technology and infrastructure development to the advancement of nations. Within this field, Chapter 13 explores the role of science, technology and innovative industries in national development. Many European and Asian countries offer pertinent learning experiences worth considering by developing nations. Typically, such economies have little or no natural resources, but have emerged as economic giants within a few decades. These nations have thrived on the formulation and execution of strategic policies that are based on technologies and innovations. Such policies have included the establishment of forward-looking public institutions that deal with scientific research and technological development, the expansion of the countries' educational systems to create a literate society with highly skilled personnel, and robust research and development culture to support its pursuit of nurturing a new system of economic growth based on technologies and innovations. Chapter 14 discusses the role of Information and Communications Technology (ICT) in national development against the backdrop of the wide recognition that the future of the world depends upon our willingness to harness ICTs to advance our development. This chapter discusses the theoretical perspectives on ICT and national development and, using Ghana as a case study, pertinent institutional policy and regulatory frameworks are presented. In addition, trends in ICT development are discussed alongside the identification of the country's experience in using ICTs to promote and enhance national development. The chapter identifies the application of ICTs to specific economic sectors and highlights lessons learnt through these applications. Finally, it identifies the challenges in implementing ICTs for the country's development and makes recommendations on ways of addressing these challenges. Chapter 15 contends that infrastructure is the mainstay of any country and that, without it, economic growth will be severely inhibited. It asserts that African countries that are able to reduce their infrastructure deficits in terms of transportation, energy, water and sanitation can grow their competitiveness to a similar level to that observed in Asia and the Middle East. Developing adequate and efficient infrastructure will enable African economies to increase productivity, especially in manufacturing and service delivery. Improved and efficient infrastructure has contributed to social development in healthcare and education, and reduced societal inequalities through a more equitable distribution of wealth. This chapter suggests how policy makers can fix the infrastructure problem and also addresses a number of options for financing infrastructure.

Private Sector and Financial Markets

CHAPTERS

16. The Private Sector as an Engine of Economic Growth
17. The Effect of Global Capital Markets on Developing Countries' Economic Growth
18. The Role of Stock Markets in National Development: The Case of the Ghana Stock Exchange
19. The Role of the Central Bank in Reforming the Financial Sector

The sixth theme examines the roles of the private sector, financial markets and central banks in economic growth and national development. Under this theme, Chapter 16 explores the significance of the private sector in economic growth, highlighting the origins of the private sector and economic growth, and the highs and lows of the private sector through different economic cycles. This is followed by an examination of the perceived notion that the private sector has always been a dominant force in national economies. Subsequently, the chapter presents how a strong private sector could be built in a developing economy, with a focus on Ghana and how the sector could contribute to national growth. Finally, conclusions are drawn for the attention of developing economy governments, policy makers and private sector organisations and the relevant stakeholders. Chapter 17 examines the trends in emerging market growth over the last few decades. It begins with a discussion of the development of markets specifically in Africa as well as the growth and contribution of these markets to the global economy. In addition, it explores the prospects and potential of African markets as developing economies continue to evolve into stronger and more influential forces in the future on the global stage. Subsequently, it assesses the likelihood of Africa being the hotspot for investment funds in the medium to long term. Chapter 18 adds to the subject by covering the contribution of financial markets in the development of emerging economies, using Ghana as a case study. It traces the history of the Ghana Stock Exchange (GSE), its perceived benefits, its performance over the years and some criticisms levelled against stock markets in general. In light of the period of existence of the operations of the GSE, the chapter examines the impact that it has had on national development. The authors opine on the strides made by the GSE in its 20 years of existence. They evaluate its capital-raising capability compared with the huge financing needs of the burgeoning companies in Ghana and assess its impact on the Ghanaian economy. They also discuss the pace of development of the Stock Market and compare this with other parts of the financial market. An interesting question that is posed is whether it is time to re-examine current strategies and market practices, given Ghana and indeed Africa's inability to tap into this potential in spite of the huge potential for growth. Recommendations are subsequently made on how to increase participation on the GSE and enhance the pace of development of the capital market industry. Using Ghana as a case study, Chapter 19 examines the role of the central bank in financial sector development, a critical component of the development process. Given the rudimentary nature of the financial system, following its establishment, the central bank embarked on a policy of reforming and deepening the financial sector as part of the overall development agenda. As part of this agenda, the government, through the central bank, facilitated the establishment of a number of development banks for specific purposes such as: assisting industry; financing agriculture; providing loans for housing, industrial construction and companies producing building materials; providing consumer loans and credit for small to medium-sized enterprises (SMEs) and co-operatives; and providing credit and long term loans to businesses and individuals. To include the rural population in the banking sector, the central bank actively promoted and set up the rural banking system. The objectives were to institutionalize financial intermediation in the rural areas, mobilize rural savings for on-lending to agricultural and cottage industries, and inculcate the banking habit among rural households. Two major financial sector reform periods are highlighted and the overall impact of the reforms on the financial sector and national development is subsequently presented.

Marketing, Branding and Service Delivery

CHAPTERS

20. Marketing and Economic Development
21. Branding and National Development
22. Enhancing Service Delivery for National Development

Theme seven focuses on the roles of marketing, branding and service delivery in national development. Chapter 20 argues that in developing economies, the 'more prestigious' fields, such as banking, finance, human resources and the conventional arts, science and business professions such as law, medicine and accountancy are highlighted, while marketing is treated with neglect, if not disdain. Yet marketing holds a key position in these countries. It suggests that while marketing may generally lag behind in most areas of economic life in developing economies, it is the most effective stimulus of economic development, especially in its ability to develop entrepreneurs and managers. Moreover, marketing provides what is the greatest need of a developing country: a systematic discipline in a vital domain of economic activity, a discipline which is based on generalized theoretical concepts, and which can therefore be taught as well as learned. In this chapter, the discussion focuses on the needs and wants people have, which society, as a consumer of marketing, hopes that marketers will supply effectively in response to changes occurring in the marketplace. Chapter 21 considers how some countries have consciously used national branding to change their growth and prosperity agenda. Historically, branding has been used to transform the lives of many products and made them big success stories, influencing patronage, sales, aspirations and image. However, this concept of branding has been extended to countries in their quest to transform and accelerate their developmental agenda and change their image for the better. Others have adopted branding in their attempt to attract focused attention, both internally and externally, and, as a result, have targeted specific investment opportunities to help boost their economies. Some nations have specifically focused on country branding and have even gone to the extent of setting up specific country brand offices solely to drive their national branding exercise. Some countries have successfully used nation branding to propel their tourism industries. Today, tourism is a major foreign exchange earner for such countries, contributing substantially to their economies. These examples are analysed and lessons are drawn which developing economies can use in terms of employing effective branding as a strategy to enhance national development. Chapter 22 postulates that efficient and effective service delivery can facilitate national development. Services are now inextricably linked to our contemporary world. The service sector is central and is a significant contributor to the GDP of many industrialized and developing countries. The service sector, which includes trade, transportation, food and lodging, communications, education, government, financial services, medical services, etc., generates many millions of new jobs and fuels economic activity. In the subsequent sections, the chapter discusses concepts relating to service quality, implications of services for positioning and the characteristics of services. Furthermore, insights are provided into how a nation can build and sustain positioning advantage with services. Recent developments in services marketing are presented and related to the context of a developing economy. In addition, the implications of enhanced service delivery for national development are highlighted and recommendations are made for the consideration of managers and policy makers in developing countries.

To gain profound insights into the thematic areas discussed above, each chapter was written by an expert or a team of experts in the particular subject and, consequently, the book represents a compilation of chapters that will be an invaluable source of reference for governments, policy makers, consultants, scholars, business executives, students and all individuals keen on gaining a greater understanding of the key determinants of national development, especially as it relates to Ghana and other developing economies, based on findings from the extant literature and historical perspectives.

PART I
LEADERSHIP, GOVERNANCE, POLICY AND STRATEGY

2

Leadership, Governance and National Development

Samuel Aning, Nana Kegya Appiah-Adu and Kwaku Appiah-Adu

Abstract

This chapter examines the influence of sound leadership and good governance on national development. It begins with a definition of leadership and a discussion of the leadership challenge facing developing nations. This is followed by a description of the various styles of leadership and their advantages and disadvantages. Next, the principles and features of good governance are explored. Also addressed are the concept of national development and the challenges faced by developing countries as they make concerted efforts to achieve growth and advancement in various areas of their economies. In this regard, the role of culture in national development is also highlighted. Relevant examples of effective leadership and good governance as well as lessons to be learnt from these examples are presented throughout the discussions. To conclude, the implications of the findings for national leaders, policy makers and practitioners of development are discussed with their appropriate recommendations for all stakeholders aspiring to see their nations make significant strides towards national development.

Introduction

The concept of leadership is a requirement in all fields of endeavour and, given the challenges of the global economy, all the more so for many developing countries. Leadership means different things to different people and it is always important to define it appropriately within the right context relative to the subject area.[1] Effective leadership is required to ensure that the vision of countries and societies is achieved. Vision is important for national development because, without it, there is no direction. Indeed, conventional wisdom suggests that where there is no vision, the people perish. It is the vision that would give an overview of the objective to be achieved relative to national development. It would clarify what a nation seeks to aspire to and the development paradigms that must form the basis for the achievement of that vision.

It is important in our discussion to ascertain whether leaders are born or made. Our history books are replete with examples of many of our kings who are considered great leaders for what

---

1   Rost (1993: 6).

they did, or their vision for the kind of society of which they were a part. One wonders whether they were successful because of the society in which they lived and the times and seasons during which they were leaders or whether it was by force of their singular strength of character and responsiveness to the challenges they faced.

We contend that it is a mixture of the times and seasons in which they lived, the support from society, the preparation for the leadership positions they were given and their response to challenges that set them apart and made them examples for today.[2] The challenge for Ghana and other developing economies within Africa is that the next generation of leaders to take our countries well beyond the twenty-first century will need to be created. We are supportive of the view espoused by those like Patrick Awuah that 'the question of transformation in Africa is a question of leadership'.[3]

Naturally, we ask additional questions! Why leadership and not bravery, wealth and education, contacts and connections? What is the greatest critical factor for ensuring development and why is leadership important? Africa lies in a region that is resource-rich and yet wracked by civil wars, ethnic strife, security challenges, issues relating to poverty, hunger, corruption, disease and under-development. What will leadership alone do for Ghana and many countries like it?

What is Leadership?

There have been many definitions of leadership and from reading the extant literature on leadership, it is interesting to discover that there is no one clear definition for this word. Different definitions range from describing qualities of leaders to what leadership styles are, making its meaning sometimes ambivalent. For the purposes of relating leadership to national development, we wish to provide the following definitions in order to place our discussions into context.

Leadership is the ability to lead, direct and encourage others, to share and work towards the achievement of a shared vision or goal aimed at bettering the lives of a given community or society. It has also been defined by Susan Ward as the art of motivating a group of people to act towards achieving a common goal.[4] Interestingly, Ward qualifies this definition by adding that it captures the essentials of inspiration and preparation, given that the leader is the inspirer or director of the action.[5]

Similarly, F. John Reh also states that a leader is a person who has a vision, drive and a commitment to achieve that vision, and the skills to make it happen,[6] while Chad Brooks of *Business News Daily* argues that while the definition of leadership is the act of leading others, getting people to do so is easier said than done.[7] Greenleaf believes that a leader initiates, provides the ideas and the structure, and takes the risk of failure along with the chance of success, knowing that the path

---

2   Kwame Nkrumah is a well-known leader in Ghana who led his country to independence and postulated that unless Ghana's independence was linked to total liberation of the African continent, its freedom would be meaningless. There have been other leaders such as Kofi Abrefa Busia, John Agyekum Kufuor, John Rawlings and John Mills whose responses to the challenges they faced are indicative that leadership requires training.

3   Quotation from a lecture given by Patrick Awuah, President of Ashesi University in Arusha Tanzania in 2007. See http://www.ted.com/talks/patrick_awuah_on_educating_leaders.html.

4   See http://sbinfocanada.about.com/od/leadership/g/leadership.htm.

5   Ibid.

6   http://management.about.com/od/leadership/a/whatisaleader.htm.

7   http://www.businessnewsdaily.com/2730-leadership.html. The article tries to answer the question of what is leadership.

is uncertain or even dangerous.[8] Greenleaf's definition of leadership seems to underline the fact that not only do leaders matter but also that they are essential or critical to success.[9]

The above definitions are clearly different from the perceptions of leadership in different parts of the world. It is a matter for discussion whether the above is all that leadership is in reality. The perception that a leader must look and act in a certain way has long shaped perceptions in some societies as to who becomes leader. In some traditional societies, leadership is by birth, denying potentially active and experienced personalities with requisite leadership skills the opportunity to lead. In addition, those who become leaders as a result of birth are not always the best to lead their people, given that a privileged upbringing that does not expose them to the realities of life. Leadership is refined through challenges, including personal and collective experiences. These experiences expose the depth of knowledge and skill that makes an individual truly a leader.

The Challenge of Leadership

Leadership is inherently associated with and inextricably linked to the concept of challenge. In other words, when one takes on a leadership role, one automatically takes on a challenge. Clearly, one way of assessing the effectiveness of leadership is to set it within the context of challenge. Thus, it is plausible to suggest that leadership is about how one responds to the challenges that confront an office holder, the constituency that one represents and how the identified challenges are turned around in order to benefit society as a whole.

Within the context of national development, there are many challenges that confront any leader of a developing country. Robinson (2012) refers to this challenge as being able to realize the crisis and to create enough reasons relative to the imminence of change and its importance.[10] In addition, there are challenges that would be internal to any leader in relation to what is right or wrong or best in any given circumstance. These would usually tax the leader's management skills. Further challenges include social pressures from those closest to the leader and pressures from political parties and other politically significant interest groups that wield some form of authority and control.

In Ghana, political pressures have emanated in recent times from a politically active group within parties known as foot soldiers, from chiefs and their subjects clamouring for anything from roads, ministerial positions and other social amenities. In other developing countries, particularly in Africa, key leadership challenges have stemmed from ethnocentrism, relationships with the military and other security agencies, and how they can be subjected to democratic control. There have indeed been instances where the retirement of generals or high-ranking military leaders has caused chaos.[11] The history of West Africa is replete with several coup d'états and has led to situations where democratically elected leaders have tended to treat security forces with some measure of fear. This continues to be a major issue as every administration works hard to promote military leaders whose loyalty to a particular administration can be guaranteed.

---

8   Greenleaf (2002: 29).

9   See Jones and Olken (2005: 838), who believe that leadership can be responsible for sustained economic growth or decline in a nation.

10   Robinson (2012: 45).

11   In the Democratic Republic of Congo, the M23 rebel movement is led by a former high-ranking General, Bosco Ntaganda, who is wanted by the International Criminal Court. The conflict that occurred in Cote d'Ivoire saw the military playing a significant part, as it did in Liberia and Sierra Leone.

Figure 2.1   Leadership Insight Quadrant

The Concept of Quality Leadership

The concept of quality leadership is an interesting one that distinguishes high-performing businesses from low/non-performing ones. Although the concept is in business, there are similarities to running countries and lessons can be learned from Paul Elkin's concept.[12] Elkin states that it is the insight of leaders that drive success of their organizations. He defines insight as *the power of seeing into a situation: understanding, penetrating; also some intuition.* His concept of insight has been re-created in the Figure 2.1.

According to Elkin, strategic perspective is the means through which a leader demonstrates vision and sets the direction of the organization and, in other cases, the country. The market focus refers to the means through which a leader ensures superior positioning compared to the competition. Every country the world over is competing for attention in order to sell its products and enhance opportunities for its citizenry. How a leader manages to sell his or her country as a centre of attraction for tourism, education, health, manufacturing and other notable feats is the market focus.

Results orientation refers to the achievement of objectives through collective effort and how the collective effort is harnessed to do so. The harnessing of potential deals with prioritization, team activities and inspirational leadership and empowerment.

Leadership Styles and Governance Systems

Closely related to the above is that the style that any leader selects is supportive of good governance and ultimately national development. We recognize that there are many leadership styles that are supportive of effective governance structures, strong institutions and the setting

---

12   Elkin (1998).

of agendas that lead to development. There are, of course, leadership styles that impede development, hence the need to discuss the styles of leadership briefly as a precursor to institutionalizing good governance.

The discussion of leadership styles naturally raises the argument as to whether leadership is a trait and whether there is a relationship between upbringing and leadership. Critical factors in leadership involve relationships, management, skills and group or national expectations relative to the challenges that a nation faces. While there are many different theories about leadership styles, we will limit ourselves to the following:

- the autocratic leader;
- the democratic leader;
- the delegative or laissez-faire leader;
- the transformational leader;
- the telling leader;
- the selling leader.

The Autocratic Leader

An autocratic leader is one whose leadership is characterized by total control over all the decision-making processes with little or no input from subordinates. Autocratic leaders operate more like military leaders or commanders who give orders which must be followed without deviation from the directives given. An autocratic leader is one who will usually make use of the phrase 'obey before complain'. Some world leaders who have exhibited signs of autocracy have included Benito Mussolini, Adolf Hitler, Muammar Gaddafi, Idi Amin and others like them whose will was what held sway when they were in power. While this form of leadership is not wholly negative, it is the least desirable in governance systems, especially when transformation and development are the ultimate goals for the country.

Ghanaian political history outlines the military leaders and Ghana's first President as examples of leaders whose period of leadership clearly showed signs of autocracy. In the case of Kwame Nkrumah,[13] he is credited with leading Ghana to independence and setting the stage for the development of the country into a modern African state. This notwithstanding, he is accused of passing laws such as the Preventive Detention Act (PDA) of 1958, which was used to pursue political opponents and incarcerate them without trial. Furthermore, he is accused of creating a personality cult known as the Young Pioneer Movement. Peter Antwi Boasiako,[14] writing on Nkrumah, stated that through a series of amendments to the constitution, Nkrumah ensured the existence of a one-party state, where his party (the CPP) was the only legal party in the country. Nkrumah's reputation is supported by the CPP,[15] which defends some of his actions as having been necessary to deal with the spate of bombings that the country was experiencing and could therefore be related to the laws that many Western nations today have to put in place to deal with the growing threat of terrorism.

---

13   Kwame Nkrumah (1909–72) was Ghana's President from 1960 to 1966. He was a charismatic leader whose support was extensive throughout the country.

14   See http://www.modernghana.com/news/302052/1/how-nkrumah-disintegrated-ghana-with-cruelty-and-d.html.

15   See http://www.conventionpeoplesparty.org/?q=node/80.

Similarly, Jerry John Rawlings[16] was seen as a dictator principally because of the way he assumed power uninvited and ruled as a virtual autocrat from 1981 to 1992, and then from 1992 to 2000 as a democratically elected leader. During the period when Rawlings was the President of Ghana, he was accused of exercising tendencies that have been described as autocratic. This has been attributed to his military background. To his credit, though, he did not attempt to extend his stay in power when his party lost the 2000 elections and for a leader who had been in power that long, that is laudable.

Although autocratic leadership is not desirable, it has some form of benefits and major disadvantages. For instance, in situations where law and order breaks down without clear-cut direction as to what ought to be done, an autocratic leader can take the decisions and ensure the restoration of calm and order. In such cases, autocratic leaders would dispense with the decision-making processes and would give instructions relevant to the challenge faced, and where feasible would take control and manage the implementation process to achieve quick and desirable results.

Overall, however, autocratic leadership is not ideal. The world has changed and successful development and nation building is not within the skills and experience of an individual. Even if the ideas for successful development are held by an individual, a nation is built by teamwork. In addition, national development requires that the vision for what a nation ought to become is shared through effective communication in order to ensure collective action and willing support. Furthermore, autocratic leaders tend to be involved in all aspects of a business, including day-to-day issues, without keeping a strategic focus. They get things done through threats, force and micro-management. As a result, the subordinates of such leaders often tend to be resentful and work only under close supervision. Where the leader is egotistical, sycophancy and bootlicking get people unmerited favours, adversely affecting the achievement of meaningful national development.

The Democratic Leader

The democratic leadership style is based on the principle of inclusiveness and openness where, as much as possible, everyone is brought on board and ideas are generated, synthesized and implemented relative to the general good. This style of leadership is great for constantly changing conditions that require dynamism to deal with situations as they emerge. In such cases, the ideas of all are tapped in order to deal with the challenges faced. Ideas are collated and synthesized and decisions are communicated to the entire group.

This system of leadership supports team-building, developing trust and building on the talents and skills available to a team. It is especially helpful when there is the need to take a decision that is complex and requires broad consensus, commitment and effective communication. The drawback of this system of leadership is that it can be extremely slow in taking a decision, so it is not ideal for making decisions in an emergency. Nevertheless, leadership is about leading and the democratic leader retains ultimate responsibility for the final decision taken.

Ghana's John Kufuor[17] is an example of a democrat who worked hard to ensure the rule of law. He endured criticism very well and tried to reconcile the country after 20 years of rule by one person. He is credited with stepping down when he needed to, raising GDP from £2.6 billion

---

16   Jerry John Rawlings is one of the longest serving leaders of Ghana. He took over the reins of power in a military coup in 1979 and executed a number of a number of people, including three former leaders, one of whom he had overthrown. He returned to power in another coup and ruled the country until he handed over power in 2001.

17   Kufuor was Ghana's President from 2001 to 2009 and assumed the reins of leadership after Jerry Rawlings.

to £11 billion within eight years, halving poverty, increasing school enrolment and providing free meals in some schools.[18]

The Delegative or Laissez-faire Leader

The delegative leadership style is based on non-interference, with little or no guidance to subordinates in the belief that office holders will do well irrespective of being given well-defined goals and guidance from the appointing authority or the individual with the ultimate decision making power. The laissez-faire leader allows all decision making to be undertaken by subordinates and does not clearly define the roles they are to play within a group. As a result, there is no allegiance to a clearly defined vision and this affects motivation to achieve.

Given the political leaders that Ghana has had since independence, one president who could be described as a laissez-faire leader is Dr Hilla Limann. He was regarded as a laid-back leader who gave his appointees the authority to make and implement decisions, some of which were to his own detriment. It is reported that Limann under-rated the risk of a coup when his own security advisors hinted to him of a plot to overthrow his government, that he insisted there was no evidence of a potential coup attempt and therefore no legal justification to hold anyone in custody under such a pretext. This eventually cost him his presidency and pushed him into oblivion in terms of Ghanaian politics. Another illustration of Limann's laissez-faire leadership style is that while he had a ruthless opposition to contend with, making his rule difficult, factions emerged within his own party. As a result, his party members in Parliament spearheaded the rejection of his first budget and some of his members of his party attempted to challenge his authority in court.

The Transformational Leader

The transformational leadership style is based on recognition of challenges, having a clear vision as to what ought to be done and getting the right team in place to inspire them to achieve the vision. This vision, which is a picture of what the future would look like, is kept in constant view in order to motivate and inspire subordinates to work towards it. The vision may be developed by the leader and shared with the team or may be developed jointly with the team.

To keep the vision alive, the leader communicates the ideals and takes every opportunity to explain and achieve buy-in from all stakeholders. Gaining buy-in and commitment from stakeholders is a critical success factor in every leadership situation. In this manner, the transformational leader encourages as many people to share the vision as possible and obtains the support required to achieve the required results. Transformational leaders are willing to show by their action that they are committed and motivated for the general good.

Transformational leaders face the challenge of mainly seeing the ultimate goal without identifying the pitfalls along the way. While such leaders have the energy and willingness to go the extra mile, they sometimes overlook the details required to achieve their vision or under-estimate the period or timeline for achieving their goal. This tendency for such potential pitfalls to derail the leader's efforts has to be borne in mind and addressed by giving consideration to the steps along the way to the top of the success ladder in a systematic fashion, without sacrificing the ultimate goal of realising one's set goal.

---

18   See   http://www.telegraph.co.uk/news/worldnews/africaandindianocean/ghana/3659680/Ghana-says-goodbye-to-President-John-Kufuor-a-good-man-in-Africa.html.

Kwame Nkrumah of Ghana is considered to be a great transformational leader of his time, given the challenges he faced and the impact he made on the African continent as a whole. The foundation he laid for education, health and agriculture and his far-sightedness in other critical areas was indeed commendable.

Nelson Mandela of South Africa is another transformational leader who showed magnanimity and moral persuasiveness through exemplary leadership in developing the building blocks of the new rainbow nation. When he died, several leaders around the world who attended his funeral attested to his exemplary leadership. The thawing of relations between the USA and Cuba was also facilitated by the handshake between Raul Castro and Barack Obama at Mandela's funeral.

The Telling Leader

In Elkin's conceptualization of leadership, the telling leadership is a high task and low relationship type of leadership that involves close monitoring and control of subordinates. This ensures that the leader is able to effectively take remedial or corrective action if something goes wrong. Such a style supports the use of standard procedures without room for alternatives and is generally meant to meet deadlines or achieve targets.

The Selling Leader

Elkin defines this leader as a high-task, high-relationship individual who shows concern for both the assignments or tasks and subordinates. Such leaders are open and friendly, and are able to ensure that deadlines are met and staff recommendations taken on board. They also allow individuals to set their own goals within the organizational framework.

Clearly, each of the leadership styles identified above will work well within a system of governance that allows the leadership styles to have pre-eminence, thrive and succeed. The discussion now turns to governance and what good governance is in order to assess whether the style can be influenced by a system of governance for national development.

Leadership and Culture

In this section, we want to assess whether the culture of a given society has an impact on leadership and its leaders, and consequently governance. Culture refers to the way of life of a people or society, those distinctive defining aspects that give it identity and prominence, such as language, religion and music. It has also been defined as a way of life of a group of people – the behaviours, beliefs, values and symbols that they accept generally without thinking about them and that are passed along by communication and imitation from one generation to the next.[19]

Indeed, cultural norms are developed as a result of our socialization processes and hence the leadership tenets that are expected of individuals of position and influence within society. In Ghana, there is general consensus within each ethnic group as to what a traditional leader ought to do while in office. It is worth noting that most traditional leaders uphold behavioural patterns that have been practised by their predecessors for years. For instance, most chiefs do

---

19   See http://www.tamu.edu/faculty/choudhury/culture.html.

not eat in public and cannot do certain things that ordinary people do. This is because some of these 'taboos' are considered culturally inconsistent with the position they hold. Therefore, to what extent does culture build and develop leaders?

The report on 'Cultural Influences on Leadership and Organisations: Project Globe' stated clearly that 'what is expected of leaders, what leaders may and may not do, and the status and influence bestowed on leaders vary considerably as a result of the cultural forces in the countries or regions in which the leaders function'. This research project brought 170 social scientists and management scholars from 61 cultures throughout the world to examine the interrelationships between cultural practices and organizational leadership, and their impact on leadership effectiveness.[20] Clearly, this research supports the view that culture does have a significant influence on leadership.

Having said that, it is important to ask whether the culture in certain parts of the world promotes peace and development while engendering war in others. Culture, in the opinion of the authors, is dynamic and susceptible to changes over time, especially in cases where there is interaction with other cultures. The challenge occurs when a particular culture is seen as immensely superior and its leaders are unwilling to change or learn from others in order to instil improvement and development.

Therefore, for Africa in particular to develop, the cultural practices that are supportive of autocracy, where the leader cannot go wrong or should not go wrong must change so as to include openness, discussion, consultation, consensus building and critical feedback. While change is strongly recommended, it must of necessity be in a manner that allows new principles to be assimilated and imbibed by the existing culture in order to change entrenched practices and bring about a positive impact. The truth of our current reality is that cultural changes are inevitable given the exchanges resulting from globalization. Schein believes that leaders and the people they lead will therefore need to become learners.[21]

Good Governance

This section of the chapter discusses governance and the critical elements that must be identified to make the governance system a sound one. It is widely acknowledged that good governance is crucial to and indispensable in the socio-economic advancement of any country, and there are ample examples to support this assertion, as reflected in the experiences of many prosperous nations the world over. Interestingly, governance and leadership go hand in hand as the leadership style of the person at the helm is influenced by the type of governance system that a nation practises.

Francis Fukuyama describes governance as 'a government's ability to make and enforce rules and to deliver services, regardless of whether that government is democratic or not'.[22]

---

20   See the introduction to the 'Cultural Influences on Leadership and Organisations: Project Globe' at http://www. google.com/url?sa=t&rct=j&q=&esrc=s&source=web&cd=2&cad=rja&uact=8&ved=0CCwQFjAB&url=http%3A%2F%2Fle adership.wharton.upenn.edu%2Fl_change%2Fpublications%2FHouse%2FCultural%2520Influences%2520on%2520Leaders hip%2520-%2520House%2520.doc&ei=CJQGVdmXNYHcUqm7gdAC&usg=AFQjCNHlcNu6qWWC8RYLE993zrh3Zg5h TQ&bvm=bv.88198703,d.d24.

21   Schein (2010: 365).

22   Francis Fukuyama, 'What is Governance?', http://www.cgdev.org/files/1426906_file_Fukuyama_What_Is_Governance. pdf, p. 3.

If the systems and processes are of a nature that is good and meets the aspirations of the general populace, this is called a good governance system.[23] The important issue here is the process and the end result – that a need is met.

Governance is defined by the World Bank as 'the manner in which power is exercised in the management of a country's economic and social resources for development'.[24] The critical factor is the public and how issues that affect everyone are handled for the benefit of all. The United Nations Development Programme (UNDP) has advanced a definition of good governance that includes certain key characteristics.[25] There is the belief that the implementation of a governance system with these characteristics will lead to a good system of governance. This is encapsulated in the model that has the key characteristics of accountability, consensus orientation, participation, transparency, responsiveness, the rule of law, equity and inclusiveness, as well as efficiency and effectiveness.

In order for a governance system to be participatory, all actors within the economy will have to be involved in a manner that allows their views to be carried over or be considered as part of the decision-making process. This form of participation will also need to be representative of all interest and gender groups. In addition, the system will have to be accountable to the stakeholders by ensuring the inclusion of a communication system that is informative. This system of accountability must be transparent by outlining the use to which the public resources have been put. This builds understanding and support for decisions that are meant to be in the public interest; where some sections of the population are negatively affected, they understand because the feedback system is informative and transparent.

The rule of law and how the law is applied, irrespective of who is affected, is a key part of any good governance system. The legal systems must be applied in a manner that is fair and consistent with similar cases and instances. Furthermore, the application of the law must be based on the equality of all individuals before the law. In addition, the process of building consensus is an integral part of a good governance system. Indeed, in any nation, there are differences in opinion and in order to ensure that everyone is supportive of the policies and programmes to be implemented, building consensus is important. To guarantee continued support, governance systems also need to be responsive to the needs of the people. It is inappropriate to give communities clamouring for water something else (such as a road) because that is what the leadership believes the people want.

Another key feature of good governance relates to the use of resources in a manner that meets the needs of stakeholders in the best way possible at the best price. Equity relates to fairness in sharing public resources in a manner that includes all the sections of society such that no section feels excluded.

---

23   http://web.worldbank.org/WBSITE/EXTERNAL/COUNTRIES/MENAEXT/EXTMNAREGTOPGOVERNANCE/0,co ntentMDK:20513159~pagePK:34004173~piPK:34003707~theSitePK:497024,00.htm.

24   World Bank, 'Managing Development – The Governance Dimension', http://www-wds.worldbank.org/external/ default/WDSContentServer/WDSP/IB/2006/03/07/000090341_20060307104630/Rendered/PDF/34899.pdf, p. 1.

25   http://www.unescap.org/pdd/prs/ProjectActivities/Ongoing/gg/governance.asp.

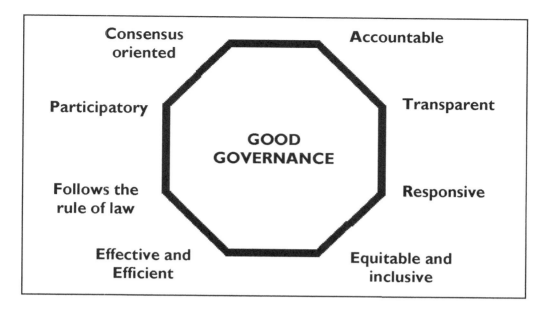

Figure 2.2   Good Governance Diagram[26]

The National Development Challenge

The concept of a national development challenge is one that faces many resource-rich countries in Africa. Many African countries are endowed with natural resources that should, if well managed, support effective national development. However, in spite of the resource-rich status of the African continent, the people are poor and grappling with serious infrastructural, economic and health challenges that are less prevalent in other parts of the world. In relation to HIV/AIDS, for instance, there are an estimated 34 million people living with the disease in developing countries. Sub-Saharan Africa accounted for 69 percent of new infections and nearly half of all HIV-related deaths in 2011.[27]

In addition, there are serious development challenges in areas such as energy, delivery of potable water to many homes, sustainable agriculture and job opportunities for the youth. Africa's population is seen as a very young one, with many of its citizens being well below 40 years old. Many of these young people cannot find jobs because there are few avenues for expression. In a recent lecture in Ghana, the Nigerian Minister of Finance, Dr Ngozi Okonjo-Iweala, defined the development challenge ahead of Africa when she stated that 'the unemployment rates today are over 20 percent in several countries – Nigeria (23 percent), South Africa (24.5 percent)'. She added that numbers are even greater relative to youth unemployment, which averages well over 40 percent in many African countries.[28]

In a region where there is so much unemployment and many young people without the requisite skills for national development, there is the danger that the planned developments

---

26   See http://www.unescap.org/pdd/prs/ProjectActivities/Ongoing/gg/governance.asp.

27   See http://www.worldbank.org/en/results/2013/04/03/hivaids-sector-results-profile.

28   *Business and Financial Times*, 26 February 2013, p. 9.

would suffer further should there be instability. In West Africa, long periods of war in Sierra Leone and Liberia left their mark on some young people, who gained no skills other than using a gun during the period of instability. Although currently there is relative peace in both countries, unemployed former combatants have been blamed for being active in combats in Cote d'Ivoire and other countries in the region. These sentiments were also expressed in the statement of the UN Under-Secretary General for peacekeeping operations.[29]

Without the ability to identify the soft issues that impinge on development targets, laudable attempts at ensuring change in a positive manner would be undermined or stillborn. Indeed, in order to achieve notable and long-lasting change in a nation's fabric, a leader needs to be able to achieve a delicate balance by successfully combining soft issues, such as culture, values and leadership style, with hard factors, such as the implementation of a robust national development plan and its associated strategies, a sound national governance structure, and effective systems and processes in the efficient running of the nation's institutions.

The Place of Culture in Development

Culture is a very popular subject in countries the world over. In the vast majority of African countries, the appreciation and study of culture and cultural practices constitutes an integral part of the educational system. The idea is that the best of our cultural practices are to be handed down through the generations so that they can be maintained and improved upon as part of the national development. To ensure the safeguarding of what are considered to be good cultural practices, several institutional and individual constituents of society are involved in the process of handing down such precepts. These include government organizations, private institutions, traditional rulers, national and community opinion leaders, family heads and scholars, among others.

Changing long-held beliefs and practices is a leadership and national development challenge because it must be acknowledged that aspects of culture are not useful today and tend to impede development. For instance, the perception that a woman was only good for the kitchen is no longer a belief that has wide acceptance. Allowing such an outmoded view to be practised today would have starved our development efforts of teachers, nurses, doctors and many more technical staff in various fields of endeavour. Some countries in other parts of the world now practise cultural renaissance as a way of reviving good and cultural practices that are supportive of national development. Similarly, it is necessary to identify new trends that impede national development.

The cultural challenge that faces many leaders hinges on the recognition of the good precepts within the culture and doing away with those beliefs that inhibit development. Practices such as female genital mutilation, the unsolicited presentation of gifts to people of importance during festive occasions such as Easter and Christmas, the lavish showering of gifts on personalities of influence on occasions such as birthdays and the celebration of milestone anniversaries, nepotism and the like adversely affect transparent and effective governance. In addition to such practices, there are many more that are detrimental to national development.

However, in spite of the above, the successful leader must outline the development paradigm and framework within which to operate. Wholesale copying without innovative and relevant adaptation can be dangerous because the most successful countries experience development relative to their local realities and conditions. There is no doubt that in Africa and other developing economies, leadership must take note that some cultural practices impede development and that there must be a time dimension to all that has be achieved.

---

29   See http://www.un.org/News/Press/docs/2013/sc11068.doc.htm.

Conclusions

In this chapter, an attempt has been made to discuss the key issues that influence national development. We believe that leadership is an important ingredient in moving any nation forward. Over the years, the world has witnessed great leaders who have been shining examples of what the ideal leader ought to be. Having stated this, however, there is no leader who can operate without a national vision, clearly determining for himself or herself and his or her nation what is in the best interest of the nation. In Singapore, the nation recognizes Lee Kwan Yew, and Malaysia has great respect for Dr Mahathir Mohammed; both clearly had vision and inspired their nations to achieve.

The second ingredient is the governance system that enables the most support for visionary leaders and participation by the citizenry. Sadly, this has been the biggest stumbling block for many developing nations. The critical link between the leadership and the systems of governance that allows for the achievement of set objectives has been missing. While many leaders start on a good note and achieve political power on the back of a popular vote, the desire to stay in power at all costs means that some leaders have destroyed the very system that allows for feedback, participation and effective evaluation. Many leaders have also destroyed trust in multi-ethnic societies by appointing leaders only from their ethnic group, thereby fuelling discontent. In addition, the creation of one-party states and the lack of alternatives given to people has undermined the governance systems in many countries.

The final issue is a national development outline or document indicating the key issues that a country faces and the approaches for dealing with them, which every citizen can support. The development of such documents should be conducted in a manner that ensures consensus building, ownership and commitment to implementation. Many countries are littered with projects that were not continued by successors of previous leaders. A largely non-partisan or multi-partisan national development document will ensure that the key issues are known and will place an obligation on leaders to ensure implementation or receive a vote of no-confidence from the citizens on the day of reckoning when the time arrives for the electorate to exercise their franchise. Clearly, when a leader is aware that there will be a day of judgement and yet refuses to implement what is stated in the national agenda, he or she would be signing his or her own death warrant.

References

Elkin, P. (1998). *Mastering Business Planning and Strategy: The Power of Strategic Thinking*. London: Thorogood Publishing.

Greenleaf, R.K. (2002). *Servant Leadership: A Journey into the Nature of Legitimate Power and Greatness*. New York: Paulist Press.

Jones, B.F. and Oklen B.A. (2005). Do leaders matter? National leadership and growth since World War II. *Quarterly Journal of Economics*, 120(3), pp. 835–64.

Robinson, P. (2012). *High Performance Leadership*. New Delhi: Positive Revolution Publishing.

Rost, J.C. (1993). *Leadership for the Twenty-First Century*. New York: Praeger.

Schein, H.E. (2010). *Organisational Culture and Leadership*, 3rd edn. San Francisco, CA: Jossey-Bass.

Smith, J.R. (2012). *The Leadership Code*. London: Alphabet Media Publishing.

Spillane, J.P. (2005). Distributed leadership. *Educational Forum*, 69(2), pp. 143–50.

Storey J. (ed.) (2004). *Leadership in Organisations: Current Issues and Key Trends*. London: Routledge.

Taylor, A.A. (2006). *Sam Jonah and the Remaking of Ashanti*. Johannesburg: Pan Macmillan.

Weir, T. (2012). *Unlocking Leadership Potential*. Dubai: Emerging Markets Leadership Centre.

Internet References

http://management.about.com/od/leadership/a/whatisaleader.htm.

http://sbinfocanada.about.com/od/leadership/g/leadership.htm.

http://www.businessnewsdaily.com/2730-leadership.html.

http://www.cgdev.org/files/1426906_file_Fukuyama_What_Is_Governance.pdf.

http://www.modernghana.com/news/302052/1/how-nkrumah-disintegrated-ghana-with-cruelty-and-d.html.

http://www.tamu.edu/faculty/choudhury/culture.html.

http://www.ted.com/talks/patrick_awuah_on_educating_leaders.html.

http://www.un.org/News/Press/docs/2013/sc11068.doc.htm.

http://www.unescap.org/pdd/prs/ProjectActivities/Ongoing/gg/governance.asp.

http://www.google.com/url?sa=t&rct=j&q=&esrc=s&source=web&cd=2&cad=rja&uact=8&ved=0CCwQFjA
B&url=http%3A%2F%2Fleadership.wharton.upenn.edu%2Fl_change%2Fpublications%2FHouse%2FCultu
ral%2520Influences%2520on%2520Leadership%2520-%2520House%2520.doc&ei=CJQGVdmXNYHcUq
m7gdAC&usg=AFQjCNHlcNu6qWWC8RYLE993zrh3Zg5hTQ&bvm=bv.88198703,d.d24.

http://www.google.com/url?sa=t&rct=j&q=&esrc=s&source=web&cd=1&cad=rja&uact=8&ved=0CB4QFjA
A&url=http%3A%2F%2Fwww.worldbank.org%2Fen%2Fresults%2F2013%2F04%2F03%2Fhivaids-sector-
results-profile&ei=-wIHVcGuKcP6asK6gKAP&usg=AFQjCNFYljlntSJCP0_IsJ0Ss56OyBlfUg&bvm=bv.881
98703,d.d2s.

3

Strategic Thinking and Economic Development: The Case of a Developing Economy

Kwaku Appiah-Adu and Sam Aning

Abstract

This chapter examines the significance of strategic management for economic development in developing economies and provides an array of techniques for assisting executives to adapt organizations to the marketplace in order to achieve their key objectives. Applied appropriately, strategic management can facilitate consensus decision making and compatibility. Nevertheless, accomplishment in organizational strategy is largely contingent on the appropriate mental perspective instead of specific tools, because tools alone can often become an obstacle to innovative thinking, especially in environments which are highly volatile, requiring consistent change and adaptation of strategy to changing circumstances. Strategic management works best when appreciated as a means of learning as opposed to a holy grail to observe. Therefore, the objective of this chapter is to outline strategic thinking using Ghana as an example for managers in developing countries to innovate and think strategically in relation to the peculiar challenges within their markets. It is expected that this chapter will contribute to understanding the implementation of strategic thinking processes in different environments.

Introduction

In the turbulent conditions and dynamic pace of modern-day business, executives often need to respond swiftly to change. Various frameworks have been developed to assist managers in responding to change. Strategic management comprises tools for establishing an organization's long-term direction, formulating plans based on internal and external conditions and taking the relevant action to achieve those objectives. The frameworks of strategic management are believed to produce information, to engender a thorough consideration of alternatives, to avoid surprises, to nurture ideas, to foster motivation and to improve internal communications and other commendable organizational characteristics.

Figure 3.1   Strategic Thinking Chart

However, mastery of strategy goes beyond the use of these tools; it is a mental approach (Crosby, 1991; Martin, 2007; Mintzberg, 2008; Jacobides, 2010; Simons, 2010). An innovative, strategic application of the mind is difficult to promulgate. The tools of strategic management are expected to foster problem resolution, yet the tools can also become ends in themselves to the detriment of what they are expected to achieve. As such, embracing strategic management by completing forms and going through the motions of planning is not the only crucial point, but must also be backed by the ability to reason strategically.

The purpose of this chapter is to outline the different facets of strategic thinking and clearly identify what it is, and use the experience of Ghana as an example for managers in developing countries to innovate and think strategically in relation to their peculiar challenges within their markets. This will contribute to dynamism in responding to the unstructured nature and volatility in the markets of developing economies, especially those in Africa.

Strategic thinking therefore consists of ideas, processes and tools, of finding new and innovative approaches to problem solving and using policy initiatives and approaches that allow for effective implementation, monitoring and refining. The fact that strategic management is no panacea for changing the fortunes of organizations and other bureaucracies does not suggest that its methods should be ignored in economic development. This chapter postulates that in developing economies particularly, if applied appropriately as a foundation to creative and consensus thinking, strategic management tools may provide additional insight into the way forward for both public and private sector organizations.

Strategic Thinking: The Conceptual Framework

The framework for strategic thinking in relation to a developing economy and the examples given indicate that the starting point is always recognition that there is an issue that requires resolution. However, the strategy to be developed must as a matter of consequence take cognizance of the internal strengths and weaknesses of the organization with regard to the opportunities and threats within the environment. In this way, strategies to be implemented would be better developed and targeted to overcome the challenges. As a result, this thinking is a continuous process and where necessary the cycle can always be repeated to achieve the right strategy.

Strategy

Although various definitions of strategic management have been proposed, the common theme shared is that it comprises the following ingredients:

*   specific objectives;
*   environmental appraisal;
*   strategy formulation;
*   evaluation of alternative strategies;
*   explicit assumptions;
*   management review and decision;
*   integrated plan;
*   action programmes;
*   performance; and
*   review.

Indeed, strategy is management's game plan for fortifying the organization's position, satisfying customers and realizing performance targets (Thompson and Strickland, 2003; Ackerman, Eden and Brown, 2004; Johnson, Scholes and Whittington, 2008; Porter, 2008; Paladino, 2010). An effectively formulated and implemented strategy is one that augments a market position adequately and is supported by a sufficiently strong organization to produce excellent performance, notwithstanding the challenges of unanticipated events, including intense competition and internal difficulties. This applies to private, public and non-profit organizations.

Strategic decisions are integrated and all-embracing. They impact on the whole organization and involve most if not all of its components. Strategic decisions are of great significance to an organization's progress and must be accorded the importance they merit. Examples in the business arena are new market entry, new business development, mergers and divestments. To be successful in strategy, managers must first understand the organization concerned, its capabilities, markets and potential markets. Next, they must analyse the external environmental variables that influence the ability of the organization to reach its chosen destination. Finally, they must establish and maintain a match between the external and internal variables. This match can be achieved by involving key groups within and without the organization who can influence its activities significantly.

Organizational success is purported to stem from being selective and from allocating resources appropriately among competing opportunities to maximize the impact of the organizational competencies. Failure is attributed to lethargic response in response to shifts in environmental conditions. It is not possible for an organization to sustain success without a well-conceived approach to adapt its internal variables to external influences.

From Strategic Planning to Strategic Management

The subject has become complicated over the years. Initially, the basis of an effective strategy was long-term planning. During the 1960s, several large organizations developed strategic planning units for this function. The new way involved a search into new areas of business that the firm should seek to enter, as opposed to the previous approach of projecting the present into the future, an approach that was considered as too simplistic/positive (Drucker, 1974).

Strategic planning was not perceived as a dynamic way of providing a platform for organizational advancement due to the sophisticated business environments that made it virtually impossible to project distant outcomes too far into the future (Parker and Stacey, 1994; Courtney, Kirkland and Viguerie, 1997; Neilson, Martin and Powers, 2008). Consequently, by the 1970s, the subject had started shifting from strategic planning to strategic management. Instead of a focus on internal and external analysis and the formulation of grandiose plans, implementation and evaluation took the centre stage as chief elements of an organization's success (Ansoff, Declerk and Hayes, 1976). These are the action and assessment components of strategy, without which planning alone is bound to be ceremonial, with minimal real-world effect.

In advocating implementation as a significant element, strategic management highlights the political dimension of running organizations. Since decisions about strategy emanate from both organizational politics and objective analysis, effective managers should negotiate, bargain and form coalitions in order to achieve successful implementation of strategy (Benveniste, 1989; Piercy, 2002; Balogun and Hailey, 2008). Consequently, the strategic management process may be conceptualized as comprising five major components that are *iterative* and not strictly sequential in nature. These are as follows:

*   *Mission and Goals:* understand the special purpose for which the organization exists and form a vision of where the organization should be aspiring to.
*   *Analysis:* examine the external situation and internal resources.
*   *Formulation:* develop a strategy to position the organization strongly, capitalizing on the capabilities and opportunities in the marketplace.
*   *Implementation:* evaluate performance and make appropriate adaptations based on knowledge and learning gained and also in line with changing conditions.

Strategic Thinking

New developments continue to emerge and some proponents tend to prefer the terminology *strategic thinking* in organizations (Stacey, 1992; Wilson, 1994; Martin, 2007). This preference stems from the fact that, strictly speaking, strategy cannot be managed. Indeed, in the face of dynamic and stormy conditions, organizations usually rely on informed intuitions and what has been learned from experience. Executives need to make decisions against the background of conflicting or incomplete information. They need to innovate and apply their practical skills to determine and find solutions to problems.

It is worth noting that informal strategies have always existed in people's minds. Still in our modern world of business, good fortune and inspiration can be more consequential than sticking to a formal strategic management prototype. Not surprisingly, several organizations continue to do well without explicit adherence to strategic management tools. Although formal methods may *augment* informal processes, the challenge is that structured approaches can *inhibit* strategic thinking. What is required is a sublime blend of analytical and intuitive stills. The strategic thinker must be creative, broad-minded, inspired and able to manage effectively. Staying ahead of change also involves co-operation and commitment to being watchful and open to receive new ideas. Some of these intuition skills are inconsistent with scientific strategy theory and are not easily imparted and replicated.

Strategic management methodologies can be a stimulant to strategic thinking – unless the methodologies degenerate into rituals that inhibit the innovativeness of mind rather than stimulating them. Lamentably, the field tends to lean towards a methodological bias (Daft and Buenger, 1990; Cherulinam, 2008). Even the practical books tend to be silent on the challenges inherent in strategy preparation and implementation, with scientific tools that play down the human element and place too much emphasis on the numbers (Freeman and Gilbert, 1988; Piercy, 2002; Bower and Gilbert, 2007; Jacobides, 2010; Simons, 2010). While no expert can claim to know all about effective strategic management in order to offer a foolproof model, strategic management cannot be considered a mere mechanistic process.

Strategy and Management in Developing Economies

Drawing on expectations that innovative thinking can be learned and reproduced, strategic management concepts have become quite popular in many organizations. This view of management founded on piecemeal transformation and benign environments appears increasingly outmoded. Thus, the new convention in developing economies is for executives to behave like entrepreneurs with strategic management offering guidance.

Strategic management is considered as a way to strengthen organizations in developing economies (Brinkerhoff, 1991; Blunt and Jones, 1992; Appiah-Adu, 2000). Many public and private sector organizations in developing economies are not helped by the civil service attitude of their executives. Strategic management is an appropriate means of assisting private and public sector executives in developing countries to be more responsive to their customers or clients.

Against this background, international development partners have initiated many programmes during the last decade to transfer the skills of strategic management. An illustration of this is the United Nation's Development Programme's National Long-Term Perspectives Studies project. This project aimed to place emphasis on long-term focus in contrast to short-term tactical issues (Ozgediz, 1990) and also attempted to foster strategic thinking in development policy within developing economies (Adesida, Caiquo and Brito, 1994). A second example is USAID's Implementation Policy Change (IPC) project (Brinkerhoff, 1995). This was implemented in several countries, with schemes lasting from about one month to three years. Under these initiatives, host country organizations usually worked with IPC advisors to re-examine and re-affirm their mandates, to identify their internal capabilities and constraints with regard to their business environments and to conduct a stakeholder analysis among others.

At the government level in some developing economies of Africa and South America, recent programmes include Growth and Poverty Reduction Strategy programmes aimed at providing guidance and support in the areas of strategic planning, socio-economic growth and poverty reduction. The Canadian government has also implemented initiatives aimed at helping developing economies to improve their policy management systems. An example is the Canadian International Development Agency's (CIDA) Central Governance Project, a joint effort by the governments of Ghana and Canada. The knowledge gained from the project being implemented in Ghana is being shared with other African countries such as Liberia and Malawi.

A fundamental basis for these initiatives is the notion that strategic management is culturally transferable, globally applicable and has universal value. This is not to say that the techniques will work similarly in every part of the world. The conventional view is that strategic management is likely to be more effective in industrialized or developed economies compared to emerging or transition economies. This is not attributable to the cultural inclinations of strategic management tools; rather, the tumultuous socio-economic environments of developing economies hamper an organization's efforts to adhere to its strategic plan (Austin, 1990; Courtney, Kirkland and Viguerie, 1997; Appiah-Adu, 2000; Jacobides, 2010). Clearly, until the recent financial and economic challenges experienced in some Western economies, key elements for determining growth such as interest rates were always stable. This has not been the case in many developing countries in Africa.

Like their counterparts in industrialized countries, executives in developing economies have to work harder to monitor and adapt to changes in the market environment. Nevertheless, this is an area where they are found wanting. Executives in developing economies tend to focus more on tactical issues as opposed to strategic issues. Indeed, this behaviour might be a reaction to the turbulence in their environments. Managing within the context of turbulence usually entails a re-allocation of resources planned for strategic management to critical functional areas. A myopic focus and failure to think and act with a view to the long term spell the beginning of a downward spiral for the organization. In periods of scarcity and re-allocation, rigid management systems do not usually allow for the use of resources for innovation or new thinking that may have the capacity to change trends.

Strategy Remedy or Strategy Cliché?

An organization that is successful must have a sound strategy in one form or another, since a distinguishing feature of organizational success is to follow a plan that yields fruit. On the other hand, a declining organization by definition has an inferior strategy or otherwise it would not be in decline. Lamentably, what constitutes a sound strategy is not easy to define. While there are many axioms and tools in strategic management, there are no rigid rules to shape the course of action.

Let us reflect on the notion of strategic innovation. Conventional wisdom advocates that organizations become successful by stretching themselves by breaking the frame (Hamel, 1994; Hamel, 1996; Balogun, Hailey, Johnson and Scholes, 2008; Paladino, 2010). Executives tend to benefit from daring their organizations to contend for greater heights rather than settling for the status quo. A few years ago, no one in Ghana probably thought that packaged water would ever become big business in the country. Today, we know that the innovative ideas of companies such as ASTEK Company Limited can work. A less revolutionary plan constrained by the conventional boundaries would not have discovered this new market.

It must be understood, however, that breaking *the frame* is not a ubiquitous tenet. There can also be worth emphasizing what is well known and has been effective in the past, that is, *sticking to the knitting* (Peters and Waterman, 1982). It takes time to optimize around a new strategy and organizations are often better off being patient. As a framework for decision making, the existence of a strategy provides managers with a focus. Owing to the guidelines it places on options and choices, the strategy helps executives to understand and manage complexity and uncertainty.

Focusing on alternatives may turn out to be useful in developing economies, which are characterized by turbulent socio-economic conditions and where resource limitations may drive executives to respond to every shift in the marketplace. In Ghana, three excellent examples of companies that have been highly successful at applying the 'sticking to the knitting' strategy are Combert Impressions Limited, Multimedia Broadcasting Company Limited and Land Tours Company Limited.

Combert Impressions Limited is a premium-quality print services provider that has positioned itself as a full service provider, offering design, editorial and print services to its clients. Multimedia Limited, an indigenous Ghanaian company, is a leader in the media and entertainment business, operating radio stations, interactive media assets and marketing and events management services. Multimedia Limited completely changed the face of media in Ghana with the launch of its flagship radio station Joy FM. Land Tours Company Limited is a full service destination management company based in Ghana, with a primary focus of providing ground-handling services and a seamless travel experience for its clientele. The company's tours consist of an array of interests and experiences, ranging from cultural and educational to adventure/eco and customized programmes to cater to customers' needs and interests.

These companies have systematically honed and embellished their expertise in the provision of 'products' and services in their respective areas of business and are currently head and shoulders above the competition in the West Africa sub-region.

'Sticking to the knitting' is not always the best way forward because a conservative approach can degenerate into counterproductive, reactive objection to favourable change. However, what separates winners (such as Combert Impressions Limited, Multimedia Limited and Land Tours Company Limited) from losers among those who adopt such a strategy is the ability to reinvent themselves using well-established principles of success in a unique way that leaves their competitors always struggling to catch up. The challenge with strategic management is that the domain provides limited guidance about what type of strategy is best in a particular set of prevailing conditions. Detecting an effective strategy is easy in retrospect – it can be done simply by examining the best-performing organizations. The task is more difficult when judging ahead of time. Good reasoning and understanding are required more than quantitative tools to resolve this issue.

Strategic Management Tools

Notwithstanding the difficulties associated with strategic management, strategic thinking remains a useful component of the management function and organizational development. While it may be superfluous to claim that organizational success stems from having the *correct* strategy, it is still plausible to suggest that managers would do well to assess their organization and the opportunities presented to it. Making an effort to anticipate events is better than leaving things to chance.

Managers who employ strategic management techniques believe that it hones their focus, enhances their insight into the environment, increases their willingness to change, and provides a host of tangible and intangible benefits (Appiah-Adu, Morgan and Katsikeas, 1996; Appiah-Adu, 2000; Kaplan and Norton, 2008; Kim and Mauborgne, 2009). Nevertheless, few managers know how to generate superior outcomes using these techniques. The tendency is to be caught in the trappings of strategic management, never addressing the challenging, innovative tasks required to perform the work effectively. When the tools become a ritual, they pose a danger of stifling the organization instead of providing a platform for its advancement.

Organizations in developing countries are more likely to face enormous difficulties in carrying out the daily responsibilities of management, let alone addressing strategy. Within this context, strategic management techniques can become the objects of strategy in themselves, and the essence of strategy is lost, a point which may be better understood by giving further consideration to the techniques of strategy.

Mission and Goals

Strategic management is founded on the basis that proficient organizations have a continuity of purpose and agreement on basic ideals and what is to be accomplished. In tumultuous conditions, a self-identity can foster managed change by offering a focal point for all those in the organization. A key task of strategic management is to stimulate this feeling of team purpose.

The essence of having a mission in organizations operating within developing economies cannot be overemphasized because of the tendency for managers to be snowed under by daily operational functions. It is important for executives to be aware of this and for them to purposely attend to the wider longer-range mission of their organizations periodically.

In the past decade, the IPC project has included mission-improvement efforts in many developing economies. For instance, in Ghana, workshops have emphasized the distinction between mission-propelled governance and the existing bureaucratic approach. As democracy in Ghana advances, there would have to be a change from fanatically sticking to procedures to a stronger emphasis on results. Examples of other development partners' efforts which have focused on mission improvement include the World Bank-funded institutional renewal projects for Ghana's tertiary institutions and the support given by the UK's Department for International Development (DfID) for the Forestry Commission and its strategic business units. Furthermore, other efforts have been made by the African Project Development Facility and the erstwhile Enterprise Support Services for Africa to help small and medium-sized firms to develop appropriate strategies to enable them to compete effectively in their respective marketplaces.

One issue that cannot be ignored is how to create mission statements, which usually entail a summary of the organization's strategic intent and business direction. These statements are now in vogue as a means of keeping organizations on course. Modern-day mission statements place emphases on teamwork, innovation, quality, continuous improvement and customer benefits, among other values (Van Wart, 1995; Davenport, 2006; Neilson, Martin and Powers, 2008, Paladino, 2010). Nonetheless, mission statement instruments are not easy to use in practice. Mission documents tend to be standard, insipid and divorced from the real abilities of the organization, with the consequence that the lofty words they contain are rarely taken seriously.

This does not suggest that the notion of mission statements is flawed; rather, it demonstrates that establishing commitment among employees for a united purpose is difficult to achieve. Organizations with striking mission statements commit major resources to forums to get their employees to gain a deeper appreciation in order to win their backing for each distinct component of the mission. A more difficult aspect may be to demonstrate commitment to the mission through behaviour. An artificial mission is worse than having none because it breeds staff cynicism, which has a negative impact on the organization.

Analysis

Strategic management urges executives to analyse their organization and the external environment for market opportunities. One favourite tool for conducting this scan is the Strength, Weaknesses, Opportunities and Threats (SWOT) analysis. The essence is to find matches between the organization's capabilities and opportunities while working around weaknesses and threats. This tool has been used extensively in both the public and private sectors. For instance, the IPC project has tried to promote capacity for SWOT analysis in a number of developing economies, with favourable outcomes. Participants in forums to build a network of businessmen and women in West Africa assert that SWOT analysis is amongst the most beneficial analytical tools they applied (Orsini, Courcelle and Brinkerhoff, 1996; Davenport, 2006; Hitt, Ireland and Hoskisson, 2006).

Nevertheless, this technique must be employed with an appreciation of its shortcomings. While there is no theoretical foundation for identifying the key internal and external variables, nor is there an objective method for measuring their significance. One employee's perception of an internal capability can be another employee's internal weakness.

Views concerning external opportunities and threats may also be influenced by similar misperceptions. Generally, executives tend to see dangers more readily compared with opportunities and, consequently, in analysing the environment, executives wrongly overplay the negative and understate the positive. A high-performing organization is likely to be complacent about the marketplace, causing executives to believe that the external environment is benign, although in reality it might not (Milliken and Lant, 1991; Courtney, Kirkland and Viguerie, 1997; Hitt, Ireland and Hoskisson, 2006; Simons, 2010).

Strengths, weaknesses, opportunities and threats are all subject to human belief and action. The characteristics and conditions of an enterprise sometimes vary in response to what people think they are. The issue is that the outcomes of SWOT analysis can be different and discretionary or highly dependent on who is conducting the analysis. Efforts should therefore be made to address this difficulty by including a variety of stakeholders in strategy formulation.

Formulation

Strategy is now viewed as a process to be negotiated, not engineered. This change in focus places emphasis on stakeholder analysis, participation and co-operation. Stakeholder analysis seeks to answer questions such as: on whom is the organization dependent for survival? Among the stakeholders, who are the winners and losers from a given strategy? Who has not been included? Who can be excluded without causing harm? What should be done to win the backing of all critical groups? The buy-in of stakeholders for a selected stance to the future results in sound strategies. In developing economies, it is well acknowledged that key players must be involved for most projects to advance and have an impact (Kinsey, 1988; Appiah-Adu, 2000; Cullen, 2008; Appiah-Adu and Aning, 2012). In our contemporary world, stakeholder analysis becomes even more critical as a more democratic tool for making decisions.

It is worth mentioning that in formulating strategy, every effort should be made by executives in developing economies to identify stakeholders and include them in the process. Amongst many executives in these economies, further illumination is provided when they recognize the significance of working together with key stakeholders (Ink, Klaus and Boynton, 1994; White, 2004; Appiah-Adu and Singh, 2011). For instance, in West Africa, stakeholders' analysis turned out to be highly beneficial in formulating a regional plan for making livestock. In the absence of strategic management tools, the traditional approach to decision making would have excluded private sector groups. However, in this particular initiative, the ground rules were altered to provide input from stakeholders, which ultimately resulted in a more effective livestock plan. The challenge here is to be able to identify key stakeholders rather than all potential groups. It is also important for executives to do something positive about what they consider to be interests of their stakeholders, otherwise they risk falling short of expectations. Where managers get caught in the trapping instead of the substance of stakeholder involvement, it may isolate groups and cause more difficulties. Stakeholders need to be given the required attention for this tool to be effective.

Implementation

A fundamental component of successful strategy implementation is organization culture (patterns of shared values). A culture-strategy fit is a potent lever for changing behaviour and facilitating job performance in a more strategy-supportive fashion (Thompson and Strickland, 1995; Piercy, 2002; Mankins and Steele, 2005; Balogun and Hailey, 2008; Paladino, 2010). Executives are encouraged to utilize both intangible and tangible methods of building solidarity. Managing organization culture entails working on changing any dimensions of treasured beliefs that are hampering the implementation of strategy. The challenge here is to identify which types of culture result in which level of performance in what kinds of organizations within what environments.

Success in examining and changing values in an organization is vital as they influence the organization's policies (Eisenhardt and Sull, 2001; Piercy, 2002; Mintzberg, Lampel and Quinn, 2007; Simons, 2010). It is worth noting that a strong group culture is no guarantee for effective strategy implementation. This is a difficulty in many developing economy organizations, which are stifled by deeply entrenched retrogressive cultures. The long-term failure of many technical assistance programmes over the last few decades is, in part, attributable to the inability of the local workforce to adjust to new thinking and ways of doing things. Undoubtedly, favourable progress is possible. While new culture behaviours can be established through management effort, they are hard to sustain and to replicate in other contexts.

Implication for Managers

Strategic thinking is about a winning strategy that ensures that organizations remain consistently successful irrespective of the challenges and the volatility in the marketplace. Thus, while a set of tools, systems and processes might be helpful, it is neither the tools nor the systems in themselves that provide the strategic edge.

Managers have to remember that failure to innovate and think ahead on a consistent basis in relation to the challenges within developing economies would make it difficult for them to realize progress. The market dynamics are always changing and predictability based on well-known variables may not always exist or be possible. Consequently, a knack for reading the trends and having a flexible attitude that allows for consistent thinking and innovation is what is required. Such activity would allow for aligning the internal organizational imperatives to the external challenges and dynamics so that relevant interventions are developed to ensure success (Appiah-Adu and Singh, 2011).

The same applies to the public sector, where cuts in the budget have become the challenge to meeting organizational targets. Such consistent thinking, combined with alignment, prioritization and effective communication, is also required to achieve organizational objectives (Appiah-Adu and Aning, 2012). When this has been done effectively, there is the need for implementing the new idea. While issues of resource adequacy would always be a challenge for many managers within the developing country context, this can be overcome by effective prioritization during the strategy formulation process.

Conclusions

Quite clearly, strategic thinking, which is described as the ability to learn from the environment while adopting a wider perspective, is a distinct attribute of sound management. Reaching conclusions based on a holistic standpoint is critical because of the changing environment that most organizations will encounter as we evolve in the twenty-first century.

Moreover, there is no arguing that many managers in developing economies tend to approach their situations compartmentally rather than being strategic. Instead of being concerned with what is happening within their environment, they place undue emphasis on internal matters. As a result of shrinking budgets, strong competition, rapid technological change and fluctuating demand for their offerings, this myopic stance is completely at odds with what is required in emerging developing economies.

Any approach that prevents managers from dwelling needlessly on mundane practices is expedient. Strategic management can be a useful aid, but, conversely, it can be a drag if it is used routinely. A challenge lies in the fact that strategic management tools tend to be reductionist, splitting strategy into distinct tasks. Finishing these tasks can override the real challenge of crafting the sophisticated, holistic scheme of an organization's game plan. Rigid or haphazard thinking, even about strategic thrusts, is at odds with the holistic, integrated perspective that is required. Rather than resolving an organization's difficulties, strategic management could even exacerbate the problems by shifting an organization's focus from maintenance operations that themselves are the subject of poor management.

How one can avoid the trappings of strategic management and focus more on the substance of strategic thinking is not easy to decipher. However, the various project experiences in developing economies provide some interesting pointers. In developing countries, indications of where lessons have been learned suggest that strategic management has been most effective when applied in a consensual manner. A rigid method often tends to be regressive (Ink, Klaus and Boynton, 1994; Eisenhardt and Sull, 2001; Neilson, Martin and Powers, 2008; Jacobides, 2010). Provided that the strategic tool is tailored to the conditions of an organization and country, it turns out to be beneficial as a means of assisting managers to adopt a holistic, long-term standpoint or think strategically. While there is no magic formula for successful strategies, the prudent application of strategic management tools can often be a step in the right direction.

References

Ackerman, F., Eden, C. and Brown, I. (2004). *The Practice of Making Strategy*. London: Sage Publications.

Adesida, O., Caiquo, B. and Brito, J. (1994). African futures: Challenges, achievements and the way forward. *Futures*, 26(9), pp. 903–11.

Ansoff, H.I., Declerk, R.P. and Hayes, R.L. (eds) (1976). *From Strategic Planning to Strategic Management*. London: John Wiley.

Appiah-Adu, K. (2000). Managerial perceptions of strategic planning benefits: A study of Ghana. *Journal of African Business*, 1(3), pp. 7–28.

Appiah-Adu, K. and Aning, S. (2012). Enhancing government's policy management and decision making system: Ghana's central governance reforms project. *Canadian Public Administration Journal*, 55(1), pp. 125–47.

Appiah-Adu, K., Morgan, R. and Katsikeas, C. (1996). Diagnosing organisational planning benefits: The efficacy of formalisation. *Journal of Strategic Marketing*, 4(4), pp. 231–8.

Appiah-Adu, K. and Singh, S. (2011). The role of strategy in national development: A marketing perspective. Paper presented at the 1st World Marketing Forum, Accra, June.

Austin, J.E. (1990). *Managing in Developing Countries: Strategic Analysis and Operating Techniques*. New York: Free Press.

Balogun, J. and Hailey, V. (2008). *Exploring Strategic Change*. London: Prentice Hall.

Benveniste, G. (1989). *Mastering the Politics of Planning*. San Francisco: Jossey-Bass.

Blunt, P. and Jones, M.L. (1992). *Managing Organizations in Africa*. Berlin: Walter de Gruyter.

Bower, J.L. and Gilbert, C.G. (2007). How managers' everyday decisions create or destroy your company's strategy. *Harvard Business Review* (February), pp. 72–9.

Brinkerhoff, D.W. (1991). *Improving Development Program Performance*. Boulder CO: Lynne Reinner.

———. (1995). Technical cooperation for capacity, building in strategic policy management in developing countries. *American Society for Public Administration*. Section on Internal and Comparative Administration, Occasional Paper Series (September).

Cherunilam, F. (2008). *Strategic Management*. Upper Saddle River, NJ: Prentice Hall.

Courtney, H., Kirkland, J. and Viguerie, P. (1997). Strategy under uncertainty. *Harvard Business Review* (November), pp. 67–79.

Crosby, B.L. (1991). 'Strategic management and strategic planning: What they are and how they are different?'. Technical Note No.1 (Washington DC: US Agency for International Development. Implementing Policy Change Project).

Cullen, J.B. (2008). *International Management: A Strategic Perspective*. Upper Saddle River, NJ: Prentice Hall.

Daft, R.L. and Buenger, V. (1990). Hitching a ride on a fast train to nowhere: The past and future of strategic management research. In J.W. Frederickson (ed.), *Perspectives on Strategic Management*. New York: Harper Business, pp. 81–103.

Davenport, T.H. (2006). Competing on analytics. *Harvard Business Review* (January), pp. 98–107.

Drucker, P.F. (1974). *Management: Tasks, Responsibilities, Practices*. New York: Harper & Row.

Eisenhardt, K.M. and Sull, D.N. (2001). Strategy as simple rules. *Harvard Business Review* (January), pp. 102–16.

Freeman, R.E. and Gilbert, Jr., D.R. (1988). *Corporate Strategy and the Search for Ethics*. Upper Saddle River, NJ: Prentice Hall.

Hamel, G. (1994). Breaking the frame: Strategy as stretch and leverage. In H. Thomas et al. (eds), *Building the Strategically-Responsive Organization*. Chichester: John Wiley & Sons, pp. 45–97.

———. (1996). Strategy as revolution. *Harvard Business Review* (July), pp. 62–77.

Hitt, M., Ireland, D. and Hoskisson, R. (2006). *Strategic Management*. Upper Saddle River, NJ: Prentice Hall.

Ink, D., Klaus, R. and Boynton, P. (1994). *Implementing Policy Change Project: Mid-term Evaluation*. Washington DC: Academy for Educational Development.

Jacobides, M.G. (2010). Strategy tools for a shifting landscape. *Harvard Business Review* (January–February), pp. 76–84.

Johnson, G., Scholes, K. and Whittington, R. (2008). *Exploring Corporate Strategy, Text with Cases*. Upper Saddle River, NJ: Prentice Hall.

Kaplan, R. and Norton, D. (2008). Mastering the management system. *Harvard Business Review* (January), pp. 62–77.

Kaplan, R. and Kaiser, R.B. (2009). Stop overdoing your strengths. *Harvard Business Review* (February), pp. 100–103.

Kim, W.C. and Mauborgne, R. (2009). How strategy shapes structure (a structuralist approach vs. a reconstructionist approach). *Harvard Business Review* (September), pp. 72–80.

Kinsey, J. (1988). *Marketing in Developing Countries*. London: Macmillan.

Mankins, M. and Steele, R. (2005). Turning strategy into great performance. *Harvard Business Review* (July), pp. 65–72.

Martin, R. (2007). How successful leaders think. *Harvard Business Review* (June), pp. 60–67.

Milliken, F.J. and Lant, T.K. (1991). The effect of an organization's recent performance history on strategic persistence and change: The role of managerial interpretation. *Advances in Strategic Management*, 7, pp. 129–55.

Mintzberg, H. (2008). *Tracking Strategies: Towards a General Theory of Strategy Formation*. Oxford: Oxford University Press.

Mintzberg, H., Lampel, J. and Quinn, J. (2007). *The Strategy Process, Concepts, Contexts and Cases*. Upper Saddle River, NJ: Prentice Hall.

Neilson, G., Martin, K. and Powers, E. (2008). The secrets to successful strategy execution. *Harvard Business Review* (June), pp. 60–70.

Orsini, D.M., Courcelle, M. and Brinkerhoff, D.W. (1996). Increasing private sector capacity for policy dialogue: The West African Enterprise Network. *World Development*, 24(9), pp. 1453–66.

Ozgediz, S. (1990). Strategic planning – Concept and issues. In R.O. Echeverria (ed.), *Methods for Diagnosing Research System Constraints and Assessing the Impact of Agricultural Research. 2. Assessing the Impact of Agricultural Research.* The Hague: ISNAR.

Paladino, B. (2010). *Innovative Corporate Performance Management: Five Key Principles to Accelerate Results.* New York: John Wiley & Sons.

Parker, D. and Stacey, R. (1994). *Chaos, Management and Economics: The Implications of Non-linear Thinking.* London: Institute of Economic Affairs.

Peters, T. and Waterman, R. (1982). *In Search of Excellence: Lessons from America's Best Run Companies.* New York: Harper & Row.

Piercy, N. (2002). *Market-led Strategic Change.* Oxford: Butterworth-Heinemann.

Porter, M. (2008). Five competitive strategies that shape strategy. *Harvard Business Review* (January), pp. 23–41.

Simons, R. (2010). Stress-test your strategy. *Harvard Business Review* (November), pp. 92–100.

Stacey, R.D. (1992). *Managing the Unknowable: Strategic Boundaries between Order and Chaos in Organizations.* San Francisco: Jossey-Bass.

Thompson, Jr., A.A. and Strickland III, A.J. (2003). *Strategic Management: Concepts and Cases,* 13th edn. Chicago: Irwin.

Van Wart, M. (1995). The first step in the reinvention process. *Public Administration Review*, 55(5), pp. 429–38.

White, C. (2004). *Strategic Management, Competitiveness and Globalisation: Concepts and Cases.* Upper Saddle River, NJ: Prentice Hall.

Wilson, I. (1994). Strategic planning isn't dead – it changes. *Long-Range Planning*, 27(4), pp. 12–24.

4

Policy Management and National Development

Judy Cavanagh, Kwaku Appiah-Adu and Samuel Aning

Abstract

This chapter begins with an examination of government and public policy followed by the subject of national development and some of its antecedents and consequences. Next, policy management reform as a development strategy is explored. In an effort to understand the policy management concept, the roles of different policy actors, particularly the executive and legislature arms of government, are discussed. To appreciate the policy process in detail, an in-depth analysis of the steps involved in policy conceptualization, analysis, formulation, implementation, monitoring and evaluation as well as feedback into objective setting is undertaken. Examples of the policy cycle are drawn from advanced countries, emerging economies and developing nations to illustrate how robust the system must be for a government to reap the full benefits of effective policy management processes. Finally, the chapter calls on governments and policy makers to commit to the institutionalization of policy as a means to sustainable national development.

Introduction

> Good governance is about harnessing a country's resources to achieve the results any citizen living in the 21st century has a right to expect. One of Africa's biggest leadership and governance challenges going forward is to master its own robust statistical system. Political sovereignty begins with data autonomy.
> (Mo Ibrahim, 2012)

Countries all over the world are investing in the improvement of policy capacity within their public service. Ghana has made the same investment. As the country's democratic process continues to evolve, it is important that efforts are made to continuously strengthen the government's decision-making apparatus.

Every organization has processes for doing what it should do, whether these are formally documented or not. The processes and the people who manage them are fundamental building blocks leading to the establishment of a formal, coherent, consistent policy management and decision-making system. This involves political and bureaucratic leadership exercising rigour and discipline in all stages of policy development and implementation.

From 2003 to 2009, as part of the overall public sector reforms, Ghana engaged in a massive undertaking to articulate its executive decision-making system, with subsequent training and support to civil servants to implement it. The scope was broad and included the participation of the Office of the President, the Cabinet Secretariat, the Office of the Head of the Civil Service and the Ministries, Departments and Agencies.

This chapter proposes to illustrate how the 'Ghana Central Governance Project' and its successors increased the knowledge and skills within the civil service to develop and manage a robust public policy process. It suggests that good policies and implementation equal good governance, which equals good national development.

Governance and Public Policy

Being wealthy does not ensure high-quality governance, just as being an emerging or developing economy does not automatically translate to poor governance.

The complexity of governance is difficult to capture in a single definition. There are many elements and indicators that are involved to determine if a country has 'good' governance. Most rest on three dimensions: authority, decision making and accountability. The Institute on Governance provides a working definition:

> Governance determines who has power, who makes decisions, how other players make their voices heard and how account is rendered. (Institute on Governance, 2011)

Governance takes into account legal and constitutional accountability, responsibilities and needs to reflect cultural traditions and norms. The Worldwide Governance Indicators project defines governance as:

> Governance consists of the traditions and institutions by which authority in a country is exercised. This includes the process by which governments are selected, monitored and replaced; the capacity of the government to effectively formulate and implement sound policies; and the respect of citizens and the state for institutions that govern economic and social interactions among them. (Institute on Governance, 2011)

The establishment of a formal, coherent, consistent policy management and decision-making system is a vital component of governance for the implementation of sound policies that are in the best interests of the country and its citizens.

Public policy is a statement of goals and a means of achieving these goals that affect the lives of people with regard to their values, what is desirable and what is feasible based on good judgement and intuition supported by evidence and analysis. The decision must be generally accepted by society with the conviction that it would make life better. Public policy is used to address community wants and needs. It ensures the provision of goods and services, for example, education, health and infrastructure. More elaborate definitions of policy have been provided in the literature pertaining to public policy as follows.

According to a review by Milton Yinger (1980), in William Jenkins' *Policy Analysis: A Political and Organizational Perspective* (1978), a policy is 'a set of interrelated decisions taken by a political actor or group of actors concerning the selection of goals and the means of achieving them within a specified situation where those decisions should, in principle, be within the power of those actors to achieve'. Thus, Jenkins understands policy making to be a process and not simply a choice.

In his book entitled *An Introduction to the Policy Process* (2001), Thomas Birkland contends that there is a lack of a consensus on the definition of policy. He outlines a few definitions of policy:

- 'The term public policy always refers to the actions of government and the intentions that determine those actions' (Cochran et al., 2008).
- 'Public policy is the outcome of the struggle in government over who gets what' (Cochran et al., 2008).
- Public policy is 'Whatever governments choose to do or not do' (Dye, 2007).
- 'Public policy consists of political decisions for implementing programs to achieve societal goals' (Cochran and Malone, 2005).
- 'Stated most simply, public policy is the sum of government activities, whether acting directly or through agents, as it has an influence on the life of citizens' (Peters, 2001).

The policy process involves gathering information, developing the idea and testing available options, proving advice through consultation and making the decision, which is usually political (Hayes, 2007). A good policy must be practical, in the interest of the public, well communicated and effectively implemented because a well-developed policy can fail if it is not properly put into practice (Thatcher and Evia, 2008).

Ghana's Governance Trends

Ghana is making good progress towards its goal of becoming a middle-income country by 2020. It has had five consecutive democratic elections and two peaceful transitions of power since 1992. With economic growth rates consistently topping 6 percent over recent years, Ghana has nearly halved the number of its citizens living in extreme poverty (Foreign Affairs, Trade & Development Canada, 2015).

Ghana registers in the top tier of African countries when it comes to the quality of governance. The Mo Ibrahim Foundation produces a government quality index to measure statistically and to be able to compare increases or declines in African countries' governance year on year. It assesses national governance against 57 criteria, capturing the quality of services provided to citizens. The focus is on the results that the people of a country experience rather than state policies and intentions. There are four overarching categories defined as the cornerstone of a government's obligations to its citizens:

- Safety and Rule of Law;
- Participation and Human Rights;
- Sustainable Economic Opportunity;
- Human Development.

The sixth Ibrahim Index of African Governance (2012) ranked Ghana seventh overall out of 52 countries. Ghana ranked second out of 16 countries in West Africa. It received its highest score in the Safety and Rule of Law category and its lowest score in the Sustainable Economic Opportunity category. In the past decade, Ghana's overall governance scores continue to improve (Mo Ibrahim Foundation, 2012: 2).

The World Bank's Worldwide Governance survey (World Bank Survey, 1996–2012) comprises aggregate scores from six indicators:

- Voice and Accountability: the extent to which a country's citizens are able to participate in selecting their government, as well as freedom of expression, association and a free media.

- Political Stability and Absence of Violence: the likelihood that the government will be destabilized or overthrown by unconstitutional or violent means, including politically motivated violence and terrorism.
- Government Effectiveness: the quality of public services and the civil service and the degree of independence from political pressures, and the quality of policy formulation and implementation and the credibility of government's commitment to such policies.
- Regulatory Quality: the ability of the government to formulate and implement sound policies and regulations that permit and promote private sector development.
- Rule of Law: the extent to which agents have confidence in and abide by the rules of society, and in particular the quality of contract enforcement, property rights, the police and the courts, as well as the likelihood of crime and violence.
- Control of Corruption: capturing perceptions of the extent to which public power is exercised for private gain, including both petty and grand forms of corruption, as well as 'the control' of the state by elites and private interests.

The Worldwide Governance Indicators, Country Data Report for Ghana, 1996–2011 (see Table 4.1) shows substantial improvements in governance, even if at times starting from very low levels. Percentile ranks indicate the percentage of countries worldwide that rank lower than Ghana, so that higher values indicate better governance scores.

Table 4.1   Worldwide Governance Indicators

Worldwide Governance Indicators	1996 Percentile	2011 Percentile
Voice and Accountability	40	64
Political Stability and Absence of Violence	36	51
Government Effectiveness	53	52
Regulatory Quality	38	57
Rule of Law	40	55
Control of Corruption	50	55

National Development

In many developing countries, the main thrust of national development is to transform the economy for enhanced growth and job creation in order to support the delivery of social services to the people of that country, regardless of their geographical location or social and economic circumstances.

Many countries achieve this through accelerated human resource development, agricultural modernization, value-added processing of natural resource endowments and leveraging the multi-sector infrastructure platform. The development of a national plan usually takes into consideration historical economic and social challenges that have impeded development. National development strategies often include regional integration aimed at promoting regional trade including investments in energy and other forms of infrastructure, harmonization of trade and investment regulations and policies, removal of non-tariff barriers and trade facilitation with a view to expanding the markets for the country's goods and services.

Since Ghana attained independence in 1957, all governments have pursued, with varying degrees of success, several policies and programmes to accelerate economic growth and raise the living standards of the people. With the return to constitutional rule in 1992, successive governments have provided policy frameworks and development plans to guide the overall economic and social development in line with the provisions of the country's constitution.

Policy Management Reform as a Development Strategy

Policy management reform as a systematic approach to addressing one dimension of poor governance emerged in the late 1990s. Similar reforms are modest in number both in Africa and internationally. These reforms are successful only if the Office of the President and Cabinet Offices are fully engaged. Previously, donors generally avoided technical assistance programmes in these offices, probably on the premise of them being 'too political'. Typically, developing countries were offered a broad menu of governance interventions, including civil service reform, functional reviews and cross-cutting policy reforms (e.g. poverty reduction, national development planning), but only rarely did donors fund management initiative taking into account the policy and decision-making processes at the heart of government (Manning, 1999).

There is a link between governance and the policy environment on the one hand, and national development strategies and effective use of policies on the other. Policies can facilitate or hinder the ability of individuals and organizations to perform – and can ensure or prevent the delivery of public services. National development is a fine balance between economic growth policies and human development policies. It must take into consideration cultural relevance, accountability, transparency, laws and policies that guide decision making and strong administrative systems.

It is for this reason that the Ghana Central Governance Project (along with its successors) was initiated in 2003. This reform was essential given that the government's ambitious policy agenda depended, to a significant degree, on the ability of the system to move coherently and effectively from policy strategy to detailed policy options, to budgeted programmes and to concrete results. It required a skilled civil service steeped in policy analysis and development to realize this agenda.

Policy Management: The Roles

The late Dr Bingu wa Mutharika, former President of the Republic of Malawi stated in the Foreword to the draft 'Guide to Executive Decision-Making Processes (2009)' that the credibility of every government is measured by its commitment and ability to deliver on its policies. The reason for developing a guide was to ensure that there was a systematic approach to procedures that govern all policy and decision-making processes of the government. The civil service has the duty to serve the ideals of the government in meeting the aspirations of its citizens by supporting the government's policy agenda. President Bingu wa Mutharika captured the roles of the main 'actors' in the process. He stated that it is the role of the executive (including Cabinet ministers) to make and champion government policies and to provide an institutional mechanism for prioritizing and implementing the policies. Parliament makes national laws that give the policies legal authority, while the judiciary interprets and enforces the law. It is, however, important to note that not all policies require legislation. The interface of all the branches in policy management helps to ensure that the implementation of policies is to the benefit of the general public.

He further elaborated on the roles in the system – ministers, as part of the executive, are accountable for achieving results; principal secretaries (administrative heads of the sector ministries) and staff in the ministries need to understand the process of executive decision making and adhere to its procedures, including robust development of documents for executive consideration, in order to promote the development of sound policies that benefit citizens.

In addition to the above, it must be noted that there are other players/stakeholders in the policy development process. In Africa, these are traditional rulers and chieftaincy institutions, civil society, leading academics, 'think tanks' and international development partners. Depending on the issue being discussed, consultation strategies need to be implemented with the appropriate stakeholders.

Policy Management: The Steps

For the purposes of this chapter, five steps are identified in the policy development and management process (Institute of Public Administration of Canada, 2011). At all steps, coordination across government ministries, departments and agencies (MDAs) is vital. In most developed countries, management of the policy process rests within a department in the Office of the President/Prime Minister. It is often referred to as 'the centre' or as a 'central management agency' and, in addition to its policy management functions, it works with the civil service to ensure that the President's/Prime Minister's national priorities are effectively reflected in government policies, programmes and budgets and monitors implementation by MDAs. Its work is reported through a chief of staff/clerk to the Privy Council to the President/ Prime Minister and the Cabinet.

The five steps are interactive with each other and continuous. They are as follows:

1. Agenda Setting – policy planning exercise at the political level with administrative support. It is important that the priority setting is performed on an annual basis and takes into consideration outcomes from planning processes.
2. Policy Formulation – this includes identifying the issue, how one understands and how one defines a problem. It is critical to properly diagnose the issue; research includes evidence-based facts, statistics, knowledge of economics and relevant social science, internet searches, etc.; consultation needs to occur early in the process as it is critical in informing solutions that work and builds acceptance for the outcome; developing options, with impact analysis, for executive consideration supports decision makers in reaching informed decisions. Typically, this work is captured in a document known as a Cabinet Memorandum.
3. Decision Making – this rests with the President and the executive. A well-presented document that is prepared by the administration and outlines options, analysis and recommendations informs decision making.
4. Implementation and Communications – administration develops and implements the policies. An implementation plan focuses on achieving results and outlines the activities, roles and responsibilities, timelines, human and financial resources. A communications plan outlines who will say what to the public and how it will be conveyed. It requires being aware of the political and wider context and anticipating various responses.
5. Monitoring and Evaluation – performance indicators are in the implementation plan. Monitoring and evaluation ensures that policy decisions are acted upon and coordinated, and assesses what worked and what did not. It is carried out at various stages of implementation in order to make changes if there are problems. Typically the monitoring oversees that the implementation is on course and the evaluation assesses the outcomes and impacts in relation to the objectives and intended outcomes.

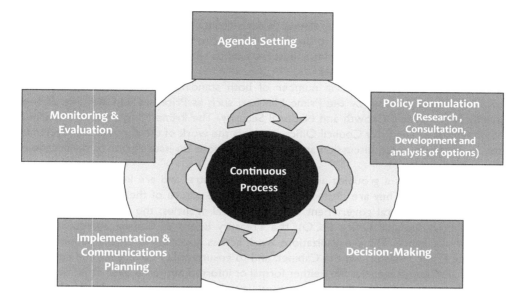

Figure 4.1   Continuous Process Chart

National Development and Policy Management

Many nations provide strong examples of the link between national development and strong policy management. For the purposes of this chapter, the following countries are cited: Canada, Malaysia, and Singapore. These countries were selected because the authors of this chapter have had first-hand experience within their central government agencies, interacting with both senior and middle-level staff at the centre of government during work careers, study and work tours. Subsequently, lessons drawn from their experiences in these countries were applied within the context of a developing economy, that is, Ghana.

CANADA

On 1 July 1867, the Dominion of Canada started a process of increasing autonomy from the British Empire that was completed in the Canada Act of 1982. Canada remains a constitutional monarchy with allegiance to the Queen of England. It is the second-largest landmass after Russia and has the world's longest border, with the USA. It has a small population of approximately 34 million people residing in 10 provinces and three territories. It is governed as a parliamentary democracy and a constitutional monarchy with Queen Elizabeth II as its head of state.

For the First and Second World Wars, the Canadian government had 'war cabinets' that were provided with secretarial support. It was not until 1940 that a more formalized process was put in place to support the Prime Minister and Cabinet ministers, and to this day, its imprint on shaping the present-day machinery of government is evident (Savoie, 2004: 24–30).

The Cabinet is the body of advisors for the Prime Minister that sets the federal government's policies and priorities for the country. The Cabinet system performs several functions such as securing agreement among ministers on government priorities and parliamentary actions by the government, providing a forum for ministerial debate on issues of general interest as well as giving adequate information to ministers in relation to decisions for which they will be held responsible and providing adequate information to the Prime Minister to carry out his or her responsibilities and leadership role. The Cabinet holds annual retreats to set government priorities from which policies and the budget are developed.

The Cabinet system includes a number of both standing and ad hoc committees. The types of committees are set by the Prime Minister, such as Priorities and Planning, Economic Prosperity & Sustainable Growth and National Security. The Prime Minister appoints ministers to the committees. The Privy Council Office supports the work of the committees. Committees are the forum for in-depth discussion and recommendations on issues prior to deliberations by the Cabinet.

Central agencies as a grouping are known as the 'centre' and are key actors in the policy management process. They are distinct as a result of the nature of their central coordinating/directive role. The federal government has four central agencies: the Prime Minister's Office (PMO), the Privy Council Office (PCO), the Treasury Board of Canada Secretariat and the Department of Finance. These organizations work across government departments to provide advice to the Prime Minister and the Cabinet, and to ensure policy coherence and coordination on their behalf. Central agencies have either formal or informal authority over other departments and often direct their actions. Line departments, on the other hand, provide services directly to Canadians and do not have the authority or mandate to direct other departments in their operations (Savoie, 2004).

The PMO serves the political interests of the Prime Minister and is staffed by partisan loyalists who serve at the pleasure of the Prime Minister. The size and structure of the PMO reflects the needs of the Prime Minister. Generally the PMO assists the Prime Minister by providing advice on priorities, the political implications of policy initiatives, and political strategy and tactics. It can plan and coordinate new policy initiatives of interest to the Prime Minister and monitor emerging issues. It also organizes the Prime Minister's time, manages communications, including preparations for Question Period in the House of Commons, and liaises with ministers, caucus members and the political party machinery across the country. Staff complements have varied from 40 to 200 over the years (Smith, 2009).

The PCO reports directly to the Prime Minister. Unlike the PMO, public servants who offer non-partisan but politically sensitive service and advice staff the PCO. The Clerk to the Privy Council and Secretary to the Cabinet heads the PCO. The Clerk is the head of the public service and is appointed by the Prime Minister. Staff complements also vary and in 2009 had close to the equivalent of 1,000 full-time employees. The PCO has three main roles: (1) to provide non-partisan advice to the Prime Ministerand ministers who functions lie within the Prime Minister's portfolio; (2) to support the Cabinet decision-making processes; and (3) to act as the principal link between the Prime Minister and the public service.

The deputy ministers (chief directors/principal secretaries) report to the Clerk of the Privy Council. It is through them that the expectations of a disciplined decision-making system are maintained and accountability for results of government priorities is realized. It is also the deputy ministers' expectation that the Clerk to the Privy Council keeps them informed of Cabinet decisions and overall government strategic direction and priorities.

The Treasury Board, established in 1867, is a Cabinet committee responsible for accountability and ethics, financial, personnel and administrative management, comptrollership and approving regulations and most Orders-in-Council. The Treasury Board Secretariat (TBS) is the administrative arm of the Treasury Board. Its role is to ensure continuous improvement in managing government resources to meet its objectives. It oversees resource planning and expenditure management by making recommendations on the allocation of funding for programme expenditures in light of government priorities, fiscal targets and results achieved.

It also develops and maintains accountability frameworks within which Parliament approves resources and departments report on their use. In addition, it had a mandate to provide leadership for government-wide initiatives for improving services to Canadians. It is responsible for traditional comptrollership functions such as financial, contract, accounting and programme evaluation. It provides leadership in embedding results-oriented performance management principles and values in departments and agencies. And finally, it provides leadership, coordination and broad direction in the use of information technology (IT) across government. It focuses on three areas: infrastructure, service to the IT community and innovation.

The Department of Finance assists the minister in developing the government's financial fiscal framework in which overall spending takes place and advises the minister on fiscal policy, taxation policy, industrial policy, development policy and trade agreements. It provides annual forecasts of the growth rate of the economy. These forecasts guide the department when it predicts the government's revenues, expenditures and debt requirements for the coming years. It also examines the potential effects of proposed government policies on the economy. The department does not have the same coordinating role as other central agencies, but it has considerable authority through its role in developing the budget. It is involved in almost all policy decisions, because the allocation of funds from the fiscal framework is almost always required in order to proceed with a policy initiative (Smith, 2009).

Canada integrates strategic planning with the Cabinet decision-making system, the budget process and results-based management. A well-established process has penetrated the system and is coordinated by the Privy Council Office. Guidelines are published on developing policy and financial requests – the rigour in analysis, steps taken for review by senior officials and Cabinet committees and ultimately Cabinet decision-making and implementation. Standardized formats, guidelines and other tools are provided to civil servants.

Central Agencies are engaged at the start of policy development. Early drafts of Memorandums to Cabinet (MCs) are shared with the appropriate PCO, Department of Finance and TBS analysts. This helps to ensure that the proposal is aligned with the government's overall agenda and to identify any policy, fiscal and implementation issues that should be addressed before the document is submitted. Drafters of MCs are also responsible for ensuring that other affected departments and agencies are adequately consulted in advance about upcoming proposals and that coordination across portfolios is pursued. These consultations ensure that cross-cutting issues are recognized and properly addressed in proposals, and that other ministers are prepared for Cabinet discussion. The Clerk's meetings with deputy ministers also provide an opportunity to review high-priority policy issues in advance of their consideration by the Cabinet.

Once MCs have addressed, as appropriate, the input received through central agency and departmental consultations, and have been reviewed by senior departmental officials, they are submitted to the sponsoring minister for approval and signature before being submitted to the PCO. The documents are reviewed by the appropriate central agency and then by a Cabinet committee. After the Cabinet committee deliberations, a Committee Recommendation (CR) is prepared as to what decisions should be taken by the Cabinet or by a committee that has been delegated the ability to ratify or approve the other committee's recommendations. The CR is submitted to the Cabinet for its consideration. The Cabinet issues a Record of Decision (RD). CRs and RDs are circulated by the PCO to all ministers and deputy ministers. It may be necessary, following a Cabinet decision, to obtain a source of funds or to obtain Treasury Board approval prior to implementation. All announcements are coordinated with the PMO and the PCO.

Evaluation is the systematic collection and analysis of evidence on the outcomes of programmes to make judgements about their relevance and performance and to examine alternative ways to deliver them or to achieve the same results. The Centre of Excellence for Evaluation (CEE) in the TBS provides functional leadership, including advice and guidance in the conduct, use and advancement of evaluation practices across the federal government. Federal department and agency deputy heads lead and support policy and programme improvement, expenditure management, proposals to the Cabinet, public reporting and lead evaluation.

Government accountability also takes place during the annual reporting cycle for government expenditure that establishes events leading up to the tabling of various documents and processes in Parliament relating to the government's budget and expenditure plans. Reports submitted, such as the *Public Accounts of Canada*, which are the audited financial statements for the recently completed fiscal year, and the *Departmental Performance Reports*, which provide organizational detail on results and performance from the recently completed fiscal year, are ways for Parliament and the public to keep the government accountable. An *Economic Fiscal Update* that updates information outlined in the budget is prepared about six months after the budget was tabled. The last document to be tabled each year is the departmental *Report on Plans and Priorities*, a forward-looking document prepared by each department and agency (excluding Crown corporations). It outlines an organization's plans and priorities for the coming fiscal year and the next two years.

No system stays the same. Each system adjusts to the leadership style of the Prime Minister, but the underpinnings of the Cabinet decision-making system stay the same. The PCO coordinates the Cabinet decision-making process. The desire is to have the review of documents and issues addressed in advance of Cabinet meetings so that ministers can spend their time on priority issues and deal with strategic interventions. The bureaucracy usually 'grumbles' about the centre and its rules and processes, in particular perceived interference and timelines. However, one could argue that having a system in place for over 70 years has resulted in Canada being a country of relatively stable economic and social strength. One example is Canada's ability to endure the global fiscal crisis that still grips the world while maintaining its social safety net.

SINGAPORE

The Republic of Singapore is a South-East Asian city-state off the southern tip of the Malay Peninsula. An island country made up of 63 islands, it is separated from Malaysia by the Straits of Johor to its north and from Indonesia's Riau Islands by the Singapore Strait to its south. The British obtained sovereignty over the island in 1824 and Singapore became one of the British Straits Settlements in 1826. Occupied by the Japanese during the Second World War, Singapore declared independence, uniting with other former British territories to form Malaysia in 1963, although it was separated from Malaysia two years later. Since then, it has experienced a massive increase in wealth and is one of the Four Asian Tigers. It is the world's fourth-biggest financial centre and its port is one of the five busiest in the world. Its economy depends heavily on exports and refining imported goods, especially in manufacturing, which constituted 26 percent of its GDP in 2005.

Singapore is a unitary multi-party parliamentary republic with a Westminster system of unicameral parliamentary government. The People's Action Party has won every election since self-government in 1959 and governs on the basis of a strong state and prioritizing collective welfare over individual rights such as freedom of speech. In terms of purchasing power parity, Singapore has the third highest per capita income in the world. There are slightly over five million people in Singapore, of which 2.91 million were born locally (2010). The population is highly diverse; the majority are Chinese, with Malays and Indians forming significant minorities. Reflecting this diversity, the country has four official languages: English, Chinese, Malay and Tamil. One of the five founding members of the Association of Southeast Asian Nations (ASEAN), the country is also the host of the Asia-Pacific Economic Cooperation (APEC) Secretariat and is a member of the East Asia Summit, the Non-Aligned Movement and the Commonwealth.

In Singapore, most if not all policies are developed by the Cabinet, which is the highest policy formulating body of the government. The Cabinet provides overall direction and management of the government and has collective responsibility to Parliament. Ministers have civil servants who advise and assist them in policy development. When a minister or the Cabinet crafts a policy at the political level, the responsibility of the civil servant is to provide required information, advice and past experience to the Cabinet, and this is subsequently assessed prior to recommending a suitable policy. Regarding policy making, the Prime Minister is the prime mover and holds sway in terms of policy development.

In the exceptional circumstances where policies are not formed at the Cabinet level, they may result from the initiative of public servants. In this case public servants identify the issues and make recommendations to the Cabinet. However, generally, public servants tend to be an apolitical group of technocrats who provide professional advice on effective policy formulation and implementation. One other group that participates in the policy process is the middle class – directly via their appointments to statutory boards and advisory committees and indirectly via their involvement in professional and business organizations.

When a policy is developed, the next stage is implementation. The issues requiring consideration are as follows: the identification of implementing agencies; the allocation of responsibilities and resources among the different implementing agencies; and the monitoring of tasks to ensure that implementation is carried out. Unlike many emerging economies that face hurdles to effective policy implementation owing to lack of resources and political will, Singapore's public sector facilitates the effective implementation of public policy.

The reasons given for Singapore's sound policy implementation are as follows: political leadership; political leaders' commitment to and support for the policies developed by providing the necessary human capital, legislation, funding and equipment to the relevant implementing agencies; a meritocracy that ensures that the institutions are sound and equipped with qualified and competent personnel; and a low level of corruption in the public service.

Additional factors believed to account for the effective implementation of Singapore's public policies are: regular national campaigns by political administration as a channel of policy implementation and agent of attitudinal and behavioural change amongst Singapore's nationals; the social discipline of Singaporeans, where citizens adhere to policies formulated by democratically elected government with the aim of achieving national goals; and, finally, Singapore's small size advantage, which reduces logistical and communication challenges faced by larger countries and facilitates relatively successful policy implementation.

The last component of the policy management process is evaluation. Policy evaluation can be difficult to undertake because there are several challenges associated with such evaluation exercises. However, Singapore has been highly successful at policy evaluation through the application of an integrated performance strategy. The government has focused on achieving strategic results through a whole-of-government balanced scorecard, which is a strategic tool used by public agencies to develop and execute strategies associated with the formulated policies. The approach clearly defines strategies for achieving results through work processes and careful management of two key resources, namely, people and finance. Monitoring and evaluation is conducted via a scorecard that has performance indicators and enables agencies to carry out continuous monitoring and evaluation. This whole-of-government scorecard has helped Singapore to manage its resources better, foster a greater sense of community and identity as a nation, make its homeland more secure and continually provide better opportunities for its citizens.

MALAYSIA

Malaysia is a federal constitutional monarchy in South-East Asia. It consists of 13 states and three federal territories. Land borders are shared with Thailand, Indonesia and Brunei, and maritime borders exist with Singapore, Vietnam, and the Philippines. The capital city is Kuala Lumpur, while Putrajaya is the seat of the federal government. In 2010 the population was 28.33 million. Malaysia has its origins in the Malay Kingdoms, which, from the eighteenth century, became subject to the British Empire. Malaysia achieved independence on 31 August 1957. Since independence, it has had one of the best economic records in Asia, with GDP growing an average of 6.5 percent for almost 50 years. The economy has traditionally been fuelled by its natural resources, but is expanding in the sectors of science, tourism, commerce and medical tourism.

The country is multi-ethnic and multi-cultural, which plays a large role in politics. The government system is closely modelled on the Westminster parliamentary system and the legal system is based on English common law. The Constitution declares Islam to be the state religion while protecting freedom of religion. The head of state is the King, Yang di-Pertuan Agong. He is an elected monarch chosen from the hereditary rulers of the nine Malay states every five years. The head of government is the Prime Minister. Malaysia contains the southernmost point of continental Eurasia, Tanjung Piai. Located in the tropics, it is a diverse country with large numbers of endemic animals, fungi and plants. It is a founding member of the ASEAN and the Organisation of Islamic Cooperation, and is a member of Asia-Pacific Economic Cooperation, the Commonwealth of Nations and the Non-Aligned Movement.

In Malaysia, development planning (policy management) is a purposeful, thorough, time-bound endeavour instigated and supported by central government with the aim of generating and upholding situations that will speed up socio-economic advancement in the nation within the remit of the Economic Planning Unit (EPU) of the Prime Minister's office.

The history of national development in Malaysia can be traced back to the country's first Five-Year Development Plan, which was instituted in 1955. Since then, nine development plans have been implemented, each with objectives consistent with the changing requirements of the Malaysian socio-political and economic situation. Development goals in the 1950s focused on the transformation of the traditional industries. In the 1960s, the focus moved to improvements in infrastructure and agriculture. Until then, social services and the development of infrastructural network constituted the major primary pillars of the socio-economic advancement programme following the attainment of independence from British rule.

Malaysia's policy management (development programme) system comprises planning, implementation and evaluation. The Economic Planning Unit (and other central agencies) is the fulcrum on which the planning (policy planning) responsibility hinges, whereas the Implementation Coordination Unit (and its appropriate staff agencies) plays a similar role with respect to implementation. These two bodies are amalgamated at different stages during the course of planning (policy planning). For instance, inter-agency planning groups are formed to handle identifiable sector issues associated with the development of the plan. The inter-agency planning groups are part of the policy network serviced by the Economic Planning Unit, while the Implementation Coordination Unit is one of the working members.

In Malaysia, policy management (development planning) comprises both fiscal and monetary incentives and solicits significant private sector input, particularly in the financial, industrial and trading sectors. Public sector participation is largely linked to the improvement of infrastructure, agriculture, health, education, public housing and manufacturing. The public sector encapsulates the government at the federal, state and local levels as well as statutory bodies. In order to successfully implement its development policies, the government uses the Outline Perspective Plan (OPP), Five-Year Plans and the Annual Operating Plan.

A strong focus is placed on policy monitoring so that government policies are invariably consistent with the objectives and strategies of Malaysia's development plan. As a result, the government can detect and deal with any problems in the implementation of the policy.

For policy implementation, all Malaysian government agencies comply with the Prime Minister's directive to ensure that development projects are implemented in tandem at all levels. The National Development Council, chaired by the Prime Minister, is established at the federal level. The Minister of Finance and other ministers responsible for development are members of this council. This council is assisted by a working committee known as the National Development Working Committee, chaired by the chief secretary to the government. The main purpose of this committee is to ensure that all decisions made by the National Development Council are carried out efficiently and effectively, and to monitor the implementation of development policies so that they are executed in conformity with the goals of the national development plan.

Minutes of the Ministerial Development Committee, chaired by the secretary-general, and constituting ministries' departmental heads are presented to the Implementation Coordination Unit for monitoring and evaluation. A working committee known as the State Development Working Committee, which is chaired by the state secretary, supports the State Development Council, chaired by the chief minister of a specific state and members consisting of state departmental heads. At the district level, the District Development Committee chaired by the district officer with members consisting of departmental heads at the district has been set up.

At the national level, the development council meets biannually, whereas the Working Committee and the committee at the ministry level meet monthly. The State Development Council meets quarterly, whilst the State Development Working Committee and the District Development Committee meet monthly. The Secretary of the National Development Council is the Director General of the Implementation Coordination Unit, whilst the secretariat for the National Development Working Committee, the State Development Council and the State Development Working Committee are all officers reporting directly to the director general of the Implementation Coordination Unit. The director general reports to the Prime Minister.

Impact evaluation concludes the policy planning process, while monitoring of policies at the implementation level only takes into account factors regarding activities associated with the policies. Impact evaluation assesses both external and internal dynamics. While factors influencing policy implementation can be worked out during the course of monitoring, impact evaluations facilitate the analysis of project effectiveness as regards policies and strategies. The outcomes of impact evaluation are utilized in terms of providing inputs to the planning process. The corresponding ministries and agencies carry out impact evaluation at the programme/project level. At the macro level, the Implementation Coordination Unit examines impact evaluation. It also oversees the coordination of development policies, programmes and projects at the federal level, and provides feedback to the planning process.

The Implementation Coordination Unit of the Prime Minister's department is responsible for overall policy monitoring and has constructed different monitoring systems to meet different plan conditions. The monitoring of development policies usually entails regular gathering and examination of physical and economic data. The process can be segregated according to different categories of organization/management, specifically what is needed by implementers to manage the daily execution of policy-related projects and what is needed by central agencies for national monitoring and evaluation.

Evaluating policy implementation is vital in detecting the reasons for the variances between predicted and achieved results. Consequently, an effective monitoring system makes it possible for institutions to determine challenges in implementation and the causes of any differences between predicted and achieved results to and ensure that these findings are systematically presented to executives with suitable recommendations.

A robust and comprehensive policy planning and implementation process is inextricably linked to national development programmes in Malaysia. Execution of the plan is reinforced by sound implementation systems and ensuing policy planning practices make use of feedback from impact assessment at the macro and micro stages. Malaysia's example highlights the role of the planning, implementation and evaluation cycle, which, combined with the vision of the country's leaders, has been critical in ensuring that development gains trickle down to all in the nation.

Developing Public Policy Capacity: Ghana

The Ghana Central Governance Project (GCGP) 2003–9 was part of the overall public sector reform to improve central government policy decision-making systems. It achieved this goal through a wide-ranging set of reforms in the areas of policy management, human resources management and management information systems. Gender equality was a cross-cutting theme.

When the project started, there was considerable enthusiasm within government as a new political party had taken over the reins of government. As with all new administrations, these were exciting times for the new government as it laid out its vision and development agenda. It needed strong political leadership and a civil service to implement its agenda and to enable Ghana to recapture its lost glory of running one of the most efficient and vibrant civil services in the world. The incoming President was sworn into office in January 2001. With the decision to pursue a Highly Indebted Poor Country (HIPC) status and the development of the Ghana Poverty Reduction Strategy (GPRS), the new government refocused its agenda on five medium-term priority areas:

- infrastructure development;
- modernized agriculture centred on rural development;
- enhanced social services, with a special emphasis on education and health;
- good governance;
- private sector development.

The new government had no prior experience in governing. While many ministers had considerable private sector management experience, most had little or no prior experience in the public sector, much less of policy development and management and its need for national development.

Capacity for strategic planning generally, and for public sector reform, was limited. MDAs suffered from a shortage of skilled workers, but, institutionally, emphasis was placed (when it was placed) on research and statistics, not policy development and analysis. Consultants, funded by donors, did the majority of policy development work. There were little or no links (other than with the Cabinet Secretariat) to the Office of the President.

The government also inherited a large number of public sector reform initiatives that fell under the umbrella of the Public Sector Reform Programme and were coordinated through the National Institutional Renewal Programme. Many argued that the public sector reforms were constrained by complex processes and management capability within the Government of Ghana (GoG) to oversee complex processes of technical and institutional change.

The GCGP was a bilateral project between the GoG and the Canadian government funded by the Canadian International Development Agency (CIDA). It was managed by the Institute of Public

Administration of Canada (IPAC) and BearingPoint LLG in collaboration with the GoG. The main goal of the project was to enhance the government's policy management and decision-making processes in the Office of the President, the Cabinet Secretariat and the MDAs.

There were a number of important, specifically Ghanaian, achievements throughout the project – for example, the policy training modules that were developed in partnership with the University of Ghana Business School and ultimately delivered by the Civil Service Training Centre, the Cabinet Memorandum Manual and supporting training for developing memoranda, a Transition Planning Guide processes and templates used by the civil service in 2008 and a Management Information System (MIS) to support policy development, email and communications within and with the Office of the President.

The project was aimed at providing mechanisms for ensuring the optimal delivery of the President's and government's priorities by formalizing the decision-making process. It improved the support at both the political and administrative levels by Central Management Agencies (CMAs), and stronger policy coordination between the Office of the President, CMAs and MDAs.

Partners and beneficiaries included the CMAs with oversight responsibilities such as the Office of the President, Cabinet Secretariat, the Office of the Head of Civil Service and the National Development Planning Commission and Finance. MDAs were also partners and beneficiaries.

Building Policy Capacity in the Ghana Civil Service, 2003–9

In the World Development Report 1997, capacity building in the public sector needed to address the three dimensions of human capacity, organizational capacity and institutional capacity. The report further defined these three dimensions of capacity as follows:

> *Human capacity: individuals with skills to analyse development needs; design and implement strategies, policies and programs, deliver services and monitor results.*

> *Organizational capacity: groups of individuals bound by a common purpose, with clear objectives and the internal structures, processes, systems, staffing, and other resources to achieve them.*

> *Institutional capacity: the formal 'rules of the game' and informal norms – for example, in collecting taxes, reporting on the use of public resources, or regulating private business – that provide the framework of goals and incentives within which organizations and people operate.*

Through work teams, seminars, training, study visits, application of tools and the development of products, the GCGP succeeded in building capacity in terms of policy development and management. The project design drew on the strengths and resources of all partners. There was a Project Management Committee that provided oversight and direction. It was made up of the Chief of Staff, the Head of the Civil Service (OHCS), the Cabinet Secretary, the Director of International Development, CIDA, the Head of the Policy, Coordination, Monitoring and Evaluation Unit (PCMEU), the Special Advisor to the President, the Canadian Project Director and the IPAC Project Director. Daily implementation was the responsibility of the Coordination Team, co-led by the Ghanaian and Canadian Project Directors. It also included the Head of the PCMEU, an OHCS Director and the GCGP Policy Analyst. The Coordination Team met weekly to review progress of activities and assign responsibilities.

The Head of the Civil Service and the interest and support of chief directors provided the necessary leadership for staff involvement. The chief directors also participated in seminars, workshops and study visits, and provided feedback on the products and implemented various aspects such as the performance management system and transition planning. Ghanaian work teams participated in the creation and delivery of products for policy, human resources/training and MIS. All the work teams were inter-ministerial and the officials selected were considered subject matter experts. These teams contributed significantly to the sustainability of the products and learning. Hundreds of civil servants participated in seminars and training.

Policy Development and Management Capacity Building: Highlights

Using work teams, seminars, training, study visits, the application of tools and product development resulted in engaged civil servants who acquired the knowledge and skills in policy development and management. They gained a better understanding of the need for discipline and rigour in the system in order to advance the goals for national development.

Product Development

A FRAMEWORK FOR GHANA'S POLICY MANAGEMENT

At the outset of the project, 'A Framework for Ghana's Policy Management and Decision Making System' was developed. The need for the Framework was identified by the Office of the President as a blueprint for a coherent policy management and decision-making system from which other incremental process improvements could be derived or anchored. The Framework was meant to accelerate efficiency in Ghana's policy management and accountability process, and ultimately its governance.

CABINET MEMORANDUM MANUAL

One of the significant successes was the adoption by Cabinet of the Cabinet Memoranda Manual (CMM) as the guide for the development of Cabinet Memoranda and public policy. Prior to the institutionalization of the use of the CMM, there were huge differences in the quality of Cabinet Memoranda submitted to the Cabinet for its consideration.

The CMM set out detailed standards and requirements for preparing documents for consideration by the Cabinet and Cabinet Committees. It laid out the process for submitting and reviewing proposals from MDAs. The CMM required the assessment of the economic, social, technological, cultural and demographic impacts of the policy, all of which were very important for national development. Furthermore, the financial implications, gender analysis and guidelines for developing communications strategies for disseminating the policy were part of the analysis. The CMM included a section on security measures for Cabinet documents.

A 'HANDBOOK FOR MINISTERS' (DRAFT)

The Cabinet Secretariat drafted a 'Handbook for Ministers' with technical support from the GCGP and by gathering information from other jurisdictions and a study visit to Canada. In advanced jurisdictions, there are guidelines for ministers and leading politicians on job descriptions, codes of conduct and other key guidelines regarding the nature and scope of their work, as well as the expectations of the public regarding their conduct while in public office.

The Handbook sets out similar guidelines. It includes the responsibilities of a minister, issues relating to good governance, transparency and accountability relationships with colleague ministers and with civil servants. A Code of Conduct for a ministerial portfolio was also developed.

JOB DESCRIPTIONS: POLICY POSITIONS

It was the intention of the OHCS that the Policy, Planning, Monitoring and Evaluation Directorates (PPMEDs) within the ministries needed to be reinvigorated and restored to the distinctive role they used to play in the civil service in Ghana's early days. Job descriptions were developed for positions based on the knowledge and skills required for a policy analyst. By its very nature of being situated in the Office of the President, the role of the PCMEU as a coordinating, reporting unit to the President and the Cabinet had a special need for specialized staff. Job descriptions were developed for policy advisors, policy analysts and monitoring and evaluation specialists. These were used in order to hire the right staff.

PERFORMANCE MANAGEMENT SYSTEM

A performance management system was established and implemented. It enabled the Head of the Civil Service to objectively measure, monitor and evaluate the performance of the chief directors and directors of the ministries.

MONITORING AND EVALUATION GUIDELINES: CENTRAL MANAGEMENT AGENCIES

The PCMEU in collaboration with central management agencies – the Office of the Head of the Civil Service, the National Development Planning Commission, the Ministry of Finance and Economic Planning, the Ministry of Local Government and Rural Development and the Ghana Statistical Service – developed tools consisting of templates and guidelines for quarterly reporting to the Office of the President. The PCMEU coordinated a process for the monitoring and evaluating of the government's priority policies and programmes. These tools were used from 2003 to 2008. The robust utilization of the tools and the completed forms, with additional activities being used to cross-check the veracity of the information submitted (e.g. field trips) and the feedback process (provided by the PCMEU to the ministers, chief directors and heads of departments and agencies), made the exercise of monitoring and evaluation very useful in reporting to the President and the Cabinet on the implementation successes (or not) of priority projects for national development.

TRANSITION PLANNING GUIDE

A comprehensive set of guidelines was developed to guide transition planning in Ghana. In most developed countries, even if the change involves one political party succeeding itself, it is expected that a formal transitional process will take place in order to ensure that institutional memory is retained and that there is a smooth transfer of power. The Transition Planning Guide provided guidance on issues relating to the activities, timing and responsibilities of both the outgoing and incoming Presidents as well as the bureaucracy (mainly the Cabinet

Secretariat and the civil service). To make the work highly practical, user-friendly templates were developed in order to facilitate the implementation of the transition plan. The Cabinet approved the use of the Transition Planning Guide. In 2009, ministries used the templates in the preparation of 'Hand Over Notes'.

MANAGEMENT INFORMATION SYSTEM

To support vibrant policy development, a state-of-the-art IT infrastructure was established in the Office of the President. The intention was to establish connectivity between the presidency and the MDAs for collaboration and sharing of information through an IT program, the Hummingbird suite. A secure networking and messaging infrastructure was also installed at the Office of the President.

Computers and supporting hardware were distributed in the Office of the President and the Cabinet Secretariat as well as some MDAs in order to transmit and receive messages between the offices to allow for coordination, collaboration and sharing of information. Training in basic IT skills, – email usage, Internet skills and Microsoft Office productivity tools (Word, Excel and Outlook) – took place for selected staff from all registries at the Office of the President. In addition, plans were advanced for Internet connectivity with high security among the selected MDAs and the Office of the President.

A portal was established in the Office of the President with appropriate links to other MDAs, where required, in order to access information and display the information in a way that it was of use to the Office of the President. It was beneficial for the purpose of monitoring and evaluating the performance of the President's priorities. CABTRACK, a software system, was developed for tracking the receipt of Cabinet Memoranda, the decisions and implementation status.

Training and Knowledge Transfer

The training and knowledge transfer activities took place in a participatory and practical manner with emphasis on case studies, group discussions, individual simulation exercises, study visits and seminars with civil servants from Canada, the UK and the USA.

PRACTICAL PUBLIC POLICY TRAINING

The Office of the Head of the Civil Service in collaboration with the University of Ghana Business School (UGBS) and Queen's University in Canada developed and delivered a comprehensive set of three training modules in public policy development:

- Module one: Policy Development and Analysis.
- Module two: Context and Framework of Policy.
- Module three: Policy Implementation, Monitoring and Evaluation.

The curriculum provided core knowledge in policy making from the economic, social and political perspectives as well as cultural realities. It offered civil servants a better understanding of the framework for decision making in order to appreciate the available policy instruments and methods for effective development, monitoring and implementation of policy.

SEMINARS

Civil servants from the Office of the President, the Cabinet Secretariat, CMAs, chief directors, gender desk officers and PPMEDs participated in seminars on Cabinet decision-making processes, policy development and analysis.

The interactive seminars included Canadian and Ghanaian civil servants (and, in some cases, practitioners from the UK and the USA) who were invited to share knowledge and experiences on different aspects of executive decision making and policy development and management in their countries. Ghanaian practitioners made comparative presentations on the existing Ghanaian system.

STUDY VISITS

To gain first-hand information from their Canadian counterparts on modern governance, study visits were organized for senior officials from the Office of the President, the Cabinet Secretariat, the OHCS, CMAs and chief directors. A team of IT specialists working on MIS also learned new methods of document and knowledge management. Participants visited Canadian institutions such as the PMO, the Cabinet Secretariat, the Privy Council and the TBS. The visits helped participants to update their knowledge and share experiences on best practices, some of which were adapted to translate the lessons learnt for the purposes of national development.

POLICY NETWORK FORUM

As part of the process of consolidating and strengthening policy development in the fabric of the civil service, a policy network forum was established. Its purpose was to provide an opportunity for the exchange of information on policy issues and to consolidate contacts and relationships between government officials in charge of policy across the various MDAs. It was also an opportunity for past and present participants of various training programmes to discuss topical policy issues in a multi-sectoral manner. Many more activities and processes were undertaken to build capacity in the civil service in policy development and management. It primarily occurred through the inclusive process of planning, developing and implementing products and training, as well as knowledge transfer activities.

One key to national development is the inclusion of as many citizens as possible. Gender representation was considered in all activities. Gender balance, where possible, was a key factor in the three work teams: the policy, human resource and MIS teams. Gender balance was also an important consideration in the selection of civil service personnel for seminars, study visits, policy training and product development. Skills were acquired on gender analysis and mainstreaming as part of the training on the preparation of Cabinet Memoranda.

Institutionalization for National Development

There is not a single way to do things. An insistence that one approach fits all does not work. The heart of good governance is cultural relevance, accountability, transparency, laws and policies that guide decision making and strong administrative systems. By 2002, the Ghanaian civil service had been 'assessed to death' through various public sector reform projects. Scepticism amongst civil servants remained high due in part to the fact that many capacity building undertakings never deliver tangibles, but instead spend a lot of money on studies rather than on what the people consider to be essential. Too often, capacity-building initiatives fall prey to the desire to cast off what went before. The GCGP had successfully expanded the community of interest and participation that augured well for the institutionalization of elements of the reforms:

- the Chief of Staff, the Cabinet Secretary and the Head of the Civil Service were actively engaged in the project;
- the Cabinet Memorandum Manual identified a fledgling disciplined approach to policy development and management;
- for civil servants, the training and knowledge transfer were extensive;
- buy-in was high amongst chief directors and civil servants;
- Ghanaians developed the products.

After six years of intensive effort and visions of a formalized, disciplined system for policy management and decision making, there was a change of government. The ruling party lost the election in 2008 and the party it had succeeded regained the reins in 2009. Transitions of power are fundamental moments in governance. After intense, exciting political campaigning, a victorious party emerges and in a short period of time must assume the responsibilities of power. There are common characteristics in transitions, but the single most important one is the personality, character and values of the incoming President. It is the President who sets the tone and standards, chooses key advisors and articulates key issues. It is his or her demands for rigour and discipline from ministers and the public sector that will or will not make a difference.

In the first year, the new government accepted in principle the usefulness of the Cabinet Memorandum Manual as a guide, but not all tenets of the CMM were implemented; nor was the CABTRACK system continued. With an understanding of the importance of coordination at the 'centre', it re-structured the PCMEU in the Office of the President into two units: the Policy Harmonisation Unit and the Policy Monitoring and Evaluation Unit. The Civil Service Training Centre, using the modules that were developed by the UGBS, undertook the policy training. The training continued for a while and the civil service placed policy training on its annual programmes. Due to the lack of funds, a training programme for rigorous policy development is no longer being delivered. The hope of a 'policy analyst' cadre of civil servants who were trained did not come to fruition. After the first year, the MIS system lapsed and was not replaced with an alternative similar system.

The new government, as all governments tend to do, started another public sector reform initiative. In a government article, 'The New Approach to Public Sector Reform', Holm-Graves (2011) states that the new government decided to approach reforms in the public sector in a different way compared to the past. It established the New Approach to Public Sector Reform. The ministers assume primary responsibility for tapping into resources for reforming various public sector areas as well as specific sector programmes. It is led by the President and coordinated by the Cabinet with the support of the Ministry of Public Sector Reform.

Central governance issues are barely being catered for or addressed in this new approach. However, under a 'Capacity Development Mechanism', which is supported by the Canadian International Development Agency, the Office of the President may re-introduce some of the products developed under the Central Governance Project, for instance, the adoption and institutionalization of a Handbook for Ministers.

One of the products of the Central Governance Project was a transitional planning guide that was developed in 2008 in anticipation of elections that were to be held during that year. From December 2008 to January 2009, for the first time in Ghana's history, a formalized system was created to indicate what was required of both the political and bureaucratic leadership during a change of government. Even if the change involves one political party succeeding itself, it was expected that a formal transitional process would take place in order to ensure the retention of institutional memory and a smooth transfer of power. The process and standardization for handing-over notes was subsequently used.

Elements of the transitional planning guide were used in drafting the Presidential (Transition) Bill that was enacted in June 2012. It is classified into four broad sections. The first section is the role and responsibilities of the transition team that specify its composition, functions, meeting schedules, sub-committees and an advisory council. The second section covers handing-over notes and assets, addressing the availability of such notes, an inventory of assets and leaving the official residence. The third section is the election of the Speaker of Parliament and swearing-in of the President. The fourth section is entitled 'Miscellaneous' and focuses on transitional provisions.

Guided by the Presidential (Transition) Act, it is expected that the judicious use of the transition planning guide will not only facilitate the smooth transition of power from one administration to another, but will also help to institutionalize the process. All things being equal, since a formal approach to power change will take place every four or eight years, it is expected that critical success factors will be noted, challenges will be catalogued and the lessons learnt will come in handy to improve the transition guide and make it even more useful during subsequent transition processes.

The institutionalization of policy development and management processes for national development is not easy. Governments have the ability to put their 'stamp' on existing processes by building on the capacity acquired through policy reforms and, for that matter, any other constructive government reform programme. With the fundamentals of good public policy and management, new administrations should seize the moment and consolidate the gains already realized.

In the situation of Ghana and the experiences of many other developing countries, the weakness (which can surely be rectified) is the lack of political will to implement effectively what preceding governments have successfully started. Though serious capacity issues have been identified in the public sector, unfortunately, even those who are trained in public policy and management are not drawn upon so that the theoretical and initial practical skills acquired can be utilized.

Conclusions

The current policy demands facing Ghana and other developing nations require continued strengthening of the policy management and decision-making processes. With strong political will and commitment, a transparent and disciplined policy management system as evident in developed countries can continue to transform developing nations' socio-economic achievements, consolidate their democracy and bring about sustained national development through good governance.

A robust and comprehensive policy planning and implementation process is inextricably linked to national development programmes in other countries. Execution of the national development priorities is wholly reinforced by sound implementation systems, and the ensuing policy planning practices make use of feedback from impact assessment at the macro and micro stages. The examples of Canada, Singapore and Malaysia highlight the role of policy management when combined with vision of the country's leaders as being critical in ensuring that development gains trickle down to all in the nation.

In Ghana's case, it was the first Sub-Saharan African country to gain independence from colonial rule. Ghanaian civil servants had a unique and early opportunity to receive strong tutelage under the auspices of many advanced Commonwealth countries. As a result, there are many world-class Ghanaian civil servants who are well known, which reflects well on the country. Ghanaians therefore enjoy the goodwill of many emerging nations and command high levels of respect in these countries. It is not surprising that the first Sub-Saharan African to head the United Nations was a Ghanaian. Although Ghana ranks in the top 10 on the Mo Ibrahim Index of African Governance, it must continue to strive to be first! Without the continued systematic implementation of a policy development and management system based on the issues raised above, Ghana and many developing countries will continue to grapple with development challenges that undermine the ultimate goal of attaining first world status.

References

Birkland, T. (2001). *An Introduction to the Policy Process*. New York: M.E. Sharpe.

Cochrane, C. and Malone, E. (2005). *Public Policy: Perspectives and Choices*. Boulder, CO: Lynne Rienner.

Cochrane, C., Mayer, L., Carr, T. and Cayer, J. (2008). *American Public Policy: An Introduction*. Belmont: Thomson-Wadsworth.

Dye, T. (2007). *Understanding Public Policy*. Harlow: Pearson.

Evans, G. and Manning, N. (2001). 'Policy management at the centre of Government: Symptoms and cures', revised paper, first delivered at the *First Dusseldorf Seminar on the Centre of Government*, University of Dusseldorf, 23–6 November.

Foreign Affairs, Trade & Development Canada (2015). www.international.gc.ca/development/where we work/Sub-Sarah Africa/Ghana.

Guy Peters, B. (2001). *The Future of Governing*. Lawrence: University Press of Kansas.

Hayes, R. (2007). Community activists' perceptions of citizenship roles in an urban community: A case study of attitudes that affect community engagement. *Journal of Urban Affairs*, 29(4), pp. 401–24.

Institute on Governance (2011). http://log.ca/en/about-us/governance/governance-definitions.

Institute of Public Administration of Canada (2008). *Ghana Central Governance Project, Project Implementation Plan 2003*, Ghana Central Governance Project, End of Project Report 2008.

——. (2011). Developed for 'Policy Boot Camps' first nations public service secretariat and the Institute of Public Administration of Canada, 2011.

Manning, N. (1999). *Making the Cabinet Work: Institutional Arrangements for Strategic Decision-Making in Government*. Washington DC: World Bank.

Mo Ibrahim Foundation (MIF). 2012 Ibrahim Index of African Governance, p. 4, http://www.moibrahim foundation.org.

Savoie, D.J. (2004). *Governing from the Centre: The Concentration of Power in Canadian Politics*. Toronto: University of Toronto Press.

Smith, A. (2009). The roles and responsibilities of central agencies. *International Affairs, Trade and Finance Division, Library of Parliament*, 23 April 2009, pp. 4–5.

Thatcher, B and Evia, C. (eds) (2008). *Outsourcing Technical Communication: Issues, Policies and Practices*. Amityville, NY: Baywood Publishing.

World Bank. http://worldbank.org/governance/wgi/index.asp.

World Bank Survey (1996–2012). http://info.worldbank.org/governance/wgs/index.asp#home.

World Development Report (1997). *World Development Report 1997: The State in a Changing World*. New York: Oxford University Press.

Yinger, M.J. (1980). Review *Policy Analysis: A Political and Organizational Perspective*. W.I. Jenkins. *American Journal of Sociology*, 85(5), pp. 1256–8.

Internet References

www.ghana.gov.gh/index.php/news/features/4691.
www.tbs-sct-gc.ca.
www.wikipedia.org/wiki/History of Canada.

PART II
THE PUBLIC SECTOR

5

The Public Sector as an Enabler of National Development

Anne Richmond

> *Without good governance – without the rule of law, predictable administration, legitimate power and responsive regulation – no amount of funding, no amount of charity will set the developing world on the path to prosperity.*
>
> *Kofi Annan, UN Secretary General, press release, 2 September 1997*

Abstract

This chapter examines the ways in which the public sector enables national development, in part by exploring the ways in which in developing countries it is failures or lack of capacity in the public sector that are seen as the main barriers to development. Some recent comparative literature and case studies on the role of the public sector (and of alternatives) are examined, and practical examples of how the public sector can work in the area of labour market development are discussed. Several conclusions are drawn: that the public sector is a critical enabler of development; that the capacity of the public sector for this purpose can be measured in terms of policy, implementation and efficiency abilities; and that the motivation of individual public servants is a key factor. Finally, the chapter suggests that while lessons can be drawn from the experience of other countries and other historical periods, ultimately each country must find solutions that suit its unique characteristics.

Introduction

This chapter focuses in depth on the public sector in relation to national development. Chapter 4 established the main terms definitions of governance as elaborated by the World Bank and defined national development as 'to transform the economy for enhanced growth and job creation in order to support the delivery of social services to the people of that country, regardless of their geographical location or social and economic circumstances'. Chapter 7 describes the role of national institutions in creating the necessary conditions for development, citing the public sector (and, more specifically, the public or civil service) as a key institution.

The logic seems clear: the public sector is generally understood as that part of the economy which is publicly owned – in practice, government and government-controlled entities – and which provide benefits and services (public goods) to all. Services include law and regulation of business, commerce, natural resources and trade; public order and justice; public health and education; regulation and/or provision of transportation and, in some cases, productive enterprises in different industries ('State Owned Enterprises'). Public services that create a fair and regulated environment for production and trade are clearly necessary to the development and growth of private sector enterprises and industries which produce and trade in goods and services, employ citizens and generate revenue, some of which returns to the public sector in the form of taxes and fees.

Hence, the public sector is inherently an enabler of development. And, indeed, it is the failures and gaps in the public sector that act as a critical barrier to development for many countries. This chapter will review some of the literature and some practical experience in terms of the role of the public sector as an enabler of development, what steps are taken to improve its functioning and remove barriers to development, and how a public sector may respond in practice to 'enable development', with the particular example of its role in labour markets.

The first and most important lesson is that despite the recurrent hopes in the communities of development and development partners, there is no single right or best approach. A public sector may most effectively enable national development in ways that are unique and specific to a country's history, culture(s) and the prevailing economic climate, using a strategy that would not be effective in another country or indeed at a different time in that country's history.

A second observation is that despite the consensus of more than 20 years' standing that good governance is crucial for development – and that good governance is expressed largely in the capacity of a state's public sector – development cooperation spends limited time, resources and effort on developing that capacity and far more on either direct provision of service, essentially replacing the public sector, or on complex conditionality.

The Role of the Public Sector in Enabling Development – And its Failures

The general purpose of development was articulated in the 1970s as 'the realisation of the human personality', and a graduated set of needs starting with those most basic to life (nutrition) and then passing through a hierarchy of needs – to address successively 'undernourishment, unemployment and inequality', and, once those are met, further needs such as those relating to educational and political participation, freedom from repression and others (Seers, 1972). This is the basis for the focus of development (as in the Millennium Development Goals) on poverty and other basic needs as a first step.

The connection between this formulation for development and the role of the public sector is clear, given that the public sector is generally responsible for maintaining the conditions within which people can live, nourish themselves, be physically safe, work, etc., and have reasonably equal opportunities to do so. But there is a practical question as to whether the development of the public sector can or should then precede the further development of the state.

The size and scope of the public sector is often thought to correspond more or less directly to the degree of economic development: as development (and specifically, urbanization and industrialization) increases, the demands on and size of the public sector grows in concert. A 2001 study by Boix (2001) at the University of Chicago examined data from 65 developing countries and found that urbanization and industrialization create pressure to increase the supply of common goods, particularly infrastructure and skills development. This contributed to the growth of the public sector, but political structures and democratic choice also affected the rate of growth. In particular, authoritarian regimes and democratic systems with very low participation rates tend to have much smaller public sectors. However, this article also notes important connections between a developing economy, which creates a demand for greater public goods and hence public expenditure, which in turn can support further economic development.

So there appears to be a strong connection between the size of a public sector and the degree of development, but size is not necessarily an indicator of the role, scope or capacity of the public sector to support development. What is meant by capacity? One definition, developed by Charles Polidano, is 'the ability of the permanent administrative machinery of government to implement policies, deliver services and provide policy advice to decision makers' (Polidano, 2000). His attempt to develop a generalizable index to measure capacity provides useful thinking about the role and thus, depending on capacity, the ability of the public sector to support development. He describes two main strategies for states to lead development (or indeed any type of change): 'despotic' (whereby the state imposes its decisions, even against opposition) and 'infrastructural' (a more pervasive strategy which affects individual and social behaviour and mobilizes resources effectively).

Infrastructural power of the state is a characteristic of developed countries. In weak states and developing countries, the state is limited in its ability to exercise infrastructural strategies, with non-state actors (tribes, social classes, etc.) retaining much of this type of power. Polidano suggests three measureable dimensions of public sector capacity: *policy capacity* (the ability to structure and coordinate the decision-making process of government); *implementation authority* (the ability to carry out decisions and enforce rules); and *operational efficiency* (cost-effectiveness and quality of services to citizens). He also cautions that capacity exists only in relation to an environment: the capacity of a public service may be severely limited by external factors such as economic crises, political instability, ethnic fragmentation and aid dependency, any of which may overwhelm or subvert the operation of the public sector.

So, some of the critical questions about the public sector's role in enabling development can be considered in terms of these three dimensions of capacity:

- Policy: do the government and the public sector have the resources and skill required to understand and make critical decisions regarding its actions?
- Implementation: is the public sector realistically able to deliver goods and services, and regulate the behaviour of others?
- Efficiency: is the public sector making the best use of resources to deliver the best possible services?

For many developing countries, the answer to the above three questions is clearly 'no' or 'not fully', and this is where failures of the public sector and consequently a lack of enabling support to development are found. One description runs as follows:

> In many developing economies, the public sector is poorly managed and lacks the capacity to provide social and infrastructural services. The crux of the problem lies in a paucity of resources and weak or inadequate incentives for the public officials to deliver services efficiently. Quite often, delivery of services is biased in favor of the 'well-connected' few at the expense of the large majority and the poor in society. Therefore, many developing countries face a growing need to reform their public institutions to provide better performance incentives to their public officials and to reduce the service delivery bias by ensuring greater transparency and accountability in decision making. (Kulshreshtha, 2008)

This formulation underpins much recent development assistance aimed at improving public sector governance, institutions and capacity. Development partners have looked to improved financial management, decision-making processes, greater transparency and accountability of plans and policies, the rule of law and various strategies to improve public sector management, including privatization, civil service reform and, in the case of assistance from the World Bank, governance reform in specific sectors of the economy, usually health, education and social services.

Strategies for Addressing Weaknesses in the Public Sector to Better Enable Development

The critical role of the public sector and more broadly 'effective governance' in successful development is increasingly recognized by development partners and lenders, as seen in the World Bank's development and governance strategy that has evolved since the 1990s. Governance improvement has become a conditional element of much development support since the 1990s, often focused on specific reforms of the recipient country's public sector. A study exploring the impact that donor-defined good governance requirements have had on Bangladesh (Parnini, 2009) identifies some of the catalysts for and barriers to development, and the degree to which donor-driven public sector reform has been beneficial.

For development partners (donors and lenders), good governance and public sector reform are intended to improve government's ability to deliver goods and services to meet citizens' expectations. However, the core question is whether the development partner's agenda actually meets local citizens' needs. While aid is a declining proportion of Bangladesh's total revenues, key poverty-reducing investments (infrastructure, services, etc.) remain the responsibility of the public sector which has inadequate tax revenues or private support to deliver. The World Bank has set the tone for public sector reform in Bangladesh and, as a whole, development partners have focused on four areas over more than 20 years of support for public sector reform:

- administrative capacity building;
- policy capacity strengthening;
- institutional reform;
- civil service downsizing.

In practice, however, Parnini describes largely negative impacts resulting from a universalist model and top-down strategy aligned with conditional funding. For example, state-owned enterprises were closed (throwing hundreds of thousands out of work) to liberalize industry and allow foreign-owned enterprises to enter the market. Administrative reforms within the civil service were imposed and had limited buy-in and little beyond cosmetic impact. Decentralization and delegation of authority led to widening levels of corruption. Parnini's contention is that the state must have autonomy and leadership to run its own affairs and to negotiate on a more equal power basis with donors and funders.

A different perspective on the role and capacity of the public sector to support or impede development comes from a recent OECD report 'Contracting out Government Functions and Services' (OECD, 2009). The report examines the impact of an initiative by a group of OECD member countries and international organizations, the Partnership for Democratic Governance (PDG) to assist states in post-conflict and fragile situations to build their governance and improve service delivery to citizens. However, as the title of the report notes, the efforts focused far more on bypassing the actual public sector of the countries involved and creating service delivery through contracts than on building the capacity of the public sector of these fragile states. As noted above, the public sector delivers basic services to citizens and creates the environment that enables development, both in terms of realizing basic human needs and of supporting further economic and social development. In the cases examined by the OECD, different types of public services were contracted out: provision of primary healthcare; security and justice; core government functions (financial management); and, in the case of Afghanistan, virtually every aspect of the public sector.

In the case of healthcare, experiences with performance-based contracted delivery of healthcare in five countries (Afghanistan, Cambodia, Guatemala, Liberia and South Sudan) proved to be somewhat effective in terms of delivering services to citizens and in potentially fostering confidence in the government in these fragile states. However, these positive results came with many caveats: the importance of clear government leadership and stakeholder involvement; the need for a functioning basic healthcare infrastructure; strong management capacity and robust record keeping by governments.

A second area for 'contracted out' service delivery explored through the PDG is security and justice. The OECD review provides a useful summary of three basic delivery mechanisms for justice and security (as with any public good or service), normally found in various combinations in functioning states:

- state delivery of the goods and services through its institutions and agencies;
- the state contracts out delivery to service providers;
- non-state networks provide services either by law or by practice.

Contrasted with this, in fragile states, security and justice are provided 'privately':

- through state institutions and agencies, but on the basis of fees paid to the organization or individual;
- by private security companies offering security as a product;
- by criminal organizations delivering security as part of a criminal enterprise.

One of the findings of the review was the importance and effectiveness of 'non-state networks' in delivering justice and security. For example, the state-sponsored local justice system in the Philippines effectively deals with petty crime and disputes, ensuring much greater access to justice than the formal court system. In contrast, many developing countries offer little to no effective access to the formal justice system for the majority of citizens, due to cost and lack of assistance (for example, only one legal aid association in Sierra Leone, serving only two cities). Formal recognition of and support given to such non-state networks can therefore significantly increase the quality and accessibility of security and justice services even where states have very limited formal capacity and can help to counter the private provision of justice. As with the contracting out of health services, one of the drawbacks to the contracting out of security is the capacity of the state to effectively manage contracts, and the vulnerability to 'capture' by a private company. One example of effective contracting out is Cape Town in South Africa, which contracts with a private security company to monitor public spaces in association with the police force and the local government. But this is in a country with strong management capacity and robust governance.

A particular example of the contracting out of core government functions and services is South Sudan. When the peace agreement was signed in 2005, the challenge of building a government and public sector 'from the ground up' was created. The two most important areas were financial management (given the large amount of donor and development funds coming in) and health service delivery (considering the urgent needs of the population). Most fiduciary functions (government accounting, project accounting, procurement and audit) were immediately contracted out under the supervision of key donors and continued to be supplied under contract. Health services were largely contracted out to non-governmental organizations (NGOs) under arrangements which delegate the overall management of healthcare delivery within a specified state to a contracted NGO.

The impacts of these choices on the development of the government of South Sudan were described in the OECD report. In terms of the fiduciary services contract, the responsible ministry (the Ministry of Finance and Economic Planning) did not have and was not able to build capacity to effectively manage the contract or ensure that the service providers gave it the information it needed to make effective planning and budgetary decisions. Essentially, the contracted providers were working for and in the interests of development partners, and did not understand or effectively support the needs and capacities of a government, leading to poor performance and calls for further externally provided services. Subsequent developments in this area have emphasized capacity building for government staff and recognition of the longer-term need to build robust and sustainable public sector capacity.

The contracting out of healthcare was, at the time that the OECD review was written, still in its early stages with limited results on which to base conclusions. An early concern, however, was that the services for the four states where contracts were underway were more costly than could reasonably be expected to be sustainable across all states and after the initial three-year funding period. The authors observed that a more modest and sustainable 'in-house' solution to providing basic services to larger populations more quickly (it took almost three years for the initial contracts to be negotiated) might be more effective.

Overall, the experience with contracting out in the case of South Sudan revealed a number of issues relevant to the question of the role of public service in development:

- Government capacity to define the services it requires and to manage contracts in order to ensure they are delivered is critical to effectiveness. Hence, 'contracting out' is not a solution for lack of government capacity to understand and manage, only for a lack of delivery capacity.
- Lengthy procurement, approval and contracting processes required by donors and development banks may be beyond the capacity of governments to manage and may actually impede securing effective support, particularly to meet immediate and urgent needs.
- Programmes designed by contractors may be overly broad or ambitious in scope and not sustainable, and may be very high cost relative to other potential approaches.
- Most critically, in South Sudan there was initially far too little emphasis on building and sustaining ongoing public sector capacity, with some projects including no capacity building at all and none incorporating an 'exit strategy' towards eventual handover to a functional national capacity.

Another example of the contracting out of core public services in the OECD review is the case of Afghanistan, where a wide range of public sector functions and services were contracted out and supported through donors, starting in 2001. Among the key findings of this review, similar to those from South Sudan, were the following:

- Government leadership and ownership is critical for identifying needs and for deciding on how those needs will be met. Governments should be accountable for the decisions they have made and should hold contracted service providers accountable for their performance.
- Capacity building for the national public sector and clear exit strategies for all contracted providers are critical and should be emphasized.
- The wider the range of services contracted out, the longer it takes to build the capacity of the public sector. In Afghanistan there have been so many development partners eager to provide 'support' to so many areas that there is little practical coordination and limited focus on building capacity, with each project focused on the delivery of a specific service (sometimes in competition).

Overall, the examples of 'contracting out' of services and capacities which should be part of the public sector do not make a compelling case for this as a strategy for enabling national development in the long term. While the hope is that NGOs and others could provide services (such as healthcare) immediately without the need to build up national organizations, in practice this has not proven to be the case, with complex procurement processes leading to significant delays in on-the-ground delivery. More significantly, this strategy does not necessarily leave any sustainable legacy. Again in the case of healthcare and security, services may be designed and delivered without reference to national conditions or resources and may very quickly become unsustainable. So in terms of the 'measures of capacity', bypassing the public sector to achieve *implementation* capacity may not even be effective in the short term and definitely not in the longer term.

Another dimension of capacity for the public sector is *policy*. The case of South Sudan is instructive: the contracting out of a core function (finance) had the predictable result of not only failing to build ongoing capacity in the public sector, but also failing to deliver the services required for government operations and accountability. More broadly, without adequate policy capacity, the contracting out of implementation is impractical as governments are not able to adequately define their needs and manage the contracts. As to the final dimension, efficiency, it also appears from the case studies that the available resources were not used to their fullest extent for the benefit of the country's citizens.

It appears that the public sector does need to have some measure of capacity in order to service as an enabler of development. But Paul Collier (UNESCO, 2009) calls for a radical re-thinking of the provision of public services in post-conflict states based on experiences with traditional public service delivery models in Africa. He contends that the 'traditional' model, inherited from colonial governments and similar to a 1950s European model, with government ministries responsible for the monopolistic direction and delivery of social services such as health or education has proven to be unsuited to an African context, particularly in post-conflict or fragile states. The main reason for this is the absence of an institutionalized norm of 'public service' motivating the workforce, supported by appropriate compensation and a sense of national public interest.

In contrast, Collier claims many public servants are now motivated by self-interest, leading to absenteeism, low productivity and minor corruption, a norm that becomes self-replicating and self-sustaining as new generations of idealistic young entrants become self-seeking. He observes the limited alternatives to self-motivation (driven by a sense of public service/national interest) with limited capacity for financial incentives (due to both pay scales linked to age, rank, seniority and equality, and the difficulties of measuring 'performance'). In a nutshell, this creates a non-functioning public sector, which development partners prefer to bypass, channelling funds for public services through UN agencies and NGOs. His suggestion of an alternative approach is the creation of 'Independent Service Authorities': a public agency, independent of the civil service but responsible for implementation (similar to a central bank), with a board of directors including non-government appointees.

In this approach, the public sector does need to have *policy*, *implementation* and *efficiency* capacity (as discussed above), but the institutional arrangements are different. Government and the core civil service retain *policy* responsibility in order to set the parameters for the operation of the agency and maintain full accountability and transparency, while arm's-length agencies, operating quasi-independently, are responsible for *implementation* and for achieving *efficiency* objectives. So the direct public service – or core civil service – is no longer responsible for implementation and efficiency, but it should be noted that the degree of policy capacity would likely have to be much greater in order to ensure that government can adequately manage the service authorities. As with wholesale contracting out, there does not appear to be a shortcut that eliminates the need for a well-functioning public service.

While Collier suggests that perverse motivation (self-interest versus public interest) drives poor performance and lack of capacity for the public sector to support development, and proposes an alternative implementing model, Rocco Macchiavello looks specifically at public sector motivation and development failures with an economic analysis of the impact of public sector wages on motivation. He finds that the difference between public and private sector wages (the 'Public Sector Wage Premia' (PSWP)) does have a relationship to both the efficiency of public sectors and the degree of corruption in ways that may not be immediately apparent, but that are borne out in research (Macchiavello, 2008). A key factor for effective public sectors, he says, is the motivation of individuals seeking public sector jobs. Where the PSWP is low or inverse, meaning that public sector wages are lower than those in the private sector, individuals choose public service due to 'public sector motivation', which in turn drives them to work more efficiently, which improves the performance of the public sector, supports development and enables the private sector to develop and increase wages there.

Conversely, where public sector wages (and in many countries this includes a range of significant benefits) are higher than those of the private sector, there is no bias towards selection for those with 'public sector motivation' and, given the right conditions, individuals are likely to be self-interested, open to corruption and less likely to create better-performing public services which support development and the growth of the private sector. At the same time, public sector wages should not be so low as to encourage opportunistic behaviour by employees who are unable to make a living on their official earnings. Macchiavello suggests a number of other policy considerations stemming from this research, including that in poor countries with high PSWP, decentralized and distributed authority is likely to result in the use of such authority for private gain, whereas in richer countries with low PSWP, delegation of authority may be an additional positive motivating factor for improved performance by public sector employees.

So, to summarize, lack of capacity in the public sector is a barrier to enabling development. Lack of capacity in policy (as discussed in Chapter 4) leads to the inability to effectively define issues and make decisions. Without policy capacity, governments cannot credibly manage implementation, by whatever means, and are unlikely to demand or deliver efficiency. And where the public sector cannot deliver public goods and services, the credibility and legitimacy of government is called into question, thus eroding the framework upon which private enterprise and human development rest. Strategies that circumvent the role of the public sector do not enable development in either the short term or the long term. However, building the capacity of the public sector is neither easy nor short term, and there are no universally applicable solutions. The research into motivation provides an interesting direction for further study.

How the Public Sector Enables Development: Examples from the Labour Market

What would a public sector be doing if it was enabling development? Obviously this is too general a question to answer, but a short discussion of the role that the public sector plays in the labour market may illustrate some of the issues raised in this chapter. In labour market terms, 'development' can be defined as increasing the formality of employment as enterprises grow, trade and investment increase and productivity rather than subsistence becomes a goal. The government's role in labour markets is often portrayed as leadership in 'job creation' – either through the outright creation of jobs and employment in the public sector or through policies and legislation that stimulate the creation of jobs in the private sector. In developing countries, the majority of employment may be in the informal sector, which is inherently less subject to government control and influence.

Neoliberal positions would argue that the public sector should play as limited a role as possible in employment so as to not to distort market forces. This has also been the position of decision makers in some developing countries, who argue that the priority is to have jobs and then worry about the quality of them later. In contrast, others would argue that the public sector has an important role to play in ensuring that employment is effectively defined and regulated in order to reduce the risks of too-rapid development and that economic benefits are equitably distributed.

The World Bank has elaborated the MILES Framework (see Table 5.1) as a way to describe the demand and supply factors in the labour market, enabling analysis of the binding constraints to the creation of more, and better, jobs (Nallari, 2011).

Table 5.1   The MILES Framework

Factor	Policy issues
Macroeconomic conditions	• Conditions for growth
	• Macroeconomic stability
Investment climate	• Regulatory environment
	• Government transparency
	• Taxes
	• Financing
	• Infrastructure
	• Legal environment
Labour market policies and institutions	• Labour market regulation
	• Wage setting
	• Non-wage costs
Education and skills	• Basic education
	• Higher education
	• Training and lifelong learning
Social protection	• Social risk management programs
	• Social insurance

It is clear from this that the capacity of the public sector is critical to enabling development in terms of job creation and a sustainable labour market. Policy capacity is required to develop legislation and regulation, implementation capacity to deliver services (such as education and infrastructure) and efficiency capacity in order to use the available resources to best effect. It is also apparent that development of the labour market would be severely impacted by the absence of a public sector.

Labour market regulation in particular is an area of intense interest in terms of its potential impact on economic development. A paper by Richard Freemen reviewed some widely held assumptions of development from the 1970s against actual experience in the 1980s. First, the rural–urban differential, where conventional wisdom holds that the high price of labour in urban areas and the relative size of the public sector contribute to a major distortion of high public sector urban wages against low, rural, agricultural wages. However, the impacts of structural adjustment in development during the 1980s meant that by the early 1990s, urban public sector wages were 'too low for the state effectively to provide law-and-order, property protection and related public activities' (Freeman, 1993). Another issue was the belief that high degrees of public ownership reduced progress in development, against which the experiences of China and Singapore were contrasted.

Second, the expectation that development necessarily leads to income inequality, particularly in the earlier stages, was examined. However, in the case of Malaysia (a democracy) and Korea and Taiwan (at the time, military dictatorships), rapid development did not lead to significant income inequality due to massive investment in education and consequent moves to higher value-added production. Finally, the supposition that labour market rigidities, specifically labour regulation and union rights, have a negative impact on development is debunked. Unfortunately, this is partially due to the fact that regulations such as minimum wages were lightly enforced and hence had limited impacts on developing economies, but conversely while unionization had a slightly limiting impact on employment, there were positive correlations with reduced turnover, increased training and higher productivity. His conclusion was that many assumptions regarding the negative impact of labour market institutions on development were not borne out by experience and that no single model of economic development, or set of institutions, was effective across all countries and times.

A more recent review of Asian labour markets (Zhu and Benson, 2011) looks at the impact of different institutions and regulations on countries at differing stages of development and political/economic characteristics: large-scale, developed economies (Japan and Korea); small-scale developed economies (Hong Kong and Singapore); developing socialist market economies (China and Vietnam); and developing capitalist market economies (India and Malaysia). This review explores the vulnerability of national systems that base economic development solely on economic growth, considering the dramatic impact of the 1997–8 Asian financial crisis which led to significant growth in unemployment.

For the large-scale developed economies, recession (starting in the 1990s in Japan) has had a long-term impact on labour markets, leading to high youth unemployment, a decline in full time/permanent jobs and a rise in temporary and casual jobs, reduced quality of employment and income equality, and an increase in informal employment. However, it is important to note that these changes are in relation to a prior state characterized by highly formalized, secure and permanent employment. Governments have been challenged to balance demands for greater labour market flexibility (to re-build competitive industries) with protection for workers. Legislation and policy have focused on pension reform, childcare, training and education and legal protection to attempt to support individual workers to be more employable.

The two developed city economies, Hong Kong and Singapore, were hit hard by the Asian economic crisis of 1997–8 and subsequent trends in globalization. Despite differences in terms of their political systems, both countries responded similarly to citizen demands to focus on protection and re-skilling of workers. Hong Kong's training effort included a government agency (the Employment Re-training Board) and introducing a skills qualification framework to provide for the recognition and transferability of skills. Singapore also adopted a new manpower policy and expanded opportunities for training and education. However, for both economies, the net impact was for greater bifurcation of the labour markets and greater inequality, with a high-wage and low-wage gap.

The developing 'socialist market' economies of China and Vietnam have some common features, including a relatively large agricultural workforce (45 percent in China and 55 percent in Vietnam). Steps to open the economies to trade and foreign investment have led to significant economic growth in both countries, while retaining a socialist political system with one-party rule. The major employment transition over the past two decades has been the rise of non-state enterprises and a growing private sector. This diversity of ownership contributes in turn to inequality in terms of wages and conditions of work, leading to an expanded role for trade unions in negotiating wages and monitoring working conditions. New labour legislation introduced in both countries has led to the increasing formalization of labour contracts, minimum standards, working hours, dismissal, social insurance and dispute resolution mechanisms. These are seen by government as a way to achieve social stability and harmony in a period of economic transition. As with more developed countries, government also invested heavily in training, upgrading and re-skilling to ease transition in the economy and build for high productivity.

India and Malaysia, as developing capitalist economies, experienced varying stresses as a result of the Asian economic collapse. Both countries, though very different in size, have both high-end, multinational and globally competitive enterprises, and large numbers of low end, unskilled, rural and agricultural enterprises. For the majority of workers, the crises led to fewer opportunities for formal employment and reduced investment by firms in human resource development. Overall, the pace of economic development and the degree to which the benefits of development were shared were equally impacted by the crises.

Overall, the authors of the study conclude that while each country has responded somewhat uniquely to the challenges of transition and developing economies, there is some necessary balance between supporting and protecting workers, and ensuring that businesses have the flexibility to develop and respond to increased trade and openness. The trade-off appears to be in terms of social stability: where the governments of Singapore, Hong Kong, China and Vietnam have invested more in mechanisms (such as skill re-training and expanded labour rights) to temper inequality in order to protect stability, other governments with a more diverse and pluralistic political approach have not. The broader lesson for development may be that the role of the public sector, specifically in terms of regulation of the labour market, may not impact the pace or direction of development, but may influence how it is experienced. At the same time, more open, pluralistic political systems may not have the capacity to intervene as strongly.

A review of employment laws in developing countries (Djankov and Ramalho, 2009) cites 2004 as a landmark year in the analysis of labour regulation in developing countries, with three major studies on 85 countries exploring the impact of rigid employment laws on economic development. Prior to this, most research on the impact of labour regulation was carried out in developed countries. In general, labour regulation falls into three areas: employment law (individual contracts of employment and conditions of work); collective bargaining (formation of trade unions and industrial relations); and social security (unemployment, disability, sickness, etc.). According to Djankov and Ramalho (2009), there is persuasive evidence from the studies to suggest a positive association between more flexible labour regulation and economic growth and poverty reduction. Conversely, more rigid labour legislation is strongly associated with slower economic growth, higher unemployment, larger informal sectors and higher youth unemployment. The authors contend that governments intervene in the labour market based on a belief that such markets are prone to unfair operation to the detriment of workers, and that laws are needed to establish a fair labour market.

Evidence from the range of countries noted above illustrates the impact that the public sector has on enabling development from the perspective of labour markets. A connecting theme is the potential of different policy strategies to impact not just on the pace of development, but also its nature – not just enabling the creation of jobs, but also influencing the types of jobs that are created and who gets them.

The role of the public sector in labour market regulation is particularly interesting in light of the pervasiveness of the informal economy in most developing countries. The informal sector may make up a significant part of the economy and, as a country develops, it may even grow as earlier forms of economic organization (such as family-based systems) decline and subcontracting rises. In Malaysia, despite concerns about poor conditions of work, instability and lack of security for workers, the informal sector is also seen as an 'entry point' for new business creators and as a major employer for low-skilled workers (Ramasamy and Rowley, 2011). Returning to the World Bank MILES Framework, it is easy to see that increasing the formalization, quality and quantity of jobs in any country requires a multi-pronged approach, largely resting on improved capacity in the public sector. Hence, simple solutions to the 'problem' of informal employment are unlikely to be found, and the lack of capacity of the public sector is one of the constraints to development.

Lessons Learned and Implications for Developing Economies

To return to the quote at the beginning of this chapter, 'without good governance – without the rule of law, predictable administration, legitimate power and responsive regulation – no amount of funding, no amount of charity will set us on the path to prosperity'. To paraphrase: without a well-functioning public sector, development is not possible. However, describing and achieving a well-functioning public sector that enables development is no easy task.

A key lesson is specificity. There does not appear to be a universal answer, and the degree to which external models and strategies have been imposed on countries mirrors the degree to which those strategies have failed. Equally, attempting to bypass the public sector and go 'straight to delivery' does not appear to be effective, even in the short term. Success comes from attending to the capacity of the public sector in all three dimensions: policy, implementation and efficiency. A public sector with capacity in these areas is able to understand and make decisions regarding obstacles to or opportunities for development, deliver appropriate services and do so in a cost-effective and sustainable way. The examples of different responses to the Asian economic crisis of the late 1990s illustrate that each country's response was rooted in its own particular circumstances and objectives.

A further lesson is that the internal culture of the public sector and especially the motivation of those working in it are of prime importance. Many developing countries work with largely inherited or externally imposed structures which may not adequately incorporate, or may distort, pre-existing cultures of obligation and expectation so that the 'ideal' of a politically neutral and public-interest- minded public servant is difficult to achieve. There is a wealth of literature on this subject but, again, no easy answers. An important first step is to acknowledge the realities: that the structure of jobs and payment systems for the public sector in developing countries may not be appropriate for attracting and sustaining people prepared to work 'in the public interest', and that alternative approaches rooted firmly in the national context are needed.

References

Boix, C. (2001). Democracy, development, and the public sector. *American Journal of Political Science*, 45, pp. 1–17.

Collier, P. (2009). Rethinking the provision of public services in post-conflict states. Centre for the Study of African Economies, Department of Economics, University of Oxford, September.

Djankov, S. and Ramalho, R. (2009). Employment laws in developing countries. *Journal of Comparative Economics*, 37(1), pp. 3–13.

Freeman, R.B. (1993). Labor markets and institutions in economic development. *American Economic Review*, 83, pp. 403–8.

Kulshreshtha, P. (2008). Public sector governance reform: The World Bank's framework. *International Journal of Public Sector Management*, 21(5), pp. 556–67.

Macchiavello, R. (2008). Public sector motivation and development failures. *Journal of Development Economics*, 86, pp. 201–13.

Nallari, R. (2011). *Labour Market Policies: Frontiers in Development Policy*. Washington DC: World Bank.

OECD (2009). *Contracting Out Government Functions and Services: Emerging Lessons from Post-conflict and Fragile Situations*. Paris: OECD.

Parnini, S.N. (2009). Public sector reform and good governance. *Journal of Asian and African Studies*, 44(5), pp. 553–75.

Polidano, C. (2000). Measuring public sector capacity. *World Development*, 28(5), pp. 805–22.

Ramasamy, N and Rowley, C. (2011). *Labour Markets in Malaysia. The Dynamics of Asian Labour Markets: Balancing Control and Flexibility*. Abingdon: Routledge.

Seers, D. (1972). What are we trying to measure? In N. Baster (ed.), *Measuring Development: The Role and Adequacy of Development Indicators*. London: Frank Cass, pp. 21–36.

Zhu, Y. and Benson, J. (2011). *Labour Markets in Asia. The Dynamics of Asian Labour Markets: Balancing Control and Flexibility*. Abingdon: Routledge.

6

The Impact of Sound Public Financial Management on National Development

Gheysika A. Agambila

Abstract

This chapter begins with an attempt to understand the concept of public financial management. Next, the significance of public financial management systems is established. This is followed by a definition of national development as distinct from economic growth and the use of growth indicators as a yardstick to measure the overall well-being of a nation. Subsequently, an effort is made to establish a relationship between national financial management and national economic development. Finally, the implications of sound public financial management for national development are espoused, drawing on examples from industrialized nations, emerging economies and developing countries. In this regard, selected public financial management policies and their individual effects or combined effects with other policies are examined with recommendations as to what the best permutations and combinations could be for developing countries.

Introduction

The objective of this chapter is to examine the impact of various public financial management policies on the economic development of Less Developed Countries (LDCs), particularly those of Africa. We define public financial management as the gamut of government policies relating to money, interest, credit, financial institutions, spending, taxation and the markets. There are many factors which promote economic development. Models have been developed to explain the factors that influence growth in economic development variables, such as growth in real income per capita. Ramsey (1928) developed one of the earliest models of economic growth. Solow (1956) and Swan (1956) propounded their growth theories relying on Ramsey's earlier work.

Public Financial Management

Public financial management (PFM) entails the development of laws, organizations and systems to enable sustainable, efficient, effective and transparent management of public finance. Public financial management includes all components of a country's budget process – both upstream (including strategic planning, medium-term expenditure framework and annual budgeting) and downstream (including revenue management, procurement, control, accounting, reporting, monitoring and evaluation, audits and oversight). Good public financial management systems are important for democratic governance, macro-economic stability, effective use of available resources and poverty reduction. Good PFM systems can also help prevent corruption and foster aid effectiveness. A sound PFM system is a precondition for making it possible to effectively channel resources to service delivery, for example, basic education and health services. Ineffective PFM systems, on the other hand, can hamper development and increase the risk of corruption.

National Development

There are many indicators of national development. The most commonly used indicators are those published by the United Nations in the *Human Development Index*. A form of national development is that development which is confined to the economy of a nation, that is, national economic development. Economic development is in turn measured by many indices. The most commonly used indicator of economic development is growth in gross domestic product (GDP) or national income (gross national income (GNI)). Per capita measures for GDP and GNP are used to control for population size to enhance cross-country comparisons. GDP is a measure of the monetary value of all production within the territory of a country; it makes no distinction about the ownership of that production. GDP and GNP measures do not consider the distribution of the benefits of production or income. A Gini coefficient will provide an indication of the level of income inequality in a country.

While Ghana and many developing countries use GDP, many developed economies with multi-national companies prefer to use GNP in order to capture the value produced by their companies regardless of the location of operations of these multi-nationals. A large GDP is not necessarily associated with national development if a country's economy is characterized by significant income inequality and/or a high dependence on an enclave industry that drives the high GDP figures. As such, a small country with oil wells operated by foreign multi-nationals will have a high GDP, even if the citizens of that country never benefit from the revenue gained from the oil extraction. Thus, there are African countries such as Angola and Equatorial Guinea that have large GDPs based on oil production, but whose economic development as measured by the Human Development Index lags behind many less natural-resource rich countries.

Public Financial Management and National Development

The chapter aims to relate, empirically, national financial management and national economic development. Finance is the blood of industry. Therefore, the development of industry (both of goods and services) and the development of financial policies and institutions must go hand in hand. If finance is the blood of industry, it follows that constraints on the quantity of this blood or its flow will hinder industrial development, and hence economic development. There are many elements of national financial management. A principal element of public financial management is fiscal, that is, the taxing and spending policies of government and how these may affect economic growth. This chapter reviews the many facets of public financial management and assesses their impacts on economic development.

Implications for Developing Economies of Selected Public Financial Policies

LIBERALIZATION OF THE MARKETS

In the 1970s and 1980s, many developing countries were plagued by macro-economic instability. When they sought the assistance of the Word Bank and/or the International Monetary Fund (IMF), they were encouraged to adopt the Bretton Woods institutions' prescription for economic recovery: a Structural Adjustment Programme (SAP). The implementation of SAPs was a part of the 'Washington Consensus' on the requirements for economic development.

In Africa, Ghana embarked on its SAP in 1985; Nigeria followed in 1986. While the full SAP dose has been blamed for accentuating poverty and income inequality, it is not debatable that price liberalization was an essential policy for development. Prior to the adoption of SAPs, many countries were saddled with controlled or fixed-price systems that bred corruption, shortages and inefficiencies.

The experience with price liberalization, especially with regard to consumer goods, suggests that the removal of price controls is an important public financial policy that can promote economic development. Liberalization must not be taken to mean the absence of a role for government or the substitution, arbitrarily, of government action for private sector action. Public financial management must have a place and a balanced approach that considers a proper role for the private sector.

MOBILIZATION OF FINANCIAL RESOURCES

A policy of liberalizing the markets by itself will not necessarily promote economic development. A related financial policy is the mobilization of financial resources to enable both public and private investment in order to promote economic development.

Public financial policy that promotes the development of commercial banks, rural banks, savings and loan associations and an insurance industry will provide the fuel for economic development. Such a policy will also include removing fixed interest policies and permitting foreign financial institutions operating in the country to repatriate a portion of their profits.

Stock Markets

The development of stock markets is part of a policy of mobilizing financial resources for development. Some authors (Demirguc-Kunt and Maksimovic, 1996; Levine and Zervos, 1998; Miller, 1998; Singh, 1997) have indicated that stock markets have played an important role in the development of countries. There is a historic relationship between industrial and stock market development.

The requirements for stock market development are consistent with the sound public financial management required to promote economic development. These include macro-economic stability (low inflation, low budget deficit, etc.) and a vibrant private sector. Stock markets also allow citizens to share in the profitability of companies (both foreign and national) operating in the country. By being a vehicle for citizen participation in the economy, a stock market promotes economic literacy and a national commitment to peace and development. These intangibles play a role in the economic development of nations.

A stock market must not be viewed as an unmitigated good with no downside. While a stock market allows funds to flow into an LDC economy (an advantage), it can also allow such funds to exit just as fast (a disadvantage). Short-term speculations and foreign company policy dominance over domestic subsidiaries of such companies are additional risks involved in the establishment of stock markets in LDCs. The objective of sound public financial policy should therefore be to address these anticipated risks.

Mitigation of Failures in LDC Financial Markets

Even as public financial policy liberates the markets and mobilizes financial resources for development, it should also be directed at mitigating the failures that characterize LDC financial markets. Joseph Stiglitz et al. (1993) identified them as follows:

- the 'public good' nature of monitoring financial institutions;
- the externalities of monitoring, selection and lending;
- the externalities of financial disruption;
- missing and incomplete markets;
- imperfect competition;
- the inefficiency of competitive markets in the financial sector;
- uninformed investors.

PUBLIC EXPENDITURE POLICY

Public expenditure can promote economic growth. The US addressed its problem of economic depression by applying Keynesian prescriptions. Through a programme of public spending for public works and later military expenditures made necessary by the Second World War, the economy climbed out of depression. These prescriptions have been followed since then. In recent times, the USA, led by its President, Barack Obama, has pursued an economic stimulus programme by spending to prevent the collapse of financial institutions and industrial companies (such as the automobile manufacturing companies). Similar measures were taken by Prime Minister Gordon Brown of the UK in bailing out distressed organizations in the country (e.g. financial services firms). Although public spending under conditions of under-utilized resources such as severe economic recession or depression can stimulate aggregate demand, this must be done within targets for budget deficits and inflation.

Studies indicate that high levels of spending in excess of revenues, measured by budget deficits, can be a drag on development. In the 1970s and 1980s, Brazil and Argentina pursued policies of inflationary spending to spur economic growth. These policies culminated in macro-economic crises in these countries. In a study of 10 industrialized countries, Karras (1994) found that there was a negative relationship between budget deficits and economic growth. Easterly and Schmidt-Hebbel (1994) have also made similar findings. Other studies involving African countries have drawn similar conclusions.

Ghana's deficit in 2013 was 12 percent of GDP and has been considered as a macro-economic indicator that must be lowered if the country is to remain on track with its development agenda. While some government spending as a public financial management policy is good, more of such spending is not, *ipso facto*, better.

Another element of government spending that impacts economic development is the object of this public expenditure. African countries suffer from physical and social infrastructure deficits. These countries need roads, railways, ports, energy plants, etc. as a foundation for their economic development. Adam Smith in his book entitled *An Enquiry into the Nature and the Causes of the Wealth of Nations*, which was first published in 1776, identified 'public works' or what we call today infrastructure as the third most important duty of government. Smith postulated that such infrastructure was necessary 'to facilitate commerce in general'.

In 1920, the British Colonial Governor in pre-independence Ghana, Frederick Guggisberg, raised a loan on the London money market. Between 1920 and 1928, this loan financed major infrastructural projects such as railways, roads, 36 hospitals (including the iconic Korle-Bu Teaching Hospital) and schools. Ghana's economic development has been positively impacted by these public spending policies.

In addition to this physical infrastructure, African countries need massive investments in such forms of social infrastructure as education and health. One of the features in the development of the Asian Tigers was their investment in human capital. No nation has developed on the back of an uneducated population. While such investments can promote economic development, it is not clear whether high spending on public servants and politicians can similarly promote economic development.

POLICY ON PUBLIC SECTOR SALARIES AND WAGES

A public financial management approach that permits a continual growth of the public sector and dedicates a large proportion of tax revenue to the maintenance of the public sector will deny funds for investment. Limited investment in economic development will necessarily limit a country's ability to grow rapidly. Large public sectors have been associated with low levels of economic growth.

GOVERNMENT BORROWING

The whole agenda of the World Bank and IMF programme has been modelled on the Marshall Plan, which saw the USA spending in Europe in order to revive the economies of these nations. The thinking was therefore that if lending to governments and the concomitant spending could spur economic growth in Europe, why not developing countries? The Keynesian model only works where there is widespread under-utilization of resources, as was the case with the Great Depression in North America and Europe. LDC governments need to borrow to finance infrastructure and engage in other judicious public investments to spur economic development. But LDC government borrowing must be carried out under a financial policy that establishes debt sustainable targets and ceilings.

NATIONAL DEBT

Large national debt (debt as a percentage of GDP) implies devotion of significant financial resources to service this debt. Where the debt is of domestic origin, the debt service represents a transfer of resources from the general population to the better-off in the country. With a large external debt, the country will be transferring resources to foreign countries that are wealthier than the LDCs. Among highly indebted African countries, debt service has been observed to constitute more than a third of the national budget, while spending on basic social services, by contrast, has been less than 10 percent of the budget (World Bank, 2001).

It was in recognition of large LDC debt burdens being a constraint on development that the World Bank and the IMF established the Highly Indebted Poor Countries Initiative to provide a mechanism for a combination of debt forgiveness and re-scheduling so that such countries could focus more resources on poverty alleviation.

MACRO-ECONOMIC STABILITY

Governments should pursue financial management policies that will ensure low inflation, reasonable budget deficits and the prevalence of positive real interest rates for savers. Such a financial policy requires that government domestic borrowing be limited in order to avoid crowding out the private sector, whose development is crucial to national economic development. If real interest rates are low or negative, many citizens will not save and others will prefer to take their money out of the country (capital flight). According to the World Bank, savings and investments have increased in the case of some countries that have pursued policies to allow real interest rates to rise (World Bank, 1987, 1990).

Judicious and selective government interventions in the financial system, such as those pursued by South Korea and Taiwan, can spur economic growth. These interventions must have as their prime objective access to credit by SMEs. Long-term macro-economic strategies, objectives, measures or growth can be jeopardized by external shocks. LDC governments must therefore pursue policies to buffer their economies against the inevitable global uncertainties or external shocks, such as commodity price volatility and unstable official development assistance (ODA) and foreign direct investment (FDI).

TAXES

Tax administration as part of public financial policy must at least conform to Adam Smith's four canons of taxation. Smith referred to them as 'maxims' and they are summarized as follows:

- Canon of equality: economic justice; the rich should pay more. 'The subjects of every state ought to contribute towards the support of the government, as nearly as possible, in proportion to their respective abilities; that is, in proportion to the revenue which they respectively enjoy under the protection of the state.'
- Canon of certainty: there should be no arbitrariness in tax administration: 'that a very considerable degree of inequality … is not near so great an evil as a very small degree of uncertainty'.
- Canon of convenience: payment of the tax should be convenient to the taxpayer. The mode and timing of the tax payment should be convenient.
- Canon of economy: the cost of collection should be minimal. The taxpayers should not be too widespread and therefore the tax should not subsequently be difficult to administer.

The heavy reliance by LDC governments on indirect taxes is probably due to their ease of collection compared to direct taxes such as individual and corporate income taxes. This fiscal policy is consistent with Adam Smith's canon of economy.

LDC governments should invest in information systems that capture SMEs currently classified as the 'informal sector'. Developing countries should also pursue a policy of expanding the tax net to ensure that those who can afford it pay their fair share of taxes. This will represent a realization of Smith's canon of equality. An expanded tax net will provide more revenue for development investment.

Tax incentives to attract FDI should be promoted as an avenue to attain economic development. Care should be taken, however, so that such foreign companies do not unduly benefit from such tax incentives. Many African countries have instituted tax incentives such as tax holidays, exemptions from import duties and VAT, and rapid depreciation of assets to attract FDI, particularly in the extractive industries such as mining, oil and gas. But by competing with each other on the provision of these incentives, they have been in a 'race to the bottom'. One consequence is that many mining companies in Africa hardly pay corporate income taxes. In these cases, governments' principal revenue from the extractive industries has been royalties.

PROPERTY TAXES

Property taxes do not generally constitute a significant source of tax revenue in LDCs. In many industrialized countries, by contrast, property taxes are a significant source of revenue, particularly for local-level governments in a multi-level government system. Since property is usually owned by the wealthy, taxation of property will constitute a tax that meets the canon of ability to pay. Moreover, property tax revenue, if used to provide social services targeted at poverty reduction, will represent a progressive tax. In some industrialized countries, the property tax has been found to be regressive where landlords are able to shift the tax burden to tenants of lower income.

STATE-OWNED ENTERPRISES

Many African countries have state-owned enterprises (SOEs). Most of these SOEs have operated inefficiently, below installed capacity and at perennial losses. Under these circumstances, many SOEs operate on the basis of central government subsidies. However, these subsidies are provided at a high opportunity cost and lead to situations where schools and hospitals are not built. Moreover, roads and other forms of infrastructure and amenities are not provided.

MILITARY SPENDING

Between 1960 and 2000, the LDC share of military expenditures has skyrocketed from 8.3 percent to 27.5 percent (UNDP, *Human Development Reports*, 1992 and 1997; Todaro and Smith, 2009). The general consensus since Emile Benoit's studies is that military expenditure is negatively correlated with indicators of economic growth. Studies by David Lim (1983) and Alfred Maizels and Machiko Nissanke (1986) support the conclusion that LDC defence or military spending is inimical to economic growth. In a study of four ex-British colonies of West Africa, Agambila (1993) found a negative correlation between military expenditure and GDP. Financial policy focused on economic development must limit military expenditure to national security threats that have been analytically assessed.

PROVISION OF FINANCIAL RESOURCES FOR SMALL BUSINESSES/THE INFORMAL SECTOR

Micro-enterprises are important for the overall development of African economies. However, a major constraint on the development of such enterprises is finance. As part of a concerted programme of economic development, a policy to ensure that financial resources at affordable interest rates are available should be pursued. One way of accomplishing this objective is to reduce the risk of lending to micro-enterprises. A proper house/building address or location system and a credit rating system that can track borrowers are important building blocks in a financial system that will reach SMEs.

The needs of farmers, small producers, artisans (mechanics, carpenters, etc.), street vendors and other traders (particularly women) that are not met by commercial banks mean that other sources of funding are required. These small operators need financial institutions that can reach low-income neighbourhoods and rural areas far removed from the large urban centres where the commercial banks are wont to be concentrated to skim the cream of the bankable population. Without government intervention to assist these micro- and small enterprises (MSEs), they are left at the mercy of usurious money lenders or have to resort to rotating savings and credit associations. These associations are called *susu* in Ghana and their interest rates are not conducive to long- and/or medium-term investments.

Consequently, the establishment of Micro-Finance Institutions (MFIs) such as rural banks and savings and loans associations are policy initiatives that can unleash financial resources to MSEs and spur their development, and hence national economic development, all other things being equal.

Conclusions

There are a number of financial policies that have been shown in empirical studies to affect economic development. These policies should not be pursued in isolation, but must be part of a complete strategic approach to development. There is widespread human interest in economic development, particularly the factors that promote such development. This chapter has attempted to summarize empirical evidence on the relationship between national financial management and economic development. Within the broad concept of financial management, this chapter has narrowed its focus on fiscal policies, that is, on the taxing and spending policies of governments.

These policies are inextricably linked and must therefore be pursued holistically. Price liberalization has been shown to promote economic development by improving consumer choice and production efficiencies. Policies that encourage financial intermediation such as commercial banking and stock markets have mobilized finance for development. Public expenditure policy focused on improving physical and social infrastructure, while critical to economic development, must be undertaken within resource constraints. Deficits occasioned by profligate public expenditure on social and physical infrastructure can act as a drag on economic development. Similarly, it is important that the public sector wage bill be maintained at reasonable levels. A country's public sector is analogous to corporate overhead and must therefore be minimized, and limited to those sectors providing critical social services such as health, education and communal security.

While public debt is often necessary in developing countries to finance long-term infrastructure projects, an unsustainable debt burden can be a burden on development. However, kleptocratic governments in LDCs siphon off either natural resource revenues or public debt proceeds. In the latter case, unsustainable public debt burdens are assumed without the commensurate infrastructure or development to account for the accumulated public debt. While macro-economic stability cannot by itself promote economic development, it is the foundation upon which the superstructure of economic development is built. Even as taxes provide the needed revenue, they must conform to classical and modern principles of taxation. SOEs have often been a means to igniting and spurring industrialization in LDCs with limited private capital. SOEs can, however, be a drag on economic development if persistent poor management bleeds the public purse. In such cases, the state would be better off privatizing such enterprises. The state will be better off if its citizens acquire the enterprises being privatized. Military spending in LDCs often acts as a drag on economic development and should be minimized. Most LDCs are characterized by a large informal sector. Financial policies that enhance the growth of the informal and SME sectors will promote broad-based economic development. Economic development is therefore achieved through a concert of financial policies orchestrated by the government.

References

Abedian, I. and Biggs, M. (eds) (1998). *Economic Globalization and Fiscal Policy*. Cape Town: Oxford University Press.

Agambila, G. (1993). Militarization among the ex-colonies of West Africa. Unpublished PhD dissertation, New York University.

Anin, T.E. (2003). *An Economic Blue Print for Ghana*. Accra: Woeli Publishing Services.

Benoit, E. (1978). Growth and defense in developing countries. *Economic Development and Cultural Change*, 26, pp. 271–80.

Demirgue-Kunt, A. and Maksimuvil, V. (1996). Stock market development and firm financing choices. *World Bank Economic Review*, 10(2), pp. 341–69.

Easterly, W. and Schmidt-Hebbel, K. (1994). Fiscal adjustment and macroeconomic performance. In W. Easterly, C.A. Rodriquez and K. Schmidt-Hebbel (eds), *Public Sector Deficits and Macroeconomic Performance*. Oxford: Oxford University Press.

Ekanem, A. (2009). South Korean industrialization strategies: Lessons for Nigeria. *International Journal of Economic Development Issues*, 8(1–2), pp. 230–43.

Karras, G. (1994). Macroeconomic effects of budget deficits: Further internal evidence. *Journal of International Money and Finance*, 13, pp. 190–210.

Levine, R. and Zervos, S. (1998). Stock markets, banks and economic growth. *Amercian Economic Review*, 88(3), pp. 537–58.

Lim, D. (1983). Another look at growth and defense in less developed countries. *Economic Development and Cultural Change*, 31, pp. 377–84.

Maizels, A. and Nissanke, M. (1986). The determinants of military expenditures in developing countries. *World Development*, 14, pp. 1125–40.

Miller, M.H. (1998). Financial markets and economic growth. *Journal of Applied Corporate Finance*, 11(3), pp. 8–15.

Ramsey, F.P. (1928). A mathematical theory of savings. *Economics Journal*, December, cited in R.M. Solow, *Growth Theory: An Exposition*. Oxford: Clarendon Press, 1970, Chapter 5.

Singh, A. (1997). Financial liberalization, stock markets and economic development. *Economic Journal*, 107(2), pp. 771–82.

Smith, A. (2012). *An Enquiry into the Nature and the Causes of the Wealth of Nations*. Ware: Wordsworth Editions Ltd.

Stiglitz, J.E., Jaramillo-Vallejo, J. and Park, Y.-C. (1993). The role of the state in financial markets. *Annual Conference on Development Economics* (supplement), pp. 19–61.

Swan, T.W. (1956). Economic growth and capital accumulation. *Economic Record*, 32(63), pp. 334–61.

Todaro, M.P. and Smith, S. (2009). *Economic Development*. Harlow: Pearson.

World Bank (1987). *World Development Report*.

——. (1990). *World Development Report*.

——. (2001). *World Development Report*.

PART III
CULTURE, INSTITUTIONS AND PEOPLE

7

Institutional Building and National Development

Kwaku Appiah-Adu, Samuel Aning and Nana Kegya Appiah-Adu

Abstract

This chapter begins with the theoretical and comparative perspectives of the rationale for strong institutions in a country, followed by a discussion of national development strategy as a subject. Next, the chapter examines how effective national institutions can contribute to national development and, in this regard, an effort is made to improve understanding between strong institutions and economic growth. The last section undertakes a detailed analysis of institutions that impact on growth and national development. These include a productive and proactive public sector, strong labour market institutions, the rule of law and protection of property rights, integrity of governance and social inclusion that results in political stability. To conclude, the chapter calls on developing countries to understand the fact that building effective institutions that contribute to economic growth and national development is a critical issue that their governments need to appreciate in word and deed if they are to realize socio-economic advancement.

Introduction

It is generally acknowledged that one factor that underpins any country's remarkable growth is a set of institutions that facilitate the formulation and execution of effective development focused policies and strategies (North, 1990; Acemoglu et al., 2005). When sound policies are facilitated by solid institutions, the foundations for strong economic growth are not only laid but also ultimately advanced. Moreover, effectual public institutions engender favourable economic conditions for investment, which in turn positively impacts upon factor accumulation, technological advancement and efficiency improvements.

The Rationale for Strong National Institutions:
Theoretical and Comparative Perspectives

The state has a role to play in economic transformation. The experiences of thriving countries in Africa, Asia and South America suggest that, through their institutions, countries play a cardinal role in guiding and fostering national development. History indicates that many of the countries we classify as developed today received government support to stimulate and expedite their take-off and catch-up processes. Excellent national institutions not only encourage business investments and capital flows but also enhance the quality of public infrastructure and the policy environment. The outcome is a constructive effect on national development. Sustainable national advancement calls for the rule of law, an impartial judiciary, representative political institutions as well as effective laws and regulatory institutions in the key economic sectors.

The foregoing hypothesis underlines the link between the early roles played by the government and capacity building in the economic growth process. Detecting the capacity shortfalls of national institutions and tackling them exhaustively will ensure that these institutions provide services productively and enhance performance to accomplish socio-economic advancement.

A nation will be characterized by effective public institutions when there is synergy in all domains of the composition of national institutions. The key lessons which should be considered when developing strong national institutions entail the following:

a) The institutional configuration must support national priorities.
b) Institutional arrangements must be goal-focused and related to the goals identified.
c) Appropriate conditions must be created, including legislative framework, designation of authority and leadership at all levels.
d) Detailed activities, such as awareness generation, education, public engagement, research, training and data generation, and inventories must be part of the package since they encourage synergy among institutions.

The ability of a developing country to deliver capacity giving consideration to the foregoing principles is an assured recipe for socio-economic advancement. Hence, this capacity-building model is a critical factor for national development. It results in a type of development that stands the test of time. This kind of transformation transcends performing tasks; rather, it has much to do with transforming attitudes and mindsets.

Summarizing the issues, national institutions have a propensity to be more effective when they enjoy public legitimacy, are accessible, have an open organizational culture, ensure the integrity and quality of their members, have diverse membership and staff and gender balance, consult with civil society, have a clearly defined mandate, have an all-encompassing jurisdiction, have the power to monitor compliance with their recommendations, treat human rights issues systemically, mobilize adequate budgetary and external resources, develop effective international links, handle specific and collective complaints speedily and effectively, report annually on all aspects of their work and are accountable to Parliament (Chognuru and Joly, 2012).

National Development Strategy

The experience of the past two centuries demonstrates that when an economy is growing in leaps and bounds, it is an indication that politicians, public servants, labour and business executives are working within the configuration of a collaborative strategy. When the growth of an economy begins to slow down or retrogress, it is an indication that it does not have a national development strategy. A country's strength is conveyed in its devotion to the grand political ideals of modern civilizations – liberty, protection of its people and the environment, economic transformation and social justice – and in its ability to put together its resources and develop strategies to attain these goals. Not one of the aforementioned ideals can be attained merely through market forces. A country may facilitate economic development through an open market that promotes resourceful allocation of factors of production, yet is factually the result of a considered approach of improving living standards, embraced by a country utilizing the state as its primary institutional apparatus of joint action. It is the outcome of a country's strategy whose major players are businesspeople, where capital accumulation and the integration of expertise into production is the viable means of accomplishment, and where the government is accountable for facilitating interests and formulating policies adopted and founded on a national accord that entails the nation's principal social groups that are devoted to the country's advancement.

In the democracies of today, the state is the country's mechanism of collective action with the government or the bureaucracy, which are led by individuals or elected officials governing in the name of the citizenry. The strategic character of economic development evolves, first, from a country's requirements and prospects to co-ordinate its endeavours to improve its living standards and, second, from the strong link between this transformation and the accomplishment of other primary political goals. While development may, in the short term, usually occur at the expense of environmental protection and social justice, the link is unequivocal in the medium term. In addition, the significance of a national development strategy may be attributed to the fiercely competitive nature of free markets. Currently, within the context of globalization, where business and technological competition among countries transcends the whole rationale of international relations, the essence of national strategy becomes evident merely by observing or scanning the media. Each nation's local news indicates that a sizeable proportion of its politicians' energies focus on how to best encourage the nation's socio-economic advancement. Furthermore, regarding economic relations, primarily in the area of trade and to a certain extent technological and financial relations, countries experience intense competition, with each government fighting tooth and nail to protect the interests of its local companies (Bresser-Pereira, 2006).

How Effective National Institutions Contribute to National Development

On this issue, all echelons of a country's institutions must be considered. First, there are the constitutional bodies – the executive, legislature, judiciary, independent constitutional bodies as well as implementing agencies and local government institutions. Second, there are individual institutions like a ministry or a service – and the collaboration amongst the various institutions and services are to be given consideration so that a policy or decision does not encounter opposition or resistance when being worked on in different institutions: for instance, at the constitutional level, the process that starts from the political party manifesto to introduce a reform to the implementation of Parliamentary Act that needs to be enacted to achieve the required reform; or at the administrative level, the decision to transform the tools for enhanced service delivery, where sufficient and judicious financial resources, internal re-engineering, sensitization and training of participating civil servants will have to be co-ordinated in a coherent and rigorous way.

Moreover, it is contended that sound institutions are those that provide the enabling environment for socio-economic advancement, thus making the government's contribution valuable. It is held that effective institutions contribute to the ability of a nation to create wealth and grow economically (Acemoglu and Robinson, 2010). The authors maintain that the main cause of differences between the productive countries and the less productive ones is not the geography, but the institutions. They also argue that an institutional paradigm that unleashes growth does exist, which suggests that there are institutional settings that do not engender economic development. Their analysis covers both historical and contemporary cases. A contemporary case is Eastern Europe following the collapse of communism vs. post-Soviet states like Uzbekistan, while an historical case is how the South American and North American colonial masters organized themselves and the effects of these differences on their current levels of wealth, or why the Industrial Revolution spread so disproportionately across Europe (Western Europe vs. Eastern Europe).

The authors have shown this in Figure 7.1 below, which outlines that where the national ideal and vision are well articulated, and this is understood and imbibed by well-established institutions with the right culture (work ethic and attitudes) supported by effective systems and processes, there would be a corresponding effect on national development.

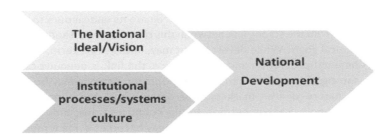

Figure 7.1   National Development Chart[1]

Wherein lies the distinction? Ineffective institutions do not facilitate growth and are typified by unprotected property rights, no respect for the rule of law, entry barriers and policies that inhibit the proper functioning of markets and discourage the creation of a level playing field. Regarding the area of political institutions, it is characterized by the concentration of power in the hands of a tiny minority, on which there are limited restraints, inadequate checks and balances and 'rule of law'.

Conversely, effective institutions facilitate growth and are typified by protected property rights, law and order, business friendly markets and investor-friendly governments that provide an enabling environment via public services and policies that are appropriately enforced, the upholding of contracts and to a large extent access by the majority of the populace to socio-economic opportunities such as education, health and business. In the political institutions arena, this converts into extensive involvement of the populace, controls on politicians, checks and balances as well as law and order. It is noteworthy that this is accompanied by some level of political centralization so that the government is capable of enforcing the rule of law and a clear vision of development that rises above regional disparities. This institutional paradigm is able to facilitate socio-economic advancement because it promotes investments, rationalizes the influence of markets with sounder resource allocation, and encourages the entry of productive businesses and the ability to finance start-up companies; it also spawns extensive participation owing to universal education, open market entry and wide-ranging property rights.

Nevertheless, history indicates that the undesirable paradigm (ineffective) has been more common compared to the desirable archetype (effective). It may be revealing to explore why this is the case. We need to note that free markets and economic transformation generate victors and the vanquished (such as organizations that lose their privileged positions when innovations or new approaches are instituted in the marketplace). This means that the creation of effective institutions may cost some people or organizations directly in the business or political sphere. It is vital to emphasize along with Acemoglu and Robinson (2010) that growth is complemented by investment in innovation and 'creative destruction': such 'creative destruction' is dreaded by

---

1   CASA Institutional and National Development Model (2012).

those who may lose out as a result, especially political losers, who are a principal obstacle to the evolution of effective institutions. Having said this, there are instances of growth in settings of ineffective institutions, when the top echelon in the nation has purposely allocated resources to highly productive pursuits that it controls or has permitted the development of stronger institutions under their influence. However, the extent to which such growth will last over the long term is questionable and the prosperity created is likely to remain in the hands of a tiny minority, so does not achieve much in terms of poverty reduction and general development. Adopting this stance, one would argue that creating strong institutions may sometimes call for the eradication of existing ones and transformation.

The degree of influence that capacity development could have on creating robust national institutions is determined by several variables, of which the capacity for successful change management is critical. It is important to tackle the innate complexities of the context because capacity building, whether deliberate or not, can result in role and responsibility shifts. These can threaten deep-seated interests in an institution and traditional power structures and call for modifications in beliefs, attitudes and behaviour. Given this, it seems that in order to facilitate a robust capacity-building process, it is essential to create the right political and socio-cultural incentives and marshal strong political commitment and ownership.

The Role of Institutions in the Policy Management Cycle

Although generally the development of growth-oriented national economic policies, strategies and activities underpins the plans of the majority of countries across the globe, only a few are able to achieve effective implementation. Several nations have formulated and continue to formulate policies directed towards developing human resources, financial and monetary consolidation, efficient market-based allocation, proactive allocation to emerging industries with superior growth prospects, and well-thought-through policies that jointly strengthen one another, transforming bearish economic conditions into bullish economic phases. Nevertheless, the issue with many of these nations is that the implementation of these impressive policies on paper has suffered (Appiah-Adu and Aning, 2012). This is reflected in the following ways: the policies are only partly executed or are not executed at all. In some cases, the policies are withdrawn shortly after their launch, while on other occasions, the valuable effect of the policy is nullified by new policies that are inconsistent or at odds with the existing one. A disciplined approach to the execution of sound policy is not achievable where there are no solid institutions to support the effective implementation of the policies. Any country that has succeeded in attaining national growth has demonstrated two critical traits – robust planning and excellent implementation.

Poorly resourced institutions stalled national development in many economies because they hampered the execution of well-conceived economic policies. A weak public sector, particularly the civil service and local government, will have a negative impact on the execution of accelerated growth policies, for example, fiscal consolidation (Ghesquiere, 2007). The absence of effective and transparent government has resulted in a situation where nations have been unable to build sound health, education and labour market systems for a productive and competitive human capital base or to facilitate resilient banking systems and capital markets that engender economic growth and national development.

It has been suggested that the absence of political commitment is the cause of poor execution of dynamic growth-oriented policies. Some of the symptoms of the lack of political commitment are unwieldy bureaucracy that makes the setting up of new business expensive and laborious, obdurate labour markets, the charity of government towards unprofitable public sector institutions and the tolerance of high inflationary conditions in spite of laudable national policy objectives. Nevertheless, fundamental to weak policy execution is almost invariably a poorly working social pact about what comprises an even-handed sharing of the benefits and costs (profits and losses) from national development.

Frivolous consent in support of ambiguous values frequently disguises deep-seated disharmony within society about the apparent allocation of the gains and losses associated with national development. As a result of the difficult task of convincing societal opinion and the media, policies are often hardly executed. If a government can overcome this challenge, it becomes relatively easier to implement policies.

Institutions have been defined as the 'rules of the game' that establish the incentives and shape the behaviour of organizations and people in society (North, 1991). Institutions may represent informal ideals and standards, for instance, those that determine official conduct. Alternatively, institutions may be characterized by formal systems such as a nation's constitution, laws, regulations and internal procedures. Institutions are usually created by human beings and embedded in history. They establish the incentives that facilitate the co-ordination and workings of society in a systematic manner, and this is sometimes achieved via contracts. Effective institutions generate the shared accord that is essential in order to enable the execution of judicious policies in furtherance of national development. Institutions are the apparatus of governance.

Understanding How Effective Institutions Impact on Economic Growth

Conventional wisdom suggests that sound institutions have a direct effect on factor accumulation and productivity improvement. Regard for the rule of law, a trustworthy judiciary system and due recognition for property rights are factors that promote investment. Institutions that support development ensure that there are safeguards against the plundering of the national wealth and abuse of individual property rights. Where such institutions do not exist, concerns about losing these benefits inhibit investment in material and human resources and labour input.

Institutions that foster growth also permit workers and businesses to benefit from the prospects provided by technological advancement or international business transactions (World Bank, 2002). Sound institutions as reflected by adaptable labour markets, clear entry and exit guidelines for businesses, and access to capital and skills provide individuals and businesses with the platform to benefit from free market prospects. In the absence of effective institutions, accelerated reform of the economy to higher-value enhancement endeavours and the ensuing productivity increases are hindered.

Several slow-growing economies did not possess the institutions that facilitate the continuous execution of socio-economic policies that are conducive to phenomenal rates of material and human resource development, labour market involvement, technological advancement and productivity improvements. Sound economic plans and institutions are inexorably linked. Indeed, both are prerequisites for the attainment of economic growth and national development.

Interestingly, research has shown that 75 percent of the level of per capita income spanning various nations could be attributed to variations in institutions (Acemoglu et al., 2005). Nations that are well developed economically usually have solid institutions, whereas economically weak nations usually have weak institutions. In the study by Acemoglu et al. (2005), the measure of a nation's institutions is captured via perceptions of a country's regard for the rule of law and the integrity of its public service. One striking illustration of the function of economic policies as fashioned by different national institutions is evidenced in the economic growth and national development of South and North Korea since the early 1950s (Weil, 2005).

Institutions that Impact on Growth

A country that aspires to achieve sustainable economic growth needs to develop resilient institutions that engender favourable conditions to attract investment and also facilitate the nurturing and thriving of businesses. Key among these institutions are the following: a productive and proactive public sector, the rule of law and protection of property rights, the integrity of governance and political stability engendered by unity.

A PRODUCTIVE AND PROACTIVE PUBLIC SECTOR

In this context, the civil service, the government and the public service as a whole need to be highly efficient and effective (*The Economist*, 23 March 2006). Recruitment, promotion and retention should be based on merit. In countries such as Canada, Singapore, Malaysia and the UK, the civil service is held in high esteem. Its salary and benefits package are comparable to that of the private sector. Government is able to maintain this policy of rewarding the civil servant because every effort is made not to overstaff the service. When a country has several high-performing and successful institutions, these organizations are able to instil into their public servants a culture of efficient and effective service delivery to the nation's citizens.

One country that has been able to obtain the best from its public service is Singapore. The country has created a number of strategic institutions that have ensured that in all areas of the economy, Singapore is well placed to take maximum advantage of opportunities presented to it. It would be insightful to examine some of these institutions.

First, the Economic Development Board (EDB) is the principal governmental organization responsible for formulating and implementing Singapore's development plans, and has developed a reputation for competence since its establishment in the early 1960s. The management of the EDB has been instrumental in promoting investment, negotiating terms and synchronizing a one-stop shop for global businesses that selected Singapore as their base for exporting worldwide. Employees are carefully recruited with an emphasis on willingness to learn, high levels of motivation and top performers (Lee Kuan Yew, 2000). The breadth and depth of the skillset of the EDB has served as a key institutional link that sustains the array of economic strategies aimed at enhancing foreign direct investment in Singapore (Schein, 1996).

Second, the Monetary Authority of Singapore (MAS) facilitated the development and implementation of sound banking policies, and also encouraged the deepening of the country's financial markets. Not surprisingly, Singapore has become a global financial centre where financial services accounted for 12 percent of GDP in 2011. An insightful lesson learnt here is that the MAS adopted a gradual approach in its efforts to regulate the financial services industry, emphasizing high capital adequacy for financial institutions and prudently scrutinizing these institutions for non-performing assets and conformity to related policies. Such judicious monitoring engendered confidence amongst investors and may also be the reason why in economic terms Singapore fared better than its neighbours, suffering limited harm within its financial sector during the Asian financial crisis of the late 1990s (Peebles and Wilson, 2004).

Third, the agency responsible for collecting taxes, which had under-performed in the late 1980s, was transformed into a statutory board in the early 1990s and was re-named the Internal Revenue Authority of Singapore (IRAS). The new arrangement is that the government pays the

IRAS a performance-related fee for its functions. The work of the tax authority was enhanced through business process improvement, adoption of technology and the introduction of self-assessment by taxpayers. These changes helped to wipe out a huge pile-up of tax assessments that had accumulated over decades and also led to a great improvement in staff motivation.

LABOUR MARKET INSTITUTIONS

In many industrialized nations, the government tends to play an umpiring role between capital and labour as a means of tempering industrial conflict. In 1919, the term 'tripartism' became embedded in the constitution of the International Labour Organization as a way of integrating the obligations of organizational performance and national growth on the one hand with social justice on the other. Some countries have formally established remuneration commissions that develop a structure for methodical pay settlements and to forestall pay negotiations from igniting inflation in a contracting labour market. Constituted by representatives of government, unions and employers, and usually chaired by a non-aligned person, the commission's decisions are arrived at through compromise (Mauzy and Milne, 2002). Prior to making its decisions every year, the commission examines the movement of economic indicators and thereafter advises the government on the guiding principles for pay adjustment for various industries. These guiding principles may be quantitative or qualitative, but in today's increasingly market-focused economic environment, the tendency is more towards a multi-dimensional pay system. Where quantitative measures are proposed, public sector organizations usually observe the guidelines. When it is effective in the discharge of its duties, the pay commission tends to provide the government with a number of advantages. These include the commitment to shared growth, offering government an avenue for learning from organizations about the business environment, market experiences and global competition. In achieving collaboration between employers and employees, industrial action is reduced significantly, in effect generating an attractive marketplace that is favourable to investment and productivity improvement.

THE RULE OF LAW AND PROTECTION OF PROPERTY RIGHTS

One critical public good that every government needs to proffer is the *rule of law*. The rule of law is a critical ingredient in any system of governance that is supportive of human rights and the entrenchment of fundamental freedoms. Indeed, the rule of law refers to fair legal systems and processes that are implemented or enforced in a manner that is impartial or retroactive. When the law is applied appropriately, it gives assurance to potential investors that their activities are safe and are guaranteed legal protection.

Important questions that potential investors would ask include the following. Are contracts enforced in a low-cost manner? Are private property and an individual's personal security protected from predation by the more powerful? In the context of the rule of law, disputes are resolved via a sound and neutral judiciary based on clearly established laws, not via subjective pronouncements or discretionary powers as might be acquired through political influence. Moreover, nobody can be penalized if the person has not broken the country's laws and where one trespasses the law, punishment can only be meted out in a recognized court of law. Regard for the law and the enforcement of its tenets in effect prevents influential people from unscrupulously snatching assets belonging to private citizens. It is believed that the failure of nations to put in place robust, easy-to-implement contract enforcement is one of the major reasons for a lack of development in the past and present (North, 1990).

Economic strength and growth are built on a framework that facilitates law and order. The stringent application of the law and appropriate punishment for lawbreakers engender confidence that society and its assets will be safeguarded if there is a breach of their rights. Preserving the tenets of parity in the context of the law may call for leaders to be bold, hardnosed or seemingly callous depending on the circumstances.

Developing a world-class judiciary system may take decades. Any judicial reform has to be developed from first principles in order to be sustained and to stand the test of time. First, on the issue of human resources: there must be a dispassionate and transparent process of recruiting the most competent and committed individual to the position of chief justice; this person must be awarded a commensurate compensation package and he or she must be acknowledged as a leader and role model by the judges; furthermore, the recruitment of judges must be based on merit. Second, regarding systems, the court processes must be transformed with information technology driving change. Third, amendments to the regulations and routines must be instituted to forestall any lags and maintain the timeliness of justice. Upholding discipline and fairness is the hallmark of an excellent institution in the judicial system and, moreover, this must be combined with speed, proficiency and cost-effectiveness.

Exercising the law resolutely and objectively can contribute to economic growth in diverse ways. Regard for labour laws facilitates the strengthening of good relations between employers and employees. It bolsters government and positively influences the furtherance of the policy and institutional environment. It offers guarantees to potential investors that their assets would be safeguarded and agreements honoured. Moreover, the low crime levels help to make the country the preferred investment destination for global enterprises seeking to expand overseas. It engenders assurances in the stability of the financial system.

THE INTEGRITY OF GOVERNANCE

It is universally acknowledged that one main impediment to socio-economic development is corruption. It is a canker that eats away the institutional underpinnings on which development hinges. This does not infer that development is unattainable where corruption exists. In the nineteenth century, New York City made economic advances without totally stamping out corruption. The same can be said of China, Taiwan, Japan and South Korea if we want to cite relatively recent examples. However, corruption, which is described as the exploitation of public influence for personal benefit, is detrimental in many respects. It gives rise to lethargic attitudes towards administrative processes as public servants attempt to extract bribes before attending to issues on their desks and undermines the judiciary. Where corruption is rife, citizens concentrate their efforts on recycling existing resources instead of innovating to generate additional wealth, which calls for confidence and access to business prospects. Corruption erodes citizens' confidence in genuine regulation, generates arbitrariness that results in ambiguity and exacerbates the cost of doing business. Governments that aim to encourage existing businesses in their country to expand and also attract investment from foreign businesses should strive to minimize incentives and opportunities for corruption using a variety of strategies (Tanzi, 1998).

Integrity of governance should begin with government leaders. Any attempts to wipe out corruption should start with the main culprits at the top echelons of government. High standards should be set by the government for itself, ensuring that there is accountability and probity associated with government expenditure. As far as the law is concerned, nobody in the country should be untouchable. Leaders should be prepared to defend themselves in the law courts if a case is brought against them. The media would have to respect a court's decision if it is ordered by the courts to retract claims of corruption levelled against a leading public official and/or pay financial compensation to the official if the media is found guilty of defaming the person.

Irrespective of a person's position in society or government, there must be uniformity in the application of the law to all. Firm leadership is fundamental to maintaining high moral principles. Total backing must be offered both in word and deed by national leaders to anti-corruption agencies in order for them to apply the rules. Any effort to corrupt a public official should be punished by law, and if a guilty verdict is established against a public official, the person should be prosecuted and have his or her appointment terminated. Such disincentives facilitate accountability and probity.

Using the carrot-and-stick approach, the disincentive of chastisement is balanced by the incentive of high compensation packages akin to analogous positions in the business world. This is regarded as crucial if accountability and probity are to be maintained (Mauzy and Milne, 2002). While this strategy makes it possible to draw first-class human resources to the public sector, it also helps to prevent enticements to abuse one's public office for personal benefit.

Every effort has to be made to seal loopholes that provide an opportunity for corruption. In the public sector, unambiguous guidelines regarding recruitment, promotion and retention based on meritocracy are published in order to minimize the use of discretion in these areas. In order to avoid conditions where public officials spend huge sums of money on re-election, a government may institute a policy to govern campaign periods. Integrity should be given a high priority by the government. In this context, investigators should be given enough authority to examine the financial statements of suspects and their family or close business associates, and confirmation that a suspect's lifestyle is inconsistent with his or her income provides enough proof of corruption. Moreover, it is mandatory for subpoenaed witnesses to appear before investigators or law courts in order to be examined.

POLITICAL STABILITY ENGENDERED BY UNITY

Unity among the diverse amongst ethnic groups within a country is critical for national development. In any country, different people may have varied inclinations and choices. The government should be tolerant of different groups of people regardless of their racial, ethnic or religious background. Every effort must be made to ensure that minority groups are not marginalized and that, as far as possible, they are fairly represented. In many countries, national service is one mechanism that helps to develop unity and harmony amongst its different groups of citizens. Misapprehensions and tensions associated with labour can be prevented through a blend of appropriate policies. Deliberate policies have to be instituted to reduce social inequalities and release vitality for economic quests. Favourable macro-economic indicators result in political and socio-economic stability, which, in turn, are principal considerations when businesses are making a decision to invest in a foreign country.

Conclusions

Developing countries need to appreciate that building institutions that contribute to economic growth and national development is a critical issue that their governments continue to grapple with. Developing nations that are characterized by robust policy management and decision-making systems, high regard for the rule of law, a strong reputation regarding integrity in governance, and a sound social inclusion culture that engenders political stability, possess a splendid combination of attributes that support and ultimately result in economic growth and national development. Though these attributes may comprise a mix of official and informal standards and rules, they determine prospects and incentives that come the way of businesses and citizens. Several countries have squandered huge resources in their efforts to take control of current output or in other fruitless pursuits. For countries that have been transformed from developing to developed status, one of the underpinning pillars has been their set of institutions. In such countries, institutions channel citizens' energies toward the development of material and human resources and improved labour productivity, the acquisition and diffusion of innovation via modern technologies, and the shifting of financial and human resources to industries that generate enhanced value. The foregoing should constitute the set of goals of all developing economies aspiring to transform their economies from a survival stage to a thriving and sustainable phase.

References

Acemoglu, D., Johnson, S. and Robinson, J. (2005). Institutions as the fundamental cause of long-run growth. In P. Aghion and S. Durlauf (eds), *Handbook of the Economic Growth*. Amsterdam: Elsevier, pp. 1499–542.

Acemoglu, D. and Robinson, J. (2010). The role of institutions in growth and development. In D. Brady and M. Spence (eds), *Leadership and Development*. Washington DC: World Bank, pp. 135–64.

Appiah-Adu, K. and Aning, S. (2012). Enhancing government's policy management and decision making system: The case of Ghana's central governance reforms project. *Canadian Public Administration Journal*, 55(1), pp. 125–47.

Bresser-Pereira, L.C. (2006). Estrategia Nacional de Desenvolvimento. *Revista de Economia Politica*, 26(2), pp. 203–30.

Chognuru, J. and Joly, C. (2012). Capacity development: Building effective national institutions. Technical paper presented to the Consultative Group Meeting, Accra, Ghana, June.

Ghesquiere, H. (2007). *Singapore's Success: Engineering Economic Success*. Singapore: Thomson Publishing.

Lee Kuan Yew (2000). *From Third World to First: The Singapore Story 1965–2000*. Singapore: Singapore Press Holdings.

Mauzy, D. and Milne, R. (2002). *Singapore Politics: Under the People's Action Party*. London: Routledge.

North, D. (1990). *Institutions, Institutional Change and Economic Performance*. New York: Cambridge University Press.

Peebles, G. and Wilson, P. (2004). The economic vulnerability and resilience of small islands states: The case of Singapore. Chapter 11 in L. Briguglio and E. Kisanga (eds), *Economic Vulnerability and Resilience of Small States*. Malta: Formatek Ltd, pp. 187–231.

Schein, E. (1996). *Strategic Pragmatism: The Culture of Singapore's Economic Development Board*. Cambridge MA: MIT Press.

Tanzi, V. (1998). Corruption around the world: Causes, consequences, scope and cures. *International Monetary Fund Working Paper*, WP/98/63.

Weil, D. (2005). *Economic Growth*. Boston: Pearson Education, Addison Wesley.

World Bank (2002). *Building Institutions for Markets. World Development Report*. New York: Oxford University Press.

National Culture and Economic Development

8

Kwaku Appiah-Adu

Abstract

This chapter focuses on a subject that has continuously engaged the minds of development scholars and practitioners. It begins with an examination of the importance of national culture, followed by the role of economics in today's world. Theoretical foundations regarding the potential links between economics and national development are laid. A question that is asked in this regard is whether certain types of culture perform better economically, and within this context the concepts of values and attitudes are discussed in detail. Subsequently, there is a focus on how these issues are pertinent to the economies of the developing world, with an attempt to determine how we can propel national development through culture. Finally, the chapter proposes a holistic approach to the culture-national development relationship.

Introduction

In simple terms, national culture encapsulates people's values, attitudes and beliefs. The subject explored in this chapter addresses how a country's cultural characteristics impact policies and institutions that favour economic growth, thereby helping to shape the incentives and prospects that promote economic development. Moreover, cultural attributes such as assiduousness, determination to excel, being receptive to new ideas, trust and capacity to co-operate may have an express influence on factors considered to have a direct impact on economic development. It is argued that if policies and institutions favouring growth are not in place, it is hardly likely that cultural features would have a significant impact.

The Importance of Culture

Culture, in the context of this book, is simply described as the mindsets of people. Curiously, culture is hardly discussed in the literature pertaining to economic development. On the contrary, the part played by institutions has assumed ever-increasing importance over the last 30 years. It has been argued (Myrdal, 1968) that institutions are a key antecedent to economic development. In addition, Myrdal emphasized the significance of values and attitudes in highlighting and interrelating to institutions. He indicated how attitudes that are widespread in conventional, largely rural communities hampered economic development. Indeed, he suggested that economists were unwilling to discuss attitudes owing to a desire to be politically correct.

The unwillingness to discuss culture may also be attributed to other factors. For economists, the more quantifiable a field is, the better it lends itself to discussion. Moreover, culture is harder to scrutinize objectively: when an economy has achieved growth, one may subliminally examine its cultural attributes in a discriminatory manner. Furthermore, the trend of causality may be unclear since economic development can change people's culture. Yet still economic development and its key fundamental values may leave us in two minds. The influential economist Keynes (1930) regarded the cultural attributes that foster economic development – an emphasis on how to improve things in the future instead of living for today, the deification of hard work and the adoration of money – repugnant and went on to state that, unfortunately, until the goal of economic development had been attained, avarice and precaution might be our gods for a little longer.

During the late 1980s and 1990s, the concept of values was extensively discussed. The search for reasons for the accelerated growth of some Asian economies attracted interest to cultural attributes. These high-growth Asian economies were characterized by a good work ethic and frugality. These attributes were a reflection of values that had been stressed by Confucius several centuries earlier. The outstanding results of the economies of these Asian 'Tigers' understandably engendered some pride in Asians who had been made to feel that their culture was inferior to that of Western societies. Many Asians sought a sense of identity and, indeed, even within this context, some felt unease at the universality of the expression 'Asian' for values that were only reflective of a section of Asia and not the whole continent. That said, many agree that highly successful socio-economic systems and their future improvement combine facets of both Eastern and Western practices.

Nevertheless, clear cultural values, attitudes and beliefs may distinguish a country from other, economically less successful countries. For this reason, governments may deliberately develop a national crusade over a sustained period to expressly influence citizens' attitudes and behaviours, as the government of Ghana did during the first decade of the twenty-first century through the establishment of a Ministry of Information and National Orientation. Some African and South American governments have embarked on campaigns to instil time-consciousness into the fabric of their societies, having commissioned research that revealed the adverse impact of lateness on national economic performance. In some Asian countries, nationals have been charged to maintain hygienic conditions in all aspects of national life, handle public property with care, keep public spaces clean, maintain healthy sanitary conditions in public washrooms, and be hospitable to tourists and one another. Primarily, a government may mould and reinforce values, regarding them as an inextricable component in executing policies and influence national institutions. Clearly identifiable values may form the ideology of a government and the set of beliefs that envelope its policies and institutions. They also play a part in branding the country globally and facilitate the attainment of national unity in a country. Clearly articulated cultural and social changes can help a country to achieve success.

In some societies, governments may be less oriented to play such an influencing role; indeed, the society may perceive it as patronizing. While governments that adopt this approach may be derided by other countries, particularly those in 'very free' societies, it is possible that a government can encourage churches, schools and other parallel organizations to play this function. To explore the functions of roles and attitudes, it would be insightful to ask what are the cultures and mindsets that (tend to) foster growth-oriented institutions? Is there a set of values that can instigate action and validate it? Within a variety of national contexts, this chapter attempts to examine different sets of values that have been instrumental in facilitating growth in some countries that have moved from the league of under-developed countries to the category of developed nations.

Today's World

In today's world of globalization where capital can cross national borders so effortlessly, investment funds can be transferred from one nation to another swiftly to take advantage of new business opportunities, economic development is achievable in the most unexpected of places. In our current environment, as was never the case previously, it is possible for any country in the world to realize economic growth.

Key to attracting investment is to position the country as investor-friendly not only in perception but also in reality and to facilitate investment via modern technology. Obviously, the country must meet the conditions required to attract investment. However, if the country has a stable government, has demonstrated that it upholds the rule of law and has a business-friendly environment, these enabling conditions should provide the basis to power the country's engine of steady economic growth.

One snag is that not all deprived countries are capable of meeting these requirements. Indeed, in some places, the situation is as if there is a curse that is preventing economies in those locations from growing or flourishing. However, even if the major conditions are largely fulfilled, that is, the government is conscientious and officially the nation is friendly to foreign investors, there may be other dynamics that cause investors to have cold feet and retreat, and head off to another destination to invest their money. Perhaps there are criteria for economic development, more comprehensive and nuanced than the provisions commonly stipulated, that focus on the country's culture and its customs. In other words, economic development could possibly be influenced by those nuances that are jointly referred to as culture.

Economics with Culture

As a subject and functional area, economics has undergone a significant transformation since its inception. The discipline, based on its technical principles and specific measures, has recorded a series of solutions for failing markets. Nevertheless, how economics relates to culture, which as a concept is not that orderly, is still an issue that is yet to be fully resolved.

This has not always been the case. During its inception period, economics encapsulated elements of human behaviour in exposition. In his seminal work entitled *An Inquiry into the Nature and Causes of the Wealth of Nations* (1776), Adam Smith, widely regarded as one of the foremost proponents of economics theory and practice, postulated that each individual, stimulated by the quest to fulfil his own desires, provides towards the public interest in a structure that regulates itself. Smith was visionary enough to acknowledge that the 'pursuit of personal interests' encompassed much more than merely enriching oneself. Consequently, his article 'Theory of Moral Sentiments' focuses on what is known as cultural values in modern times. Decades later, John Stuart Mill (1956 [1843]) reiterated Adam Smith's idea by arguing that cultural considerations on individuals could have a greater effect on them than the quest for individual financial prosperity.

At the beginning of the twentieth century, the German sociologist, philosopher and political scientist Max Weber (2001 [1905]) proposed more precise insights into how culture and religion could influence economic performance. He posited that the Protestant work ethos, buttressed by Reformation doctrines that the quest for prosperity was an obligation, instilled the qualities required for optimum economic productivity. He argued that this was one of the major reasons why, comparatively, Protestants were more productive than Catholics throughout Europe (comparing Great Britain and Germany on the one hand with Ireland, Spain, Portugal and Italy on the other hand at the start of the twentieth century).

In the interim, the standpoint of economists was undergoing profound transformation. Economic development was now a real possibility and economics had discarded its dour hypothesis propounded by Malthus (1798) earlier in the eighteenth century that population explosion confined human beings to waning living standards since it was deemed that, with the world's total wealth being constant and a limit to what the world could produce, in no time, most of the world's population would be relegated to scrambling for crumbs from the table. Nonetheless, the phenomenal growth of Western economies during the nineteenth century clearly indicated that the underlying set of assumptions needed to be altered. Consequently, economic theory was guided by the new perception that there was growing affluence and an ever-increasing pool of economic resources to benefit from. This had positive implications for under-developed countries and also meant that such nations had the opportunity of becoming upwardly mobile and joining the league of highly developed economies.

Following the optimism provided to the under-developed that they could become members of the developed league of nations, economists since the 1930s have spent much more effort on developing models associated with issues like the management of inflation, exchange rates, interest rates, employment, rents, income policies, price stability and markets. Economists have also been honing their formulae to investigate the hypotheses that the subject has been developing. The major focus of economics has been in estimating the effect of diverse economic and business variables on market crises in order to put in place a reliable spectrum of principles for better forecasting and management of these crises.

Curiously, in the midst of its fascination with models, formulae, mathematics, forecasting and their associated variables, the attention of economics on culture has been diminishing. Its premise is that human beings are susceptible to the universal concepts of supply and demand, maximization of profit and other fundamental economic variables, regardless of where they live in the world. The systems it has devised to analyse and manage economic situations are independent and have little room for the vagaries of human behaviour (Hezel, 2009). Today, paradoxically enough, with the proponents of globalization trumpeting new hope for countries striving to break the back of poverty, economics does not proffer much to assist them on how this can be achieved. In other words, the discipline's desertion of its initial interest in culture has dumbfounded those who would have benefited most from its assistance in this present time.

Is Culture Really Important?

Clearly, some nations excel whereas others regress or at best remain stagnant irrespective of the fact that they all have in place the essential economic features. For instance, in Asia, there are some nations with a strong resource base and a well-educated society but that are averse to development. Moreover, what accounts for the slow economic growth rates of the Pacific nations? In the same vein, there are many African countries that still remain under-developed in spite of the numerous financial assistance programmes and packages they have received from various development partners to develop their economies over the past half-century.

In explaining such differences, development economists may focus on the various requirements that must be fulfilled for an economy to take root and grow. Some of these criteria are: a stable political system; good governance as a prerequisite of development; entrenchment of the rule of law where laws are not only explicit but are also enforced and contractual agreements are respected; and public officials who are honest and efficient. In addition, land and rental values should be reasonably priced for business prospects, with foreign investment actively promoted and a painless process for applying for a business permit.

While the above criteria are of critical importance, they do not directly address the basic issue regarding the effect of culture on national development. In her seminal book *World on Fire* (2004), Amy Chua asserts that some cultural groups excel in commerce compared with the rest of the population, in spite of the fact that they are in the minority in their society. This can be seen in many societies across the world and the question is what accounts for this?

Some interesting revelations are made by Chua in her book. For example, it is observed that though ethnic Chinese in the Philippines constitute less than two percent of the population, they command 60 percent of the country's private sector, including the nation's four leading airlines and the majority of the nation's financial institutions, leisure, hospitality and tourism firms, and large retail outlets. Interestingly, the Philippines is not the only place where Chinese ethnic minorities have made a significant impact; indeed, they have also assumed control over commerce in other countries around the world. Some of the regions the Chinese have impacted upon include South-East Asia, particularly Burma, Indonesia, Malaysia and Thailand. Still closer to China, the Chinese have excelled in Majuro, the Solomon Islands and Tonga. Today, they are making significant inroads to Africa. Not surprisingly, this success has sparked sporadic remonstrations from native citizens.

A cursory observation of the success of minority groups across the globe reveals that the Chinese are not the only group to have achieved this feat in 'foreign' lands. Regardless of geographical location, there are several instances of successful minorities around the world. In Latin America, people of Caucasian lineage have tended to dominate the economy compared to citizens of darker complexion. In the former Yugoslavia, the Croats succeeded in various fields of the economy and consequently were characterized by a higher standard of living compared to the majority of Serbs. In Russia, following the divestiture of state enterprises, the immediate aftermath revealed that the overwhelming majority of billionaires resulting from the divestiture were Jews. In addition, in many West African countries, the Lebanese are a dominant force in the fields of trade and commerce, whereas in East Africa, the Indians are renowned as the leading entrepreneurs.

While some ethnic minorities tend to achieve huge success in countries where they are not considered natives, this prosperity can trigger fierce protests against these groups that are perceived as minorities in the countries where they have settled. Although since the 1990s and early 2000s, the concept of globalization has been touted as a phenomenon that would cause the world to shrink to a small village and would synchronize consumer behaviour, revolutions have taken place in many countries and continents across the globe to wrest economic power from powerful entrepreneurial minorities.

Examples of continents where such revolts have occurred include Africa (e.g. Ethiopia, Rwanda and Zimbabwe), Asia (e.g. Indonesia) and Europe (e.g., Serbia). A closer examination of the underlying reasons reveals that the fundamental motivation was to rectify what the majority considered to be an imbalance through confiscation of assets, expulsion of ethnic minorities or, in the most extreme case, through wars of genocide. The whole world would testify that these disturbances not only resulted in human atrocities but also caused further destitution after hostilities ceased. The nations that had sought to reclaim the wealth they felt was justly theirs degenerated into deeper poverty after the failure of the indigenous citizens to whom trade and commerce were passed on to make them viable.

In spite of the above challenges, the call to a globalization that will provide all ethnic groups with equal opportunities continues to be trumpeted. If this promise has substance and can be fulfilled, it offers tremendous optimism to many. However, it is mere rhetoric and with little promise of fulfilment, the likelihood of uprisings based on ethnicity spawned by frustration will remain a real threat.

Reasons for the Distinctions

Given the evidence in the foregoing sections, it is plausible to suggest that some cultural groups seem to perform comparatively better than others. If we accept this proposition, then what accounts for the distinctions? The actual aim of this question, clearly, is to ascertain what might be done to offset these inequalities and annul the relative demerits that some cultures appear to manifest in this era of globalization.

In Gregory Clark's book *A Farewell to Alms* (2008), in which he expertly covers the economic history of the world, one of the subjects examined is the differences in cultures. Clark posits that it was not coincidental that Great Britain, rather than any other nation, was the birthplace of the Industrial Revolution. While his book focuses more on the precursors to the Industrial Revolution as opposed to the momentous effect of this cutting-edge revolution on ensuing history, he indicates that it occasioned what he terms the 'Great Divergence'. So, while the Industrial Revolution certainly provided significant innovations in production and operations technology, many nations were thrust deeper into poverty just as many nations were propelled to higher levels of prosperity. From the mid-nineteenth century, the zenith of the Industrial Revolution, the disparities in national income and standard of living around the world became even more pronounced compared to the earlier periods leading up to the Industrial Revolution and it seems that these disparities have been widening further as the years have gone by.

It is argued that there was a reason why Great Britain was uniquely placed to be the country for the Industrial Revolution to take off. A critical analysis of the impact of the Industrial Revolution shows that its influence varied from one part of the world to another. Did Great Britain precipitously make a quantum leap that was fuelled by innovation derived from a few energy-propelled equipment of the Industrial Revolution? Not really. Instead, according to Clark (2008), it was a step-by-step process occurring over a period of few centuries leading up to the nineteenth century. Clark contends that the Industrial Revolution would not have occurred had it not been for the changes in values that had taken place centuries before. Following the signing of the Magna Carta in the thirteenth century which curbed royal authority, Great Britain was characterized by a period of political stability, as well as solid economic and legal institutions frequently hailed as prerequisites for economic advancement.

On their own, however, such institutions do not spawn economic prosperity. Though political stability, effective markets, a trustworthy legal system and predictable land values were fundamental conditions, they were not sufficient for the economic leap that Great Britain witnessed when successful production and operations innovations were introduced through the birth of the Industrial Revolution. That said, the aforementioned prerequisites undoubtedly did result in the steady development of precisely such an array of profound cultural transformations, in particular, an appreciation of competitiveness and robust work values that were essential for rapid technological revolutions to have a sound effect on a people. At the beginning of the Industrial Revolution, Great Britain was characterized by a society that was losing its penchant for hostilities, a nation with an increasing middle-class population, where people had to be productive in order to obtain a competitive edge over their colleagues, a people who were increasingly well educated and tolerant. This bundle of attributes, usually related to the middle class, provided many with advantages in surviving and, indeed, in certain cases thriving, just as speed of response, powerful legs and an excellent aim might have in a previous era and different setting. Undoubtedly, these attributes served the people of Britain well.

Since all of this preceded the Industrial Revolution, when innovative production and operations management took off in a big way in the early nineteenth century, the people of Great Britain were able to utilize them to grow their economy several times over. On the other hand, when India had the opportunity of experiencing the Industrial Revolution, the outcomes were completely different. The engine-propelled cotton mills that had stimulated such an astounding economic surge in Great Britain were brought to the doorstep of India, but the country never truly experienced the same competitive edge.

Evidently, given the cultural attributes of British workers that resulted in a superior work ethic, British-operated mills were many times more cost-efficient than Indian-managed mills, with the comparative efficiency levels completely eclipsing the argument that hourly rates for British employees were four times those of their Indian compatriots (Hezel, 2009). For the Indians to make up for their comparative low productivity per employee and also to position themselves to achieve optimal output, the solution would be to hire more personnel. However, this resulted in higher staff costs relative to staff costs in a British mill, ultimately rendering the Indian-managed mill less productive. Thus, in the final analysis, a major determining factor of the difference between these sets of workers was the people and the inherent values which had been cultivated during their lifetime.

Values and Attitudes

Is there a relationship between culture and national development via economic performance? A number of writers have attempted to explore this association over the last half-century. These include Weber (1905), Banfield (1958), Putnam (1993), Landes (1998), Chua (2004), Guiso, Sapienza and Zingales (2006), Clark (2008) and Hezel (2009).

In their thought-provoking publication, Luigi Guiso, Paola Sapienza and Luigi Zingales (2006) present thought-provoking submissions as to which values are most critical when considering national development. They contend that until recently, writers on the subjects of culture and development had been hesitant to surmise that culture had the potential to influence national development. To a large extent, this caution stems from the precise conception of culture: it is so general and the contexts within which it can be discussed within national development are so pervasive (and nebulous) that it is not easy to develop straightforward, contestable propositions. Nevertheless, of late, improved methods and additional information have facilitated the identification of distinctions in human inclinations and convictions, linking them to different degrees of cultural heritage (Henrich et al., 2001; Bornhorst et al., 2005). These occurrences offer an approach to including discussions and rationalizations in economics that are rooted in culture. In addition, these cultural issues can be critically examined in an attempt to deepen our appreciation of economic events.

A study of the literature indicates that the political scientist Edward Banfield was one of the first writers to suggest that there was a possible association between culture and national development. This was espoused in his book written in 1958 and entitled *The Moral Basis of a Backward Society*. Banfield ascribes the lethargic expansion of southern Italy's economy to the undue quest for myopic egocentricity by citizens who have never had faith in anyone else apart from those in their family. Building on this observation, Robert Putnam (1993) provides further confirmation that parts of Italy that had free city status much earlier are far healthier societies today compared to areas of southern Italy that never had the opportunity to experience such public institutions. Where such establishments are successful, citizens are willing to invest in social capital. The building of trust is crucial in this regard, and it is postulated that such trust takes place over a lengthy time period as members of society grow in terms of their appreciation of something else other than their own relatives.

Another author, David Landes, in his book entitled *The Wealth and Poverty of Nations* (1998) infers that cultural traits more than any other attributes have a strong influence on the prosperity of national economies. He postulates that prudence, perseverance, conscientiousness, tolerance and integrity are the cultural characteristics that differentiate success from failure. He opines that Max Weber was not wrong when he alluded that social mindsets and meanings have a pivotal influence on which nations will perform successfully in economic terms and which ones will perform abysmally.

In a relatively recent working paper written by Guido Tabellini (2005), a bold attempt was made to present tangible evidence of the effect of culture on national development. Drawing on a culture construct developed from a suite of four values (trust, belief in the importance of individual effort, generalized morality and autonomy), Tabellini discovered that annual gross domestic product (GDP) per capita and economic growth tend to be higher in those regions of Europe that are characterized by higher degrees of these four cultural values.

Clearly, all the foregoing simply corroborates what Clark (2008) endeavours to submit and Chua (2004) advocates: that state-of-the-art technology single-handedly will not be sufficient to transform an economy and raise the standard of living of a society. The inculcation of a set of attitudes, along with the associated tenets and behaviours, constitutes a large component of the paradigm. Conventional learning and training may play a role, but perhaps not so much because it provides additional knowledge and sharpens competences as because it instils a fresh vision of the world and associated ideals.

For developing countries around the world, these findings present interesting lessons. At a point in time, economists believed that adequate capital, particularly garnered through a country's savings, might propel the country into a trajectory of economic advancement. Recently, the trend has been to place emphasis on both political and economic establishments in order to guarantee a fertile terrain for the imminent abundant economic harvest. However, a recent school of thought has seen many writers leaning towards the cultural facet of economic development, positing that the creation of such political and economic institutions may have spanned generations. Even when they are in place, there may be a need for a further nurturing of values and attitudes before a nation is ready for economic development. Where do African nations stand in all this?

In the Context of the Developing World

Several regions of the world are deemed as being impervious to advancement. In this regard, one's mind quickly goes to the greater part of Africa, some areas in South America, the Middle East and a few South-East Asian nations. Obviously, in several of these nations, there is an absence or at best a shortage of trustworthy institutions, starting with stable government and the rule of law, that are necessary conditions for development in keeping with present-day norms. There is also the Pacific region, where economic growth rates have not been encouraging in the last couple of decades. Assuming that the research findings of the writers mentioned in the preceding sections are authentic, that is, historical experiences of a society engender a bundle of values and beliefs that promote national advancement, it might be instructive to benchmark typical developing economies against this cluster:

- *Belief in the importance of individual effort.* African societies tend to lean more towards communalism and the subservience of individual to group interests. Though globalization has provided the continent with high levels of exposure to all parts of the world, Africans are still hardly known for individualism or the value system that fosters it.
- *Frugality.* This was connected with parsimoniousness, which was considered as a vice as opposed to a virtue in African culture. On the contrary, the investment in social capital – by means of donations to a festival within one's society or homage to a traditional ruler – called for excessive charity.

- *The principle of hard work.* In some parts of the developing world, assiduous relentless work executed daily and weekly is considered to be a value, whereas in other parts, such traits are not considered to be so important. The latter is particularly evident where seasonal work such as farming could call for intense surges of arduous labour, but would be followed by long intervals of leisure. This is particularly evident in communities or societies where the labour required for subsistence is restricted to a short period per day. That said, in other societies, particularly in the developed world and some developing countries, citizens have to spend several hours working to make ends meet and this is the expectation of the culture of the societies in which they live.
- *Self-sufficiency.* In the developed world, most citizens tend to be self-sufficient during their working lives and, in addition, both governments and individuals put in place schemes to make workers comfortable after retirement. In such societies, the fact that limited emphasis is placed on the extended family system promotes the need to be self-sufficient. While many developing countries are becoming exposed to Western lifestyles and thus appreciate the need to take measures to become self-reliant, such traits are not particularly high on the range of virtues in some societies. Indeed, in many rural areas, lifestyles are skewed in the reverse trend towards traditionalism in accordance with plans required for subsistence in small communities.
- *Trust.* This may vary from culture to culture depending on how well advanced political and social institutions in societies are. In such societies, the people tend to have trust in their institutions. Conversely, in societies without well-established political and social institutions, it may be much more difficult for the people to develop trust in existing institutions.
- *Universal uprightness.* This represents the effective use of ethical standards in one's dealings with all in society and not only in relation to a selected few or one's relatives. Depending on a community's dominant religious beliefs, this may vary from area to area, though this tendency might not have been distinct during the era marked by traditions. Nevertheless, there was a compelling force to foster such norms in many parts of the world where religious beliefs were embraced by the people.

Generally, it seems that Africa, like most of the developing world, does not rank prominently in the cultural mindsets and meanings that have been recognized as beneficial in fostering national development in our modern world. This is not to unduly condemn the cultures of Africa or those of other developing economies. Nor is it to allude that the developing world is bedevilled by vices or political volatility or many of the other ills that afflict less-endowed countries and regions. There is no doubt that the customary value clusters of developing countries, particularly in rural communities, were well matched to subsistence in times past. Nonetheless, the same value cluster that provided these small communities with the impetus to build and sustain coherence and succour previously may not be appropriate to developing a progressive economy. In other words, the developing world clearly cannot be said to enjoy the same cultural benefits that propelled Britain to affluence following the Industrial Revolution, the USA to prosperity after the Second World War, or which have given Jewish, Chinese, Indian and Lebanese entrepreneurs the competitive advantage they have experienced despite leaving their native lands to live in another country.

How Can We Propel National Development through Culture?

Drawing upon what the founding fathers of economics, ranging from Adam Smith to the present-day proponents, perceive as the underlying prerequisites for attaining tangible national development, is it possible to create and nurture a cluster of values to engineer national development? If so, what is required to achieve such a goal? Can we fast-track this process or would nations working to achieve a quantum leap towards development have to wait for decades for this to come to pass, as some of today's leading industrialized nations did?

It is widely held that enhanced education for the nation is the best step to take in order to address the issue of development. Yet, others argue that studies on the effect of education do not substantiate the assertion that only education will provide the solution (Chua, 2004). It is further suggested that additional effort has to be made to examine the links between culture and national development, and if it became possible to establish the association between the two variables, there would be other moderating variables such as the role that ethnic groups or regional clusters would play in influencing the relationship. This contention is made against the background that in many countries, the playing field between regions and ethnic groups is not level and, consequently, efforts to create a level playing field, even through education, will be an agonizingly protracted process, which may take decades to yield the desired results.

One factor that has been strongly identified as a determinant of national development is productivity or worker output and that this is the case in each industry, whether it is a manufacturing, services or high-technology venture. A study that vividly demonstrates this assertion was undertaken by Clark (2008), who tracked and compared the industrial productivities of Indian workers and Japanese employees at the beginning of the twentieth century. His findings indicated that by the 1930s, Japan had outpaced India in terms of productivity, largely controlling the market. During this era, the comparatively higher level of productivity of the Japanese was ascribed to their higher levels of discipline, which in turn was attributed to their cultural values.

An increasing number of writers tend to agree that national development requires more than merely injecting investment or financial resources – indeed, more than innovation, the most up-to-date technology and trustworthy national institutions. A collection of cultural values appropriate for present-day business also tends to be a vital component. While it is one thing to say that culture influences national development, the exact delineation of these values is yet to be universally agreed upon, much less the development of the most suitable set of strategies for instilling such values in developing societies. In the meantime, the need to encourage the various arms of government (the executive, the legislature and the judiciary) and their major stakeholder (the population at large) to work together to create a level playing field is an issue that nations eager to advance cannot afford to ignore if they are to achieve permanent and lasting national progress.

For the time being, while many developing economies make the effort to grow economically, those that truly demonstrate good governance in their national affairs do enjoy appreciable degrees of financial assistance from development partners that are eager to promote economic advancement in such countries, which then tend to become role models for other developing economies to emulate. In addition to such assistance, what is required for development to really take root is the cultural environment considered critical to drive the intensity and speed of growth that can turn around the fortunes of a country permanently.

Currently in some societies, particularly those that are close-knit, small and highly traditional, instead of perceiving money as a channel to building on one's financial fortunes, there may be other more important purposes for its use within society. In some cultural environments, economic dynamics may be constrained by other factors, for instance, those that may provide a person with benefits other than merely increasing their wealth. These factors could be classified as collateral, reputation and camaraderie:

- Collateral is frequently reflected in land ownership, usually considered by many as the ultimate reserve (contingency) and perhaps the most significant currency of all assets. In a society where a high premium is placed on land ownership, it is not easy to persuade an owner of this asset to offer his land in exchange for a prospect to make decent returns in a business undertaking. Many in such cultures facing such a situation may prefer not to take up the business opportunity at all.

- Reputation may be the reason why a person declines a prospect to invest in a business opportunity, but instead makes a huge donation towards a religious or community function or project. The reward for this person is an escalation in reputation or a higher status in the community.
- Camaraderie, or a sense of belonging, is the rationale for giving a percentage of one's income to a family member so as to deepen family ties, an attribute that is considered to be of great importance by many in developing economies.

It could not be said that any of the above 'virtues' is unacceptable; however, holding dear the values of collateral, reputation and camaraderie does not necessarily signify the suite of values that will produce business tycoons or magnates and foster the accelerated advancement that developing economies strive for today. While it is appreciated that certain traditional values are treasures with deep roots that still resonate within many societies and are in themselves socially laudable in every respect, choices like these can be baffling to the modern-day investor in that they appear to defy what one would clearly consider as compelling business opportunities that would help a whole society to move up the trajectory of prosperity and at the same time create even better opportunities for the wealthy to further consolidate values, such as land security, reputation and cohesion. Nevertheless, what is 'inconsequential' from one cultural perspective is not essentially so in the context of another culture. This is where cultural values influence business, financial and economic preferences, where one society's analyses that inform decisions on the choices available flout what other cultures would consider 'realism' or good judgement. Perhaps this is where it is necessary to begin the discussion on national development.

This begs the following question: what transpires when people originally from close-knit, small and highly traditional societies re-locate to fast-moving, technologically advanced countries? What is the impact of this new environment on the suite of cultural values that have the propensity to hinder economic development? Many citizens from rural societies of the developing world who have emigrated to the Western World could be studied to examine the pace at which their cultural values are transformed. A study of these diaspora citizens could shed further light on the effect of the new cultural environments on them and help us to address specific details regarding how the cultural transformations required to enhance national development can be fast-tracked.

A Holistic Approach to the Culture and National Development Relationship

National economies are said to go through four phases of development: factor-driven; investment-driven; innovation-driven; and wealth-driven (Porter, 1990). It is contended that collectivism comprising interdependence, sacrificing for the group, relational social exchange and national goal congruency are useful when a nation is in the early phases of economic development (Bhawuk et al., 2010). The writers also suggest that the cultural values that contribute to success in the first two stages of economic development may lead to failure as a result of group-think in the third and fourth stages, and that failure can be avoided by substituting group-think with team-think.

Associated with the above are the concepts of individualism and collectivism, both of which comprise the following elements: self (Markus and Kitayama, 1991; Bhawuk, 2001); interaction between individuals and other groups (Triandis, McKuster and Hui, 1990; Kim, 2000); interaction between individuals and society as a whole (Mills and Clark, 1982); and how individuals engage in social exchange with other individuals (Bhawuk et al., 2010).

Research findings suggest that collective cultures usually engender enduring institutions and policy-influencing systems (Crocker et al., 1984). It is therefore not surprising that in cultures characterized by collectivism such as Japan, strategies such as quality circles and suggestion systems have been actively used and supported in efforts to develop organizational creativity (Min Basadur, 1992). Again, in Japan, Korea, Singapore and other Asian nations, institutional and national building is stimulated and buttressed by the shared destiny that people identify with in collective cultures. In such cultures, people are prepared to make sacrifices for the common benefit. For instance, Japanese consumers tend to save far more compared to their American counterparts, despite the fact that returns on savings are generally lower than interest paid on savings in the USA, and this personal sacrifice exhibited by the Japanese makes the cost of capital in the country one of the lowest in the world (Synodinos, 2001).

It is contended that the two World Wars influenced the ensuing economies of the Western world. Similarly, it is postulated that colonization and the Second World War have impacted East Asian economies, and that though free market concepts developed internally within Western nations, free market practices were foisted upon Asian countries by colonial powers (Kim, 1995). While this imposition transformed some of the cultural practices of these nations, a situation that is still evolving today, it has been observed that the focus on relationships, an attribute of collectivism, is still deep-seated. Indeed, Japan, which is characterized by industrialization, modernization, capitalism and urbanization, still places great emphasis on human relations, with some suggesting that the advancement of Japan is primarily attributed to its maintenance of human relations (Misumi, 1985).

In addition, Kim (1995) noted that newly industrialized countries such as Taiwan, South Korea, Singapore, Japan and Hong Kong that were all conventionally agricultural societies were effective in fostering collective values that were congruent with their traditional norms and still performed creditably. The desire for these collectivist countries to be economically emancipated from the Western world spurred them to cultivate deeper national compatibilities. This is reflected in the use of widely embraced phrases such as Singapore Inc., Korea Inc. and Japan Inc. (Bhawuk et al., 2010). The Asian achievement was engendered by the collective effort inspired by nationalism against the backdrop of national adversity. The consciousness of joint fate has been the driving influence for novelty and transformation in these nations. Porter (1990) avers that a combination of challenge and pressure, not tranquil conditions, has driven organizations and countries to develop. This is observed during the first two phases of economic development when the ability of collectivist cultures to attain economic goal congruency via collective norms can be a major factor in determining economic success and in competing with other countries.

The first of Porter's four economic stages is the factor-driven economy where competitive advantage is derived from basic factors of production. It is argued that the focus on these factors tends to restrict a nation in terms of the types of industries it can develop. While countries exploit the benefits derived from their factors of production, not many are able to gravitate towards a more advanced stage, with Hong Kong, Japan, Korea, Singapore and Taiwan amongst the few nations that have been successful in doing so. Porter (1990) warned that a factor-propelled economy is one with feeble roots for sustained productivity growth, citing nations grappling with poverty in Africa, Asia and South America as typical of this group.

During the second stage (investment-driven economy), a nation's competitive advantage is derived from high levels of investment in technology, education and management systems to improve production capabilities. It is this mix of factor benefits and enhanced production capability that positions the country as a tried and tested industrial economy. Other characteristics associated with this stage include a transformation in the workforce from semi-skilled to better-educated with higher pay. While the higher labour costs would have an adverse effect on the nation's competitiveness over time, during the initial phase of development, the higher productivity compensates for the higher labour costs. It is this higher productivity that facilitates the exceptional economic growth, and the corresponding rise in domestic discretionary earnings can be saved, re-invested into the economy or spent by consumers.

It is postulated that cultural norms that result in collective and national goal congruencies have a significant impact in factor and investment-propelled economies, which is substantiated by the advancement of several East Asian nations since the early 1980s. Driven by the vision of national development, these nations rapidly attained higher productivities in sectors where they had factor benefits and ploughed the profits back in order to develop the local labour force and technology. Therefore, it is reasonable to suggest that collectivist cultural norms can result in a strong economic performance. Nonetheless, it does not necessarily hold that the cultural norms that have a positive impact during this stage of economic development will guarantee success once the economy shifts to the innovation-propelled stage, which gets more complex as globalization and fiercer competition set in. The reason is that strong performance can create an attitude that blinds a nation to the need to change policies, structures and values to be competitive in today's dynamic world. Such attitudes, which are characterized by extreme conformity, can simply result in group-think, which is disadvantageous to businesses and nations when they need to be innovation-focused.

When countries are successful in the context of an investment-propelled economy, they are compelled to gravitate towards the innovation stage, since the prior economic achievement increases the cost of factor production (for instance, labour), thus beginning to erode their competitiveness, and this is further exacerbated by globalization. In addition, the local environment assumes more complexity owing to higher living standards, which necessitates higher-quality innovative products. In order for organizations to remain competitive, they must become creative in the products offered to customers and proactive in their strategies. Group-think is not beneficial during this stage. Owing to acute group-think by policy makers and firms, countries tend to lose their ability to compete during the innovation phase. Since cultural effects cannot be completely eradicated and it may be counterproductive to do so, it is proposed that the concept of team-think is encouraged to facilitate organizations to be more prosperous during the innovation and wealth-propelled phases of economic development.

It is postulated that there are two routes for culturally collectivist countries to cultivate team-think and thus gravitate towards innovative and wealth-propelled economies. One route is obtainable before group-think becomes entrenched, while the other route is a response to failure emanating from group-think and is applicable after group-think has become embedded.

Route one is most associated with countries that are rapidly becoming industrialized and some of their firms start evolving as global market leaders, or when production costs make relocating them offshore more beneficial. During the late 1980s, many Japanese firms such as Canon, Honda and Toyota were rising above their respective competitors. Moreover, during this period, Sony and other firms were relocating their production plants to South East Asian nations such as Thailand and Malaysia. This was the opportune period for government to begin modifying policy regarding the services sector rather than safeguarding the manufacturing sector through duties and other benefits. Manufacturers are expected to become more creative in order to maintain a competitive advantage. Toyota and some other Japanese firms responded proactively by building multi-faceted teams to develop new products and market them in less than 24 months (Ward et al., 1995).

Route two is more applicable to nations that have prospered economically during the first two stages of economic development, yet are struggling in the third phase owing to group-think at the policy formulation level and in entities where executives continue to advance identical strategies notwithstanding failures in the worldwide business environment. When nations are in crisis, it is more difficult to alter their course, since citizens still think that determinants of past success should hold, not recognizing that business conditions are now different and that successful competition requires new methods. Team-think enables businesses and countries to garner different viewpoints, which is vital in identifying new prospects and impediments and in developing synergies.

An interesting question is how organizational practices impact upon government policy makers. Policies that compel organizations in the factor and investment-driven phases to dwell on narrow specialization focus in certain areas of business should be eased and the revised policies should offer variety for companies in order for them to respond appropriately to the evolving environmental challenges. In addition, while during the early phases of economic development, governments formulate policies which emphasize resource conservation or optimization, during the stages of innovation and wealth-driven economies, the emphasis must be on setting a wider course for businesses so that they can investigate the requisite variety of choices available.

The notion of varied opinions and participation has been presented as a key strategy for successful organizational performance (McDaniel and Walls, 1997). Instances of this principle can be discovered in Asian culture. Taking China as an example, the country initiated the 'three-in-one' concept as its industrial policy to facilitate collaboration amongst managers, workers and technicians for scientific and technological creativity (Wang, 1994).

Policies can be formulated at the national stage to enforce the advancement and entrenchment of requisite variety. For instance, the multi-language policies in Singapore and India have helped them to improve their human capital and provide offerings to a wider market. Malaysia has also been adamant that the possession of Tamil and Mandarin languages skills in addition to Bahasa Malaysia and English is critical, given the access it offers to the Chinese and Indian markets. Thus, Mandarin and Tamil language lessons have been included in the curricula of national schools in Malaysia.

It is held that diverse groups lower the likelihood of group-think by virtue of their composition. Diversity is reflected in both objective measures (e.g. demographic) and subjective assessments (e.g. values, norms, attitudes and cultural behaviour) (Adler, 2002; Bhawuk et al., 2002). Clearly, using the combined objective and subjective variables yields is most desirable and organizations need to be mindful of this fact so as to take full advantage of the essential competencies of their human capital. While it may take longer for disparate individuals to arrive at decisions, the probability that they would investigate the comprehensive range of options is greater (Triandis, Kurowski and Gelfand, 1994). Organizations that utilize this approach are better positioned to identify emerging opportunities in the marketplace and respond ahead of their competitors.

Drawing upon Neck and Manz's (1994) study of self-managing teams, team-think illustrates group decision-making processes that are derived from the fundamental forbears of group-think, but guides groups to constructive decision making. Compared to group-think, team-think is regarded as a more productive approach to decision making and also enhances team performance. Among the indicators of team-think are: discussion of shared misgivings; acknowledgement of the inimitable characteristics of participants; an awareness of weaknesses; the free articulation of apprehension; and the encouragement of different opinions.

The cultural values of the participants are crucial to the development of team-think. The process maximizes the potential results of each decision that a team makes since it allows variety, critical thinking and assessment of all potential options. Consequently, team-think can help entities to address the challenges associated with innovation and wealth-driven economies. Each nation has several cultures, though typically there is a prevailing culture. Organizations are drivers of national advancement and while they work to extend the boundaries of production, governments also seek to encourage such expansion, but may unintentionally develop policies that are counterproductive to the expansion of the economic boundaries.

Conclusions

Drawing upon and amalgamating organizational paradigms, the economic development process and culture principles, this chapter has sought to draw conclusions on the possible link between culture and national development.

It is suggested that all cultures have a propensity to be positively linked to economic success and they have to discover their own means to move from one phase of economic development to the next level. Indeed, collectivist cultures that epitomize most developing economies could strive for economic development without forgoing their cultural norms. Overall, culture can have a positive effect as a facilitator of economic development and, moreover, the negative influence of culture can be minimized by employing mechanisms that are consistent with cultural norms (Azfar, 1992). Anti-cultural traditions usually are not firmly embraced or embedded, and so get misrepresented over time or are eventually discarded.

Collectivist nations can make progress in the early phases of their socio-economic development, but do not tend to do well in advancing their economies to the innovation and wealth-driven phases because of the absence of team-think. The limitations caused by dominant group-think can be complemented by the norms of team-think. Collectivism is important in sustaining national goal congruency and if a delicate balance is achieved, economic development is relatively easier to attain. The development of national economic goal congruency is a prerequisite for national development, as performed by countries like Japan, Korea, Singapore and Taiwan.

Research has shown that collectivism is a determinant of prosperity and it is contended that the relationship between individualism and economic success might have altered in the last three decades since it was found that individualism had a significant impact on wealth. The effort to identify culture as the cause of economic failure is an unproductive academic exercise that should be discarded, given the historical and theoretical findings contesting it (Greif, 2000; Kennedy, 2010).

History demonstrates that cultural norms that are held responsible for economic failures in today's world have been significant determinants of wealth in times past. The view that East Asian nations have become prosperous only recently is false, since they have been wealthy in the past. For instance, in the fifteenth century, Malacca, which is a segment of Malaysia, was a major economic power and was the world's leading seaport, accommodating up to 2,000 vessels each day (Elegant, 1999). Likewise, the most effective agricultural system and the best merchant sea vessels were designed and constructed by the Chinese during the Song era in the eleventh century.

It is vital for the economies of developing nations, most of whom exhibit collectivist cultures, to grow if the global economy is to prosper. While it may seem apt to propose that developing countries with collectivist cultures need to transform their cultures and fashion them in line with those of Western nations, it is contended that such an attempt will lead to a fiasco and backfire. Clearly, the soundest approach is to maintain the critical components of collectivist cultures and yet gravitate towards the later phases of economic development propounded by Porter (1990), using team-think with divergent participants and viewpoints in decision-making processes. It has been succinctly captured by Gullen (2001) that economic development involves the amalgamation of politically viable, conceptually acceptable and economically practicable blends of local and international resources in order to foster progress.

References

Adler, N. (2002). *International Dimensions of Organizational Behaviour*, 4th edn. Cincinnati, OH: South-Western.

Azfar, K. (1992). *Asian Drama Revisited*. Karachi: Royal Book Company.

Banfield, E. (1958). *The Moral Basis of a Backward Society*. New York: Free Press.

Bhawuk, D. (2001). Evolution of culture assimilators: Toward theory-based assimilators. *International Journal of Intercultural Relations*, 25(2), pp. 141–63.

Bhawuk, D., Munusamy, V., Bechtold, D. and Sakuda, K. (2010). Globalisation, culture and economic development: A cultural model of economic success and failure. Presentation at the *Asia-Pacific Economic and Business History Conference*, Wellington, NZ, February.

Bhawuk, D., Podsiadlowski, A., Graf, J. and Triandis, H. (2002). Corporate strategies for managing diversity in the global workplace. In G. Ferris, M. Buckley and D. Fedor (eds), *Human Resource Management: Perspectives, Context, Functions, and Outcomes*. Englewood Cliffs, NJ: Prentice Hall, pp. 112–45.

Bornhorst, F., Ichino, A., Schlag, K. and Winter, E. (2005). Trust and trustworthiness among Europeans: South-north comparison. Unpublished.

Chua, A. (2004). *World on Fire: How Exporting Free Market Democracy Breeds Ethnic Hatred and Global Instability*. New York: Knopf Doubleday Publishing Group.

Clark, G. (2008). *A Farewell to Alms: A Brief Economic History of the World*. Princeton: Princeton University Press.

Crocker, O., Charney, C. and Chiu, J. (1984). *Quality Circles: A Guide to Participation and Productivity*. New York: Methuen Publications.

Elegant, S. (1999). A pyrrhic victory. *Far Eastern Economic Review*, 162(23), p. 45.

Greif, A. (2000). The fundamental problem of exchange: A research agenda in historical institutional analysis. *European Review of Economic History*, 4(3), pp. 251–84.

Gullen, M. (2001). *The Limits of Convergence*. Princeton: Princeton University Press.

Guiso, L., Sapienza, P. and Zingales, L. (2006). Does culture affect economic outcomes? *Journal of Economic Perspectives*, 20(2), pp. 23–48.

Henrich, J. Boyd, R., Bowles, S., Camerer, C., Gintis, H., McElreath, R. and Fehr, E. (2001). In Search of homo economicus: Experiments in 15 small-scale societies. *American Economic Review*, 91(2), pp. 73–9.

Hezel, F. (2009). The role of culture in economic development. *Micronesian Counselor*, 77 (June).

Kennedy, P. (2010). *The Rise and Fall of the Great Powers: Economic Change and Military Conflict from 1500 to 2000*. New York: Random House.

Keynes, J. (1930). Economic possibilities for our grandchildren. In *The Collected Writings of John Maynard Keynes*, vol. 9, Essays in Persuasion. London: Macmillan (1972).

Kim, U. (1995). *Individualism and Collectivism: A Psychological, Cultural and Ecological Analysis*. Copenhagen: Nordic Institute of Asian Studies.

Kim, U. (2000). National development and East Asian values: Cultural perspective. In I. Norland and D. Pham (eds), *International Conference Asian Values and Vietnam's Development in Comparative Perspectives: Selected Papers*. Hanoi: National Centre for Social Sciences and Humanities, pp. 135–54.

Landes, D. (1993). *The Wealth and Poverty of Nations*. New York: Norton and Company Inc.

Malthus, T. (1798). *An Essay on the Principle of Population*. London: J. Johnson Publishing.

Markus, H. and Kitayama, S. (1991). Culture and the self: Implications for cognition, emotion and motivation. *Psychological Review*, 98, pp. 224–53.

McDaniel, R. and Walls, M. (1997). Diversity as a management strategy for organisations: A view through the lenses of chaos and quantum theories. *Journal of Management Inquiry*, 6(4), 363–75.

Mill, J. (1956) [1843]. *A System of Logic*. London: Longmans, Green and Co.

Mills, J. and Clark, M. (1982). Exchange and communal relationships. In L. Wheeler (ed.), *Review of Personality and Social Psychology*. Beverly Hills, CA: Sage Publications, pp. 121–44.

Min Basadur (1992). Managing creativity: A Japanese model. *Academy of Management Executive*, 6, 29–40.

Misumi, J. (1985). *The Behavioural Science of Leadership: An Interdisciplinary Japanese Research Programme*. Ann Arbor: University of Michigan Press.

Myrdal, G. (1968). *Asian Drama: An Enquiry into the Poverty of Nations*. London: Penguin.

Neck, P. and Manz, C. (1994). From group-think to team-think: Toward the creation of constructive thought patterns in self-managing work teams. *Human Relations*, 47(8), pp. 929–52.

Porter, M. (1990). *The Competitive Advantage of Nations*. New York: Macmillan.

Putnam, R. (1993). *Making Democracy Work*. Princeton: Princeton University Press.

Smith, A. (1776). *An Inquiry into the Nature and Causes of the Wealth of Nations*. Available at: http://www.econlib.org/library/Smith/smWN.html.

Synodinos, N. (2001). Understanding Japanese consumers: Some important underlying factors. *Japanese Psychological Research*, 43(4), pp. 235–48.

Tabellini, G. (2005). *Culture and Institutions: Economic Development in the Regions of Europe*. CESifo Working Paper No. 1492.

Triandis, H., Kurowski, L. and Gelfand, M. (1994). Workplace diversity. In H. Triandis, M. Dunnette and L. Hough (eds), *Handbook of Industrial and Organisational Psychology*. Palo Alto, CA: Consulting Psychologists Press Inc, pp. 769–827.

Triandis, H., McCusker, C. and Hui, C. (1990). Multimethod probes of individualism and collectivism. *Journal of Personality and Social Psychology*, 59, pp. 1006–20.

Wang, Z. (1994). Culture, economic reform, and the role of industrial and organisational psychology in China. In H. Triandis, M. Dunnette and L. Hough (eds), *Handbook of Industrial and Organisational Psychology*. Palo Alto, CA: Consulting Psychologists Press Inc, pp. 689–725.

Ward, A., Liker, K., Cristiano, J. and Sobeck, K. (1995). The second Toyota paradox: How delaying decisions can make better cars faster. *Sloan Management Review*, 36(3), pp. 43–62.

Weber, M. (2001) [1905]. *The Protestant Ethic and the Spirit of Capitalism*. London: Routledge Classic.

Human Capital and National Development

9

Ebenezer Ofori Agbettor

Abstract

Leapfrogging from a developing nation status to one that is fully developed by 2020 is the desire and goal of most Ghanaians ever since the government of Ghana laid out its bold Vision 2020 national development blueprint in the 1990s. Central to the attainment of this vision is the creation of an excellent human capital base that is skilled, knowledgeable, healthy, flexible and mobile. To this end, governments of Ghana over the years have embarked on various initiatives that have aimed to transform the way human capital is developed to achieve national development. Conclusions drawn from the evaluation of the perspectives of various philosophers and economists on human capital will serve as an invaluable resource to policy makers, administrators and educationists.

Introduction

The capacity and abilities of human beings in making a difference have no known comparison or boundaries. The inventions from the time of Adam and Eve up to now can be described as mind-blowing. Nations that exploit the tools of innovation and creativity of humanity will continue to move the frontiers of development for the benefit of their citizens. Money, buildings, cars, land, oil, gold, timber, etc. may have their value and importance, but they do not come anywhere near the value of human capital. Human beings make or break societies and organizations, so prudently managing and exploiting such great potential is not a matter of choice, but is *obligatory* for every serious nation that seeks to achieve real national development.

Modern economists are of the view that natural resources such as forest minerals, climate, water power, etc. play an important role in the economic development of a country. A country which has abundant natural resources is in a position to develop more rapidly than a country which is deficient in such resources. However, they emphasize that the presence of abundant resources is not a sufficient condition for economic growth. Physical factors are passive factors of economic growth; they are to be combined with the human resources of a country which are active factors of economic development.

In pursuit of Ghana's national development goals, it is exigent that the country invests and develops its human capital to ensure that a trained, skilled and well-educated workforce is created. From a resource-based perspective, human capital can be effectively leveraged as a source of competitive advantage to boost a country's productivity, economic performance and sustain its competiveness as it makes the shift from a manufacturing-driven economy into one that is information and communication technology (ICT)-driven and knowledge-based.

The key task in moving towards the status of a developed nation lies in Ghana's ability to develop its human and intellectual capital to produce an adequate supply of knowledge workers who are flexible, agile and mobile with the relevant knowledge and skills required by industry and the nation at large.

Human Capital

There is need for us to look at the definition of *human capital* in the *Oxford Dictionary*: the concept is conveyed as the skills, general or specific, acquired by an individual in the cause of vocational and technical education training and the industrial workplace after training. Howitt (2005) defines it as 'the skill and knowledge of human beings'. It is also defined as the endowment of abilities to produce that exists in each human being. It can be increased through formal education, on-the-job training and improved health and psychological well-being. To be more precise, if the people of a country are well educated, well nourished, skilled and healthy, they are said to have more human capital. It takes human capital to organize and rationalize the contributions of other factors of production before a result-oriented productive goal can be achieved in any industrial setting.

Fundamentally, it is that intangible factor of the production that brings human intellect, skills and competencies in the production and provision of goods and services. It is that human capability and productivity engendered through knowledge and skills acquired from vocational and technical education, training and experience and facilitated by an environment. Elements of human capital would include knowledge, skills, attitudes and motivation belonging to an enterprise or society and engaged in the development of that enterprise or society to fulfil its objectives.

THE IMPORTANCE OF HUMAN CAPITAL

Human capital is the fundamental source of economic growth. It is a source of both increased productivity and technological advance. In fact, the major difference between developed and developing countries is the rate of progress in terms of human capital. Ghana needs human capital to staff new and expanding government services in order to introduce new systems of land use and new methods of agriculture, to develop new means of communication to carry forward industrialization and to build the education system. Galbraith (1998) is right in saying that 'we achieve greater economic growth from investment in men and improvements brought about by improved men'.

More and more nations are realizing that in order to stay on top in the global economy, they need to place more emphasis on retaining and developing their people. It is the collective attitudes, skills and capabilities of people that contribute to the success and growth of a nation. People are essential assets who contribute to the development and growth of a nation. Hence, in the world of rapid technological advancements, nations are looking at building relationships with people and are appreciating the financial impact of their people, who are referred to as human capital.

HUMAN CAPITAL FORMATION

Human capital formation is described by Harbison (1962) as 'the process of acquiring and increasing the number of person who have the skills, education and experience which are critical for the economic and political development of a country'. Human capital formation is the act of increasing the productive qualities of the labour force by providing more education and by increasing skills, health and notarization levels.

In Ghana, the political and civic rights of the citizenship are more often highlighted against social citizenship and the responsibilities that accompany this. The life of Kojo Mensah, who was six years old at the time of independence, differs greatly from that Amina Atta, who was six years old in 1979, and Yao Adjah, who turned six in 1998. These hypothetical citizens are 62, 40 and 21 years old respectively. The 62-year-old was fortunate enough to have 'free' university education and is now faced with the fact that the right to an adequate pension is not guaranteed by his Ghanaian citizenship. Amina, now 40 years old, knew only arbitrary government in her formative years and is now becoming familiar with democratic discourse, albeit in its raw form. Political opponents refer to each other as enemies and leaders of political parties raise the spectre of their parties 'ruling' forever after democratic elections, as if we live in a feudal medieval state.

As emotive as these issues may be, they are now being discussed. Blows may fly at some party meetings and conventions, but that is an indication of how far we have to climb on the ladder to a truly just and civil society. Amina may find the courage to become engaged in the political process or may leave as some of Kojo's peers did to try their luck elsewhere. The 21-year-old Yao has lived through eight years of multi-party democracy and is uncontaminated by arbitrary arrests, disappearances and the like. What a near-idyllic political life! Will it get better for Yao or worse? An uncle in England is paying his older brother's university fees. His mother had 'free' university education. What will his prospects be in terms of health, education and employment? What is a citizen to expect and what can the nation truly expect from him or her in the future? What investment did the state make in these individuals when they were young?

Currently, we are told that 50 percent of the state's internally derived revenue pays the salaries of government employees. Not much is left for every duty that a government owes its citizens. Ghana's economy is still largely pre-industrial and true commercial agriculture and food self-sufficiency is yet to be achieved. There is no culture of investment in the life of the ordinary Ghanaian outside of limited social security for public sector employees. Most people attribute the absence of investment culture in Ghana to poverty. The problem is more complex than that. The Nobel Prize-winning Grameen Bank of 2006 and others like it have demonstrated that poverty in itself is no barrier to full participation in the financial system.

Ghana's population of 24,223,431, as per the Ghana Statistical Service, of which women constitute 12,421,770, with men at 11,801,661, is worth looking at in terms of the available human resources in the country. According to the Ghana Statistical Service, the intercensal growth rate for the country has declined from 2.7 percent per annum to 2.4 percent per annum. Table 9.1 gives Ghana's population trends from 1891 to 2010. At the time of the first census in 1891, the population of Ghana was less than 1 million, at 765,000. Since 1960, the growth of the population has always exceeded 2.3 percent.

Table 9.1   Ghana's Population (1891–2000)

Year	Population	Percentage change from previous census	Average annual growth rate
1891	764,613	–	–
1901	1,549,661	765,048	7.3
1911	1,503,991	(45,750)	-1.5
1921	2,298,433	794,522	4.3
1931	3,163,568	865,135	3.2
1948	4,118,450	954,882	1.6
1960	6,726,815	2,608,365	4.2
1970	8,559,313	1,832,498	2.4
1984	12,205,574	3,646,261	2.6
2000	18,412,247	6,206,700	2.7
2010	24,233,431	5,821,184	2.4

Source: Ghana Statistical Services compiled by author from National Population Censuses.
Note: Bracketed numbers signify negative change.

Aful-Dadzie (2011) poignantly paints a picture of Ghana's rapid population growth by comparing Ghana to Portugal. In 1960 'Ghana's population stood at just 6.8 million compared to 8.9 million of Portugal. From 1960 to 1990, Portugal's population increased by just 10.6% to 9.8 million; while that of Ghana increased by 120.5% to 14.9 million, and surpassed Portugal. By 2009, Ghana's population had reached 23.8 million, an increase of 59.3% over 1990. In 2009, Portugal's population on the other hand stood at 10.6 million, an increase of just 7.4% over 1990'. The growth rate and total population in the two countries gives us food for thought in relation to a nation's human capital and national development.

The quality of population as measured by health standards, educational levels and technology is vitally important in influencing a nation's cultural and economic progress. A country which has developed the skills and knowledge of its people can exploit its natural resources, build social economic and political organizations, and carry forward national development. The less developed countries of the world are now making investment in people in order to increase their skills, abilities, ideals, health and on-the-job training opportunities. These productive investments have a strong bearing upon increasing human capabilities, which is called human capital.

The nation's assets are not only embodied in its citizens within its geographical borders, but all over the world. One challenge as a nation is to evaluate all our human capital and plan to derive the greatest sustainable advantage over the next developmental horizon. The country's constitution must guarantee the same rights and responsibilities to all its citizens irrespective of their country of residence at any given time; otherwise, we effectively have a constitutionally supported apartheid policy in our own country. If the population of a nation is educated, efficient, patriot, skilled and healthy, it makes significant contribution to national development. On the other hand, if a country is overpopulated and the labour force is unemployed, uneducated, unskilled and unpatriotic, it can place serious hurdles on the path of economic development. According to Schultz (1961), there are five ways of developing human capital:

a) The provision of health facilities which affect one's life expectancy, strength, vigour and vitality.
b) The provision of on-the-job training which improves the skills of the labour force.
c) Arranging education at the primary, secondary and higher levels.

d) The provision of study programmes for adults that are not organized by firms including extension programmes, notably in agriculture.

e) The provision of adequate migration facilities to families to adjust to changing job opportunities.

Problems of Human Capital Formation in Ghana

The main problems of human capital formation in Ghana in brief are as follows.

HIGH POPULATION GROWTH RATE

The population of almost all developing countries of the world including Ghana is increasing faster than the rate of accumulation of human capital. This is demonstrated by the fact that expenditure on education in most developing countries has been approximately 2.5 percent of GDP for the last five years. Ghana's sector expenditure on education, which ranges between 20 and 25 percent of GDP, is considerably high relative to the figures of some developing economies.

DEFECTIVE PATTERN OF INVESTMENT IN EDUCATION

Successive governments in Ghana have tended to give priority to primary education in order to increase the literacy rate. Secondary education, which provides the critical skills needed for economic development, remains neglected. Another problem related to investment in education is that in the public and private sectors, there has been a mushroom growth in the number of universities without an allied attempt to improve their standard of education.

MORE STRESS ON THE PROVISION OF BUILDING AND EQUIPMENT

Another major problem in Ghana is that the politicians and administrators place more stress on the construction of buildings and provision of equipment than on the provision of qualified staff. It has been observed that foreign qualified teachers and doctors are appointed in rural areas where they are of little use.

SHORTAGE OF HEALTH AND NUTRITION FACILITIES

For many years now in Ghana, there has been a shortage of trained nurses, qualified doctors, medical equipment, medicines, etc. The limited availability of health facilities poses a threat to millions of people. The people are faced with unsatisfactory sanitary conditions, polluted water, high fertility and death rates, urban slums, illiteracy etc. All these deficiencies affect the health of the people and reduce their life expectancy.

LIMITED FACILITIES FOR JOB TRAINING

On-the-job training or in-service training is critical in empowering the youth with new or improved skills. However, the lack of facilities like structured programmes, training centres, equipment, etc. in Ghana is militating against the acquisition of skills by the youth, who could contribute immensely to national development.

STUDY PROGRAMMES FOR ADULTS

Study programmes for adults, introduced in Ghana to provide basic education and increase the skills of farmers and small industrialists, have not achieved the expected level of success as interest shown by adults in getting such training is limited.

HALF-HEARTED MEASURES IN CREATING EMPLOYMENT OPPORTUNITIES

The government of Ghana has taken some steps to increase employment opportunities through initiatives like the establishment of a National Youth Employment Programme and encouraging domestic and foreign investment to increase employment through the setting-up of technical and vocational training centres Laudable as they are, these initiatives have been subject to their fair share of mismanagement and corruption, thereby rendering them ineffective.

NO MANPOWER PLANNING

Owing to the non-availability of reliable data, there is little manpower planning in Ghana. As a result, there is no matching of demand and supply in relation to different types of skills. The result is that large numbers of skilled and highly qualified persons remain underemployed. The frustration and discontentment felt by unemployed or underemployed graduates and postgraduates result in a brain drain from the country. This represents a huge loss of resources to Ghana.

NEGLECT OF AGRICULTURAL EDUCATION

In Ghana, where agriculture is the major sector of the economy, very little attention is paid to the education of farmers in the use of modern agricultural practices and equipment. Unless attention is given to the provision of adequate agricultural education and training in the fields, farmers will not be able to improve their economic status.

Perspectives of Human Capital

Perspectives of human capital that have been clearly articulated over a period by known authorities have been briefly couched and provide as follows:

a) The first view is based on the individual aspects. Schultz (1961) recognized human capital as 'something akin to property' against the concept of the labour force in the classical perspective.

b) The second view is based on the accumulation process involved in human capital. This perspective stresses the knowledge and skills obtained throughout educational activities such as compulsory education, post-secondary education and vocational education (De la Fuente and Ciccone (2002) as cited in Alan, Altman and Roussel (2008)).

c) The third view is closely linked to the production-oriented perspective of human capital. Frank and Bernanke (2007) define human capital as 'an amalgam of factors such as education, experience, training, intelligence, energy, work habits, trustworthiness, and initiative that affect the value of a worker's marginal product'. Sheffrin (2003), who holds a similar view, defines it as 'the stock of skills and knowledge embodied in the ability to perform labour so as to produce economic value'. In essence, human capital is a synonym for knowledge embedded in all levels, such as an individual, an organization and a nation.

THE CHARACTERISTICS OF HUMAN CAPITAL

a) Crawford (1991) suggests that compared to physical labour, human capital includes expandable, self-generating, transportable and shareable characteristics. He asserts that, to begin with, the expandable and self-generating characteristics of human capital are closely linked to the possibility that the stock of knowledge increases individuals' human capital.
b) In addition, Crawford explained that the transportable and shareable characteristics of human capital mean that the original holder of knowledge can distribute his or her knowledge to others.

Human Capital and National Development

The World Bank describes Ghana as a middle income economy and is ranked as a lower middle-income economy and an emerging economy. The Ghanaian economy grew by 7.7 percent in 2010 and by 14.4 percent in 2011. In 2012 the total value of goods and services produced was valued at US$40.71 billion. Should this national income be distributed amongst the population, each Ghanaian would receive almost US$1,550 (World Bank Data, 2013).

The Gross Domestic Product (GDP) in Ghana increased by 6.7 percent in the first quarter of 2013 over the same quarter of the previous year. Historically, from 2000 until 2013, Ghana GDP annual growth rate averaged 7.6 percent reaching an all-time high of 19.1 percent in June 2011 and a record low of 2.2 percent in September 2009. In Ghana, the annual growth rate in GDP measures the change in the value of the goods and services produced by the country economy over the period of a year. Data for Ghana GDP annual growth rate has been provided in Appendix 1.

The continuous growth of the Ghanaian economy has only benefited a few Ghanaians and some foreigners who make huge profits and earn huge salaries. This is particularly the case in the mining and financial sectors. The majority of Ghanaians have not benefited from three decades of economic growth and the change in their status from poor to a lower middle-income country.

The importance of economic development cannot be overemphasized. Despite the tremendous material gains produced by the innovation of humanity, poverty, disease and deprivation still run rampant in Ghana. The fact that the majority of people still experience hunger is a poignant reminder of the crucial role that economic development plays in determining social conditions in civil society.

Economic development depicts a wide range of actions, including but not limited to growth in GDP, growth in the per capita income of citizens, increased employment opportunities, improved quality of life and living standards in relation to basic necessities like food, water, shelter and healthcare. Economic development is therefore the cumulative change in employment, per capita income, quality of life and GDP of a nation that is self-sustained (Mathur, 1999: 204). In general, economic development is important because production relations to a large extent define social, legal, cultural and political interactions within any society. In producing material goods, people produce and reproduce their own social relations, ensuring that the social, political and economic spheres of human life coalesce.

Although research by Rankin (2002) shows the influence of social capital on economic activity, economic relations still remain the infrastructure that grounds the superstructure of civil society. Social capital is a 'feature of social organisations, such as networks, norms, and social trusts that facilitate coordination and cooperation for mutual benefit' (Krishna and Shrader, 1999: 3). In particular, the issue of economic development in the developing world is of great importance to the global economy. The future of emerging markets could lead to either a sustained period of global economic growth or a fragmented system of economic development characterized by high tariffs, trade impasses, unhealthy competition and higher prices for basic commodities (Errunza, 1983).

MACROECONOMIC EFFECTS OF HUMAN CAPITAL

At the macro-economic level, human capital plays an integral role in economic development in a number of ways. A study conducted by Baldacci, Clements, Gupta and Cui (2004) analysed data from 120 developing countries collected from 1975 to 2000. The results of this study show a positive relationship between years of education and economic development in developing countries. They demonstrated that 'the impact of education on growth is more pronounced in low-income countries, where an increase in 1 percentage point in the composite enrolment rate is associated with a 0.1 percentage point increase in per capita GDP growth. This effect is 1.5 times that in middle-income countries' (Baldacci et al., 2004: 16). They determined that geographically the effect of human capital is highest in Sub-Saharan Africa and lowest in Eastern Europe and Central Asia.

Becker, Murphy and Tamura (1990) demonstrated that the rate of return on investment in human capital rises rather than falls as the stock of human capital increases. This happens because 'education and other sectors that produce human capital use educated and other skilled inputs more intensively than sectors that produce consumption goods and physical capital' (Becker, Murphy and Tamura, 1990: 13). The intensive use of human capital accounts for increased productivity and technological growth that stimulates economic growth in terms of growth in GDP. Since the rate of return on human capital continues to increase productivity, it follows that an increased stock of human capital raises investments in developing new technologies by expanding the education-intensive research and development industry, facilitating technological innovations at the heart of economic expansion (Becker, Murphy and Tamura, 1990). This makes human capital an endogenous driver of economic growth.

A Historical Perspective

THE HISTORY OF HUMAN CAPITAL

Many great philosophers and economists have contributed to the development of the concept of human capital. The modern theory of human capital dates as far back as the seventeenth century. In 1691, Sir William Petty was credited as being the first economist to understand the economic importance of human beings. He evaluated the value of human capital by placing a value on labourers and estimated the cost of life lost in wars and other deaths. Petty's method and logic greatly appealed to many of his followers, who used his method of calculating national wealth for about 100 years after his death.

About 50 years later, another economist, Philip Cantillon (1759), made an additional contribution towards the concept of human capital. His estimation was based on the cost of maintaining the slave and his offspring rather than on the slave's earnings that he created. In 1853, William Farr, who was more sophisticated in his approach, proposed that the net value of a person's earnings, which he defined as earnings less living expenses, should be taxed. He attempted to find a system of taxing the population and felt that each member of the community should contribute to the public expenditure in a fixed proportion in relation to the amount of property in his possession during that year. He felt that it was equivalent to wealth and physical property.

In 1867 Theodore Wittstein proposed that William Farr's theory on the net future of a person's earnings should be utilized to calculate compensation for those who lost their lives. Then, in 1930, Louis Dublin and Alfred Lotka, who were into life insurance, claimed that William Farr's theory on the present value of net future earnings could be used in mortality statistics too. Many others were early contributors to the literature on human capital economics by suggesting in various ways that human beings are an investment which generates a return. Among them were Adam Smith (1776), Jean Baptiste Say (1821), John Stuart Mill (1909) and Henry Sidgwick (1901).

In his definition of capital, Fisher (1897) compared human beings to physical commodities. Many early researchers and economists refused to acknowledge this concept and labelled it as 'sentimentalism'. In around 1900, Alfred de Foville attempted to estimate the value of human stock in France. He applied Petty's method and subtracted consumption. At about the same time, Barriol, a Frenchman, used Farr's method to determine the social value of man in France, but did not deduct consumption. He calculated using different age groups. Solomon Huebner, the founder of the American College of Life Insurance at the University of Pennsylvania, stated in 1914 that human life value should be afforded the same scientific treatment as is applied to conventional capital. To this day, the certificate of the Certified Life Underwriter states that the recipient is an expert in insuring human life value.

Through the centuries, the application of what today would be called human capital theory has been applied to address many issues of public policy. Most of these issues remain the subject of that theory today. Some explanation of the exact role of human capital in economic growth and the development of an economy has been provided by early writers on the subject. In the traditional neoclassical growth models developed by Solow and Swan in the 1950s, the output of an economy grows in response to larger inputs of capital and labour (all physical inputs). Non-economic variables such as human capital or human health variables have no function in these models.

In the mid-1980s, a new paradigm was developed in the literature, mostly due to Paul Romer (1986), which is now commonly known as 'endogenous growth models'. By broadening the concept of capital to include *human capital*, the new endogenous growth model argues that the law of diminishing-returns-to-scale phenomenon may not be true in the case of African economies. In simple terms, what this means is that if the nation that invests in capital also employs educated and skilled workers who are also healthy, then not only will the labour be productive, but it will also be able to use the capital and technology more efficiently. This will lead to a so-called 'Hicks neutral' shift in the production function and thus there can be *increasing* rather than *decreasing* returns on investments. In other words, technology and human capital are both 'endogenous' to the system.

Indeed, the advent of 'endogenous growth models' with human capital has certainly enhanced the understanding of the mystery of the rapid and long sustainable high-growth performances of some African economies. Although there are many variables that can represent human capital and the health conditions of the people of a nation, in order to keep the analysis simple while, at the same time, capturing the basic broad thrust of these two variables, this chapter will touch on total literacy rate and life expectancy.

EMPIRICAL EVIDENCE

The adult literacy rate in Ghana was 71.5 percent in 2010, with males at 78.3 percent and females at 65.3 percent. Ghanaian children begin their education at the age of three or four, starting from nursery school to kindergarten, then elementary school (primary school), junior high school and senior high school, and finally university. The average age at which a Ghanaian child enters primary school is six years. The level of education of the adult Ghanaian is observed to be very low, to the effect that the highest level of education of most adults in basic education (see Table 9.2). In 2006, about 53 percent of adult Ghanaians aged at least 15 years old have participated in or completed basic education, compared to 31 percent with no education. Only 16 percent have 'tasted' or completed at least secondary education.

Table 9.2   Education Attainment by Economic Status in 2006 (%)

Level of education	Adult population
No education	31.1
Basic education	52.8
Secondary	10.1
Vocational/technical	3.8
Tertiary	2.2

Source: Calculated from the fifth round of the Ghana Living Standards Survey 5, 2006.

Using the people within a country to create a competitive advantage is one of the overlooked tools in Ghana today. We are familiar with institutions trying to mould people to fit the organization rather than creating an organizational model that fits the strengths and weaknesses of its people. Various governments over the past years in Ghana have embarked on numerous initiatives in their aim to prove how critical they view the nation's human capital. Some of these are as follows:

*   Legislation allowing private participation in providing education, hence the emergence of private educational institutions such as universities, colleges, training centres, primary and secondary schools.
*   Providing free/subsidized education for primary and junior secondary school education. Others are mooting the idea of extending free education to senior secondary schools.
*   Expanding the infrastructure of educational institutions, particularly buildings.
*   The provision of interventions like school feeding programmes, capitation grants, providing laptops/computers to teachers and students, vocational training/skills for the youth – catering, sewing, computer hardware and software, etc.
*   Instituting a best teacher's award.
*   A universal national health insurance scheme.

A comprehensive human resource development system is essential for ensuring an efficient and motivated people/workforce capable of contributing to the ultimate success of a nation. China is now leading the pack, with India, the USA, Japan, South Korea and Singapore all leveraging on managing human capital to achieve different levels of sustainable competitive advantage at one point in time. Yes, Ghana is on course, but we still have some way to go, so we ought to re-double our efforts to achieve Vision 2020.

Ghana has a universal healthcare system, the National Health Insurance Scheme (NHIS), and life expectancy at birth is 66 years, with males at 64 years and females at 67 years (see Table 9.3), while infant mortality is 39 per 1,000 live births. The total fertility rate is about 3.57 children per woman. There are about 15 physicians and 93 nurses per 100,000 individuals. In 2010, 5.2 percent of the country's GDP was spent on health. Although Ghana's universal healthcare system has been described as the most successful healthcare system on the African continent by some commentators, it is saddled with some inherent challenges.

Table 9.3   Ghana: Life Expectancy at Birth, Total (Years)

Year	2008	2009	2010	2011	2012
Life expectancy	63	63	64	64	66

Source: World Bank Data (2013).

Africa is the only region, to my knowledge, in which the life expectancy has been *declining* over the past two decades, and it looks like the continent's life expectancy will continue to decline for the foreseeable future. According to a recent conference on African population issues held in Ethiopia, the average life expectancy in Africa has declined by almost 15 years over the past two decades (BBC News, 2002). The biggest reason for this trend is the infectious disease AIDS and other infectious diseases, which are pushing life expectancy to extremely low rates in several African countries. In both Botswana and Malawi, for example, life expectancy is below 40 years according to the BBC report. By 2005, according to the conference, life expectancy for Africa as a whole was only 48 years, compared to 74.9 and 81.2 years for European men and women respectively (BBC News, 2002).

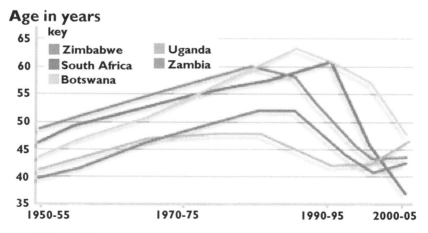

Figure 9.1   AIDS in Africa: Life Expectancy Chart

The consequences of such a drop in the life expectancy rate resulting from the AIDS epidemic is far-reaching as investments in the population's education and health will impact economic activity only in the short run.

Lessons from These Perspectives

The many great philosophers and economists who have contributed to the development of the concept of human capital provided great insight into the various facets of the subject. Learning from the various perspectives provided seems to pull together the philosophers under broad areas covering the individual, the organization and society.

THE INDIVIDUAL

A healthy and highly skilled and educated citizen of a nation stands a possibility of increasing individual income resulting from the individual productivity (Becker, 1993; Denison, 1962; Schultz, 1961, 1971; Sidorkin, 2007). The highly skilled individuals in Ghana and abroad tend to attract high earnings resulting from high value addition. This also tends to enhance the possibility for individuals or workers to move to a higher level in the internal market (Sicherman and Galor, 1990).

THE ORGANIZATION

The aggregate of healthy, highly skilled and educated workers ensures 'collective competences, organisational routines, company culture, and relational capital' (Edvinsson and Malone, 1997), which guarantees the bottom line for the organization.

SOCIETY

The total aggregate of healthy, highly skilled and educated citizens ensures the possibility of human capital that advocates and supports 'democracy, human rights, and political stability' (McMahon, 1999), which are the constituents of social consciousness within the community (Beach, 2009). Consequently, the link between human capital and social consciousness is based on a close inter-relationship resulting in socio-political development (Alexander, 1996; Grubb and Marvin, 2004; Sen, 1999). Tom Peters, co-author of *In Search of Excellence*, also gives great insight into the various areas of learning, which are as follows:

a) *Development of 'human capital' should always be the top priority.* This is imperative in an age in which imaginative brainwork is de facto the only plausible survival strategy for individual enterprises of consequence and higher-wage nations in their entirety.
b) *Maximizing 'gross domestic development' of the workforce.* This factor, driven at the level of the individual enterprise, is the key source of growth, productivity, wealth creation and social stability.
c) *Top decision makers must become obsessed about continuous training.* This must be placed at the top of the enterprise's agenda.

d) *The chief 'training' officer must be placed at a level of seniority comparable to that of the chief financial officer or chief information officer.*

e) *We must maximize the rate of development of women leaders at every level.* Among other reasons, evidence suggests that women are more likely than men to champion the imperative of maximizing human asset development.

f) *The educational infrastructure must be up-ended to underpin support for the creative jobs that will be more or less the sole basis for employment*, economic growth and wealth creation. Central to this would be a dramatically enhanced, appreciated, compensated and accountable role for teachers; teaching should be a career of choice for a nation's best and brightest.

g) *A radical re-orientation of leadership education and development throughout the enterprise/education/continuing education institution must occur.* The MBA and executive education must have open-heart surgery – aimed at shifting the focus from finance and marketing to human resources.

Implications for Developing Economies

In order to raise capital for investment in our citizens, we must attach the idea of investing to already-present cultural ideals and values like children and education. Every family wishes the best for its children and most Ghanaians still recognize that education is the most reliable path to a brighter future, with greater opportunities for success and individual autonomy. We should not only think out of the box, we must throw the box away. We must find the political will to seek answers to our problems from within ourselves. Our development policies must transcend relationships with development partners. First it was the Paris Club (an informal group of creditor nations whose objective is to find workable solutions to payment problems faced by debtor nations), now China beckons and all African heads of state arrive in Beijing with the outstretched hands of perennial recipients.

True national development must guarantee upward mobility for citizens and thus reduce poverty from generation to generation. National development is a 'life course' issue, not a matter of improving everyone's lot today, as some of our politicians view it. True development must be 'citizenry development' in which human capital accumulation is a public priority. This begins with children. A concerted focus on children is the 'sine qua non' of sustainable national transformation if Ghana is to become a knowledge-based productive and competitive society. Even poor families invest in their children. So should the state, because the future truly belongs to the children of today and we should help them shape it to their maximum advantage.

Ghana should institute an early childhood investment programme in the 0–5 age group. All families, irrespective of their financial status, would be encouraged to establish investment accounts which are matched by government funds and invested over the long term. The ratio of the match is less important than the partnership between the state and its future. There could be accounts primarily for secondary or university education. The concept could take numerous forms, but the concept and its universality are crucial to planting the seeds of a broad-based capital market with the involvement of ordinary citizens. This will create an incentive for parents to begin planning much earlier for their children's education and future. An initiative like this would attract more funds from Ghanaians abroad to invest directly in the future of the country through their children, nieces, nephews, grandchildren and others. This would potentially generate investment capital for supporting other needs such as a bond market. Most important in all of this would be the contagion effect over time, which would grow to involve other investment habits among the population in general. Other positive dimensions including tax incentives and improved identification and location of citizens for the purpose of general revenue collection would arise from such efforts. This is a conceptual proposal and no attempt is made to present a fully designed programme.

We are reminded that a well-educated and skilled citizenry is the surest guarantee of a sustainable future. We must overcome our past failures, learn from them and rely more on our own human capital to secure a brighter national future. We must invest earlier in our citizens in order to ensure that all the rights and responsibilities of the citizenship are fully expressed and protected. In this way, our children will own the future of their countries. 'There are only two lasting bequests we can hope to give our children. One of these is roots, the other wings' (Manus Ulzen, 2013).

Conclusions

Human capital has been identified as a key stimulus of economic development. This chapter has demonstrated that when the highlighted strategic approaches are adopted in developing countries, they can efficiently harness human capital to create competitive advantages and surplus value, which could be used to upgrade technology and diversify economic activity, facilitating national development. In a nutshell, improving equity and the population's access to healthcare and education will greatly enhance the quality of human capital of a nation.

The truth of the matter is that the key task in moving towards a developed nation status lies in Ghana's ability to develop its human and intellectual capital to produce an adequate supply of knowledge and healthy workers who are flexible, agile and mobile with the relevant knowledge and skills required by the nation's industry for national development.

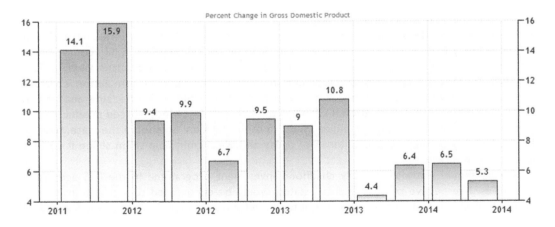

Figure 9.2   Ghana's GDP Annual Growth Rate Chart
Source: www.tradingeconomics.com, Ghana Statistical Service.

References

Aful-Dadzie, K. (2011). The leading root cause of unemployment. *Daily Graphic*, 6 August.

Alan, K.M.A., Altman, Y. and Roussel, J. (2008). Employee training needs and perceived value of training in the Pearl River Delta of China: A human capital development approach. *Journal of European Industrial Training*, 32(1), pp. 19–31.

Alexander, K. (1996). *The Value of an Education*. Concord, MA: Simon & Schuster.

Baldacci, E., Clements, B., Gupta, S. and Cui, Q. (2004). Social spending, human capital, and growth in developing countries: Implications for achieving the MDGs. IMF Working paper, WP/04/217, Fiscal Affairs Department.

Barriol, A. (1910). La valeur sociale d'un individu. *Revue économique internationale* (December), pp. 552–5.

BBC News (2002). Life expectancy still falling, 11 February, http://news.bbc.co.uk/2/hi/africa/1814609.stm.

Beach, M.J. (2009). A critique of human capital formation in the U.S. and the economic returns to sub-Baccalaureate credentials. *Educational Studies: A Journal of the American Educational Studies*, 45(1), pp. 24–38.

Becker, G. (1993). *Human Capital: A Theoretical and Empirical Analysis with Special Reference to Education*, 3rd edn. Chicago: University of Chicago Press.

Becker, G., Murphy, K. and Tamura, R. (1990). Human capital, fertility and economic growth. *Journal of Political Economy*, 98(5), pp. 12–37.

Cantillon, P. (1759). *The Analysis of Trade, Commerce, Coin, Bullion, Banks, and Foreign Exchanges*. London.

Crawford, R. (1991). *In the Era of Human Capital*. New York: HarperCollins.

Davidson, P. and Honig, B. (2003). The role of social and human capital among nascent entrepreneurs. *Journal of Business Venturing*, 18(3), pp. 301–31.

Denison E.F. (1962). The sources of growth in the US. New York Committee for Economic Development.

De la Fuente, A. and Ciccone, A. (2002). *Human Capital and Growth in a Global and Knowledge-based Economy*. Report for the European Commission, DG for Employment and Social Affairs.

Dublin, L. and Lotka, A. (1930). *The Money Value of Man*. New York: Roland Press Co.

Edvinsson, L. and Malone, M.S. (1997). *Intellectual Capital*. London: Piatkus.

Errunza, V. (1983). Emerging markets: A new opportunity for improving global portfolio performance. *Financial Analyst Journal*, 39(5), pp. 51–8.

Farr, W. (1897). Equitable taxation of property. *Royal Statistical Society*, XVI, March, pp. 1–45.

Fisher, I. (1897). Senses of 'Capital'. *Economic Journal*, VII, June, pp. 199–213.

Frank, R.H. and Bernanke, B.S. (2007). *Principles of Microeconomics*, 3rd edn. New York: McGraw-Hill Irwin.

Foville, A. de (1905). Ce que c'est la richesse d'un peuple. *Bull Institut Internal Statis.*, XIV, pp. 62–74.

Galbraith, J.K. (1998). *Created Unequal: The Crisis in American Pay*. New York: Free Press.

Grubb, W.N. and Marvin, L. (2004). *The Education Gospel: The Economic Power of Schooling*. Cambridge, MA: Harvard University Press.

Harbison, F.H. (1962). Human resources in development planning in modernising economies. *International Labour Review*, LXXXV(1), pp. 435–58.

Huebner, S. (1914). The human value in business compared with the property value. Proceedings of the Thirty-Fifth American Convention National Association of Life Underwriters, July, pp. 17–41.

Howitt, P. (2005). Health, human capital and economic growth: A Schumpeterian perspective. Seminar paper for the Pan American Health Organization.

Krishna, A. and Shrader, E. (1999). Social capital assessment tool. Prepared for the Conference on Social Capital and Poverty Reduction, World Bank, Washington DC, 22–4 June.

Manus Ulzen, T.P. (2013). Political will and the future of our democracy. *Business in Ghana*, 7 April.

Mathur, V. (1999). Human capital-based strategy for regional economic development. *Economic Development Quarterly*, 13(3), pp. 203–16.

McMahon, W.W. (1999). *Education and Development: Measuring the Social Benefits*. New York: Oxford University Press.

Mill, J.S. (1909). *Principles of Political Economy*. New York: Longmans, Green & Co.

Mun, S.H. and Jorgenson, D.W. (2000). Education policies to simulate growth. In G.W. Harrison, S.E.H. Jensen, L.H. Pedersen et al. (eds), *Using Dynamic General Equilibrium Models for Policy Analysis.* New York: Elsevier, pp. 223–57.

Petty, W. (1769). *Tracts Relating Chiefly to Ireland.* Dublin, p. 31.

Rankin, K. (2002). Social capital, microfinance, and the politics of development. *Feminist Economics,* 8(1), pp. 1–24.

Romer, P. (1986). Increasing returns and long-run growth. *Journal of Political Economy,* 94, pp. 1002–37.

Say, J.B. (1821). *A Treatise on Political Economy.* London: Longman, Hurst, Rees, Orme, and Brown.

Schultz, T.W. (1961). Investment in human capital. *American Economic Review,* 51(1), pp. 1–17.

———. (1971). *Investment in Human Capital.* New York: Free Press.

Sen, A. (1999). *Development as Freedom.* New York: Anchor Books.

Sheffrin, M.S. (2003). *Economics: Principles in Action.* New Jersey: Prentice Hall.

Sicherman, N. and Galor, O. (1990). A theory of career mobility, *Journal of Political Economy,* 98(1), pp. 169–92.

Sidgwick, H. (1901). *The Principles of Political Economy.* London: Macmillan & Co.

Sidorkin, M.A. (2007). Human capital and the labour of learning: A case of mistaken identity. *Educational Theory,* 57(2), pp. 159–70.

Smith, A. (1937). *The Wealth of Nations.* New York: Modern Library.

Solow, R. and Swan, T. (1950). The theory of economic growth: A 'classical' perspective. *Quarterly Journal of Economics,* 70, pp. 65–94.

Wittstein, T. (1867). *Mathematische Statistik und deren Anwendung auf National-Okonomic und Versicherung-Wissenschaft.* Hanover: Hahn'sche Hofbuchland-lung.

Appendix 1

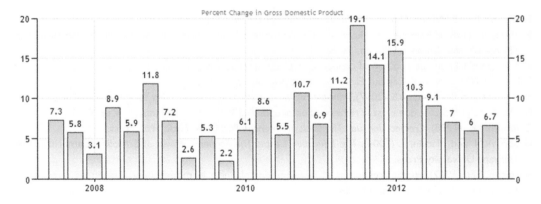

Figure 9A.1   Ghana's GDP Annual Growth Rate

Source: www.tradingeconomics.com, Ghana Statistical Service.

GDP	INDICATORS	Last		Previous	Highest	Lowest	Forecast		Unit	Trend
GDP	40.71	Dec/2012	39.20	40.71	1.20	39.74	Dec/2012	USD Billion	
GDP GROWTH RATE	-3.10	Mar/2013	2.10	7.80	-5.90	1.72	Dec/2013	Percent	
GDP ANNUAL GROWTH RATE	6.70	Mar/2013	6.00	19.10	2.20	9.50	Dec/2013	Percent	
GDP PER CAPITA	402.70	Dec/2011	360.32	402.70	188.15	405.82	Dec/2012	USD	
GDP PER CAPITA PPP	1,871.14	Dec/2011	1,637.76	1,871.14	444.63	1,890.24	Dec/2012	USD	

PART IV
NATURAL RESOURCES

10

Harnessing Land Resources for Economic Development

Wordsworth Odame Larbi

Abstract

Land is the basic asset on which the wealth of most nations is built. In Ghana, as in many African countries, the concept of land is a complex phenomenon that is not regarded simply as an economic or environmental asset, but as a social, cultural and ontological resource which defines the construction of social identity, the organization of traditional religious life and the production and reproduction of culture. It is both a natural resource as well as a marketable commodity. Land also provides a more attractive form of investment in developing economies where alternatives in manufacturing and the service industry are both few and subject to great risks. In rural economies, land forms the main source of livelihoods. The contribution of land and its resources to economic development lies in the property rights that exist in the land. These rights define the ownership, control, use and management of land. Property rights evolve over time and may be driven by economic, social, environmental or political considerations. They may exist in both formal and informal economies although in either situation it is required that they are well defined and enforceable. Through a combination of factors such as conquest, migration and long-undisturbed occupation, purchase and colonialism, a complex system of property rights regime has evolved in Ghana. These are mediated through the land administration system, which provides the framework and infrastructure through which property rights are managed. This chapter explores the complex relationship between property rights, land administration, land governance and economic development. It identifies critical challenges that militate against unleashing the full potential of property rights for the social and economic development of the country. These include a debate as to whether customary land tenure is an enigma to economic development or not, constraints of extant legal framework as well as lacuna in the law, challenges of establishing the land administration infrastructure and the governance system. Key recommendations include bold political will to take decisions that can transform some of the fundamental conceptions about customary land, co-operation and collaboration of all stakeholders to build the land administration infrastructure and improve upon the land governance system.

Introduction

Land is the basic asset on which the wealth of most nations is built. It represents the main form of wealth accumulation and the principal source of economic and political power (Doner, 1972: 18; Deininger, 2003). It is also the basic instrument of overall development policy, performing both an indirect, facilitating role and a direct and active one (Doebele, 1983). Approximately 60 percent of the population of Africa derives its livelihoods and income from farming, livestock production and related activities (AUC-ECA-AfDB, 2010). Thus, there is a need to appreciate the importance of land both as a natural resource as well as a marketable commodity. A fundamental principle upon which ownership of land in Ghanaian traditional communities is based is collective ownership by a community or group. The character of the group or community is usually dependent on the structure of the political or social organization of the community, which in turn reflects the nature of landholding. The group may be a stool or skin, clan or family. The general acclaim is that 80 percent of land in Ghana is owned by these groups, commonly referred to as customary land. The remaining 20 percent are state lands under the management and control of the Lands Commission. Land in the Ghanaian traditional setting and culture is not regarded simply as an economic or environmental asset, but as a social, cultural and ontological resource which defines the construction of social identity, the organization of traditional religious life and the production and re-production of culture. In spite of these characteristics a striking feature of the customary system of land holding is that it is a dynamic institution which responds to the needs of the community at any stage of development.

Over the years, due to diverse influences such as conquest, migration and settlement, colonization and government policies, a complex system of land tenure arrangements has evolved. These arrangements underpin the organization of several socio-economic activities, livelihoods, gender relations, sustainable development, economic growth and socio-political stability. These issues are mediated through a land governance structure which also provides the framework for dealing with any disputes associated with land issues. Land governance has thus assumed importance in recent times as many of the land-related disputes, some of which develop into full-blown conflicts, are traceable to the governance structures that have superintended and mediated land tenure relations over the years.

This chapter considers secured property rights in land, and the contribution it makes to economic development and poverty reduction. It also explores the challenges militating against achieving secured property rights in land and the consequential adverse effects on socio-economic development. It further explores the implications of complex interrelation of various factors on the evolution of property rights in land and the eventual impact on economic development of the country. It concludes with proposals for dealing with challenges and setting a policy context for land-based economic development.

The contribution of land and its resources to the economic development of any nation cannot be underestimated. So too are the property rights that define the ownership, control, use and management of these rights. Land uses such as agriculture, pastoralism, access to and control of common resources such as grazing lands, water resources, urbanization and its land requirements for housing, industrial development, recreation, social and physical infrastructure are all underpinned ultimately by property rights in land and socio-economic relations between people and land. These are also influenced by government policies which ultimately define the parameters of the governance structures and institutions. It is noted that although land is central to sustainable livelihoods in Africa, development initiatives in many countries do not always take comprehensive account of this reality (AUC-ECA-AfDB, 2010). It is important that appropriate measures are taken to ensure that land plays its primary role in the development process and more particularly in social reconstruction, poverty reduction, enhancing economic opportunities for women and the vulnerable, strengthening governance, sustainable management of the environment, reducing land-related conflicts or promoting conflict resolution and driving agricultural modernization. Recent emerging issues that demand attention because of their implications on land rights, sustainable livelihoods and sustainable economic development include climate change, large-scale land-based investments and the achievement of four of the Millennium Development Goals, which have direct bearing on land rights. These are to:

- eradicate extreme poverty;
- promote gender equality and empower women;
- ensure environmental sustainability; and
- develop global partnerships for development.

Achieving these goals calls for a critical examination of land in all of its facets – tenure, governance, valuation, use, development and control. It calls for the establishment of a land governance structure and infrastructure that supports the complex land ownership system in order to promote an efficient and effective land administration system that supports land market operations.

The impact of global warming on climate change is expected to affect land use systems, although its extent and magnitude is still unfolding and may take time for the full impact to manifest itself. Nevertheless, direct impacts such as reduced availability and scarcity of water, saline intrusion, increased temperatures, biodiversity loss and desertification as a consequence of more frequent droughts are known to reduce productivity of land (AUC-ECA-AfDB, 2010: 10). In dealing with these, the use of appropriate mitigation measures, appropriate adaptation responses and links with other economic decisions such as subsidies, physical and social infrastructure development, and affordability as well as policies that protect the poor and the vulnerable are called into play. The more vulnerable in society usually bear the brunt of the impact. Thus, the effects of global warming and climate change are likely to have more adverse effects on adaptation strategies and are likely to accelerate poverty where the appropriate policy responses are not formulated and implemented.

Land also provides a more attractive form of investment in developing economies where alternatives in manufacturing and the service industry are both few and subject to great risks. In rural economies, land forms the main source of livelihoods. As noted by Toulmin and Quan (2000), land has a particularly significant role to play in securing the livelihoods of poorer rural people. There is competition among land users and land uses. The processes of allocating land for various uses, either through market forces of demand and supply or through government policies in supply-led situations, are critical to the successful operation of the land market. These are influenced by accessibility to land for development, ownership and control over land resources, and the security attached to land tenure and land rights. Equally important are the policies put in place to regulate dealings and tenures in land. Land and its tenure and administration therefore form one of the important pillars underpinning the socio-economic development of many developing economies. Apart from competing for the scarce land resources that are available, compatibility among various uses are underpinned and determined by the national, regional and local spatial frameworks that influence the highest and best uses to which each piece of land can be put. There is a connection between land and other areas of economic and social policies such as gender, environment, poverty and available economic opportunities which should be explored for a better understanding of the land–economic development nexus. This should encompass the various land tenure systems, the social, political, economic and cultural frameworks within which land issues are managed, and the policy instruments adopted to intervene in the operation of land markets.

The Historical Context of Property Rights in Land in Ghana

The land question in Ghana, like many other Sub-Saharan African countries, has its origins in the geopolitical, economic, social and demographic factors that have shaped African societies over the years. They have defined the nature of property rights and greatly influenced the land tenure relations and governance, land use, management and environmental considerations. Primarily land in pre-colonial times has been appropriated through four main mechanisms, namely conquest, migration and long-undisturbed occupation of virgin land, purchase and deeds of gift, and colonialism.

CONQUEST

Throughout Ghana, communities and traditional states have always asserted their hegemony over land through conquest during pre-colonial warfare. The Ashantis, Denkyiras, Dagombas, Gonjas, etc. all have historical records of conquering other native states and annexing the lands of the vanquished states. The implications of these war exploits were that any citizen of a defeated native state occupying any land anywhere within the domain of the defeated state had the land automatically annexed and placed under the control and jurisdiction of the conquering state. They eventually became stool or skin lands. These lands were not mapped, so what were the extent and limits of these lands? What were the boundaries? How are these boundaries determined in modern times? Ancient boundary marks such as rivers, trees, hills, footpaths and anthills lacked precision in several areas and posed challenges to the determination of the limits of land. Bentsi-Enchill (1964: 13) argues that the absence of established boundaries resulted from the small population of the communities relative to the land they occupied and an absence of any pressing demand to demarcate boundaries as well as large areas of unoccupied land between communities. The author recalls that during boundary demarcation exercises under the Ministry of Lands and Natural Resources' Land Administration Project Phase I in 11 customary land areas, the paramount chiefs had to depend on people and settlements close to the boundaries for the boundaries to be identified for demarcation.[1] With population increases, pressure on land has increased, leading to considerable tension over land. It has become a critical requirement of the governance system and the land administration infrastructure to have the boundaries demarcated and surveyed. Without that, it becomes difficult to administer the land, which then undermines the economic and social benefits of good land administration.

MIGRATION AND LONG-UNDISTURBED OCCUPATION OF VIRGIN LAND

A study of the migration patterns in Ghana shows that the current configuration of traditional states and ethnic composition has been the result of intense migration of communities which eventually settled among other indigenous early settlers – see, for example, Field (1940) and Manoukian (1964). Some people settled on unoccupied land and appropriated the land through cultivation and settlement, according to the 'strength of their cutlasses'. Others negotiated with earlier settlers for permission to occupy land, which was usually granted with or without conditions. Such arrangements (with varying deviations) underlie the relationship between some communities such as the Mamprusis and the Kusasis of the Upper East Region,

---

1   The 11 areas are Wasa Amenfi, Wasa Fiase, Asebu, Dormaa Ahenkro, Anum, Fieve, Gulkpegu, Sandema, Gbawe, Ejisu and Juaben.

Nanumbas and Konkombas in the Northern Region, the Abiriws and Akropong in Eastern Region and the people of Fintey, who are saddled between the Akwamus and the Anums also in the Eastern Region. The tenurial arrangements for this co-existence were not usually clearly defined, nor were the actual extent and limits of the land occupied or to be occupied defined. What is clear is that the earlier settlers always asserted that the late arrivals were given use rights over the land and such rights could never mature into ownership. This creates problems where the latter settlers begin to assert full ownership rights over their settlements without reference to their 'benefactors'. Over time, the populations of these settlements have grown, expanding the original settlements and appropriating new lands for economic activities such as farming, hunting and wood gathering. This phenomenon has the potential to create disputes regarding how much land should be occupied and what the limits of such lands should be. The effects are incessant disputes, which occasionally erupt into violent conflicts. The recurrent conflict between the Kusasis and Mamprusis, the 1994 Nanumba–Konkomba conflict, the recurring Peki–Tsito conflict, the Alavanyo–Nkonya conflict and the recent Abiriw–Akropong conflict can all be traced back partly or in whole to these earlier settlement arrangements. It is reported that the chiefs of the Nkonya and the Alavanyo have signed a peace declaration to end the protracted decades-long land dispute between the two communities and to ensure peaceful coexistence between them (*Daily Graphic*, No. 19190, 1 July 2013). It is submitted that subsequent to the accord, every effort should be made to demarcate the boundaries between the two communities, otherwise it is doubtful whether the accord will last. There are a number of other festering yet latent disputes, which have not yet developed into conflicts. Some of these were unearthed during the customary boundary demarcation exercises mentioned above. Such conflicts were noted in the Volta Region between the Fieve clan and the Mafi Traditional Authority in the Sogakope area, the Gbawe Kwatei Family and the Sempe and Jamestown Stools in Accra (in both situations, the tensions were so severe that the exercises could not take off), between Wasa Amenfi, Sefwi Bekwai and Sefwi Asanwinso, and between the Anums and the Akwamus in the Fintey area. Despite efforts at mediation, some of the tensions and disputes were so entrenched that they stalled the exercise. Such conflicts or festering disputes undermine the peaceful occupation and use of land, which then affects sound socio-economic development, prevents effective investment in land development and creates unfavourable conditions for the management of the environment. Such conflicts have the capacity to entrench poverty. It may be necessary to set up early warning mechanisms to systematically track these simmering conflicts so that they do not develop into full-blown conflicts, while efforts are made to resolve these disputes through alternative dispute resolution mechanisms (such as mediation, negotiation and arbitration) and the effective determination and demarcation of the boundaries.

PURCHASE AND DEEDS OF GIFT

These mechanisms for acquiring customary rights in land by communities are not many and the absence of effective recording of such grants makes the analysis problematic. However, some anecdotal evidence confirms purchase as a mode for acquiring customary land. The Jackson Commission of Inquiry into Ningo Lands, for example, held that the Shais bought the land they occupy at Ayikuma and Dodowa from the people of Larteh. It is also known that under customary practices, land had been gifted to families who had displayed gallantry during warfare. These are not adequately recorded except by oral tradition. The extent of land given to such families is not usually known and the boundaries are not clearly defined – a recipe for disputes.

COLONIALISM

The interaction between traditional leaders and European adventurers which eventually evolved into colonization and the establishment of colonial administration and domination of traditional authority in the then Gold Coast played a profound role in the evolution of a complex system of land tenure. It led to the development of a legal-plural environment and profound changes to the traditional arrangements for managing land in societies that did not have chieftaincy as the dominant customary system for managing land. Such societies were described as acephalous and were predominant in the Upper East and Upper West Regions. The colonial administration established chieftaincy systems in these communities and administered land through them, instead of the *Tendamba*, who were the recognized customary authorities over land. Among the Gas in the south, chieftaincy arrangements were strengthened and the land was administered through chiefs instead of through the *Wulomei*. Colonialism introduced compulsory acquisition of land for national development (the origin of the concept of state lands in Ghana) and directed the policies for managing land which has affected the way in which land is managed in the country. McAuslan (1985: 1) argues that colonialism was basically about land tenure. Platteau (1992) adds that the policy with regard to land was probably the most important factor in determining the relationship between colonial governments and the African. One of the legacies of colonialism is the operation of Western tenurial arrangements alongside customary or indigenous systems, not only in Ghana but also in Sub-Saharan Africa as a whole. Nevertheless, traditional land tenure systems which do not allow private land rights to be fully recognized still predominate in most of the countryside, particularly in the Francophone countries (Platteau, 1992: 83). In Southern and Eastern Africa, for example, customary tenures operate mainly in rural areas. In Northern Africa and parts of West Africa, Islamic laws have a wider influence on land tenure (Acquaye and Asiama, 1986). In West Africa, Napoleonic land laws operate in former French colonies as a result of the French policy of assimilation and later association. French colonial land laws refused to recognize the existence of an indigenous customary system of land tenure and were entirely based on notions of exclusive private property and proof of title to land through a process called immatriculation and formal registration (Platteau, 1992). In Anglophone West Africa, however, customary land tenure operates alongside Western tenurial systems, even in the urban areas. Customary laws were not harmonized with colonial policy. What emerged in the end were different layers of tenure systems where the local tenure systems were overlaid by national legislation, introduced by the colonial powers, which were based on very different principles geared towards a different set of interests (Delville, 2000; Toulmin et al., 2002) with different consequences.

Hence, contrary to what might have been thought, the main impact of British colonial land policies has not been the replacement of African land tenure by private property rights in land. Rather, they resulted in a complex tenurial system shaped by both customary land laws and the British conveyancing system which is still in operation today and still determines the relationship between people and land, as well as the allocation of land for competing uses. Many developing countries trying to industrialize have to confront the issue of how land tenure and land polices influence the location and localization of industries, and how land markets shape economic activities, underwritten by secured and certain property rights. The challenge is to recognize that 'although land is central to sustainable livelihoods in Africa, development initiatives in many countries do not always take comprehensive account of this reality' (AUC-ECA-AfDB, 2010).

Land Tenure and Secured Property Rights to Land

Many human endeavours and enterprises find expression in spatial dimensions on land. Land lies at the heart of social, cultural, spiritual, political and economic life in most of Africa. Land and natural resources are therefore key assets for economic growth and development. They are vital to livelihoods, income and employment, factors which ultimately contribute to peace and security. Thus, the types of rights and interests that land users have and the certainty, clarity and security associated with those rights form the basic property rights for land-based economic development. Secure property rights provide not only the necessary certainty to do business, but, when held in the forms of transferable land titles and used as collateral, also enable access to credit and contribute to the development of financial systems (AUC-ECA-AfDB, 2010).

Land tenure is the nature of and manner in which rights and interests over various categories of land are created or determined, allocated and enjoyed (AUC-ECA-AfDB, 2010). In Africa, land tenure is governed by two regimes: customary systems and statutory systems. Customary land tenure comprises the right to use or dispose of use rights over land which rests neither on the exercise of brute force nor on evidence of rights guaranteed by government statute, but on the fact that they are recognized as legitimate by the community, the rules governing the acquisition and transmission of these rights being usually explicitly and generally known, though not normally recorded in writing (Bower, 1993; Larbi, 1995; Delville, 2000). Under these arrangements, the right to cultivate a piece of land is an inseparable and, in principle, inalienable element of being a member of the land-holding community (Deininger, 2003). Thus, it is the community's recognition and assurance that an occupier of land has the right to use the land that gives legitimacy and security of tenure (Larbi and Kakraba-Ampeh, 2013). Since the main mode of transmitting land rights in customary systems is unwritten, it is tempting to describe land transactions emanating from such modes as informal. Article 267(1) of the *1992 Constitution of Ghana* provides that all stool land in Ghana shall vest in the appropriate stool on behalf of and in trust for the subjects of the stool in accordance with customary law and usage. This recognition moves customary land transactions from informality to formality. Section 4 of the Conveyancing Act 1973 (NRCD 175) provides for the recording of oral grants of interest in land under customary law, incorporating the essential features of the transaction and incorporating an adequate plan of the land if available. The customary system of land tenure provides an egalitarian nature of land allocation mechanism prevailing at the customary or village level (Platteau, 2000) and to the extent that they are not recorded in formal state registers may be so described as informal (Larbi et al., 2004). However, they are recognized as legal land transactions, otherwise rural people will find themselves in a position of permanent illegality and insecurity, especially in forest areas where the gap between formal law and local practice is greatest (Delville, 2000).

THE IMPACT OF POPULATION GROWTH

As noted above, an increasing population puts considerable pressure on land, necessitating the need for more defined property rights to land, exercised over well-defined boundaries. This is because increased population tends to increase the value of land. The population of Ghana has grown steadily from 12.3 million in 1984 to 18.9 million in 2000 and has doubled over a 26-year period to 24.6 million in 2010. Population density has also increased steadily from 51.5 persons per square kilometre in 1984 to 79.3 in 2000 and reaching 103.4 in 2010. Inter-censal growth rate was 2.9 percent in 1984, 2.7 percent in 2000 and 2.5 percent in 2010. Correspondingly, the urban proportion of the population has also been growing steadily – it was 32 percent in 1984, 43.8 percent in 2000 and 50.9 percent in 2010. Thus, currently more than half of the total population live in towns and cities. Table 10.1 below shows the population characteristics of the regions as at the last census in 2010.

Table 10.1   Regional Distribution of the Population in 2010

Region	Land area (km²)	Total population	Urban population (%)	Population density (persons/km²)	Inter-censal growth rate (%)
All regions	238,533	24,658,823	50.9	103.4	2.5
Western	23,921	2,376,021	42.4	99.3	2.0
Central	9,826	2,201,863	47.1	224.1	3.1
Greater Accra	3,245	4,010,054	90.5	1,235.8	3.1
Volta	20,570	2,118,252	33.7	103.0	2.5
Eastern	19,323	2,633,154	43.4	136.3	2.1
Ashanti	24,389	4,780,380	60.6	196.0	2.7
Brong Ahafo	39,557	2,310,983	44.5	58.4	2.3
Northern	70,384	2,479,461	30.3	35.2	2.9
Upper East	8,842	1,046,545	21.0	118.4	1.2
Upper West	18,476	702,110	16.3	38.0	1.9

Source: Ghana Statistical Services.
Note: An urban area in Ghana is defined to be a settlement of 5,000 people or more.

The figures do not at a glance portray any stress that the steady increase in population may have on land resources, nor does it seem to pose a threat in the near future. However, the fact that it is increasing steadily is worrisome. The national figures obscure the pressures in areas of high population concentration, where there is indeed stress on available land resources. As shown in Table 10.1 above, the population densities in the Greater Accra, Central, Eastern, Ashanti and the Upper East Regions, which are above the national average, present a worrying trend. It becomes more serious when the concentration in some peri-urban areas around the major cities of Accra, Tema, Kumasi, Tamale and Bawku are considered. Such growth imposes tremendous pressure on land resources. In the absence of clear and certain property rights to land, increasing population density tends to exacerbate the struggle over property rights and the propensity to resort to disputes over land. Increasing population density is therefore a pointer to the need to establish mechanisms, institutions and structures for clarifying property rights, demarcating boundaries, resolving land-related disputes and for authoritative recording of rights and interests in land. This in turn may lead to the emergence of institutions that facilitate a more precise definition of property rights or the emergence of costly conflict over land rights (Deininger, 2003). Security of property rights to land can offer significant benefits to land users, communities and the entire nation in terms of equity, investment, credit supply and reduced expenditure of resources on defensive activities such as prevention of conflicts. However, due to the sensitivity and sentiments attached to land, a stronger political will is required to deal with these issues.

Thus, in general land tenure and property rights evolve over time. The evolution may be determined or facilitated by factors such as population growth, economic development, migration, warfare, institutional frameworks, scope for investment and the transferability of property rights.

The evolution could further be affected by the possible threats to dispossession or conflict which can influence the potential or increasing output from the land through land transfers. Secure property rights provide incentives for investment in land and land resources. It is necessary to establish systems that help to clarify property rights, especially in situations of high population density, increased demand for land-related investments or other factors that increase the value of land. Rights and interests in land provide the bundle of property rights and define the nature of legitimate uses that can be made of land, and therefore the benefits to be derived from doing so (Deininger, 2003). The bundle of rights and interests in land are exercised over the physical land and are geographically defined. They are also defined by the extent or duration as well as limitations imposed by landowners, governments, communities or society at large. Secured property rights should therefore be defined with sufficient precision and should be enforceable at low cost so as to instil confidence in economic actors. Even though the legitimacy of property rights and the security associated with them are generally provided and determined by the community and the customary arrangements defined by the particular land-holding community, the state also defines generally the parameters within which the rights can be safely exercised. In addition, the state provides the framework for the formal definition, enforcement and how the rights eventually evolve in line with changing economic conditions. This in turn provides a basis for determining the level of tenure security enjoyed by individual land owners and their ability and willingness to exchange such rights with others (Denininger, 2003). The framework provided by the state thus forms part of the infrastructure for socio-economic development. The infrastructure includes the need to physically demarcate and delineate boundaries of all property rights holders, including individual plots, maintenance of the boundaries at all times, the establishment and maintenance of accurate records of land ownership, and all the associated transactions and encumbrances and servitudes that run with ownership of the land, the protection of the rights against intruders and adverse claimants, and the enforcement of the rights, as well as the mechanism for the resolution of disputes that may arise. Tools of the infrastructure includes accurate maps and plans, well-constructed geographical information systems that shows parcels of land over which rights are exercised and all the attributes of such parcels, including information on ownership, tenures, permitted uses, servitudes, etc. Such information may be provided in registers or in a computerized system and are fundamental tools used in land market operations as well as inputs for the planning and provision of public services.

Property Rights, Land Administration and Economic Development

It has been indicated above that secured property rights form one of the bedrocks of economic development. According to Besley and Ghatak (2009), property rights (of which land rights is a component) can be grouped into three bundles: use rights which include an owner's right to use a good or asset for consumption and/or income generation; transfer rights which include the right to transfer to another party in the form of a sale, gift or bequest; and the right to contract with other parties by renting, pledging or mortgaging or allowing other parties to use it. Property rights are therefore very important for economic growth and development, particularly where they are well defined, secured and enforced. Nations prosper when private property rights are well defined and enforced (O'Driscoll and Hoskins, 2003). Property rights also define social relations and how society is generally shaped. The way in which property rights are managed also affects environmental conservation, particularly where the rights are not properly managed and enforced. Even under customary tenurial arrangements, it is the egalitarian tenurial system (which defines the property rights at the local level) that sustains social cohesion and security at the community level (Kasanga, 2002). Property rights are therefore key elements of the social fabric of most societies, as well as a critical determinant of investment. They define the nature of legitimate uses that can be made of land and the benefits to be derived from doing so (Deininger, 2003).

Property rights evolve over time (Besley and Ghatak, 2009) and may be driven by economic, social, environmental or political considerations. They may exist in both formal and informal spheres, although in either situation, it is required that they are well defined and enforced. They may exist as individual private property rights or may be communal property rights. They may also exist as customary rights. Irrespective of the form in which the property rights exist, they affect resource allocation by shaping the incentives of individuals to carry out productive activities involving the use of the right, undertake investments that maintain or enhance its value, and also to trade or lease it for other uses (Besley and Ghatak, 2009).

The functioning of property rights as a means for economic development and wealth creation is underpinned by the existence of an efficient and effective land administration system through which property rights are defined, recorded, protected and enforced. Such a system is supported by appropriate and efficient mechanisms for dispute resolution, which may be at the customary or national level and are necessary for guaranteeing land tenure security. Adequate land tenure security benefits all land market participants, including the poor, who have fewer resources to acquire and defend land rights in insecure tenure environments (Bruce et al., 2006). The importance of secure land rights underscores the need for public involvement in the establishment and guaranteeing of property rights to land so as to eliminate the need for individuals to dissipate resources in trying to establish their own systems and to create systems skewed towards and manipulated by the rich and influential in society. The cost and equity advantages of a systematic approach to the establishment of a land administration system cannot be overemphasized. It provides a network effect through the availability of consistent, accurate, reliable and up-to-date information to support other administrative units such as land use planning, infrastructure planning and other service providers. The system provides a best practice platform where public participation, transparency and good governance exist.

A land administration system provides the structure and processes for the determination, archiving and delivery of land rights, and systems through which general oversight on the performance of the land sector is managed (AUC-ECA-AfDB, 2010). It provides a country with the infrastructure to implement land policies and land management strategies (Williamson et al., 2010). It offers several benefits to its beneficiaries. It provides the mechanism through which land and property rights are ascertained. A good land administration system offers greater security of tenure, reduces the chances of losing the land or being evicted, opportunities for investing in the land, an environment within which it is easy to sell the land and often at a higher price, and access to credit by using the land as collateral. Land use can easily be planned and managed at both the local and national levels, and it becomes easy to raise revenue from the land through fees and taxation (UN-Habitat, 2012). As indicated above, the land administration system should be able to define property rights with sufficient precision and should be enforceable at low cost. This will instil confidence in economic actors in the land market. To achieve this requires considerable investment in technical infrastructure, such as boundary demarcation, and the generation and maintenance of maps and land records, social infrastructure, such as the courts and dispute resolution mechanisms (Deininger, 2003), and human capacity in terms of well-trained and motivated staff to run the system. Can the land administration system in Ghana be said to be delivering these benefits to the citizenry in support of land market operations and the economy as a whole? The National Land Policy (1999) described the land administration system as weak, characterized by a lack of a comprehensive land policy framework, reliance on inadequate and outdated legislation, a lack of adequate functional and co-ordinated geographical information systems and networks, as well as of transparent guidelines, poor capacity and capability to initiate and co-ordinate policy-actions, let alone resolve contradictory policies and policy actions among various land delivery agencies. It therefore means that the land administration system in Ghana is not delivering the expected benefits. It is for this reason that the *Land Administration Project* was introduced in 2003 with the objective of developing a land administration system that is efficient, fair, effective and transparent and that guarantees security of tenure. Even though the project has been ongoing for the past 10 years, real results that will deliver re-engineered processes and procedures for efficient and effective services are still some way off. Rent seeking and corruption are still rife in the land administration system in both the customary and public sectors.

On the contrary, insecure and undefined property rights undermine the effective functioning of property markets. They constitute a disincentive for investment by individuals and corporate institutions as they cannot realize the fruits of their investment and efforts (Besley and Ghatak, 2009). For example, a study by Goldstein and Udry (2005) into variation in security of tenure within informal property rights administered by a customary system in Ghana found that cultivators without political power (those who do not hold any form of customary 'political' office) are less confident of their rights compared to those who hold such 'political' office (leadership at the community level). They leave their land to fallow for significantly shorter durations (for fear that the land will be allocated to someone else), resulting in significant loss in profits per unit of land. Yet security of tenure is a precondition for a working land market (Bruce et al., 2006). Rights to land must be publicly recognized, enforceable and not arbitrarily violated.

Rigid and inflexible approaches to land administration have created a situation where land transactions are undertaken outside the formal land administration system without any appropriate documentation or legal rights. Undefined and insecure property rights cannot be integrated properly into the formal land administration system. They thus lead to the creation of parallel, extra-legal and informal system where transactions are done outside officialdom. Such a system leads to costs that individuals have to incur to defend their property, which is unproductive and a disincentive to investing in the land. The 2010 population and housing census indicated that there are about 3,392,745 houses in the country. Anecdotal analysis suggests that just about 300,000 (including farmlands) constituting 8.8 percent of these properties are registered either under the deeds registration system or the land title registration system. Thus, more than 90 percent of properties are not registered under any system. De Soto (2000) refers to such properties as 'dead capital'. Owing to the absence of formal rights, many land transactions take place in the informal system, denying the state of accurate and up-to-date information on properties and property ownership, revenue in the form of rent, and taxes. Ultimately, they adversely affect the land development process and the socio-economic development of the country.

Unleashing the Potential of Property Rights: The Challenges

The contribution of secured property rights and an efficient and well-functioning land and property market to economic development were analysed in the previous section. The analysis showed that Ghana is not reaping such benefits. The next question then is what are the constraints and challenges and how can they be dealt with? Sometimes the constraints are placed on the customary system of land ownership. It needs to be stated, however, that opinions are divided as to whether customary/traditional systems of land tenure are inimical or supportive to the efficient operation of the land or property market. Trollip (2012), writing about communal property rights in South Africa, notes that 'tribal tenure is a guarantee that the land will never be properly worked'. Goldstein and Udry (2005) also note about the situation in Ghana that the process of acquiring and defending rights in land is inherently a political process based on power relations among members of the social group. In other words, membership in the social group is, by itself, not a sufficient condition for gaining and maintaining access to land. A person's status can and often does determine his or her capacity to engage in tenure building. Customary systems create uncertain property rights which are disincentives for investment by individuals. The flipside is that customary systems provide a safety net which ensures that those who need land have access to land. A United Nations report on urban land policies and land use control measures in Africa noted that the structure of the land market is burdened with customary land-holding practices which impede land transactions (United Nations, 1973). Ababio-Appah (1981) concluded from his study of 'land ownership in the economic development of Ghana' that the poor performance of Ghana's economy after the Second World War was due to several obstacles in the system of land ownership and native institutions which are the vehicles in which the ownership forms manifest themselves. In the words of Ababio-Appah, 'we cannot change the land ownership system without first changing the native institutions in the country' (1981: 206). Acquaye and Associates (1989) also argue that the customary land-holding systems in Accra, among other things, present major problems regarding the development of inner-city lands. Brobby (1992) comes to the same conclusion. The United Nations (1973: 21) summarizes the position this way: 'the clouded unmarketable land titles resulting from customary land tenure systems militate against the development of a workable urban land market' (see also Platteau, 1992). These assertions seem to conclude that customary systems do not lead to the efficient operation of land markets. They have influenced some of the state interventions in the land market by promoting the individualization of property rights in land.

However, it has been increasingly recognized that there is indeed a market in customary land tenure and that customary systems are able to respond to economic opportunities. This is exemplified by the response of land owners in the Eastern Region during the pioneering stages of the cocoa industry. Hill (1963) records actual sales of lands in the Akyem Abuakwa traditional area to migrant Akwapim and Krobo farmers that were properly documented and registered. Where farmers lacked the financial resources to purchase the land, owners and farmers negotiated and agreed on tenurial arrangements that were mutually beneficial to both parties. Eventually, the 'abunu' and 'abusa' systems of share-cropping tenancy evolved. Deininger (2003) also notes that customary tenures are beneficial and support the economic functioning of land markets, as well as providing social safety nets for sustainable livelihoods. Indeed, security of tenure within the customary system of land ownership is guaranteed by the fact that the community recognizes and confirms the rights that individual members of the community have in the land, and the entire community bears responsibility in protecting those rights irrespective of whether the rights are supported by documentary evidence or not. *The Voluntary Guidelines on Responsible Governance of Tenure of Land, Fisheries and Forests in the Context of National Food Security* notes, among other provisions, and in relation to customary tenure systems that:

> *States should protect indigenous peoples and other communities with customary systems against unauthorized use of their land, fisheries and forests by others. Where a community does not object, States should assist to formally document and publicize information on the nature and location of land, fisheries and forests used and controlled by the community. Where tenure rights of indigenous peoples and other communities with customary tenure systems are formally documented, they should be recorded with other public, private and communal tenure rights to prevent competing claims. (FAO, 2012: 15)*

Evidence across the country supports the proposition that viable land markets are capable of operating within the customary system of land ownership. What is lacking and constraining the efficient operation of such a market is an efficient and transparent governance system and an efficient land administration infrastructure. These two issues will now be examined.

The land governance system refers to the processes by which decisions regarding access to and use of land are made, the manner in which those decisions are implemented, and the way in which conflicting interests in land are resolved or reconciled (AUC-UNECA-AfDB, 2010: 20). It thus comprises the policy, legal and institutional frameworks within which land ownership, control, tenures and use rights are managed. Since land governance entails control over land rights, it is a means of accumulating and dispensing political and economic power and privilege through patronage, nepotism and corruption both in the customary or traditional system or the formal system. Nor does it matter whether the land is owned by the state or the traditional authority. *The Voluntary Guidelines on Responsible Governance of Tenure of Land, Fisheries and Forests in the Context of National Food Security* (2012) provides that 'states should provide and maintain policy, legal and organizational frameworks that promote responsible governance of tenure of land, fisheries and forests. These frameworks are dependent on, and are supported by broader reforms to the legal system, public service and judicial authorities' (FAO, 2012: 7). The *National Land Policy of Ghana* (1999), which provides the framework for the administration of land, identifies numerous constraints that militate against the effective and efficient operation of the land governance system. These include: general indiscipline in the land market; indeterminate boundaries of stool/skin lands resulting from a lack of reliable maps and plans; use of unapproved, old or inaccurate maps leading to conflicts and litigation between stools, skins and other land-owning groups; compulsory acquisition by government of large tracts of land which have not been utilized and for which payment of compensation has been delayed; difficult accessibility to land for agricultural, industrial, commercial and residential development purposes due to conflicting claims of ownership and varied and outmoded land disposal procedures; lack of consultation with land owners and chiefs in decision-making for land allocation, acquisition, management, utilization and development; and, lastly, lack of consultation, co-ordination and co-operation among land development agencies. Other serious governance issues relate to a lack of accountability and transparency in the management of customary lands and the revenues that accrue therefrom, resulting in many disputes over ownership and control over customary lands. The net effect is insecure tenure, which affects confidence in the operation of the land market, sometimes with multiple sales of the same piece of land to more than one person.

The legal framework for land governance currently comprises more than 100 pieces of substantive and subsidiary legislation (*National Land Policy*, 1999) as well as judicial decisions of the courts of Ghana. Some of the legal provisions are outmoded and do not support the effective functioning of the land market. For example, the Administration of Lands Act 1962 (Act 123) sets ceilings for the acquisition of land for agricultural purposes. It provides in section 12(2) that 'except as provided in subsection (4), and despite anything to the contrary in any other enactment, a grant of a farming right to land subject to the Act shall not exceed:

a) in the case of land for poultry rearing or the cultivation of cereals, a term of ten years; or
b) in the case of ranching or the cultivation of mixed or permanent crops, a term of fifty years'.

Subsection (3) is even more instructive. It provides that 'except as provided in subsection (4), a grant of a stool land to any one person and the aggregate of the grants shall not exceed as regards:

a) mining rights, 51.80 km^2 for a grant or, in the aggregate, 155.40 km^2;
b) timber rights, 103.40 km^2 for a grant or, in the aggregate, 621.60 km^2; and
c) the right to collect rubber, to cultivate the products of the soil, other than timber, or relating to the pursuit of animal husbandry,
   for an individual, 2.59 km^2 or in the aggregate 7.77 km^2;
   for a body corporate or unincorporated body of persons established or registered in Ghana 12.95 km^2 or in the aggregate 25.90 km^2'.

Subsection (4) referred to above provides for the President to waive the above restrictions in situations where he is satisfied that special circumstances exist that render compliance with the limits prescribed by the section prejudicial to the national interest or to the interest of a stool. Records available at the Lands Commission and some unregistered land transactions that have come to the notice of the author indicate that these provisions have been breached.

Table 10.2   Major Registered Stool Land for Agricultural Purposes in the Ashanti and Brong Ahafo Regions (2001–10)

District	Region	Type of lessee	Population	Land size (km²)	Remarks
Adansi	Ashanti	Individual	115,378	0.67	–
Ahafo Ano South	Ashanti	Individual	121,659	0.36	–
Asante Akyem North	Ashanti	Corporate	140,694	4,000	Biofuel. Exceeds the legal limit
Ahafo Ano North	Ashanti	Corporate	94,285	0.49	–
Sekyere East	Ashanti	Corporate	62,172	2.03	–
Sekyere East	Ashanti	Individual	62,172	0.86	–
Sekyere Central	Ashanti	Individual	71,232	0.83	–
Ejura Sekyedumase	Ashanti	Individual	85,446	6.57	Exceeds the legal limit
Mampong	Ashanti	Individual	88,051	0.73	–
Mampong	Ashanti	Corporate	88,051	10.97	Teak plantation
Kintampo North	Brong Ahafo	Corporate	95,840	8.25	–
Atebubu – Amantin	Brong Ahafo	Individual	105,938	2.59	Mixed farming
Atebubu – Amantin	Brong Ahafo	Corporate	105,938	8.45	Mixed farming
Nkoranza South	Brong Ahafo	Corporate	100,929	124.71	Exceeds the legal limit
Sunyani West	Brong Ahafo	Individual	85,272	2.26	Stool land vested
Yendi	Northern	Corporate	199,592	120	Biofuel. Exceeds the legal limit
Ahanta West	Western	Corporate	106,214	200	State land divested. Rubber plantation
East Gonja	Northern	Corporate	135,450	1,000	Not yet registered. Exceeds the legal limit

Source: Land data: *Lands Commission, Regional Offices.* Northern Region and Western Region data is included for emphasis and does not represent the only transactions that have taken place in those regions. Population data: *Ghana Statistical Service,* 2010 Population and Housing Census.

    Given the nature of scattered rural settlements in southern Ghana, any land size in excess of 20 ha is considered to be large-scale acquisition because it has the tendency to displace many settlements. Clearly, Table 10.2 shows that the legal provisions have been breached in five of the allocations to which the Lands Commission has granted concurrence and registered. This is inappropriate and does not augur well for good land management practices. Yet officials of the Lands Commission have called on the government for regulations on how much land can be granted for specific purpose (see *Daily Graphic,* No 19197, 9 July 2013). If those charged with enforcing the law themselves do not know that the law exists, then it is anybody's guess what is happening to the many transactions going on in the informal market. Perhaps it is time to debate the continued validity of such policy, given the government agricultural policies to promote large-scale commercial farming as provided in the *Food and Agriculture Sector Development Policy II* (FASDEP II) and Ghana's *Medium Term Agriculture Sector Investment Plan* (METASIP).

Other legal provisions such as the compilation of register of deeds registered under the Land Registry Act 1962 (Act 122) in preparation for title registration as provided by section 13 of the Land Title Registration Act 1986 (PNDCL 152) has been found not to be implementable. This is due to the quality of the plans in the registered deeds and the technical requirements that such a plan must satisfy to enable the land to be registered, i.e. to be placed on the folio of the title register. The essence of the provision was to provide a seamless transition from deeds registration to title registration. This transition never worked and created a lot of confusion between deeds registration managed at the time by the Lands Commission and title registration managed by the Land Title Registry. The Ministry of Lands and Natural Resources stepped in during 2006 and issued a directive to the Lands Commission to stop the registration of deeds in respect of lands in the Greater Accra Region which had been declared compulsory land title registration areas. Furthermore, Article 267(5) of the Constitution prohibits the creation of freehold interest howsoever described in stool lands. Again the revenue accruing from stool lands should be paid to the Administrator of Stool Lands and disbursed according to a formula prescribed by Article 267(6) of the Constitution: 10 percent as an administrative charge and the remaining 90 percent should be taken as 100 percent and disbursed as follows – 25 percent to the land-owning stool through the traditional authority, 20 percent to the traditional authority and 55 percent to the district assembly within the area of authority of which the stool land is situated. There have been agitations by traditional authorities for a review of the percentages, the argument being that the district assemblies are not able to account properly for their share of the revenue.

Despite the plethora of laws, there are still aspects of customary land ownership and tenure that are not governed by any legal provisions. These include the management of family and clan lands. Article 295 of the Constitution has defined stool land to include 'any land or interest in, or right over, any land controlled by a stool or skin, the head of a particular community or the captain of a company, for the benefit of the subjects of that stool or members of that community or company'. The High Court in *Kludze v Lands Commission* (unreported) in 1994 ruled that this definition of stool land does not cover family and clan lands, and therefore the legal requirements to subject family and clan land grants to the concurrence of the Lands Commission do not apply. Equally, the limits on sizes of lands to be granted as discussed above, the subjection of the management of family lands to the concurrence procedure, the prohibition of freehold grants, and the collection and disbursement of family land revenue from family lands do not apply. The implication is that the existing legal framework does not provide certainty and clarity, which are essential requirements needed for the efficient and effective functioning of the land market, as land acquirers have to ascertain whether a particular land is stool land or family land in order to know which law would apply. This is not always easy to work out.

The evolution and individualization of property rights (either through leaseholds or freeholds) necessarily involve the resolution of disputes mediated through a number of institutions either at the customary level or through judicial processes. One of the determinants of an efficient property market is the efficiency and efficacy for resolving disputes. Land disputes are principally of two types: boundary disputes and declaration of title. Boundary disputes occur where both parties to the dispute agree that each party has land in the disputed area, but disagree on where the boundary should be. These are relatively straightforward to resolve generally, but could also be intractable, especially between communities, as has been discussed above. Title disputes may be caused by chieftaincy disputes, different claimants and conflicting court judgements. Apart from the delays, there are instances where more than one judgement has been given in respect of a particular land. A full discussion of chieftaincy conflicts and conflicting court judgements is beyond the scope of this chapter. Suffice to say that the importance of conflicting judgements is that they create uncertainty in property rights, which in turn creates difficulty for land owners, land acquirers, land administration institutions and the general public to deal convincingly in the land market. Several instances have occurred where real estate developers have had to purchase the same land from more than one purported owner. These uncertainties undermine the confidence of the public in the land administration system, pushing people to adopt extra-judicial processes to protect and defend their land rights. This has given rise to the phenomenon of land guards, which is a reflection of the loss of public confidence in documentary proof of title to land and recourse to physical possession as a defensive mechanism.

Land Administration Infrastructure

Land administration is defined as the process of recording and disseminating information about ownership, value and uses of land and its associated resources (Williamson et al., 2010). The land administration infrastructure comprises all the processes involved in identifying land, ownership and control, defining interests and different tenures in land, collecting data and organizing information or inventories. Williamson et al. (2010: 95) argue that land administration is basically about processes, not institutions. This is because land administration systems cannot be understood, built or reformed unless the core processes are understood. If the processes are well organized and integrated, the structure of the agencies and institutions that manage them is much less important. Each element of the core areas of land administration (cadastral, registration, valuation, land use, etc.) needs first to be designed and built, then managed through regular updating to offer efficient services in support of land market operations. The processes in Ghana are tortious in all the core areas. The procedures are not clear and lack transparency. They are long, winding and frustrating to go through. They have been disincentives to many to pursue the registration of their rights and interests in land, and are mainly responsible for the large number of unregistered properties ('dead capital') in many urban areas in the country. Many actors are therefore driven to operate in the informal market.

Unleashing the potential of property rights in land for economic development and in order to use secure land rights as a poverty reduction mechanism calls for a clear strategy for dealing with the constraints discussed above. The strategies may include the following:

- Gather the political will to reform the land administration system in the country at both the customary and national levels. This is key to any successful intervention and in dealing with corruption in the system.
- Clarify the position and relationship between primary and secondary settlers, and clarify property rights held by each group to reduce the incessant disputes over land. This requires political will and a high level of co-operation from traditional authorities to achieve the desired results. Communities should be prepared to shift from entrenched positions to ensure that land is put to its highest and best uses, communities co-exist in peace and land-related disputes are reduced.
- Take a systematic approach and strategy for demarcating boundaries between communities – at the paramount, divisional stool levels and individual communities in the family land areas. This will remove some of the sources of protracted litigation and create the certainty required for defining property rights.
- Streamline the processes and procedures for land registration by eliminating redundant requirements. Currently the processes of preparing parcel plans for registration have duplications, which impose unnecessary costs on actors in the registration processes.

- Improve transparency in the land administration system through the publication of the processes and procedures for registration. This requires improved supervision in the public sector and holding individuals accountable for their actions.
- Improve the governance system for land administration at both the customary and the public levels, including the management of revenue at the district assemblies.
- Undertake comprehensive staff audit and staff training to change the attitude of staff of land administration institutions and other public sector staff towards work and make the client the focus of operations.
- Systematically review the issue of conflicting court judgements to remove ambiguity and uncertainties surrounding the implementation of such judgements.
- Build the capacity of customary land owners in land management and assist them to reduce the sources of land disputes at the customary level. It should be possible to criminalize the multiple sale of the same piece of land to more than one person even though the courts have not had the boldness to call customary land authorities to order where they are found to be culpable.

Conclusions

Secure land and property rights are vital to the socio-economic development of individuals, corporate institutions and nations. On the one hand, as land rights evolve from customary tenures through the commodification and commercialization of property rights, its value rises. It becomes an attractive investment venture, particularly in developing countries where investment opportunities are relatively few. Proprietary rights in land become sharpened and some customary tenures may mature into actual ownership. Clarifying property rights may emit both positive and negative consequences. Secured property rights may serve as good investment opportunities in agriculture, forestry, residential, infrastructure, industrial and other urban land uses, offering employment and housing to many, as well as providing social safety nets. A country may take off smoothly in its industrial development. Well-defined and secured property rights also enhance the land development process, which becomes well-defined with clear determination of outputs.

On the other hand, the process of evolution of property rights, the ascertainment of clearer ownership and control over land and the determination of appropriate tenures may be associated with uncertainties, litigation and sometimes conflicts which can throw all the potential benefits and opportunities into complete disarray. The history of evolution of land rights indicates that this is not unusual. What is needed is to have the appropriate governance structures for successful mediation of such disputes and mechanisms for enforcement. Again, where property rights are not properly clarified, the land development process also becomes more complex and difficult to manage. Good institutional structures for mediating and clarifying the rights are required. Decisions about investment in land become difficult. Enthusiasm by actors in the land market falls and they resort more to self-help than to relying on documentary proof of title. The socio-economic consequences become bizarre. The governance system should provide mechanisms for successfully mediating such disputes.

Unleashing the potential value in land for economic development requires a land administration system that is efficient and effective, and which exhibits the characteristics of a good land governance system to transform the negative outcomes into positives. It should also create a sustainable land administration infrastructure that accurately defines property rights in land and supports the operations of the land market. A lot needs to be done about the land administration infrastructure and governance system in Ghana to reap the associated benefits.

It is anticipated that the *Land Administration Project* embarked upon by the Ministry of Lands and Natural Resources will re-engineer the land administration processes and procedures, complete the institutional reforms already started to achieve real seamless processes, and establish a transparent land governance system both in the customary and formal sectors to support the operations of the land market. Some decisions will require strong political will to deliver the required outputs. The collaboration of all participants in the land market, particularly the customary land owners, surveying professionals, real estate developers and public sector institutions is required for the establishment of good governance structures for successful land rights evolution to contribute to the socio-economic development of the country.

References

Ababio-Appah, N.W. (1981). *Land Ownership in the Economic Development of Ghana 1945–1975*. Lund: University of Lund Press.

Acquaye, E. and Asiama, S.O. (1986). Land policies for housing development for low-income groups in Africa, *Land Development Studies*, 3, pp. 127–43.

Acquaye, E. and Associates (1989). *Study of Institutional-Legal Problems Associated with Land Delivery in Accra*. Final Report, Accra, Government of Ghana, UNDP, HABITAT.

Asante, S.K.B. (1975). *Property Law and Social Goals in Ghana: 1844–1966*. Accra: Ghana Universities Press.

AUC-ECA-AfDB (2010). *Framework and Guidelines on Land Policy in Africa: A Framework to Strengthen Land Rights, Enhance Productivity and Secure Livelihoods*. Addis Ababa: ECA Publications.

Bentsi-Enchill, K. (1964). *Ghana Land Law: An Exposition, Analysis and Critique*. London: Sweet & Maxwell.

Besley, T. and Ghatak, M. (2009). Property rights and economic development. In D. Rodrik and M. Rosenzweig (eds), *Handbook of Development Economics, Volume 5*. Amsterdam: North Holland, pp. 4525–95.

Bower, P. (1993). Land tenure policy and development, in tenure *n*. the holding of office or of land or other permanent property or of accommodation, etc.: the period or condition of this. Paper presented at a conference on international land tenure organised by the Royal Institution of Chartered Surveyors, December, 1993, University of East London, London, RICS.

Brobby, K.W. (1992). *Improving Land Delivery System for Shelter*. Final Report of Land Policy Consultancy, Accra, Government of Ghana, UNDP & HABITAT.

Bruce, J.W., Giovarelli, R., Rolfes, L. Jr, Bledsoe, D. and Mitchell, R. (2006). *Land Law Reform: Achieving Development Policy Objectives*, Washington DC: World Bank.

De Soto, H. (2000). *The Mystery of Capital: Why Capitalism Triumphs in the West and Fails Everywhere Else*. London: Black Swan.

Deininger, K. (2003). *Land Policies for Growth and Poverty Reduction*. Washington DC: World Bank.

Delville, P.L. (2000). Harmonising formal law and customary land rights in French-speaking West Africa. In C. Toulmin and J.F. Quan (eds), *Evolving Land Rights, Policy and Tenure in Africa*. London, Department for International Development/International Institute for Environment and Development/Natural Resources Institute, pp. 97–121.

Doebele, W.A. (1983). Concepts of urban land tenure. In H.B. Dunkerley (ed.), *Urban Land Policy: Issues and Opportunities*. New York: Oxford University Press.

Doner, P. (1972). *Land Reform and Economic Development*. Harmondsworth: Penguin.

FAO (2012). *The Voluntary Guidelines on Responsible Governance of Tenure of Land, Fisheries and Forests in the Context of National Food Security*. Rome: FAO/CFS.

Field, M.J. (1940). *Social Organization of the Ga People*. London: Crown Agents.

Goldstein, M. and Udry, C. (2005). Addressing unequal economic opportunities: A case study of land tenure in Ghana. In *Development Outreach*, Washington DC: World Bank Institute, September edition.

Hill, P. (1963). *The Migrant Cocoa Farmer of Southern Ghana: A Study in Rural Capitalism.* Cambridge: Cambridge University Press.

Kasanga, K. (2002). Land tenure, resource access and decentralisation in Ghana. In C. Toulmin, P.L. Delville, and S. Traoré (eds), *The Dynamics of Resource Tenure in West Africa.* London: IIED.

Larbi, W.O. (1995). Urban land policies and the delivery of developable land in Ghana. Unpublished PhD thesis, University of Ghana.

Larbi, W.O., Antwi, A. and Olomolaiye, P. (2004). Compulsory land acquisition in Ghana – Policy and praxis, *Land Use Policy,* 21(2), pp. 115–27.

Larbi, W.O. and Kakraba-Ampeh, M. (2013). Securing land rights and improving land use at the grass roots: Innovative approaches to secure customary land rights in Ghana. Paper presented at the Annual World Bank Conference on Land and Poverty, World Bank, Washington DC, 8–11 April 2013.

Manoukian, M. (1964). *Akan and Ga-Adangme Peoples.* London: International African Institute.

McAuslan, P. (1985). *Urban Land and Shelter for the Poor.* London: Earthscan.

Ministry of Lands and Forestry. (1999). *National Land Policy.* Accra: MLF.

O'Driscoll, G.P. and Hoskins, L. (2003). Property rights: The key to economic development. *Policy Analysis,* 482(7), pp. 1–17.

Platteau, J. (1992). *Land Reform and Structural Adjustment in Sub-Saharan Africa: Controversies and Guidelines.* Rome: FAO.

——. (2000). Does Africa need land reform? In C. Toulmin and J.F. Quan (eds), *Evolving Land Rights, Policy and Tenure in Africa.* London: Department for International Development/International Institute for Environment and Development/Natural Resources Institute, pp. 51–73.

Trollip, A. (2012). Communal property stands in the way of economic growth, http://www.bdlive.co.za/articles/2012/07/09/athol-trollip-communal-property-stands-in-way-of-economic-growth;jsessionid=43A717FFFEB0B10447F51135I4999857.present1.bdfm.

Toulmin, C., Delville, P.L. and Traore, S. (eds) (2002). *The Dynamics of Resource Tenure in West Africa.* London: International Institute for Environment and Development, GRET, Currey and Heinemann.

Toulmin, C. and Quan, J.F. (eds) (2000). *Evolving Land Rights, Policy and Tenure in Africa.* London: DFID/IIED/NRI.

UN-Habitat (2012). *Handling Land: Innovative Tools for Land Governance and Secure Tenure.* Nairobi: UN Habitat, IIRR, GLTN.

United Nations (1973). *Urban Land Policies and Land Use Control Measures, Vol 1: Africa.* New York: United Nations.

Williamson, I., Enemark, S., Wallace, J. and Rajabifard, A. (2010). *Land Administration for Sustainable Development.* Redlands: ESRI Press Academic.

11

Management of Energy Resources for National Development: The Trinidad and Tobago Model

Anthony E. Paul and Atiba Phillips

This chapter was prepared in 2005 as a paper to help inform the ongoing discussion in Trinidad and Tobago (T&T) on how to best use the development of recently discovered, large natural gas fields for national sustainable development. Although issues in T&T have progressed since, the context then is familiar to countries where oil and natural gas are being discovered in abundance, as is the case in Africa, so the original paper is produced intact, in the hope that it might help with ongoing discussions in new producer countries. However, we have added a brief epilogue to illustrate how some of the recommendations were either implemented or not, alongside some of the consequences. The epilogue also contains select examples of the current state of T&T, looking at instances of the application and non-application of the recommended initiatives made in the paper and some of the outcomes. These examples are very limited, as this is not the primary intent of this chapter.

The purpose of the chapter is to illustrate how lessons learnt from one boom in production and prices in an extractive industry within a single location might be applied to a second such boom in just over 25 years, in that same industry and location, to increase the benefits from the extracted resource and support sustainable development. Given the nature of the extractives industry and the state of development of T&T at the time of the report, the findings and recommendations might be applied to other resource-rich countries that are experiencing similar booms at this time. Hopefully, these new producers, learning from the lessons of T&T and others, will be able not just to emulate T&T, but to surpass it in the level of value retention from the resources and in creating sustainable economies.

This original paper built on previous work done by Anthony E. Paul and which is included in the Vision 2020 for the T&T Energy sector (2004), some of which was subsequently included in the National Development Plan for T&T (2007).

Abstract

In this chapter we look at the case of the small twin-island developing nation of T&T, and trace the story of this nation's energy sector through the period 1972–2005. The saga of this period tells a tale of energy-based boom and bust and then boom again, all within a very short timeframe, which had a significant impact on the economic and social life of the nation as a whole.

We then try to understand the underlying reasons for the downturn in the economy that occurred after the boom of the 1970s and use this experience to distil certain key deficiencies in the economic activity set of the time. Recognizing that the country is again experiencing an energy-driven period of buoyancy, we ask the question: 'What lessons can be learnt now towards the achievement of more sustainable development?'

To this end, we look at the models that have been put forward in the past for the economic development in the Caribbean; we look at their underlying assumptions and the outcomes which they have intended versus what has actually been observed. The assumptions of these models are then contrasted with the attributes of the current economic environment towards the establishment of a more appropriate frame of analysis.

We also examine the experiences of other nations that have in the past and presently are experiencing success in navigating the global economic landscape, and suggest a new model framework which we propose can guide developing nations towards the ideal of sustainable economic growth. The framework promotes the use of the productive (energy) sector to build local capability in human resources, enterprises and capital markets by investing in innovation systems and technology infrastructure buttressed by an enabling policy environment emphasizing local content and the creation of a learning environment.

Having introduced the concept, we then relate it to specific T&T institutions in both commercial and factor markets (education, research and development (R&D), etc.), and put forward specific policy and tactical recommendations, which can be derived from the general framework. These recommendations take the form of targeted market and non-market actions, which can be immediately taken to improve that country's ability to use its current windfalls from the energy sector to diversify its economy and pave the way towards sustainable development.

Introduction

Many developing countries possess a primary export industry, which disproportionately contributes to their gross domestic product (GDP) and national wealth. Examples of these include the oil industry in Venezuela, precious minerals in Angola, columbite-tantalite (coltan) in the Congo and natural gas in T&T. Furthermore, these industries are often based on non-renewable natural resources, which will only sustain the economies linked to them for a finite period, as technological substitutes advance and reserves dwindle.

The heightened activity throughout the value chain within these sectors in recent times has increased levels of revenue growth for producer countries and has provided a window of opportunity through which local capability can develop. However, a prototypical feature of these economies is their unstable nature due to dependence on fluctuating world commodity prices, changes in preferential market access arrangements, depleting reserves and a host of other possible market structure shocks. These changes invariably have detrimental social and economic effects for the nations and societies in question.

In this context, the central concerns of this chapter are as follows:

1. How can developing economies with characteristic flagship primary export industries enhance their sustainability and diversify their economies?
2. How can these countries/economies capture more of the value that they create in a manner that allows them to diversify and sustain their economies?

The text illustrates, within the context of the energy-based economy of T&T, that economic activity, including schemes of attracting foreign direct investment (FDI), must be orchestrated in a co-ordinated and targeted manner towards the goals of developing indigenous strategic and technological *human resource capability*, the engendering of *local ownership and control* of the nation's economic and productive assets and the engendering of a *learning environment*.

In this light, a framework of analysis is suggested which can guide developing nations towards the ideal of sustainable economic growth. The framework promotes the building of local capability in human resources, enterprises and capital markets by increasing equity participation in global businesses operating locally, by investing in innovation systems and technology infrastructure and by enhancing the policy environment to emphasize local content and the creation of a learning environment.

A key finding in the text, as a subset of engendering a learning environment, is the imperative of market awareness and ability of the local productive system to innovate. More than relating innovation capacity to 'the formal activity being undertaken by the R&D system and science base' or the 'ability of a productive system to learn', we suggest further that for a production system to be truly innovative, it must possess a deep understanding of the market(s) into which it sells its product/service. We posit that it is only through this knowledge that true innovation can occur, in response to the dynamic and ever-present need to better satisfy intermediate and final 'consumers'.

The text also introduces into the discussion the concept of 'innovation chains' and 'innovation systems', a concept which disaggregates economic activity into its component parts – e.g. education, research, technology development, product development, production *and marketing* (for the production chain) – emphasizing that the success of the system depends on the creation of greater links between the traditionally distinct economic institutions, mainly through policy arrangements, which will result in the desired outcomes of creativity, innovation and entrepreneurship, through worker training, market knowledge and technology transfer.

We conclude, in summary, with certain key action items which we think can move developing nations closer towards the ideal of sustainable development:

- Develop and institute credible local content policies describing how local value-added is defined and measured, and the specific activities to which they apply, also explaining the monitoring mechanisms in place as well as the penalties for non-compliance.
- Develop more thoughtful policies and strategic criteria for choosing partner companies as well as for encouraging local businesses so as to engender market and technology pull effects, as well as deep synergistic links throughout the economy.
- Enter into deep equity arrangements with external partners so that technology and business know-how can be transferred.
- Augment the local skill base through a co-ordinated programme of attracting skilled expatriate nationals to local opportunities in business and technology.

The Iconic Case of T&T

We have chosen to use as an example the case of T&T for several reasons:

1. T&T exhibits the characteristic profile of a post-colonial developing country which relies heavily on a single export facing industry to make the major contribution to national wealth and GDP.
2. Its dominant productive sector is natural resource-based and has been subject to the fluctuations and vagaries of the global market over the last 30 years, which has thrown the host economy into prototypical booms and busts.
3. T&T's energy sector is foreign investor-led and thus much of the value and returns created by the sector do not remain in-country.
4. The local skill base has mainly been developed in the operational and maintenance (low value-added) aspects of the sector, while the strategic managerial, marketing and technology aspects have been provided by external partners.

Thus, in this chapter we trace the story of this small twin-island developing nation's energy sector from 1972 to the present.

The T&T Energy Economy

In 1973/4 and again in 1979/80, global oil prices increased to unprecedented levels. This fact, coupled with unprecedented oil finds of the south-east coast of Trinidad, had a profound impact on the T&T economy. The nation's GDP increased sixfold from US$1,309 million to US$8,140 over the period 1973 to 1982 and foreign currency reserves also jumped from US$47 million to more than US$3 billion.

The government of the day invested heavily in laying certain types of physical infrastructure including electricity, water, roads transport and, most notably the Point Lisas Industrial Estates, which it used to found a number of energy-intensive downstream industries such as urea, steel, fertilizer, methanol and ammonia.

The energy-based projects, however, did not perform as anticipated. In the case of ammonia, for example, actual prices turned out to be much lower than predicted and thus returns on these investments under-performed all forecasts. In the case of steel, due to a number of factors, including technical inefficiency, substantial cost overruns and an anti-dumping charge from America, the iron and steel plant ran into significant financial difficulties.

By 1990, energy prices had reversed their upward spike and the country's GDP had decreased by 20 percent compared to its 1982 levels. The external debt rose to over US$2 billion and foreign reserves plummeted to US$492 million (from over US$3 billion in 1982). With a serious balance of payments crisis on its hands, the government was forced to turn to the World Bank for help. The country even endured an unprecedented attempted political coup in that year (1990), which was a testament to the political and social tensions brought about by the economic hardship of the time. The country's former dependency on the buoyancy of the global oil market, its inability to diversify the economy and limited strategic investment in its human capital had become its undoing.

The Theories Underpinning the Energy Economy

The economic and industrial development of the Caribbean, particularly T&T, has been influenced by two main schools of economic thought:

1. Noted economist and Nobel Prize-winner Arthur Lewis put forward the model of 'Export-led Industrialization by Invitation' for Caribbean territories.
2. Historian, economist and former Prime Minister Eric Williams pursued his 'Point Lisas Model" for the development of T&T.

THE ARTHUR LEWIS MODEL

The tenets of the Arthur Lewis model are as follows:

- Given the inability of agriculture to sustain high levels of employment in the region, industrialization was needed, *complementarily*, to achieve 'full employment'.
- Domestic and regional markets were too small in terms of population and the level of domestic savings was not sufficient for investment at the level needed to resolve the unemployment problem through industrialization. Therefore, foreign investment would be required to provide access to foreign markets and to fill the domestic capital resource gap.
- Caribbean capitalists were regarded as 'risk averse', preferring the distributive trades and protected agricultural production over manufacturing production, especially for export. In order to develop the industrial sector, there was a need to invite foreign industrialists to teach Caribbean capitalists the 'tricks of the trade'.

THE POINT LISAS MODEL

This model rests on the same basic principles of Arthur Lewis' model, but with some notable distinctions. This model called for the following:

- State-led investment versus foreign-based capital.
- Quick monetarization of energy assets through large-scale conversion into early stage primary products (e.g. natural gas to methanol).
- Created out of an assumption of surplus capital and *unlimited natural resources* rather than unlimited labour.

THE MODELS IN PRACTICE

While both models assume the transfer of technology and business know-how – the 'tricks of the trade' – they both fell short of devising a specific process by which this knowledge transfer would be achieved, resulting in a lack of local innovation capacity, and limited strategic business and technology skill being developed regionally.

A Closer Look at T&T

While there was significant investment in the nation's infrastructure and physical economic assets, at the time, the government did not emphasize and ensure the concomitant deepening of the nation's strategic-managerial and technological capability in its precious human resource assets. The energy sector therefore attracted the existing re-deployable high-value human resources away from other non-energy sectors and the lack of significant new investment in skill development meant that the energy boom had a strangling effect in terms of the upgrading of other sectors of the economy and ironically further entrenched the economy's umbilical dependency on petroleum.

In addition, the lack of re-investment in a critical mass of in-country strategic and high-level managerial skill had the follow-on effect of effectively relinquishing functional control and ownership of the country's most productive assets into foreign hands. Weak policy frameworks around technology and skill transfer also prevented significant high-level skills from being built in the energy sector and then eventually disseminated to other parts of the economy.

In parallel, it must be taken into consideration that foreign firms have tendencies that are not necessarily in the best interests of their less developed host country partners. Foreign firms are predisposed to accessing international suppliers of inputs and services with whom they are familiar rather than creating excessive domestic links. This import-intensity of foreign-owned firms can often lead to balance of payments problems for the host nation (Mytelka and Barclay, 2003).

Foreign-owned firms also have a tendency to conduct the more knowledge-intensive activities at 'head office' (in the developed country), shifting only highly capital-intensive, relatively low-skilled/value-added, commodity-type activities to their operations in less developed regions.

T&T Today

Currently, global economic conditions once again are playing to the favour of the twin-island nation of T&T. Geopolitical tensions in the Middle East, an increased energy appetite in the northern developed countries, political instability in Venezuela and a host of other factors have once again conspired to bring energy prices to their highest levels in history. In tandem, there have been unprecedented finds of, this time, natural gas and consequential inflows of FDI into the petroleum sector of T&T. During the years 1996–2001, oil and natural gas accounted for 23 percent of the country's GDP, 53 percent of its export earnings and 84.3 percent of its FDI. The contribution of the natural gas sector to the government's energy revenues overtook that of oil for the first time in 2002 (Centre for Energy Enterprise Development – CEED, 2003).

T&T AT A GLANCE

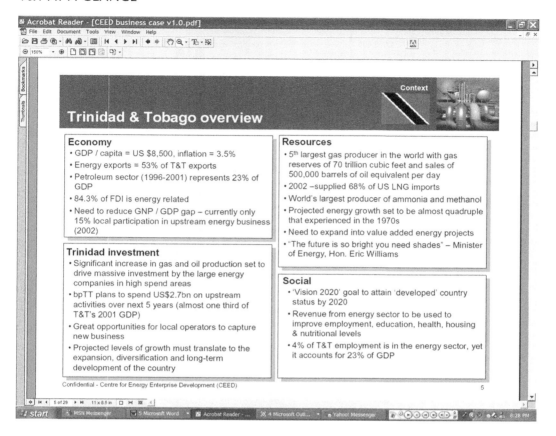

Figure 11.1   CEED Institutional and National Development Model
Note: CEED stands for the proposed Centre for Energy Enterprise Development which would provide information and consulting services to Small and Medium Enterprises in the Energy Sector.

T&T's Second Chance

Despite the country's increasingly enviable macro-economic performance, FDI in this sector has played only a small role in contributing to the stock of strategic and technological human resource skills in the country. Once again, these have generally been limited to the acquisition of operations and maintenance skills. It has not been fully involved in the transfer of industrial R&D that would lead to meaningful product and process innovation.

Particular characteristic points of concern are as follows:

*   Energy is still by far the major single productive sector of the economy.
*   The sector is now engaged in industries which extract large volumes of natural resources at high rates but yield minimum value. This because the return to economic activity early in the value chain (primary extraction) is much lower and creates fewer economic links than does the higher value-added activity further down the value chain (e.g. the creation of final products such as plastics or manufactured products).

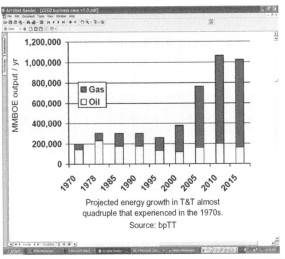

Projected energy growth in T&T almost
quadruple that experienced in the 1970s.
Source: bpTT

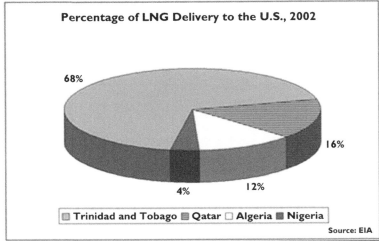

Source: EIA

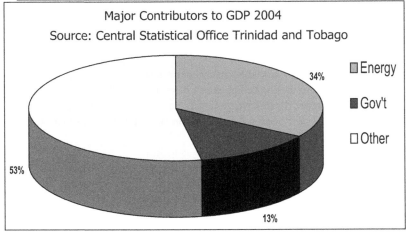

Figure 11.2   Indicators of the Performance Significance of the Gas Economy of T&T

- This sector is also referred to as the 'offshore' sector as its major investors and earnings originate and are thus remitted to foreign-based entities.
- The sector is responsible for at least 53 percent of total exports (2004), but accounts for only four percent of total employment

Indicators of the Performance Significance of the Gas Economy of T&T

The foundation of T&T's economy is pinned on a non-renewable resource, which at current production-to-reserve levels will be depleted in approximately 50 years. As the knowledge-intensity of production continues to increase dramatically throughout all sectors around the world, investments will be needed not only in R&D but also in other intangibles, such as intellectual property infrastructure, marketing, finance engineering, training and capacity development in marketing, finance, design engineering, strategy and business decision-making skills as these come to play a greater role in the production of goods and services over time.

The country thus has a window of opportunity to make the necessary adjustments and investments to avoid a second and possibly more disastrous downturn in its economy due to changing fortunes in its main productive (energy) sector.

Defining a New Outcome

In order to define a new vision for T&T, we feel it may be instructive to look at case studies of other countries that have brought themselves out of factor-driven 'plantation' economies into knowledge-based societies, taking note of the processes and guiding principles that they have employed to get there. To this end, we look briefly at two examples, the 'Asian Tigers' and the Asian model, as well as a more recent example of record-breaking development in the little nation of Qatar.

SOUTH ASIA

Hobay (1995) notes the catalytic effect that the initial arm's length contractual arrangements between foreign and local firms had on the electronics industry in East Asia (South Korea, Taiwan, Hong Kong, Singapore). The domestic forms initially provided subcontracting services to the MNE; however, within forty years some had progressed to the export marketing of their own brand of electronics. The initial training of workers resulted in the 'virtuous circle' of deepening capabilities in process and production technology, the development of domestic supplier firms the stimulation of agglomeration economies, and the creation of final good producers. This process occurred in an environment where government efficiently implemented selective intervention policies in product and capital markets, as well as in factor markets such as education, technology, information and institutional development.

Qatar (www.qatargas.com.qa)

Little noticed, Qatar has reversed the typical role of the producer country, which simply opens its territory to oil companies to explore, and takes a cut of whatever they find.

Not only does Qatar own the majority share of each LNG joint venture, but it will also own delivery ships and stakes in import terminals in Europe and the United States. The arrangement allows Qataris to profit from processes and sales far beyond its borders, elbowing into a business that was once the sole province of big oil.

'There's no doubt it is unique' says Harms. 'Their logic is pretty sound. It is to participate in every part of the value chain.'

Having highlighted these iconic examples and the core principles that are leading to increased economic prosperity for these nations, we turn now to a more in-depth focus on a country that is already at what we consider the 'goal state' – Finland. We examine its competitive characteristics, comparing it against T&T on key factors/indices.

WHY FINLAND?

Finland is a small country of approximately five million people and with no significant endowment of natural resources, but is ranked No. 1 on the World Economic Forum's Growth Competitive and Business Competitive Indices for three out of the last four years. Finland is now internationally recognized as the most competitive nation in the world.

The Business Competitiveness Index (BCI)

The BCI uses micro-economic indicators to measure the 'set of institutions, markets structures and economic policies, supportive of high current levels of prosperity, referring mainly to an economy's effective utilization of its current stock of resources'.

The BCI examines the conditions that support a high level of sustainable productivity and prosperity, measured by GDP per capita. It thus assesses the current productive potential of countries, looking at areas that affect the business environment, such as university–industry research collaboration, foreign technology licensing, government procurement of advanced technology, R&D spending, the availability of venture capital, the intensity of local competition and the quality and quantity of local suppliers.

Table 11.1 below presents selected countries and their ranking on the BCI for 2001. Two of the sub-indices are presented, one focusing on company sophistication and the other on quality of the national business environment.

Table 11.1   BCI 2001 (Selected Countries)

Country	Composite ranking	Operations and strategy	Quality of the national business environment
Finland	1	–	–
Singapore	10	15	9
Hong Kong	18	21	16
Norway	19	20	19
New Zealand	20	19	20
Chile	29	30	28
T&T	**34**	**27**	**37**
Malaysia	37	37	38
Uruguay	46	48	45
Costa Rica	50	34	52

We now compare the 2001 rankings with the 2004 rankings to give an indication of trends. Thus, Table 11.2 presents selected countries and their ranking on the BCI for 2004 with similar sub-indices included.

Table 11.2   BCI 2004 (Selected Countries)

Country	Business competitive ranking (2004)	Operations and strategy ranking	Quality of the national business environment ranking
Finland	2	7	1
Singapore	10	13	8
Hong Kong	11	15	10
New Zealand	18	20	15
Norway	20	23	14
Malaysia	23	28	23
Chile	29	33	29
Costa Rica	48	35	50
T&T	**59**	**55**	**62**
Uruguay	71	75	69

Source: Business Competitiveness Report. Published by the World Economic Forum.

Table 11.3   Growth Competitive Index (GCI) 2001–4

Country	(2004)	(2003)	(2002)	(2001)
Finland	1	1	1	2
Singapore	7	6	6	4
Norway	6	9	9	6
Hong Kong	11	15	10	13
New Zealand	18	14	14	10
Chile	22	28	26	27
Malaysia	31	29	27	30
Costa Rica	50	51	49	35
T&T	**51**	**49**	**47**	**38**
Uruguay	55	50	48	46

Table 11.4   GCI Sub-indices 2003 (Selected Countries)

Country	Growth competitive index ranking	Macro-economic environment index ranking	Public institution index ranking	Technology index ranking
Finland	1	2	2	2
Singapore	6	1	6	12
Norway	9	4	16	13
New Zealand	14	13	5	23
Hong Kong	15	15	10	37
Chile	28	35	19	31
Malaysia	29	27	34	20
T&T	**49**	**47**	**56**	**47**
Uruguay	50	89	29	51
Costa Rica	51	63	49	46

Source: Global Competitiveness Report. Published by the World Economic Forum.

Table 11.5 presents a comparison of comparative advantages of Finland vis-à-vis T&T.

Table 11.5   A Comparison of Competitive Advantages of Finland vis-à-vis T&T

Notable competitive advantages (Finland)	Notable competitive disadvantages (T&T)
Research & education:	Research & education:
High level of tertiary enrolment	Low level of tertiary enrolment
University/industry research collaboration	Lack of university/industry research collaboration
High company spending on R&D	Company spending on research and development insufficient
Technology & innovation:	Technology & innovation:
Technological sophistication	Shallow dirm-level technology absorption
Firm-level technology absorption	Poor technological readiness
Capacity for innovation	Prevalence of foreign technology licensing
Internet access in schools	Limited internet access in schools
Company operations & strategy:	Company operations & strategy:
Broad value chain presence	Narrow value chain presence
Production process sophistication	Nature of competitive advantage – factor-driven economy

Note: See Appendix for 'National competitiveness balance sheets' for T&T and Finland for 2002–4.

A New Mandate for T&T

The vision is to build a cadre of skilled managers, entrepreneurs and technologists who can participate at all business levels and better organize the local industrial sector to execute business operations locally, initially in the productive sector, where there is the biggest immediate return. The challenge will be to ensure that these skills are then transferred across all sectors and eventually to the international market such that revenue streams begin to occur which are diverse and independent of the initial 'cash crop' activity within the economy.

However, based on the experience of the T&T energy sector, we have found that in order to promote sustainability and to capture value locally, economic activity must be co-ordinated to promote the following:

- *Local ownership and equity* – promoting greater local stakes in assets and profits, greater wealth distribution and movement from a savings to an investment culture.
- *Local control and decision making* – promoting greater local control over the country's productive assets and the development of high-value, transferable skills and services for global competitiveness and sustainability.
- *The creation of a continuous learning environment* – promoting greater transfer of technology, leading to more and more relevant innovation in both products and markets.

In order to achieve this mandate, T&T must strategically invest in the development of its:

- *human resource capability* in technology and strategic business;
- *enterprise and institutional capacity* in the private and state sectors;
- *capital market*/financing and investment capability.

In pursuance of this mandate, we put forward the following framework which we suggest can guide developing nations towards the ideal of sustainable economic development.

The Suggested Development Framework

The idea of the framework is to promote the building of local capability in businesses, personnel and capital markets by investing in systems and infrastructure which are relevant to the current stage development of the host economy. It consists of the following parts:

- *Human capability development* – increasing local participation in industry by building relevant and transferable skills and knowledge.
- *Enterprise development* – building tools, processes, strategic business and technological capability that allows local businesses to grow and become competitive in the global marketplace.
- *Capital market development* – creating a financial environment conducive to business development and broad local participation in the industry.

The framework for sustainability is a series of building blocks. The technical and operational skills lead to the business being developed within the home country, which in turn leads to the development of higher value-added skills. These then enable ownership and control, which act as the catalyst for the creation of local firms of sufficient size to influence the development of financial and capital markets.

Apart from local financing, at the top of the framework pyramid is public trading. In addition to creating access to capital markets and aiding wealth creation, the growth of local capital markets will also encourage transparency and good governance in domestic institutions as they are placed under greater regulatory and public scrutiny.

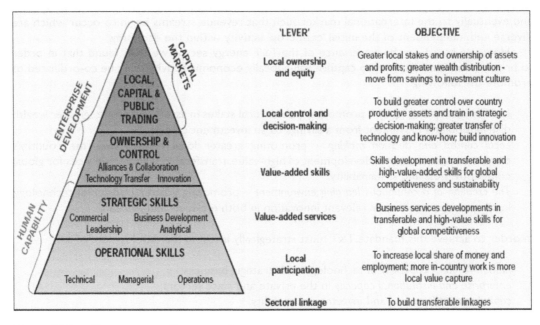

Figure 11.3   Development Framework

To achieve these ambitious goals, the government must involve itself in deep discussions involving a broad range of potential stakeholders in participatory agenda-setting processes that build bridges and broker partnerships across all actors in the system. It must foster local buy-in to a process of change, facilitating co-ordination and collaboration amongst clients and suppliers, and seek coherence in the setting of policy parameters within which innovation and development-related decisions are taken (Mytelka, 2003).

To implement the framework in the context of our prototypical (especially post-colonial) developing economy, the following six enabling levers are necessary:

* Increasing equity participation in global business.
* Investments in 'innovation systems'.
* Investments in skills development.
* The quality of the business environment.
* Investments in technology infrastructure.
* Enhancing the policy and legal framework.

Implementing the Framework: Equity Participation

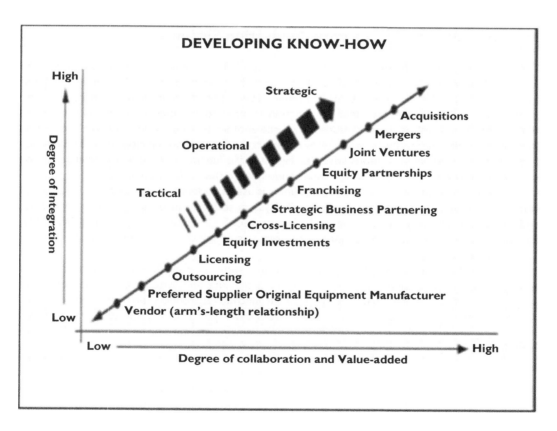

Figure 11.4   Developing Know-How
Source: Accenture.

Transitioning a traditionally less-developed economy and society forward into one which is based on innovation will entail the adoption of 'more productive company strategies [that] require more highly skilled people, better information, more efficient government processes, improved infrastructure better suppliers, more advanced research institutions and more intense competitive pressure, among other things' (Martin, 1986).

To carry out this transition, less developed regions would be well advised to employ world-class resources in the international marketplace to their advantage. This can be achieved through specific partnerships with international and organizations that are adept in the experience and skillsets being sought. As Figure 11.4 shows, at all levels of this value chain, the developing country must seek to forge deep *equity* relationships in this process of alliance (rather than simpler distribution-type arrangements) for there to be the optimal transfer of ideas and technology necessary to bolster indigenous human resource and institutional capability.

This concept of growing managerial and technological capability through acquisition/ merger/joint venture, etc. is a well-understood and practised concept in business. For example, Cisco has grown to become one of the largest and technologically advanced companies in the world through its very focused strategy of acquiring and assimilating promising smaller firms, which possess advanced technological and/or managerial competencies relevant to Cisco's strategic objectives.

Implementing the Framework: Innovation Systems

The National System of Innovation (NSI) approach is a helpful framework for understanding the process of knowledge creation, transfer, adaptation and monetization occurring within a country. In this framework the components of economic activity are identified and disaggregated. This gives a clear and consistent look into the functional roles and activities played by different parts of the economy as well as their relationships to one another (see Figure 11.5 for the 'Production Innovation Chain'). In this framework, innovation success depends on the closeness of interaction between the economic institutions which carry out these functions and the cohesiveness of the norms and policy arrangements which define and enhance their relationship.

The application of this framework to a country is useful in identifying the systemic failures that hamper the ability of an industry or productive system to learn, adapt and generate innovation and wealth. Public policy can then be applied to correct for such systemic failures (Mani, 2004) and be used as a tool in order to introduce greater streamlining to the process of economic value creation.

However, two main views of national innovation systems prevail. One is a more narrow view which focuses on the science and technology infrastructure and synergies, and the economy's ability to leverage this infrastructure to produce innovative products, processes and services. The other focuses more on the ability of the productive system as a whole to learn and adapt to changing market and economic conditions, and remain relevant and in step with the wider economic system.

Table 11.6   Implementing the Framework: Innovation System

Approaches	Scope and emphasis
Narrow definition of NSI (e.g. Nelson 1993)	This analysis emphasizes the impact that national technology policy has on firms' innovative behaviour. Innovative behaviour is measured in terms of the level of formal activity being undertaken by the R&D system and the science base. So the narrow definition of NSI includes organizations and institutions involved in searching and exploring, such as R&D departments, technological institutes and universities.
Broad definition of NSI (e.g. Lundvall 1992)	This puts the emphasis on learning rather than on the creation of knowledge itself, implying that the competitiveness of an individual firms and entire systems of innovation reflect the ability to learn. The new trends in production and in the labour market, which are increasingly knowledge-based, mean that knowledge building and learning are becoming more and more crucial for economic growth and competitiveness. It is also argued that learning, especially new skills and competencies, is essentially a collective and interactive process which cannot flourish in a purely market economy. Hence, the emphasis in this approach is more on the efficacy of the networks of firms and how they undertake innovative activity than on formal activities related to the R&D system and the science base.

Sources: Mytelka and Smith (2001); Tomlinson (2001).

However, more than relating innovation capacity to 'the formal activity being undertaken by the R&D system and science base' or the 'ability of a productive system to learn', we suggest that for a production system to be truly innovative, it must possess a deep understanding of the market(s) into which it sells its product/service. We suggest further that it is only through this knowledge that true innovation can occur in response to the dynamic and ever-present need to better satisfy market actors in basic response to the foundational capitalistic competitive drivers of increasing profits or market share.

It is in this context that we present the following visualization of a 'Production Chain' (Figure 11.5), including the post-production dynamic of 'marketing' in which we incorporate activities such as distribution and logistics, wholesaling/retailing, consumer financing, communications and branding, etc.

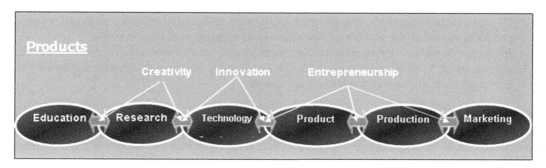

Figure 11.5   The Production 'Innovation Chain'

The innovation systems approach helps us to understand the links between commercial markets and factor markets such as education and R&D. Through this approach, it can be seen that the principles and understandings delivered through formal education must be applied to delving into new yet relevant areas of research. The goal of this research must be to develop new technologies, forms of organization, processes or products which can be taken to market. Products, services or processes must then be produced in the light of prevailing and forecasted market conditions, giving consideration to production costs, user acceptance and value delivery. Thus, we have a coherent system of innovation from education to post-consumption activity.

The key to this framework is the creation of links between traditionally distinct economic institutions, which result in the desired outcomes of creativity, innovation and entrepreneurship. These concepts are both overlapping and interrelated. We suggest here that 'creativity' occurs as a result of the understanding and tools given through education, the focused study of a particular area of research and the active attempt to bring about new technologies, processes or methods of organization. 'Innovation' is the taking of research and new or existing technologies and applying them to the creation of new products that may be offered to a market. Finally, 'entrepreneurship' is the harnessing of new technologies into products that are market-relevant and organizing their production and delivery on a scale and in a manner which is relevant to an identified market opportunity.

When applied in a country context, we can identify those parts of the innovation system that are either present, under-developed or absent. We can then assess the importance of each element to overall country sustainable development and prioritize, through policy and government spending, those aspects that are most critical and in need of immediate as well as long-term attention.

Aside from the identification of innovation chain elements that are either absent or under-developed within a country, it must be noted that the innovation chain concept, and innovation systems analysis, is not limited to the realm of production. Specifically, we expand the concept and approach of innovation systems to encompass the 'set of mechanisms institutions and technologies that facilitate trade'. These are market elements that affect the *environment* in which goods and services are traded. The market elements referred to here include the following:

- *Financing elements–* the ability of firms to access the capital needed to provide services to the market and the availability of financing to the enable or catalyse the rate of consumption by consumers.
- *'Market structure' elements –*the physical (or virtual) ability of customers to access desired products as well as the amount of risk assumed in engaging in market activity.
- *Facilitation elements –* those structural or institutional mechanisms which make it easier for individuals or firms to participate in market activity, e.g. information databases, chambers of commerce and investment promotion companies.

As argued earlier, innovation can take place with respect to these and a host of other strictly non-production functions, and the mapping of these (and other) market elements constitutes an 'innovation chain' for *markets* (see Figure 11.6). It is in fact true that innovations in these (market environment/market structure) realms may well bring more value to the producer and to the market itself than is possible through product or process innovation.

Developing nations in particular seem to be under-served in terms of their human and institutional capacity to innovate in these fundamental market realms. Arguably, this is an under-exploited area of innovation possibility which developing nations would do well to focus on with respect to their value and wealth generation efforts in the future.

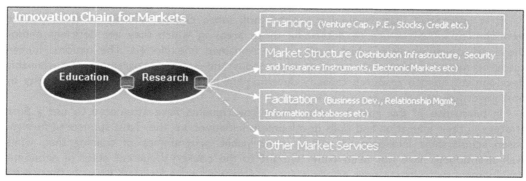

Figure 11.6   The Innovation Chain for Markets

Implementing the Framework: Innovation Systems and Skills Development

To achieve the goal of fostering a cadre of successful innovative domestic companies, the broadening and deepening of the skillsets of the indigenous workforce into areas of endeavour that formerly constituted the sole domain of the multinational corporation (MNC) will be required. Functions such as business development, commercial analysis, strategy, market analysis, political risk analysis, negotiation, mergers and acquisitions, financial trading and knowledge management must now be carried out in local educational and innovation-hybrid institutions. This is so that domestic firms can be supplied with the range of human resource skillsets necessary to fuel market activity along all aspects of the industry value chain, from incorporation to long-term asset management.

Figure 11.7 shows an expanded view of some of the links in the human resource development chain. It illuminates the various routes through which human resources may become available to firms and institutions which carry out commercial activity.

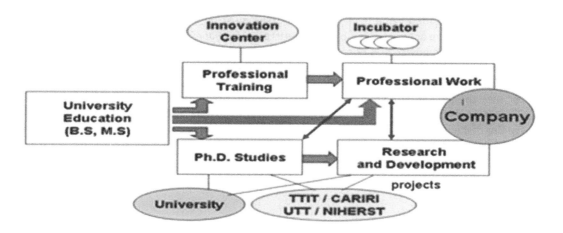

Figure 11.7   The Human Resource Development Chain

It is imperative that developing nations look more closely at their human resource development infrastructure to determine those areas in which they are deficient and/or those private–public links which have so far remained unexploited. The national human resource must be the cornerstone of any serious and holistic programme of sustainable development; human resource capacity development must be given the highest priority by host governments.

In pursuance of this goal, however, many governments have attempted to use a push strategy in their education and skills development initiatives, i.e. they have sponsored foreign-based scholarships initiatives as well as mass public programmes of training that, while well-intentioned, have not been truly relevant to the country's current state of economic development or to its strategic priorities for development going forward. As such, these push strategies have invariably resulted in the crippling phenomena of 'brain drain' as graduates find their skillsets mismatched to the opportunities and priorities of the local economy. Thus, they seek employment in other territories that sre better able to accept and reward their new-found competencies.

We therefore advocate pull strategies, in which the proscribed training and development activities are directly related to current and anticipated market opportunities as well as country development priorities.

The Quality of the Business Environment

Factors such as the state of cluster development, the availability of business financing, the extent of bureaucratic red tape (in management culture as well as in government), the extent of unionization and labour relations as well as the independence of the judiciary all affect the ability of the productive sector to efficiently carry on the business of wealth generation.

In addition to these macro-elements, there are other more micro business support elements that can significantly affect the ability of small and medium-sized firms to survive and thrive in the modern global economy. Especially in developing economies, accurate and timely information on current and planned activity and on the potential for increasing the national share of added value is crucial. Businesses must be fed with the best-trained minds and bodies and have access to one or more *enterprise development centres*, which provide such businesses with the advice and consulting services needed to allow them to upgrade business models to meet MNC contractor requirements and other international standards. It would also provide them with access to the tools and incentives necessary to encourage innovation, foster new thinking and bolster overall industry competitiveness.

Figure 11.8 shows a cross-section of some of the various institutions (from educational to funding) which are connected to and in support of start-up companies as well as small and medium-sized enterprises.

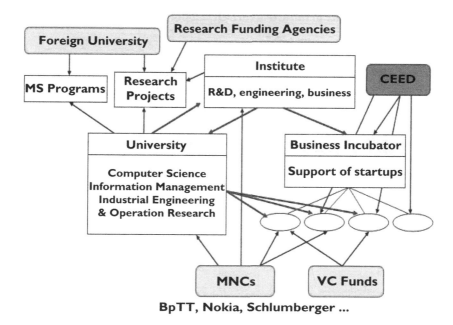

Figure 11.8   The Network of Support for New and Existing Small- and Medium-Sized Enterprises

Note: CEED stands for the proposed Centre for Energy Enterprise Development which would provide information and consulting services to Small and Medium Enterprises in the Energy Sector.

Implementing the Framework: Technology Infrastructure

Pulling information from the national competitiveness balance sheets for T&T and Finland for 2002/3 specifically in the area of technology, the following table gives a broad comparison between the two countries on key areas.

It is clear that one of the important levers that Finland has used to elevate itself into the competitive elite in the world is a large investment of effort into the integration of the latest technologies and methods into every aspect of its economy and value chain. These aspects have contributed to Finland becoming a more robust society and are ones in which T&T's developing economy, despite its windfall of energy earnings, remains notably weak.

In order to build its technology infrastructure, the following are some of the measures that should be set as metrics to gauge the success of any programme of infrastructural development:

* Growth in R&D investments.
* Human resource development leading to increases in the supply of business and technical professionals through enhanced educational, research and product development institutes.
* Updating of patenting legislation and an increase in indigenous patenting activity.
* The growth of knowledge intensive industries and an increase in hi-tech exports.
* Specific policy support for the growth of sustainable local business.
* Government R&D labs and institutes linked to both public and private enterprises.
* Financial incentives and schemes for the local generation of technology.
* Increased venture capital availability and venture creation vehicles.

Table 11.7   Measurements of Infrastructure Development

Finland		Trinidad & Tobago	
Technology		**Technology**	
3.01 Technological sophistication	1	3.13 Quality of competition in the ISP sector	100
3.02 Firm-level technology absorption	1	4.22 Tertiary enrollment	85
3.08 University/industry research collaboration	1	3.16 Laws relating to ICT	79
3.16 Laws relating to ICT	1	3.12 Internet access in schools	78
3.18 Tertiary enrollment	1	3.14 Government prioritization of ICT	72
3.12 Internet access in schools	1	3.15 Government success in ICT promotion	70
3.06 Company spending on research and development	2	3.01 Technological readiness	62
3.14 Government prioritization of ICT	3	3.06 Company spending on research and development	61
3.21 Internet hosts, 2002	3	3.02 Firm-level technology absorption	54
3.15 Government success in ICT promotion	5	3.08 University/industry research collaboration	54
3.17 Utility patents, 2002	7	3.18 Cellular telephones, 2003	54
3.20 Internet users, 2002	7	3.19 Internet users, 2003	52
3.19 Cellular telephones, 2002	10	3.21 Personal computers, 2003	52
		3.03 Prevalence of foreign technology licensing	51

Implementing the Framework: Policy Enhancements

Here we suggest some high-level and preliminary actions which are designed to help developing nations along the path of sustainable development:

- Develop and institute credible local content policies (especially in the dominant sector) describing how local value-added is defined and measured, and what specific activities it is applied to, as well as explaining the monitoring mechanisms in place and the penalties for non-compliance.
- Be more strategic about the type of businesses that are invited to operate nationally and the way those businesses are guided to interact with the local economy.
- Develop more thoughtful policies and strategic criteria for choosing partner companies as well as for encouraging local businesses to engender market and technology pull effects as well as deep synergistic links throughout the economy.
- Enter into deep equity arrangements with external partners so that technology and business know-how can be transferred.
- Seek to create pull effects rather than the push effects, both in terms of the creation of markets and with respect to production and supply.
- Augment the local skill base through a co-ordinated programme of attracting skilled expatriate nationals to local opportunities in business and technology.
- Conduct an innovation systems analysis of the local economy to identify those parts of the component innovation chains system that are either under-developed or absent. These must then be prioritized in terms of their possible contribution to sustainable development and then addressed through policy arrangements and government spending and guided partnerships with the private sector.

Conclusions

Developing nations must move away from their present mode of engendering 'static technological capability', which is the minimum requirement for the maintenance of a given productive system, with existing given equipment and technology. They must seek to develop a 'dynamic technological capability' which assures the long-term development of industry by giving nationals the complex set of skills and tools necessary to run the industry successfully over time and to innovate where necessary to overcome specific problems as they arise.

Host governments cannot rely on the schemes of attracting FDI alone to bring about 'productivity spillovers' (i.e. worker training, knowledge transfer and market access) and other positive externalities as extolled in theory. Developing countries must see it as being within their ability and mandate to *choose* international companies as partners in mutually beneficial and balanced processes of development and profit making. This ability becomes credible when developing countries recognize the value their respective nation brings to the MNC's global business.

T&T, for instance, is the fifth largest liquefied natural gas exporter in the world and provides 70 percent of the LNG intake of the US. T&T has an opportunity to choose partners who will move away from the traditional model and to require that more of the energy business be done locally, particularly head office functions, such as business development, analysis, commercial strategy, customer relations, markets, political risk, negotiating, mergers and acquisitions, trading and knowledge management. T&T would therefore have access to world-class business methodologies and personnel development, technologies and processes. These businesses, in turn, will develop and spawn local suppliers and contractors at a similar level, encouraging local businesses to develop their services to international specifications.

As argued by Barclay (2003), they must enact *credible selective intervention* policies, i.e. policies which seek to create an environment which identifies opportunities and mechanisms for implementation, and promotes indigenous technological and strategic business acumen in the host country. However, the response by multinational enterprises (MNEs) to intervention policies is likely to depend on whether or not they are perceived as credible, i.e. 'they are seen as binding commitments made by host governments on which firms can rely on as strategic planning assumptions. The MNE will not enter into a process of mutual strategic adaptation unless it is assured that the government can and will implement consistent policies over time'.

Another shift in emphasis which is necessary to achieve the goal of sustainability is the move away from the focus on the upgrading of the individual firm or entity within the sector towards looking upon upgrading as a process of innovation across the sector as a whole. Individual domestic firms cannot compete on their own in the global economy; they must be supported by a dynamic and upgraded sectoral innovation support structure. In addition, there must be efforts to upgrade *across* sectors, actively using the innovations and systemic improvements in the energy sector to provide links and enhancements to other sectors, thus achieving the goal of economic diversification.

T&T's changing objective is now not only to increase GDP, but also to reduce dependency on oil and gas. The strategy suggested is one which is designed to create a diversified economy with increased purchasing power parity, greater equity in wealth distribution, a world-class workforce and a dynamic onshore economy satisfying local demand and exporting its surpluses.

Summary

- Post-colonial developing countries, especially those in the Caribbean, have always produced great quantities of wealth from natural resources – first in agriculture, then minerals and then services (tourism). All revenue-generating activity is based on natural resources.
- Almost exclusively, this wealth and natural resources have been developed through reliance on an external (big brother) investor.
- The foreign companies in question came with all of the business elements in-house (i.e. markets and marketing, financing, business know-how and relationships).
- In the new economy, however, many of these are disaggregated commodity services which can be sourced from one of a number of competing service providers on the international market. As a matter of operating protocol, though, critical elements of business know-how are still usually kept in-house within the multinational.
- There is now the growing ability of host counties to build indigenous business know-how by:
  - increasing their equity stake in global business operating locally and thus gain access to world-class methods and technology by participating at senior management and board-level positions within those companies;
  - re-organizing the education system (including R&D) to increase the provision of technology and strategic market skills, thereby better equipping the local workforce to take up the challenge of achieving sustainable growth.

From Theory to Practice:
Specific Tactical Recommendations for the Case of T&T

OVERALL UNDERLYING POLICY FRAMEWORK

1. Make learning and innovation among the explicit goals of FDI promotion policies.
2. Implement a credible, transparent and consistently enforced system of laws, policies and taxation regimes which send clear signals to all existing and potential investors, and which take a long-term view of the development of T&T.
3. Formalize and enforce an overall framework and policy for local content, describing what defines local value-added, how it is measured, what specific activities attract a local value-added minimums and how adherence to the policy will be monitored, with clear penalties for non-compliance.
4. Upgrade domestic intellectual property legislation/enforcement and encourage increased knowledge creation and patenting behaviour.

EDUCATION /R&D

1. Adequately fund local research institutes to enable them to afford the equipment and human resources needed to carry out a broader range of higher value-added services to industry firms (both local and foreign) and as such begin to build a reputation of world-class centres of research excellence (especially in oil and gas).
2. Increase the interaction and links between these R&D institutions (e.g. CARIRI, TTIT, NIHERST, UTT and UWI) and the energy and technology-based commercial sectors through initiatives which would encourage students and faculty of the engineering, technological and business schools to carry out research and projects based on the local energy industry.

These initiatives must be given high visibility in the business sector and act as part of an overall integrated national innovation plan in which every effort is made to seek out synergies and co-ordinate research in a systematic and directed manner, taking advantage of agglomeration benefits as they accrue.

3. Ensure that the training curriculum of the energy and technology training institutions addresses critical current shortfalls of leadership, strategic business and technological capability. Possible new areas of focus include marine management and shipping logistics, exploration and production, engineering design simulation software, international commodity marketing and planning, managing large-scale projects and financial trading.

TECHNOLOGICAL DEVELOPMENT/PRODUCT DEVELOPMENT

1. Ensure that the foreign investor who comes into T&T enhances the indigenous technology capability by devising a detailed and comprehensive plan which addresses the capabilities needed to be developed over the long term, as well as specific technologies that the foreign firm may contribute. These must be implemented to systematically develop local capabilities to the fullest extent through spread effects and supplier links (Barclay, 2003).

2. Encourage identification and exploitation of synergies, business opportunities and benefits from extensive use of computing power in the upstream services sector, one of the biggest users of computing power in the world. Operators and their suppliers should be required to build the digital infrastructure to support their work with local suppliers, using open standards and formats that enable other businesses and sectors to leverage the network to support the country's ongoing transformation to a digital economy.

3. Inaugurate a Centre for Energy Enterprise Development (CEED), which will supply small and medium-sized enterprises with accurate and timely information and metrics on current and planned activity in the sector and on the potential for increasing the national share of value-added. The CEED should provide consulting services, assist domestic firms in upgrading business models to meet MNE contractor requirements and supply the advice and tools needed to encourage innovation, foster new thinking and bolster overall industry competitiveness. Energy businesses are currently unable to access the support resources provided by state business development agencies (BDC and TIDCO), since energy businesses are excluded from their client portfolio.

PRODUCTION AND FINANCING

1. Establish a trading marketplace and trading floor for LNG, methanol and ammonia – creating a T&T gas exchange with a minimum 50 percent level of local ownership, which enables the development of the capital market and technology base.

2. Act strategically concerning the types of technology and equipment used in plant and operational processes. This would allow the local industry to understand the new technology and over time be able to localize its equipment and technology to local conditions. The learnings would be applicable industry-wide and updating training could be organized in-country.

3. Develop industry clusters in specific strategic areas, which allow agglomeration synergies to occur. These clusters can act as the drivers and beneficiaries of R&D initiatives, the combined scale can service larger contracts both at locally and internationally, and there are also training and workforce synergies which can be derived.

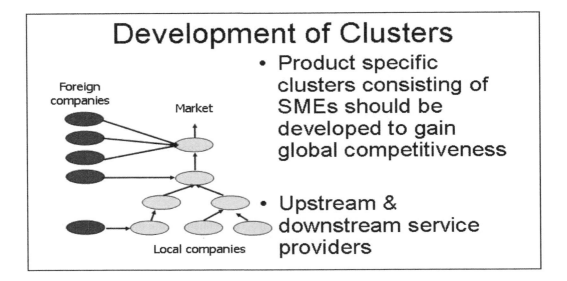

Figure 11.9   Development Clusters

4. Devise a comprehensive plan for receiving finance and in-kind donations from foreign companies which are directed at labour force upgrading (e.g. NESC and TTIT) so that companies do not regard these as an unsolicited tax and thus refuse to contribute to these schemes (Barclay, 2003).

5. Consider a regime of incentives to be offered to existing and new local firms which recognize the strategic role that local private equity plays in industrial and sustainable development.

6. Increase public ownership and access to energy businesses by enabling local investment in the sector through the amendment of the Pension Fund and Venture Capital Acts which currently prevent investment in the local energy sector. These are critical elements that could impact significantly on the growth of the local capital market. Local investment in long-term projects, rather than funds languishing in overseas reserves, could provide the country with a much-needed boost to the development of its capital market. In addition, a reduction in the Central Bank reserve requirement (currently at 14 percent) could free funds that can be used for local energy sector investment. Some of the windfalls from high oil and gas prices that are secured for the benefit of future generations in the Heritage Fund might be made available for strategic investments, including lower-risk ventures in the energy sector, thereby making hard currency (US$) available to locals at rates competitive with those available to foreign investors.

Epilogue

The strategic approach recommended in this chapter considered the characteristics of operations along the entire oil and natural gas value chain, in the light of T&T's vision of becoming a developed nation by 2020. By identifying those industry activities that were used and/or allowed for the development within T&T of the characteristics that define a developed nation, T&T was able to determine the overlap between what the country desires and what the industry provides.

The resource development approach recognized the relative importance of the three factors of production (capital, labour and resources) and especially the value of knowledge skills and the capture, aggregation and subsequent strategic deployment of capital in support of these skills. Means were found to maximize the impact of the relevant industry activities within the country and recommendations were made to put the appropriate policies and regulatory framework in place so as to ensure that these would be implemented.

The recommendations of this chapter built upon the 'Report of the Energy Sub-Committee for T&T's Vision 2020' (2004), the subsequent 'Energy Framework for Action – Vision 2020' (2005) and aligns with the subsequent 'Draft National Plan for T&T' (2007).[1]

With changing circumstances in the political leadership of T&T, different priorities within government and the variable application of policy, some of the recommendations were followed more robustly than others, with mixed results in terms of attainment of the potential benefits.

A major success came in 2013, when T&T was designated by the World Economic Forum as the first developing country to become an innovation-driven economy. This followed a series of deliberate policy decisions and investment in human and technology capacity enhancement, utilizing the revenue and experience acquired from a very successful period of oil and natural gas development.

T&T's well-established tradition of pursuit of excellence in education through ready access, quality educational institutions and systems was enhanced during the period of the natural gas boom and was extended to reach the evolving world of high technology and innovation. The National Energy Skills Centre, the UWI School of Business, the University of T&T (the vision of which is to provide education for a future world) and others were established to meet the needs of the growing energy sector, which had the financial capacity to fund their initial construction and operation, and were then extended to other sectors of the economy.

The Evolving TecKnologies and Enterprise Development Company Limited (eTecK) was given a mandate to, among other things, develop innovative businesses and build technology parks to support these along with the main campus of the University of T&T. Its Taman Park Brochure opens with the following statement:

> A new era is beginning. An era in which economies are built around knowledge, and innovation powers success. An era driven by the energy of new ideas, new connections, and the vital power of collaboration. An era in which industry and technology cross-pollinate, and the barriers to commerce disappear. A new era that's beginning at the centre of the Americas, in Trinidad & Tobago's Tamana Intech Park.

Tamana Intech Park is developed by eTecK – a state enterprise company created by the Ministry of Trade and Industry to diversify T&T national economy. eTecK is developing enterprises and services that are economically sustainable, technology-driven, environmentally accountable, community oriented and knowledge-based, always acting in the national interest.

---

1   http://www.transforme.gov.tt/sites/default/files/library/documents/Vision%202020%20Draft%20National%20 Strategic%20Plan%20Trinidad%20and%20Tobago.pdf.

References

Barclay, L.A.A. (2003). FDI – facilitated development: The case of the natural gas industry of Trinidad and Tobago. *Oxford Development Studies*, 32(4).

Downes, A.S. (2004). Arthur Lewis and industrial development in the Caribbean: An assessment. Presented at a conference on 'The Lewis Model after 50 years: Assessing Sir Arthur Lewis' Contribution to Development Economics and Policy', University of Manchester, 6–7 July.

Fagerberg, J. and Godinho, M.M. (2002). Innovation and catching up. In J. Fagerberg, R.R. Nelson and D. Mowery (eds), *Oxford Handbook of Innovation*. Oxford: Oxford University Press, Chapter 20.

Kaplan, D.E. (2003). Measuring our competitiveness – A critical examination of the IMD and WEF competitiveness indicators for South Africa. *Development Southern Africa*, 20(1), pp. 75–88.

Lundvall, B-Å. (ed.) (1992). *National Innovation Systems: Towards a Theory of Innovation and Interactive Learning*. London: Pinter.

Mani, S. (2004). A national system of innovation in the making: An analysis of the role of government with respect to promoting domestic innovations in the manufacturing sector of Iran. Available at: http://www.intech.unu.edu/publications/discussion-papers/2004-12.pdf.

Martin, M.J.C. (1986). Managing technological innovation and entrepreneurship. *Journal of Product Innovation Management*, 3(1), pp. 64–5.

Mytelka, L.K. (2003). New wave technologies: Their emergence, diffusion and impact. United Nations University, Discussion Paper Series.

Mytelka, L.K. and Barclay, L.A.A. (2003). Using foreign investment strategically for innovation. *European Journal of Development Research*, 16(3), pp. 531–60.

Mytelka, L.K. and Smith, K. (2001). Innovation theory and innovation policy: Bridging the gap. Paper presented to DRUID Conference, Aalborg, 12–15 June.

Nelson, R. (1993). National innovation systems: A comparative analysis. University of Illinois at Urbana-Champaign's Academy for Entrepreneurial Leadership Historical Research Reference in Entrepreneurship.

Phillips, A. (2004). Master's in Business Administration project document – British Petroleum's continuing investment in the energy sector of T&T and the tools used by the company to hedge its risk, as part of a consortium of companies, to embark on the Atlantic LNG project.

Social and Economic Planning Division, Ministry of Planning and Development (2002). *Transforming T&T into a Developed Country – Profile of Comparator Countries: The First Step*.

Tomlinson, M. (2001). The supply and demand of high-technology skills in the United Kingdom. In *Innovative People Mobility of Skilled Personnel in National Innovation*. Paris: OECD.

Vision 2020 Energy Sub-committee (2004). *Vision 2020 Energy Report, Trinidad and Tobago*.

World Economic Forum (2004). *Energy Industry Agenda Monitor*.

World Economic Forum & IESE Business School (2003/2004). *Global Competitiveness Report*.

12

Mineral Resource Policy Dynamics and the Contribution of Mining to Ghana's Development

Toni Aubynn

Abstract

The expectation that the exploitation of a country's natural resources would catalyse the development of that country is age-old and widespread. Ghana is endowed with significant natural resources, including minerals, forests and hydrocarbons. The debate as to whether the exploitation of these natural resources, particularly, mineral resources, have benefited the development of the country still rages on. This chapter contributes to the debate and discusses a range of issues that have bearing on how Ghana can harness the benefits of its natural resource extraction for national development. Based on the available data, literature and the author's own experience in the field, the chapter comes to the conclusion that while mining has greatly supported the economy of Ghana over the years, the benefits seem to be overly skewed to the centre, with no significant propelling forces to ensure effective impact at the actual mining regions. Similarly, given that only four of the country's minerals have been mined commercially over the years, compared to hundreds in South Africa, for example, the study underscores the imperative for managing the seemingly exaggerated expectations of how Ghana's mineral exploitations can carry the burden of development. The chapter challenges both critics and supporters of the mining industry to improve their understanding of the mechanisms that allow for increased developmental benefits of mining and advocate the deepening of the integration of mining into the economy through local supply chain development.

Introduction

Ghana is a currently a lower-middle income economy with a per capita income of about $1,100 and a population of 24 million (Government of Ghana, 2013). That Ghana has been blessed with a host of natural resources goes without saying. Under its former name of the Gold Coast, Ghana has historically been touted as being adorned with gold and other natural resources.

Therefore, on the face of it, the expectation that Ghana would develop on the back of its natural resource endowment sounds natural and not misplaced.

The question is: are the expectations of benefits from Ghana's natural resources exaggerated or realistic? To what extent has Ghana benefited from the extraction of its mineral resources? Current discussions on the benefits of mining have centred heavily on mineral taxes and rents (Ayee et al., 2011; Collier and Hoeffler, 2005; Ousman et al., 2012). In other words, what policies has Ghana adopted to ensure the sustainable and beneficial exploitation of its mineral resources? How have recent significant hikes in global commodity prices impacted on Ghana's economy? How can mining serve as a true catalyst for Ghana's development?

This chapter seeks to provide some answers to these critical questions. It discusses a range of issues that have bearing on how Ghana can harness the benefits of its natural resource extraction for national development. It relies on available data largely at the Ghana Minerals Commission, the Ghana Chamber of Mines, the Ghana Statistical Services, the Bank of Ghana, the International Council on Minerals and Metals (ICMM) and other literature on mining as well as the author's own experience in the field.

The chapter begins with a brief discourse on mining and development and an analysis of Ghana's mineral production, and places it within the context of the extent of endowment and the level of commercial extraction. This analysis reveals a problematic basis for the levels of expectation in terms of how much Ghana's solid minerals extraction can 'solve the developmental challenges of Ghana'. It then takes a historical tour of the country's mining policy trajectory which effectively reveals the excessive emphasis on revenue generation over the years and effectively no efforts at comprehensively integrating mining into the development framework of the country. It further examines the contribution of mining to the economy since the implementation in the 1980s of a comprehensive macro-economic programme, well known as the Structural Adjustment Programme (SAP), and provides some suggestions on how the extraction of Ghana's mineral resources can play a true catalytic role in the country's development. This chapter therefore contributes to a further and better understanding of mining and its contribution to the socio-economic development of the country, and also underscores the imperative for managing the seemingly exaggerated expectations of the solid minerals sector.

Mining and Development

The discourse of development and mining was and is still centred on two theoretical frameworks: first, the concept and practice of *development, growth* and the environment; and, second, whether the endowment of natural resources is a curse or blessing – the *resource curse* thesis. It must be said at the outset that I do not use the term *development* as that which is self-evident, terminal and needed by all poor societies regardless of their particular needs, circumstances or history. On the contrary, I problematize the notion of development and propose to understand development as a practice, an arena of constant negotiation and change, a struggle which is historically constructed and may take unprecedented turns, but which usually involves interactions among different social actors.

Linked to the concept of development and growth is the concept of *sustainable development* (SD), which has evolved through the constant search for a more comprehensive concept of development that takes into consideration quality, equity and longevity, which are highly relevant to the understanding of the relationship between mining and development. In orthodox development thinking, development is seen in terms of increases in economic output and the capacity of the national economy to generate annual increases in its gross national product/gross domestic product (GNP/GDP).

Several scholars have since kicked against this unilateral focus on growth as a measure of development. In a collection of articles and contributions, Silvana De Paula and, Gary Dymski (2005) make a frantic effort to emancipate development theory from the straitjacket of neoclassical thoughts and provide a more sophisticated understanding of development. They ground development theory in a more accurate analysis of social change and in so doing propose policies that seek to deliver not only higher economic growth, but also social change and social justice. Several decades earlier, Dudley Seers (1969) had pointed out that it was very slipshod of development economists to confuse development with economic development and economic development with economic growth. According to Seers, to understand a country's development one needs, it was necessary to raise and answer a number of pertinent questions:

> What has been happening to poverty? What has been happening to unemployment? What has been happening to inequality? If all these have declined from high levels, then beyond doubt this has been a period of development. (Seers, 1969: 5)

Even though these concerns are now rudimentary to the development discourse, the problems (poverty, unemployment and inequality) that constitute the objects of Seers' checklist are still relevant some 46 years later.

There is currently a growing consensus that the most ideal form of development is that which is sustainable. Constanza writes:

> [B]ut we must be careful to distinguish between 'growth' and 'development' ... Economic growth, which is an increase in quantity, cannot be sustainable indefinitely on a finite planet. Economic development, which is an improvement in the quality of life without necessarily causing an increase in [the] quantity of resources consumed, may be sustainable. Sustainable growth is an impossibility. [SD] must become our primary long-term policy goal. (1991: 85)

SD has evolved from an esoteric concept into a vital principle embraced by many business entities, governmental and non-governmental organizations (NGOs). The concept has come to overshadow the traditional concept of development and has assumed a prominent place in policy discussions. The definition of SD by the World Commission on Environment and Development (WCED), often called the Bruntland Commission, still remains the most popular. In its final report, the Commission defined SD as an approach to progress or 'development which meets the needs of the present generation without compromising the ability of future generations to meet their own needs' (WCED, 1987: 363). Elkington (1994) has functionalized the definition into the triple bottom line (TBL) – People, Planet and Profit – which basically goes beyond the traditional measure of profit, return on investment and shareholder value to include environment and social dimensions. O'Fairchealaigh (2010) argues that as a non-renewable resource, mining is by its nature neither sustainable nor unsustainable.

This chapter does not undertake a detailed one-on-one application of Elkington's TBL principle in a strictly evaluative sense. However, it adopts it as a guide to interpreting mining's financial contribution as a key avenue for SD by which the natural capital of a country can be transformed into human capital, including social development that transcends generations while maintaining a minimal impact on the environment.

The other theoretical lens through which mining and development has been viewed is the 'Resource Curse' framework. Indeed, at the heart of development is the harnessing of resources including natural, human and financial resources for the transformation and improvement of society. From this obviously expected point, it has been commonly assumed that because countries like Canada, the USA and Australia were built on mining, mineral development is an automatic development driver (Slack, 2010). In other words, mineral endowments must almost necessarily be a blessing to the host. This assumption has largely been questioned by the 'Resource Curse' thesis, which argues that natural resources have negative effects on economic growth and development (see Auty, 1993, 1998 and 2000; Sachs and Warner, 1997).

Proponents of this thesis argue that countries with abundant natural resources tend to be poorer and experience slower economic growth than their resource-poor counterparts. Adherents of this line of thought are not persuaded on the issue of the role of mining as a growth engine, particularly because most mining in developing countries is a capital-intensive enclave industry, foreign-owned and operated largely by expatriates with little integration to the local economy. The 'Resource Curse' thesis questions the wisdom of placing extractive activities at the core of any policy that seeks to achieve SD. While there may be theoretical and even empirical evidence supporting this line of thinking, I subscribe to the views of a group of scholars like Davis (1998 and 2011), Brunschweiler and Bulte (2008), and Wright and Czelusta (2007), who question the basis of the generalization of the 'Resource Curse' thesis. They argue that the reported negative outcomes of mineral economies are case-specific, with mixed and heterogeneous economic performance.

In my view, economic theory provides no convincing explanation as to why resource abundance should be inherently dysfunctional. Many economies, including those of Botswana and South Africa, have grown and developed precisely because of the abundance of mineral resources. One cannot agree more with Davis (1998: 220), who observes that 'when the entire mineral economies are examined, the heterogeneity and inter-temporal variability of their performances prevents any generalisation of development pattern'. Indeed, Auty (2000) and Auty and Mikesell (1998) admit that the additional rent and foreign exchange obtained from the export of commodities should provide a source of additional investment and higher economic growth. The International Council on Minerals and Metals (ICMM) in its Resource Endowment and Partnership for Development studies takes a more positive outlook and argues that a search for the impact of mining on society should not focus largely on problems, but rather on solutions and success stories that can be replicated through appropriate policies. This chapter proposes that, contrary to the popularly held view that Ghana has not benefited from its mineral endowments, the facts on the ground suggest that Ghana is (a potentially) 'blessed' rather than 'cursed' country.

Mineral Types and Ghana's Position

There is no doubt that Ghana is richly endowed with mineral resources. Ferrous and other precious minerals such as gold, diamonds, bauxite, manganese and, to a lesser extent, iron ore have long been associated with Ghana. A recent airborne geophysical survey indicated the 'occurrences' of more than 28 minerals, including, platinum, uranium, tantalite and rare earth in the country (Ghana Geological Survey, 2011). Table 12.1 indicates the various minerals in the country and distinguishes between those which have been commercially exploited over the years versus those that have not, even though their existence is not in doubt.

Table 12.1   Mineral Resources in Ghana

Commercially exploited	Not fully exploited	
Gold	Kaolin	Andalusite and Kyanite
Diamonds	Salt	Barite
Manganese	Clay	Beryl
Bauxite	Marble	Chromites and Asbestos
	Mica	Columbite
	Limestone	Copper
	Iron ore	Lead
	Zinc	

Source: Based on Ghana Minerals Commission 2012.

Table 12.1 makes two very simple but interesting revelations: first, although Ghana is endowed with substantial amounts of mineral resources, only four of them, namely gold, manganese, bauxite and diamonds, have been ever commercially exploited with a potentially significant impact on the economy. In addition, available statistics at both the Minerals Commission and the Ghana Chamber of Mines suggest that by merchandise value, gold receipts alone constitute close to 95 percent of the total export value from the minerals sector. Therefore, based on export value, Ghana may well be described effectively as a mono-mineral economy, contrary to the long-held impression that the country mines an array of mineral resources from which huge returns must be expected.

From the perspective of the country's position in the league of global and regional gold producers, Ghana's predominance in terms of gold production within the West African sub-region is unquestionable, at least for now. However, the same cannot be said of Ghana when it is considered from the global and continental standpoint. For example, in 1975, South Africa produced over 32 million ounces of gold, representing two-thirds of the world's gold production of 47.5 million ounces (www.goldsheetlink.com). Ghana produced less than 500,000 ounces that year, not enough to warrant an appearance in the top 10 global gold producers. It was not until 1992 that the country crossed the million ounces production mark (1.2 million ounces) and in 2005 produced a little over two million to take twelfth position globally, representing 2.5 percent and, from a continental perspective, a distant second to South Africa, which produced 11 percent of the global gold. It is important to note that Ghana has since increased its output of gold and, in 2012, contributed over 3 percent of global production and placed itself eighth on the list of producers, maintaining its second position on the African continent while closing the gap between itself and South Africa.

The above analysis serves to caution against what could be described as the exaggerated expectation by citizens about gold production in Ghana and the allied expectation for it to be the key source of revenue mobilization and national and local development. In other words, economic managers and mineral producers should manage expectations and hold a realistic view on the extent to which solid minerals production in Ghana, on their own, can undergird the country's development.

Mining Policy Trajectory

What policies has Ghana adapted to ensure the sustainable and beneficial exploitation of its mineral resources? The concept of *policy* is not a self-evident one, even if it has been relatively widely used in the literature (Guimaraes, 1991; Roberts, 1991). Policies are broadly speaking 'rules of the game' (Brinkerhof and Goldsmith, 1992; Gill et al., 1992). They are the rules of the game governing decision making by socio-economic actors such as individual firms as producers or consumers. Friends et al. (cited in Ham and Hill, 1993: 11) see policy in terms of a 'stance which, once articulated, contributes to the context within which a succession of future decisions will be made'. A policy is thus a purposeful course of action designed and implemented with the objective of shaping future outcomes in ways that would be more desirable than would otherwise be expected. Since Ghana's independence in 1957, variants of mining and allied policies have been implemented with the aim of ensuring the effective exploitation of the country's mineral resources as well as maximizing the benefit thereof. This section examines the trajectory of mining policy and its implication on mineral production and economic development.

PRE-AND IMMEDIATELY POST-INDEPENDENCE MINING POLICIES

It is not known exactly when mining began in Ghana. The earliest records indicate that gold mining had been carried out by the natives of the forest and the coastal regions of Ghana for a thousand years before the Phoenician landed on the west coast of Africa around the fifth and sixth centuries (Acquah, 1995; Dumett, 1999). Drawing on abundant archives and some oral tradition, Dumett (1999) observes that native mining operations in the Wassa area have been in place for over 100 years and further examines the relationship between mining and colonialism, including the beginning of European capitalistic gold mining in the then Gold Coast. Indeed, mining of the Banket Reef at Tarkwa is said to have preceded the South African Banket (the Witwatersrand) by about seven years. Tsikata (1997) suggests that the existence of large mineral resources, including gold, diamonds bauxite and manganese, was among the key reasons for Britain's imperial adventures in Ghana during the nineteenth century, even though the country's influential position in mining dwindled steadily over the years.

There have been several estimates of the historical production of gold by Ghana. One estimate put it at approximately 2,488 metric tons (80 million ounces) between the first documentation of gold mining in 1493 and 1997 (Kesse, 1985; Ghana Chamber of Mines, 1998). The World Bank asserts that Ghana accounted for 36 percent (8,153,426 ounces) of the total global production of gold during the period 1493–1600 (Tsikata, 1997). Yet, it is believed that regular shipments of gold from the ports of Ghana, then the Gold Coast, between 1471 and 1880 were over 14.4 million ounces (Acquah, 1995; Dumett, 1999). While these estimates may well have been exaggerated, they clearly underscore the significant extent of gold production by the country over the years.

Ghana's first real mining policy is believed to have been formulated under British colonial rule during the latter half of the nineteenth century when large-scale mining by British and other foreign investors began. Prior to this, and until the passage of the Mercury Ordinance Law in 1932, which effectively prohibited indigenous mining, gold and, to a smaller extent, diamond mining was predominantly an indigenous activity. According to Tsikata (1997: 9–13), the central focus of the colonial mining policy, which was largely influenced by British mining interests, was on four factors, namely:

1. to establish a legal and administrative framework to facilitate mineral operation;
2. to ensure security of tenure for grantees of mineral rights;
3. to help manage problems which would arise in the relations between mining companies and representatives and members of local mining communities;
4. to raise revenue for the colonial government through the levying of duties and income tax.

Clearly, the central aim of the colonial mining policy was to ensure self-sufficiency for the British Empire and to guarantee that imperial rather than the indigenous Ghanaian mining interests were taken care of. The development of manganese and bauxite mining is a clear case in point of the selfish objectives of the colonial administration. Manganese mining in Ghana is believed to have started in 1916 at the request of the British War Time Ministry of Munitions in order to meet the increasing wartime needs for the metal (Graham, 1982).

Similarly, even though concession had been granted as early as 1926 for the mining of bauxite in the Awaso area of western Ghana, production did not start until the early 1940s, when other sources of the commodity had been cut off from the Allied Forces during the Second World War. Furthermore, it is largely believed that beneath the promulgation of the Mercury Ordinance in 1932, which effectively criminalized indigenous gold mining, was the need to rope in more of the local labour force into the European-dominated mining sector (Akabzaa and Darimani, 2001).

By mid-1950s, the fortunes of the mining sector had begun to dwindle, largely due to the growing struggle for independence that had created some disquiet among investors and increased the level of political risk in the country. The immediate post-colonial government took steps to reverse the situation. In 1960, the government appointed a commission to investigate the prevailing situation in the mining industry in Ghana (Tsikata, 1997). The commission's recommendation culminated in the Minerals Act 1962. The intention of the policy can be summarized as maximizing government revenue, control of mineral resources and the generation of employment. According to Tsikata (1997), the key points of the Minerals Act 1962 are as follows:

- All minerals in their natural state were vested in the President for and behalf of the people.
- Government was held to have the sole right to export minerals.
- The power of control of land rights was vested in the state.
- The power to grant and determine the type of mineral rights was vested in the state.

Since then, and until the mid-1980s, the country has adopted various forms of state-controlled economic management policies and has maintained permanent sovereignty over minerals in their natural state (Leith, 1996; Walde, 1983). For instance, through the policy of nationalization and renegotiation of existing agreements, the government gained control over five gold mining operations (the Tarkwa, Prestea, Bibiani, Dunkwa and Konongo mines) and one manganese operation, hitherto owned by British companies, through the creation in 1961 of the State Gold Mining Corporation (SGMC) and the Ghana National Manganese Corporation (GNMC). The government's influence took a further turn towards consolidation when, in 1972, it enacted an Act that allowed it to acquire majority shares in mining companies. This culminated in the acquisition of a 55 percent share in the Ashanti Gold Fields Corporation (AGC),[1] the Ghana Diamonds Company (GCD) and the Ghana Alcoa Bauxite Company (GABC), and took over the African Manganese Company's (AMC) operations at Nsuta.

---

1   The British company Lonrho had previously owned AGC. The share structure after this acquisition was 55 and 45 percent respectively for the governments of Ghana and Lonrho.

It is important to comment quickly on the question of land rights under the 1962 Act vis-à-vis mineral rights as they have implications for the benefits of mining on the affected local communities. The 1962 Act vested the control of land and mineral rights in the state. The broad exercise of control over land by the state meant that the state had absolute control over stool and skin lands.[2] Even though the Act required the payment of compensation to the communities for the loss of land, no evidence exists that compensation was ever paid to the chiefs. In my view, therefore, any future policy that recognizes community land ownership and indeed ensures that 'fair and adequate' compensation is paid for the loss of access to the use of such resources would represent a significant improvement in the relationship between resource extraction and local communities.[3]

Economic Growth and Decline

The 1950s and 1960s witnessed significant growth in terms of the key commodities of the country, namely cocoa and gold, largely due to the high quality and improved prices of cocoa, the massive infusion of input subsidies and private investment and also high gold prices. This greatly expanded the foreign exchange base and the overall production of the country. Gold production reached a peak of 0.9 million ounces produced from about 30 mines in the country in 1960 (Barning, 1990)

Since Ghana's independence in 1957, mineral production has experienced varying fortunes, often responding to the prevailing policy and political framework. In the 1960s, Ghana produced about 0.9 million ounces (about 27,000 kg) of gold, 0.4 million tonnes of manganese, 0.5 million tonnes of bauxite and 3.2m carats of diamonds per annum (Ewusi, 1987; GLSS, 1989). However, by the mid-1970s, things had begun to change for the worse. The production of manganese had declined so much so that by 1983, output was less than 0.2 million tonnes. Similarly, gold production plummeted from 920,000 ounces in 1960 to 236,000 ounces in 1983.

In spite of the relative abundance of natural and human resources, a combination of internal and external factors steadily brought the economy of Ghana into decline in the late 1960s. By the second half of the 1970s, the economy was in a shambles and was desperately in need of some form of redemption. The average annual GDP growth rate between 1975 and 1983 was -3 percent, while the per capita GDP growth rate was -7 percent. Agricultural output was also declining at a rate of 0.3 percent annually. The output of cocoa, the lifeline of the country's economy, had fallen from an average annual of about 0.5 million tonnes in the 1960s to less than 0.2 million tonnes between 1975 and 1983. Again, by 1983, mineral production had also fallen drastically. A case in point was gold, whose output fell to one-third of its 1960 level by 1983, by which time only four mines were in operation. In addition, roads and general infrastructure were in a deplorable condition (Tabatabai, 1986: 404; Leith and Lofchie, 1993).

The pace of decline accelerated in the 1970s. Between the latter half of the 1970s and the early 1980s, the economy was virtually at a standstill. National income per annum fell by around 0.5 percent between 1970 and 1982, while real income per capita fell by over 30 percent. The poor performance of Ghana's economy during the immediate post-independence years is particularly striking given that at the time of independence, the country had a real GDP per capita of over US$450 (in 1995 prices), which was more than 40 percent higher than in Botswana (Roe and

---

2   Stool and skin lands are lands owned by the communities, but are held in trust by the local community chief. Over 80 percent of the lands in Ghana are customarily held by the traditional authorities: stools (mid-Ghana southwards) and skins (in northern Ghana).

3   However, the current Minerals and Mining Law 2006 (Act 703) provides for compensation to be paid for loss as to the use of the land, even though the mechanism to effectively evaluate loss of use of such assets remains to be clarified.

Samuel, 2007). By 1985, Ghana's GDP had declined to US$313 and Botswana had outpaced Ghana and was growing at 7.9 percent, while Ghana's growth rate was only 1.4 percent. The economic situation in the early 1980s is given in Table 12.2.

Table 12.2   The Annual Growth Rate of Selected Economic Indicators, 1981–3 (%)

Indicator	Year		
	1981	1982	1983
GDP (at market prices)	-3.8	-6.1	-2.9
GDP per capita	-5.1	-7.4	-17.1
Agriculture	-2.6	-2.2	-5.7
Industry	-16.0	-17.0	-12.5
Service	3.3	-3.7	5.0
Export (US$ value	-15.0	-10.6	-49.3
Import (US$ value	12.3	-44.3	-38.0
Inflation: wholesale prices	49.8	36.0	128.9
Inflation: consumer prices	116.5	22.3	122.8
Gold output (in ounces)	-2.8	0.9	-15.6

Source: Tabatabai (1986: 4).

The Era of SAP and Beyond

Various studies of the decline in Ghana's mineral production during the 1970s and early 1980s have concluded that the cause was less due to the absence of ore than the overall impact of the macro-economic malaise of the country, as well as the production constraints in the sector (Barning, 1990; Hutchful, 1996). The unfavourable macro-economic environment coincided with increased concerns over political unrest and the possibility of expropriation or sudden changes in taxation policies, as well as the prevailing laws on repatriation of profits, which precluded large-scale foreign direct investment (FDI) (Warhurst and Bridge, 1997: 2).

The Provisional National Defence Council (PNDC) was a military cum civilian junta, which took over power from the People's National Party (PNP) government of Dr Hilla Limann through a coup d'état on 31 December 1981 under the leadership of Flight Lieutenant Jerry John Rawlings. The political and economic exigencies of the time, including the continuing decline in most economic indicators, made a compelling case for the government to adopt a pragmatic rather than a dogmatic approach to resolving the country's socio-economic quagmire. Consequently, the PNDC government overturned its initial populist, mass-mobilization-based self-reliance policy and, in early 1983, began negotiations with the International Monetary Fund (IMF) and the World Bank for economic assistance and policy guidance.

On 21 April 1983, the government of Ghana launched the SAP, locally christened the 'Economic Recovery Programme' (ERP), under the financial support and supervision of the IMF and the World Bank. The programme was a constellation of macro-economic policies designed to bring the country's domestic and external imbalance to an equilibrium (Engberg-Pedersen et al., 1996; Lall, 1995; World Bank, 1988). Recognizing the enormous economic potential and strategic value of the mining sector, the government needed to take steps, under the SAP, to resuscitate the sector. The policy challenge for Ghana under the SAP was to revitalize the mineral sector and find a balance between the investors' objectives of profitability and the government's objectives of revenue generation and positive social and environmental externalities.

MINING LEGISLATIONS

The current legislative framework for mining in Ghana in the post-1980s is laid down in the Minerals and Mining Law 1986, PNDCL 153 (Law 153), as amended by the Minerals and Mining Amendment Act 1993 (Act 475), modified by the provisions of the 1992 Constitution of Ghana and, since 2007, amended and replaced by the Minerals and Mining Law 2006 (Act 703). Within the current legal framework, all minerals in Ghana are vested in the President on behalf of and in trust for the people of Ghana. Thus, regardless of who owns the land upon or under which minerals are situated, the state is the owner of all minerals occurring in their natural state within Ghana's land and sea territory, including its exclusive economic zone. According to the law governing mining in Ghana, the exercise of any mineral right requires a licence to be granted by the minister responsible for mining, who acts as an agent of the state for the exercise of powers relating to minerals.

New institutions such as the Minerals Commission and the Environmental Protection Agency (EPA) were established in 1986 and 1994, respectively. The Minerals Commission in particular has the authority under the constitution to regulate, manage and advise the government on the utilization of mineral resources and co-ordinate policies in relation to minerals. It also seeks to ensure a one-stop shop for investors in the minerals sector in order to reduce the existing complex bureaucracy and administrative inertia. The new mining law also regularized the activities of small-scale mining.

INVESTMENT INCENTIVES

In order to attract venture capital into the mining industry in Ghana, the government undertook a review of its tax and incentive regimes in respect of mining and introduced what may be described as relatively generous investment incentives for mining companies, including the following:

*   Reduction of corporate tax from 50–55 percent prior to the implementation of the SAP to 45 percent in 1986 and later scaled down further to 35 percent in 1994. In 2002, corporate tax was further reduced to 25 percent, but was reversed to its 1992 level of 35 percent in 2012 (Government of Ghana, 2012).
*   Exemption from payment of customs import duties in respect of plant, machinery, equipment and accessories imported specifically for mining.
*   Increase in the capital allowance from 20 percent prior to the SAP in the first year of production and 15 percent per annum subsequently to 75 percent and 50 percent, respectively, in 1986. In 2002, the capital allowance was revised further to 80 percent in the first year and 50 percent subsequently in a reducing balance approach. Like the other fiscal impost, the capital allowance has since 2012 been changed to a flat rate of 20 percent for a fixed period of five years.
*   A negotiable foreign exchange retention regime of a minimum of 25 percent.[4]

The government, through the SAP, provided finances for the purchase of spare parts and materials, and for the rehabilitation of infrastructure such as roads and railways. This new climate led to increased investment in the mining sector, making it a major springboard for the economic recovery of the 1980s up to the mid-1990s. In the next section I will examine in some detail the contributions of the mining or minerals sector to the economy of Ghana.

---

4   Under this programme, mining companies could retain up to 75 percent of their profits anywhere and in any currency. Prior to this, companies operating in Ghana were required by law to keep nearly 80 percent of their profits in the country. Under the new regime, each mining company negotiates directly with the government the exact percentage that can be retained outside the country, but this can be no higher than 75 percent.

Contribution and Benefits Stream

The mining industry globally has been generally criticized for not contributing 'enough' to their host countries. In Africa, and Ghana in particular, the criticism has been heightened in recent decades when commodity prices, particularly gold, experienced an unprecedented bull rally (Africa Union Commission and United Nations Economic Commission for Africa, 2009; United Nations Economic Commission for Africa, 2011). The impression created, especially by anti-mining non-governmental organizations (NGOs) and a certain section of the media is that mining is not only destructive but also does not make any meaningful contributions to the social and economic benefit of the country. This impression of extreme environmental degradation associated with the mining industry has often overshadowed the contribution it makes to the economy. This section presents a critical examination of the socio-economic impact of the mining sector in Ghana at the macro level, highlighting some of the main concerns raised by critics of the industry. I will focus on the sector's contributions to investment or capital inflow to the economy, domestic revenue, foreign exchange and employment. Unfortunately, time and space would not allow for discussions in this chapter of issues relating to the environment, community and corporate social responsibility that are also of immense importance to the discourse of mining and development.

Capital Injection and Production of Minerals

During the decade prior to 1985, the mining industry virtually stagnated. There were no significant new investments into the country in general and the mining sector in particular. However, largely as a result of the policy measures described above, coupled with favourable global market prices for some minerals during the 1980s, substantial donor re-capitalization for the mining industry, notably gold, has occurred. Between 1983 and 2012, the mining sector injected cumulatively over US$12.5 billion in FDI into the economy of Ghana for exploration and the establishment of new mines, as well as the expansion and rehabilitation of already-existing ones. This is significant from the standpoint of overall investment in Ghana and also against the background of the dearth of FDI in Africa.

Table 12.3   Gross FDI in the Mining Sector (in $ millions)

Year	Mining sector
2000	231.78
2001	275.53
2002	315.59
2003	545.62
2004	638.33
2005	797.52
2006	586.74
2007	670.22
2008	765.30
2009	762.26
2010	770.00
2011	780.10
2012	1,444.00

Source: Minerals Commission (2013).

As can be seen in Table 12.3, FDI in the mining sector since 2000 has represented between 40 and 65 percent of the total investment in the country. In 2000, for example, the FDI into the mining sector in Ghana represented over 60 percent of the total FDI of the country. Undoubtedly, this has come with enormous spin-off benefits, including the provision of support infrastructure (roads, houses, schools, hospitals and the extension of electricity), on-the-job training opportunities for Ghanaians and transfer of technology. These are benefits that will remain in the country long after the mining companies are gone. The increased investment, following the implementation of the SAP, has led to the revitalization of exploration activities and the arrival and the establishment of mining operations in Ghana by global leading gold mining companies, such as the South Africa-headquartered Gold Fields and Anglogold Ashanti and the US-based Newmont Gold (all of which were among the top four global gold mining companies).

By 1999, there were 128 companies engaged in gold exploration in Ghana, including 20 foreign companies. All the state-owned mines have been divested or privatized. In 1992, for instance, the state sold to the public 25 percent of its shares in the Ashanti Goldfields Company, the largest gold mining company in the country and the only one then listed on the New York Stock Exchange. Since 1983, about 14 new mines have been opened with private funding in addition to the five already in operation.

Table 12.4   Minerals Production (1980–2012)

Year	Gold (ounces)	Diamond (carats)	Bauxite (M/t)	Manganese (M/t)
1980	437,669	1,227,071	224,501	368,593
1981	349,870	1,016,580	179,598	260,409
1982	335,724	893,016	63,530	176,871
1983	311,707	529,767	52,676	177,154
1984	282,641	450,049	53,421	243,260
1985	283,819	505,295	122,512	325,905
1986	447,796	878,943	273,602	498,996
1987	328,939	435,900	196,255	295,061
1988	374,051	277,966	284,527	259,614
1989	418,070	160,729	347,065	333,743
1990	522,517	484,877	381,373	364,373
1991	946,269	702,172	352,921	325,964
1992	1,006,943	596,236	338,244	353,476
1993	1,251,010	584,848	423,747	294,789
1994	1,396,887	746,949	426,128	271,989
1995	1,630,309	627,319	512,977	245,432
1996	1,550,814	714,717	473,218	161,690
1997	1,644,622	698,585	504,401	273,224
1998	2,353,000	823,125	442,514	348,406
1999	2,257,681	680,343	355,260	638,937
2000	2,315,000	627,000	503,825	638,937
2001	2,205,473	870,490	715,455	1,212,338
2002	2,115,196	924,638	647,231	1,132,000
2003	2,208,154	927,000	494,716	1,509,432
2004	1,794,497	911,809	498,060	1,593,778
2005	2,149,372	1,062,930	726,608	1,714,797
2006	2,244,680	970,751	885,770	1,658,701

Table 12.4   **Minerals Production (1980–2012) (*concluded*)**

Year	Gold (ounces)	Diamond (carats)	Bauxite (M/t)	Manganese (M/t)
2007	2,486,821	837,586	748,232	1,156,339
2008	2,585,993	598,042	693,991	1,089,021
2009	2,930,328	354,443	490,367	1,012,941
2010	2,970,080	308,679	512,208	1,194,074
2011	2,924,385	283,369	400,069	1,827,692
2012	3,166,483	215,118	752,771	1,490,634

Source: Minerals Commission, 1980–1999; Chamber of Mines Annual Reports, 2000–2012.

In terms of production, the mining sector has witnessed a phenomenal growth since the implementation of mining sector policies under the SAP. As indicated in Table 12.4, the production of almost all minerals (with the exception of manganese) has at least doubled compared to their 1983 outputs. Gold, by far the major mineral (by export value), has increased more than tenfold to nearly four million ounces from its immediate pre-1980 level. Also, over 1,000 small-scale mining concessions have been granted following the legalization of small-scale mining (Minerals Commission, 2013).

Domestic Revenue Generation

One of the major benefits from mining is the generation of domestic revenue for the state. The current Minerals and Mining Law of Ghana (Act 703), with its recent amendments in 2012, requires large-scale mining operators to contribute five percent of their gross revenue as royalties to government. Eighty percent of this amount is retained by the central government, 10 percent goes to the Minerals Development Fund and one percent goes to the Office of Stool Lands Administrator to cover administrative expenses, while the remaining nine percent is allocated among the District Assemblies, traditional councils and affected stools. In addition, mining operators are required to pay 35 percent of their profits in corporate tax and dividends for the government's statutory 10 percent free carried interest in all private mining companies.[5]

---

5   There was also a proposal in the 2012 national budget for a 10 percent windfall profit tax which was later suspended by the government

Table 12.5   The Contribution of the Mining Sector to Domestic Revenue (1990–2012)

Year	Corporate tax	Mineral royalties	PAYE	Reconstruction levy	Total IRS (GRA)	Percentage of mining revenue ot total revenue
1990	2,825,941,158	1,893,436,000	–	–	52,818,068,300	8.94 percent
1991	821,844,979	3,021,277,000	–	–	61,485,625,496	6.25 percent
1992	455,051,883	4,545,804,000	–	–	74,931,531,366	6.67 percent
1993	4,393,447,293	7,485,121,000	2,649,306,000	–	113,236,997,000	12.83 percent
1994	7,214,082,000	12,783,689,000	4,810,802,000	–	166,595,941,000	14.89 percent
1995	20,392,973,000	20,911,926,000	7,951,763,000	–	275,513,201,000	17.88 percent
1996	9,160,528,000	35,527,027,000	16,834,543,000	–	424,491,908,000	14.49 percent
1997	9,868,796,000	34,594,950,000	25,022,023,000	–	605,782,577,000	11.47 percent
1998	14,450,773,000	49,841,242,000	31,016,506,000	–	785,436,693,000	12.13 percent
1999	31,117,108,000	48,620,419,161	27,839,260,000	–	901,663,758,000	11.93 percent
2000	15,789,167,000	118,736,935,173	59,243,800,000	–	1,409,445,273,000	13.75 percent
2001	24,812,893,000	127,358,386,430	76,111,678,000	4,251,467,579	1,950,162,751,000	11.92 percent
2002	23,501,158,000	153,452,471,032	101,457,668,000	26,474,633,878	2,757,747,781,032	11.06 percent
2003	68,137,702,000	194,387,579,429	141,049,450,000	16,785,882,702	3,824,078,389,429	10.99 percent
2004	100,331,114,000	215,743,706,000	134,357,711,000	36,346,622,100	5,333,114,704,000	9.13 percent
2005	269,889,639,000	235,951,903,000	194,058,939,000	22,957,004,700	6,446,385,048,000	11.21 percent
2006	404,361,775,000	316,254,789,000	216,525,776,000	11,085,262,400	7,333,916,866,000	10.20 percent
2007*	47,415,690	40,882,042	34,587,597	–	901,242,340	14.42 percent
2008*	73,554,697	59,004,892	47,139,242	–	1,222,272,177	15.32 percent
2009*	124,600,880	90,415,902	103,061,985	–	1,731,633,034	18.21 percent
2010*	241,578,780.28	144,697,000	132,469,709.91	–	2,441,331,841.81	21.29 percent
2011*	649,902,536	222,024,706	161,822,107	–	3,746,024,194	27.61 percent
2012*	893,773,828	359,392,853	207,495,934	–	7,461,202,977	20.72 percent

Source: Minerals Commission (2013).

Note: * Contributions for 2007–11 are in GH¢. All others are in Cedis.

The collection of these taxes over the years has placed the mining sector as the leading contributor to the domestic revenue of Ghana. Table 12.5 shows the revenue contribution to the state by the mining companies. Government receipts from the mining sector have generally reflected the general production levels, price and the tax rate at any particular period, and have evidently been increasing over the years. Between 1995 and 2003, for example, the total annual average contribution by the sector to Ghana's domestic revenue was approximately $40 million, representing an average of approximately 10 percent of total government domestic receipts. This was within the period of a dramatic fall in the gold price, which reached a 20-year low of $255 per ounce (Table 12.5) and unimpressive gold production levels. Since then, Ghana has witnessed significant growth in receipts from the mining sector, which peaked in 2011 at 27 percent ($708 million) of the country's domestic receipts.

Figure 12.1   Trends in the Gold Price (1995–2012)
Source: www.kitco.com.

Foreign Exchange

In terms of foreign exchange or receipts from merchandised exports for Ghana, mineral exports ave maintained a consistent leadership as the country's number one earner since 2000. The share of minerals to the total foreign exchange earnings of Ghana has increased from 14 percent in 1990 to an average of 41 percent since 1993, outpacing cocoa as the country's most important foreign exchange earner (Institute of Statistical and Social Research, 1996–2010; Bank of Ghana, 2010). Between 1995 and 2002, for instance, the annual average export earning of Ghana was approximately $1.7 billion, of which mining contributed about $690 million. In 2012, mining earned over $4.0 billion or 42 percent of the gross merchandise exports value for Ghana. Gold has always made up a gigantic position by all indicators in the mining industry and has contributed between 86 percent and 95 percent of the earnings from the country's total mineral exports since 1986.

Critics of the industry have questioned the extent to which the high levels of foreign exchange earned from mineral exports are retained in Ghana (Akabzaa, 2001; Akabzaa and Darimani, 2001). However, the available records at the Minerals Commission, the Ghana Chamber of Mines and the Bank of Ghana indicate that on average, mining companies have returned more of their export proceeds than they are statutorily required to do (Ghana Chamber of Mines, 2012; Aryee, 2014). This is contrary to the commonly held view that mining companies retain their earnings in offshore accounts.[6] As we have noted earlier, mining companies are permitted by the Minerals and Mining Laws of Ghana to operate external accounts in order to purchase operational inputs that are not available in Ghana and also amortize their foreign loans. The amounts to be held in these accounts are negotiated directly by individual companies with the government. So far, retention amounts approved by the government of Ghana since the mid-1980s have ranged between 25 percent and 80 percent.

---

6   The former Governor of the Bank of Ghana, Dr Paul Acquah, confirmed this in a speech he delivered at the 79th Annual General Meeting of the Ghana Chamber of Mines. See the Ghana News Agency report on 9 June 2006, http://ghanadistricts.com.

Table 12.6   Total Mineral Revenue and Mineral Revenue Returned (2009–12)

Year	Total mineral revenue ($)	Mineral revenue returned ($)	Percentage of mineral revenue returned
2009	2,384,836,583	1,812,255,608	76 percent
2010	3,290,792,703	2,222,901,896	68 percent
2011	4,245,370,284	3,173,491,961	75 percent
2012	4,525,657,336	3,268,084,143	73 percent

Source: Ghana Chamber of Mines (2013).

Table 12.6 shows that since 2009, mining companies have kept an average of about 27 percent of their exports in overseas accounts and have returned approximately 72 percent to Ghana. For instance, according to the Bank of Ghana (2001), between 1998 and 2000, of the total export earnings of $756 million for minerals, a quarter of it ($177 million) was repatriated to Ghana. This amount has since increased to reflect production and price dynamics. In 2012, the sector returned approximately $3.2 billion, representing 73 percent of total mining export receipts. Clearly, mining companies returned far more than what is required by law. The significant return of foreign exchange through the local commercial banks and Ghana's central bank (the Bank of Ghana) has contributed immensely to the relative stability of the local currency, the *cedi*, and the overall balance of payments of the country.

The situation can also be viewed from the perspective of the potential Dutch Disease implication of foreign exchange inflows to a resource-based economy such as Ghana's (Auty, 2000; Burda and Wyplosz, 1997). The Dutch Disease thesis has been generally explained in terms of how the tendency for a huge surrender of foreign exchange inflow from a dominant export sector such as mining can negatively affect the exchange market between the local currency (the *cedi*) and the US dollar.[7] The logic is that the disproportionate influx of dollars is likely to strengthen the local currency against the dollar, with the effect that the price of imports will decrease, with the resultant negative impact on the local industry's competitiveness. So far, there is no evidence of the Dutch Disease syndrome in the mining sector (Addy, 1998; Aryee, 2001). Perhaps the negotiated surrender levels were consciously designed to limit the potentially negative effects that a dominant resource industry could have on the national economy.

Contribution to GDP and Integration into the Economy

The GDP of a country is a measure of the total final outputs of goods and services produced by the economy within the country's territory. Typically, mining provides only a modest direct contribution to a country's GDP (ICMM, 2012: 7). In Ghana, the data suggest that the contribution of mining to GDP has seen steady improvements since the implementation of SAP in the 1980s. Figure 12.2 depicts the contribution to GDP by the mining sector. In 1991, the industry contributed a little over one percent to Ghana's GDP. Since 1992, mining has contributed an average of five percent to Ghana's GDP and, like all other indicators, this has steadily improved since the 2000s, reaching a high of 14 percent in 2012.

---

7   A renowned economist, Tadeusz Rybczynski (1995), explains Dutch Disease from the perspective of wage differentials through factor price equalisation. He draws attention to the internally generated Dutch Disease that could be applied in the case of mining versus agriculture sectors.

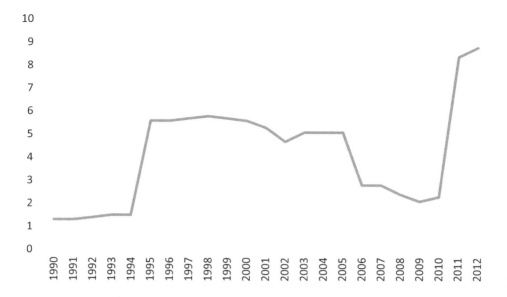

Figure 12.2   Share of Mining and Quarrying in GDP (%)
Source: ISSER (2005), (2008), (2012).

This may be even more significant if one looks at it in relation to exports (as clearly shown in Table 12.7) and also considering that in South Africa, which is well known as a major mining country, mining contributed approximately eight percent to the country's GDP in 2010. However, the level of integration of mining into the overall economy of Ghana is not yet clear. To understand the extent of the link of minerals sector to the rest of the economy, it is necessary to look at the per unit contribution to exports per unit of GDP. To do this, the per unit contribution of GDP to exports of minerals is compared with the other key sectors of the economy as well as with other key mining countries. The basic assumption is that the higher the per unit contribution of GDP to exports, the lower the integration with the national economy and vice versa.

Table 12.7   Average Per Unit Contribution of GDP to Exports by Key Sectors of the Economy (2000–2012)

Sector	Contribution to GDP (%)	Contribution to exports (%)	Per unit contribution of GDP to exports
Agriculture	38	34	0.8
Mining	6	41	6.8
Services	29	5	0.2
Others	27	20	0.7

Source: Based on ISSER (2000–2012); GSS, (2005), (2008).

It must be admitted that there are questions over the links between the mining sector and the rest of the national economy. In other words, to what extent does Ghana add value to its minerals or utilize minerals as raw materials to fuel the economy?

Table 12.6 and column 3 of Table 12.7 indicate the per unit contribution of the sectors by GDP to exports. As can be seen from Table 12.7, services, with the lowest per unit contribution to exports by GDP (0.2), is the sector with the highest link to the economy. On the contrary, a comparatively high per unit contribution of GDP to export (7) by mining is indicative of a weak link between the sector and the rest of Ghana's economy. The picture is similar when an inter-country comparison is undertaken. Table 12.8 suggests that among the selected countries where mining is key to their economy, the mining sector in Ghana has the weakest link to its overall economy. Thus, although Ghana is not as heavily dependent on mining as Botswana, Papua New Guinea and Namibia, its higher index of GDP contribution to exports compared to those of the aforementioned countries confirms the weak link thesis.

Table 12.8   The Contribution of the Mining Sector to GDP and Exports for Some Major Mining Countries (2010)

Country	Contribution to GDP (%)	Contribution to exports (%)	Per unit contribution of GDP to exports
Botswana	33	84	2
Canada	0.9	12	4
Ghana	13	42	7
Guinea	25	84	4
Namibia	11	54	5
Papua New Guinea	25	72	3
South Africa	8	48	5.1
Zimbabwe	15	31	6

Source: ICMM (2012).

The relatively low contribution of mining to GDP, coupled with the weak link to the economy, may partly be explained by the absence of the industrial base for the manufacture of inputs required by the mining industry, which is notably technology-intensive, thereby requiring them to be imported. The steady increases in the mining GDP numbers may, however, reflect the gradual increase in local participation in mining support services areas such as drilling, exploration and explosives, cement, lime and high-density polyethylene pipe (HDPE) manufacturing and supplies in the sector. As was noted above, over 95 percent of the gold produced in Ghana is shipped outside as exports with minimal added value. Effectively less than 5 percent of Ghana's gold and diamond production (mainly from the small-scale artisanal sector) is processed into consumables (jewellery) in Ghana. Certainly, beneficiation is an area that mining policy makers should seriously consider if more benefits are to be accrued to the country.

Employment Generation

To what extent does mining contribute to employment in Ghana? Critics of the industry argue that open-pit mining lacks the capacity for employment generation. This is due largely to its capital-intensive nature and short life span. This is true to some extent. For example, the closure of the Tarkwa and Prestea underground operations in 1999 and 2002, respectively, led to over 2,000 job losses. Similarly, the closure of the Teberebie surface operations, after less than 10 years of operations, also led to about 500 labour redundancies, although it is believed that about

70 percent of the retrenched labour force were engaged by emerging operations at Damang, Tarkwa and Akyempim (Aubynn, 1997a and 1997b). These have often created some nostalgia for underground mining which is believed to employ more labour and have minimal competition for agricultural lands.

Conversely, it could be argued that the breath of the technology of open-pit mining has been rather timely, allowing for new operations in areas such as Damang Wassa, Akyempim, Iduaprim, Teberebie (in the Western Region), Amansie, Chiraano, Kenyaasi, Nkawkaw and Akyim, which were not known to produce gold, to be brought on stream and actively benefit from the production of gold. This provided a conduit to absorb the teeming mass of underground miners who would have been retrenched following the evidently poor performance of the country's underground mines.

In terms of numbers, the massive retrenchment occasioned by the implementation of the SAP had an initial debilitating effect on employment in the mining sector. Before the 1980s, the sector was estimated to have directly employed about 27,000 Ghanaians. By 1987, this number is believed to have shrunk to 15,000, largely due to the massive retrenchment exercise at the Obuasi Mines. Employment in the mineral sector surged back to about 23,000 by 1995. However, by 2004, the number had reduced to approximately 18,000 Ghanaians, which was attributable to the closure of the Teberebie Mines and redundancies at the Damang Mines.[8] According to the 2012 Annual Report of the Ghana Chamber of Mines, the sector directly employed approximately 23,000 people. The Minerals Commission put this figure significantly higher at 27,000 to include other mining contractors. The Chamber of Mines has long estimated that the mining industry indirectly offers employment that amounts to five times this number through local purchases and the awarding of various kinds of contracts (Ghana Chamber of Mines, 2001; *High Street Journal*, 16 April 2001). These estimates may be an understatement if we consider the large army of youth employed in the informal, unregulated artisanal mining sector of Ghana, which has been variously estimated at 500,000–1,000,000.

Furthermore, incomes from this sector are high relative to those in other sectors, with the potential for high savings and higher standards of living. As has been noted above, the high incomes translate into significantly high pay-as-you-earn (PAYE) tax for the government as well as high social security (SSNIT) contributions.

From the above, it is clear that the special attention paid to the mining sector under the SAP has yielded good dividends for the country in terms of employment, foreign exchange earnings for the country and capital injections. It remains to be seen how these dividends translate into social improvement and SD.

Challenges and the Way Forward

This section looks at the challenges that currently constrain the efforts at optimizing the existing potential for mining to significantly catalyse the SD of Ghana. There are a myriad of issues that need to be addressed. Some of the issues raised here are not peculiar to Ghana and may be found in many resource-based developing countries.

---

8   This estimate includes employees in the exploration area, contractors and suppliers to the large-scale mining companies. It does not include artisanal and small-scale miners.

MISALIGNMENT OF PERCEPTION AND REALITY

An unpublished report of a commissioned study by Africa Practice (2013), a British-based strategy and communications consultants, confirmed the negative view held by a section of the Ghanaian community, particularly NGOs, about mining. Although the outcome of the study was not too surprising, it somewhat confirmed the irony of the mining industry that while it maintains a fundamental position in the very existence of life and humanity, it is menacingly plagued by strong negative perceptions as if mined products were no longer relevant to human survival. Yet the very existence and survival of humanity is fundamentally based on what is mined or grown. The strongly negative perception of the industry transcends even the high level of officialdom and decision makers. For example, a recent statement on an Accra-based *Joy FM* by the former Head of Policy Monitoring and Evaluation at the Presidency of Ghana, Dr. Tony Aidoo, reflects the contradictory public position of some policy makers whose policies, on the one hand, advocate for mining investment in the country:

> Large-scale mining has not befitted Ghana in any way. It has only led to the destruction of Ghana's arable agrarian lands … We should reduce the scale of an industry that does not give us value … . Between those large-scale miners and small-scale (illegal), I'll go for small-scale miners and tell these foreigners to get out.[9]

Dr Aidoo is believed to have further commented that 'we do not get more that 5 percent from mining related activities'. Two key, somewhat contradictory effects arise out of this situation. First, there is *subtle and sometimes overt dislike for industry*. This physiological fall-out may not be specific to the mining sector, but may also reflect the apparent ambivalence towards the private sector in Africa which Greg Mills (2010: 13) aptly describes as 'ranging from suspicion to outright hostility'. Porter and Kramer (2011) have wondered why sometimes political leaders set policies that undermine competitiveness and sap growth. It is quite intriguing that governments go out of their way to canvas for investment in the mining sector, but sometimes turn to vilify the same sector that evidently supports the economy. It is also amazing that where the facts about the contribution of mining are clearly available, powerful critics and NGOs and sometimes key people in government chose to conveniently ignore them in order to give credence to the suggestion that 'mining contributes nothing to the country'. These sometimes unfounded criticisms only reflect a certain level of discomfort with the private investment in the mining sector, which is often accused of extraversion and capital flight. This type of attitude and posture clearly contradicts the fact that Ghana is ranked among the highest 20 percent in the global Mining Contribution Index (ICMM, 2012). It may well be the case that Ghana does not want its natural resources to be developed because of its perceived (and certainly not real) negative impact. But this must be clearly transmitted in order to avoid sending confusing signals that undermine business certainty for both existing operators and prospective investors and the markets. Public pronouncements by government officials may be construed as the official posture of government which, for all intents and purposes, may sound contradictory. It is therefore absolutely imperative to align the understanding of mining and its respective benefits and challenges between industry players and policy makers as well as the general public.

Another aspect of the fall-out of the misaligned perception described above is the *exaggerated public expectation* of the extent to which mining can contribute to Ghana's development. As has been noted in the previous section, there is a misaligned perception between the extent of the country's natural resource endowment and the actual minerals commercially developed.

---

9   *Graphic Online*, 4 December 2013, emphasis added.

The phrase 'Ghana has so many minerals' is common and widespread, and is often repeated even at the pulpit and in social discussions. The strong perception that the country mines a myriad of minerals in commercial quantities has often generated inordinate expectations that the sector can offer more than it has historically delivered. Yet, weighed against existing data including international publications on mining in Ghana (for example, Roe and Samuel, 2007; ICMM, 2012), there is a significant discordance between the perception and the reality. Even on the strength of its effectively mono-mineral position in terms of exploitation and value, Ghana is still ranked among the highest 20 percent in the global Mining Contribution Index (ICMM, 2012). It needs to be conceded, however, that headline contributions by the mining sector in Ghana have not necessarily translated sufficiently into improvements in the quality of life of Ghanaians in areas such as healthcare, infrastructure and education, particularly in mining areas. For example, most of the mining areas of Obuasi, Ayamfuri, Bogosu, Tarkwa and Damang currently host some of the country's worst roads and poorest educational delivery.

The challenge is for both the industry and the government to instigate a 'reality check' and embark on educating the public on what can realistically be expected from the exploitation of the country's minerals in order to manage their expectations. There is also the need for the government to redirect policy to ensure that sufficient revenue streams are devoted to improving healthcare and infrastructure, as well as creating visible opportunities for the people in areas affected by mining. The current practice where only about 5 percent of the total royalty receipts effectively returns to the areas affected by mining with no clear definition of its usage is woefully inadequate and justifies the cry for physical development in those areas.

Excessive Focus on Rents and Taxes and Lack of Integration into the Economy

As can be gleaned from earlier sections of this chapter, successive policies on mining in Ghana have largely focused on revenue generation and, to a certain extent, employment. Clearly, the priority of mining (and cocoa and timber) in revitalizing the national economy under the SAP was precisely to attract more FDI and also to generate more income for the country. We have also observed the limited integration of mining into the overall economy of the country in spite of its significant contributions to local revenue and foreign exchange generation. There is no dispute about the need for the extractive industry to generate revenue for the state; however, such a narrow focus on taxes is not only unsustainable but also renders the country vulnerable to the vicissitudes of global commodity prices.

At the heart of these lapses in Ghana's past policy focus is an opportunity to develop and deepen a well thought-out approach to integrating the mining industry into the overall economy of Ghana. This will require a clear vision on what the country seeks to do with its mineral resources. An integration of the value chain of mining into the economy will fortify the country not only against the unstable behaviour of global commodity prices but is also likely to generate more employment and higher income for the state. The call for beneficiation of the country's minerals has been made several times. Some industry experts have suggested that value addition through a large-scale refinery for gold is simply not feasible in Ghana due to insufficient infrastructure, including power, and inadequate quantities to sustain such a refinery in the country.[10] One way out is for the government to convert 5 percent of royalty receipts

---

10   Informal conversation with three mining beneficiation experts at suggests that the approximately four million ounces of gold produced annually by Ghana is not enough to set up a viable large-scale refinery especially given that it is cheaper

from minerals production into in-kind payment (in gold) to serve as the basis for the regular supply of gold to the jewellery industry.

However, given the significant leap in the country's attempt at bauxite beneficiation, including the establishment of the aluminium smelting company VALCO in the country's port city of Tema, Ghana should focus on eventually processing all its bauxite production in the country. The country's manganese production, which has historically been washed and shipped in raw form, could be processed at least into sinter before export.

The current efforts at integration (also known as 'local content') are based on Legislative Instrument LI. 217,3 which, while setting the right tone, appears to put the onus too heavily on operating companies for its success. The suggestion here is for a close multi-stakeholder responsibility, including the government, the donor agency and the industry. In particular, the government must have a clear strategy on assisting the capacity building of local entrepreneurs to effectively participate in the mining food chain. A special fund to support this initiative should be set up and should be funded by the key stakeholders mentioned earlier and with leadership from industry and government.

INEFFECTIVE INFRASTRUCTURE

An efficient rail transportation system is a *sine qua non* to effective bulk mineral production and haulage. The absence of an effective rail network has meant that bulk minerals such as bauxite and manganese have to be hauled by road. The country's only bauxite mine at Awaso in the northern part of the Western region presently hauls its bauxite over 240 km by road to the Takoradi port. This not only has a negative impact on the country's roads but also has serious safety and cost implications. Manganese production at Nsuta, although relatively nearer to the port of Takoradi, has to struggle with frequent breakdowns on the 60 km fragile remnant of the rail lines. Clearly, improvements in and modernization of the country's railway and port networks are an urgent imperative not only for the efficient operation of existing mines but also for development of the Ghana's iron ore potential.

Conclusions

This chapter has discussed a range of issues that affect Ghana's ability to effectively harness the benefits of its natural resource extraction for national development. We have discussed the question of the extent to which Ghana benefits from the extraction of its mineral resources. Based on the available data, literature and the author's own experience in the field, the chapter has underscored the significant contribution made by the mining sector to the broader economy of Ghana over the years. This position is supported by the ranking of Ghana among the highest 20 percent in the global Mining Contribution Index (ICMM, 2012). It could even be said that Ghana's recent rapid move into the lower middle income category of countries has largely been propelled by mining and other extractive industries.

It is however true that the country faces the challenge of ensuring that a sufficient revenue stream from natural resource extraction is devoted to creating visible benefits such as the delivery of healthcare, infrastructure and opportunities for the people in communities where mining takes place. In the present scheme of things, benefits from the mining sector seem to be overly skewed

---

to refine in South Africa and Britain. Some argue that a minimum sustainable quantity of 7 million ounces of gold will be required annually.

to the central economy, often causing people to believe that the industry has not benefited the country as a whole.

The historical over-concentration on rents and taxes from mineral extraction, especially at the production stage of mining has not led to sufficient benefit extraction from the activity. An integration of the value chain of mining into the economy is important to fortify the country against the unstable behaviour of global commodity prices and also to generate more employment and higher income for the state. The appreciation of the benefits of mining in the country should not be restricted only to the actual production stage, but must also be broadened to include the entire life-cycle exploration, construction, operation, closure and post-closure as proposed by the ICMM (2012).

In this way, the full picture of the contribution by the industry could be better appreciated. Similarly, given that only five of the country's mineral reserves have been mined commercially over the years, compared to hundreds in South Africa, for example, the chapter underscores the imperative not only for the diversification into other minerals, including industrial minerals such as kaolin, limestone and dimension stone, but also for managing the seemingly exaggerated expectations of how Ghana's mineral exploitations can carry the burden of development.

References

Acquah, P. (1995). Natural resources management and sustainable development: The case of the gold sector of Ghana. United Nations Conference on Trade and Development (UNCTAD).

Addy, S.N. (1998). Revival of the mining sector. *Resources Policy*, 24(4), pp. 229–39.

Africa Practice. (2013). *Ghana's Mining Sector Stakeholder Perception Study*. Ghana Chamber of Mines.

Africa Union Commission and United Nations Economic Commission for Africa (2009). *Africa Mining Vision*. Addis Ababa: AUC-UNECA

Akabzaa, T. (2001). Boom and dislocation: The environmental and social impacts of mining in the Wassa West district of Ghana. *Third World Network Africa*, December.

Akabzaa, T. and Darimani, A. (2001). Impact of the mining sector investment in Ghana: A study of the Tarkwa mining region. *Structural Adjustment Participatory Review International* (SAPRI) Network.

Aubynn, A. (1997a). Liberalism and economic adjustment in resource frontiers: Land-based resource alienation and local responses: Reflections from Western Ghana. Working Paper, Institute of Development Studies, University of Helsinki.

———. (1997b). Economic restructuring dynamics and environmental problems in Africa: Empirical examples from the forestry and mining sectors of Ghana. Institute of Advanced Studies UNU.

Ayee, J., Soreide, T., Shukla, G.P. and Minh Le, T. (2011). Political economy of the mining sector in Ghana. Working Paper, World Bank.

Aryee, B.N. (2001). Ghana's mining sector: Its contribution to the national economy. *Resources Policy*, 27, pp. 61–75.

———. (2014). Strengthening the impact of the mining sector on development: Supporting more Ghanaian mining companies to push the industrialisation and structural transformation agenda. A presentation by Minerals Commission at the National Policy Dialogue on Economy-wide Consequences of Ghana's Dependence on Minerals. *Third World Network Africa*, March.

Auty, R.M. (1993). *Sustaining Development in Mineral Economies: The Resource Curse Thesis*. New York: Routledge.

———. (1998). *Resource Abundance and Economic Development*. Helsinki: WIDER.

———. (2000). How natural resources affect economic development. *Development Policy Review*, 18, pp. 347–64.

Auty, R.M. and Mikesell, R.F. (1998). *Sustainable Development in Mineral Economies*. Oxford: Clarendon Press.

Bank of Ghana (2001). *Bank of Ghana Annual Report 2000*.

Barning, K. (1990). A review of mineral exploitation activities in Ghana 1984–1990. In K. Barning (ed.), *Symposium of Gold Exploitation in the Tropical Rainforest Belt of Southern Ghana.* Accra: Minerals Commission.

Brinkerhoff, D. and Goldsmith, A. (1992). Promoting the sustainability of development institutions. A framework for strategy. *World Development*, 20(3), pp. 369–83.

Brunschweiler, C. and Bulte, E. (2008). Linking natural resources to slow growth and more conflict. *Policy Forum, Science* (www.sciencemag.org), 320, 2 May.

Burda, M.C. and Wyplosz, C. (1997). *Macroeconomics: A European Text.* New York: Oxford University Press.

Collier, P. and Hoeffler, A. (2005). Resource rents, governance and conflict. *Journal of Conflict Resolutions*, 49(4), 625–33.

Davis, G.A. (1995). Learning to love the Dutch Disease: Evidence from the minerals economies. *World Development*, 23(10), pp. 1765–79.

——. (1998). The mineral sector, sectoral analysis, and economic development. *Resources Policy*, 24(4), pp. 217–28.

——. (2011). The resource drag. *International Economics and Economic Policy*, 8, pp. 155–76.

De Paula, S. and Dymski, G. (2005). *Reimagining Growth: Towards a Renewal of Development Theory.* London: Zed Books.

Dumett, R. (1999). *El Dorado in West Africa: The Gold Mining Frontier, African Labour and Colonial Capitalism in the Gold Coast, 1875–1900.* Athens, OH: Ohio University Press.

Elkington, J. (1994). Towards the sustainable corporation: Win-win business strategies for sustainable development. *California Management Review*, 36(2), pp. 90–100.

Engberg-Pedersen, P., Gibbon, P., Raikes, P. and Udsholt, L. (eds) (1996). *Limits of Adjustment in Africa.* Copenhagen and Oxford: Centre for Development Research.

Ewusi, K. (1987). *The Impact of Structural Adjustment Programme in a Developing Country: The Case of Ghana's Experience.* Tema: Ghana Publishing Corp.

Ghana Chamber of Mines (1998). The impact of mining on local economy. Annual report of the Chamber Mines, Accra, Ghana.

——. (2001). Annual report of the Chamber Mines, Accra.

——. (2012). Annual report of the Chamber Mines, Accra.

Ghana Geological Survey (2011). Annual report.

Ghana Minerals Commission (2012). The role of the Minerals Commission in positioning mining as a catalyst for development. A presentation at the Ghana Chamber of Mines Mining for Development Forum. Movenpick Ambassador Hotel, 17 May.

Ghana Statistical Service (GSS) (2005) Ghana in figures, Accra.

——. (2008) Ghana in figures, Accra.

Gill, M., Perkins, D., Roemer, M. and Snodgrass, D. (1992). *Economics of Development*, 3rd edn. New York: W.W. Norton and Company.

GLSS (1989). *Ghana Living Standard Survey.* Accra: Statistical Service.

Government of Ghana (2012). *Budget Statement and Economic Policy of the Government of Ghana for the 2012 Financial Year.*

——. (2013). *Public Expenditure and Financial Accountability (PEFA) Performance Review.* Final Report, ECORYS, June.

Graham, R. (1982). *The Aluminium Industry and the Third World: Multinational Corporations and Underdevelopment.* London: Zed Books.

Guimaraes, R.P. (1976). *The Ecopolitics of Development in the Third World: Politics and Environment in Brazil.* Boulder, CO: Lynne Reinner Publishers.

Ham, C. and Hill, M. (1993). *The Policy Process in the Modern Capitalist State.* New York: Harvester Wheatsheaf.

Hutchful, E. (1996). Structural adjustment in Ghana 1983–1994. In P. Engberg-Pedersen, P. Gibbon, P. Raikes and L. Udsholt (eds), *Limits of Adjustment in Africa.* Copenhagen and Oxford: Centre for Development Research.

ICMM (2012). The role of mining in national economies. October.

Institute of Statistical and Social Research (ISSER) (1996–2010). The state of Ghana's economy. University of Ghana.

Kesse, G.O. (1985). The mineral and rock resources of Ghana. *Journal of African Earth Sciences*, 7, pp. 601–10.

Lall, S. (1995). Structural adjustment and African industry. *World Development*, 23(12), pp. 2019–31.

Leith, J. (1996). *Ghana: Structural Adjustment Experience*. San Francisco: International Centre for Economic Growth.

Leith, J. and Lofchie, M. (1993). The political economy of structural adjustment in Ghana. In H. Bates and A. Krueger (eds), *Political and Economic Interaction in Economic Policy Reform. Evidence from Eight Countries*. Oxford: Blackwell.

Mills, G. (2010). *Why Africa is Poor and What Africans Can Do about It*. Johannesburg: Penguin Books South Africa.

Minerals Commission (2013). *Minerals Commission 2012 Annual Report*.

O'Fairchealaigh, C. (2010). Mining company contractual agreements in Australia and Canada: Implications for political autonomy and common development. *Canadian Journal of Development Studies*, XXX (1–2), pp. 69–86.

Ousman, G., Mutambatsere, E. and Ndiaye, G. (2012). Gold mining in Africa: Maximizing economic returns for countries' Working Paper Series, African Development Bank No. 147, March.

Porter, M.E. and Kramer, M.R. (2011). Creating shared value: How to reinvent capitalism and unleash a wave of innovation and growth. *Harvard Business Review*, 89(1–2), pp. 62–77.

Roberts, G. (1991). *A New Dictionary of Political Analysis*. New York: Routledge, Chapman and Hall Inc.

Roe, A. and Samuel, J. (2007). *The Challenge of Mineral Wealth: Using Resource Endowments to Foster Sustainable Development*. London: ICMM.

Rybczynski, T.M. (1995). Factor endowment and relative commodity prices. *Economica*, 22(88), pp. 336–41.

Sachs, J. and Warner, A.M. (1997). Natural resource abundance and economic growth. Centre for International Development and Harvard Institute for International Development, Harvard University, Cambridge MA, November.

Seers, D. (1969). The meaning of development. IDS Communication 44, Institute of Development Studies.

Slack, K. (2010). The role of mining in the economies of developing countries: Time for a new approach. In J. Richards (ed.), *Mining, Society, and a Sustainable World*. London: Springer.

Tabatabai, H. (1989). Economic stabilization and structural adjustment in Ghana, 1983–86. *Labour and Society*, 11(2), pp. 390–425.

Tsikata, F.S. (1997). The vicissitudes of mineral policy in Ghana. *Resource Policy*, 23(1–2), pp. 9–14.

United Nations Economic Commission for Africa. Minerals and Africa's Development (2011). *The International Study Group Report on Africa's Mineral Regimes Africa*. Addis Ababa: Economic Commission for Africa.

Walde, T. (1983). Permanent sovereignty over natural resources: Recent developments in the minerals sector. *Natural Resources Forum*, United Nations, New York, July.

Warhurst, A. and Bridge, G. (1997). Economic liberalisation, innovation and technology transfer: Opportunities for cleaner production in the minerals industry. *Natural Resources Forum*, 21(1), pp. 1–12.

WCED (1987). *Our Common Future*. Oxford: Oxford University Press.

World Bank (1988). *World Development Report*. Washington DC.

Wright, G. and Czelusta, J. (2007). Resource-based growth, past and present. In D. Lederman and W.F. Maloney (eds), *Natural Resources: Neither a Curse nor Destiny*. Washington DC/Palo Alto: World Bank/Stanford University Press.

PART V
SCIENCE, TECHNOLOGY
AND INFRASTRUCTURE

13

The Role of Science, Technology and Innovative Industries in National Development

Samuel Nii Odai

Abstract

Science, technology and innovation form a group of key related inputs that play a significant role in achieving national development and are part of a cocktail of essential strategies. Certainly, there are many other factors that affect national development and several metrics for describing what national development means. Generally the level of national development is discussed qualitatively in terms of the level of industrialization and quantitatively in terms of gross domestic product (GDP). The Asian Tigers provide relevant learning experiences worth considering and emulating by other developing countries. As a typical poor agrarian country through the 1950s, South Korea's example as a country with little or no natural resources, suffering many atrocities and yet emerging as an economic superpower within four decades is extremely impressive. The country started developing and implementing national strategic policies, which were based on technologies and innovations. South Korea had only two public institutions dealing with scientific research and technological development at the turn of the 1960s. Despite this limitation, the country managed to expand its educational system to create a profoundly literate society and highly skilled labour force, and a strong research and development culture to support its quest for the creation of a new system of economic growth based on technologies and innovations.

Introduction

Science, technology and innovation (STI) have always been at the centre of almost every human development. They have contributed to all areas of modern civilization, namely, aerospace, agriculture, biomedicine and telecommunications to mention just a few. In the twenty-first century, STI has acceptably become synonymous with modern developments. The World Bank (2010) notes that 'innovation in all its forms, particularly technological innovation, has become a crucial driver of growth, enhancing competitiveness and increasing social well-being in all economies of the world'. It is thus not surprising that almost every nation propounds the application of STI for the development of their economies and subsequently their communities. Questions that deserve some attention are as follows: 'when did STI actually come into existence?' and 'are they modern terminologies created in the twentieth century or have they evolved in the last few centuries?'

In fact, history (Egbogah, 2012) makes us aware that technology has always been at the heart of human existence and that man has always used appropriate means to confront his daily challenges through the application of appropriate 'technology'. Man, throughout history, has dealt with newer and more complex issues by adopting new measures – that is, innovation. In discussing innovation, our ancestors of generations past knew that 'doing the same things in the same ways leads to the same results' – that is, lack of innovation.

Man, in the prehistoric ages, is known to have applied appropriate 'technology' to 'conquer' nature and to preserve the human race. Even though modern man considers most of the apparatus available to man in the prehistoric ages as archaic and crude, these types of apparatus really helped man to overcome his immediate environment and the forces of nature, thus enabling him to perpetuate the human race and to build more stable societies. This is because the inherent survival instinct in man continuously gives birth to new ways of doing things – innovations.

Science, on the other hand, which provides the theoretical and evidential explanation of the types of matter available for use, why they can be used, when they break down or the laws and conditions under which they work optimally, also continues to evolve and hence gives answers to many questions relating to technological developments.

Modern history considers the second half of the twentieth century to be the period of the emergence of tremendous modern technologies and innovations. The growth of modern technologies and innovations has been sustained in even greater proportions in the twenty-first century. The period from the second half of the twentieth century was critical in the history of the nations of the world. This is because the Second World War had just ended and the United Nations had also come into existence, with many nations picking up the pieces left after the Second World War and devising means to come out of extreme poverty and hardship. Another historical landmark of the same period is the liberation from colonial powers and the self-realization of several states in the Third World – especially Africa and South-East Asia. The emergence of modern technologies and innovations coincided more sequentially with this period. There was also the point of departure when the gap between the economies of Asian countries and Sub-Saharan African countries started diverging, with the Asians giving birth to the 'Asian Economic Miracles'. Singapore, Taiwan, South Korea and Malaysia have most often been cited as examples of such countries.

Many historians and scientists alike have contributed to the discourse in trying to explain the bases for the birth of the 'economic miracle' in Asia. This chapter will focus mainly on the South Korean story and will raise a few examples of other nations. History tells us that South Korea is a country with a dearth of natural resources, which also suffered several atrocities as a result of the Japanese occupation and the Korean War. It is reported that by the end of the Korean War in 1953, the GDP per capita of the country stood at US$67. However, through the Korean government's 'outward-looking development strategy', well-educated and well-disciplined work force, and technological innovation, GDP jumped to US$20,050 in 2007, confirming the birth of the 'Korean Economic Miracle' (Suh and Chen, 2007; Chung, 2011).

South Korea and the South-East Asian countries are typical examples of nations that have been transformed through technological innovations. Most have managed to build strong economies and have transformed their communities through prudent technological innovative policies.

Singapore is one such country that moved from a GDP of US$400 in 1959 to nearly US$30,000 by the year 2000 (Lee, 2000). Interestingly, South Korea is also known to have had very similar GDP figures to the West African country of Ghana at the turn of the 1960s. However, through strategic and sustained investments in education, STI policies, research and development (R&D), and the implementation of technological innovative policies, South Korea has grown its economy from about US$80 in 1960 to nearly US$26,000 by 2013 (Chung, 2011; World Bank, 2014a).

This chapter explores the key historical lessons which contributed to this strong growth. It considers four main sections, namely, STI personalities, STI processes, STI industries and STI progress. The section on STI personalities raises a series of discussions on the groups of people and institutions needed to build a sustainable STI system. The section on STI processes explores the necessary ingredients and structures needed to create a conducive environment for receiving, developing, using and commercializing STIs. The section on STI industries examines the technological and innovative industries that manufacture the technology or that use technology to manufacture, as well as their impact on the economic transformational process. The final major section on STI progress is intended to provide a way forward in terms of how the lessons learnt can help transform national economies using STI. Throughout this chapter, the interplay between the personalities and the other sections will be pronounced because the personalities are the carriers and leaders of activities in the processes and progress phases of STIs for development.

STI Personality

An STI personality is a key person or institution that plays a key role in developing 'technology vision', leading the way in policy development and recommending STI strategies for national development. In developing STIs, personalities are keenly involved in assessing national developmental demands and eventually international trends and demands. When this process is strategically undertaken with the government's support, it lays the necessary foundation for strong industrialization and economic development.

The World Bank (2010), in describing the role of governments as technology personalities, notes that 'governments have traditionally played an important role in promoting technology, sometimes by directly supporting the development of technologies (in space, defence, and the like) or more indirectly by creating a climate favourable to innovation through various incentives or laws'. This statement by the World Bank summarizes the case of South Korea, as will be discussed in later sections: the government consciously made the initial investments, developed the necessary policies and strategies, and created a conducive environment for innovative industries to flourish.

The 'economic miracle' of Asia was not an accident, but rather was as a result of conscious national developmental strategies, some of which are discussed in the sections below. Dr Henry A. Kissinger, a former US Secretary of State, in his foreword to the book *From Third World to First World* by Lee Kuan Yew, stated: 'the institutions of the West developed gradually while those of most new states were put into place in elaborated form immediately. In the West, a civil society evolved side-by-side with the maturation of the modern state' (Lee, 2000). This suggests that modern economies can be consciously put in place within a short period by harnessing technological innovation. This conscious fast national development is the example of the 'Asian Economic Miracles' that are discussed in this chapter.

TECHNOLOGY VISION

Every nation aspiring to make meaningful progress in sustainable development must have a clear vision of the innovative technology needed or desired for this purpose. This can be possible and best sustained when there is a technology vision bearer. Such a person or institution usually 'carries' the vision, works with a group and sees to the development and implementation of such a technological innovative strategy. A technology vision bearer has the aim of moving a set of systems from one level to another. The vision bearer identifies gaps that need addressing and then helps the nation to keep pace with the identified technology or go into technology commercialization for wealth creation. In the case of South Korea, the country needed to come out of poverty and develop. Thus, through its government machinery, it launched its First Five-Year Economic Development Plan in 1962, followed by subsequent plans, which created extremely high demand for new technologies (Chung, 2011). This marked the birth of a new way of creating wealth for an originally poor agrarian nation.

Kissinger in Lee (2000) describes the role of Lee Kuan Yew in the national development of Singapore: 'Every great achievement is a dream before it becomes reality, and his vision was of a state that would not simply survive but prevail by excelling. Superior intelligence, discipline, and ingenuity would substitute for resources.' Kissinger clearly dispels any doubt about the role of personalities in national development. Like South Korea, Singapore had no natural resources to serve as 'natural collateral' for its development, but instead depended heavily on vision, superior intelligence, discipline and ingenuity. Under the visionary leadership of Lee Kuan Yew, Singapore refused to become a client state of its more powerful and resource-rich neighbouring nations, and through the prudent implementation of strategic policies transformed the nation into a rich economy.

In the case of South Korea, government is acknowledged as the major personality for bearing the STI vision and hence developing policies to give life to the vision. The government of South Korea in 1962 started with a focus on light industries, manufacturing items such as shoes, textiles and bicycles, with a gradual shift towards more sophisticated commodities in 1967, following the First Five-Year Economic Development Plan in 1962. This was followed by several other government policies, eventually leading the nation out of poverty and becoming a global high-tech hub.

STI-SUPPORTING AGENCIES

It is necessary to mention that the personalities of STI (as used in this chapter) are not limited to persons, but include institutions and agencies championing the course of STI through the development of policies and the communication and implementation of the policies. In this context, a Ministry of Science, Technology and Innovation is a necessary organ in policy development and lobbying for the creation of the necessary environment for the development of STI. If a cabinet minister heads this ministry, it definitely goes a long way to help make STI a government priority, leading to the attraction of the necessary attention and funding. The existence of STI development agencies or STI commissions plays a tremendous role in operationalizing the policy and ensuring that the various components of STIs are fairly considered during implementation.

South Korea is a good example of a nation that has assigned specific bodies to oversee policy implementation and the development of technology and innovation. In 1967, the Science and Technology Promotion Act and the Science Education Act were enacted, forming the legal basis for the government's policies for science and technology development. The South Korean government established the Korea Institute of Science and Technology (KIST) in the same year. The KIST is broadly considered to be the first organization in Korea for R&D. The Ministry of Science and Technology (MOST) was created the following year to be responsible for science and technology policy. The Act establishing the Korea Advanced Institute of Sciences was enacted in 1970, and this paved the way for the founding of the Korea Advanced Institute of Sciences (KAIS, currently KAIST). The KAIS is known to be the first Korean institution to have introduced the US-graduate education system into Korea. The government, in a bid to provide leadership in R&D, established various Government-supported Research Institutes (GRIs) in the 1970s to assist industries in absorbing and adapting technologies. This conscious comprehensive arrangement suggests that in order for countries to actualize their STI vision, they need to do more than put in place appropriate policies by moving on to establish public and private supporting institutions that help to create new knowledge and facilitate the acquisition and dissemination of that knowledge (Chung, 2011).

Currently in South Korea, the National Science and Technology Council, and the Ministry of Science, ICT and Future Planning are overseeing the nation's Framework Act on Science and Technology. As discussed in an information note by the Hong Kong Legislative Council Secretariat (LCS), the Act mandates the South Korean government to develop plans for the science and technology sector every five years. It is interesting to note that South Korea released its latest basic plan in July 2013. This plan recommends using government funding to support domestic R&D projects. This is expected to raise South Korea's innovation capacity, create 640,000 new jobs and increase the contribution of basic science research to the growth of GDP over the next five years (LCS, 2014).

Following the successful start and setting-up of the appropriate environment for the growth of STI in the 1960s, South Korea's industrial policy started shifting in the 1980s from technology learning to technology development (Chung, 2011). In addition, the government started focusing its efforts on promoting and facilitating private industrial R&D while allowing the private sector to take the lead in planning and financing. This strategy adopted by the South Korean government shows that, in order to ensure long-term sustainability, the private sector must play a major role.

As the technology vision bearer, the South Korean government initially financed 80 percent of R&D, while the business sector contributed only 20 percent. In addition, the government created an enabling environment by offering attractive incentives such as duty-free imports for research equipment and materials, and tax incentives to encourage the private sector to develop their technology by importing what they needed to make a more meaningful impact (Baek and Jones, 2005). All these initiatives did not make the desired impact until foreign companies started restricting technology licences to Korean companies because they were becoming their global competitors. It was around this time that Korean companies began to invest heavily in R&D, which then became important 'collateral' for their access to foreign technology (Kim, 1997). Interestingly, by 2004, the financing ratio for R&D had been reversed, with almost 80 percent from the private sector and 20 percent from the public sector. The lesson for developing countries is that governments should be the main initial financier and performer of R&D because the private sector is usually less well endowed financially. This was the case in South Korea, but with the efforts of the government and other STI personalities, prudent policies were implemented, leading to the reversal of the roles.

STI Processes

STI processes are about the putting together of the various ingredients needed for the comprehensive development of STI for national development. The processes include formal education, R&D, technology transfer, etc., which form the cocktail of necessary activities for sustainable harnessing of STI potential for national development.

As mentioned earlier, South Korea lacks natural resources; however, through effective human skills development, hard work and dedication, the country is now the fourteenth richest nation in the world according to data released in July 2014 (World Bank, 2014b). To drive its people out of poverty and move the nation towards prosperity, South Korea has followed prudent economic policies, which underlie the success it enjoys. Since 1962, it has dynamically developed the human skills needed to propel the economy by injecting massive capital into establishing more universities and creating the enabling environment for private sector participation in the delivery of higher education. In particular, the heavy investment in science and technology to promote STI-driven industrial development has paid off.

As discussed previously, South Korea had its first policy in 1962 towards strategic national development, and by 2007 the outcome had already become overwhelmingly evident. As recent as the 1980s, apparel was the top export commodity from South Korea, with semiconductors occupying the ninth position and automobiles missing from the top 10 items. Following positive strategic policies coupled with short- to long-term goals, by the year 2000, semiconductors and automobiles occupied the top two positions, respectively, in exports from South Korea. By 2007, it had become automobiles first and semiconductors second. Education in all its forms is a necessary ingredient for this endeavour (Chung, 2011).

GENERATING INTEREST IN STI

The process of creating a modern STI environment should start with consciously engaging young brains from the basic and high schools in science and mathematics. It is important that governments create and sustain appropriate environments in their nations for the study and appreciation of science. Since science is not an abstract subject, it requires equipped laboratories for hands-on experience. This is a sure way of creating interest in young minds. Well-resourced zoos are great opportunities for young people to admire nature and develop the necessary interest in it. It is at the zoos that children learn another dimension of nature and appreciate the world in a broader sense. Next to well-resourced zoos, science and specialized museums are very good avenues for young minds to be engaged in appreciating and learning about science and technology. Educational documentaries can create remarkable levels of interest and awareness in STIs. These triggers are necessary to generate the necessary level of sustained interest in science as an area of study and research in the formative years of young people.

Most often, society does not take advantage of creating the necessary interest in STIs in young minds. There are generally delays in interest generation until the youth enters university, at which stage the level of curiosity in STIs has almost waned and the focus is on passing exams. Definitely, more advocacies by STI personalities and governments would go a long way towards creating and sustaining this interest.

BUILDING A STRONGER BACKBONE FOR STIS

After generating the necessary interest in STIs, the necessary backbone for sustaining STIs in a nation is a well-planned and endowed higher education system, which serves as the cradle of knowledge generation and dissemination. A higher education system where the focus is not mainly on undergraduate teaching but on postgraduate research is desirable in this quest. This serves as the STI knowledge generation point that supports the government agenda for national development. Thus, dedicated postgraduate training with a focus on building the desirable human resource capacity to develop, manage and maintain STI systems is the backbone to depending on

STIs for national development. The steady supply of these groups, including a maintenance arm, by well-endowed educational institutions is critical. It is necessary to establish in this discussion the importance of having a critical mass in place for the proper functioning of any STI venture before any meaningful lasting progress can be made in STIs for development. In 1945, when it was liberated from Japanese rule, South Korea had only one national university. However, between 1951 and 1953, seven national universities were established, so South Korea does not have very old universities like those in other developed cultures. Counting progress made by South Korea as at 2004 indicates the nation had 411 higher educational institutions (made up of 61 public and 350 private), with a total student enrolment of 3.5 million (Pillay, 2010). Several of these institutions are technology-based, while some are specifically corporate universities. These institutions form the foundation of the technological innovations in the Asian economic powerhouse. There is no doubt that South Korea has successfully transformed itself into one of the most dynamic technological and innovative economies in the world and it is ranked first in the 2014 Global Innovation Index (Bloomberg, 2014).

A primary difference between South Korea and Sub-Saharan Africa countries is the relevance of the tertiary education provided. Employers in Nigeria and Ghana lamented a 'total lack of practical skills among technology graduates' (World Bank, 2010). It has also been reported that there is a shortage of highly skilled labour for innovation prevailing throughout the developing countries from Africa (World Bank, 2009). According to the World Bank, this then makes it difficult for industries to depend on locally graduating students for technology positions, and this is a major bottleneck in providing the highly skilled labour required by industry for industrial development. For many developing countries in Sub-Saharan Africa and Asia, traditional apprenticeship training by the informal sector is responsible for more skills development than all other types of training combined (Adams, 2008); for example, according to Atchoarena and Delluc (2001), 80–90 percent of all basic skills training comes from traditional or informal apprenticeship in Ghana. South Korea, on the other hand, managed to reduce the illiteracy rate from 10.6 percent in 1970 to 0 percent by 1980 so as to ensure the raising of a well-informed labour force and general citizenry (Naim, 2001). This has been the foundation of its success.

A critical need in Sub-Saharan African countries is closer collaboration between local industries and tertiary institutions for the provision of placements for the training of students to develop that highly skilled labour required by industry. This is because technologically innovative industries depend more on skilled labour that has gone through formal education than on apprenticeship. Therefore, more collaboration with industry in the formal education establishment is necessary to provide the necessary support in the training of Ghana's human resources.

RESEARCH AND DEVELOPMENT IN STI

Investing in that critical backbone of dedicated higher education with emphases on postgraduate training and research is the starting point in STI R&D. It is a fact that the strength of STI R&D of a nation is equal to the strength of STI practice in that nation. R&D is the real foundation of almost every innovation in technological advancement in modern industrialization and civilization. It is in these R&D units that R&D is carried out, leading to actual production. R&D units have become integral parts of most industries since the second half of the twentieth century. This unit has become the nerve centre where technologies are developed and prototypes are built and tested. Without R&D units, the percentage of recalls in technology products delivered to consumers will be extremely high, so this unit is not a luxury, but the necessary 'womb' for STI development. In modern industrial practice, all top industries that develop the great technologies for domestic and industrial use have very advanced R&D units.

Science and incubating parks have come to stay, and they serve as another wing of STI processes. Provision of technology parks, business incubators, technology transfer centres, etc. support the commercialization of essential knowledge. Silicon Valley in California in the USA is a testimony to this development. Other countries have also followed suit, with tremendous outcomes, as shown in the software industry in Mumbai, India. In fact, providing the necessary support for innovation is at the root of the creativity needed in STI developments.

The government of South Korea created GRIs in the 1970s to help industries adopt new technologies. These GRIs have been at the forefront of R&D and are recognized for two major impacts: they assisted industries in acquiring new technologies and they contributed to the building of local R&D capability by bringing back many established scientists and engineers from abroad. It was a time of great opportunity for native Koreans to return home and help build their country. This meant that Western experience and technology were transported into Korea with the arrival of this cohort. This contributed to the boom of STI growth. These GRIs have been the source of most of the STI knowledge available in South Korea and have contributed to the telecommunications, machinery, chemicals, metals, electronics and energy industries (Kim, 1997). The GRIs also worked strongly with private industries in building the necessary technological foundation for the industrial development of South Korea. These investments in education and R&D have had a positive effect on knowledge accumulation and a positive impact on employees' productivity (Cardoza, 1997). Significant progress was made in R&D such that there was a sharp increase in the R&D expenditure of private firms from $3.36 billion in 1990 to $8.95 billion in 1995, accounting for almost 81 percent of the total R&D expenditure, while the number of private R&D organizations grew from one in 1970 to 2,270 in 1995 (Naim, 2001). South Korea alone had five companies out of the Top 10 R&D Companies from Developing and Emerging Economies in 2007, followed by Brazil with two and then China, Russia and Taiwan with one each (see Table 13.1). In the same group, Samsung had the highest R&D expenditure of over US$6.5 billion in 2007, as shown in Table 13.1 (World Bank, 2010).

Table 13.1   Top 10 R&D Companies from Developing and Emerging Economies (2007)

SN	Company	Country	Industry	R&D expenditure (US$ millions)
1	Samsung (9)	South Korea	Computing, electronics	6,536
2	Hyundai Motor (62)	South Korea	Auto	1,197
3	LG Corporation (63)	South Korea	Other	1,952
4	Petrobras (117)	Brazil	Chemicals, energy	879
5	Cia Vale do Rio Doce (140)	Brazil	Minerals	717
6	Petrochina (142)	China	Chemicals, energy	699
7	Kia Motors (148)	South Korea	Auto	649
8	Korea Electric Power (149)	South Korea	Other	649
9	Hynix Semiconductor (150)	Taiwan	Computing, electronics	635
10	Gazprom (159)	Russian Federation	Chemicals, energy	605

Source: Jaruzelski and Dehoff (2008).
Note: The figure in parentheses is the position among the global 1,000.

South Korea's strategic investments in R&D from the 1960s have yielded significant outputs in terms of the number of patents registered over the years. In 2013, South Korea was fourth only to the USA, Japan and Germany in terms of the number of patents registered by the US Patent and Trademark Office. This performance bears witness to the great investment made by the South Korean government and business sector in R&D (see Table 13.2).

Table 13.2   Number of Patents Granted by the US Patent and Trademark Office (2013)

SN	Country	Number
1	USA	**147,666**
2	Japan	54,170
3	Germany	16,605
4	Korea Republic	15,745
5	Taiwan	12,118
6	Canada	7,272
7	China	6,597
8	France	6,555
9	UK	6,551
10	Israel	3,152

Source: US Patent and Trademark Office, available at http://www.uspto.gov/web/offices/ac/ido/oeip/taf/cst_all.htm.

It is important to mention that universities also play a key role in the R&D processes by, first, supplying the trained scientists and engineers needed for the R&D sector and, second, undertaking R&D themselves in their research laboratories. Therefore, the quantity and quality of universities in developing countries directly influence domestic R&D and subsequently STIs for national development. The world ranking of universities gives some indication of the quality of universities and consequently national R&D strength. With all the investment it has made into education, South Korea is reaping the benefits, being ranked nineteenth globally, with its universities making up 1.6 percent and 1.8 percent of the top 100 and the top 500, respectively (World Bank, 2010).

South Korea's investments in STI R&D have made great impact in raising STIs to an internationally competitive level. This is evidenced by the profound increase in the number of scientific publications in internationally recognized academic journals. The Science Citation Index shows that the country's contributions to scientific publications increased to 25,494 in 2007 from an insignificant 171 in 1980. No doubt, the country was the twelfth largest producer of scientific publications in the world in 2007 (Chung, 2011).

TECHNOLOGY ACQUISITION

In the whole cycle of technology development and consumption, technology acquisition and transfer are critical, and these require a clear goal and, more especially, personality receivers. Technology acquisition is generally preceded by appropriate STI policy and strategy, technology identification and selection for purpose. Typically, technology acquisition may occur in one of two ways: through partnerships or procurement. Technology procurement may involve the outright purchase of technology for use, while partnerships usually involve working together with the technology provider for a period of time until the receiving personalities or institutions have successfully acquired the technology.

For sustainability purposes, modern technology acquisition always has built into it a technology transfer component. This includes a conscious arrangement to have technology suppliers and recipients working together in the process (Kim, 1997) because sustainable technology transfer is not vacuum-friendly. This requires the existence of arrangements with identified people and institutions to receive the technology and to also become the repository and channels for the consumption, production and maintenance of the technology locally. Without this arrangement, most technology acquisitions will fail with the departure of the original developers and providers of the technology. In the case of South Korea, following the initial policy of 1962, it adopted a strategy of importing and adapting foreign technology, as will be described in the section below.

It is important to mention that as far as possible, the option of partnerships is a more sustainable acquisition process than outright acquisition when dealing with heavy industrial or new technology. This is where the whole STI processes, including education, R&D and science parks, are recognized as vital.

STI Industries

The government of South Korea in 1973 selected six strategic industries – chemicals, electronics, machinery, non-ferrous metals, shipbuilding and steel – for focus and development. Along with this strategy, the government also decided to expand the GRI system to establish more GRIs to support the STI industry (Shin et al., 2012). This has yielded profound results in the STI industry in the country.

The STI industries in Korea are varied in terms of size and products, as indicated above. The South Korean STI industry has grown enormously; by 2005, South Korea had 24 companies among the Global 1000 companies and was second only to Taiwan among developing economies (see Table 13.3). The country has expanded and diversified its STI industry into automobiles, chemicals, electronics, energy, industrials, shipbuilding, software, telecoms, etc. The prudent implementation of STI policies from 1962 onwards has resulted in the building of such a strong STI industrial nation. As discussed earlier, this confirms that the point of departure from the Sub-Saharan African countries started from the 1960s when South Korea begun the implementation of such strategic policies.

Table 13.3   The Number of Developing Economy Companies among the Global 1000
in 2007

Rank	Country	Number	Industry
1	Taiwan	30	Computing and electronics, software, industrials
2	South Korea	24	Electronics, software, telecom, automobiles, chemicals, energy, industrials
3	China	10	Petrochemicals, automobiles, industrials
4	India	6	Automobiles, health, industrials, other
5	Israel	5	Software, health
6	Brazil	4	Natural resources, aerospace, power
7	Hong Kong, China	4	Consumer goods, industrials, chemicals, energy
8	Singapore	3	Computing, electronics
9	South Africa	2	Industrials, chemicals, energy
10	Hungary	1	Health
11	Russian Federation	1	Chemicals, energy
12	Slovenia	1	Health
13	Turkey	1	Other

Source: Jaruzelski and Dehoff (2008).

Samsung, the leading company in South Korea, has progressively grown to become a leading global company in terms of R&D expenditure and annual revenue. It spent a staggering US$10.4 billion in 2013 on R&D, leading to the company being ranked second in the top 20 R&D spenders and the third in the 10 most innovative companies globally in 2013 (Jaruzelski and Holman, 2014). The high-tech industrialization in South Korea is championed by a few major companies. These companies also make significant investments in R&D. As of 2011, the top five companies in R&D investments in the country were Samsung Electronics, LG Electronics, Hyundai Motors, Hynix and GM Daewoo Auto and Technology. It is reported that 20 of the largest companies accounted for 55.73 percent of the total manufacturing R&D, the top 10 companies 50.2 percent and the top five companies 44.3 percent. The case of electronic components is quite impressive, with the top 20 companies accounting for 91.4 percent (Chung, 2011). This confirms why most of these top companies in Korea also appear in the global 1,000.

Table 13.4 shows that currently, the 10 biggest companies of South Korea are made up of nine STI companies with only one financial company (CNBC, 2014). This is led by Samsung Electronics, which stands as the world's biggest technology firm by revenue, has currently overtaken all the big names in electronics and has become a household name in smartphones (the Galaxy family), LCD/LED technologies, etc.

Table 13.4   South Korea's 10 Biggest Companies

Rank	Company	Market capital (US$ billions)	Remarks
1	Samsung Electronics	165.2	World's biggest technology firm by revenue; listed company in South Korea. World's biggest maker of memory chips, smartphones and televisions. Founded in 1969
2	Hyundai Motor	49.8	World's fifth-biggest car maker, based on annual vehicle sales: top car maker in South Korea. Founded in 1967
3	POSCO	32.6	World's fourth-biggest steel maker. Founded in 1968 as a joint venture between the South Korean government and tools manufacturer TaeguTec
4	Kia Motors	29.2	South Korea's second-largest car maker and a subsidiary of the Hyundai Motor Group. Founded in 1944 as a manufacturer of steel tubing and bicycle parts, the company started producing vehicles in 1957
5	Hyundai Mobis	26.1	Subsidiary of the Hyundai Motor Group and the country's leading maker of auto parts. Founded in 1977 as Hyundai Precision Industry to produce containers; turned focus to autos and launched the Galloper brand vehicle in the 1990s
6	LG Chem	20	South Korea's largest chemical maker and one of the leading suppliers of car batteries. Founded in 1947 as Lucky Chemical Industrial and merged with LG Petrochemical in 2007
7	Hyundai Heavy Industries	19.8	World's largest shipbuilding company. Founded in 1947 as a construction business by Hyundai Group and moved into shipbuilding in the 1970s. By 1974, the company had built the world's largest shipyard
8	Samsung Life Insurance	18.8	The biggest life insurer in South Korea with about 26 percent of the local market share. Founded in 1957
9	Shinhan Financial Group	18.2	South Korea's largest banking firm and the only financial company to make the top 10 list. Founded in 2001 as a holding company for 11 subsidiaries
10	SK Hynix	16.4	Formerly known as Hynix Semiconductor Inc; the world's second largest memory chip maker. Founded in 1983 and changed its name to SK Hynix, after SK Telecom paid $2.98 billion for a 21 percent share in the firm

Source: CNBC (2014), available at http://www.cnbc.com/id/48237596#.

South Korea is enjoying amazing successes today because the First Five-Year Economic Development Plan of 1962 came with a big stimulus package to help grow the country's STI industries. The government announced an 'Automobile Industry Promotion Policy' and the Automobile Industry Protection Act. This Act created the legal bases for protecting the automobile industry. This was done mainly to create favourable conditions for the growth of the local automotive industry by legislating that foreign automobile companies could only operate in the country through joint ventures with local industries. This spurred the industry towards quick growth by benefiting mainly from the involvement of Japanese car makers and to some extent from their US counterparts.

In 1962, following the Automobile Industry Protection Act, most of the co-operation between South Korean companies and their international partners started as joint ventures. All these ventures were only in relation to assembling, with the parts being imported from their international partners. Chronologically, Toyota started collaboration with the predecessor of the now General Motors Korea in 1960 through a technical licensing agreement. But Toyota withdrew in 1970, paving the way for General Motors to come in. The predecessor of Kia Motors (although it had started initially in 1957) was established in 1962 through a joint venture with Mazda of Japan in 1964 in assembling cars; the predecessor of SsangYong was also established in 1962 through technical co-operation with the Nissan Motor Company of Japan, and the Hyundai Motor Company came in 1968 through technical co-operation with the US Ford Motor Company (Wikipedia, 2014).

These successful ventures and technology transfers provided the strong foundation for the take-off of the automobile industry. The Korean automobile industry now holds a prominent position in the national economy. As of 2005, it accounted for 8.9 percent of the total employees, 11.5 percent of the gross output, 10.2 percent of the value-added amount and 10.3 percent of the total export amount in Korea's manufacturing sector. Direct and indirect employment creation effects reached up to 1.57 million employees, accounting for 10.38 percent of the total employment. According to the Korean Automobile Manufacturers Association (KAMA), by 2012, the auto industry was ranked first in terms of employment, production and added value of the Korean manufacturing industry with shares of 10.7 percent, 11.4 percent and 10.6 percent, respectively (KAMA, 2013).

Currently, the Korean automobile industry is one of the largest in the world and is quickly becoming the fastest-growing one in the global markets (Lee, 2011). KAMA (2013) reports that, in 2012, Korea maintained its fifth place among automobile-producing countries in production with a 5.4 percent share of global production, following China, the USA, Japan and Germany (see Table 13.5). The industry posted its largest record in export volume of 3.171 million units, and export value (including auto parts) stood at U$71.8 billion in 2012. Hyundai Motors and Kia Motors are leaders in the automobile industry.

Table 13.5   The Global Top Five Countries in Vehicle Production

Ranking	2011			2012		
	Country	Production (units)	Share (%)	Country	Production (units)	Share (%)
1	China	18,418,876	22.8	China	19,271,808	22.8
2	USA	8,661,535	10.7	USA	10,331,619	12.2
3	Japan	8,398,630	10.4	Japan	9,942,711	11.7
4	Germany	6,311,318	7.8	Germany	5,649,269	6.7
5	South Korea	4,657,904	5.8	South Korea	4,557,738	5.4
Global total		80,732,000	100.0	Global total	84,702,000	100.0

Source: KAMA (2013).

Another equally important industry that is well developed and a global leader is the IT industry, which is made up of the semiconductors, LCD and electronics industry. History makes us aware that the year 1959 marked the beginning of Korea's electronics industry, when GoldStar (now LG Electronics) produced the first radio set under its own brand in Korea. This radio set was based on the Sanyo model (the Japanese electronics producer) with major components imported from West Germany. This was the beginning of the industry in the country as production was based on imitation of foreign technology. The Korean electronics industry has grown tremendously since then, with its companies accounting for very high shares in the global market (Suh, 2004).

The electronics industry of South Korea is a major player in the national economy. South Korea has now overtaken Japan as the world's leading producer of LCDs and can boast of Samsung and LG, which have made bold investments and are now the two leading companies in the global LCD market. The display industry creates high added-value industries and many jobs. Korea is a home to solid industrial foundation and companies including, Samsung Electronics and LG Electronics. With their global strength in LCD TVs and mobile devices, Korea can be said to be a major leader in STI industries (Invest Korea, 2014).

Apart from the LCD industry, the Korean semiconductor industry is a major leader in the national economy, exporting a record US$57 billion of products in 2013. Having grown its economy through strategic policy implementations, South Korea is currently the world's No. 1 producer of memories even though its semiconductor industry is ranked second globally, supplying 15.8 percent of the entire global semiconductor market as reported by Invest Korea for the year 2013 (2014).

The South Korean STI industry with its humble beginnings in the 1960s has progressively grown to become a global competitor. The industry has produced companies with international repute, like Samsung, LG, Hyundai and Kia, that are having a great impact on the national economy. These industries have benefited from focused leadership that consciously placed innovative industries on the national agenda and created a conducive environment for their growth. South Korea is indeed an example of a country that has developed its economy using science, technology and innovation.

STI PROGRESS

The section on STI progress has intended to look at the way forward by bringing all the historical examples considered, the lessons learnt and their implications, and then draw lessons from them. It is important to first of all emphasize that for a producer of technology, technological results provided for existing problems of consumers are usually in the form of products. And these technological products are exchanged for money. This alone could be motivation for countries seeking dependence on STIs for development to appreciate how providing innovative solutions to society can generate wealth. Two major ingredients are discussed in this section to sum up all the thoughts raised in the discussions in this chapter. The first major ingredient is the creation of the necessary enabling environment for flourishing STI industries. The necessary inputs for such an enabling environment include the STI personality constituting the technology visionary and the STI agent for leading the way in the development and implementation of appropriate policies, including low-interest loans, tax incentives and duty-free imports of selected capital goods. The Automobile Industry Protection Act used by the Koreans could be an appropriate tool to help build indigenous STI capacity and industries. The appropriate ministry of science and technology, and STI commissions and agencies should champion these strategies.

The second ingredient is the government championing STI processes, including the generation of interest among the youth, and the promotion of higher education and R&D for high-tech industries with the government being the main provider of direct financial support to public and non-profit institutes, universities and other educational institutions. Heavy investments in R&D and training are the necessary means towards ensuring that the highly skilled labour force with the requisite technological know-how is available to feed into the STI industry. Industries should endeavour to make a committed effort to take up the responsibility of creating opportunities for students-in-training to spend some time in their specific industries as part of their training.

The governments of developing countries should create the enabling environment necessary for local industries to flourish by building on the education and R&D features of the STI processes. STI policies for industrial development should consider the advantage of encouraging more ventures with local industries to ensure strong technology transfer to the local people. Governments must include tax incentives, duty waivers and concessions as an 'attraction package' in a bid to attract more international STI firms to their countries. It is definitely more strategic to develop gradually, having short- to medium-term developmental plans (e.g. five-year plans) to start with, such as the assembling of STI equipment. As in the case of South Korea, it started with light industries, manufacturing items such as shoes, textiles and bicycles, with a gradual shift towards more sophisticated commodities. This could be a good example to emulate.

STI is a sure way to create wealth and development in national economies. It needs strong government support in order to succeed. Sub-Saharan African governments can learn a lot from the experiences of South Korea and Singapore and should become more pragmatic in creating more 'do tanks' than 'think tanks' and 'talk tanks'.

References

Adams, A.V. (2008). Improving skills in the informal sector: Policies, providers, and outcomes. Presentation at the World Bank Labour Market Policy Course, 'Jobs for a Globalizing World', World Bank, Washington DC, 31 March–11 April.

Atchoarena, D. and Delluc, M.D. (2001). *Revisiting Technical and Vocational Education in Sub-Saharan Africa: An Update on Trends, Innovations, and Challenges.* IIEP/Prg.DA/01.320. Paris: International Institute for Educational Planning.

Baek, Y. and Jones, S.J. (2005). Sustaining high growth through innovation: Reforming the R&D and education system in Korea. OECD Economics Department Working Paper 470, OECD, Paris.

Bloomberg (2014). Most innovative in the world 2014: Countries. http://www.google.com/url?sa=t&rct=j&q=&esrc=s&source=web&cd=3&cad=rja&uact=8&ved=0CC4QFjAC&url=http%3A%2F%2Fimages.businessweek.com%2Fbloomberg%2Fpdfs%2Fmost_innovative_countries_2014_011714.pdf&ei=ChzBU5ysBoPfOLXogfgN&usg=AFQjCNEOgFzhmZBg1YhmSV9r16WdvFv9JA&sig2=mc15_hTA9pTX6tjxtAr2XA.

Cardoza, G. (1997). Learning, innovation and growth: A comparative policy approach to East Asia and Latin America. *Science and Public Policy*, 24(6), pp. 377–93.

Chung, S. (2011). Innovation, competitiveness, and growth: Korean experiences. Annual World Bank Conference on Development Economics 2010, International Bank for Reconstruction and Development.

CNBC (2014). South Korea's 10 biggest companies. http://www.cnbc.com/id/48237596#.

Egbogah, E.O. (2012). The role of science and technology in national development: The miracle of Malaysia and the future for Nigeria. *Petroleum Technology Journal*, 1(1), 1–12.

Invest Korea (2014). The industries that make Korea competitive. http://www.investkorea.org/ikwork/iko/eng/cont/contents.jsp?code=10202.

Jaruzelski, B. and Dehoff, K. (2008). Beyond borders: The Global Innovation 1000. *Strategy and Business*, 53 (Winter). http://www.strategy-business.com/article/08405.

Jaruzelski, B. and Holman, R. (2014). The top innovators and spenders. http://www.strategyand.pwc.com/global/home/what-we-think/global-innovation-1000/top-innovators-spenders#/tab-2013 [accessed 3 July 2014].

Jung, S.C. (2008). The Korean automobile industry's production network in China. In M. Ariff (ed.), *Analyses of Industrial Agglomeration, Production Networks and FDI Promotion, ERIA Research Project Report 2007–3*. China: IDE-JETRO, pp. 331–67.

KAMA (2013). *Annual Report 2013: Korean Automobile Industry*. Seoul: KAMA.

Kim, L. (1997). *Imitation to Innovation: The Dynamics of Korea's Technological Learning*. Cambridge, MA: Harvard Business School Press.

LCS (2014). Hong Kong Legislative Council Secretariat information note: Innovation and technology industry in South Korea, Israel and Belgium. http://search.legco.gov.hk/LegCoWeb/Search.aspx?lang=en&searchtype=simple&keyword=IN04 percent2F13–14.

Lee, C.Y. (2011). The rise of Korean automobile industry: Analysis and suggestions. *International Journal of Multidisciplinary Research*, 1(6), pp. 428–39.

Lee, K.Y. (2000). *From Third World to First. The Singapore Story: 1965–2000*. New York: HarperCollins.

Naim, S.T.K. (2001). Science and technology for industrialization. *Journal of Science for Development*, 7(1–2), pp. 59–75.

Pillay, P. (2010). Linking higher education and economic development: Implications for Africa from three successful systems. Centre for Higher Education Transformation, Wynberg, South Africa.

Shin, T., Hong, S. and Kang, J. (2012). Korea's strategy for development of STI capacity: A historical perspective: Policy reference 2012–01. Science and Technology Policy Institute.

Suh, J. (2004). The industrial competitiveness of Korea's IT industry. http://www.google.com/url?sa=t&rct=j&q=&esrc=s&source=web&cd=1&ved=0CBwQFjAA&url=http%3A%2F%2Ffaculty.washington.edu%2Fkaryiu%2Fconfer%2Fseoul04%2Fpapers%2FSuh.pdf&ei=iArDU9iXE8OuOanbgKgO&usg=AFQjCNGPO5NiKthzbtkED2Z2qqY4kdvnKw&sig2=36rYQd6He-HHjkQzRMu8Zw&bvm=bv.70810081,d.ZWU.

Suh, J. and Chen, D.H.C. (2007). Korea as a knowledge economy – Evolutionary process and lessons learned. Korea Development Institute and World Bank Institute.

US Patent and Trademark Office (2013). Patents by country, state, and year – All patent types. http://www.uspto.gov/web/offices/ac/ido/oeip/taf/cst_all.htm.

Wikipedia (2014). http://en.wikipedia.org/wiki/Automotive_industry_in_South_Korea.

World Bank (2009). *World Development Report, 2009: Reshaping Economic Geography*. Washington DC: World Bank.

——. (2010). Innovation policy: A guide for developing countries. https://openknowledge.worldbank.org/bitstream/handle/10986/2460/548930PUB0EPI11C10Dislosed061312010.pdf.

——. (2014a). Data on world development indicators. http://data.worldbank.org/country/korea-republic?display=graph.

——. (2014b). World Development Indicators database: Gross domestic product 2013. http://www.google.com/url?sa=t&rct=j&q=&esrc=s&source=web&cd=6&ved=0CFAQFjAF&url=http%3A%2F%2Fdatabank.worldbank.org%2Fdata%2Fdownload%2FGDP.pdf&ei=c0nBU-rDA43DPJz8gKAO&usg=AFQjCNElwhnm5v2jnwU2M-1JvCc0IXLXsw&sig2=0m3KkH3BrmBxDwAsNoAyHg.

14

Information Technology and National Development

Osei K. Darkwa

Abstract

This chapter discusses the role of Information Communication Technology (ICT) in national development. It begins with a background to ICT development in Ghana followed by theoretical perspectives on ICT and national development. Next, the pertinent institutional policy and regulatory frameworks are presented. In addition, trends in ICT development are discussed alongside the identification of Ghana's experience in using ICTs to promote and enhance national development. The chapter identifies the application of ICTs to specific sectors of the economy and lessons learnt through these applications. Finally, it identifies the challenges in implementing ICTs for the country's development and makes recommendations on ways of addressing these challenges.

Introduction

The future of the world depends upon countries' willingness to harness ICTs to advance their development. Meanwhile, the speed with which ICT is developing and its impact on socio-economic activities cannot be overemphasized. The United Nations Development Programme (UNDP) defines ICT as including the full range of electronic technologies and techniques used to manage information and knowledge. Today, ICT cuts across all aspects of human life and has become the main catalyst for development and the key to transforming traditional economies into knowledge-based economies the world over.

Today's knowledge economy based on ICT offers countries a tremendous opportunity to leapfrog the earlier stages of development and to move swiftly and directly on to the global economic stage, with all of its benefits and, of course, all of its new problems that need attention (World Bank, 2006). In other words, countries do not need to evolve slowly from agriculture to industry to service and then to the knowledge (or K) economy: nations can move directly from what we are now, where we are now, to the new ICT-based K-economy. Today, one can say with a fair degree of certainty that ICT is the key that can open the doors of the new global economy and its benefits to us. A nation unable to join this new economic order and unable to harness the power of ICT is effectively locked out of the new global economy and is forced to remain a marginal player on the global economic stage. Current transformation taking place in the Knowledge Economy (KE), sometimes known as the weightless or the digital economy, is driven by ICT.

The 1996 Information Society and Development (ISAD) conference in South Africa introduced the African development community to the potential of ICTs and served as a launch pad for the African Information Society Initiative (AISI), a framework for using ICTs in Africa to accelerate economic and social development. The 2003 world summit held in Geneva adopted the Geneva Declaration of Principles on Information and Knowledge Society, a generalized framework to facilitate the development of an Information and Knowledge-based economy by countries. Since then, several ICT-led initiatives have been launched on the continent to help propel African countries towards the information society.

Background to ICT Development in Ghana

As is well documented, Ghana was the first African country south of the Sahara to attain political independence in 1957. This was a unique occasion since it was the first time in history for a black African country to successfully wrench itself free from the shackles of colonial domination to self-government and independence. To quote one of the famous phrases of Ghana's first President, Dr Kwame Nkrumah, the man who led the country to independence, 'we are free, we are free at last. At long last the battle has ended and Ghana our beloved country is free forever'.

To Ghanaians, this achievement signified the dawn of a new awakening in the history of Africans in particular and all people of African descent. It marked a turning point in Africa's history and gave impetus to the liberation movements in other sister African countries. To Africans, it was the beginning of the possibility of realizing their long-cherished hopes and aspirations to free themselves from the yoke of colonialism. Ghana earned the accolade of 'Torch bearer and star of Africa'.

Nkrumah had a vision to free Ghana and the rest of Africa from colonial domination through pan-Africanism, a socio-political world view which sought to unify and uplift both native Africans and those of the African diaspora. Nkrumah and other African leaders focused most of their energies on institution building, nationalism and the need for black pride.

When Nkrumah declared Ghana's independence and outlined his pan-Africanist vision, the information age was not born. The great writers of his time, writers such as Immanuel Wallerstein and Basil Davidson, were silent about technology. From Nkrumah's declaration of 'self-government now' during the days of the colonial struggle, we know that he was a 'man in a hurry'. He had no time to waste and was perhaps determined to make up for the time lost during colonial rule. Even though the information age was not born during the time of Nkrumah, we know from his speeches and writings that he was fascinated by technology. He believed in the power of science and technology to transform society and to leapfrog the earlier stages of development. He once declared that 'we shall achieve in a decade what it took others a century'. He had a natural attraction to large technological projects. The Akosombo Dam, the Tema Motorway and plans for nuclear energy are three examples of his visionary projects. At the ground breaking of Ghana's first atomic reactor in 1964, he said 'we cannot afford to sit still and be passive onlookers of technological change'. In forming the Ghana Academy of Science, he urged Ghanaians to 'take part in the pursuit of scientific and technological research as a means of providing a basis for our socialist society'.

Nkrumah laid the foundation for the development of the country's technological infrastructure. And the leaders who came after him have always emphasized the importance of ICT in transforming the country's national development. For example, a renowned physicist once remarked that 'we paid the price of not taking part in the Industrial Revolution ... because we did not have the opportunity to see what was taking place in Europe. Now we see that ICT has become an indispensable tool. This time we should not miss out on this technological revolution. The message for Ghana is that we need to embrace information, knowledge and technology. If we Ghanaians fail to take advantage of information technology, we will be further marginalized in the world' (Allotey, 2000).

ICT and National Development: Theoretical Perspectives

There is a general belief that ICT has the potential to transform our society in various ways and contribute to the improvement of socio-economic conditions (Mann, 2004; Sahay, 2001; Heeks and Arun, 2006). The question before us is to what extent can ICT contribute to national development? Various writers have expressed their views on this topic (Avgerou, 1998; Heeks and Arun, 2006; Sein and Harindranath, 2004; Wilson and Heeks, 2000). Even though the literature discusses various theoretical frameworks regarding ICT and national development, three broad theoretical perspectives have emerged: modernization, dependency and human-centredness (Sein and Harindranath, 2004). The modernization perspective argues that developed countries are equipped with the resources (capital, technology, etc.) to attain a certain level of growth, while developing economies lack the ability to break out from indigenous mode of production due to a lack of knowledge and resources (Sein and Harindranath, 2004). This perspective sees ICT as a tool that can overcome the limitations of developing countries and assist them to attain a certain level of economic growth and leapfrog the earlier stages of development.

Based on these perspectives, Sein and Harindranath (2004) present an integrative framework that builds on the modernization, dependency and human-centredness position. Drawing on other theoretical models proposed by Orlikowski and Iacono (2001) to explain how ICT is viewed, they concluded that the way in which ICT is viewed represents a hierarchy when applied to national development. Drawing on another framework proposed by Malone and Rockart (1991) to explain the impact of ICT on national development, they identified three ways in which new technologies impact society-first order or primary effect (where society substitute the old technology with the new), the second order or secondary effect (where we see an increase in the phenomena enabled by the technology) and the third order or tertiary effect (where the new technology brings about societal change and generates new businesses).

Sein and Harindranath's model draws on four conceptualizations of ICT in national development: as a commodity, as supporting development activities, as a driver of the economy and directed at specific development activities. The three conceptualizations (ICT views, ICT impact and ICT use) affect national development. In a related study, Sein (2005) develops four paradigms of ICT in development-functionalism, social relativism, radical structuralism and neo-humanism.

The functionalist perspective (regarded as the most common perspective in ICT for development) sees foreign experts from donor countries as the main drivers of the ICT intervention, with the government of the host country playing a passive role. This perspective sees ICT as a tool and the end instead of a means to an end.

The social relativism perspective takes a modernization view of ICT in development. Here the main actors or roles of ICT are from outside the host country but are termed more as facilitators and partners than as consultants. Technology is adapted to suit the situation of the host country. One of the key players under this perspective is the NGO community.

Radical structuralism takes a neutral view of ICT and views the main actors from either outside or inside the host country in the form of activists or partisans for the 'exploited' class. According to Sein (2005), call centre outsourcing provides a classic example of this perspective.

The neo-humanism perspective views the main actors of ICT from within the host country in the form of activists whose aim is emancipation. Sein cites initiatives such as knowledge networks, e-Democracy and locally developed software by local personnel as classic examples of this perspective.

Other theoretical approaches have been introduced to explore ICT innovation in the context of developing countries. For example, Avgerou (1998, 2001, 2003) presents two perspectives regarding the nature of the ICT innovation process in developing countries: as transfer and diffusion, and as socially embedded action. According to the author, ICT innovation in developing countries is a process of diffusion of knowledge, transferred from advanced economies and adapted to the conditions of a developing country. The author draws on the ICT for development literature to elaborate on the role of culture in ICT innovation, a perspective he labels progressive transformation and disruptive transformation. This is illustrated with literature on telecentres.

With the progressive perspective, ICT is considered an enabler of transformations in multiple domains of human activities and has been promoted by major international development agencies to help in understanding the impact of ICT in development (Avgerou, 2003; UNDP, 2001; World Bank, 1999). On the other hand, the disruptive perspective is premised on interest and struggles for power as a necessary part of ICT innovation in developing countries and considers ICT-enabled development as a contested endeavour involving action with unequal effects on different categories of population and laden with conflict (Avgerou, 2003).

Taken together, these theoretical perspectives provide an insight into the various ICT policies and development initiatives in the country and the sub-region. For example, the UN ECA Pan-African Development Information Systems (PADIS) initiative (with its goal of establishing low-cost and self-sustained nodes to provide access to email in most African countries), the Leland initiative by USAID (with a goal to provide African countries with connections), the Acacia Project sponsored by the International Development Research Centre, the development of national e-strategies to deploy, harness and exploit ICTs for socio-economic development at the local, national and sub-regional levels, the Millennium Development Goals (MDGs), and the New Partnership for African Development (NEPAD) Action Plan, where ICT projects and initiatives have been initiated to speed up sub-regional/regional connectivity and inter-connectivity reflect the above theoretical perspectives. They represent aspects of the above frameworks where the main actors are foreign and local experts who are the main drivers of ICT intervention in the country.

Institutional Policy and Regulatory Frameworks

For a holistic development of the ICT industry, there is the need for a policy and regulatory framework to drive development in the field. As noted by the UNDP Human Development Report (2001), 'it is policy, not charity that will ultimately determine whether new technologies become a tool for human development everywhere'. Since independence, the government has formulated numerous policies to guide the development of telecommunications and information technology in the country. The First Telecommunications Project (FTP) was enacted in 1975. This enabled the installation of several telecommunication facilities (such as electronic exchanges, the construction of an earth station, and the construction of microwave radio links for telephone and television from southern to northern Ghana).

The next major policy was the Accelerated Development Program (ADP). The policy was geared toward reforming the regulatory structure and the improvement of the quality of communication services. Other policies such as the National Communication Authority Act 2008, Act 769; the National Information Technology Agency Act 2008, Act 771; the Electronic Transactions Act 2008, Act 772; and the Electronic Communications Act 2008, Act 775 have all been enacted to boost ICT development in Ghana. Together, they provide a detailed legal and regulatory framework for the advancement of the ICT sector in Ghana and the legal basis of subsequent ICT policies that have shaped ICT developments in the country: the ICT for Accelerated Development (ICT4AD) and National Telecom Policy (NTP). Of the two, the ICT4AD is more detailed and elaborate and will be discussed below.

The Ghana ICT for Accelerated Development (ICT4D) Policy

To show its commitment to the development of ICT in the country, the government established the National ICT Policy and Plan Development Committee to develop an ICT-led socio-economic development policy to aid Ghana's developmental effort and move the economy and society towards a knowledge-based information society within a reasonable timeframe. The policy is 'to be integrated within government's three-pronged development strategy for its second term, which revolves around (i) the development and enhancement of the nation's human resource base, (ii) the continued rejuvenation of the Private Sector, and (iii) the entrenchment of Good Governance' (ICT4AD, 2003). The policy is the latest in a series of government initiatives to be enacted as a 'road map' for developing an information society for the country.

Based on all the national strategic framework documents – the Vision 2020, Ghana Poverty Reduction Strategy (GPRS) (2002–4) and the Coordinated Programme for Economic and Social Development of Ghana (2003–12) – the policy statement sets out the road map for the development of Ghana's information society and economy. It acknowledges the role that ICT can play in moving Ghana from where it is today to a knowledge-based economy. The 14 priority areas of the policy focus on: accelerating human resource development; promoting ICTs in education; facilitating government administration and service delivery; facilitating the development of the private sector; developing an export-oriented ICT product and service industry; modernizing agriculture and developing an agro-based industry; developing a globally competitive value-added services sector; deploying ICTs in the community; promoting national health; rapid ICT and enabling physical infrastructural development; legal, regulatory and institutional framework provisions; research and development; promoting foreign and local direct investment drive in ICTs; and facilitating national security and law and order (ICT4AD, 2003).

Trends in ICT Development

Since the country's independence, successive governments have recognized the importance of ICT to socio-economic development and have put several measures in place to promote its development. Over the years, several strides have been made in developing the country's ICT infrastructure so as to bridge the digital divide between Ghana and the developed world. For example, plans to implement broadband services and the Global Mobile Personal Communications by Satellite (GMPCS) systems as well as the local manufacture and assembling of handsets and auxiliary equipment have been implemented. A national communications backbone infrastructure network has been put in place to provide open access broadband connectivity nationwide. Ghana (in addition to Ethiopia, South Africa and Mauritius) is part of the pilot phase of the Pan-African E-network project, a joint initiative between the Indian government and the African Union (AU) to develop ICT infrastructure across the continent. This initiative, the largest infrastructure project in Africa's history to date, connects all the 53 African countries through satellite and fibre optic networks to promote tele-medicine and tele-education programmes. According to the Data Development Group of the World Bank, ICT infrastructure in Ghana is progressing as compared to other low-income countries globally and above the 1.1 percent average for Sub-Saharan Africa. Prominently featuring among these initiatives is the development of a national fibre optic network called Voltacom.

To strengthen the country's physical ICT infrastructure, a new Eastern Corridor Optic Fibre Network to complement the existing fibre infrastructure to enhance broadband connectivity is being developed. This will link the 12.3 Terrabytes submarine cable capacity (SAT-3, Main One, GLO-1, WACS and ACE) to provide the country the necessary fibre backbone. In addition to the above, the country's existing WIMAX system is being upgraded to Long-Term Evolution (LTE), a 4G standard for wireless communication of high-speed data for mobile phones and data terminals. The goal of LTE for the upgrade is to increase the capacity and speed of wireless data networks using new digital signal processing techniques and modulations. This technology will reduce data transfer latency compared to 3G architecture. A new Data Centre is being constructed near the Kofi Annan ICT Training Centre at the estimated cost of GH¢41.5 million to provide data hosting services. Other facilities such as the Technology Parks Business Centre which is to be set up in the free-zone area of Tema is being upgraded to a Next Generation Tech Park through funding by Exim Bank China.

ICT TRAINING

Several training institutions have emerged to produce the human capacity needed to fuel the emerging ICT industry in the country. Prominent among them are the Kofi Annan ICT Centre of Excellence, which is a joint Ghana/India project, the Ghana Technology University College and the Ghana Multi-Media Centre, which functions as an incubator facility to nurture creative and innovative ICT ideas. A Research and Educational Network (REN) has been established to bring Ghanaian universities and local research institutions such as the Council for Scientific and Industrial Research (CSIR) and the Ghana Atomic Energy Commission to promote the country's research agenda.

INTERNET SERVICES

Ghana is privileged to be among the first countries in Africa to achieve connection to the Internet thanks to the pioneering work of Network Computer Systems (NCS), which introduced the Internet in Ghana in 1995. The company is credited with registering the gh.com domain name. Today, Internet penetration is estimated to be around 10 percent. Dial-up was the primary mode of connection to the Internet when it was introduced to Ghana. Today, Asymmetric Digital Subscriber Line (popularly known as ADSL), broadband and wireless service have become available in most parts of Ghana. Over 150 new Internet Service Providers (ISPs) have been licensed, even though only a few remain active. Most government ministries and Parliament are connected to the Internet. All the major banking institutions, international organizations operating in the country (e.g., the World Bank, The World Health Organization and the UNDP), Embassies and High Commissions are connected. A sizable number of non-governmental organizations (NGOs) are connected as well, according to a recent National Communication Authority (NCA) research. However, connectivity is not impressive in the private sector, particularly amongst small and medium-sized enterprises.

Sectoral Application Initiatives

Today, the use of ICT has been integrated into virtually every facet of commerce, education, governance and civic activity in developed countries and has become a critical factor in creating wealth worldwide. A number of core sectors have been selected to explore how ICTs have impacted on those sectors over the years. These include education, health, business, governance and commerce.

APPLICATION OF ICT TO THE EDUCATIONAL SECTOR

Global interest in the use of new technologies to support educational initiatives has increased dramatically, in part driven by targets associated with the Millennium Development Goals and the World Summit on the Information Society. In 1971, futurist writer Alvin Toffler predicted the rapid pace of change that the information age would bring to education, especially higher education. He envisioned a shift from conventional degrees to what he termed 'learning contracts'. Since then, numerous authors have written about the impact of the information revolution on education. The digital age has changed conventional university practices and has introduced unconventional and new ways of doing things. Educational institutions have made progress in using information technology to transform their operations. For example, old manual library catalogues have been replaced with computer terminals; digital and virtual libraries have either replaced or complemented physical libraries; faculty offices have been computerized; instructional technologies using LCD projectors and computers have replaced the blackboard; instructional mode has changed from face-to-face delivery to a mix of delivery platforms ranging from correspondence to web-based. Most importantly, the four-walled notion of a campus has changed considerably. Higher education itself is changing. Education has now become an ongoing part of life. This has led to the notion of lifelong learning. Technology-enhanced education appears to the one of the viable options to address changing educational needs.

Today, network portals have emerged to provide educators with a central point from which to access various educational tools, and pedagogical changes have emerged due to the use of information technology in higher education. The digital age has made it possible for virtual collaboration, the use of technology to bring people together to achieve their goals using both asynchronous and synchronous tools such as email, calendars, links and bulletin boards, streaming media, narrated slideshows, the web, audio or video conferencing. We now have the technology to provide education to multitudes of people who would otherwise have gone without it. The digital age gives us the capability to communicate with anyone, anywhere at a rapid speed. Society stands to benefit if higher education is based on the strategic use of information and communication technologies.

In her book *In the Age of the Smart Machine: The Future of Work and Power*, sociologist Shoshana Zuboff (1988) clearly documented that the old forms of work were being radically transformed by 'the smart machine', the computer. The twenty-first century is the age of the smart machine, and the forms of work and power and communication it is creating. If Ghana is to take its rightful place in the global economy, its educational system will have to turn out graduates who understand and use the smart machine. Former President John Kufuor, in his complimentary endorsement of the White Paper on the new educational reform, endorsed the expansion of education and the proposed Open University. The Open University is one way to maximize the use of the 'smart machine' as well as achieve the goal of increasing access and enrolment, improving the quality of education and cutting increasing educational costs. This has been demonstrated by some of the earlier open universities such as the University of South Africa (UNISA), the Indira Gandhi

National Open University in India and the Open University in the UK. For example, the Indira Gandhi National Open University (IGNOU) now has over three million students enrolled. It is ranked as one of the top 10 Indian universities for the quality of its teaching and it operates at a fraction of the cost of India's conventional universities.

If we move in this direction, higher education will become for most students institutions without walls. The smart machine will be the classroom, lecture hall, seminar room, library or laboratory. The university student can be anywhere in the nation, anywhere in the world, and yet be part of a learning community, a virtual community, the smart machine keeping teachers and students in easy and regular communication. What the Open University movement around the world has demonstrated is that teaching and learning of quality can go on without the buildings, without requiring students to leave their communities and their families and their responsibilities in order to learn. The computer and all of the new communication technologies can connect students scattered throughout Ghana with their teachers and their teachers can be anywhere – in Ghana, the US, the UK or anywhere in the world that has instruction that Ghanaians want and need. In addition, various e-educational networks have emerged to explore the role of technology-enhanced education. The emphasis here is on e-educational networks designed to support e-learning in schools, such as the African Learning Network supports school networks (e.g. SchoolNet), university networks (e.g. VarsityNet), networks of research institutes (e.g. African Knowledge Network Forum – AKNF) and networks for marginalized people (e.g. Out of School Youth Network – OosyNet).

APPLICATION OF ICT TO HEALTHCARE SERVICES

Healthcare is undoubtedly one of the most fundamental needs in Ghana and elsewhere considering the country's multiple medical problems. In fact, three out of eight MDGs are related to healthcare. Goal 4 calls for a reduction in child mortality. The target here is to reduce the mortality rate among children under five by two-thirds. Goal 5 calls for an improvement in maternal healthcare. The target here is to reduce the maternal mortality ratio by three-quarters. Goal 6 deals with combating HIV/AIDS, malaria and other diseases. The target is to halt and begin to reverse the spread of HIV/AIDS. Without a comprehensive strategy to address the challenges inherent within the healthcare system, Ghana as a country cannot achieve any of the above global health targets by the time the MDGs are fully implemented, which is around the corner.

Like healthcare systems in other parts of Africa, the Ghanaian health system has not been able to respond fully to the multiple health challenges confronting the people of this country. The low quality of health services, the inefficient use of scare health resources, the shortage and uneven distribution of health resources and the lack of adequate medical information on patients are some of the factors that have been cited as challenges confronting our healthcare system. These challenges are not new; they have been with us since the days of Hippocrates and Florence Nightingale. For example, Florence Nightingale wrote of the appalling absence of information about causes of death in the Crimean War, noting how this lack prevented appropriate understanding and approaches to healthcare in that conflict. How far have we come since the days of these two medical icons?

One plausible way out of the numerous medical challenges confronting the continent is to explore how the power of ICT could be leveraged to address the challenges inherent in healthcare delivery, training and medical education. Information technology holds the potential to revolutionize healthcare practice in Ghana and other parts of the world. ICT applied to healthcare delivery could help increase the efficiency, effectiveness and quality of health services. The use of ICT in healthcare delivery will enable knowledge to be exchanged, as well as providing the basis for networks of professionals to be supported by their peers and educators. This quest to apply ICT to healthcare services has given birth to new areas in healthcare such as telemedicine, tele-health, tele-pharmacy, medical informatics and other emerging fields. Telemedicine is the delivery of healthcare and the exchange of healthcare information across distances using telecommunications technology. The term was first coined in the 1970s by Thomas Bird to refer to healthcare delivery where physicians examine distant patients using telecommunications technologies. The term 'tele-health' is used in a broader context to refer to the application of telecommunications to the healthcare environment.

Over the past few years, telemedicine has become popular as a medium of healthcare delivery in various parts of the world. Telemedicine applications and technologies represent an opportunity to improve the delivery of healthcare in Africa. Since telemedicine is an emerging field, most health professionals need to be been trained in the art and science of telemedicine. Without adequate training of healthcare providers, the success of the technique will be limited. Training has to focus on the level of skills needed by healthcare providers in order to apply telemedicine effectively. Thus, training in the technology and its application is crucial for the success of telemedicine in Africa. To achieve an effective outcome, there is the need to identify the training needs of each medical facility interested in applying the technology. This will ensure that the training is tailored to the needs of specific institutions.

The Ghana ICT4AD discussed earlier presents 14 ICT pillars. The ninth pillar which addresses ICT in healthcare indicates that ICT will be utilized to support the activities and operations of the health delivery system throughout the country. In order to do this, all healthcare institutions will be networked to collate information, share data and communications online; the healthcare system will be re-structured at the primary, regional and tertiary levels by providing a national databank to support online national healthcare information, administration and management; full Internet connectivity and access for healthcare professionals at all levels will be established; ICT skills acquisition will be made mandatory for all healthcare professionals; Health Management Information Systems will be established for all levels of healthcare through the use of ICT; a proposed National Health Insurance-driven health service will be enabled through the use of ICT; and ICT will be utilized to provide education and to combat major national health threats such as HIV/AIDS, malaria, etc.

APPLICATION OF ICT TO GOVERNANCE

In the olden days, people met at a common place to deliberate on issues affecting the community. This was the era of direct democracy. Over time, it became nearly impossible to practise this form of democracy. Thus, society witnessed a transition from this form of government to a system where each community elected officials to represent its interests. This gave birth to a system of indirect or liberal democracy. In Ghana and most African countries, before the advent of colonial rule, different systems of political administration were practised, from patriarchal democratic gerontocracies to monarchical rule in centralized societies. As is well documented in most history books, most African countries were colonized at some stage in the history of their development. With the exception of Liberia and Ethiopia, all the remaining African countries were colonized. The 1940s saw an intense struggle on the part of Africa to extricate itself from the shackles of slavery and colonial domination. By the end of the 1960s, most African countries had attained political independence. Since then, various systems of government have been tried across the continent. One common aspiration by most African countries is to establish a democratic system of government based on common values shared by people throughout the global community irrespective of cultural, political, social and economic differences. The creation of a democracy that is appropriate to African conditions is one of the challenges facing Africa in the twenty-first century.

With the advent of the ICT revolution, there has been a transition from representative democracy (traditional democracy) to electronic democracy (e-democracy), a term used to refer to the broad use of the Internet in politics, advocacy, elections and governance. In its broadest sense, e-democracy refers to how the Internet can be used to enhance democratic processes and provide increased opportunities for individuals and communities to interact with government E-democracy uses information technology to let the governed participate in government. The purpose is to enhance political democracy or the participation of citizens in democratic forms of communication. The general expectation is that e-democracy will lead to the transformation of the way politics is practised and the way in which governments interact with citizens by providing new avenues in order to enable citizens to participate in the political process.

E-government (sometimes referred to as digital or online government), on the other hand, is generally regarded as the use of ICT to automate governmental processes. The UNDP defines it broadly as the use of ICT to promote more efficient and effective government, facilitate more accessible government services, allow greater public access to information and make government more accountable to citizens. It is simply the online mirror of the offline world. Where it is fully deployed, delivery models such as Government-to-Citizen (G2C) or e-Service (the application of IT to transform the delivery of public services), Government-to-Business (G2B) or e-Business (the application of IT to operations performed by government), Government-to-Government (G2G) and Government-to-Employees (G2E) have been employed.

The adoption of e-government on a massive scale will put essential public goods at the disposal of citizens. This will reduce overall transaction costs and better efficiency in government processes. People seeking governmental services will not be limited by bureaucratic delays and excessive red tape, since most of the necessary services will be placed online. Processes will be more transparent as information will be readily available online with minimal interference from established and ineffective governmental bureaucracies. This eliminates the role of intermediaries, brings citizens closes to the government and puts them directly in touch with government processes. It is expected that this process will lead to better allocation of national resources and systems of government that are better able to meet the needs of economically and socially disenfranchised populations.

At the local government level, local authorities in other parts of the world are increasingly using the Internet to deliver information and services electronically, 24 hours a day. Such local bodies are using interactive websites to enable users make comments, ask questions, make online payment for government services (such as property taxes and parking tickets) or submit applications online. Through the use of information technology, e-local government places citizens and customers at the heart of services in terms of the way in which local government services are delivered. Such approaches lead to a better, more cost-effective and accessible services for citizens interested in utilizing the services. Such innovation leads to local government efficiency.

The main catalyst for e-government and e-local government is due to advances in ICT including the Internet and the successful embrace of ICT by several countries. Even though a number of African countries have embarked upon measures to transfer responsibility and authority from central ministries to local governments or community representatives, the pace of development has been slow. The concept is yet to be popularized among government bureaucrats. Through support from the World Bank and other development partners, Ghana has launched an e-Ghana project to generate increased employment in the IT-enabled services (e.g. business processing outsourcing (BPO), data entry and processing, contact/call centre operations and software development). To facilitate the process, the government has created the Ghana Multimedia Incubator Centre (GMIC), under the auspices of the Ministry of Communication, to spearhead the development of human resource in the areas of BPO centres and medical transcription. The success of the above proposals is contingent upon having a solid technological infrastructure in place.

APPLICATION OF ICT TO COMMERCE

Traditional commerce is defined by *Webster's Dictionary* as the exchange or buying and selling of commodities, especially the exchange of merchandise, on a large scale, between different places or communities, extended trade or traffic. This type of commerce has been with us for quite a while. However, over the years, advances in the banking system (such as the electronic transmission of funds over computer networks) and the development of the information revolution has led to the emergence of a new type of commerce known today as electronic or e-commerce. In fact, there is no universal definition of e-commerce, which is generally described as any type of business or commercial transaction that involves the transfer of information across the Internet. Generally, there have been two major waves in the evolution of e-commerce.

The first wave lasted from the mid-1990s to 2003. This is the era of the dot.com boom (from the mid-1990s to 2000) and the dot.com bust (after 2000–2003). This first wave happened predominantly in the US, with most of the web presence (websites) in the English language. This was the era of low-speed Internet and limited bandwidth.

The second wave of e-commerce emerged after 2003. This is the era when companies such as Amazon.com and eBay.com were able to re-invent themselves and became profitable in operating in the virtual environment. It was more international in scope, with several countries participating and the use of multiple languages. Faster, cheaper Internet connections were realized during this era.

Three types of infrastructure are needed to create e-commerce: platform-technological infrastructure; process infrastructure; and an infrastructure of rules and regulations. The emergence of a global economy, the development and growth of electronic funds transfer, the evolution of electronic data interchange, automation, the emergence of value-added network, and major advances in science and technology have contributed to the evolution of electronic commerce.

Largely ubiquitous in the developed world, e-commerce's pace of development in Africa has been rather slow. Even though more African countries (e.g. South Africa, Kenya, Nigeria and Ghana) have entered the e-commerce arena, more needs to be done to increase the pace of the countries' involvement. With the emergence of websites such as eShop Africa, and an online payment system through organizations such as eTranzact and banks such as Zenith and Ecobank, Ghana is expected to capture a share of the e-commerce market. E-commerce will certainly change the way in which business is conducted in the country. However, there is a need to address challenges such as limited access to the Internet, the low penetration of electronic payment systems, the high cost of computer hardware and a host of others, in order to make e-commerce a viable business option in Ghana and many other African countries.

APPLICATION OF ICT TO BANKING SERVICES (M-BANKING)

Mobile banking (also referred to as m-banking or SMS banking) generally refers to the use of a mobile device to perform banking transactions through either Short Messaging Service (SMS) or Mobile Internet. Tiwani, Rajnish and Buse, who have written extensively about the technique, regard it as the provision of banking and financial services with the help of mobile communication devices. The mobile banking service makes it possible for clients to access balance information, pay bills, transfer funds and do business at nearby ATMs and banking centres. It is free (one may be charged for web access by one's mobile carrier), secure and allows one to manage one's accounts at one's own convenience.

M-banking has changed the way in which traditional (bricks and mortar) banking is conducted by offering similar banking services, but on more flexible terms. The M-banking service is more cost-effective than traditional banking. The low cost of using existing infrastructure makes such channels more amenable to use by low income customers, most of whom lack formal addresses, have limited credit histories and live in rural communities. One of the most successful M-banking services in Africa is M-Pesa, a service launched by Safaricom and Vodafone in Kenya and other Eastern African countries. M-Pesa agents have been registered in selected parts of the country. Over 3.5 million people have registered to use the service. To send money, one contacts an agent with cash that is credited to a virtual account. A text message is then sent to the desired recipient, who cashes it at an agent's outlet. The recipient is charged a small commission. Vodafone hopes to reach the base of the pyramid through this innovation.

In Ghana, most of the banks offer an M-banking service. Some of the telecom companies have launched a similar service with limited success. For example, MTN's mobile banking service allows customers to open and access accounts using their mobile handsets. The availability of such a service has enabled MTN's numerous mobile phone subscribers, many of whom are under-banked or unbanked, to be involved in mobile banking. This has given rise to a new trend called *mobile airtime* on the continent. Pioneered by MTN, the technique is based on using pre-paid phone airtime vouchers as virtual currency. This enables users to use part of their phone's airtime to exchange for goods and cash. Airtel, another telecom company, has launched a similar service.

A report by the UK's Department for International Development (DfID) and the Information for Development Program (InfoDev) entitled *Mobile Banking Knowledge Map and Possible Donor Support Strategies* deals with the status, opportunities and challenges of m-banking in the developing world. Released in July 2006, it elaborates the likely impact of m-banking on the unbanked – those without access to banking services. The report identifies three main barriers to the emergence and growth of m-banking. The first relates to uncertainties over the speed and nature of customer adoption. Second is the lack of inter-operability with existing payment systems. The third concerns regulatory barriers, i.e. lack of openness to new models and lack of policy certainty. Clearly, efforts should be made to address the above barriers to enable the widespread use of m-banking services in the country.

Challenges Facing ICT in Development

Much has been written about the challenges facing Ghana and the African continent in our quest to becoming an information society. A number of challenges have been outlined.

INADEQUATE TELECOMMUNICATIONS SERVICES

To a large extent, the destiny of ICT development in Ghana depends on the services provided by the telecommunications industry. Unfortunately, these organizations have not been able to provide the necessary services that will propel the country into the information age. The country's telecommunication infrastructural expansion has failed to meet the country's demand for emerging services voice and data services. For example, the cost of Internet services is still high. Moreover, service distribution has been uneven. While most urban areas have access to services, this is almost non-existent in most rural areas. This means that most rural areas do not benefit from the information revolution (Bhatnagar and Schware, 2000). The availability of affordable broadband services is vital to ensure Ghana's competitiveness as an ICT destination. Online promotion firms are emerging. This limits the extent to which businesses could be promoted online. The lack of adequate ICT infrastructure to support high-quality and high-speed Internet connection is one of the major obstacles to the country's ICT development. Given the global connectivity maps, it is evident that Sub-Saharan Africa is the least-connected part of the world. Without adequate ICT infrastructure to move information rapidly, Africa could be marginalized. There is the need for the launching of a national information and communication infrastructure plan on a massive scale geared towards increasing access to ICT infrastructure, reducing bandwidth costs and facilitating access to the Internet. This will help to achieve universal service and access to basic and value-added communication services in the country. The deployment of the national backbone infrastructure and new technologies such as WiMAX and LTE will assist in addressing the infrastructure gap. Due to this, all efforts should be made to ensure the accelerated deployment of ICT broadband access across the country at affordable costs in order to promote investment in ICT.

HIGH INTERNET SUBSCRIPTION

Another challenge has been with start-up fees and the monthly subscription charges. The average cost for a broadband service is close to $70 per month. Most individuals and small businesses cannot afford to pay such a fee. The expectation is that with an increase in the number of ISPs and the introduction of new technology, these fees will drop to an affordable range.

HUMAN CAPACITY BUILDING

The lack of human capacity building to support the ICT industry is another major challenge confronting Ghana. Most of the critically needed skillsets to advance the ICT industry are not readily available in the country. Even though a number of specialized institutions have emerged to provide training to fill in the ICT skills gap, more needs to be done if Ghana is to be placed on the global information map.

HIGH COST OF ICT PRODUCTS

The cost of most ICT products is still above the means of the average Ghanaian. This is because most ICT products are imported. The time has come for the country to begin thinking about a local assembling industry to drive ICT development in Ghana.

INADEQUATE FINANCIAL RESOURCES

Financial resources are vital for the growth of the ICT industry in Ghana. Raising these to develop the ICT sector has always been a major challenge. We know that the government alone cannot raise the necessary capital to develop the sector. The Information and Knowledge Society requires the involvement of all stakeholders in the formulation and implementation of policies and strategies. This entails public-private partnerships and the involvement of international development agencies.

MAINSTREAMING GENDER AND ICT

Gender gaps in ICT are narrowing in more highly developed information societies. However, Ghana is yet to integrate gender mainstreaming activities with national ICT policies/strategies. Measures should be taken to ensure that ICT policy is gender-sensitive and gender-mainstreamed. Government support is needed to ensure gender equality. The Ghana Strategic Document for ICT and Gender recognizes the importance of gender mainstreaming in ICT and emphasizes the importance of new technologies on gender and, in particular, on the economic and political spheres of women's lives. As stated in the document, 'we, as a nation must appreciate the fact that ICT has become the threshold of national development and it is therefore important we involve all citizens to avoid any technological divide between men and women'. In addition, the role of gender in ICT mainstreaming is captured as part of the 15 pillars of the national ICT4D document. These pillars cover policy and decision making, infrastructure, education and private sector development, and particularly recognize the role of women in all sectors of the economy, especially at the micro-levels.

POLITICAL WILL

Invariably, the decision to develop our information infrastructure is primarily a political decision. The full value of information technology will only be realized if it is brought forcefully into the mainstream by powerful political, academic and business advocates. The brief history of the evolution and application of ICT in the country and other parts of the world clearly depicts the importance of political support for success. The evidence to date clearly suggests that the acquisition of new communication technologies will transform the country's economy and improve the lives of the people. Consequently, we encourage the government of Ghana to make ICT a strategic direction in its development plans. Proactive strategies are required to ensure that the economic and social benefits of ICTs extend to all, and these strategies must include proper attention to enabling conditions and capacity building. In order to reach all sectors of society, ICT strategies should not merely focus on high-end technologies such as the Internet, but also on the full range of ICTs (including, for example, radio) and on related synergies.

Conclusions and Recommendations

The use of ICT will continue to grow in Ghana and other parts of the world. Ghanaians have embraced ICT. This can be measured by the increased investment in ICT infrastructure, the growing number of Internet cafes in major cities and district centres, the proliferation of ISPs in urban centres, improvement in the country's telecommunication infrastructure, the deployment of innovative technologies, increased funding of ICT-related projects, the formation of major technology-oriented organizations, the establishment of technology-oriented training institutions and universities, and the enactment of new government policies to regulate the field. These changes and investments have revolutionized our traditional institutions and have brought dramatic transformation to Ghanaian society. Today, the impact of information technology can be keenly felt in several sectors of Ghana. Notwithstanding the progress made, more still needs to be done by the government by embarking on an aggressive human capacity building programme to address the country's human capacity shortfall in the area of ICT. For Ghana and Africa as a whole, the prospects as an ICT destination over the next 50 years are optimistic. The golden age of technology is here and Ghana should lead the African continent to the technological finishing line.

References

Avgerou, C. (1996). Transferability of information technology and organisational practices. In M. Odedra-Straub (ed.), *Global Information Technology and Socio-economic Development*. Nashua, NH: Ivy League, pp. 106–15.

——. (1998). How can IT enable economic growth in developing countries? *Information Technology for Development*, 8(1), pp. 15–28.

——. (2001). *Information Systems and Global Diversity*. Oxford: Oxford University Press.

——. (2003). The link between ICT and economic growth in the discourse of development. In M. Korpela, R. Montealegro and A. Poulymenakou (eds), *Organizational Information Systems in the Context of Globalization*. Dordrecht: Kluwer, pp. 373–86.

Avgerou, C. and Walsham, G. (eds) (2000). *Information Technology in Context: Studies from the Perspective of Developing Countries*. Aldershot: Ashgate.

Bhatnagar, S.C. and Bjørn-Andersen, N. (eds) (1990). *Information Technology in Developing Countries*. Amsterdam: North-Holland.

Bhatnagar, S.C. and Odedra, M. (eds) (1992). *Social Implications of Computers in Developing Countries*. New Delhi: Tata McGraw-Hill.

Bhatnagar, S.C. and Schware, R. (2000). *Information and Communication Technology in Rural Development: Case Studies from India*. Washington DC: World Bank Institute.

Frempong, G. (2009/2010). Ghana ICT sector performance review 2009/2010. Towards evidence-based ICT policy and regulation 2, 8

Harindranath, M.K. and Sein, G. (2007). Revisiting the role of ICT in development. Proceedings of the 9th International Conference on Social Implications of Computers in Developing Countries, São Paulo, Brazil, May.

Heeks, R. (2001). Understanding e-Governance for development. Paper no. 11, Government Working Paper series, Institute for Development Policy and Management, University of Manchester. http://www.sed.manchester.ac.uk/idpm/publications/wp/igov/igov_wp11.htm.

Heeks, R. and Arun, S. (2006). Social outsourcing as a development tool: Outsourcing to social enterprises for poverty reduction and women's empowerment in Kerala. Proceedings of DSA Annual Conference, Reading, UK, November.

ICT4AD (2003). An integrated ICT-led socio-economic development policy and plan development framework for Ghana. Volume 1. Compiled by the Government of Ghana and the Economic Commission for Africa.

Mann, C.L. (2004). Information technologies and international development: Conceptual clarity in the search for commonality and diversity. *Information Technologies & International Development*, 1(2), pp. 67–79.

Orlikowski, W.J., Walsham, G., Jones, M.R. and DeGross, J.I. (eds) (1996). *Information Technology and Changes in Organizational Work*. London: Chapman & Hall.

Orlikowski, W. and Iacono, C. (2000). Research commentary: Desperately seeking 'IT' in IT research: A call to theorizing the IT artefact. *Information Systems Research*, 12, pp. 121–34.

Sahay, S. (1998). Implementing GIS technology in India: Some issues of time and space. *Accounting, Management and Information Technologies*, 8, pp. 147–88.

——. (2001). Introduction to the special issue on 'IT and healthcare in developing countries'. *Electronic Journal on Information Systems in Developing Countries*, 5, pp. 1–6.

Sahay, S. and Avgerou, C. (2002). Special issue on IS in developing countries. *The Information Society*, 18(2), pp. 73–6.

Sahay, S., Nicholson, B. and Krishna, S. (2003). *Global IT Outsourcing: Software Development across Borders*. Cambridge: Cambridge University Press.

Sahay, S. and Walsham, G. (2005). Scaling of health information systems in India: Challenges and approaches. IFIP WG9.4 8th International Conference.

Sein, M.K. (2005). Paradigms of ICT-in-Development. Proceedings of the IFIP9.4 Conference, Abuja Nigeria, May.

Sein, M.K. and Ahmad, I. (2001). A framework to study the impact of information and communication technologies on developing countries: The case of cellular phones in Bangladesh. Proceedings of the BITWorld International Conference. Cairo, Egypt, 4–6 June.

Sein, M.K. and Harindranath, G. (2004). Conceptualising the ICT artefact: Towards understanding the role of ICT in national development. *The Information Society*, 20, pp. 15–24.

UNDP, Human Development Report, 2001.

World Bank (1999). *World Bank Development Report: Knowledge for Development.* New York: Oxford University Press.

——. (2006). *Information and Communications for Development.* Washington DC: World Bank.

Wilson, G. and Heeks, R. (2000). Technology, poverty and development. In T. Allen and A. Thomas (eds), *Poverty and Development: Into the 21st Century.* Oxford: Oxford University Press, pp. 403–24.

Zuboff, S. (1988). *In the Age of the Smart Machine: The Future of Work and Power.* New York: Basic Books.

15

The Impact of Sound Infrastructure on National Development

Charles K. Boakye

Abstract

Modern infrastructure is the backbone of any country and without it economic growth is severely inhibited. It is established that African countries have a considerable infrastructure deficit and lag behind all other developing regions in relation to transportation, energy, water and sanitation. Reducing this deficit will help to grow Africa's competitiveness to levels like those observed in Asia and the Middle East. Increasing urbanization, growing populations and consumer markets, and broader ties to the global economy are making the need for African economies to invest more in new growth poles imperative. Because infrastructure underpins the basic services in any country, it offers both great opportunities for business, employment and the general competitiveness of an economy, while also presenting intensely political challenges. Developing adequate and efficient infrastructure will enable African economies to increase productivity, especially in manufacturing and service delivery. This in turn will create more jobs, attract investment opportunities and encourage the efficient use of natural resources. Improved and efficient infrastructure has contributed to social development in healthcare and education, and reduced societal inequalities through a more equitable distribution of wealth. Money alone is not the answer – but with good planning, the necessary finance can be attracted to fund infrastructure. To fix infrastructure, policy makers must have the end in mind – creating new growth poles, housing and industrial centres, and moving away from the preponderance of highly informal to formal systems – such that the desired funds are attracted from not only insurance, pension and micro-finance sources but also land financing, credit systems and rising incomes from increased job creation. Very little money can be attracted into an economy that is overly dominated by informal systems. To bridge Africa's infrastructure gap, investments must be driven by increasing urbanization and agglomeration trends across the continent, creating the scope for exceptional growth in infrastructure projects, real estate and other sub-sectors. This potential, which is still largely unknown to African governments, is one of the most economically feasible ways of advancing infrastructure, as has been demonstrated in the Middle East and Asia. Key issues relating to infrastructure delivery are established: that infrastructure is evolutionary, based on time, inherently spatial and a long-term fix and therefore requires a considerable amount of trust; and prosperity and density of urban space go together. A number of options for financing infrastructure are addressed.

Introduction

This chapter examines infrastructure development in three key sectors: transportation (roads, rail, aviation and ports); water and sewerage systems; and urban development and housing. While most regions of the world have achieved some success, progress in Africa is generally lethargic; the transport sector reveals mixed results, water and sanitation are slow, while housing has shown negative results. The write-up reviews the impact of these developments on Africa's competitiveness and explores the link between infrastructure development and the continent's competitiveness. It explains the important role that infrastructure plays in improving social welfare in general and in the equitable distribution of income among people and regions. For example, the promotion of adequate basic rural roads or water supply effectively entails a transfer of wealth among the population.

Considerations highlighting the importance of growth pole projects on the continent as a tool for accelerating infrastructure development are explored, focusing on paths forward regarding co-ordination, financing and risk challenges as a way of improving new urban planning systems. Also highlighted is the need for a long-term national development plan, comprehensive policy mix and strong leadership to drive infrastructure development. This chapter argues that, at the regional level, urgent attention should be given to the development of regional infrastructure to achieve economies of scale. It recognizes that the construction industry is an integral part of any country's infrastructure delivery mechanism and if the sector is not developed, no sustainable infrastructure delivery can be achieved. Manufacturing which is integral to economic development should be developed to obtain cheap construction materials for infrastructure, thereby bringing down the cost of infrastructure, and scarcely any country in the world has developed without passing through this route. The benefits of industrial transformation are several, including rapid productivity growth, stable, well-paid jobs, fostering of innovation and the facilitation of trade integration through exports.

An effort is made to explain that infrastructure systems must be designed to protect the natural environment and withstand both natural and man-made hazards, using sustainable practices – to ensure that future generations can also use and enjoy it. Sustainable development will not only preserve the high quality of life and environment, but will also improve conditions in the future. The last section of this chapter addresses the important question of where to obtain the resources to finance large infrastructure projects. It identifies several examples of how countries in the Americas, Europe, Middle East and Asia have financed infrastructure, and suggests that it is the turn of African countries to apply lessons learned to enhance their programme.

Infrastructure and National Competitiveness

Infrastructure plays a critical role in enhancing a country's competitiveness and lowering the cost of doing business. Competitiveness refers to how nations come together and compete, and depends on how institutions of state work. Firms in countries with inadequate infrastructure are burdened with high costs of doing business as they have to try to provide infrastructure themselves, suffer potentially huge inefficiencies, or are simply unable to conduct activities for which infrastructure services are a prerequisite. Well-developed infrastructure networks are a prerequisite for linking less-developed communities to markets in a sustainable way. Effective modes of transport – including quality roads, railroads, air transport and ports – enable entrepreneurs to convey their goods and services to markets in a secure and timely manner, facilitate the movement of labour to their workplaces and encourage foreign direct investment.

Infrastructure is also critical for the promotion of inclusive and sustainable growth. Rural infrastructure – notably feeder roads and distribution systems – enable individuals, households, communities and small businesses to embark on income-generating activities thanks to improved access to electricity and links to markets. The World Bank flagship report – *Africa's Infrastructure: A Time for Transformation* (2010) – finds that Sub-Saharan Africa has the weakest infrastructure in the world, leading to an ironic situation where some African countries pay more than twice as much for basic services as people elsewhere. The report argues that well-functioning infrastructure is essential to Africa's economic performance and that improving efficiencies and reducing waste could result in major improvements in the lives of Africans on a global scale. The report said that in order to catch up during the next 10 years, most states would need to devote more than a third of their GDP to infrastructure development and stressed the need for a massive effort to overhaul Africa's infrastructure. Another report entitled *Infrastructure Productivity: How to Save $1 Trillion* (2013) from the McKinsey Global Institute (MGI) and McKinsey's infrastructure practice shows how pragmatic steps can boost productivity in the sector. It called for steps that do not require re-inventing the wheel, including eliminating waste, improving the selection of projects, streamlining their delivery and other best-practice examples from around the world, which would make a decisive difference if scaled up globally. The report added that to spur change programmes and capture potential savings, governments must move beyond a project-by-project view and look at the potential effects on the entire network in a programmatic approach and upgrade systems for planning and delivery.

Inadequate infrastructure has raised the transaction costs of business in most African economies. According to the *African Competitiveness Report* (2013), African countries exhibit the lowest levels of productivity of all low-income countries and are among the least competitive economies in the world. Inadequate infrastructure has been estimated to shave off at least two percent of Africa's annual growth. With adequate infrastructure, African firms could achieve productivity gains of up to 40 percent over current growth rates. Productivity growth and increasing competitiveness are therefore higher in countries with an adequate supply of infrastructure.

Adequate infrastructure that works properly is crucial for Africa's economic integration, such as networks designed in such a way as to link production centres and distribution hubs across the continent, as exists in developed economies. To achieve this calls for the construction of an efficient and secure national and cross-border physical infrastructure as well as a coherent system of regulation for business transactions. Developing adequate and efficient infrastructure will boost Africa's competitiveness and productivity, especially in manufacturing sectors, enable access to regional markets, lower the cost of doing business, and facilitate trade and foreign direct investment, as well as deepen economic and social integration and create employment opportunities. The job creation and the growth of attractive investment opportunities will consequently encourage the efficient use of natural resources. Improved and efficient infrastructure will also contribute to social development in the areas of health and education and will reduce societal inequalities through a more equitable distribution of national wealth.

The State of Key Sectors

The World Bank's 1994 World Development Report defines infrastructure as the combination of fundamental systems that support a community, region or country. It includes everything from water and sewer systems to road and rail networks, to the national power and natural gas grids. African countries suffer from a pronounced infrastructure deficit. Compared with other regions, these countries have a low stock of infrastructure in all sectors, except information and communication technology (ICT), whose potential is gradually being fully harnessed. Ineffective links between different transport modes, deteriorating air connectivity, poorly equipped ports, ageing rail networks and inadequate access to all-season roads are key problems confronting

Africa's transport system. Coupled with burdensome trade regulations, these deficiencies have constrained gains in domestic productivity and present a critical bottleneck to stronger regional integration. The key infrastructure sectors are described below.

THE TRANSPORTATION SECTOR

Reliable transport infrastructure in all its four sub-sectors (roads, railways, airports and seaports) is an essential component of every country's competitiveness. Africa's prolonged under-investment in transportation has resulted in a dilapidated transport infrastructure. Indeed, the Africa Competitiveness Report (2013) notes that compared with other developing countries, excluding the provision for maintenance, African countries on average invested 15–25 percent of GDP in transport infrastructure over the period 2005–12, while India and China invested about 32 percent and 42 percent of GDP, respectively, within the same period. This under-investment has resulted in a decrepit infrastructure and considerably higher transport costs (by as much as 100 percent in Africa) compared to other low-income developing countries. This poses a fundamental constraint to Africa's global competitiveness and economic growth. It is particularly crucial for landlocked countries, for which transport infrastructure is a prerequisite to opening up production zones. The continent's 15 landlocked countries are constrained in transporting their produce to markets and in importing goods because of the lack of multi-modal infrastructure that can accommodate their particular requirements. Reliable transport must be in place for companies to import and export goods, fill orders and obtain supplies. For example, 78 percent of Burkina Faso's trade is carried by four main roads and rail corridors linking the country to the gateway ports in Benin, Côte d'Ivoire, Ghana and Togo according to the Africa Competitiveness Report (2013). Eighty percent of the economic activity in Senegal is concentrated in Dakar. In South and East Africa, port congestion and shipment delays undermine the ability to acquire imported production inputs, with resulting production losses and higher production costs.

ROADS

Although roads are the predominant mode of transport for freight and passengers in Africa, major deficits exist in road infrastructure throughout the continent. A significant percentage of Africa's road network is unpaved, isolating people from basic education, health services, transport corridors, trade hubs and economic opportunities. Access to the road network is uneven, with both urban and rural areas largely underserved. A number of countries including Ghana and Nigeria have started Bus Rapid Transit (BRT) systems to address their urban transport challenges. A BRT transforms a bus so that it functions virtually as a train car, with dedicated lanes and similar comfort and features to a subway station. A kilometre of BRT costs 10 times less than a subway and can be built much faster. Limited competition in the trucking industry keeps road freight tariffs unnecessarily high, while red tape along international trade corridors slows the movement of freight below 12 km an hour even though truck speeds can average 60 km per hour. The urban–rural disparity in road networks is a concern across the entire continent. The unequal access makes the flow of goods and services to and from rural areas difficult and expensive.

Rural roads are indispensable for poverty reduction. Together with the development of corridors, rural roads provide economic opportunities and access to markets. Accordingly, emphasis should be given to developing rural roads so as to enhance access, and also to upgrading urban roads with a focus on those with cross-border connections. Only 40 percent of rural Africans live within 2 km of an all-season road, compared to some 65 percent in other developing regions. Improving road accessibility in rural areas is critical to raising agricultural productivity across Africa. Making provisions for adequate road maintenance, both corrective and preventative, is vital, as this ensures the sustainability of investments. In addition, it will be essential to address the overloading of vehicles by means that include harmonized legislation in the form of regional axle load control acts and enforcing axle load limits and control. To stem the incidence of road fatalities and resulting sizeable losses to the economy, road safety programmes need to be enhanced and adequately funded as road accidents double the direct cost of congestion. Adequate maintenance plans are also prerequisites for sustainable infrastructure. Maintenance is not only corrective but also preventative because it inspects assets and reduces the risk of failure. Costs associated with statutory maintenance can be substantial, even considerably larger than the value of the asset, yet providing for these maintenance costs is crucial. Without adequate maintenance, infrastructure deteriorates quickly and is unsustainable.

RAILROADS

Outdated infrastructure and limited maintenance have resulted in a significant reduction in usable track and undermined the effectiveness of railways across Africa. Inefficient and inadequate railroad networks contribute to the high costs of doing business in the continent. North Africa, particularly Egypt, boasts the oldest railway network in Africa, but it has had only a few upgrades since its inception. In West Africa, as evidenced by Senegal and Ghana, the rail network has deteriorated substantially in recent years because of a lack of investment. Addressing these deficiencies will require investments in the sector which, in turn, will ease pressure on road networks. A regional approach should be taken, with an emphasis on establishing uniform rail gauges to enable trains to cross country boundaries. Currently African countries have several different gauges and consequently even when the railway is linked, for example, in Cote d'Ivoire and Ghana, trains cannot move between these two countries. A customs regulatory framework for the cross-border movement of goods and services will also need to be agreed in order to facilitate railroad transportation across Africa. It is interesting to note that the sector is being addressed by regional economic development blocks. ECOWAS, for example, is spearheading the development of a West African high-speed railroad that would link a number of countries from Nigeria through Ghana to Senegal.

AIR TRANSPORT

The importance of air transport for trade, particularly for landlocked countries, cannot be overemphasized as it is the most convenient means of freighting light and perishable goods. It is imperative that countries enhance this sector's development so as to improve connectivity and safety and to reduce costs in order to promote intra-African and global trade. By providing a quick link to export markets, air transport enables the trade of time-sensitive, perishable exports such as cut flowers, vegetables, fruits, meat and fish, which are becoming increasingly important foreign-exchange earners for African countries. Air transport in Africa, while crucial, is expensive by international standards because of a lack of infrastructure and regulatory systems. Regulatory challenges relate mainly to the liberalization of airspace. Despite some countries having liberalized their airspace after the Yamoussoukro Declaration of 1988, several countries such as Angola and the Democtratic Republic of the Congo have not. Improvements in infrastructure have the potential to open up production zones and facilitate product delivery while reducing their costs.

PORTS

Many African ports have serious capacity problems that are accentuated by an ineffective inland transport system. Enhancing port infrastructure substantially reduces the cost of production for enterprises. Countries should put in place measures to address the serious port capacity problems and deal with the inefficiencies that slow down processing times and result in higher charges than those of nearby ports. Accordingly, as a result of the recent Dakar Port Container Development Project, Senegal has been able to expand its exposure to international markets.

WATER RESOURCES, WATER SUPPLY AND SEWERAGE SYSTEMS

Wide hydro-climatic variability, inadequate storage, rising demand and a lack of trans-boundary co-operation undermine the African water sector. Less than 60 percent of Africa's population has access to drinking water and only a handful of countries are on track to reach the Millennium Development Goals (MDGs). With more than 60 trans-boundary rivers in Africa, developing large-scale infrastructure to manage water use and avoid conflicts is a formidable challenge. Over the last 40 years, only four million hectares of new irrigation have been developed, compared to 25 and 32 million hectares for China and India, respectively. Most cities do not have adequate environmental infrastructure to serve the existing population, so meeting future growth demands presents a challenge requiring significant policy reforms, capacity development and very substantial capital investments. The lack of adequate and safe water supply combined with poor sanitation and drainage facilities in urban areas presents the most serious environmental health threat from waterborne diseases, particularly to those poorly housed in slums. In many cities the solutions are well understood, but the capital investment required, for example, for sewerage and waste treatment facilities is considered to be just too high and unaffordable.

URBAN DEVELOPMENT AND HOUSING SYSTEMS

Africa is urbanizing rapidly – generally a good thing on a sparsely settled continent that is more rural than any other region of the world. The demand for food created by cities pulls surrounding rural areas out of subsistence farming by offering a nearby market for agricultural goods. At the same time, the agglomeration effect kindled in cities greatly enhances economic productivity. These valuable benefits hinge on effective infrastructure as well as serviceable urban–rural links. But most of Africa's infrastructure has not kept pace with urbanization. The weak financial base of African cities and ineffective urban planning and malfunctioning land markets are key constraints. Africa's rapid urbanization is putting significant pressure on existing infrastructures and the ability of cities to offer housing and services to all citizens. Although urbanization is usually associated with rising incomes, better living standards and improved human development, these economic and social advantages will not come automatically. In order to fully benefit from the advantages of rapid urbanization, governments need to formulate efficient, affordable and environmentally sustainable urban plans. Brand new cities will rise, while existing ones will expand to accommodate growing populations.

Historical Perspectives and Lessons

URBANIZATION AND ENVIRONMENTAL IMPROVEMENT

Global trends in urbanization and environmental improvements are generating a worldwide demand for improved urban infrastructure and a greater emphasis on supporting environmental initiatives. Urbanization has accelerated progress towards the MDGs, but careful planning is essential to prevent the growth of slums, pollution and crime that can derail achievements, according to the 2010 Annual progress report on the MDGs, which focused on urbanization and was presented during the World Bank and the International Monetary Fund (IMF) meetings. The report's lead author, Jos Verbeek, urged governments not to be troubled by urbanization as it provides higher incomes than workers would earn on a farm and yields further opportunities to climb the income ladder. If managed well, it can be a force for good; virtually no country has graduated to a high-income status without urbanizing and urbanization rates above 70 percent are typically found in high-income countries, said the report, which noted that urban poverty rates were relatively low and declining in all regions between 1990 and 2008, and poverty and inequality affect access to and the affordability of modern infrastructure services (see Figure 15.1).

About 2.7 billion people in the developing world live in urban areas and 96 percent of the additional 1.4 billion people in the developing world will join them by 2030. Growth will not only be in today's megacities of Shanghai or Mumbai, but also in secondary cities such as Accra in Ghana, Huambo in Angola, Fushun in China and Surat in India. The report says that many emerging urban centres are still taking shape, providing policy makers with a unique but rapidly closing window of opportunity to get their cities right. The report warned that if the forces of urbanization are not managed speedily and efficiently, slum growth can overwhelm city growth, exacerbate urban

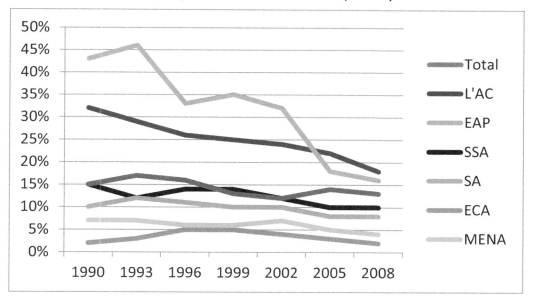

Figure 15.1   **Decreasing Poverty Rates**
Source: World Bank Staff calculations and Household surveys

poverty, derail MDG achievements and reduce, if not eliminate, cities' comparative advantage regarding attainment of the MDGs. Generally, about one billion people live in urban slums in poor countries worldwide, and their numbers are projected to grow by nearly 500 million by 2020. These populations are growing fastest in Sub-Saharan Africa, South-East Asia and western Asia, and as much as 62 percent of Africa's urban population live in slums. According to Hans Timmer, Director of the World Bank team that produced the report, slums are the result of an unfettered approach to urbanization. If planning is done right, there cannot be the emergence of slums. A key message of the report is that governments should provide basic services for people in slums just like in rural areas or cities. In Laos, for example, the government has given squatters long-term leases to public land, formalizing their status on the land they already occupied. The Vietnamese government is trying to provide slums with better services by adjusting planning standards to make them more realistic and cheaper. The report emphasizes the importance of planning, making markets accessible to other neighbourhoods in the city, other cities and export markets, and financing for large infrastructure projects.

DEVELOPING MANUFACTURING CAPACITY

The rapid growth of Japan's economy owes as much to the development of the nation's infrastructure as to technological progress. Since the Second World War in particular, infrastructure development has made a major contribution to economic advances that have, in turn, improved living conditions in cities that have seen huge influxes of population and a heavy concentration of urban functions. Public investments in cities have also helped develop an infrastructure that promotes local growth and assists correct regional disparities in economic development. Thus, infrastructure development has been pursued by provincial governments throughout the nation as a basic means of enriching lifestyles and maintaining Japan's economic vitality. Infrastructure development needs to be supported by a comprehensive manufacturing policy mix to reinforce the backward and forward links of infrastructure investments in the economy. An analysis of historical patterns of economic development in 13 developed countries by the Nobel Prize-winner Simon Kuznets (1971) identified a shift of resources from agriculture to industry as the defining feature of economic growth patterns. His findings are, among others, that: (i) the rise in the industrial sector as a share of an economy is largely due to increased manufacturing, which rises from between 11 percent and 15 percent in the initial decades of development to over 30 percent of GDP in later stages, and thus comes to account for about two-thirds of the rise in the economy; (ii) this shift corresponds to a decline in the contribution of the agricultural sectors to GDP; (iii) of the other sub-sectors in the industrial sector, transportation and public utilities rise moderately; and (iv) among the sub-sectors of the service sector, only the share taken by government services tends to rise in most countries.

The economic development patterns of industrialized countries were also studied by Hollis Chenery and his comparative cross-country analysis extended to developing countries. Chenery's main focus was to find out how the transformation of production structures affects rates of growth and the distribution of the benefits of growth, and what effect policies designed to accelerate this shift have had. One of Chenery's major findings is that the post-war experiences of newly industrialized countries indicate a high correlation between industrialization and rising income, and that as per capita income rises, there is a rise in the share of manufacturing in total output and employment. He concluded his work by stating that development is conceived as the successful transformation of the structure of an economy. A definition of structural transformation includes changes in consumption patterns in relation to increased income, changes in comparative advantage of different productive factors, productivity growth and the effects of government policy on resource allocation. The structure of an economy is linked to its composition and the magnitude of its productive factors, namely labour, capital and natural resources, and their allocation to different uses within sectors. Changes in economic structure can be recognized by shifts in the allocation of productive resources among the various sectors.

A structural transformation from agriculture to manufacturing in the total aggregate production of an economy is inevitable, since the demand for manufactured goods is more elastic than that for agriculture goods when income rises. Consequently, growth in the manufacturing sector is higher than in agriculture, which thus implies that the manufacturing sector accounts for an increasing share of GDP when income reaches a certain level. This means that manufacturing's contribution to GDP is one of the most important indices of the development phase. Observing from the Japanese experience, gross manufacturing production correlates strongly with trade patterns, which can also be used as an important variable in the characterization of the development phase. Fifty years after the end of the Second World War, Japan, which was devastated by the war, ranked second globally in terms of economic power. Most of this infrastructure was constructed and brought into operation in the 40 years following the war. Clearly, its development required a perceived demand, as well as the determination to encourage the enterprises, capital, technology, manpower and organizations needed to implement it. The country responded appropriately to these requirements and the result is now widely seen as one of the most successful examples of a nation's industrialization.

NATIONAL DEVELOPMENT PLAN: A SINE QUA NON TO DEVELOPMENT

A comprehensive national development plan is a *sine qua non* for sound infrastructure development. Infrastructure development needs a compelling national-level vision backed by leadership to ensure sustainable investments. Currently most infrastructure investment decisions are made without the benefit of a national vision. Such a strong national development plan must originate with strong national leadership and be shared by all levels of government without neglecting the contribution of the private sector, which is paramount. Without a strong national development vision crafted to cover a minimum period of 25 years, infrastructure cannot be effectively planned and efficiently executed. The plans should complement broad national goals of economic growth and leadership, resource conservation, human resource development, energy requirements and environmental stewardship. Plans should be synchronized with regional land use planning and related regulation and incentives to address the growing demand for increased infrastructure. Countries that have had successful infrastructure development can also be associated with strong visions, for example, China 2000, Dubai 2020, Abu Dhabi 2030, China 2050 and Japan 2050. Added to the national vision is the need for well-funded research and development at the national level and made available to all levels of government to develop new, more efficient methods, personnel and materials for building and maintaining a nation's infrastructure.

A LONG-TERM FIX

Infrastructure development is a long-term delivery. Once established, infrastructure, be it a road, railway, airport, seaport, harbour, power plant or telecommunications facility, continues to influence local industry and inhabitants for an extended period. These projects take a number of years to plan, a further few years to construct, and can then remain in service for more than 100 years if adequately maintained. Decisions on investment therefore require a long-term perspective and should depend on predicted future levels of economic activity. In other words, infrastructure development should be considered in view of the long-term development path of an economy. It is thus crucial to decide when, where and what infrastructure elements should be constructed in terms of their possible long-term influence on both national and local economies. Resource allocation must therefore be properly handled in national economic plans or development plans according to a broad, long-range perspective. As such, this definition of infrastructure highlights its important attribution, the inter-generational resource transfer. The primary beneficiaries of investment in infrastructure by the present generation may well be the next generation, since developments take a long time to mature. So, for example, railways, airports, hydroelectric dams and cities projects will provide timely benefits to future generations. This attribute is being recognized as increasingly important as sizable investment is urgently needed in environmental protection and improvement work, not only locally but also in the global context. This emphasizes the point that basing infrastructure investment on market principles is not always appropriate, since the contemporary market cannot reflect the values of future generations.

MANAGING FUTURE CLIMATE CHANGES

Infrastructure represents such a major investment that it is important to build in order to cope with future changes. This means that recognition of likely future climate changes, their impacts and appropriate adaptation measures should occur at the planning stages. However, most infrastructure is designed, built and maintained on the premise that the future climate will be similar to that experienced in the past. Today's infrastructure services, whether they are cities, transportation, water, flood control systems, etc., must be able to withstand both current and future challenges. Both structural and non-structural methods must be applied to meet challenges. Infrastructure systems must be designed to protect the natural environment and withstand both natural and man-made hazards, using sustainable practices, to ensure that future generations can use what is built today. Efforts must be made to raise the bar in infrastructure excellence to enable it to weather the debilitating effects of climate change. Advances in dealing creatively with unplanned urban growth, land degradation, inefficient use of water and energy will not only have immediate, short-term benefits but will also make livelihoods and nations more resilient in the face of the impacts of climate change.

BUILDING SOUND INSTITUTIONS

Institutional competence and capacity are important determinants of the performance of infrastructure providers in every sector. Institutions make a difference and they reveal how far reforms can go to match the requisite facilities. Generally, reforms are needed in regulatory systems, finance, land, building and construction materials, and last but not least in the construction and labour sectors. Infrastructure expansion and economic growth depended greatly on a continuing improvement of the absorptive capacity of society, which is a function of many factors, including law and order, political stability, the work ethic, the strength of manpower, technology and management, and most crucially on the provision of physical infrastructure. Infrastructure therefore becomes a fine opportunity to increase the disposable income of citizens and predict future levels of economic activity.

As value systems and even societal structure change over time, infrastructure planning inevitably involves predicting future structural changes in society. For example, investment in a transportation project today will have a long-term impact on future generations; that is, the impact will spill over into the economic structure, production and consumption patterns of subsequent generations.

This inescapable interaction between current investment in infrastructure and future economic structures is worth anticipating, and the experience of advanced countries may have a certain relevance to infrastructure planning in today's developing countries. Ideally, an investment package would be accompanied by complementary labour policies to enhance productivity and maximize investment benefits. Nationals of poor African countries are among the least paid people in the world, and this trend must be reversed if sustainable infrastructure is to be developed and patronized. In a globalizing world, the cost differences of infrastructure delivery and maintenance in developed and developing countries narrows down and therefore the purchasing power of the labour force should be increased to enable them to pay for the delivery and maintenance of infrastructure of international standards. Thus, decisions on investment should not only depend on the long-term view of the economy, but also on value judgements by society with regard to income transfer and distribution.

It can be seen today in Asia's rapidly expanding economies that a lack of infrastructure often becomes a major constraint on private sector activities, reduces the state's revenues and curtails the citizen's welfare and standard of living. The cases of Japan, Thailand, Indonesia and China suggest that a smooth transition may require substantial investment and careful allocation of national resources in infrastructure. To strengthen the nation state, build up the private sector and boost the consuming market, government must craft a tripartite recovery programme for the state, the corporate business class and citizenry aimed at establishing a more secure environment, developing infrastructure, reforming business and financial practices, and giving work to the unemployed.

ECONOMIC EVALUATION OF LARGE PROJECTS

As infrastructure is built or rehabilitated, life-cycle cost analysis should be performed to account for initial construction, operation, maintenance, environmental, safety and other costs reasonably anticipated during the life of the project, such as recovery after disruption from natural or man-made hazards. Life-cycle cost analysis, maintenance and planned renewal will result in more sustainable and resilient infrastructure systems and will ensure that they can meet the needs of future users. All available financing options must be explored and debated.

Strategies for Developing Countries

Strategic infrastructure development can generally be described as developments of strategic economic or social importance to the state that contribute significantly to the fulfilment of the national development plan in a sustainable manner. The most strategic investments are functional and create the greatest impact in terms of economic growth, social uplift and sustainability. Infrastructure will only drive sustained economic growth when it is properly aligned with the country's priorities and systems, some of which are the construction sector and skills development, growth poles and slum avoidance, and the unique role of housing as an economic stimulator and infrastructure financing tool.

CONSTRUCTION SECTOR AND SKILLS DEVELOPMENT

The construction industry is an integral part of any country's infrastructure and industrial development, and activities in the sector signal the general direction of an economy, indicate how resources are put into infrastructure development and demonstrate the extent to which development is maintained. Generally, the state of the construction sector in any nation is an indicator of the economic development of that country. If Africa wants to raise the game in its infrastructure, the construction industry is the vehicle and the absorptive capacity of the sector must be assessed and addressed. Within the sector, various strata of construction personnel are assessed: high-level engineers, architects, planners, surveyors, etc.; middle-level technicians; and lower-level skilled and unskilled manpower. Civil engineers are the main professionals that take the lead in infrastructure delivery, just as doctors take the lead in the health delivery system and teachers the educational system. Generally, civil engineering is the crucial skill needed for Africa's infrastructure development and particularly to drive waste management, urban development and housing, roads and railways, water resources, water supply and irrigation, sewerage and waste management systems. Not enough construction professionals are produced and a significant portion of them migrate overseas or are attracted to more lucrative career sectors, particularly banking and finance.

The construction industry is a major sector of the economy of most nations. The industry is a large consumer of minerals and mineral-based materials ranging from aggregates, cement and tiles to structural steel, glass and ceramic bathroom fittings. This holds true for both industrialized and emerging countries where a major proportion of total demand for industrial minerals is generated by the construction sector. The British Geological Survey 2001 publication, *Minerals for Development – Industrial Minerals Workshop Papers*, reports that in 1990, construction raw materials were estimated to make up about 40 percent of the total value of construction output in the UK, or some £20 billion. Industrial minerals serve as basic raw materials for the manufacturing sector where the added value may be several times the cost of the mineral or where the mineral itself forms an essential part of an industrial process. Fortunately, Africa has all these minerals too and in larger quantities. A major constraint in harnessing industrial minerals in Africa is closely related to the fact that the importance of industrial minerals to the economic development of Africa is still not clearly understood. As a first step, Africa needs to prepare a comprehensive databank for industrial minerals deposits, which contain information on resources and reserves, quality, production, demand, and imports and exports for each commodity.

THE GROWTH POLE CONCEPT

Most countries normally follow the natural physical development pattern which does not always lead to development and there is a need for selectivity in deciding what investments to pursue, where they should be located, and how these would impact the growth potential of the region and the national economy. This is where growth poles are so important. The growth pole approach to economic development looks at how infrastructure that will be developed for an investment resource in, say, oil and gas, tourism, mining or agriculture can be used to encourage spillovers into other sectors. They are built on the assumption that there is a need for simultaneous, co-ordinated investments in many sectors to encourage self-sustaining industrialization that could increase market size, thereby attracting more investment and employment. This could manifest itself through a development corridor or a special economic zone, or urban development in an agglomeration economy. Agglomeration is simply the advantages that accrue to industries when production is concentrated at a given location and thus further enhance the efficiency of production.

A recent World Bank Research paper, *Infrastructure for Growth in Ghana: A Spatial Approach* (2013), indicates that a 10 percent increase in firm concentration boosts output by 0.5 percent. In other words, activities clustered in space can generate synergies, which could unleash a virtuous spiral of growth. Growth poles are thus successful and innovative approaches that link infrastructure investments to the development of industries and that can set into motion a reinforcing cycle of forward and backward links. By bringing together investors from both the public and private sectors to share risks, growth poles can reduce the costs of infrastructure projects and incentivise the local private sector's participation in these projects. The underlying assumption about the benefits of growth poles is that they increase market size so that it becomes profitable for private firms to invest. Private sector investments in turn lead to more jobs, higher wages and economies of scale. Growth pole projects also often attract foreign direct investment, are built across borders and have spillover effects beyond national economies. Thus, they can also be a boon to regional integration.

The core idea of the growth poles theory is that economic development is not uniform over an entire region, but instead takes place around a key industry linked mainly through direct and indirect effects. The expansion of this key industry implies the expansion of output, employment and related investments, as well as new technologies and new industrial sectors. The growth pole idea is an opportunity to solve most of a country's development challenges by starting all over, avoiding all the mistakes and undertaking all the reforms needed in that one place and, if successful, replicated throughout the entire country. The growth pole concept has created a large middle class in many countries, and nations such as China, India, Dubai, Qatar, Shanghai, Abu Dhabi, Malaysia and Indonesia benefited from investments from several other sectors.

The Chinese government, for example, has capitalized on the growth pole concept to create a large consuming middle class. The result was that from the late 1990s to 2010, more than 400 million Chinese were lifted out of poverty, mainly on the backbone of tremendous infrastructure development and the growth of new cities, and an even larger middle class is expected to be developed by 2030. The Chinese have used the growth pole concept to transform villages into urban settlements and by 2030, more than 200 cities planned for one million residents each will be built. China's leadership has charted equally ambitious plans for the future. Its goal is to bring the entire nation's urban infrastructure up to the level of infrastructure in a middle-income country, while using increasingly efficient transport logistics to tie the country together. The government used substantial infrastructure spending to hedge against flagging economic growth.

IMPROVING SLUM AREAS

As a result of Africa's rapid economic and population expansion, over a third of African inhabitants currently live in cities. The population of African cities is projected to increase by up to 85 percent in 20 years, with Lagos and Kinshasa overtaking Cairo as the most populous cities on the continent. Ominously, in this new urban growth, city slums are growing dangerously fast too – faster indeed than urban growth itself. Kofi Annan, the former Secretary General of the United Nations, said that 'the locus of global poverty is moving to the cities, a process now recognized as the *urbanization of poverty*' and efforts must be made to invest in the poor. According to the Africa Progress Panel Report (2012), across Africa cities are growing at twice the rate of rural villages. By the end of 2012, 72 percent of urban dwellers resided in slums and their living conditions were worse than in rural areas. In order to fully benefit from the advantages of rapid urbanization, governments need to address these challenges by formulating efficient, affordable and environmentally sustainable urban plans. African cities require the expansion of housing capacity through the development of low-cost residential properties as well as commercial buildings. Brand new cities need to rise, while existing ones should expand to accommodate growth in populations, and the growth pole idea gives the opportunity to improve on slum areas of the city which normally occupy some of the most prime urban lands.

HOUSING AS A STIMULUS AND MULTIPLIER

African countries should use housing as a great stimulus to kick-start growth in their countries. Generally, the housing sector has historically been the sector that economies rely on for recovery during times of recession because it fuels three key powerful effects on the rest of the economy. First, housing is a source of long-term finance as it is typically the largest investment most individuals make in their lifetime. Second, construction has a trickle-down effect on employment and is a great source of relatively high-paying jobs for real estate brokers, engineers and lawyers to name just a few, as well as for lower-skilled workers. Finally, investment in a new home usually necessitates demands for purchases of different consumables like furnishings, appliances, services and even clothing.

Housing is one of the most effective ways of stimulating consumption and production activity in other sectors of the economy. The stimulus occurs because of the multiplier effect that marks any spending done in the economy, whether by private spenders or by the government. New incomes turn into another round of spending, subject to some saving by the income earners that again turns into incomes for others, triggering more new spending, and the process repeats itself ad infinitum. As such, the total additional income resulting from any new spending would be several times the size, i.e. a multiple of the original amount spent. How much the original spending is actually multiplied depends on how much is saved at each round of the income-spending cycle, how much of the spending goes to domestically produced goods and services, as against imports, and how easily the spending permeates the rest of the economy. However, if the money was spent, for example, to buy a new presidential jet, to import rice from Thailand or the road contract awarded to a Chinese firm, then it is foreign incomes that would be multiplied, not that of the implementing country. State funding for housing infrastructure, whether new construction or rehabilitation, is a powerful tool to create jobs, boost economic growth and increase public revenues while addressing the housing challenges across Africa. Creating productive employment for Africa's rapidly growing young population is not only an immense challenge but also the key to future prosperity.

Financing Large-Scale Infrastructure Projects

The 2010 study carried out by the World Bank and African Development Bank entitled *Africa Infrastructure – A Time for Transformation* estimated that Sub-Saharan Africa will need to invest up to US$93 billion annually until 2020 for both capital investment and maintenance if the rest of Africa is to achieve levels of infrastructure comparable to Mauritius. The reality, however, is that the figure is grossly underestimated and aggregating country-specific figures gives a budget eight times as much. Given the substantial amounts involved, governments have to be innovative in the search for sustainable approaches to infrastructure finance and development, and would do well to create conditions for public-private partnerships (PPPs). The private sector will necessarily need to play an increasingly important role, and efficiency gains from performance improvements in infrastructure provision are themselves a significant source of finance, while the development of infrastructure bonds as a financing vehicle will need to be encouraged.

As indicated previously, Africa's development strategies should be shaped by a long-term vision, where all elements affecting the country's development are considered coherently, giving each factor a chance for consideration, and the importance of links between infrastructure planning and the long-term development policy will then be apparent. The preparation of long-term planning facilitates long-term finance and governments should encourage inflows of long-term finance to productive sectors of the economy. Short-term solutions are unsustainable. Besides loans, bonds and micro-finance initiatives, there are a few non-traditional sources that African countries can use to mobilize funds. While national resources must be used to complement, encourage and leverage investment from the regional and local government levels as well as from the private sector, users of the infrastructure must be willing to pay the appropriate price for their use. This section explores other ways of raising finance besides the traditional sources: development aid, bonds, pension funds, foreign direct investments, etc.

TAX AND RESOURCE MOBILIZATION

Many infrastructure projects have largely been financed by borrowing from multi-lateral or international institutions. Developing countries need to understand that the sources of aid and financing given out by development partners for infrastructure in developing countries are taxes paid by their citizens. While aid remains a short-term necessity for most African countries, the long-term goal must be to increase the domestic savings rate to reduce dependence on external investment sources. In order to undertake this evolution, African countries must ensure the efficacy of resource mobilization both domestically and internationally. Resource mobilization in the form of tax policy and administration must be tailored in such way that they not only yield adequate resources to government but are also fair and effective in order to promote economic growth. Increasing tax yields represents a challenge for African tax authorities, but this is a crucial part of mobilizing domestic resources for development. Tax policy plays a major role in financing infrastructure and accelerates national development as taxes are the cheapest means of funding public investments. Tax is also key to the social contract between citizens and the state: citizens as taxpayers want assurance that everyone pays their fair share and that the revenue collected is being spent wisely on their behalf. Citizens are far more likely to pay taxes when they feel that politicians are honouring the social contract and that tax policies are legitimate and applied fairly. However, tax injustices are rife across Africa as they are in many countries around the world. If poorer countries are to escape from aid dependency, the grip of external debt and from poverty more broadly, it is essential that their revenue authorities have the capacity to collect taxes efficiently and in ways that are just and equitable.

African tax policy makers face formidable barriers in devising progressive, pro-poor tax regimes. Some barriers arise from domestic factors such as the scale of informal businesses, the power of political and wealthy elites to secure tax exemptions, and special tax treatments while also resisting and evading progressive taxes on wealth and property, and the under-resourcing of national and regional tax departments. The large proportions of the micro-businesses that predominate in the economy and operate outside the formal system reduce labour productivity, as they are not captured in national accounting and reduce the government's revenue. Tax exemptions to infrastructure providers are also generally unhealthy because they are distortionary and unfair as they have an effect of shrinking the tax base, i.e. less revenue to government. Seeking to bring the informal sector into the taxed formal sector offers opportunities not just for increased tax revenues, but also for higher levels of productivity, faster growth rates and enhanced social inclusion. If, however, the costs of entering the sector are too high for small firms and particularly for the micro-businesses that currently dominate most informal economies, then most are likely to choose to remain outside the system (Jütting and de Laiglesia, 2009).

BUILDING A VIABLE BANKING SYSTEM

An efficient financial system is a *sine qua non* for sustainable infrastructure delivery and conscious efforts should be made to develop the banking, financing and insurance sectors to address infrastructure needs. Almost every country that has achieved success in infrastructure delivery has established a state investment bank to streamline bureaucracy, channel low interest funds to development projects and help to restore business prosperity, particularly in the banking sector. A number of countries in challenging times set up investment funds owned by the state with the purpose of investing the state's resources across various low-risk asset classes both locally and abroad. There are several examples the world over, including the United States Reconstruction Finance Corporation, the Abu Dhabi Investment Authority, the Government of Singapore Investment Corporation, the South Korea Investment Corporation, etc. The investment banks are normally responsible for building a portfolio of global infrastructure investments as well as contributing to the growth of the economy through participation in local developments. Their investments target large-scale public systems that are vital to countries' economies, including transportation, communication, utilities and power and social infrastructures.

The Reconstruction Finance Corporation (RFC) was a former US government agency established and chartered by the US Congress after the Great Depression with the primary objective of providing liquidity to and restoring confidence in the banking system. The then banking systems, the vast majority of which were small and particularly susceptible to local economic difficulties, experienced pressures during the economic contraction of 1929–33, leading to widespread bank failures. The RFC gave $2 billion in the form of credit to state and local governments to shore up banks, railroads, mortgage associations and other businesses, and these loans were nearly all re-paid. The programme was continued by President Roosevelt and played a major role in reversing the Great Depression by setting up the relief programmes that were taken over by *The New Deal*. The RFC established eight new corporations and purchased an existing one in hydro-power, steel, cement, rubber plants, inter-state highways, etc. to push a manufacturing programme that would support the follow-on infrastructure plan. The RFC was abolished as an independent agency by an Act of Congress and was transferred to the Department of the Treasury to wind up its affairs in June 1954. It was totally disbanded in 1957.

CREDIT CREATION AND CAPITALIZING AFRICAN BANKS

According to the World Bank, Africa as a continent holds 15 percent of the world's oil reserves, 40 percent of its gold, more than 50 percent of its bauxite, about 80 percent of the platinum group of metals and a significant portion of its iron ore reserves, among others. A study by Boakye (2010) estimated Ghana's gross mineral wealth to be in excess of $1 trillion, arising from only four commodities: gold ($300 billion); iron ore ($250 billion); bauxite ($250 billion); and oil and gas ($200 billion). Other reports estimate that Sierra Leone with 10 billion tons of iron ore at average 52 percent grade, together with large deposits of bauxite, gold and oil, has gross reserves in excess of $2 trillion. Guinea with 40 percent of the world's bauxite reserves has gross mineral wealth valued at more than $12 trillion. Nigeria's oil and gas reserves and the Democratic Republic of the Congo, with almost every mineral on earth, have several trillion dollars of mineral wealth.

State institutions do not have high enough credit ratings to inject liquidity into the banks and therefore the capitalization of African banks must begin with African mineral reserves, with infrastructure and manufacturing sectors as the vehicle. National investment banks should be established to issue credit at low interest rates to commercial and other banks tapping into the productive capacity of the country. The value of credit should be based on the country's mineral wealth and the ability of the government to perform in creating credit over the long term for the development of the economy. The value of credit should be related to the quantity, quality and volume of the raw material, and the physical life of the investment, the amount that can be processed over a given period of time and the ability to re-pay the debt in a timely fashion. African states should take active part in the recapitalization process. To undertake this process, governments must create an entity which will be mandated to recapitalize the banks via selected instruments. African states must also bring a large proportion of the populace into the formal sector, provide better identification of citizens and create a demand for housing, mortgages and consumption. Going forward, the rewards will be linked to long-term performance and value creation, not excessive risk-taking. But the government should not be a permanent investor; over time, it will dispose of these investments in many orderly ways.

LAND FINANCING AND BENEFIT CAPTURE

Developing countries can make use of urban land within the city to finance its infrastructure. If infrastructure throws off externalities that raise productivity and profitability elsewhere in the economy, then the public sector must profit from the investment project. It is economically appropriate for the state to capture part of the land value increment it creates through its investment. The correspondent tax would also capture increases in land value that occur in the economy and which are not the result of investment decisions of landowners – what is called unearned increments to land value. In other words, society will take for itself part of the income it creates in land for landowners. It is a great source for funding urban infrastructure and its main attraction is the upfront generation of funds which reduces the burden of borrowing. Land developments are essentially priced to reflect costs of accommodating growth; the higher the quality of infrastructure proposed, the higher the land value. Cities such as the new Shanghai and Dubai were built based on land benefit capture. Many cities in China have financed more than half their infrastructure investments from land leasing, and they borrow against the value of land on their balance sheets to finance the rest.

George E. Peterson of the World Bank in his book entitled *Land Leasing and Land Sale as an Infrastructure-Financing Option* demonstrates how several cities have carried it out. For example, the Shanghai city authorities raised more than $100 billion from land leases for its makeover programme, about half the necessary investments to transform Shanghai. Cairo raised $4.57 billion from the sale of 5,400 hectares of desert land without financial cost to the government. In Mumbai, $1.2 billion was obtained from only 13 hectares. More recently, similar sums were raised in Cape Town, Bangalore, Khartoum, Luanda, Bogota and Istanbul from land leases to finance infrastructure. Land benefit capture is easier to implement when the land is under public control. In China, nearly all land is owned by the state and this allows the government an unusual degree of freedom to think in the longer term. To enhance infrastructure delivery, developing countries should make efforts to convert most lands from private and traditional control to state control, and the policy of returning state lands to stools and families should be discouraged.

Table 15.1   Magnitude of Land Financing in Select Projects of Developing Countries

Location and activity	Land financing amount and use of proceeds	Comparative magnitude
Cairo, Arab Rep. of Egypt: auction of desert land for new towns (May 2007, 2,100 hectares)	US$3.12 billion: to be used to reimburse costs of internal infrastructure and build connecting highway to Cairo Ring Road	117 times to urban property tax collections in country; equal to approximately 10% of total national government revenue
Cairo, Arab Rep. of Egypt: private installation of 'public' infrastructure in return for free transfer of developable desert land (2005–present)	US$1.45 billion of private investment in internal and external infrastructure plus 7% of serviced land turned over to government for moderate-income housing	Will provide a range of urban infrastructure services for more than 3,300 hectares of newly developed land without financial cost to the government
Mumbai, India: auction of land in the city's new financial centre (January 2006, November 2007, total 13 hectares) by Mumbai Metropolitan Regional Development Authority (MMRDA)	US$1.2 billion: to be used primarily to finance projects in metropolitan regional transportation plan	10 times MMRDA's total capital spending in year 2005: 3.5 times total value of municipal bonds issued by all urban local utilities in India in the past decade
Istanbul, Turkey: sale of municipal bus station and former administrative site (March and April 2007)	US$1.5 billion in auction proceeds to be dedicated to capital investment budgets	Total municipal capital spending in fiscal 2005 was US$994 million; municipal borrowing infrastructure investment in 2005 was US$97 million
Cape Town, South Africa: sale of Victoria and Albert Waterfront property by Transnet, the parastatal transportation agency (November 2006)	US$1.0 billion, to be used to recapitalize Transnet and support its investment in core transportation infrastructure	Sale proceeds exceeded Transnet's total capital spending in year 2006; equal to 17% of five-year capital investment plan prepared in 2006
Bogota, Colombia: betterment fees, *contribucion valorizacion*	US$1.0 billion collected in 1997–2007; US$1.1 billion planned for 2008–15; used to finance city street and bridge improvement programme	Finances 50% of street and bridge improvements; other sources of financing: US$50 million loan from the International Finance Corporation; US$300 million peso-linked bond issue

Source: Peterson (2007).

Conclusions

This chapter has demonstrated that although Africa has made improvements in increasing its infrastructure stock in recent years, it remains underdeveloped relative to other emerging regions. Improved infrastructure will increase Africa's competitiveness and productivity, lower the cost of doing business, facilitate trade and investment, create employment opportunities and deepen social integration. There are clear ways to create more and better infrastructure that African countries need to harness. First, a comprehensive long-term national development plan is necessary for sound infrastructure development, backed by strong leadership, local resource mobilization and a viable national construction industry. Infrastructure investment decisions require a long-term perspective and depend on predictable levels of future economic activity, increasing prosperity, expansion of jobs and rising incomes, but basing infrastructure investment on market principles is not always appropriate, since the contemporary market cannot reflect the values of future generations. This section also explained that infrastructure systems must be designed to protect the natural environment and withstand both natural and man-made hazards using sustainable practices in order to ensure that future generations can use and enjoy it. Infrastructure represents such a major investment that it is important Infrastructure represents such a major investment that it is important to build to cope with future changes and the appropriate adaptation measures should occur at the planning stages.

Efforts must therefore be made to raise the bar in infrastructure excellence to avoid the debilitating effects of climate change. Infrastructure also needs to be supported by a comprehensive manufacturing policy mix to reinforce the backward and forward links of investments in the economy. Manufacturing which is integral to economic development should be developed in order to obtain inexpensive construction materials for infrastructure, thereby bringing down the cost of projects. The chapter has covered the growth pole approach to economic development and how infrastructure developed for an investment resource can be used to encourage spillovers into other sectors and unleash a virtuous spiral of growth. Other countries have effectively utilized the growth pole concept to create a large consuming middle class which must be emulated by African countries. Housing is historically the key sector signalling an economy's recovery because of the production activity, consumption capacity and the multiplier effect that marks any spending done in the economy. An efficient banking and financial system is a *sine qua non* for sustainable infrastructure delivery and stepwise efforts are required to develop the banking, financing and insurance sectors to address investment needs. Finally, the ability to secure long-term financing depends on the preparation of a sound long-term planning. African countries must wean themselves from financing projects with aid from development partners and focus on the long-term goal of building capacity for local resource mobilization.

References

The African Competitiveness Report (2013). Developing Africa's infrastructure for enhanced competitiveness.

Akatsuka, Y. (1999). *Systems for Infrastructure Development: Japan's Experience*. Tokyo: Japan International Corporation Publishing.

British Geological Survey (2001). Minerals for development – Industrial Minerals Workshop Papers.

Chenery, H. (1986). *Industrialization and Growth: A Comparative Study*. Oxford: Oxford University Press.

Foster, V. and Briceno-Garmendia, C. (2010). *Africa's Infrastructure: A Time for Transformation: International Bank for Reconstruction and Development*. Washington DC: World Bank.

Jütting, J. and de Laiglesia, J. (2009). *Towards More and Better Jobs in Developing Countries*. Paris: OECD.

Kesse, G.O. (1980). Industrial mineral resources of Ghana.

Kuznets, S. (1971). *Economic Growth of Nations*. Cambridge, MA: Harvard University Press.

McKinsey Global Institute (MGI) (2013). *Infrastructure Productivity: How to Save $1 Trillion a Year*.

Peterson, G.E. (2007). *World Bank Land Leasing and Land Sale as an Infrastructure-Financing Option*. Washington DC: World Bank.

Verbeek, J. (2012). World Bank Staff calculations and household surveys (2012). Annual progress report on the MDG.

World Bank (1994). World Development Report 1994. Infrastructure for development.

——. (2010). Annual progress report on the MDGs, the World Bank and the International Monetary Fund (IMF).

——. (2013) Infrastructure for growth in Ghana: A spatial approach. Research paper.

Electronic References

American Society of Civil Engineers (2005). Report card for America's infrastructure. http://www.asce.org/reportcard/2005/page.cfm?id=203.

Boakye, C. (2010). Addressing housing, money and job creation in Ghana. http://www.infrastructureghana.org/news_upcomingevents/Addressing%20the%20Challenges%20of%20Housing%20and%20job%20Creation%20in%20Ghana.html

Christensen, J. (2012). Africa's lost tax revenue, lost development opportunities. http://concernedafricascholars.org/bulletin/issue87/christensen

Reconstruction Finance Corporation (n.d.). http://www.princeton.edu/~achaney/tmve/wiki100k/docs/Reconstruction_Finance_Corporation.html.

World Bank (2013). World Bank launches new fund to help African countries negotiate best-possible deals for their oil, gas, and minerals. http://www.worldbank.org/en/news/press-release/2012/10/05/world-bank-launches-fund-african-countries-negotiate-deals-for-oil-gas-minerals.

PART VI
THE PRIVATE SECTOR AND FINANCIAL MARKETS

16

The Private Sector as an Engine of Economic Growth

Kwaku Appiah-Adu and Osei Boeh-Ocansey

Abstract

This chapter examines the significance of the private sector in economic growth. It begins with an exploration of the origins and definitions of the private sector and economic growth. Next it traces the history of the private sector in industrial and developing economies, and the highs and lows of the sector through different economic cycles. This is followed by an examination of the perceived notion that the private sector has always been a dominant force in national economies. Subsequently, the chapter presents how a strong private sector could be built in a developing economy with a focus on Ghana and how the sector could contribute to national growth. Finally conclusions are drawn for the attention of developing economy governments and policy makers, as well as the private sector organizations and relevant stakeholders.

Introduction

In the past, for most developing countries under colonial rule, the vast majority of the working population (about 97 percent) was employed in the public sector, making the government the employer of the day (Villars, 2014). Most of these employees were amongst the well educated in society at that time. Only a few people went into commerce, which now constitutes a sizeable proportion of the private sector, because it was perceived that only those who could not further their education went into trade, since that sector was mainly characterized by buying and selling, which did not require much skill to venture into.

The situation was not any different even after most countries gained independence from their colonial masters because not much emphasis was placed on the private sector. The government still remained the largest employer, employing most of the adults in the employable group or bracket. Post-independence, many governments initiated the idea of creating state-owned enterprises, but these were still managed by public servants. For instance, decisions and directions still emanated from government as to how to run operations and other work affairs.

Over time, few educated people in developing countries saw the need to go into the private sector to produce and sell, create employment and also to gain experience in the management of one's own business. The private sector back then was weak because people went into it just to make a profit, winning or losing with not much formal training. However, with population growth, exposure, continuous change in governments and a new world economic order, together with interactions and experiences drawn from other nations, the private sector seems to be gaining much strength to stay in business and people are also realizing the fact that this sector is not only for the uneducated, as had been the perception previously.

This realization really came into full force in the 1980s as many developing countries embarked on economic reforms through the structural adjustment programmes prescribed by the Bretton Woods institutions comprising the World Bank and the International Monetary Fund (IMF). During the 1990s, the private sector began increasing its participation in the delivery of essential services partly because of the heavy fiscal burdens of state-owned enterprises and partly because of the increased commercial opportunities in emerging markets for private investors. While governments maintained their role of managing policy and regulatory frameworks, they allowed more private sector provision of services.

The Significance of the Private Sector as an Engine of Economic Growth

The private sector is an economic term and can also be referred to as the citizen sector. It is the part of the economy that is run by private groups or individuals without being controlled by a state. One reason why it can serve as an engine of economic growth is the fact that the sector pays about 25 percent of its profits to the government in the form of taxes, thereby adding value to society. The private sector is more than a mere engine of growth; it is also a key mechanism for women and men to participate in and contribute to that growth by creating jobs and opportunities and providing new goods and services, including financial services.

The private sector's ability to innovate and conduct its operations efficiently allows societies to achieve more with the resources at their disposal. When the private sector brings the spark of its imagination and innovation to develop localized solutions, poor communities as well as the owners and workers in the organizations will benefit. By working with private enterprises and being open to new ideas, ways can be found to improve the reach and delivery of basic services. It is not only the private sector itself that benefits from innovation and efficiency; it has much to teach the public sector and the aid industry about delivery, logistics, reaching the most remote communities, nurturing talent and taking risks for higher returns.

Capital markets drive economic growth, tapping initiative and investment to raise incomes. Trade is also a driver of economic growth as it integrates developing countries into the global economy and generates benefits for their people. Private sector actors are increasingly being recognized as a major force in development (Carlo, 2006). They drive economic growth through investment, employment and business creation, innovation and knowledge transfer, and other multiplier effects from their operations and activities. However, ensuring that this growth is likely to contribute to long-term poverty reduction requires private companies to include the poor as producers, suppliers, employees and consumers, especially when government policy provides the necessary incentives.

Under the right circumstances, public-private partnerships that are based on the identification of complementary expertise and shared commercial and development interests are also an important tool that can harness the private sector's contribution to such inclusive growth. Besides directly contributing to economic growth, poverty reduction and jobs, the private sector also provides essential services such as infrastructure (transport, telecommunications, water and power), health, education, and finance that are important to growth and to improving people's lives. Private sector participation in infrastructure and other services has become more important over the past 20 years, as governments have sought alternatives to public funding and have looked for more efficient ways to deliver services (World Economic Forum, 2010).

A growing private sector is fundamental to moving people out of poverty. Economic growth drives poverty reduction by creating jobs. Research into households that have escaped from poverty shows that, in more than 80 percent of cases, the decisive factor was a household member finding employment (AusAID, 2014). The private sector is the main source of employment for people in both developed and developing countries. Studies estimate that the private sector is responsible for creating around 90 percent of all jobs in developing countries (World Bank, 2005). When people have jobs and stable incomes, they tend to consume more, generating higher levels of economic activity. This, in turn, creates more jobs. Even in situations where people are not employed directly in the private sector, taxes collected from businesses can be used to fund public services and social safety nets. As economies expand, so too does the tax base available to governments.

In some cases, a diverse and vibrant private sector can become an advocate for reform and increased transparency and accountability in government. An emerging middle class can build support for a more independent media, greater government transparency, increased democracy and improved government services. In fragile states, a legitimate private sector can also be a powerful advocate for peace. In general, the business community has a strong interest in peace and stability because it provides the right environment for investment and growth. The private sector also contributes to peace and stability by providing jobs, which reduce incentives for people to return to conflict.

Definition of the Private Sector

The private sector comprises organizations that have a core strategy and mission to engage in profit-seeking activities through the production of goods, the provision of services and/or commercialization. It includes financial institutions and intermediaries, micro-, small and medium-sized enterprises, individual entrepreneurs, co-operatives, social enterprises and large corporations operating in the formal and informal sectors. It is the part of a country's economic system that is run by private individuals and companies rather than being government-controlled. Most private sector firms are run with the intention of making a profit.

The private sector is larger in free enterprise economies in which the government imposes relatively few restrictions on businesses. However, in countries with more government control, the public sector makes up the majority of the economy. An industry or business may start out in one sector and move to the other. The act of turning a publicly run enterprise over to private citizens is known as privatization. Private sector companies are those that are not owned by the government, as opposed to the public sector, which consists of industries such as education and unemployment insurance.

Definition of Economic Growth

Economic growth has become a global necessity for alleviating poverty. From 1970 to 2007, every region experienced economic growth, but some grew faster, while others grew at a slower rate. In general, Asia's rate of growth was high; North America had moderate growth while Western Europe recorded low growth. Specifically, Asia's growth rate was 19 percent of the global economic growth rate in 1970, but 28 percent in 2007. The growth rate of North America was 33.3 percent in 1970 and still remained at 33.3 percent in 2007, while that of Western

Europe was 34 percent in 1970, but 25 percent in 2007. However, African countries were below the average of the world: in 1920, Africa's per capita income was 40 percent less than the global average. The gap widened to 60 percent in 1950 and almost 80 percent in 2000. According to the United Nations Economic Commission for Africa (UNECA, 2010), economic growth in Africa fell from 4.9 percent in 2008 to 1.6 percent in 2009 as a result of falling exports and the global recession (financial turmoil that originated in the USA). Though Africa had the lowest growth rate compared to the rest of the world, its performance improved substantially over the first decade of the twenty-first century, giving hope for the future (United Nations, 2010).

Economic growth has been the concern of many governments globally. This is because it is a phenomenon in human civilization. Among policy makers in advanced countries and developing nations, there have been a number of debates and discussions on how economies could grow. The reason might be due to the fact that without economic growth, economies could stagnate and nations would be unable to provide for the well-being of their citizens. Economic growth is a multi-dimensional concept. It refers to the increase in a specific measure such as real national income, gross domestic product (GDP) or per capita income. National income or product is commonly expressed in terms of the aggregate value-added output of the domestic economy – GDP. When the GDP of a nation rises, economists refer to it as economic growth (Conteras, 2007). Economic growth also describes an increase in the productive capacity of an economy as a result of which the economy is capable of producing additional quantities of goods and services.

Usually the standard of living is measured by the quantity of goods and services available to us; thus, economic growth is synonymous with an increase in the general standard of living. Economic growth is important because it keeps society moving in a positive, productive direction. It is expected that the more an economy grows, the better its society becomes. New advances in technology and industry have brought society a long way, and the likelihood is that society will continue to grow and change in the future. Clearly, nations have improved greatly because of economic growth and expansion. Economic growth is undeniably important for a country to progress not only economically, but also socially and politically. It is believed that nations which grow at a strong pace for sustainable periods of time have the ability to drastically reduce poverty, improve democratic and political stability, achieve greater quality in the natural environment, and minimize the volume of crime and violence (Loayza and Soto, 2002).

Economic growth is conventionally characterized by increases in GDP or real GDP per capita that occur over the long term (Jackson and McIver, 2001). Stern (1991) describes economic growth as evolving from the supply side, such as the accumulation of physical capital, the progress of skills, ideas and innovation, and how factors are used, combined and managed.

Economic growth can generally be described as a positive change in the level of production of goods and services by a country over a certain period of time. In other words, economic growth is the increase in value of goods and services produced by an economy. It can also be referred to as the increase in GDP. It is a relatively straightforward measure of output and gives an idea of how well-off a country is compared to its competitors and past performance. It is a beacon that helps policy makers to steer the economy towards key economic objectives. Finally, it is a measure of the well-being of a state – usually in real terms, all other things being equal.

The definitions of economic growth have been criticized on a number of grounds. The criticisms could find explanations in the rate of population, the type of goods and services produced, the type of technology used and income distribution (Fosu, 2003). Population increases may offset economic growth; thus, the output of goods and services may rise, but the number of people may also increase. If the economy and the population both grow at the same rate, the national per capita income will not change. Economists would not consider this as economic growth. It is only when the growth in national output is faster or higher than the growth in population that the national per capita income increases (Elwell, 2006). In addition, economic growth is simply an increase in the amount of goods and services in the country. Whether the increase of goods and services benefits the majority of the population or not is unknown. This depends on the composition of the goods and services. The increase may comprise military hardware, goods and services for refugees outside the economy, or building presidential palaces which may not benefit the masses directly. In this case, most people may not be better off as compared to output made up of basic foodstuffs and low-cost housing provision (Fosu, 2003; Elwell, 2006).

Economic growth tells us nothing about the way increases in productivity come about. They may result from a capital-intensive method of production, leaving the majority of the population unemployed and thus leaving many people impoverished. This may nullify the effects of economic growth (Fosu, 2003). Economic growth per capita is only an average figure, which simply means that everybody's income has risen at that rate. The income distribution might be skewed, with a few very rich people and the majority in abject poverty. In this case, more income may go into the pockets of the few rich, who may be foreigners, who usually repatriate their incomes and would not benefit the people and for that matter the economy as a whole. For the economy to grow meaningfully, the increases in output and income must be fairly and widely distributed among the majority of the people. This should be the paramount concern of policy makers (Elwell, 2006). In conclusion, even though the definitions of economic growth have been criticized on a number of grounds, it is still a good indicator of how well an economy is performing (Kuznets, 1957).

Origins of Economic Growth

In the late 1370s, some citizens of Western European nations began conceiving the idea that economies could 'grow', that is, produce a greater economic surplus which could be spent on something other than religious or governmental projects (such as road construction, railway, construction, building of dams for electric power, building of schools and hospitals). The previous view was that only increases either in population or tax rates could generate more surplus money for the country. During much of the 'mercantilist' period, growth was seen as involving an increase in the total amount of species, that is, the circulating medium such as silver and gold, under the control of the state. This 'Bullionist' theory led to policies to force trade through a particular state and the acquisition of colonies to supply cheaper raw materials, which could then be manufactured and sold.

Later, such trade policies were instead justified simply in terms of promoting domestic trade and industry. The post-Bullionist insight saw the increasing capability of manufacturing, which led to policies in the 1700s to encourage manufacturing in itself and the formula of importing raw materials and exporting finished goods. Under this system, high tariffs were erected to allow manufacturers to establish 'factories' (the word comes from 'factor', the term for someone who carried goods from one stage of production to the next). Local markets would then pay the fixed costs of capital growth and would then allow them to be exported abroad, undercutting the prices of manufactured goods elsewhere. Once competition from abroad was removed, prices could then be increased to recoup the costs of establishing the business.

Under this theory of growth, the road to increased national wealth was to grant monopolies, which would give an incentive to an individual to exploit a market or resource, confident that he would make huge profits when all other extra-national competitors were driven out of business. The Dutch East India Company and the British East India Company were examples of such state-granted trade monopolies. It should be stressed that mercantilism was not simply a matter of restricting trade. Within a country, it often meant breaking down trade barriers, building new roads and abolishing local toll booths, all of which expanded markets. This corresponded to the centralization of power in the hands of the crown (or 'absolutism'). This process helped produce the modern nation state in Western Europe. Internationally, mercantilism led to a contradiction. Growth was gained through trade, but to trade with other nations on equal terms was disadvantageous. This, along with the rise of nation states, encouraged the outbreak of several major wars.

The modern concept of economic growth began with the critique of mercantilism, especially by the physiocrats and the Scottish Enlightenment thinkers such as David Hume and Adam Smith, and the foundation of the discipline of modern political economy. The theory of the physiocrat was that productive capacity itself allowed for growth, and the improving and increasing of capital led to 'the wealth of nations'. Advocates of this view stressed the importance of agriculture and saw urban industry as 'sterile'. Smith extended the notion that manufacturing was central to the entire economy. In his comparative trade theory propounded in 1816, David Ricardo argued that trade was beneficial to a country because if one could buy a good more cheaply from abroad, then it meant that there was more profitable work to be done. This theory of 'comparative advantage' would be the central basis for arguments in favour of free trade as an essential component of growth.

This notion of growth as increased stocks of capital goods (means of production) was codified as the Solow-Swan (1956) growth model, which involved a series of equations that showed the relationship between labour, time, capital goods, output and investment. Today, the role of technological change is crucial – even more important than the accumulation of capital. The late twentieth century with its global economy comprising few very wealthy nations and many very poor nations gave rise to the study of transition from substance and resource-based economies to production and consumption-based economies. This led to the field of development economics as a subject, including the influential works of Nobel laureates Amertya Sen and Joseph Stiglitz over the years. From the above discussion, it could be said that economies could grow depending on: increases in population; increases in tax rates; international trade (manufacturing output); technological change; capital accumulation; labour productivity; and agricultural output, all other things being equal.

Historical Perspectives

HISTORY OF THE PRIVATE SECTOR IN INDUSTRIALIZED AND DEVELOPING ECONOMIES AND IN GHANA

During the 1980s, developing countries faced major challenges in developing their economies. This was due to steep increases in the levels of external debt, particularly in the non-oil countries, significant reductions in the rate of international trade with the continuing decline of the export prices of primary commodities, high levels of deficits in balance of payments and of deficits in public budgets, decrease in the development of human resources as a result of high rates of poverty, a deterioration of living standards associated with the decline in the rates of economic growth compared to the continuous rise in population growth rates, decreases in health and education levels, and also an increase in the rate of disguised unemployment. All these factors pushed some developing countries to re-think of the role of the state as a leader in the economy, even though there had been some achievements by the public sector regarding economic development (Al-Roubaiee, 2003).

Drawing from the policies of President Ronald Reagan of the USA and Margaret Thatcher of the UK, it was during these times that privatization, which was viewed as a panacea to cure the ills of many developing countries, emerged as a force to reckon with in the developing world. The result was a major reform to address the issue of inefficient state-owned enterprises and to prepare the path towards an expansion role for the private sector. In the re-structuring that ensued, there was a major reconsideration of the state's role in developing countries, which had hitherto gone unchallenged (Al-Roubaiee, 2003). This support for a larger role for the private sector was due to a common belief that privatization could decrease the level of unemployment and increase efficiency in state-owned firms, and also that privatization would lead to a decrease in the subsidies that the state-owned firms were receiving from the state.

Indeed, though in the 1980s many African economies, including Ghana, embarked upon economic reforms and structural adjustment programmes to liberalize their economies, a close examination of the situation in Ghana indicates that the private sector had not achieved the phenomenal growth rate one would have expected to produce Ghanaian multi-national companies. Discussions with key officials of the Private Enterprises Federation, the Association of Ghana Industries and the Ghana Employers' Association reveal that the private sector has not achieved high growth rates due to historical factors and the liberalized policy environment. In the case of the historical factors, informant interviews showed that because of the political economy nature of Ghana's industrial policy, the private sector has tended to be largely marginalized except for a few transnational corporations, but one would argue that the private sector needs to add value, otherwise the government is hardly likely to invite the sector for its inputs on policy. It also needs to be noted that poverty reduction, growth and sustained economic development can only be obtained through economic sustainability and, in this context, the governments of many developing economies have failed.

HIGHS AND LOWS OF THE PRIVATE SECTOR INDUSTRIALIZED AND DEVELOPING ECONOMIES

The private sector has its own share of experiences in terms of the highs and lows of operation. Among the low times are periods when government policies adversely affect business activities and production or when the government plans its budget without consulting the sector to take its views into account. However, the private sector experiences its high times when the government's economic policies are established in consultation with all key national stakeholders and some indicators such as inflation and interest rates are brought down. Good seasons are also experienced by the private sector when the government provides: financial products to private companies that lack sufficient access to private sources of capital; related advisory (technical assistance) products to make available the specialized and scarce knowledge that is essential for effective investments, such as to improve the investment climate, strengthen project performance and impact, facilitate privatization and proper risk sharing, enhance environmental, social and corporate governance effectiveness; and comfort in difficult environments to catalyse or help to attract financing from other investors.

HOW THE PRIVATE SECTOR HAS SURVIVED GLOBAL RECESSIONS AND FINANCIAL MELTDOWNS

The private sector as a body has come through hard times by implementing various mechanisms. Among these strategies are reducing inventory and overheads and increased savings, as well as firms re-organizing working time to avoid making redundancies, curbing overtime or introducing short-term working. In addition, some firms respond to recessions by increasing numerical flexibility, that is, greater numbers of part-time and temporary workers are employed instead of full-time workers in an effort to more closely match company employment levels with changes in demand for the company's products or services. Sometimes employees have to work harder for less money during recessions. Furthermore, the sector optimizes core processes by minimizing excess spending and non-core programmes, since it helps companies to direct limited resources to satisfying customer expectations and taking activities that position a company strategically not only during times of recession but also for long periods of growth. By reducing silos, business leaders improve collaboration inside and outside their enterprise, and better align goals and performance measures with overall strategy.

THE PRIVATE SECTOR AS A FORMIDABLE FORCE IN ECONOMIES

Although the private sector is often not given the attention it requires, captains of industry and entrepreneurs have generally been characterized by a determination to succeed, courage and the persistence to endure, and, consequently, the private sector has been able to maintain its relevance, has always been a strong constituency in most economies and has maintained its position as a formidable force to reckon with throughout the world. Moreover, competition from other sectors and other nations has been a driving force compelling the private sector to offer its best and strive to make advances in today's dynamic business environment.

In addition, the private sector is characterized by the establishment of development plans for all employees as well as training and formal development programmes for supervisors; leadership positions and critical roles are obvious choices for targeted career development through performance, succession planning and learning initiatives. Career development for all employees has been considered a worthwhile investment. It is believed that private sector organizations with high-quality development plans for all employees have higher revenues than companies that do not. Such initiatives make it possible for private sector organizations to remain current when faced with changes in the marketplace and the evolving needs and preferences of customers.

Also, the private sector typically has had the ability to build a foundation of competencies such as knowledge, skills and behaviours that have helped in maintaining and developing industry and commerce. These competencies have made it possible for the private sector to build job profiles and internal talent pools. Building internal talent pools helps to get things done right first time all the time and thus saves the private sector from repeating mistakes. While a common mistake made by the private sector is sometimes to eliminate entire business units without any attempt to identify and retain high-performing and high-potential employees, during times of recession, many companies have stayed the course, endured recessions and have come through much stronger when there is an improvement in the economy.

By creating wealth and generating the majority of employment through creative and genuine enterprise as well as sheer determination and perseverance, politicians, the public sector, the non-governmental sector, society and all stakeholders have had to pay attention and recognize the immense contribution of the private sector to economic growth and overall national development.

BUILDING A THRIVING PRIVATE SECTOR IN GHANA

Since attaining independence, Ghana has embarked various initiatives to develop the private sector. These initiatives have emanated from the government, development partners and the private sector operators themselves. The government's role has been to provide an enabling environment through the establishment of institutions to facilitate the growth of the private sector and the development of private sector-friendly policies and funding where possible. To this end, Ghana has always had a Ministry of Trade and Industry, has established institutions such as the Ghana Investment Promotion Centre and the Ghana Export Promotion Authority, and at a point had a Ministry of Private Sector Development. Various policies have been formulated at different times to make the country attractive to investors and to facilitate the process of establishing and doing business in Ghana.

In addition, in the past decade, successive governments have introduced many initiatives in Ghana to promote private sector growth. Some of these initiatives have been maintained as an integral part of the national governance system, while others have disappeared with the exit of their proponents. One of the initiatives that has stood the test of time and has traversed or straddled successive governments is a private sector development strategy. Many of Ghana's governments have had a strategic plan aimed at making the private sector a lead facilitator of economic growth, thus establishing the government's position regarding the significance of industry and commerce in its national development efforts.

Development partners have also tended to support the private sector through various programmes. These include the provision of grants to private small and medium-sized businesses to: support these enterprises in order to enable them to receive support from business service providers in preparing and implementing their advocacy actions; address the legal and regulatory issues that affect the ease of doing business and ultimately improve productivity; assist the Ghanaian private sector to lobby local, regional and national authorities in order to create the appropriate enabling business environment for the private sector to be profitable and competitive; strengthen the culture of business; improve access to markets; strengthen the labour markets; and support advocacy efforts by the non-state actors for an enabling environment for the private sector by targeting institutions like the Private Enterprise Foundation (PEF) and the Association of Ghana Industries (AGI).

To complement these efforts, in the 1990s, the captains of Ghana's private sector established the PEF, a non-profit, non-political, autonomous institution and a company limited by guarantee under the Ghana Companies Code (Act 179), with membership open to all private businesses and trade associations from both the formal and informal sectors of the economy. It is an apex institution whose goal is to forge consensus and provide the leadership voice for advocacy, on the initiative of the Association of Ghana Industries, the Ghana National Chamber of Commerce and Industry, the Ghana Employers' Association and the Federation of Associations of Ghanaian Exporters, with the support of the United States Agency for International Development (USAID). The Ghana Association of Bankers (GAB) was later admitted as the fifth founding member and the Ghana Chamber of Mines (GCM) was also added as a member later on.

In the last few years, the PEF has strengthened the effectiveness of the its advocacy functions and leadership for the private sector by including four new members, namely, the Ghana Chamber of Telecommunications (GCT), the Ghana Insurers' Association (GIA), the Association of Oil Marketing Companies (AOMCs) and the Liquefied Petroleum Gas Operators Association (GLiPGOA) as fully fledged members. It is instructive to note that in 2013, the name of the 'Private Enterprises Foundation' was changed to the 'Private Enterprises Federation'.

Since its inception, the PEF's achievements include: gaining national prominence as the leading private sector advocate by participating in key national advisory, policy planning, formulation and monitoring committees; building consensus in the country by organizing a Conference in North Carolina in the USA for a cross-section of the Ghanaian political and business landscape, comprising government leaders, Members of Parliament (including members of the Opposition), business leaders, academia and civil society representatives, leading to the introduction of the National Economic Dialogue between the government, the private sector, academia and civil society to discuss and share ideas on private sector development and national economic issues.

Other achievements of the PEF over the years are as follows: it was instrumental through various presentations and position papers in the establishment of the original Export Development and Investment Fund (EDIF); it played a pivotal role in extending the coverage of the EDIF to include agricultural financing; in collaboration with the Ministry of Energy, the US Department of Energy and USAID, it established the Energy Foundation, which has been instrumental in the promotion of energy-efficient policies and practices.

Currently, the PEF is working to change the regulatory and procedures for obtaining permits, certification and licensing by businesses in the country after years of research of this thorny subject. Various projects include the Agricultural Public Private Dialogue Forum that trains farmer-based organizations on advocacy. These are a few of the numerous advocacy activities that the PEF has undertaken. The PEF exists to support government and private sector efforts for the efficient allocation of the nation's resources, the provision of requisite business development services and capacity building for a sustainable private sector-led economic development. It aspires to influence government policies to effect the growth of a globally competitive and profitable private sector in Ghana.

The five main objectives of the PEF outlined by its strategic plan are as follows. First is the PEF's advocacy function, which is aimed at influencing government policies and regulations supported by empirical data emanating from research. In this regard, the PEF streamlines cross-sectoral licensing requirements in Ghana and the allocation of resources to institutions that supervise the issuance of this cross-sectoral licensing. It also advocates on topics and issues that cut across all sectors of the economy and are of interest to the private sector.

Second, the PEF offers research and publication services. These include a web-based interactive research platform linked to academia and other business-oriented research institutions that will provide pertinent information to private sector businesses, government, development partners, civil society organizations and other interested parties. Also, the PEF undertakes policy research for an effective representation to government on behalf of member associations on issues of concern to the private sector, such as government deficits and borrowings, the high levels of interest on loans, capital mobilization, infrastructural deficiencies, land reforms, the burdensome legal and regulatory framework, the complicated tax regime and multi-lateral trade agreements, among others. Again, the PEF monitors and identifies best management practices and the strategic factors accounting for enhanced enterprise competitiveness and profitability, and disseminates such best practices among member enterprises. Furthermore, it provides pertinent business information such as benchmarking local business operations with others elsewhere to ascertain efficiency, market links into the international supply chain and create a profile of the individual business to stimulate competition and attract partnerships.

The third function of the PEF is to the provision of innovative business development services. In this context, PEF prescribes customised business development services/training to private businesses for efficient and profitable operations. PEF's fourth function is capacity building and technical skills training. Here the organization provides avenues for mentoring, internships, attachments and other forms of training to help build the capacities and requisite skills needed by the business community.

The final function of the PEF involves intermediation and facilitation for agricultural investment. This covers assistance in policy formulation through public private dialogue to identify constraints and challenges and advocate profitable and pro-poor policy strategies. In addition, the PEF facilitates links between various investors, both local and foreign, with opportunities in the agricultural sector to enhance investment in commercial agriculture with protection and safeguards for small land holders and other land users.

How the Private Sector Can Contribute to National Growth

One of the objectives of a liberalized economy is to achieve accelerated growth through a vibrant and competitive private sector. The private sector would have to adopt technology and competitiveness in areas of the economy such as agriculture, industry and the service sectors. This will empower the private sector to effectively play its role as the engine of wealth creation, economic growth and national development. The strategies for achieving such objectives should focus on strengthening the partnership between the public and private sectors in attracting and channelling investments into carefully selected sectors. In selecting the focal sectors for public and private investments, the main criteria would be competitiveness and employment-generating capacity.

AGRICULTURE

The private sector needs to step up its participation in modernized agriculture and this would prepare the ground for a structural transformation between agriculture and industry. A comprehensive plan needs to be developed that recognizes the need for greater use of modern, improved and cost-effective inputs such as seeds, fertilizer and equipment. The purpose of modernizing agriculture is to make the sector more competitive through the use of modern but feasible technologies, as well as increasing and attracting investment into the agricultural sector. The productivity of agriculture should be increased to sufficiently high levels to make a meaningful impact on wealth creation and economic growth. The approach to attracting and channelling more investment into agriculture will focus on partnerships between large private organizations, the state and small holders with a view to reducing the risks which restrain each category of investors. This will engender increased productivity in agriculture to ensure food security and contribute immensely to the health and well-being of the population.

PRIVATE SECTOR-LED AGRICULTURE

There are a number of areas in which the private sector could consider in its efforts to act as a catalyst in accelerating Ghana's economic development. First is the diversification into other crops apart from traditional cocoa, especially cereals and other cash crops for export markets, such as mangoes, papayas, pineapples, cashew nuts and vegetables. This diversification could result in raised production levels and could create more job opportunities. This will have a direct impact on poverty reduction in the villages and will help to slow down the rural–urban drift. Next is the investment in aqua-culture among other technological improvements. Agriculture as a whole will always be dependent on natural conditions – land, sunlight and especially rainfall. The unreliability of rainfall with regard to its onset, duration, intensity and amount can disrupt food crop production. Technologies could be used to harvest Ghana's rain water endowments, which could yield immense benefits in agricultural productivity and poverty reduction.

Also worth considering are large-scale farming and nucleus out-grower schemes for the production of selected crops, the development and use of improved seeds/planting materials, and assistance in intensifying research to ensure that technologies are developed and disseminated appropriately to meet global market standards. Moreover, the use of weights and measures as well as grades and standards in the marketing of commodities should be promoted and supported in order to enhance commercial efficiency. Equally, private sector marketing firms can assist in marketing farmers' produce. The private sector can also step up its efforts to improve storage/warehousing and distribution networks, including refrigerated transport systems and cold storage facilities at the ports.

Irrigation strategies should be given greater attention, promoting a culture of community-based irrigation to move agriculture from reliance on the vagaries of the weather to a more scientifically managed system of assuring water all year round. As part of irrigation schemes, the private sector can go into dug-outs, hand-pump systems, valley bottom schemes, etc., which have the potential to reach smallholder farmers and are best suited for certain geographical areas. Existing irrigation facilities and infrastructure can be purchased by the private sector and expanded into small-scale community irrigation schemes and ground water development that can be leased to farmer-based organizations.

To grow agriculture and ensure that it has a significant impact on the economy, a combination of other strategies should be considered. These include: the establishment of land banks for onward sale to investors; the provision of improved breeds of animals for sale to farmers; the formation of extension service think-tanks and the provision of services to farmers cultivating commodities targeted at leading accelerated growth in the agricultural sector; venturing into industrial and domestic waste management systems that deal with the problems presented by plastic and promote composting; the establishment of fish storage facilities, including community-level facilities and setting up of small-scale fish processing industries and agro-processing industries.

ACCESS TO GLOBAL MARKETS

In this area, some of the initiatives that the private sector could consider include: the formation of marketing companies to increase access to global markets by targeting sector specific exports, and supporting local farmer based organizations to participate in foreign and domestic trade shows, fairs and exhibitions at reasonable fees; providing beneficial links along production and supply chains in targeted produce; producing standardized packaging materials and weights for sale to farmer-based organizations and assisting these organizations to get fair prices for their produce at a commission; and forming produce-buying companies or setting up satellite markets in urban centres to provide outlets for rural farmers.

SUPPORT SERVICES FOR PRIVATE SECTOR GROWTH

Support services opportunities include construction and operation of cold chain facilities from production point to the port, well-organized container terminals with security, equipment, effective operators and computerized tracking; financing, construction and maintenance of roads and railways; and participation in the investment and management of aviation infrastructure and equipment.

ENERGY, SCIENCE AND TECHNOLOGY

Opportunities in this area include: participation in energy generation in a Build, Operate, and Transfer (BOT) project involving thermal, hydro, wind and solar power; taking advantage of the gas flow from the West African Gas Pipeline to establish gas turbine thermal plants for sale to the government in a BOT arrangement; assisting Ghana's best scientists and engineers to design and manufacture a range of capital goods and machine tools, or new corrosion-resistant and energy-efficient materials; assisting in managing and developing new (and existing) energy resources; channelling resources to develop the latest environmental and sanitation solutions; building links between research and development, minimizing holes in Ghana's technological capabilities; and writing smart banking software and also software to assist the government in broadening its tax base.

INFORMATION AND COMMUNICATION TECHNOLOGY

In this area, the following initiatives could be examined: provision of an open access broadband network for the whole country to develop an ultra-high speed network – the government's role in this telecommunications initiative would be facilitative, involving access to state and local government assets (such as electricity poles, pits, pipes, road and rail easements) to be used to carry infrastructure and services; and the provision of additional telephones, particularly in rural and peri-urban communities to improve the quality of the telephone service.

TOURISM AND SPORTS

Tourism is a young but expanding industry in Ghana that has the potential to become one of Ghana's main foreign exchange earners if it is harnessed properly. The private sector could contribute to the sector's growth through the development of hotels with restaurants in known historical tourist sites and the provision of souvenirs for tourists at small fees. Moreover, historical sites can be rehabilitated to appreciable standards by operators to attract tourists, the operators keeping a fraction of the income from their operation and the rest going to the government.

Corporate bodies can pick unique sports disciplines for promotions and development. They can also build adequate and appropriate sports and recreational facilities at the local, district, regional, and national levels to be leased or rented out to sporting clubs, whether private or governmental, at reasonable fees. Links and partnerships can be established with countries and international sports agencies committed to the development of sports, thereby enhancing its contribution to national development objectives.

EDUCATION AND HEALTHCARE

In the field of education, the private skill/professional training institutions can liaise with industry to produce demand-driven skilled labour and establish effective collaboration between human resource institutions and industry. In the area of health, practising private health professionals and business players in the healthcare delivery system can go for accreditation to establish quality medical and nursing institutions that would augment the government efforts at training doctors and nurses in the country. These collaborate efforts can be built upon to establish medical centres in the districts to provide basic medical care to the communities.

Conclusions

THE STATE OF THE ECONOMY

The IMF completed a staff report on Ghana in April 2014 after discussions and studies carried out as part of the Article IV Consultations. The report stated that 'short-term vulnerabilities have risen significantly amid high fiscal and current account deficits. The international reserve position has weakened alongside mounting public debt. High interest rates and a depreciating [national] currency have begun to weaken private sector activity. The spread on Ghana's Eurobonds have risen above those of regional peers'.

The report suggested that economic growth was slowing down, decreasing from an estimated 5.5 percent of GDP in 2013 to 4.75 percent in 2014 and from higher rates in earlier years. Inflation, which in earlier years was in single digits, reached 13.5 percent at the close of December 2013 and by the end of March 2014 was 14.5 percent, 14.7 percent in April and 14.8 percent in May (*Daily Guide*, 3 and 12 June 2014, p. 11). The year-on-year inflation rate as measured by the Consumer Price Index (CPI) was 16.5 percent in February 2015 according to Ghana Statistical Service data reported by the *Daily Guide* and 16.4 percent for January 2015.

The fiscal (cash) deficit in 2013 was estimated at 10.9 percent of GDP against a target of 9 percent. In the absence of further measures, the 2014 deficit was projected at 10.25 percent of GDP. Consolidation is made more difficult by slower growth, while inflation is driven by currency depreciation and administered price increases. Monetary policy was being tightened, yet fiscal consolidation targets were missed. The government's objectives of economic diversification, shared growth and job creation, and macro-economic stability would rely on the re-allocation of resources from current to capital spending. However, the twin fiscal and current account deficits in the presence of large interest payments on rising public debt have a cumulative effect of crowding out priority expenditure and private sector activity. The cited vulnerabilities put Ghana's transformation agenda at risk and the weakening macro-economic outlook and currency depreciation expose the financial sector to credit and foreign exchange risks, to the further disadvantage of private sector development.

At a forum in commemoration of May Day 2014, the Secretary-General of the Trades Union Congress of Ghana (TUC) made a statement on the state of the economy of Ghana. In his words, the TUC's views were as follows:

First, it is our view that Ghana's economy remains fundamentally a developing third world economy. The economy is faced with challenges of under-developed infrastructure. Technology, whether in industry or agriculture, is rudimentary. Literacy is high but the quality of education is low. Our exports have coalesced around natural resources. The bulk of the workforce is trapped in low productivity employment in agriculture and services. Many citizens including those in agriculture are finding it ever more difficult to meet their daily food needs. Manufacturing base is shallow and shrinking. The social indicators, whether in the realm of access to sanitation, decent housing, safe drinking water or affordable healthcare are nothing to write home about. These are but a few of the characteristic features of our economy and society.

Second, in a country characterized by these features of under-development, economic policy should be radically different from one in which the basic necessities of life have been achieved. Addressing this fundamental ethos of under-development through a liberal or neo-liberal economic framework has never worked anywhere. The 'official' account of globalization as told by the World Bank and the IMF will tell you it is doable, and they point to South Korea and Malaysia. When in fact, we now know from many other credible sources that these countries did something different from what we have been led to believe. But after all, we have China to look up to. When Chinese officials repudiate the characterization of their development model as 'Beijing Consensus', they simply are telling us that development does not follow any linear path; it is a process of pragmatism and adaptation to both internal and external circumstances. And as a former Chief Economist of the World Bank Justin Lin, has noted, at all times in the last fifty years countries that followed dominant economic policies failed to change their economic structure; they also failed to catch up.

Third, Organized Labour believes that overcoming our development challenges requires a skilful interplay of both the visible hand of government and the invisible hand of the market. In the first two decades after independence, we sought and failed to develop using the apparatus of the state; in the process, we destroyed the private sector and killed market incentives. In the last thirty years, we have unleashed market forces, not only pushing back the state but also thoroughly deforming it. It is our view that development cannot be achieved through market fundamentalism. There are many aspects of national development for which market incentives do not exist, but that does not mean that they should not be attended to. In all successful cases of economic transformation markets were tamed for the purpose of reaching a defined goal or destination; they were however, not strangulated; they were simply governed. And in all such cases the State was a developmental, purposeful one, with efficient institutions that designed and implemented smart rules knowing its power and its limits. Unfortunately, our state has become deformed, and unable to undertake the simple task of governing. All the high and low profile corruption cases that have become all too pervasive are symptoms of a weak and failing state. We need to rescue, and rehabilitate the state, and place it at the front and centre of national development.

In tune with the neo-liberal economic orchestra, a weakening state has retreated into the comfort zones of politics leaving economic governance to market forces in the name of laissez-faire. But as history teaches us, the winds of laissez-faire are not likely to blow in the desired direction when a country is steeped in under-development. Therefore, financial liberalization has brought in more banks, which are announcing huge profits but the rest of the business community is reeling under a high interest rate regime that makes domestic production almost suicidal. A developmental state should not stand aloof; it should intervene strategically to bring down interest rates because in the long term, this business model is not in the interest of anyone including the banks themselves.

In the name of laissez-faire, we have adopted for ourselves perhaps the most liberal trade regime ever in the history of mankind. And there is pressure from within and without to liberalize further. History has no example of a country that developed in such a liberal trade environment. Our trade deficit has continued to worsen because our low-priced primary commodity exports are not paying for our manufactured imports; the terms of trade have always favoured manufactures. Three decades ago, a ton of cocoa bought one VW Beetle car. Today, we require 20 tons or more to buy one VW car. This is because cocoa beans have remained cocoa beans while VW has moved from the Beetle of the 1970s to the Touareg of today.

The trade deficit is exacerbated by two factors. One factor is that foreigners control the bulk of our exports (the raw materials). Foreigners own the gold mines and other solid mining concerns. The Jubilee oil is over 80 percent owned by foreign companies. And it is important to note that these companies have been guaranteed the right to retain up to 80 percent of their earnings outside the country. Effectively, however, some of them keep over 90 percent of their earnings in offshore accounts. This means, out of the over 40 percent of our export revenues that come from gold, no more than 20 percent of that gets retained in the country.

The other factor is the rate at which we allow transfer of foreign currencies out of the country, particularly by companies that do not themselves generate foreign currencies. Take the case of the telecom companies. These are service companies dealing in what economists refer to as non-tradeables. That is, they deal in products that do not cross national borders. What it means is that they do not bring in foreign currency beyond their initial capital requirements. At the same time, these companies generate so much domestic revenues and they are super-profitable. They are foreign owned, which also means that they need to transfer profit to their shareholders in London, Johannesburg and other foreign destinations. And they definitely cannot transfer the local currency (cedi) they generate in large quantities on a daily basis. What they do is to exchange those cedis for the dollars our hardworking cocoa farmers bring in.

In such a situation, the grand depreciation of the local currency against all major international currencies is only a matter of course. No currency can withstand such onslaught. Therefore, the challenges that confront Ghana's economy emanate directly from the economic policies that we are pursuing that have led to unbridled liberalization of the economy, made import trade super lucrative, penalizes domestic production and reduced the economy to buying and selling. Added to these, is the regime of investment rules that favour foreign investors over domestic investors, carved out strategic sectors of the economy for foreign capital and grants them mouth-watering incentives, which we are not prepared to give to domestic producers. These bad economic policies have been made worse by a number of domestic challenges including widespread corruption in high and low places, cronyism, incompetence and extreme partisanship.

Sadly, our policy makers and politicians continue to play ostrich, focusing on red herrings. They point to GDP growth when they know that growth is not creating decent employment. They are pointing to our middle income status when they know that we have come into middle income with all the characteristics of a Least Developed Country; paying the lowest wage rates and with deteriorating social indicators. Suddenly, the public sector wage bill has become the cause of all the difficulties; the evidence does not support it. Instead of addressing the many challenges that face domestic industry we are busy creating platforms for 21st century Lugards to lecture Ghanaians about the virtues of free trade and Economic Partnership Agreements when in fact all analyses show that, that the agreement will constitute a major stumbling block to national development.

THE STATE AND THE PRIVATE SECTOR: PARTNERSHIPS IN ECONOMIC TRANSFORMATION

After the Millennium Development Goals, the post-2015 UN global development agenda presents economic transformation as a consensus paradigm for Africa's development. The African Centre for Economic Transformation (ACET) in its 2014 report postulates that African economies need more than growth if they are to transform. They need to diversify their production, make their exports competitive, increase the productivity of farms, firms and government establishments, and upgrade the technology used throughout the economy with the overarching objective of improving human well-being. To attain such an ambitious and profound transformative shift would require a high-level constructive engagement and strategic relationships between the state and the private sector.

The earlier cited commentaries on recent developments about the economy of Ghana point to, and betray, a vicious interplay between market failures and government failures, as the respective shortcomings of the private sector and state are referred to in the literature. The main elements of market failure include information asymmetries, learning spillovers, co-ordination failures, increasing returns and capital market imperfections. The main elements of government failure include rent-seeking behaviour (especially corruption), inefficient public sector operations and government officials lacking the relevant knowledge to enable them to make the right choices for promotion and support among investment alternatives.

The 2014 ACET African Transformation Report postulates further that the state can promote economic transformation by providing leadership in setting a coherent vision and strategy in consultation with the private sector and other key stakeholders, and by managing the economy well and providing a business-friendly environment under conditions where there is peace and security in the country, the state is committed to a private sector-led economy and the political leadership accepts economic transformation as a priority. Managing the economy well and providing a business-friendly environment entails providing a stable macro-economic environment, managing public resources honestly and efficiently for the supply of supporting public goods and services, maintaining a favourable regulatory environment for business and producing timely, quality economic and social statistics.

Transparency and accountability institutions as well as civil society organizations including labour unions are also important stakeholders in ensuring that the unfolding close collaboration between state and business does not degenerate into corruption and crony capitalism. Similarly, co-operation between organized labour, government and business in a tripartite pursuit of industrial harmony and peace while upgrading the skills of the labour force to promote competitiveness will all contribute to the country's rapid economic transformation and the concomitant human well-being of its citizens.

The private sector in Ghana, as elsewhere in Sub-Saharan Africa, is far from being a homogeneous mix of enterprises by size, ownership and registration. The larger enterprises are foreign-owned, limited liability businesses or joint ventures, whereas the majority of small enterprises and sole proprietorships are Ghanaian (Boeh-Ocansey, 2005) with limited capital and technology investment. Foreign-controlled companies rarely participate actively and directly in national development policy matters. The private sector is widely believed to constitute the supply side of the corruption equation in economic governance in the country with a negative perceived reputation. Fostering strong working relations between the private sector, especially its intermediary organizations or trade or business associations, and third-party civil society organizations and think-tanks will enhance the contribution of non-state actors to the policy dialogue in their collaboration with a privileged state actors segment favoured by the existing information asymmetry.

References

African Centre for Economic Transformation (ACET) (2014). *African Transformation Report: Growth with Depth.* Accra, Ghana and Washington DC, USA.

Al-Roubaiee, F.A. (2003). Economic development between the state and the private sector. Available at: http://adel-amer.catsh.info/vb/showthread.php?t=4818.

AusAID (2012). *Private Sector Development Strategy.* Department of Foreign Affairs and Trade, Australian Government.

Australian Council for International Development (2014). *Benchmarks for an Effective and Accountable Australian Aid Program*, p. 7.

Boeh-Ocansey, O. (2005). Private sector development in Ghana: Sustainable employment generation, corporate governance and the informal/formal economy. Ghana Employment Policy Workshop, ILO/Ministry for Manpower, Youth & Employment, November.

Conteras, R. (2007). *How the Concept of Development Got Started.* University of Iowa Centre for International Finance and Development, E-book.

Dade, C. (2006). The privatization of foreign development assistance. *FOCAL* Policy Paper, 7 July, FPP-06–05, pp. 1–14.

Elwell, C. (2006). Long-term growth of the US economy: Significance, determinants, and policy. CRS Report for Congress, order code RL32987.

Fosu, A. (2003). Political instability and export performance in Sub-Saharan Africa. *Journal of Development Studies*, 39(4), pp. 67–83.

Jackson, J. and McIver, R. (2001). *Microeconomics.* Boston, MA: McGraw-Hill.

Kuznets, S. (1957). Quantitative aspects of the economic growth of nations: 2. Industrial distribution of national product and labor force. *Economic Development and Cultural Change*, 5(4), part 2.

Loayza, N. and Soto, R. (2002). *The Sources of Economic Growth: An Overview in Economic Growth: Sources Trends and Cycles*. Santiago: Central Bank.

——. (eds) (2010). *Series on Central Banking, Analysis, and Economic Trends, and Cycles*. Promoting high-level sustainable growth to reduce unemployment in Africa. UNECA Publications and Conference Management Section.

Report on the World Social Situation (2010). *Rethinking Poverty*. Department of Economic and Social Affairs, United Nations Publication No E.09.IV. 10.

Solow, R. (1956). A contribution to the theory of economic growth. *Quarterly Journal of Economics*, 70(1), pp. 65–9.

Stern, N. (1991). The determinants of growth. *Economic Journal*, 101, pp. 122–33.

Swan, T.W. (1956). Economic growth and capital accumulation. *Economic Record*, 32, pp. 334–61.

United Nations Economic Commission for Africa (2010). Promoting high-level sustainable growth to reduce unemployment in Africa. ECA Publications and Conference Management Section.

Villars, E. (2014). Interview with Elizabeth Joyce Villars on the history of Ghana's private sector. Accra, Ghana.

World Bank (2005). *World Development Report: A Better Investment Climate for Everyone*. Washington DC: World Bank.

World Economic Forum, in collaboration with PricewaterhouseCoopers (2010). *Paving the Way: Maximizing the Value of Private Finance in Infrastructure*. New York: World Economic Forum.

17

The Impact of Global Capital Markets on Developing Countries' Economic Growth

Clifford D. Mpare

Abstract

This chapter examines the trends in emerging market growth over the last few decades. It begins with a discussion of the development of markets specifically in Africa and of the growth and contribution of these markets to the global economy. In addition, it explores the prospects and potential of African markets as developing economies continue to evolve into stronger and more influential forces in the future on the global stage. Finally, it assesses the likelihood of Africa being the hotspot for investment funds in the medium to long term.

Introduction

The capital markets in Africa are small by global standards, but have been evolving along with the dramatic economic changes that have occurred in the majority of African countries over the last decade. We have observed unprecedented economic growth on the continent in the last 15 years, which has had a profound impact on the capital markets. Economic growth has been fuelled by the commodities super cycle, an emerging middle class, which is consuming goods at a fast clip, the re-building of infrastructure and technological changes. Capital markets are defined as organized financial markets where trading is done in various instruments including equities, government bonds, corporate bonds and other structured products.

In a developed economy, the financial markets are set up for people to participate in financial transactions. For example, individuals borrow and lend to banks. Similarly, corporations source financing and execute deal with banks, but also use the financial markets through their intermediaries, such as investment bankers and insurance companies, to change their capital structure. The capital structure of a company may be changed through the offering of shares, issuing bonds and engaging in merger and acquisition activities. Governments participate in the financial markets by lending to individuals, companies, institutions and sovereign government.

Financial markets can facilitate transactions whereby consumption can take place now, while delaying payment in the future. It is therefore a way of transferring future resources to the present by borrowing and increasing one's immediate satisfaction. Governments sometimes shift future resources to the present so as to allow greater present consumption by its citizens.

Governments can borrow in the capital markets through loans or the treasuries market with a promise to pay with interest using future cash flow expected by the government from taxes, levies, etc. One of the most common motivations for participating in the financial markets is to shift future resources to the present in order to increase present consumption and thus satisfaction.

When individuals, governments and companies have excess current resources and they do not want to consume, they may shift these to the financial markets by lending or buying ordinary shares, treasury stock and corporate bonds. These activities have a tremendous impact on the economy and individual wealth creation. It is an evolution of the former barter system that allowed transactions to take place between individuals at an agreed exchange rate. The capital markets allow the same thing to happen, but the medium of exchange is money supported by various paper or electronic instruments.

The Nobel Prize-winning economist Professor Merton Miller argued in 1998 that a well-fleshed-out set of financial markets and associated institutions means that a country will be able to reduce its dependence on the banking system as the dominant institution for financing economic growth in developing countries (Miller, 1998).

Even though banking plays an important role of intermediation, it remains fragile and crisis-prone because of the inherent maturity mismatches of credit portfolios and the instability of deposit obligations to savers. Well-developed financial markets bring diversification benefits to investors. Having a wide spectrum of financial markets available keeps a country from being over-dependent on the crisis-prone banking system. The 2007 and 2008 global financial crisis made it abundantly clear how markets are interdependent and highly correlated in the short term. In the long term, regional differences do emerge and reflect the macro-economic strength of a region.

The Stock Markets

Unlike developed economies, where trading in the stock market has a long and varied history, organized stock market systems did not exist in Africa until recently. The US stock market started in 1792, while the UK market began 100 years before that. According to research undertaken by Credit Suisse, there are 19 countries comprising about 90 percent of the global stock markets with data for the last 111 years (Credit Suisse, 2011). The US has the largest stock market and accounts for 41 percent of the global stock value, which is five times bigger than its closest rival, Japan (World Federation of Exchanges, 2010, as cited in Today Forward, 2010).

By comparison, the Ghana Stock Exchange began in 1989 and is among a number of African stock exchanges that started in the 1990s. The Nigerian market has a longer history, having started in the 1960s, but was dormant for years until the 1990s, when it re-invigorated itself and began active trading. The oldest stock market on the continent is the Egyptian market (the Alexandria Stock Exchange), which was officially started in 1883. Together with the Cairo Exchange, the market was highly active in the 1940s and ranked fifth in the world (Egyptian Stock Exchange, 2013). An experiment with the centralized government system in the 1960s nearly caused the Egyptian market to collapse.

The South African market is the largest and most sophisticated market on the continent with a current capitalization of over $800 billion (JSE, 2011). The Johannesburg Stock Exchange (JSE) opened in 1887 to cater for the gold rush that led to the need for financing of the mining companies. The JSE, which was historically dominated by resource stocks, is now a broadly diversified stock index with companies represented in all the strategic sectors.

The majority of exchanges on the continent are small and lack liquidity, making it difficult for international investors to do meaningful trading on the bourses. But it is encouraging to note that there has been progress in the trend of developing and expanding new stock exchanges. At the behest of development partners and local governments that encouraged the development of stock exchanges in a number of countries, the numbers of stock markets have increased from five in 1980 to 29 in 2013 (Ndikumana, 2001; Ntim, 2012).

The increase in the number of stock markets in Africa is an affirmation of the role of stock exchanges as intermediary institutions that facilitate financial transactions. It is also a recognition that countries can only participate in the global financial markets by having established financial systems and infrastructures. The market capitalization of African stock markets is about $1.2 trillion, which compares to $22 trillion for the US and $61 trillion for the world's total capitalization in 2013 (Demisse et al., 2008; African Development Bank, 2012; Business Insider, 2013).

Regional Integration

The African stock markets have a critical limiting factor, that is, in terms of their size and scale. Although there are 29 stock exchanges, apart from the South African market, most markets cannot compete with other jurisdictions. The idea of regional integration has come about in order to help to mitigate the shortcomings of the individual African markets. For example, the Regional West African Market that would combine the markets of Nigeria, Ghana, Sierra Leone and BRVM (Benin, Côte d'Ivoire, Senegal and Togo) into one sizeable stock exchange is an idea which was expected to come into existence in 2014 (African Development Bank, 2012); however, this has not been realized. The advantage of such a regional market would be for an investor to have access to a market with a capitalization of over $100 billion with massive potential to grow into a trillion dollar market in the next 50 years. This will further integrate the African markets into the global markets where the size and speed of transactions is of paramount importance.

Treasury Market

Government securities form the foundation of fixed-income markets in most developed and developing economies. They are the building blocks from which to derive the appropriate yield curve and establish the overall credit curve. A country can benefit from developing a comprehensive bond market provided that the appropriate operating structures are in place.

By providing an avenue for domestic funding of budget deficits other than that provided by a country's central bank, a fully developed bond market can reduce the need for direct and potentially damaging monetary financing of government deficits and can avoid a build-up of foreign currency-denominated debt. The existence of a government bond market should enable the authorities to smooth out consumption and investment expenditures in response to shocks and, if coupled with sound debt management strategies, can help governments to reduce their exposure to interest rates and currency and other financial risks. These benefits can lead to a more stable macro-economic environment.

At the micro-level, a bond market can increase overall financial stability and improve financial intermediation through greater competition and development of related financial infrastructure, products and services. Based on the above reasons, it is not a matter of whether innovative fixed-income instrument must be introduced, but rather of when and what kinds of securities should be introduced in an economy for accelerated growth. As new products are introduced on the continent, it will entail the creation of an extensive legal and institutional infrastructure that will benefit the entire financial system.

The Role of the US as a Financial Superpower

In the twentieth century, the US rapidly became the world's foremost political, military and economic power. Along with this distinction, the US is a financial superpower. The market for US Treasury securities is by far the largest, most active debt market in the world. At the end of 2013, the amount of US Treasury debt was in excess of $11.95 trillion, having risen from $5.29 trillion at the end of 2008. The market for US Treasury securities has a complex structure and involves numerous participants – the Department of the Treasury, the Federal Reserve System, government security dealers and brokers, and other holders of Treasury securities.

The US first incurred debt in 1779 when it borrowed money to finance the Revolutionary War. Total debt remained fairly small in the first half of the nineteenth century, but rose sharply following the American Civil War and the First World War. The Great Depression and government financing of the First World War led to an explosion of US debt. In recent years the US debt level has increased at an accelerated rate due to a legacy of budget deficits.

US Treasuries are regularly offered in maturities ranging from 13 weeks to 30 years. Bills – securities having maturity of one year or less – sell at a discount from their face value and do not pay interest before maturity. Investors realize a return on bills from the increase in their price to face value at maturity. Notes have an initial maturity of 1–10 years, while bonds have an initial maturity of more than 10 years and offer investors semi-annual interest payments coupons. More than half of Treasuries are in the form of Notes, while bonds and bills each represent 20 percent of the total.

The value of a Treasury coupon security is often expressed in terms of its yield to maturity or yield rather than price. The yield on a Treasury security is the constant interest rate at which the present discount value of future coupons and principal payments equals the current price of the security. In effect, the yield represents the rate of return an investor would earn if he or she held the security to maturity assuming semi-annual compounding of interest. By definition, the yield and the price move in opposite directions. A change in interest rate affects both price and yield in the secondary market.

In contrast to coupon securities, Treasury bills are quoted in terms of a discount rate, which is the difference between the face value and the market price as a percentage of the face value, scaled to an annual rate (using 360 or 364 days). The supply of Treasury securities is largely a function of the need to finance the cumulative budget of a country. The demand for those securities is determined for investment and hedging purposes. The value of Treasury securities is often summarized by the yield curve, which plots the yields of securities against their maturities.

Securities with similar maturities tend to have similar yields because they offer payments over similar periods. Securities with different maturities are also linked. Long-term interest rates generally reflect expectations about the future path of short-term interest rates. This relationship, which is referred to as the expectations hypothesis, arises because an investor can choose among several strategies, including purchasing a Treasury security whose maturity extends over his or her investment horizon or purchasing a short-term security (that is, rollover) through the investment period.

The first strategy offers a return equal to the yield on the long-term security, whereas the second strategy offers a return determined, approximately, by the average of the yields on the short-term security over the investment period. The results of the two strategies are similar, but have different risk profiles. Both short-term and long-term rates are affected by monetary policy, but long-term rates also reflect the expectations of future short-term rates and as such are more sensitive to the changes in policy interest rates.

Sovereign Debt Market in Africa

The advent of the Treasury market in Africa has taken an interesting turn in the last few years as African governments, by stabilizing their economies, have been able to tap into the Eurobond market. The development of the African sovereign debt market, in contrast to the debt markets of the US and other developed economies, has been slow. But recent attempts to integrate the African capital markets into the global capital markets have been encouraging. Although local currency bonds in Africa have existed for decades, they have generally been regarded as low-quality bonds and thus held little interest to international investors. With the advent of the Eurobond market in Africa, major global institutional investors have begun to participate in the debt market; Indeed, trade volumes have grown quickly and are now approaching the $10 billion mark.

With several African countries looking at the Eurobond market to raise much-needed capital for infrastructure and other large-scale capital commitments, the Eurobond market has become an unlikely destination for capital raising in Africa. Paul Collier, Oxford University professor and author of the *Bottom Billion*, has noted that the need for infrastructure investments in Africa is now acute. He has suggested that it is the development in infrastructure that will underpin the sustainability of the African growth story. In order to plug the wide deficit gap, African countries are accessing the Eurobond and other foreign currency-denominated debt markets. Ghana was the first Sub-Saharan African country apart from South Africa to issue a sovereign bond in 2007. The $750 million 10-year bond was issued at a coupon of 8.5 percent and was widely oversubscribed.

In 2013, issuance by African countries in the Eurobond market stood at over $8 billion, its highest level ever, due to the issuance of Egypt, Ghana, Nigeria, South Africa and one debutant issuer, Rwanda. With the low rates earned by enormous pools of capital thanks to the US quantitative easing strategy, it is believed that some of the large global funds will continue to pull some of these resources into Africa at attractive yields to help stem the tide of the infrastructure and agriculture deficits. Given the more than $40 billion annual infrastructure deficit, the development of the debt market is critical to tackling this mammoth problem. We share the opinion that global yields will stay low for the foreseeable future, lending credence to the belief that foreign investors would need to tap into the more attractive yields offered by the emerging African economies. The following supports our argument for a continuing low yield environment:

1. The end of the Cold War – resources formerly needed for defence spending are now being diverted into more productive uses.
2. Globally, central banks are preoccupied with inflation as a policy tool.
3. Corporate cost-cutting and re-structuring is taking hold at a global level.
4. Super-efficient retailing, including online outlets, promises further consumer savings as it spreads globally.
5. Privatization and de-regulation continue to spur healthy competition.
6. Globalization is fuelling a more efficient world supply chain.
7. Consumers will begin to boost the national savings rate, which will somewhat stagnate growth in terms of consumption and debt.
8. The developed countries accumulate huge mortgage and consumer debts, a phenomenon which is not characteristic of Africa.

Corporate Debt

The corporate debt market in Sub-Saharan Africa is almost non-existent. However, we believe there is enormous potential to develop this segment of the market to fulfil the insatiable needs of the pension industry, which in itself is a burgeoning industry on the continent. There is the need to invest in other asset classes besides government debt instruments in the pension fund industry. The growth of the pension fund industry has been remarkable. Pension reforms have unleashed the potential of the industry to finance many projects with internally generated funds. For example, Nigeria's pension assets have increased from $1.7 billion in 2007 to over $24 billion in 2013 (Reuters, 2013). This is an increase of over 1,300 percent in six short years. Similar observations can be made in other countries where pension reforms have been introduced.

The development of the fixed-income market today has been aided by the establishment of an efficient and safe payment and settlement system. These systems have enabled secure and instantaneous settlement of payment orders, the clearing and settlement of equity and debt instruments and record keeping in electronic form. Further regulatory changes need to be made to continue to attract foreign investors in the capital markets.

Several institutions are working hard to develop the means to strengthen the fixed-income market in Africa. The African Development Bank (AfDB) is working on a Domestic Bond Fund and Index, but the private sector beat it to the punch. The Ecobank Middle Africa Bond Index (MABI) has been developed as a proportionally volume-weighted benchmark index to measure the performance of selected Sub-Saharan African (excluding South Africa) domestic sovereign bond markets. The Ecobank MABI is governed by a clear and transparent set of rules for selecting countries and instruments eligible for the index.

The Index currently consists of sovereign bonds from the BRVM group of countries, Ghana, Kenya and Nigeria, with a further 12 countries being considered for future inclusion. It is a joint initiative of Ecobank and Nedbank.

Risk and Return Profile

Over the long haul, equities have beaten inflation, bonds and treasury bills. In the 2011 Credit Suisse *Global Investment Returns Yearbook*, the same pattern was repeated in every market for which it had long-term data. With 111 years of returns for 19 *Yearbook* countries, representing almost 90 percent of the global stock market value, the publication states with confidence the historical superiority of equities. In the US, for example, equities gave an annualized total return over the 111 years of 6.3 percent in real terms, far ahead of the 1.8 percent real return on government bonds.

The superiority of equity investment returns versus bonds, Treasury bills and inflation over the long term has been confirmed by several academic research studies (Ibbotson and Chen, 2003, 2009; Siegel, 1992). Indeed, the most prolific researched studies on this view produced by Ibbotson Associates estimates a sizeable equity premium to bonds since 1926 (Ibbotson and Chen, 2009). A London Business School publication (Dimson et al., 2011) examining the returns of the various asset classes for 19 countries over 111 years confirmed that over the long run, on average the annualized equity risk premium was 3.8 percent. Notwithstanding this, since the start of the twenty-first century, bonds have outperformed equities. Out of the 19 countries analysed, only four countries, three of which were resource-rich economies, held true to the long-term view of equity outperformance.

According to the Credit Suisse *Yearbook*, on average, the realized equity risk premium versus bonds over the period 2000–2010 was -3.2 percent per year. Government bonds have so far been the asset of choice in the twenty-first century. The question is how long will this last, given the historical norms and the unprecedented low interest environment necessitated by the 2007 global financial crisis? Clearly, any hint of the tapering off of the US Federal Reserve's quantitative easing strategy may dramatically change the landscape of the low global interest rate environment. The prospects of a change in direction of US Federal policy after several years of easing to bring the US economy back from the brink of disaster is an eminent danger to emerging markets. For investors with long memories, it can be recalled that it was the tightening move made by the US in its interest rate policy that helped to trigger the Latin debt crisis in the 1980s and the Asian crisis in the late 1990s. African policy makers must be aware of this danger and guard against it. As the old saying goes, when the US coughs, the rest of the world catches a cold. In Africa, it might be a case of severe malaria with devastating consequences.

How does the performance of Africa compare to the rest of the world from 2000 to 2009? Using Ghana's financial markets as a proxy for the Sub-Saharan region, it is observed that the equity risk premium argument holds in Ghana. On average, the equity risk premium versus the one-year bond was 1.28 (Frontline Capital Advisors Research, 2010). As has been widely reported, the African equity markets have largely outperformed the developed market bourses since 2000 (Mahony, 2007; Senbet and Otchere, 2008). For example, the average annual return for the S&P 500 index for the same time period was -0.95 percent versus the Ghana stock index performance of 22.12 percent (Bloomberg Software Service, 2010).

Conclusions

The integration of Africa into the global financial structure has not been easy given the various historical macro-economic challenges and limitations. However, over the last two decades, there has been tremendous progress in terms of political, economic, social and regulatory reforms that is gradually leading to a re-definition of the economic environment. While it is difficult to forecast the surprises that may lie ahead as Africa makes a bold statement to become a meaningful partner in the globalization of the financial services sector, it may actually benefit the most from this, as it has the furthest to go in terms of financial and regulatory reforms. Clearly, the economic renaissance in Africa will accelerate and give a big boost to capital flows into the continent. The financial services industry is expected to play a major catalytic role to drive this economic transformation as countries move towards a better financial education system and an understanding of the basic prerequisite for economic success.

References

African Development Bank (2012). *Realising the Potential of Africa's Stock Exchanges.* Issue 16.

Bloomberg Software Service (2010). Historical data.

Business Insider (2013). The combined value of the world's stock markets has reached a record high, 16 December, www.businessinsider.com/wfe-world-stock-market-capitalization-2013-12.

Credit Suisse (2011). *Global Investment Returns Yearbook.* Credit Suisse Research Institute.

Demisse, M., Onah, R. and Prasannakumar, S. (2008). Africa and emerging financial markets.

Dimson, E., Marsh, P. and Staunton, M. (2011). *Equity Premia around the World.* London: London Business School.

Egyptian Stock Exchange (2013). Frequently asked questions (FAQ), http://www.egx.com.e.g./english/faq_main.aspx#2.

Frontline Capital Advisors Research (2010). Stock, bonds, inflation and risk premium analysis.

Ibbotson, R. and Chen, P. (2003). Long-run stock returns: Participating in the real economy. *Financial Analysts Journal,* 59(1), pp. 70–80.

Ibbotson, R. and Chen, P. (2009). Are bonds going to outperform stocks over the long run? Not likely. *Morningstar Inc.*, pp. 2–6.

Johannesburg Stock Exchange (JSE) (2011). *Dual Listing on the GSE.* Johannesburg Stock Exchange Africa Board.

Mahony, D. (2007). African market reform continues – African capital markets follow the emerging world. African Alliance Presentation at ASEA Conference, Accra, Ghana.

Miller, M.H. (1998). Financial markets and economic growth. *Journal of Applied Corporate Finance*, 11(3), pp. 8–15.

Ndikumana, L. (2001). Financial markets and economic development in Africa. Department of Economics and Political Economy Research Institute, University of Massachusetts, Working Paper Series 17.

Ntim, C.G. (2012). Why African stock markets should formally harmonise and integrate their operations. *African Review of Economics and Finance*, 4(1), pp. 53–72.

Reuters (2013). Nigeria pension assets to triple in next 3 years – Regulator, http://www.reuters.com/article/2013/11/27/Nigeria-pension-idUSL5N0JB3M820131127.

Senbet, L. and Otchere, I. (2008). Beyond banking: Developing markets – African stock markets, Seminar by IMF Institute and Joint Africa Institute, Tunisia.

Siegel, J.J. (1992). The equity premium: Stock and bond returns since 1802. *Financial Analysts Journal*, 48(1), pp. 28–38, 46.

Today Forward (2010). The 15 largest stock markets and exchanges. NYSE EuroNext$_{SM}$. http://todayforward.typepad.com/todayforward/2010/04/the-15-largest-stock-markets-and-exchanges.html.

World Federation of Exchanges (2010). 2010 WFE market highlights.

18

The Role of Stock Markets in National Development: The Case of the Ghana Stock Exchange

Kwesi Amonoo-Neizer and Nana Kumapremereh Nketiah

Abstract

It is generally accepted that financial markets play a key role in the development of emerging economies. Over the past 20 years, many developing economies have experienced tremendous growth in their financial markets, as evidenced by the increased level of participation of international investors in local markets. This chapter traces the history of the Ghana Stock Exchange, its perceived benefits, its performance over the years and some criticisms levelled against stock markets in general. In the light of over two decades of operations of the Ghana Stock Exchange, the chapter examines what impact it has had on national development. The authors conclude that although the Ghana Stock Exchange has made very important strides in its 20 years of existence, its limited capital-raising capability compared with the huge financing needs of the burgeoning companies in Ghana is one of the reasons why the stock market has not met expectations in terms of its impact on the Ghanaian economy. In spite of tremendous support given by both government and development partners, the pace of development of the stock market has lagged behind other parts of the financial market, much in line with the trends in other markets. Although the potential for growth is huge, Ghana and indeed Africa's inability to tap into this potential gives rise to the following question: 'Is it time to re-examine current strategies and market practices?' The authors recommend among other things that private pension plans should be encouraged to increase participation in the stock market by increasing the allowable limits for their holding in listed equities from 10 percent to 30 percent and that there is the need for greater collaboration between regulators and market participants to enhance the pace of development of the capital market industry.

Introduction

It is generally accepted that financial markets play a key role in the development of emerging economies. Over the past decade, Sub-Saharan countries have witnessed the consistent deepening of their financial markets. Many have overcome structural weaknesses and have enhanced market credibility. The growing integration of economies has also helped speed up the process. Macro-economic stability through the strengthening of monetary and budgetary policies have been an attraction because they have led to the development of more complete and stable domestic financial markets. Better management of economies has provided an increased cushion against external shocks. These developments are encouraging because participation in financial globalization has been shown to increase economic growth rates. However, the ratio of bond and stock market capitalization to gross domestic product (GDP) still remains low in most developing economies when compared with ratios of over 140 percent for some developed economies. Corporate bond markets remain underdeveloped in many emerging economies. Further progress is needed in strengthening public debt management and fiscal discipline in domestic markets. The local investor base needs to be expanded and regulation requires improvement.

What are the Perceived Benefits of Stock Markets?

Stock markets are thought to complement banking systems by providing five functions which are vital for the funding, growth and development of economies. These are:

1. the production of information and allocation of capital;
2. the enhancement of corporate governance;
3. improvement in risk management;
4. greater mobilization of savings; and
5. offering a medium for the exchange of goods and services (Merton and Bodie, 1995).

Stock markets augment banking systems by reducing the large costs and disincentives for investors in the quest to acquire and process information on companies and their managers, and this tends to improve the allocation of capital, which in turn accelerates economic growth. Markets enable providers of capital to monitor and influence how firms use it. They also provide alternative and more effective corporate governance mechanisms, help boost savings mobilization and enhance the flow of capital to profitable projects (Stiglitz and Weiss, 1983). Stock markets play an important role in diversifying risks associated with investing in individual projects, firms, industries and geographical areas. The ability to diversify risk enables the shifting of focus to longer-term projects. These markets are deemed to be necessary for dealing with the inefficiencies created by a financial system dominated by the banking system and fill the gaps not covered by banks. A bank-dominated system may encourage rent seeking and discourage risk taking (Rajan, 1992). Bank-based systems may hinder innovation and growth.

Firms connected to dominant banks have greater access to capital and are less cash-constrained. These tend to employ conservative, slow-growth strategies and use more capital-intensive processes. Such companies tend to have lower profit margins relative to those without connections to big banks (Morck and Nakamura, 1999; Weinstein and Yatch, 1998). Banks may be less effective at gathering and processing information. Self-interest tends to promote the relationships of banks with firms they provide credit to, normally to the detriment of other stakeholders. Banks are more reluctant to remove inefficient managers with whom they have had long-standing relationships. In times of adverse shocks, markets tend to do a better job of identifying, isolating and liquidating distressed firms, and thereby preventing them from making things worse (Rajan and Zingales, 1998).

A number of studies have demonstrated that stock market development may have a positive influence on a country's growth. Using data of 42 developed and developing countries from 1976 to 1993, Levine and Zervos (1998) demonstrate that growth in stock market liquidity increases a country's per capita GDP by 15 percent. Moreover, it has been posited that firms grow relatively faster in countries with active stock markets than otherwise, with researchers establishing that stock market liberalization influences the country's growth in real GDP per capita (Demirguc-Kunt and Maksimovic, 1996).

Stock markets are expected to accelerate economic growth by providing a boost to domestic savings and by increasing the quantity and quality of investment (Singh, 1997). The widening of options to suit various risk profiles tends to increase savings by individuals. Enhanced savings mobilization may increase the savings rate (Levine and Zervos, 1998). Stock markets provide a mechanism for growth companies to raise equity capital at lower costs. They positively influence economic growth through the encouragement of savings amongst individuals and by providing avenues for the financing of companies.

Liquid stock markets reduce downside risk and the cost of long-term investments. Liquidity ensures that initial investors do not lose access to their savings during the project gestation period because they can exit easily, quickly and cheaply (Bencivenga and Smith, 1991). More liquid stock markets promote investments in the long term, potentially more profitable projects, thereby improving capital allocation.

Criticisms of Stock Markets

Critics of the stock market suggest that stock market prices do not accurately reflect the underlying fundamentals during speculative bubbles (Binswanger, 1999). Under these conditions, momentum tends to determine price movement rather than the discounted value of future cash flows. The irrationality exhibited in these periods tends to adversely affect other sectors of the economy, which become a byproduct of speculation.

Critics argue that the enhanced liquidity of stock markets may encourage short-termism and may negatively impact on corporate investors. Since investors can easily sell their shares, more liquid stock markets may weaken investors' commitment and incentive to exert corporate control. Enhanced stock market liquidity may discourage investors from having long-term commitments with firms whose shares they own and therefore may create potential corporate governance problems with implications for economic growth (Bhide, 1993).

Parmendra Sharma and Eduordo Roca (2011) also argue that stock markets in smaller economies may have been detractions and may have led to the misallocation of scarce resources. They ask the following question: 'Are stock markets practical in all situations?' In some of these countries, stock markets have been marginally successful in accomplishing their functions. They propose a gradual withdrawal of stock markets from financial systems in some of these economies and propose that scarce resources should be re-directed to strengthening the banking sector and promoting more suitable alternatives, such as micro-finance and venture capital.

The effectiveness of stock markets tends to depend on the size and liquidity. The illiquidity of stock markets in some developing economies makes them less attractive as an investment avenue and therefore leads to a stagnation of these markets. There are serious doubts about the ability of an extremely small and inactive market to produce timely and useful information, allocate resources, diversify risks and make significant contribution to economic growth.

This is compounded if there is limited ability to improve and the market is unprofitable and dependent on the government. The question then to be posed is 'does such a country really need a stock market?' rather than the normal question of 'how do we develop the stock market?'

Table 18.1   Ghana Stock Exchange Review (1991–2012)

	1991	1996	2001	2006	2012
No. of listed companies	12	21	21	32	34
Market capitalization ($ billions)	0.08	1.65	0.54	1.85	6.10
Annual trade value ($ millions)	0.26	16.03	12.72	51.68	54.23
Average daily volumes ($)	2,632	104,040	82,589	309,436	883,494
GDP ($'b)	7.33	6.76	5.97	20.33	40.08
Market/GDP (%)	3.55	10.29	9.05	3.58	15.00
Annual trade/market CAP (%)	0.33	0.97	2.36	2.79	0.89

The idea of having a stock exchange in Ghana was first recommended by the Commonwealth Development Finance Company Limited's Pearl Report in 1969. In 1971, the Stock Exchange Act was enacted and the Accra Stock Exchange was incorporated. This company was never operationalized. A 10-member committee on the establishment of the Stock Exchange was set up in 1989 under the chairmanship of the then Governor of the Bank of Ghana. The Ghana Stock Exchange was incorporated as a private company limited by guarantee in July 1989. Trading began on the Ghana Stock Exchange on 12 November 1990 and it was officially launched on 11 January 1991.

The number of listed companies was 12 in 1991, which increased to 21 by 1996 and remained static until 2001, after which it saw an increase to 32 companies in 2006. By 2012, the number of listed companies had barely moved up to 34. Market capitalization excluding the effect of dual listing has not fared much better. Market capitalization at the end of 1991 was US$0.08 billion. This figure increased to US$1.65 billion in 1996, but dropped to US$0.54 billion in 2001, before increasing to US$1.85 billion in 2006. Market capitalization was US$6.10 billion by the end of 2012.

The Ghana Stock Exchange has failed to make a meaningful impact on the Ghanaian economy during its 20 years of existence. Out of the several thousands of companies operating in Ghana, only 34 have found it worthwhile to list. Funding from banks remains a greater attraction than raising equity from the stock market. Market capitalization as a percentage of GDP was 3.6 percent in 1991, which increased to 10.3 percent in 1996, dropped slightly to 9.1 percent in 2001 and dropped further to 3.6 percent in 2006. This ratio was 15 percent in 2012, which is significantly lower than ratios of over 70 percent in more developed markets.

Trading activity has been even more sluggish. The annual trading volume was US$0.3 million in 1991, which increased to US$16 million in 1996, fell back to US$13 million in 2001 before increasing to US$52 million in 2006. The trading volume for 2012 was US$54 million. This pales in comparison with the weekly Treasury bill volume of nearly US$200 million. Annual trades as a percentage of GDP have ranged between 0.5 percent and 3 percent, a further indicator of how inactive the Ghana Stock Exchange has been since its establishment.

Table 18.2   Five-Year Performance of the Ghana Stock Exchange

	1991–1995	1996–2000	2001–2005	2006–2010
Dollar returns (%)	1.99	-46.13	352.78	32.85
Capital raised (US$ millions)	75.30	44.25	57.26	228.90
Average prices to earnings ratio	5.4	5.0	11.0	12.9
Average dividend yield	9.2	8.9	4.7	4.0

The performance of the Ghana Stock Exchange in US dollar terms was static from 1991 to 1995, dropped by 46 percent between 1996 and 2000 and then rallied significantly by 353 percent between 2001 and 2005, before increasing by 33 percent between 2006 and 2010. The price to earnings ratio averaged around five times from 1991 to 2000 before rising to an average of 11 times from 2001 to 2005. The price earnings multiples averaged 13 times earnings from 2006 to 2010. This indicates that there has been an increase in the attraction of equity investments from 2001 to 2010. However, this has not been enough of an incentive to attract more companies onto the market to raise capital.

Most companies still depend predominantly on bank loans to meet their financial needs. The question then is: 'Why do so few companies utilise the Ghana Stock Exchange to raise capital even after 20 years of operation?' What deters more companies from listing and raising capital? The total capital raised between 1991 and 1995 was US$75 million, US$44 million between 1996 and 2000, US$57 million between 2001 and 2005, and US$229 million between 2006 and 2010. The equity capital raised on the Ghana Stock Exchange during its 20 years of existence has been less than US$0.5 million. This limited capital-raising capacity compared with the huge financing needs of burgeoning companies in Ghana may be one of the reasons why the Ghana Stock Exchange has not met expectations in terms of its impact on the Ghanaian economy.

The Development of the Ghana Stock Market within the African Context

In their paper of 2007, Charles Amo-Yartey and Charles Komla Adjasi identified stock market development as one of the central planks of the domestic financial liberalization programmes in most African countries. The establishment of stock markets and the liberalization of capital accuracy are seen as part of a global trend, with most African countries having joined the bandwagon. This is expected to boost domestic savings and increase the amount and quality of investments.

In spite of these developments, questions are still being asked about the impact of stock markets on the economy in Sub-Saharan Africa outside South Africa. These include the following questions. What benefits have African countries gained from having a stock market? Are they playing an important role in allocating capital to industry? What is the relationship between stock market development and economic growth? How do we make stock markets more functional in African countries?

It is questionable whether the perceived impact of stock markets on economic growth has been achieved in Africa. Stock markets are expected to encourage savings by offering individuals an additional financial instrument that may be most in line with their risk preference and liquidity needs. However, there is no evidence that the savings rate in Africa has increased as a result of individuals participating in the stock markets. Companies are expected to be less dependent on banks as a result of raising capital on stock exchanges, but this has not been the case in the African markets.

Information gathering has been improved as a result of the existence of stock markets in Africa. Better information enhances decision making and more efficient capital allocation, resulting in higher growth rates for listed companies.

Challenges remain, such as the low level of liquidity, as shown by limited trading volumes and values. Liquidity in African stock markets is substantially below even emerging market averages. Although information and pricing mechanisms have been greatly enhanced, information deficiencies still exist in most stock markets. The regularity and content of reporting leaves much to be desired in many African stock markets. The budgetary constraints of regulatory authorities make it difficult for them to perform their functions effectively. The trading activities of insiders are not sufficiently reported or monitored and there is little clarity as to what constitutes insider trading.

There are substantial information asymmetries between majority and minority investors. As illustrated in Table 18.3 below, most markets are small with very few listed companies. Market capitalization and turnover of markets remain extremely low.

Table 18.3   Selected Statistics of the African Stock Market (2012)

	No. of listed companies	Market capitalization (US$ billions)	Market capitalization/ GDP (%)	Annual trading value (US$ millions)	Value traded market cap (%)	Value traded GDP (%)
Botswana	38	53.0	23.8	135.9	2.7	0.6
Cote d'Ivoire	37	8.1	11.6	174.2	2.2	0.3
Egypt	235	60.1	22.7	23,402.7	34.1	7.7
Ghana	34	6.1	15.0	54.2	0.9	0.1
Kenya	60	15.9	42.1	1,084.9	6.8	2.8
Malawi	14	10.6	19.9	16.2	1.6	0.3
Mauritius	88	7.1	63.7	352.8	4.9	3.1
Morocco	77	52.8	53.0	5 832.5	9.0	4.8
Namibia	33	144.15	–	494.5	0.34	6.6
Nigeria	194	57.8	21.8	4,321.6	7.3	1.6
South Africa	400	998.3	30.9	406,628.9	40.9	12.6
Tanzania	13	2.0	7.5	32.4	0.4	0.1
Tunisia	59	8.9	19.3	240.5	14.1	2.7
Uganda	15	5.9	34.9	9.9	0.15	0.1
Zambia	20	9.4	52.8	68.3	0.7	0.4
Zimbabwe	79	11.8	42.8	448.2	11.3	4.8
Malaysia	962	476.3	101.3	124,497	28.6	50.8
Mexico	152	525	25.4	118,162	25.3	6.3
Thailand	405	382.9	70.6	229,460	70.4	66.7

Enhancing the Ghana Stock Market's Role in National Development

Liquidity of the stock market has been found to be one of the main drivers of economic growth. Greater liquidity enables companies to acquire much-needed capital quickly, facilitates more efficient capital allocation and results in greater investment. An increase in activity on the stock market is expected to increase economic growth through liquidity injection, savings mobilization and equity financing for companies. The Ghana Stock Exchange needs to focus on measures to boost liquidity since turnover ratios are major indicators of the influence of the stock market on economic growth.

Improvement in trading of shares through the increase in the number of shares traded, increased frequency of trading and an improve trend in the efficiency of trading will boost economic growth. More efficient trading systems and the encouragement of new listings could boost liquidity.

Other factors are needed to boost the development of the Ghana Stock Exchange. These include macro-economic stability and a sufficiently high level of income. Well-developed banking systems complement the stock market through the existence of liquid inter-bank markets and well-developed financial intermediaries. Efficient government institutions are also key to the growth of the stock market. Law and order, democratic accountability, quality of government institutions and low political risk are essential to the growth of the Ghana Stock Exchange.

The participation of institutional investors in the market should lead to more efficient market practices and greater innovation. Private pension plans should be encouraged to increase participation in the Ghana Stock Exchange by increasing the allowable limits for their holding in listed equity from 10 percent to around 30 percent. The participation of these institutions in the Ghana Stock Exchange should drive a move towards greater transparency and market integrity, lower cost of transactions and more efficient trading systems.

The responsiveness of regulators should be more timely to promote innovation in Ghana's market. The long approval process is a huge disincentive for companies that need to raise money quickly to fund transactions. Greater collaboration is required between regulators and market participants to greatly enhance the pace of development in the capital market industry. Regulation and supervision should be strengthened, but compliance cost and the time requirement need to be managed in order not to overburden an already cash-strapped industry. Frequency of disclosure, transparency and enforcement all need to be strengthened. Regulatory requirements need to be simplified, made inexpensive and non-cumbersome.

Conclusions

This chapter began with a review of the case for stock markets and the arguments against stock markets. It then examined the performance of the Ghana Stock Exchange and placed it in the African context. It then identified some of the factors that need to be addressed to enable the Ghana Stock Exchange to play a meaningful role in national development. However, while the Ghana Stock Exchange has made very important strides in its 20 years of existence, much still needs to be done. In spite of tremendous support from development partners over the years, patronage of the market remains low. The creation of the second, third and alternative markets has not led to any meaningful increase in participation of Ghanaian companies. The focus needs to be shifted to addressing the true needs of companies and the investing public. Liquidity is low, with trading occurring in few stocks. Low volumes lead to undeveloped brokerage, research and investment management industries. The stock market as a source of funding for private sector companies remains paltry, with corporate funding being dominated by bank borrowing. The Ghana Stock Exchange has not had a major impact on economic development. This could be attributed to low levels of liquidity, which acts as a deterrent to both issues and investors.

References

Amo-Yartey, C. and Adjasi, C.K. (2007). Stock market development in Sub-Saharan African challenge. *IMF Working Paper* (August).

Bencivenga, V.R. and Smith, B.D. (1991). Financial intermediation and endogenous growth. *Review of Economics Studies*, 58(2), pp. 195–209.

Bhide, A. (1993). The hidden costs of stock market liquidity. *Journal of Financial Economics*, 34, pp. 31–51.

Binswanger, M. (1999). *Stock Markets, Speculative Bubbles and Economic Growth*. Cheltenham: Edward Elgar Publishing.

Demirguc-Kunt, A. and Maksimovic, V. (1996). Stock market development and firm financing choices. *World Bank Economic Review*, pp. 341–71.

Ghana Stock Exchange Reports (1991–2013).

Levine, R. and Zervos, S. (1998). Stock markets, banks and economic growth. *American Economic Review*, 88(3), pp. 537–58.

Merton, R.C. and Bodie, Z. (1995). A conceptual framework for analyzing the financial environment. In D.B. Crane, K.A. Froot, S.P. Mason, A. Perold, R.C. Merton, Z. Bodie, E.R. Sirri and P. Tufano (eds), *The Global Financial System: A Functional Perspective*. Boston, MA: Harvard Business School Press, pp. 3–31.

Morck, R. and Nakamura, M. (1999). Banks and corporate control in Japan. *Journal of Finance*, 54, pp. 319–39.

Rajan, R. and Zingales, L. (1998). Which capitalism? Lessons from the East Asian crisis. *Journal of Applied Corporate Finance*, 11(3), pp. 40–48.

Rajan, R.G. (1992). Insiders and outsiders – The choice between informed and arm's-length debt. *Journal of Finance*, 47, pp. 1367–400.

Sharma, P. and Roca, E. (2011). Re-designing financial systems: A review of the role of stock markets in developing economies. Griffiths Business School Discussion Papers, Griffiths University.

Stiglitz, J. and Weiss, N. (1983). Incentive effects of terminations: Application to the credit and labour market. *American Economic Review*, 75(5), pp. 912–27.

Weinstein, D. and Yafeh, Y. (1998). On the costs of a bank-centred financial system: Evidence from the changing main bank relations in Japan. *Journal of Finance*, 53, pp. 635–72.

19

The Role of the Central Bank in Reforming the Financial Sector: The Case of Ghana

Mahamudu Bawumia

Abstract

Formal banking took its roots in the colonial Gold Coast towards the end of the nineteenth century with the establishment of the British Bank of West Africa in 1897 (known as the Standard Chartered Bank (SCB) today) and Barclays (Dominion, Colonial and Overseas) in 1917. These two banks basically served the needs of the expatriate community to the exclusion of the local indigenous population. Prior to the establishment of the British Bank of West Africa, the Post Office Savings Bank was established in 1887 and was more widely used by the local population. By 1913, there were 13 branches of the Post Office Savings Bank, which grew to 32 branches by 1918. At independence, and with the establishment of the central bank, the importance of financial deepening to support the nation's development agenda was vigorously pursued by the government through the central bank. In the process, many state banks were established with direct controls on interest rates and were allocated credit to reflect government priorities. However, the financial sector, as with the overall economy, was soon to run into trouble. Nevertheless, Ghana's financial sector has seen a remarkable turnaround from the pre-1988 reform period. Two major financial sector reform programmes were implemented from 1988, one driven by the World Bank (the Financial Sector Adjustment Programme (FINSAP) between 1988 and 2000) and the other being home-grown (the Financial Sector Strategic Plan (FINSSIP) between 2001 and 2008). Both sets of reform impacted positively on the banking and financial system in many areas, but the 2001–8 reforms resulted in a major deepening of Ghana's financial sector driven by the central bank.

Introduction

The Bank of Ghana (BOG), the central bank, was established in 1957 when the Bank of Ghana Ordinance (1957, No. 34) was passed by the British Parliament. Under the Ordinance, the Bank of Ghana was established as an independent central bank with orthodox central bank functions of regulating the money supply, containing inflation and stabilizing the monetary system. As with central banks in most developing countries, the Bank of Ghana, following its establishment and given the rudimentary nature of the country's financial system, embarked on a policy of reforming and deepening the financial sector as part of the overall development agenda.

As part of the agenda of using the banking system to drive the development agenda, the government through the Bank of Ghana facilitated the establishment of a number of development banks, which were established for specific purposes. In fact, all the banks that were established between the 1950s and the late 1980s were wholly or majority owned by the government. These included the National Investment Bank (NIB) in 1963 to assist industry and the Agricultural Credit and Cooperative Bank (now called the Agricultural Development Bank (ADB)) in 1965 to assist agriculture. A merchant bank, Merchant Bank Ghana, was set up in 1972 as a partnership between ANZ Grindlays, the government and public sector financial institutions. A Bank for Housing and Construction was set up in 1974 to provide loans for housing, industrial construction and companies producing building materials. The National Savings and Credit Bank (NSCB) and the Cooperative Bank (CO-OP) were set up in 1975 to provide consumer loans and credit for small and medium-sized enterprises (SMEs) and co-operatives. The Social Security Bank (SSB) was set up in 1977 to provide credit and long-term loans to businesses and individuals. In 1975 the government issued an indigenization decree, which allowed it to acquire a 40 percent equity stake in the two foreign-owned banks (Barclays and SCB), which had been established during the colonial era.

The Rural Banking System

As the Ghanaian banking system evolved after independence, it was increasingly clear by the 1970s that the financial system was developing to the exclusion of the rural population. The Bank of Ghana, under its then Governor Dr Amon Nikoi, actively promoted and set up the rural banking system. The objectives were to institutionalize financial intermediation in the rural areas, to mobilize rural savings for on-lending to agriculture and cottage industries, and to inculcate the banking habit among rural households. In 1976, the first two rural banks were established at Agona Nyakrom and Biriwa, both in the Central Region. By 1980, there were 20 rural banks.

Rural banks are unit banks incorporated as limited liability companies. They are owned by the communities in which they are located and they operate generally within a 20-mile radius of their headquarters. To avoid the dominance of large shareholders in the community, no single individual or company was allowed to own more than 10 and 20 percent of the share capital respectively.

Rural banks were subject to the same regulatory oversight as the deposit money banks and operated under the Banking Act 1970. Rural banks had to maintain a primary reserve in the form of cash and balances with other banks of not less than 10 percent of deposit liabilities and secondary reserves in the form of treasury bills and other money market instruments of not less than 52 percent of their deposit liabilities. In addition, rural banks had to transfer a minimum of 50 percent of their annual net profit after tax to their reserve fund and seek ratification of the Bank of Ghana before the disbursement of loans above specified amounts to a single party and all loans to directors or companies in which they had an interest.

Under the policy of directed lending, rural banks were required to comply with sectoral guidelines in respect of their loan portfolio. In the mid-1980s, these requirements were 45 percent for agriculture and 30 percent for cottage industries.

Financial Sector Reform: 1984–2000

As part of a comprehensive macro-economic adjustment programme with the support of the International Monetary Fund and the World Bank, financial market liberalization in Ghana began in the late 1980s under the Financial Sector Adjustment Programme (FINSAP), with the re-structuring of distressed banks and the cleaning-up of non-performing assets to restore banks to profitability and viability. The programme set prices right and initiated structural reforms, including fiscal and monetary operations, and privatizations (including banks).

The adoption of the FINSAP was part of a strategy to move the Ghanaian financial sector from an era of financial repression towards one of financial liberalization. This included the removal of interest rate ceilings, the abolition of directed credit and credit controls, the re-structuring of seven financially distressed banks, the improvement of the regulatory and supervisory framework, the privatization of banks, the development of money and capital markets, and a move towards indirect and market-determined instruments of monetary policy.

LIBERALIZATION OF INTEREST RATES

Interest rate liberalization under the FINSAP was implemented gradually. First, the maximum and minimum deposit interest rates were abolished in September 1987 (however, the minimum saving deposit rate was temporarily maintained at 12 percent). All sectoral credit allocations were also phased out. Interest rate controls were gradually relaxed and full liberalization was achieved in February 1988. In November 1990, the Bank of Ghana liberalized all bank charges and fees. A foreign exchange auction was introduced in 1986 and the establishment of forex bureaus was permitted in 1988.

RE-STRUCTURING FINANCIALLY DISTRESSED BANKS

The re-structuring of the distressed banks involved the reconstitution and strengthening of their board of directors, the closure of unprofitable branches, the reduction in operating costs through retrenchment of staff, the cleaning of balance sheets by offloading non-performing loans granted to state-owned enterprises, non-performing loans granted to the private sector and loans guaranteed by the government of Ghana, the upgrading of managerial capacity, intensified staff training of affected banks, and providing enough capital and adequate liquidity to enable the distressed banks to operate in a self-sustaining manner after re-structuring.

STRENGTHENING OF THE REGULATORY AND SUPERVISORY FRAMEWORK OF THE CENTRAL BANK

The existing regulatory framework was governed by the Banking Act of 1970. However, this Act did not provide clear guidelines on minimum capital requirements, risk exposure, prudential limits for banks and provisioning for loan losses, among other things. A new Banking Law, the Banking Act 1989, was passed to remedy these deficiencies. The new Banking Act laid out the basic regulatory framework for the banking system: minimum capital requirements, capital adequacy ratios (banks required to maintain a minimum capital base of six percent of risk-weighted assets), prudential lending ratios, exposure limits, and uniform accounting and auditing standards. Supervisory activities of the Bank of Ghana were also strengthened and the banks were required to submit accounts for off-site monitoring. Annual on-site inspections, as well as off-site surveillance, were to be conducted to verify banks' compliance with the regulations.

Specifically, the Banking Act 1989 provided, among other things, the following:

- The minimum paid-up capital for commercial banks with at least 60 percent Ghanaian ownership was set at ¢200 million.
- Foreign banks with Ghanaian ownership of less than 60 percent had to maintain a minimum paid-up capital of ¢500 million.
- The minimum paid-up capital for development banks was set at ¢1 billion.
- All banks were required to maintain a minimum capital adequacy ratio of 6.0 percent.
- Banks were not allowed to lend more than 25.0 percent of their net worth by way of secured loans and 10.0 percent of their net worth as unsecured loans.
- Banks were not allowed to undertake non-bank activities – they could only do so through subsidiaries.

A revised Bank of Ghana Law (PNDCL 291) was also enacted in 1992 to give more supervisory powers to the central bank. These two laws together provided the legal and regulatory framework for the banking business in Ghana.

RECOVERY OF NON-PERFORMING ASSETS

A major part of the process of re-structuring the banks involved removing non-performing loans (NPLs) from their balance sheets. This was accomplished either through swapping such loans for government-guaranteed interest-bearing bonds issued by the Bank of Ghana or offsetting such NPLs against liabilities to the government. A total of ¢62 billion NPLs ($170 million or 4.4 percent of gross domestic product (GDP)) were removed from the banks' portfolios under the exercise. These NPLs were transferred to a newly created Non-Performing Assets Recovery Trust (NPART), whose mandate was to realize these assets to the greatest extent possible. In return, the government issued the distressed banks with interest bearing FINSAP bonds redeemable in annual instalments.

Table 19.1 indicates that the NPAs of the foreign-owned banks or banks with foreign equity participation (Barclays, the SCB and Merchant Bank Ghana (MBG)) were the lowest, while the NPAs of the state-owned banks (Ghana Commercial Bank (GCB), the Social Security Bank (SSB), the Bank for Housing and Construction (BHC) and the NIB) were the highest (accounting for 91.6 percent of the NPAs transferred to NPART). This was because the foreign-owned banks applied stricter commercial criteria in their lending decisions. The local banks were characterized by poor credit decisions, especially due to government encouragement to lend to the agricultural sector. The foreign banks were also able to avoid political pressures.

The experience in Ghana is that the politicians are generally not able to approach the foreign banks with propositions they know will be rejected (because they are not commercially viable), but have no qualms with presenting the same propositions to government-owned banks as the managing directors can easily be 'persuaded' to oblige. The foreign banks were also helped by a directive that all state enterprises move their accounts to GCB, the perennial government milking cow of the Ghanaian banking industry. This experience with the performance of the state-owned banks provided the rationale for the reduction of direct state involvement in the banking system under the FINSAP.

Table 19.1   Non-performing Assets Transferred to NPART by Banks (¢ Millions)

Bank	Total Amount of NPAs	% of Total
GCB	14,321	28.4
SSB	12,585	25.0
NSCB	725	1.4
ADB	1,293	2.6
NIB	6,623	13.1
BHC	12,853	25.5
Barclays	689	1.4
SCB	462	0.9
MBG	881	1.7
TOTAL	50,432	100

Source: Ziorklui et al. (2001).

INSTITUTIONAL RE-STRUCTURING AND DIVESTITURE OF GOVERNMENT SHARES IN COMMERCIAL BANKS

As was noted earlier, one of the major problems plaguing the financial sector was the domination of the sector by government banks and the attendant political influence and lack of competition. The government therefore undertook, as part of the FINSAP, to divest its shares in commercial banks in 1992. On the block for divestiture were the Social Security Bank (SSB), GCB, the ADB, the NIB, the BHC and the CO-OP. Forty percent of the SSB was sold to a strategic investor and 21 percent of shares were divested through a public offer. In February 1996, 42 percent of shares in the GCB were floated on the stock exchange. The divestiture of the ADB and the NIB stalled, while the BHC and CO-OP banks were liquidated following a cheque fraud scandal (the A-Life scandal). The government also divested 40 percent of its shares in Barclays in June 1998.

In 1995, the SSB merged with the National Savings and Credit Bank (NSCB). The money market was formalized with the creation in 1991 of a second discount house, the Security Discount Company (SDC), to compete with the Consolidated Discount House (CDH), which was created in 1987. Both were wholly owned by the banks in Ghana and were charged with carrying out inter-bank market operations. These institutions played their traditional role of facilitating the intermediation process and reducing imbalances in the money market.

Non-bank Financial Institutions

The liberalization of the financial sector resulted in a rapid growth of non-bank financial institutions (NBFIs). To streamline the regulatory framework, a Financial Institutions (Non-banking) Law (PNDCL 328) was also enacted in 1993 to govern the operations of non-banks (savings and loans companies, finance companies, discount houses, acceptance houses, building societies, mortgage finance companies, credit unions, venture capital funds, and leasing and hire-purchase companies under the oversight of the Bank of Ghana). NBFIs had not previously been covered by legislation.

The NBFI Law of 1993 provided for the following amongst others:

- The minimum capital requirement for an NBFI was set at ¢100 million.
- The minimum capital adequacy ratio was set at 10.0 percent of risk assets.
- Non-banks were not allowed to lend more than 15.0 percent of their net worth by way of secured loans and 10.0 percent of their net worth as unsecured loans.

The Banking Act of 1989 and the NBFI Law of 1993 resulted in the emergence of new financial institutions which have added diversity and depth to the financial system, including acceptance houses, discount houses, finance houses, mortgage finance, savings and loans companies, and venture capital companies (see Table 19.2).

Table 19.2   Licensed NBFIs at the end of 2000

Type of Institution	Number
Building societies	2
Discount houses	3
Finance housed	10
Leasing companies	6
Mortgage finance	1
Savings and loans	8
Venture capital funds	2
Credit unions	225
TOTAL	257

Source: Bank of Ghana.

Rural Bank Reforms

The Bank of Ghana also continued to support the development of the rural banking system. The number of rural banks increased from 20 in 1980 to 112 by 1999 (see Table 19.3).

Table 19.3   Regional Distribution of Rural Banks (1987–2008)

Region	1987	1995	1999	2008
Ashanti	20	22	21	22
Central	22	22	20	21
Eastern	19	22	19	21
Brong Ahafo	15	18	17	20
Western	10	14	12	14
Volta	12	14	8	11
Greater Accra	5	6	6	6
Upper East	2	2	3	4
Upper West	2	2	3	4
Northern	0	3	3	6
TOTAL	107	125	112	129

Source: Bank of Ghana.

The main catalysts for the increase in the number of rural banks were the 1983 Economic Recovery Programme (ERP), the pressures exerted on the Bank of Ghana in the early 1980s by the Cocoa Board to facilitate cocoa purchases in the rural areas, and the demands of prominent local citizens to have rural banks in their communities.

Rural banks have on average about 1,000 shareholders. Even though the number of rural banks is large, their regional coverage is unequal, with a high concentration in the Ashanti, Central, Brong Ahafo, Eastern regions, while the northern regions (Northern, Upper East and Upper West) are not well served (see Table 19.3).

Consistent with the financial sector reform programme (FINSAP), the sectoral lending requirements which required rural banks to allocate 45 percent of their loan portfolio for agriculture and 30 percent for cottage industries were discontinued at the beginning of the 1990s. Notwithstanding the increase in the number of rural banks, the high reserve requirements, along with high Treasury Bill interest rates, limited the ability as well as the willingness of rural banks to extend credit. With Treasury Bill rates high and close to the lending rates for agriculture, manufacturing and trading, rural banks maintained a high share of their deposits as primary and secondary reserves, ranging between 65 and 80 percent of deposits between 1994 and 1998 (see Table 19.4).

Outstanding credit (including on lent funds under externally assisted projects) increased from ¢6.8 billion in 1993 to 54.0 billion by 1998 while deposits over the same period increased from ¢13.2 billion to ¢114.0 billion. While the increase in deposits was significant (nearly nine times) rural bank deposits only accounted for 3.0 percent of total formal banking system deposits by the end of 1998.

Table 19.4   Selected Financial Indicators of Rural Banks 1993–98 (¢ Billions)

	1993	1994	1995	1996	1997	1998
Total Assets	–	–	45.3	72.5	101.8	164.3
Deposits	13.2	16	33.5	50.1	76	114
Outstanding Credit	6.8	7.8	14.4	24.3	36.4	54
Primary/Secondary Reserve	9.4	10.5	23.4	37.7	49.5	91.3
in % of Total Deposits	71	66	70	75	65	80
Shareholder Funds	–	1.3	3.2	4.7	7.4	11.4

Source: Bank of Ghana.

The distribution of loans and advances by the rural banks was heavily skewed towards salaried workers (who accounted for at least 50 percent of the total outstanding loans), while the share of credit to agriculture (between 16 and 20 percent) was relatively small. For rural banks, lending to salaried (mainly urban) workers is relatively low risk, while the experience with lending to agriculture has been very risky.

The Ghana Stock Exchange

Under the direction of the government, the first feasibility study on establishing a stock exchange in Ghana was conducted in 1968 (the Pearl Report). This recommended the establishment of a stock exchange. In 1971, the Stock Exchange Act was passed and the Accra Stock Exchange Company was incorporated. However, because of frequent changes in government and political instability, the stock exchange envisaged in the Pearl Report was not established until 1989, when the Ghana Stock Exchange (GSE) was incorporated under the Companies Code (Mensah, 1997). The incorporation of the GSE by the Provisional National Defence Committee (PNDC) government in July 1989 (and officially launched in January 1990) was a landmark event in the development of the financial sector of Ghana. The presence of a stock exchange was seen as increasing the possibilities for raising financial savings and contributing to capital formation. The GSE was also seen as a way to accelerate the government's privatization programme, allowing participation by local investors. The GSE has no shareholders, but is incorporated as a public company limited by guarantee (i.e. it is a not-for profit organization).

There are three categories of members, namely Licensed Dealing Members (LDMs), Associate Members and Government Securities Dealers (Primary Dealers (PDs)). An LDM is a corporate body licensed by the Exchange to deal in all securities. An Associate Member is an individual or corporate body which has satisfied the Exchange's membership requirements, but is not licensed to deal in securities. In 1993 the GSE was the sixth-best performer among emerging stock markets, with a capital appreciation of 116 percent. In 1994 the GSE was the best performer among emerging stock markets, with a capital appreciation of 124 percent. After a slump in performance in 1995 following high inflation and interest rates, the GSE recovered in 1998, with the GSE index increasing by 70 percent to become the best-performing market in Africa (International Monetary Fund, 2000). After the floatation of Ashanti Goldfields Corporation (AGC) in 1994, it became the most important stock on the GSE, accounting for more than 70 percent of the market. The GSE was also fairly illiquid, with a turnover rate of just four percent in 1998.

The Securities Industry Law

The Securities Industry Law (SIL) was passed in 1993 (PNDCL 333) to provide for the establishment of a Securities Regulatory Commission (SRC) to serve as a watchdog over the industry. Its main functions include maintaining surveillance over the securities market to ensure orderly, fair and equitable dealings in securities, and to license and authorize stock exchanges, unit trust and mutual funds and securities dealers and investment advisers. The SRC was charged under the SIL with the responsibility of protecting the securities market against any abuses arising from the practice of insider trading. Takeovers, mergers, acquisitions and all forms of business combinations are subject to the review, approval and regulation of the SRC (Mensah, 1997). The SRC was vested with significant powers to enable it to acquire and gather information. The SIL gave it the power to order production of books by stock exchanges and certain persons and to impose criminal sanctions on anyone who fails to obey such orders of the SRC.

Financial Sector Reform: 2001–08

The FINSAP, which was implemented between 1988 and 1999, achieved a great deal, including the liberalization of interest rates, the abolition of directed credit, the re-structuring of financially distressed banks, the strengthening of the regulatory and supervisory framework, the privatization of state-owned banks, the promotion of non-bank financial institutions, the liberalization of the foreign exchange market, the establishment of forex bureaux, and the beginnings of a capital market with the establishment of the GSE in 1990.

By 2001, a number of constraints still remained in the financial sector, including high nominal interest rate spreads, low financial intermediation, crowding-out of the private sector in the credit market, a cash-dominated payment system, a large unbanked population, the absence of a credit information system, a complex foreign exchange regime, and the absence of a clear legal framework that addressed the rights and responsibilities of borrowers and lenders. There was also a need to fashion a legislative framework that would allow Ghana to position itself as an international financial centre within the sub-region.

These issues led to the launch of a new wave of home-grown reforms, some of which were later placed under the banner of the Financial Sector Strategic Plan (FINSSP) in 2003. The stated objectives of the FINSSP were: to make the financial sector the preferred source of finance for domestic companies; to promote efficient savings mobilization; to establish Ghana as the financial gateway to the Economic Community of West African States (ECOWAS) region; to enhance the competitiveness of Ghana's financial institutions; to ensure a stronger but also 'user-friendly' regulatory regime; and to achieve a diversified domestic financial sector within a competitive environment.

Reforming the Legal Framework: 2001–08

The 2001–8 period saw a wide range of legal reforms comprehensively affecting the financial sector. These reforms were meant to build on the earlier reforms of the 1980s and 1990s under the FINSAP, to address remaining bottlenecks and to better position Ghana's financial sector to drive Ghana's agenda of accelerated growth. Among the laws that were passed in this period were the Bank of Ghana Act 2002, the Payments System Act 2003, the Banking Act 2004, the Long-Term Savings Act 2004, the Venture Capital Trust Fund Act 2004, the Foreign Exchange Act 2006, the Banking Amendment Act 2007, the Central Securities Depository Act 2007, the Credit Reporting Act 2007, the Borrowers and Lenders Act 2008, the Non-bank Financial Institutions Act 2008 and the Home Mortgage Finance Act 2008.

The Bank of Ghana Act 2002

The Bank of Ghana Act 2002 was a landmark legislation which re-established the independence of the Bank of Ghana. It should be recalled that the Bank of Ghana Ordinance of 1957, which established the Bank, provided it with statutory and operational independence. However, this independence was taken away from the central bank with the passage of the Bank of Ghana Act 1963. After 45 years of government interference in the operations of the central bank which was largely characterized by fiscal dominance, and with the economic crisis of 2000 still fresh, Parliament passed the Bank of Ghana Act 2002, which once again enshrined into law the independence of the Bank of Ghana.

Section 3(1) of the Bank of Ghana Act 2002 specifies that 'the primary objective of the Bank is to maintain stability in the general level of prices'. The Act further states that '(2) without prejudice to subsection (1) the Bank shall support the general economic policy of government and promote economic growth and effective operation of banking and credit systems in the country, independent of instructions from the Government or any other authority'. This provision has made the Bank of Ghana (on paper at least) one of the most independent central banks in the world.

The Bank of Ghana Act 2002 has re-focused the central bank on the major task of inflation control and away from the developmental activities which characterized the Bank of Ghana's operations in the past. Other provisions of the Act include the following:

- A Monetary Policy Committee will be responsible for formulating monetary policy, which should bring transparency to the central bank's operations and its communications with the public.
- Government borrowing from the central bank in any year shall be limited to 10 percent of its revenue, which ties the hands of the government and the central bank in a way that is much stricter than the 20 percent ceiling which prevails in the Central African Franc (CFA) zone countries, for example.

The statutory mandate of the central bank was rooted in a resurgence of public interest in economic policy, a heightened aversion for inflation and an awareness of how much stability, in a growing economy, contributes to raising the standard of living of its people. The prevailing concern was that instability and weaknesses in the regulatory framework had accounted for the poor performance of the private sector.

The independence of the Bank of Ghana under the Bank of Ghana Act 2002 also provided the Bank with the freedom to pursue policies in the interests of the financial sector without having to wait for the approval of the government or any other authority. This was a major breath of fresh air for the Bank. However, there are legitimate questions about the extent to which the Bank of Ghana Act demands accountability from the Bank to Parliament, for example, as is the case with the Bank of England or the Federal Reserve.

Universal Banking

Financial sector policy conducted through the licensing of banks sought to serve multiple objectives other than the fundamental goal of debt and equity intermediation. These were to develop specialized segments of banking and financial services, notably merchant banking, development banking, retail banking, mortgage banking, rural-based banking and financial institutions.

In 2003, the Bank of Ghana introduced the concept of universal banking to replace the increasingly fragmented banking system. This involves the removal of restrictions on banking activity and was introduced to allow banks to choose the type of banking services they would like to offer in line with their capital, risk appetite and business orientation. It removes, for instance, the monopoly that was given to commercial banks in the area of retail banking. It creates room for the diversification of the range of financial services that a bank can provide. It allows merchant banks, for example, to compete for retail deposits. This process was expected to lead to branch network expansion, increasing banking penetration, and also competition for deposits at the retail level. The introduction of universal banking was basically a recognition that the financial system had to become integrated and thus the old divisions between commercial banks, development banks and merchant banks had become anachronistic. Universal banking therefore levelled the playing field and opened the financial sector to competition and the entry of new banks.

The Bank of Ghana at the same time recognized that for banks to adequately perform their roles as universal banks, it was important that they were adequately capitalized to take on additional risk. The Bank of Ghana therefore raised the minimum capital requirement for banks from ¢25 billion (US$3.3 million) to ¢50 billion (US$6.7 million) for Ghanaian banks and from ¢50 billion (US$6.7 million) to ¢70 billion ($7.2 million) for foreign banks in 2003.

Along with universal banking, the central bank also adopted an open but selective licensing policy, which allowed the entry of new banks. The addition of new banks was expected to encourage faster modernization of banking operations and efficiency of the financial system in order to support the growth and diversification of the financial service industry. Competition was also expected to positively affect the tariffs that banks charge for their products and services, lower lending rates in line with credit risks, and make credit accessible to all sectors in the economy. While the entry of new banks would increase competition, the Bank of Ghana also recognized that excessive numbers within the system could dilute the franchise value of banks and increase instability. Entry therefore had to be selective, well-managed and paced over time, and clear exit rules and prudential supervision vigorously enforced to safeguard systemic stability.

The Banking Act 2004 and the Banking Amendment Act 2007

The Banking Act 2004 (Act 673) was passed by Parliament to bring the banking law up to date with international standards as well as strengthen the operational independence of the Bank of Ghana in its role as a regulatory authority and to ensure greater transparency in the regulatory framework. However, the Act was amended by the Banking Amendment Act 2007 as part of the legal framework to support Ghana as an International Financial Services Centre (IFSC), a world-class hub to facilitate the delivery of a wide range of cross-border financial services to clients in other countries in the mould of Mauritius, Singapore or London. Taken together, the Banking Act 2004 and the Banking Amendment Act 2007 have resulted in fundamental changes in the regulatory framework for banking in Ghana.

LICENSING

The Bank of Ghana now issues three types of banking licence: a Class I Licence, a Class II Licence and a General Licence. A Class I Licence allows a bank to conduct universal, development or merchant banking business as existing banks currently do. All existing banks are therefore designated as Class I banks. A Class II Licence restricts the clients of the bank to non-residents. Class II banking business is conducted in a currency other than the Ghana cedi. A bank with a Class II Licence may accept deposits and make loans or offer other financial services only to non-residents. The domestic economy is expected to benefit from the foreign direct investment, employment, fees and taxes and skills transfer. A General Banking Licence allows the bank to combine both Class I and Class II activities.

CAPITAL ADEQUACY

Holders of General and Class I Licences are required to maintain a minimum capital adequacy ratio of 10.0 percent. On the other hand, the capital adequacy ratio for a Class II licence holder will be set by the Bank of Ghana for each bank separately depending on the financial resources available to the bank in question and the nature, scale and risks of its operations.

MINIMUM CAPITAL REQUIREMENTS

The Banking Amendment Act 2007 established minimum capital requirements for Class I and General Licence banks at ¢70 billion (the equivalent of some $7.0 million), while that for Class II banks was to be determined by the Bank of Ghana from time to time. In February 2008, the Bank of Ghana set a new minimum capital requirement for obtaining a Class I Licence (universal banking) at ¢60 million (the equivalent of some $60.0 million at the time). Existing banks were required to attain a minimum capitalization of ¢60 million by 31 December 2009. However, Ghanaian-owned banks were given a longer time period to meet the new minimum capital requirement. Under the directive, banks with local majority share ownership would have to attain a capitalization of at least ¢25 million by the end of 2010 and ¢60 million by 2012. The capitalization requirement constitutes part of the Bank of Ghana's strategy to deepen the financial sector and support Ghana's drive for accelerated growth of the economy.

The Long-Term Savings Scheme Act 2004

One of the factors inhibiting capital market development and the availability of medium- to long-term loans from financial institutions in Ghana is the dearth of long-term savings. While the history of macro-economic instability and high inflation has contributed to this outcome, the absence of incentives for voluntary long-term savings is a major obstacle. It is as a result of this that the Long-Term Savings Scheme Act 2004 was passed by Parliament to provide for the operation of tax incentive-based voluntary savings plans for retirement, education, home ownership, disability or death. Between 10 and 17.5 percent of contributions by employers to various savings schemes are tax deductible by the contributor. A Long-Term Savings Scheme Agency was established under the Act to administer the scheme.

The Venture Capital Trust Fund Act 2004

The Venture Capital Trust Fund Act 2004 established a Venture Capital Trust Fund to provide financial resources for the development and promotion of venture capital financing for SMEs in specific sectors of the economy. Funding for the Trust Fund was to come from a number of sources, including 25 percent of the National Reconstruction Levy from the 2003 financial year, budgetary allocations by government, grants, fees and investment income.

Any venture capital financing company is eligible to apply for funds provided it:

1. is incorporated in Ghana as a limited liability company under the Companies Code (1963);
2. has as its sole authorized business the business of assisting the development of small businesses by making equity investments and providing managerial expertise in which it has made or proposes to make an eligible investment;
3. is managed by an investment advisor who is licensed by the Securities and Exchange Commission and is in good standing;
4. has met the minimum capital requirements;
5. has in place adequate governance, internal control and monitoring procedures for the selection and monitoring of investment projects;
6. meets any other conditions specified by the Board.

The Payment System Act 2003

One area in the financial sector which needed major reform was the payment and settlement system. It was therefore important to put in place the legal underpinning to support these reforms and move the payments and settlement system into the twenty-first century. The Payment System Act was passed by Parliament in 2003 to provide for the establishment, operation and supervision of electronic and other payment, clearing and settlement systems. The Act also provided for the rights and responsibilities of transacting and intermediating parties.

The Payment Systems Act 2003 was a response to the need to develop non-cash payment products and clearing systems in order to reduce the over-dependence on cash payments in the economy.

The Act gives the Bank of Ghana the power to establish, operate and supervise the payment and settlement system. Section 1 stipulates that:

> the Bank of Ghana may establish, operate or supervise funds payment, funds transfer, clearing and settlement systems subject to such rules as it may publish, and designate any other payment, funds transfer, clearing and settlement system operating in the country which the bank considers to be in the public interest for the Bank to supervise under this Act.

Participants in the payments and settlement system are expected to play by the agreed rules of the system. The Act states that a transfer made in accordance with the rules, without prejudice to any remedies that may exist to recover an equivalent amount in case of fraud, mistake or similar factors, is irrevocable once executed. The discharge of settlement obligations between institutions participating in the system is made through entries in the accounts of the settlement bank and such an entry is final and irrevocable.

The Foreign Exchange Act 2006

One of the key reforms in the legal framework was the review of the basic laws governing foreign exchange transactions and the subsequent passage of the Foreign Exchange Act in 2006 to replace the Exchange Control Act of 1961. A number of key issues drove this reform.

The first was the need for Ghana to rationalize its foreign exchange system to make its economy more efficient within an integrated global financial system, which has been experiencing constant capital flows. Second, when the foreign exchange regime in Ghana was liberalized by policy in the mid-1980s, this was not accompanied by a corresponding reform of the existing relevant statutes. This therefore created a situation where the policy direction on foreign exchange transactions was diametrically opposed to statutory law.

Third, Ghana is seeking to establish itself as an international financial centre within the West African sub-region. This called for a reform of all laws that could facilitate such a project. Fourth, as a member of the West African Monetary Zone, Ghana had an obligation to liberalize its capital account transactions as a precondition for entry into the common currency arrangement.

The Foreign Exchange Act 2006 signalled an open and liberal exchange and payments system for Ghana. Unlike the Exchange Control Act of 1961, which prohibited all foreign exchange dealings and transactions unless permitted by the Minister of Finance and the Bank of Ghana, the philosophy of the Foreign Exchange Act 2006 is to permit all foreign exchange transactions unless otherwise prohibited by the Bank of Ghana.

For current account transactions, the Foreign Exchange Act requires the payments in foreign currency to or from Ghana between residents and non-residents to be made through a bank. Furthermore, payments for merchandise exports from Ghana are required to be made through the bank of the non-resident exporter to the exporter's bank in Ghana. This provision is to allow the Bank of Ghana to monitor Ghana's export proceeds. Under the Foreign Exchange Act, an exporter who fails to repatriate proceeds from merchandise exports through an external bank commits an offence. However, exporters are free to utilize the proceeds of their exports as they deem fit, with the exception of cocoa and gold, where there are surrender requirements.

In the area of capital account transactions, while the Exchange Control Act placed restrictions on the issuance and transfer of securities as well as external loans contracted between residents and non-residents, the Foreign Exchange Acts liberalized the inflows of foreign exchange into Ghana for foreign direct investment purposes. Also, loans contracted by residents will no longer require the approval of the Bank of Ghana. However, there are restrictions on short-term money market investments, with non-residents being allowed to invest in instruments for three years or more provided these instruments are held for at least two years.

Broadly, with the passage of the Foreign Exchange Act 2006, there is a shift in emphasis away from controls embodied in the Exchange Control Act towards an increased focus on monitoring foreign exchange transactions. In this regard, and consistent with international best practice, banks are required to submit reports on all underlying transactions related to transactions in foreign exchange to the Bank of Ghana.

The Anti-money Laundering Act 2008

The Anti-money Laundering Act was passed in 2008 to reinforce existing mechanisms for monitoring terrorist finances and money laundering within the global financial system. This was especially important as Ghana seeks to position itself as an international financial services centre. In this regard, it was important that the necessary safeguards be put in place.

The Act provides for the establishment of a Financial Intelligence Centre (FIC) to assist in the identification of proceeds of unlawful activities and the combatting of money laundering activities. The transfer of currency physically or electronically will be subject to the Bank of Ghana regulations consistent with the Foreign Exchange Act 2006.

The Act also provides that when an individual or institution becomes aware of a transaction involving money laundering or the financing of terrorism, such an individual or institution is required to submit a suspicious transaction report to the FIC within 24 hours of becoming aware of the transaction.

Under the Act, the FIC may freeze a transaction or a bank account to prevent suspected money laundering, but is required to go to court within seven days in order for the freeze to either be upheld or denied.

The Credit Reporting Act 2008

A major constraint on accessing credit has been the existence of asymmetric information in the credit markets. Lenders generally cannot be certain about the creditworthiness of borrowers in the absence of credit information. To address this problem, the Credit Reporting Act (Act 726) was passed by Parliament in 2007. The purpose of the Act is to provide a legal and regulatory framework for credit reporting in Ghana. The availability of credit information is generally accepted to be crucial for the development and maintenance of an effective financial sector.

Borrowers tend to have a natural incentive not to reveal negative information about themselves. The lack of a credit information system therefore increases the risks of lending and causes financial institutions to provide less credit. A credit reporting system in Ghana would provide timely, accurate and up-to-date information on the debt profile and re-payment history of borrowers, and would lead to a number of benefits, including:

a) reducing information asymmetry between borrowers and lenders;
b) enabling financial institutions to make informed decisions about the allocation of credit;
c) reducing default probabilities of borrowers as they seek to meet their obligations in a timely manner;
d) improving access to credit facilities by small and medium-sized businesses;
e) enabling the central bank to monitor systematic risks on an aggregate basis; and
f) promoting financial stability and the efficient allocation of resources in the Ghanaian economy.

This Credit Reporting Act is designed to promote the orderly development of a credit reporting system for Ghana and to promote public trust in credit bureau operations. Specifically, it provides for the licensing of private credit bureaus (and gives the Bank of Ghana the authority to set up a public credit bureau), regulates the activities of credit bureaus, establishes guiding principles for the conduct of the credit reporting system and provides for credit data submission, data management and protection, and dissemination. It seeks to strike a balance between, on the one hand, the rights of borrowers and, on the other hand, the need to share credit information effectively.

The Bank of Ghana is the regulatory authority for the Credit Reporting Act and the first credit reference bureau in Ghana was licensed in 2008.

The Borrowers and Lenders Act 2008

The Borrowers and Lenders Act 2008 (Act 773) was enacted to address a major gap in the financial sector – the absence of a legal framework governing the rights and responsibilities of borrowers and lenders. Stakeholder meetings convened by the Bank of Ghana to address this issue revealed very deep suspicions held by each of the parties. Borrowers felt rather powerless in dealing with lenders (the banks). High interest rates, hidden charges, non-disclosure of pertinent information, unfair denial of access to credit and discrimination were some of the complaints raised. On the other hand, lenders complained about high default rates, the difficulty of enforcing collateral through the courts, customers pledging the same collateral to more than one bank, and the misapplication of funds.

The Borrowers and Lenders Act provides the legal framework for credit, improves the standard of disclosure of information by borrowers and lenders, and promotes a consistent enforcement framework relating to credit.

The Home Mortgage Finance Act 2008

The Home Mortgage Finance Act 2008 (Act 770) was passed to clarify and rationalize the regulatory framework for home mortgages so as to deepen the development of the home mortgage market. In this regard, this Act takes precedence over the Mortgages Act 1972 where there is a conflict between the two. The Act covers, among other things, the requirements for a mortgage, disclosure requirements for the mortgagor and the mortgagee, use of the loan, registration of mortgages, default and remedies, and sale of mortgaged properties in case of default. It is a borrowers and lenders law specifically for the home mortgage market.

The Non-Bank Financial Institutions (NBFI) Act 2008

The Financial Institutions (Non-Banking) Law 1993 (PNDCL 328) was promulgated in 1993 to provide a prudential regulatory framework for nine categories of institutions designated as NBFIs. These were discount houses, finance houses, acceptance houses, building societies, leasing and hire-purchasing companies, venture capital funding companies, mortgage financing companies, savings and loans companies, and credit unions. The Bank of Ghana subsequently issued the Non-bank Financial Institutions (Bank of Ghana) Business Rules for Deposit Taking Institutions and the Non-bank Financial Institutions (Bank of Ghana) Business Rules for Non-deposit Taking Institutions in 2000 to provide detailed prudential rules for NBFIs. While PNDCL 328 regulated certain micro-finance institutions (MFIs) such as savings and loans companies and credit unions, a good number of MFIs, including non-governmental organizations (NGOs) and some informal operators such as *Susu* collectors remain outside the scope of prudential regulation, with the attendant potential system risks.

Ghana's FINSSP identified the need to review the existing NBFI and MFI regulatory framework to ensure that they met the current challenges facing the market. The FINSSP recommended the revision of PNDCL 328 to remove ambiguities in the objectives of regulation and to liberalize the regime for the development of NBFIs. It also envisaged the progressive deregulation of non-deposit-taking NBFIs and the establishment of consistency in the regulation of deposit-taking NBFIs and banks.

The Non-bank Financial Institutions Act 2008 (Act 774) has a number of key provisions, including the following:

1. Non-bank financial services are defined under the Act as leasing, money lending, money transfer, mortgage finance, non-deposit-taking micro-finance services and credit unions. Discount houses, acceptance houses and building societies are to be phased out and converted into other licensed NBFIs under the Act.
2. The Act defines a deposit-taking NBFI as one that 'offers debt securities to the public and is in the business, directly or indirectly, of lending money or providing other financial services'.
3. Deposit-taking NBFIs would now be regulated as closely as possible to banks in view of the fact that they pose similar risks to the financial system. The Act provides that savings and loans companies, finance houses and deposit-taking MFIs will now be regulated under the Banking Act 2004 (Act 673).
4. Non-deposit-taking NBFIs such as leasing/hire-purchase companies, finance houses and mortgage finance companies are to be brought under a lower-tier prudential regulatory regime, with a view to a progressive de-regulation of non-deposit-taking NBFIs and MFIs.
5. The Money Lenders Ordinance 1941 (Cap 176), under which money lending licences could be issued by police stations, has been repealed under the Act.

The Act also seeks to promote self-regulation of NBFIs and MFIs through strong industry associations or networks such as the existing Ghana Micro Finance Network (GHAMFIN) and the *Susu* Collectors Association.

The Impact of Financial Sector Reforms on Financial Sector Developments (1984–2008)

Ghana's financial sector has seen a remarkable turnaround from the pre-1988 reform period. Two major financial sector reform programmes have been implemented, one driven by the World Bank – the Financial Sector Adjustment Programme (FINSAP) between 1988 and 2000 – and the Financial Sector Strategic Plan (FINSSIP), which was largely home-grown with significant input from stakeholders (between 2001 and 2008). Both sets of reform impacted positively on the banking and financial system in many areas.

Table 19.5   Ghana Banking System Indicators (1988–2008)

	1988	1991	1992	1998	2008
Number of Banks	10	12	13	17	24
Of which private	2	–	4	9	21
Number of branches	405	328	–	315	639
Banking System Assets/GDP	21	19	23	26	60.7
Non-Performing Loans/total credit	–	41	–	27	7.7
Asset Concentration					
4 largest banks	81	77	72	55	51.9
Public Sector Share					
Of total assets	79	73	70	37	24.9
Of total capital	–	77	76	34	31.9
Of total deposits	73	71	65	32	22.9
Of total advances	71	70	63	54	30.7
Of non-performing loans	–	–	–	84	29.8
Number of Account Holders:					
Commercial Banks					3,915,788
Rural Banks					2,827,023

Source: Bank of Ghana, IMF.

Entry of New Banks

The liberalization of the financial sector under the FINSAP resulted in an increase in the number of banks and non-banks in the financial sector with increased private sector participation. In 1988 the Ghanaian banking system comprised 10 banks with 405 branches (see Table 19.5).

In 1998, there were 17 banks in existence made up of nine commercial banks, five merchant banks and three development banks. Nine new banks were licensed since 1990 and two banks (the Bank for Credit and Commerce (BCC) and the CO-OP) were liquidated in 1993.

Table 19.6   Structure of the Ghanaian Banking Sector (December 2001)

Bank	Ownership (percent		Number of Branches	% Share of Total Assets
	Ghanaian	Foreign		
Commercial Banks				
Ghana Commercial Bank Ltd.	97	3	134	24.8
SSB Bank Ltd.	46	54	38	9.2
Barclays Bank of Ghana Ltd.	10	90	24	14.5
Standard Chartered Bank	24	76	23	16.1
The Trust Bank Ltd.	39	61	6	2.5
Metropolitan and Allied Bank	53	47	4	0.7
International Commercial Bank	0	100	3	0.6
Stanbic Bank Ghana Ltd.	9	91	1	1.2
Unibank	100	0	1	0.3
Merchant Banks				
Merchant Bank Ghana Ltd.	100	0	5	4.0
Ecobank Ghana Ltd.	6	64	4	7.1
CAL Merchant Bank	34	66	3	2.5
First Atlantic Bank	71	29	2	1.5
Amalgamated Bank	100	0	1	0.6
Development Banks				
Agricultural Development Bank	100	0	39	
National Investment Bank	100	0	11	
Prudential Bank	100	0	5	

Source: Bank of Ghana.

Of the 17 banking institutions in existence at the end of 2001, foreign investors held a majority of the shares in eight commercial banks, and three banks were state-owned (see Table 19.6). By 2009, there were 27 banks, with foreign investors holding the majority shares in 13 (see Table 19.7).

Table 19.7   Structure of the Ghanaian Banking Sector (December 2009)

Bank	Ghanaian ownership (%)	Foreign ownership (%)	Number of branches	% of total assets
Barclays	0	100	90	10.1
Standard Chartered	28.5	71.5	22	10.8
GCB	100	0	154	13.9
SG-SSB	48.3	51.7	37	4.2
ADB	100	0	53	5.0
NIB	100	0	27	4.0
MBG	100	0	21	4.9
ECO	9.9	90.1	44	9.6
CAL	94.4	4.6	13	3.2
TTB	70.5	29.5	18	2.2
FAMB	100	0	6	2.1
UTB	100	0	10	0.7
PBL	100	0	22	2.4
ICB	0	100	12	1.4

STANBIC	2.1	97.9	21	4.8
AMAL	51	49	12	2.6
UNIBANK	100	0	12	1.6
HFC	67.8	32.2	21	1.8
UBA	36.9	63.1	27	1.9
ZENITH	0	100	17	4.1
GTB	2	98	13	2
FIDELITY	100	0	14	2.6
IBG	25	75	20	3.2
BARODA	0	100	1	0.1
BSIC	0	100	8	0.2
ACCESS	4	96	1	0.6

Source: Bank of Ghana.

Assets and Liabilities of the Banking System (1993–2008)

Table 19.8 shows the trends in the assets and liabilities of commercial banks between 1993 and 2008. It can be observed that there was an increase in the total assets of the banking system from 0.31 percent of GDP in 1993 to 0.44 percent of GDP by 2000 (a 42.0 percent increase in the total assets/GDP figure) before declining to 0.38 percent of GDP in 2001. This was partly due to the economic crisis of 2000, which adversely impacted the ability of many bank customers to service their loans. Since 2001, total assets of the banking system steadily rose to 0.66 percent of GDP (a 73.0 percent increase in total assets/GDP figure) by 2008, reflecting a more vibrant banking system following the FINSSIP reforms.

The period between 1993 and 2000 also saw a shift in the composition of bank assets as lending to the private sector increased at the expense of lending to government. The loans/asset ratio increased from 0.16 in 1993 to 0.40 by 2000, while at the same time the ratio of holdings of Treasury and Bank of Ghana bills/total assets declined from 0.40 in 1995 to 0.24 in 2000, before increasing to 0.28 in 2001. This trend was reinforced after 2001, with the loans to asset ratio increasing from 0.38 in 2001 to 0.52 by 2008, while the bills/total assets ratio declined drastically from 0.32 in 2002 to 0.14 by 2008 (see Table 19.8).

Demand deposits as a proportion of total deposits increased from 48.0 percent in 1993 to 66.0 percent by 2000, before falling to 61.0 percent in 2001. By 2008, however, there was a marginal decline to 58.0 percent. Over the same period, savings deposits declined from 40.0 percent of total deposits in 1993 to 21.0 percent by 2001 and further to 15.0 percent by 2008. Nevertheless, time deposits increased over the reform periods from 12.0 percent of total deposits in 1993 to 16.0 percent of total deposits by 2000 and further to 26.0 percent of total deposits by 2008 (see Table 19.8).

Table 19.8   Banking System Balance Sheet Indicators (1993–2008)

	Loans/Total Assets	Bills/Total Assets	Demand Dep/ Total Deposits	Savings Dep/ Total Deposits	Time Dep/ Total Deposits	Total Assets/ GDP
1993	0.16	0.38	0.48	0.40	0.12	0.31
1994	0.17	0.32	0.57	0.31	0.12	0.33
1995	0.18	0.40	0.63	0.21	0.16	0.25
1996	0.23	0.27	0.65	0.19	0.16	0.25
1997	0.29	0.31	0.61	0.24	0.15	0.26
1998	0.33	0.35	0.59	0.22	0.19	0.27
1999	0.36	0.31	0.61	0.21	0.18	0.35
2000	0.40	0.24	0.67	0.18	0.16	0.44
2001	0.38	0.28	0.62	0.20	0.18	0.38
2002	0.30	0.32	0.64	0.22	0.13	0.40
2003	0.35	0.28	0.61	0.21	0.16	0.41
2004	0.36	0.28	0.61	0.21	0.14	0.39
2005	0.43	0.27	0.61	0.22	0.17	0.38
2006	0.45	0.23	0.59	0.22	0.19	0.45
2007	0.50	0.18	0.57	0.18	0.25	0.56
2008	0.52	0.14	0.58	0.15	0.56	0.66

Source: Bank of Ghana.

ASSET CONCENTRATION

At the beginning of the reforms in 1988, the banking system concentration was high, with the four largest banks accounting for 81.0 percent of the assets of the banking system. However, banking system concentration was reduced significantly, with the top four banks accounting for 55.0 percent of assets by 1998 and 51.9 percent by 2008 (see Table 19.5).

The dominant influence of the state in the banking system at the onset of the FINSAP is evident from the public sector's share of total assets (79.0 percent), total credit (71.0 percent) and total deposits (73.0 percent). The waning public sector influence after the reforms saw the public sector's share of the total assets of the banking system decline to 37.0 percent by 1998, while its share of total credit and total deposits declined to 54.0 percent and 32.0 percent respectively by 1998. By 2008, the public sector's share of total bank assets had further declined to 24.9 percent and its share of bank advances also declined to 30.7 percent (see Table 19.5).

The reform period also saw the closure of bank branches, which declined from 415 in 1988 to 315 by 1998 and 300 by December 2002. The closure of bank branches was part of the efforts of banks to rationalize their activities and close unprofitable branches. Even though the banking penetration ratio (one branch per 54,000 inhabitants at the end of 2002) is relatively high, formal banking reaches less than 10 percent of the population and the coverage varies widely. About 35 percent of the branches are in the Greater Accra region, even though this region represents less than 13.0 percent of the population, and about half of all bank branches in the interior of the country belong to the state-owned Ghana Commercial Bank.

Under the FINSSIP, there was an expansion of the bank branch network. By the end of 2008, bank branches had more than doubled from 300 in 2002 to 636 (see Table 19.5), reflecting the more vibrant banking environment.

Asset Quality

Following the FINSAP reforms and the re-structuring of the balance sheets of problem banks, there was also an improvement in the quality of the assets of the banking industry. At the end of 2000, the proportion of non-performing loans stood at 12.1 percent (down from 41 percent in 1988). However, NPLs increased to 17.4 percent in 2001 following the economic crisis in 2000. By 2008, they had further declined to 7.7 percent (Bank of Ghana, 2009).

Capital Adequacy

The capital adequacy of the banking system also saw significant improvements following the reforms. The average capital adequacy ratio (CAR) for the banking system increased from 10.73 percent in 1996 to 14.74 percent by 2001, well above the minimum 6.0 percent required by law. However, there were significant differences between banks, even though all banks met the minimum CAR. The CAR for the banking industry increased further to 15.67 percent by 2007, but fell to 13.84 percent at the end of 2008, although this was still well above the minimum requirement of 6.0 percent (Bank of Ghana, 2009).

Savings Mobilization, Interest Rates and Financial Deepening

The liberalization of the financial sector under the FINSAP and the FINSSIP brought with it expectations of increased savings, deposit mobilization, financial deepening and competition in the banking sector.

SAVINGS MOBILIZATION

The data (see Table 19.9) shows that the banking sector witnessed a growth in deposits over the immediate post-reform period, with deposits of the private sector with the banking system increasing from ¢14.0 million in 1990 to ¢427.8 million by 2000. The FINSSIP reform period of 2002–8 also saw a major increase in deposits as the economy expanded. Total private sector deposits in the banking system increased from ¢427.8 million in 2000 to ¢5.7136 billion by 2008. Time deposits similarly increased from ¢53.8 million in 2000 to ¢1.2461 billion by 2008.

The increase in total deposits was reflected in all its categories: demand, savings, foreign currency and deposits. Demand deposits of the private sector increased from ¢8.0 million in 1990 to ¢70.1 million by 2000. Between 2000 and 2008, private sector demand deposits in the banking system further increased from ¢70.1 million to ¢1.686 billion. Similarly, savings deposits of the private sector increased from ¢109.5 million in 2000 to ¢964.1 million by 2008 and time deposits increased from ¢53.8 million to ¢1.246.1 billion by 2008 (see Table 19.9).

Table 19.9   Liabilities of Deposit Money Banks (1990–2008)

	Private Sector Deposits					Public Sector Deposits			
	(GH¢ millions)								
Year	Demand deposit	Foreign currency deposits	Savings deposits	Time deposits	Total	Demand deposits	Savings deposits	Time deposits	Total
1990	8.0	–	5.5	0.5	14.0	4.0	0.1	0.6	4.7
1991	9.8	–	7.8	1.0	18.6	4.2	0.1	0.8	5.0
1992	10.7	–	11.5	1.9	24.1	6.8	0.2	2.3	9.2
1993	14.7	–	13.6	2.4	30.7	8.9	0.1	3.9	12.9
1994	21.5	–	20.0	3.3	44.9	10.6	0.6	3.4	14.6
1995	23.3	–	25.8	7.8	56.9	13.8	0.2	6.7	20.6
1996	27.3	51.6	34.9	14.2	127.9	20.9	0.2	7.7	28.8
1997	57.2	72.9	51.4	23.5	205.0	20.4	2.4	5.2	28.0
1998	74.3	67.2	67.0	42.4	251.0	23.9	0.2	6.5	30.6
1999	80.7	97.0	87.3	47.9	312.9	13.2	0.3	7.9	21.4
2000	70.1	194.3	109.5	53.8	427.8	16.1	0.4	15.1	31.6
2001	161.9	237.4	158.9	92.7	650.8	39.1	0.5	23.2	62.7
2002	269.7	355.3	228.8	104.5	958.3	81.0	1.3	25.2	107.4
2003	346.4	457.6	295.2	183.4	1,282.6	147.5	1.8	42.1	191.4
2004	526.7	568.1	395.6	211.5	1,701.9	189.7	1.7	31.4	222.8
2005	570.9	653.3	484.2	292.7	2,001.0	173.0	0.8	52.7	226.5
2006	803.1	902.4	694.3	466.8	2,866.6	251.1	1.4	70.5	323.0
2007	1,412.7	992.9	849.6	837.6	4,092.9	208.8	1.1	138.3	348.1
2008	1,686.6	1,816.8	964.1	1,246.1	5,713.6	406.2	1.3	231.2	638.7

Source: Bank of Ghana.

The 2001–8 period under the FINSSIP reform programme therefore saw a major increase in private sector bank deposits compared to the FINSAP period (1988–2000).

Interest Rates

An explanation for the increase in deposit mobilization observed under both the FINSAP and the FINSSIP may be found in interest rate developments in the pre- and post-reform periods.

A key driver of financial sector reform under the FINSAP was the negative interest rates prevailing under the regime of direct controls and the disincentive to savings and deposit mobilization that this provided. Average real savings rates reached -111.8 percent in 1983. The FINSAP reform programme, by liberalizing interest rates, resulted in an increase in nominal interest rates. However, as Table 19.10 shows, real interest rates continued to be negative, with bank savings rates averaging -10.0 percent between 1984 and 2000 and -8.8 percent between 2001 and 2008. Real bank lending rates, on the other hand, turned positive by 1989 (5 percent), increasing to 22.0 percent by 2000. However, real lending rates declined to 9.1 percent by 2008, following the general trend decline in interest rates between 2001 and 2008.

Nevertheless, the post-reform period did not result in positive real interest rates on bank products. For example, real interest rates on savings deposit accounts increased from an average of -46.0 percent between 1975 and 1986 to an average of -6.0 percent between 1987 and 2000.

Table 19.10 also shows that real interest rate spreads (i.e. the difference between banks' lending and deposit rates adjusted for inflation) were on average negative between 1983 and 2008. The FINSAP period between 1984 and 2000 saw real interest rate spreads at an average of -20.0 percent. While real interest rate spreads during the FINSSIP period (2001–8) were marginally positive, they averaged -0.9 percent. Economic theory[1] will therefore predict, as was observed, higher deposit mobilization and higher bank lending under the FINSSIP regime (2001–8) than under the FINSAP regime (1984–2000) because real interest rates paid on deposits were higher.

Financial Deepening

Key monetary indicators often used in gauging the extent of financial deepening in an economy (Tables 19.11 and 19.12) point to significant deepening of the Ghanaian financial system over the past couple of decades, especially following the financial sector reforms. The indicators thus reflect the strong contribution of the financial system to the growth of the economy over the period. However, this has happened with broadly unchanged interest rates spreads, a situation that has triggered the pursuit of vigorous market competition policies[2] by the central bank. In the process, money supply, broadly defined, rose consistently from an average of 17.2 percent of GDP during 1990–1995 to 45.8 percent at the end of 2008. This was reflected in a strong deposit mobilization over the period, rising significantly from some 11.1 percent of GDP during 1990–1995 to 36.3 percent of GDP at the end of 2008. The strong deposit mobilization supported increased growth of bank credit to the private sector from under 10 percent of GDP during the 1996–2000 period to 27.7 percent of GDP by 2008. Currency outside banks remained broadly unchanged at an average of some 7.6 percent of GDP over the period.

---

1   The McKinnon-Shaw hypothesis.

2   Including the licensing of new banks and the publication of annual percentage rates recently.

Table 19.10   Selected Interest Rates, Spreads and Inflation (1975–2000)

	12-month deposit	Average Saving Deposit	Lending Agric	Lending Other	Treasury Bills	Inflation (cpi, 2002 = 100)	Average Real Saving Rate	Average Nominal Interest Spread (Lend-Dep)	Average Real Interest Spread (Lend-Dep)
1975	8	7.5	6	125	7.8	40.4	-23.4	4.5	-25.6
1976	8	7.5	6	125	7.8	67.0	-35.6	4.5	-37.4
1977	8	7.5	8.5	125	7.8	105.9	-47.8	4.5	-49.3
1978	13	12	13	18.5	12	108.5	-46.3	5.5	-49.4
1979	13	12	13	18.5	12	18.3	-5.3	5.5	-10.8
1980	13	12	13	18.5	12	87.8	-40.4	5.5	-43.8
1981	19	18	20	25.5	18.5	100.2	-41.1	6.5	-46.8
1982	9	8	8	14	9.5	16.8	-7.5	5.0	-10.1
1983	12.5	11	12.5	19	13	142.4	-54.2	6.5	-56.1
1984	16	14.5	16	22.5	16.8	6.0	8.0	6.5	0.5
1985	17	15.5	18	22.5	16.8	19.5	-3.3	5.5	-11.7
1986	20	18.5	22.5	23	19.8	33.3	-11.1	3.0	-22.8
1987	22	21.5	30	26	19.6	34.2	-9.4	4.0	-22.5
1988	22	19.25	30	30.3	19.8	26.6	-5.8	8.3	-14.4
1989	20	17	30	30.3	19.9	30.5	-10.3	10.3	-15.5
1990	22	16	29.5	30.3	27.5	35.9	-14.6	8.3	-20.3
1991	24	15	31.5	31.5	18	10.3	4.3	7.5	-2.5
1992	22.5	13.5	26.5	29	25.4	13.3	0.1	6.5	-6.0
1993	32	18.75	39	39	32	27.7	-7.0	7.0	-16.2
1994	31	18.1	35.5	37.5	29.5	34.2	-12.0	6.5	-20.6
1995	31	26.25	38.5	40.5	33	70.8	-26.1	9.5	-35.9

1996	31.5	28.25	47	43	47.9	32.7	-3.3	11.5	-16.0
1997	32	28.5	49	44	45.6	20.5	6.7	12.0	-7.0
1998	25	16.5	42	38.5	28.7	15.7	0.6	13.5	-1.9
1999	18.75	13	36.75	34.75	34.2	13.8	-0.7	16.0	1.9
2000	26.25	18	47	47	42.0	40.5	-16.0	20.8	-14.1
2001	20	14.5	44	44	28.9	21.3	-5.6	24.0	2.2
2002	20	13	38.5	38.5	26.6	17.0	-3.4	18.5	1.3
2003	15.5	9.75	32.75	32.75	18.7	31.3	-16.4	17.3	-10.7
2004	11.25	9.5	28.75	28.75	17.1	16.4	-6.0	17.5	0.9
2005	9.5	6.375	26	26	11.5	13.9	-6.6	16.5	2.3
2006	8.75	4.75	24.25	24.25	9.6	10.9	-5.6	15.5	4.1
2007	10.75	4.55	23.75	24.25	10.6	12.7	-7.3	13.5	0.7
2008	15.5	9.0	27.25	27.25	24.7	18.1	-7.7	11.8	-5.4

Source: Bank of Ghana.

Table 19.11   Ghana: Indicators of Financial Deepening (Annual Growth Rates, %)

	1991–95	1996–2000	2001–05	2006	2007	2008
M2+/GDP	17.2	23.5	31.0	36.3	40.8	45.8
Deposits/GDP	11.1	16.0	22.1	27.5	31.6	36.3
Currency outside banks/GDP	6.1	7.5	8.9	8.7	9.2	9.4
Currency outside banks/ deposits	54.8	46.7	40.6	31.8	29.3	26.0
Private sector credit/GDP	4.8	9.9	12.9	17.7	23.4	27.7
M1/M2	0.70	0.66	0.68	0.63	0.62	0.61

Source: Bank of Ghana.

The data from Table 19.11 indicates that going by the traditional measures of financial deepening (M2/GDP, bank credit/GDP, bank deposits/GDP), some financial deepening has taken place since the liberalization of the financial sector, even though the pace was slower during the FINSAP regime.

Table 19.12   Financial Deepening Indicators (1970–2008)

	M2/GDP	Bank deposits/GDP	Credit to the private sector/GDP
1970	19	12.4	8.2
1971	19	12.6	12.6
1972	23.7	15.2	10.1
1973	22.6	15.6	5.3
1974	21.6	14.4	5.7
1975	26.5	17	5.8
1976	29.1	18.3	5.9
1977	29.7	19.5	5.0
1978	36.6	16.6	3.5
1979	22.8	14.2	2.8
1980	20.4	12.4	4.1
1981	22.9	14.7	3.1
1982	19.8	12	3.7
1983	13.2	7.8	2.7
1984	12.5	7.4	3.0
1985	16	9.7	4.5
1986	16.6	10.4	5.2
1987	17.1	10.9	4.3
1988	17.3	11.2	3.6
1989	16.9	11.1	5.6
1990	13.6	9.7	3.9
1991	13.4	9.3	3.2
1992	17.5	11.8	4.6
1993	16	12.7	4.6
1994	18.7	12.8	5.3
1995	17.5	13.1	6.5
1996	19.4	14.5	8.3
1997	18	17.7	7.3

1998	22.7	16.8	10.6
1999	23.7	16.4	14.3
2000	26.7	16.9	14.2
2001	26.9	18.7	11.8
2002	31.5	21.8	12.3
2003	32	22.3	12.6
2004	33.4	24.1	13.1
2005	31.4	23.0	14.9
2006	36.2	27.3	17.7
2007	40.9	31.6	23.5
2008	45.8	36.1	27.7

Source: Bank of Ghana.

The M2/GDP ratio was 19.0 percent in 1975 and by 1995 (20 years later) it was 17.5 percent. At the beginning of the FINSAP in 1988, M2/GDP was 17.3 percent and, after declining in the early 1990s, it increased to 19.0 by 1996 and increased significantly to 26.6 by 2000. However, this is still lower than the level of 29.6 percent attained in 1976. Under the FINSSIP reforms, M2/GDP increased from 26.7 percent in 2000 to a record high of 45.8 percent by 2008, which was indicative of a significant deepening of the financial sector.

The bank deposits/GDP ratio increased from 11.2 percent in 1988 to 17.7 percent in 1997 and declined to 16.2 percent by 2000 (still lower than the 1977 level of 19.5 percent). Following the FINSSIP reforms, bank deposits/GDP reached a record level of 36.0 percent by 2008. The private sector credit/GDP ratio increased significantly from 3.2 percent in 1998 to 14.0 percent by 2000 (following the FINSAP reforms) and further to 29.7 percent by 2008. With the increase in bank credit, Ghanaians experienced the unusual phenomenon of banks pursuing customers at their workplaces and in their homes to offer credit.

The evidence therefore shows that Ghana's financial sector has been deepened by the two programmes of financial sector reform implemented between 1984 and 2008, and the central bank has played a critical role in this process.

Conclusions

The FINSAP, which was implemented between 1988 and 2000, achieved a great deal, including:

* the liberalization of interest rates and the abolition of directed credit;
* the re-structuring of financially distressed banks;
* the strengthening of the regulatory and supervisory framework;
* the promotion of NBFIs: discount houses, finance houses, acceptance houses, leasing companies and mortgage finance companies;
* the liberalization of the foreign exchange market;
* the establishment of forex bureaux; and
* the establishment of the GSE.

The legal framework for the financial sector was enhanced with the passage of bills such as the:

* Banking Act 1989;
* Bank of Ghana Law 1992, PNDCL 291;

- Securities Industry Law 1993, PNDCL 333;
- Financial Institutions (Non-banking) Law Law 1999, PNDCL 328;
- Insurance Act 1989, PNDCL 227;
- Social Security Act 1991, PNDCL 247.

The financial sector reforms between 2001 and 2008 under the FINSSIP built on these reforms with the goal of addressing many of the constraints in the financial sector and re-positioning Ghana's financial sector as an international financial services centre in the sub-region. In this regard, reforms introduced included the following:

- the Bank of Ghana Act 2002;
- the Monetary Policy Committee (MPC) process – transparency;
- universal banking;
- the aboltion of secondary reserve requirements;
- the Banking Act 2004;
- the Banking Amendment Act 2007 (offshore banking);
- the Long-Term Savings Act 2004;
- the Venture Capital Trust Fund Act 2004;
- the Payment System Act 2003;
- the Foreign Exchange Act 2006;
- the Anti-money Laundering Act 2008;
- the Credit Reporting Act 2008;
- the licensing of the first Credit Reference Bureau;
- the establishment of a Collateral Registry;
- the Borrowers and Lenders Act 2008;
- the Insolvency Act 2003;
- the Home Finance Act 2008;
- the Non-bank Financial Institutions Act 2008;
- the Central Securities Depository Act 2007;
- the payment and settlement system reforms:
  - the real-time gross settlement system (RTGS),
  - the Central Securities Depository (CSD),
  - the Automated Clearing House (ACH),
  - cheque codeline clearing (CCC),
  - a national payment system with a common interoperable platform that is inclusive of the unbanked in rural and urban areas (e-Zwich),
  - the Ghana Interbank Payments and Settlement System (GHIPSS).

The wide-ranging reforms that were implemented in the 2001–8 period resulted in a significant deepening of the financial sector in that period compared to the 1984–2000 period (using all key measures like deposit/GDP, M2/GDP, credit to the private sector/GDP, etc.).

The ability of the Bank of Ghana and the government to undertake the wide-ranging reforms between 2001 and 2008 was primarily because the reform programme was domestically owned and an independent Bank of Ghana was mandated to drive it. It is difficult to imagine a Bank of Ghana where governors in the past constantly had to look over their shoulders (sometimes literally at the barrel of a gun) with concern with regard to the reaction of political authorities to various initiatives moving the financial sector reform process as quickly as the Bank of Ghana did in the 2001–8 period. With its newfound independence under a democratic political dispensation, the Bank of Ghana had a clear focus on the type of financial sector it desired and was willing to think outside of the box to achieve this. The fact that a reform or policy had not been implemented before anywhere else in the world was not a deterrent.

Throughout the reform process, the Bank of Ghana constantly drove home the point that Ghana should benchmark itself against the best in the world and should move away from the 'poverty mentality' towards a 'can do' attitude. It is this thinking that allowed Ghana to leapfrog many countries in the area of payment system development, for example. It is the same thinking that made Ghana the first post-Highly Indebted Poor Country (HIPC) to issue a sovereign bond (and the first country in Africa outside of South Africa and Egypt to do so), and it is this same thinking that made it the first low-income country in the world to adopt the inflation targeting monetary policy framework, and the first central bank in Africa (and one of the few globally) to obtain ISO 27001 certification.

Furthermore, Ghana's financial sector reform programme was not driven by development partners. To the extent that development partners helped (which was useful), it was complementary to ongoing efforts. With a lot more domestic ownership of its reform process, Ghana was able to move faster and accomplish a lot in the process. This reinforces the view (which I share) that the quicker that Ghana and other African countries can wean themselves from dependence on development partners on a sustainable basis, the better their prospects for development would be.

However, notwithstanding all the reforms in the financial sector, the sector still faces fundamental problems that need to be addressed going forward if Ghana is to obtain the financial sector development and low interest rate environment that other developed countries have become accustomed to. These challenges, many of which are not within the remit of central banks, include the following points.

Unique Identification Numbers for the Population

A key ingredient underpinning financial transactions in any society is *trust* or what Fukuyama (1999) refers to as 'social capital'. For example, since 1801, the motto of the London Stock Exchange has been 'My Word is My Bond' and deals were made with no exchange of documents and no written pledges being given. Transactions are based on trust and anyone breaching this is ostracized, with the attendant consequences. In this type of environment, interest rates on loans would be lower than in an environment in which the word of the borrower cannot be trusted and the probability of default is high. Banks in Ghana have complained about customers who take loans for particular purposes only to do something quite different and unproductive with the loans. It is important to note that this does not mean that individuals in the UK and other developed financial centres are necessarily more trustworthy; the difference is that they have put in place institutions and technology (like CCTV) to engender trustworthy behaviour.

In developed economies, the consequences of declaring bankruptcy, for example, are severe and will affect job prospects, ability to obtain a loan, etc. Everyone can be uniquely identified by a number on a database that is accessible for background checks. This means that the cost of defaulting on a loan is high. In Ghana and many other developing countries, unique identification numbers on such a database do not generally exist and therefore the cost of defaulting on a loan is low. Defaulters will generally switch to another financial institution or even change their name to access another loan. The establishment of a credit reference bureau, as Ghana has recently done, without a unique identification for market participants will not solve the problem either. It is therefore important to have a unique ID that cannot be faked and can also be easily authenticated offline as well as online. In Ghana, the biometric smartcard platform may provide an ideal solution to this issue.

Address System

The importance of a system of property addresses is probably one of the most underestimated requirements for the development of an economy and its financial sector. One can imagine what would happen if, for example, the address system in the US, the UK, South Korea or Japan disappeared overnight. These economies would basically grind to a halt because so much depends on residential or business addresses. For banks and other lenders, the question in Ghana and other developing countries is how to track down a defaulter. Borrowers are also aware that they cannot be tracked down and so are likely to default. It is highly imperative that countries like Ghana put in place a comprehensive address system as a matter of priority. The UK, for example, developed its postcode system in the 15-year period between 1959 and 1974. This was in response to the increasing confusion with similar street names going back to the 1840s. The six-digit postal code was finally settled on after many experiments. The availability of GPS technology and Google Maps today, together with the experiences of various countries, should make the task much easier for a country like Ghana. The absence of an address system increases the risk that premium bankers attach to a loan.

Financial Inclusion (Banking the Unbanked)

The financial system cannot develop to its potential and monetary policy cannot be effective if the majority of the population continues to be excluded from access to financial services. The importance of this to the overall development of financial systems in Africa cannot be overemphasized. This is the reason why the Bank of Ghana has placed a high priority on banking the unbanked through the facilitation of a common platform and technology (the e-Zwich biometric smartcard) for banks and other non-bank institutions to allow access to financial services by the unbanked in the context of overall payment system reform. Other technologies (like mobile phones) are also available to deliver mobile banking services and should be encouraged in the context of the central bank's regulatory framework for branchless banking.

References

Aryeetey, E. (1994). *Financial Integration and Development in Sub-Saharan Africa: A Study of Informal Finance in Ghana*. London: ODI Working Paper No. 78.

———. (1996). The formal financial sector in Ghana after the reforms. Report of a study sponsored by the World Bank Research Committee and administered by the Overseas Development Institute.

Bank of Ghana (2007). *Commemoration of Fiftieth Anniversary*, Edward Ayensu (ed.). Accra: Bank of Ghana.

———. (2009). Financial Stability Reports: Monetary Policy Committee Statistical Releases, 2002–2009.

Brownbridge, M. and Gockel, F. (1998). The impact of financial sector policies on banking in Ghana. In *Banking in Africa: The Impact of Financial Sector Reform since Independence*. Oxford and Trenton, NJ: James Currey and Africa World Press.

Fukuyama, F. (1999). Social capital and civil society. Institute of Public Policy, George Mason University.

International Monetary Fund (1991). *Ghana: Adjustment and Growth. 1983–91*. Occasional Paper No. 86. Washington DC.

———. (2000). *Ghana: Selected Issues*. IMF Country Report No. 2.

Killick, T. (1978). *Development Economics in Action. A Study of Economic Policies in Ghana*. London: Heinemann.

McKinnon, R.I. (1973). *Money and Capital in Economic Development*. Washington DC: Brookings Institution.

Mensah, S. (1997). Financial markets and institutions: Ghana's experience. International Programme on Capital Markets and Portfolio Management. Indian Institute of Management, 8–20 September 1997.

Nachega, J.-C. (2001). Financial liberalization, money demand, and inflation in Uganda, IMF Working Papers 01/118.

Shaw, E.S. (1973). *Financial Deepening in Economic Development.* New York: Oxford University Press.

Sowa, N.K. and Acquaye, I. (1999). Financial and foreign exchange markets liberalization in Ghana. *Journal of International Development,* 11, pp. 385–409.

Sowa, N.K. and Kwakye, J.K. (1993). Inflationary trends and control in Ghana. AERC Research Paper 22, Nairobi.

Tanner, A.A. (1995). Financial system restructuring: An overview of Ghana's experience. *The West African Banker,* 5, pp. 5–11.

Yahya, K. (2001). Monetary management in Ghana. A paper presented at the Conference on Monetary Policy Framework in Africa Pretoria, South Africa.

Ziorklui, S.Q. (2001). The impact of financial sector reform on bank efficiency and financial deepening for savings mobilization in Ghana. African Economic Policy Discussion Paper No. 81, February, Howard University.

20

Marketing and Economic Development

Kwaku Appiah-Adu

Abstract

In developing countries, the 'more glamorous' fields such as production, finance, human resources and the traditional arts and science professions are highlighted, while marketing is treated with neglect, if not disdain. Yet marketing holds a key position in these countries. Although marketing generally lags behind in most areas of economic life, it is the most effective stimulus of economic development, especially in its ability to develop entrepreneurs and managers speedily. Moreover, it provides what is the greatest need of a developing country: a systematic discipline in a vital domain of economic activity, a discipline which is based on generalized theoretical concepts and which can thus be taught as well as learned. In this chapter the discussion focuses on the needs and wants that people have, which society, as a consumer of marketing, hopes that marketers will supply effectively in response to changes taking place in the marketplace.

Introduction

The label 'developing economy' is used to describe the Western bloc of so-called technically advanced nations (Western Europe, North America, Japan, Australia and New Zealand). Developing economies are characterized by low per capita income, wealth concentration in the hands of a few, high population growth rates, high illiteracy levels, a high percentage of the population employed in agriculture and a high proportion of exports concentrated in staple crops and raw materials. However, in reality, these nations range from primitive, stagnant economies to rapidly developing dynamic economies. Moreover, these countries differ in terms of culture, politics and level of economic development and, hence, efforts have been made to introduce some sub-classifications. For instance, the World Bank's classification using gross national product (GNP) yields low, middle, upper-middle and high income nations. Indeed, the range of developing economies is enormous and is likely to change further in the future, so any rigid categorization is unlikely to remain legitimate for a lengthy period.

If some developing economies are regarded as more developed than others, then it is important to examine the meaning of economic development. Unfortunately, definitions have varied from 'economic growth' to 'modernization' to 'distributive justice' to a 'socio-economic change' (World Bank, 1986; Kinsey, 1988). Following the Second World War, economic growth, based on an increase in GNP, was used as a measure of development. A limitation of this approach was that a rise in GNP could be eclipsed by population growth, resulting in a lower average standard of living. In the 1960s, 'modernization' emerged as a major yardstick for assessing development, with an emphasis on social, psychological, political and educational changes. Following a realization that the improvements associated with growth were not reaching the poverty-stricken areas of society, 'distributive justice' involving an emphasis on regional planning and more public goods/services became the criterion for measuring development. Economic development now embraces a total socio-economic transformation, with improvements in industrial and agricultural sectors, material prosperity, literacy, health and gainful employment for the working-age segment in general, since this is the real measure of enhancement of overall living standards.

The Significance of Marketing in Developing Economies

Marketing generally involves a process of exchange between two parties which is concluded to their mutual benefit and satisfaction (Baker, 1983). Although its origins date back to the times of trade by barter, the marketing concept which was formally recognized in the West during the 1950s holds that a business exists to satisfy consumer needs and wants, and thus social and economic transformation are central to the marketing concept's development. Kotler's (1984) societal marketing concept which was proposed in the 1980s urges an organization to place emphasis on the welfare of society in general in addition to satisfying consumer needs and wants. Based on these concepts, marketing may be regarded as a strategic component of any society because it directly allocates resources and exerts a fundamental influence on other facets of economic and social life. Hence, it is logical to suggest that marketing is relevant to economic development and is an intrinsic part of it – and, indeed, an active agent.

Nonetheless, some authors have debated whether the organizing framework of the marketing discipline, with its origins in the industrial culture of the US and Western Europe, is applicable in developing economies (Bartels, 1983; Ross and McTavish, 1985). One standpoint is that marketing lacks applicability in developing economies because its concepts and techniques have evolved and been nurtured in buyers' market conditions, whereas most developing economies reflect sellers' markets (Dholakia and Dholakia, 1980; Bartels, 1983). The other perspective is that marketing principles and techniques are applicable in developing economies. However, the lack of availability of trained marketing personnel in these countries is viewed as impeding its ready applicability (Drucker, 1958; Mittendorf, 1982). Although the sophistication typical of marketing practices in the Western world may not be required, the fundamental objectives and functions of marketing are relevant. The latter perspective is endorsed in this chapter. In fact, marketing exists in some shape or form in any society where exchange takes place. The process is the same, but there may be qualitative and quantitative differences, such as fewer goods moving through the system, different types of goods and usually a limited variety of goods.

This debate has significant implications for marketing management in developing economies and the global character of the discipline. For example, if marketing principles and practices are found to lack applicability in these countries, it would not only exacerbate the difficulties that multi-national corporations encounter in designing global marketing strategies, but would indeed necessitate a re-examination of the discipline's organizing framework to enhance its global importance (Bartels, 1983). Against this background, several empirical efforts have been made to examine the significance of marketing in developing African economies during the last two decades. Some of the subjects investigated include the perceived usefulness of marketing concepts, the extent to which marketing activities are performed and the applicability of marketing activities (Okoroafo and Torkornoo, 1985; Akaah, Riordan and Dadzie, 1986; Appiah-Adu and Blankson,

1998; Appiah-Adu and Singh, 2008; Appiah-Adu, 2009). All these studies concluded that, indeed, marketing management activities are applicable in developing economies.

Marketing as a Business Discipline

As a *business discipline*, marketing seeks: an orderly, purposeful and planned way to find and create customers; to identify and define markets, create new ones and promote them; to integrate needs, wants and preferences, and the intellectual and creative capacity and skills of an industrial society towards the design of new and better products and of new distributive concepts and processes. On this contribution and similar ones of other founding fathers of marketing during the last century rests the swift evolution of marketing as one of the most *scientific* of all functional business.

Marketing as a Social Discipline

However, marketing is also considered as a *social discipline* in that it constitutes a dynamic process of society through which business enterprise is integrated productively with society's purposes and human values. It is in marketing that individual and social values, needs, and wants are satisfied – be it through producing goods, supplying services, fostering innovation or creating satisfaction. Marketing has its focus on the customer, that is, on the individual making decisions within a social structure and within a social value system. Hence, marketing is the process through which the economy is integrated into society to serve human needs.

The focus of this chapter is not on marketing as a functional discipline of business. This is not because the functional aspect of marketing is not important; in fact, one cannot be concerned, as many are, with the management of business enterprise without a direct concern with marketing.

The Role of Marketing

Emphasizing marketing as a social discipline places attention on the role of marketing in the economy and society. To make the chapter relevant to the business environments of developing economies, this contribution focuses on the role of marketing in economic development, particularly in a developing country with *growth* potential.

The proposition of this chapter is simple and short. Marketing has a vital role to play in respect of such *growth* areas. In fact, marketing is the critical *multiplier of* such development. Unfortunately, it is the least developed and least sophisticated part of the economic system in most developing countries. Its development, above all others, facilitates economic integration and the optimal utilization of the assets and productive capacity that an economy possesses. It mobilizes latent economic energy. It contributes to the principal needs, facilitating the speedy development of entrepreneurs and managers, while at the same time, it may be the easiest area of managerial work to get going.

International and Intra-National Inequality

In most parts of our current environment, the whole world is united and unified. This statement may sound strange given the conflicts and threats of suicidal wars that scream at us from every headline. But conflict has always been with us. What is noteworthy is that today, all of mankind shares the same vision, the same objective, the same goal, the same hope and believes in the same tools. This vision might, in a gross over-simplification, be called *industrialization*.

There is a general belief that it is possible for man to improve his economic lot through systematic, purposeful and directed effort – individually as well as collectively. It is believed that we have the tools at our disposal – the technological, conceptual and social tools – to enable man to raise himself, through sustained efforts, at least to a position that is considered to be above the internationally defined level of poverty.

And this is an irreversible fact. It has been made so by these true catalysts of revolution in our times: the mechanisms of communication – the dirt road, the truck, the radio, the television and the Internet, which have penetrated even the most remote, isolated and primitive communities. But at the same time, we have a new, unprecedented danger: that of extreme inequalities. A tiny minority of our population holds the vast majority of wealth. This is inequality of income as great as anything the world has ever witnessed. It is accompanied by very high inequality of income between those in different parts of the world, especially when we are in the process of proving that a free market economy does not have to live in extreme tension between the few very rich and the many very poor as lived in earlier societies of man. These inequalities do not augur well for the health and well-being of society and represent a potentially dangerous phenomenon.

The Significance of Marketing

Marketing is central in a liberalized developing economy. It is one of our most potent levers to convert threats into opportunities. To understand this, we must ask: what do we mean by 'developing'? The first response is, of course, an area of low income. But income is, after all, a result. It is a result of extreme agricultural overpopulation in which the vast majority of citizens have to make a living on the land which, consequently, cannot even produce food to feed them, let alone produce a surplus. It is certainly a result of low productivity. And both, in a vicious circle, mean that there is not enough capital for investment and very low productivity of what is being invested – owing mainly to misdirection of investment into unessential and unproductive channels.

Presumably, all this we know today and understand. In fact, we might have learned in recent years a great deal both about the structure of a developing economy and about the theory and dynamics of economic development. What we tend to forget, however, is that the essential aspect of a developing economy and the factor, the absence of which keeps it *underdeveloped*, is the inability to organize economic efforts and energies, to harness resources, wants and capacities, and so to convert a self-limiting static system into creative, self-generating organic growth.

And this is where marketing comes in.

Lack of Development in Developing Countries

In many developing countries, marketing is the most underdeveloped or the least developed part of the economy, if only because of the strong, pervasive prejudice against the *middleman*. As a result, these countries are stunted by an inability to make effective use of the little they have. Marketing might by itself go far towards changing the entire economic tone of the existing system without any change in methods of production, distribution of population or income. It would make the producers capable of generating marketable offerings by providing them with standards, quality demands and specifications for their product. It would make the product capable of being brought to markets instead of perishing in transit. And it would make the consumer capable of discrimination, that is, of obtaining the greatest value for his limited purchasing power.

What is needed in any *growth* country to make economic development realistic and simultaneously produce a poignant manifestation of what economic development can engender is a marketing system:

- an effective system of physical distribution;
- a financial system to make possible the distribution of goods;
- an actual marketing system, integrating the wants, needs and purchasing power of the consumer with capacity and resources of production.

One of the potential dangers of masking this need lies in the tendency to confuse marketing with the traditional trader or merchant, of which each developing country has more than enough. For a developing country, one of the most important contributions to its development is to get across the fact that marketing is something quite different. It is fundamental to disseminate the triple function of marketing:

- crystallizing and directing demand for maximum productive effectiveness and efficiency;
- guiding production purposefully towards maximum consumer satisfaction and consumer value;
- creating discrimination that rewards those who really contribute excellence and that then also penalizes the monopolist, the slothful or those who only want to take but do not want to contribute or to risk.

Utilization by the Entrepreneur

Marketing is the most easily accessible *multiplier* of managers and entrepreneurs in an *underdeveloped* growth area and, interestingly, managers and particularly entrepreneurs are the foremost need of these countries. In the first place, *economic development* is not a force of nature; it is the result of the action, the purposeful, responsible, risk-taking action, of men as entrepreneurs and managers. Certainly, it is the local entrepreneur and manager who alone can convey an understanding of what economic development means and how it can be achieved in his country.

Marketing can convert latent demand into effective demand. It cannot by itself create purchasing power. Nonetheless, it can uncover and channel all purchasing power that exists. It can therefore accelerate the conditions for a much higher level of economic activity than existed before, creating opportunities for the entrepreneur. It can then provide the spur for developing modern, responsible, professional management by creating the opportunity for the producer who knows how to plan, how to organize, how to lead people and how to innovate.

In most developing countries, markets are of necessity quite small. They are too small to make it possible to organize distribution for a single product line in any effective manner. Consequently, without a marketing organization, many products for which there is an adequate demand at a reasonable price cannot be distributed or, worse, they can be distributed only under monopoly conditions. A marketing system is required which serves as the joint and common channel for many producers, if any of them is able to come into existence and to stay in existence. This suggests that a marketing system in developing countries is the *creator of small business* and is the only way in which a man of vision and daring can become a businessman and entrepreneur himself. This is thereby the only way in which a true middle class can develop in the countries in which the habit of investment in productive enterprise has still to be fully exploited.

Developer of Standards

Marketing in a developing country is the developer of standards – of standards for products and services as well as of standards of conduct, integrity, reliability, foresight and concern for the basic long-term impact of decisions on the customer, the supplier, the economy and society. Instead of carrying on with theoretical statements, let me provide one illustration: the impact that the Standard Chartered Bank (SCB) has had on several developing countries. Although a multi-national company, the SCB caters for a wide spectrum of customers, engaging in effective marketing practices. Its impact and experience are therefore a fair test of what marketing principles, marketing knowledge and marketing techniques can achieve. The impact of such a multi-national company can be truly amazing. It forces modernization of banking premises and of facilities to expedite the service delivery process. It forces a different attitude towards the customer and towards the supplier. It forces other banks to adopt modern methods of pricing, training, providing efficient flexible service, etc. Simply to satisfy its own marketing needs, the SCB has standards of operations, quality and delivery – that is, on standards of operations management, of technical management and, above all, of the management of people, thereby expediting the progress in the art and science of bank management in these countries. Needless to say that SCB or, for that matter, Barclays or Unilever are not in developing countries for reasons of philanthropy, but because it is good and profitable business with promising growth potential. In other words, a multi-national operates in a developing country because marketing is the major opportunity in *a growth economy* – precisely because its absence is a major economic gap and the greatest need.

The Discipline of Marketing

Marketing is also vital in economic development because, among all business disciplines, it is the most learnable and teachable. One cannot forget for a moment how much one can still learn in the field of marketing. But most of what has been learnt so far can be expressed not only in general concepts, but also in valid principles.

A critical factor in this world of ours is the learnability and teachability of what it means to be an entrepreneur and manager. Indeed, the entrepreneur and the manager play a critical role in causing economic development to happen. Consequently, the world needs them in large numbers – and it needs them fast. The demand is also much too urgent for it to be supplied by slow evolution through experience or through dependence on the emergence *of naturals*. The danger that lies in the inequality today between the few people who have and the great many who have not is too great to permit a wait of decades. Yet, it takes decades, if not centuries, if we depend on experience and slow evolution for the supply of entrepreneurs and managers to adequately meet the needs of modern society.

In all the efforts of man to achieve advancement, there is only one way in which he has been able to short-cut experience in order to truly develop or really learn something significant. This way is to have available the distillate of experience and skill in the form of knowledge, concepts and generalization; in other words, in the form of a *discipline*.

The Discipline of Entrepreneurship

Many marketers today are working on the fashioning of such a discipline of entrepreneurship and management. They appear to be making more progress than most of them probably realize. Certainly they are at the cutting edge of providing an understanding of the basic problems of organizing people of diversified and highly advanced skill and judgement together in one effective organization.

But marketing, although it only covers one functional area in the field of business, has something that can be called a discipline. It has developed general concepts, that is, theories that explain a multitude of phenomena in simple statements. Marketing, therefore, already possesses a learnable and teachable approach to this basic and central problem not only of the *developing* countries but of all countries. Today the world has the same survival stake in economic development.

Marketing is obviously not a cure-all; it is only one thing we need. But it addresses a critical need. Indeed, without marketing as the hinge on which to turn, economic development will almost have to take the totalitarian form. A totalitarian system can be defined economically as one in which economic development is being attempted without marketing, indeed as one in which marketing is suppressed. Precisely because it looks first at the values and wants of the individual, and because it then develops people to act purposefully and responsibly – that is, because of its effectiveness in developing a free economy – marketing is suppressed in a totalitarian system. If we want economic development in terms of freedom and responsibility, we have to build it on the development of marketing.

In the new and unprecedented world in which we live, in a world that knows both a new unity of vision and growth and a new and potentially dangerous cleavage, marketing has a special and central role to play. This role goes beyond:

- 'getting the stuff out the back door';
- 'getting the most sales with the least cost';
- 'the optimal integration of our values and wants as customers, citizens, and persons, with our productive resources and intellectual achievements' – the role marketing plays in society.

In a developing economy, marketing is, of course, all of this. But, moreover, in an economy that is striving to break the age-old bond of man to misery, want and destitution, it is also the catalyst for the transmutation of latent resources into actual resources, of desires into accomplishments, and the development of responsible economic leaders and informed economic citizens.

References

Akaah, I. and Riordan, E. (1988). Applicability of marketing knowhow in the Third World. *International Marketing Review*, 5(1), pp. 41–55.

Akaah, I., Riordan, E. and Dadzie, K. (1986). Applicability of marketing concepts and management activities in the Third World: An empirical investigation. Working Paper, Wayne State University, Detroit.

Appiah-Adu, K. (2009). *Market Orientation and Competitive Performance: A Comparison of Firms in Industrialised and Emerging Economies.* Accra: Smartline Publishing Ltd.

Appiah-Adu, K. and Blankson, C. (1998). Business strategy, organisational culture and market orientation: Empirical evidence from a liberalised developing economy. *Thunderbird International Business Review*, 40(3), pp. 235–56.

Appiah-Adu, K. and Singh, S. (2008). Current marketing practices in Ghana. In S. Singh (ed.), *Business Practices in Emerging and Re-emerging Markets.* Basingstoke: Palgrave Macmillan, pp. 153–65.

Baker, M. (ed.) (1983). *Marketing: Theory and Practice*, 2nd edn. London: Macmillan.

Bartels, R. (1983). Is marketing defaulting its responsibilities? *Journal of Marketing*, 47 (Fall), pp. 32–5.

Dholakia, N. and Dholakia, R. (1980). Beyond internationalization: A broader strategy for marketing pedagogy. In R. Bagozzi (ed.), *Marketing in the 80s: Changes and Challenges.* Chicago: American Marketing Association, pp. 30–32.

Drucker, P. (1958). Marketing and economic development. *Journal of Marketing*, 22 (January), pp. 252–9.

Kinsey, J. (1988). *Marketing in Developing Countries*. London: Macmillan.

Kotler, P. (1984). *Marketing Management: Analysis, Planning and Control*. Englewood Cliffs, NJ: Prentice Hall.

Mittendorf, H. (1982). The role of FAO in promoting effective agricultural marketing systems. Paper presented at the 23rd Annual Meeting of the GEWISOLA, Giessen, Germany (September–October).

Okoroafo, S. and Torkornoo, H. (1995). Marketing decisions and performance in economic reform African countries. *Journal of Global Marketing*, 8(3), pp. 85–102.

Ross, C. and McTavish, R. (1985). Marketing in the Third World: Educators' views. Paper presented at a conference in Scotland (August).

World Bank (1986). *World Development Report 1986*. Oxford: Oxford University Press.

21

Branding and National Development

Vicky Wireko-Andoh

Abstract

The concept of branding is usually applied to products. Branding has transformed the lives of many products and has made them big success stories, influencing patronage, sales, aspirations and image. This concept of branding can be extended to countries in their quest to transform and accelerate their developmental agenda and change their image for the better. In this chapter we will look at how some countries have consciously used national branding to change their growth and prosperity agenda. Others have adopted branding in their attempt to attract focused attention, both internally and externally and, as a result, targeted specific investment opportunities to help boost their economies. Nations like South Africa, Malaysia, China and Kenya have specifically focused on country branding and have even gone to the extent of setting up specific country brand offices solely to drive their national branding exercise. After a bitter election dispute that left many people killed, investors with cold feet and the country's image badly battered, Kenya represents a specific example of a country that used branding to gradually instil confidence both internally and externally. Malaysia has successfully used nation branding to propel its tourism industry. Today, tourism is a major foreign exchange earner for the country, contributing substantially to that country's economy. South Africa's image both internally and externally suffered badly in the era of apartheid, virtually isolating it from the rest of the world. Today, some two decades after apartheid was dismantled, the country has used national branding to bounce back and is now Africa's biggest economic success. These examples are not only analysed but lessons are also drawn that developing economies can use to employ effective branding as a strategy to enhance national development.

Introduction

Due to the fact that branding is often associated only with products from manufacturing companies, the benefits of branding for all other areas of life are sometimes lost on us. Some of these products become so successful that, due to their visibility and the power they have on the consumer's mind, they get known and accepted long before the consumer realizes which company is behind the branded product. In other words, the consumer gets so acquainted with brands and not necessarily the companies that brought them into being. For some people, these branded products become their aspiration due to the brand's promise. The good thing, however, is that the strategies in transforming the long-term viability of brands can also be applied to individual personalities, to churches, to health institutions, to cities and of course to a country that is determined to change its image and get on the path of accelerated growth and development. This chapter seeks to answer the question that many have asked: 'Does branding have any impact on national development?'

To a large extent, national branding has succeeded in transforming and growing the economic and social prospects of nations beyond measure, a catalyst which is worth recommending to any developing country. There are many benefits towards having a consolidated brand image in a competitive marketplace, particularly in the areas of trade and tourism. Examples from China, Malaysia, South Africa and Kenya have shown that a deliberate focus on national branding can help attract both local and foreign investors as well as transform the image of the respective countries.

What is Branding?

Before we go on to discuss the topic for this chapter, let us put into perspective what branding is, what national development means and what the correlation between branding and national development is.

What is a brand? Or, better still, what is branding? There have been many definitions of brand or branding out there. Indeed, it is often believed that in order to understand branding, it is important to know what brands are. David Ogilvy, the legendary advertising copywriter and founder of the global advertising company Ogilvy & Mather, has defined brand as 'the intangible sum of a product's attributes: its name, packaging, price, its history, its reputation and the way it is advertised'. Brick marketing also defines brand as 'the idea or image of a specific product or service that consumers connect with by identifying the name, logo, slogan, or design of the company who owns the idea or image'.

Brick marketing's definition of brand goes on to state that 'branding is thought to be when that idea or image is marketed so that it is recognisable by many more people'. 'Branding is also a way to build an important company asset, which is a good reputation.' To the marketer, therefore, branding is not only to build recognition but also to build a good reputation and a set of standards that are highly respected and loved by a group of people. It is key to getting one's products out as a preferred choice.

When a woman selects the cosmetics that will make her look attractive, she goes looking for a particular brand irrespective of the cost. She believes in the product, has confidence in it and trusts that it would do something good for her compared to some others on the market. Similarly, when an architect is putting up a high-profile building, he looks for certain products with a certain name to give him the quality he is looking to see and to satisfy his client's expectations. Certain automobiles have come to be associated with quality and regarded as status symbols because of their brand names. Customers who are looking for a certain quality and durability would pay for that quality, no matter how expensive the automobile is. Brands are powerful assets carefully developed, managed and maintained. They reside in the minds of consumers for a long time. Therefore, a brand clearly is the distinguishing factor that differentiates products and services.

The Power of Branding

However, it is important to note that a brand has a name, a logo, a design, certain colours or a combination of factors that when put together can identify the goods or services of one seller and that of his or her competitor. For everyone who buys a product or a service, a brand is an important part of that product or service. This means that branding can add value. For example, many fashion-conscious women who are using a certain brand of make-up are doing so because of their belief in that product. The same product unwrapped in plain paper and packed in an unmarked packaging is likely to be seen as of low quality or inferior.

A businessman who goes to China to buy electrical goods to supply to big and small shops once talked about his first experience in China and what truly confirmed to him that branding is essentially important for both the manufacturer and the end user. He said that the first time he went to China to transact business, he went with the intention of purchasing and shipping container loads of a certain brand of electrical appliances. His business counterparts in China took him to a huge factory and warehouse where they manufactured and stocked all types of unbranded electrical goods, including air conditioners and television sets. He was somewhat disappointed when he did not find what he was looking for. To his amazement, however, he was told at the warehouse that the brand he wanted could be produced by just printing it and then embossing it on whatever number and varieties of appliances he was seeking to order. That is the influencing power of a brand. It is increasingly becoming the deciding factor on the market today as far as the selection of products and services is concerned.

Interestingly, the power of brands is alive in some cultures and stays in people's minds to the extent that in Ghana today, for example, there are those who see every newspaper as the *Daily Graphic* simply because that newspaper has been the leading name in the print media in the country for decades. Similarly, Pepsodent toothpaste, a local brand of toothpaste, has become the generic name for all toothpastes, while every mineral water is known by the name Voltic, the name for a local brand of bottled water in Ghana. Indeed, branding helps manufacturers to tell their stories of special qualities that differentiate them from other products in the same category. It gives them legal protection and helps the consumer to identify products that might benefit them, while leading them to quality goods. A great brand tends to foster/engender/carry loyalty and credibility, and invariably provides competitive advantage.

Nation Branding

Brands have personalities. A brand will project itself to a target audience. If one should juxtapose a country and a branded product, then the advantages for a nation that is seeking to position itself as a preferred destination for all manner of economic and social investment is enormous. It would mean that for such a country to embark on branding itself, it would have to focus on a clearly defined marketing and communications strategy that often guides successful product brands.

Examples of countries that have sought to create distinctive images that have yielded economic and social dividends abound. Egypt, from ancient times to the present day, has maintained a certain image – that it is the mother of civilization and has preserved such artefacts in museums to show to the world that indeed civilization started there. In Europe, Germany is seen as the country of automotive excellence, while the mention of Great Britain brings to mind a centuries-old monarchy that is well preserved to this day. The country France brings to mind images of sophistication, haute couture, fine wines and cosmetics. In the Americas, the US carries the image of a rich, powerful country with glamour and superstars. The positive strong images carved by these countries have helped them somewhat in their growth and development because the fact remains that if you get it right, you are bound to see a startling upturn in terms of trade, exports, tourism and investors. Nation branding shapes both external and internal opinions. The fact is that the brand reputation of countries is receiving attention by governments around the world in the same way as other areas of growth and development because of their potential benefits for the economic upturn of their countries.

What is National Development?

Every country has a national agenda to reach a certain goal for the long-term viability of the country and in order to bring prosperity and better living conditions to its people. This growth and prosperity is measured in terms of the gross domestic product (GDP) of the country. GDP is defined as the market value of a country's officially recognized final goods and services produced in a given period of time. It guides nations as to how well or how badly their growth prospects are. Countries with higher GDP usually fall within the higher income group, while countries with lower GDP are in the lower income bracket.

Ghana is currently said to be in the lower-middle income group with a per capita income of $1,600 (World Bank National Accounts Data files and the WHO, Ghana, 2013). Ghana's aim is to move up to the higher-middle income status within the shortest time possible. But that can only happen in a situation where there is rapid socio-economic development in the country. Such a level of development will have an impact on the economy, leading to a social change which involves job creation and therefore a reduction in unemployment, wealth creation, poverty reduction and generally better living conditions for the people. National development which therefore cuts across almost all sectors of the economy brings about transformational change in the quality of life of the population and the country as a whole.

What to Do When Creating Nation Branding

In creating nation branding, the following points need to be considered:

- Carry out a brand audit. The question of who, what, how and when? There is the need to think through who you are and who your stakeholders are. Who do your stakeholders think you are? What do you want to become in branding your country? What platforms do you have to showcase this? What do your stakeholders want? How do you communicate with stakeholders? When is the appropriate time?
- Analyse and review the data collected and identify which group can help drive the nation-branding exercise. Is it industry or farmers or services, the media, etc.?
- Develop a framework – vision, mission and values of the brand.
- Develop a visual and verbal description of the brand.
- Put together the brand strategy. The plan to drive the brand forward by asking what is unique, different or attractive for each of the stakeholders.
- Once you have the brand, remember to periodically measure, improve and refresh to keep relevant.

How Does Branding Fit into the Development Agenda of a Nation?

The question to ask at this point is whether branding a nation would have an impact or play any role in the development agenda of a country. Will putting a differentiation on a country necessarily help its growth agenda, whether economic or social? The simple answer is yes! A national effort at branding is exigent because it is always linked to the country's products, its services, its people, the governance system, the culture and, indeed, the totality of its image. A good image is always an asset. It attracts, it unearths credibility and it commands respect. It has become common knowledge that countries seeking to improve their economies by attracting investment, tourism and improving purchase decisions or trade have tended to brand themselves with colourful words and with compelling 'advertisements' for the world to hear or see them. They have given themselves jazzy descriptions, what the marketer would describe as taglines, to tell their stories in a few eye-catching words and symbols. Let us look at some known examples.

In Asia, there are varieties of nation branding, beautifully crafted in catchy taglines which, to them, say a lot about each country's potentials or attractiveness. Malaysia's tagline is 'Truly Asia', Vietnam's is 'Timeless Charm', that of the Philippines says 'It's More Fun in the Philippines', Thailand's is 'Amazing Thailand', Cambodia's is 'The Kingdom of Wonder', Brunei's is 'The Kingdom of Unexpected Treasures' and Hong Kong's simple message to the world is that it is 'Asia's World City'; Singapore has used the tagline 'New Asia' and Indonesia's theme is 'Endless Beauty of Diversity'. We see similar affectionate country descriptions when we come to Africa. South Africa says it is 'The Heart of Africa', Malawi says it is 'The Warm Heart of Africa', Ghana refers to itself as 'The Gateway to West Africa' and the Gambia says it is 'The Smiling Coast of Africa'. These simple descriptions immediately give a mental picture of what one should expect of the country.

Bearing in mind that the key to successful branding is the perception of a difference between competing brands, it is clear that all those countries named above are promoting themselves within a region or a world that is fighting for attention in the face of fierce competition from similar nations. With the most attractive of themes and messages, with colourful logos full of meaning to catch every eye, they present themselves as the best ever. In other words, they are seeking to create a brand for their countries and, in doing so, they have the aim to develop and implement a proactive marketing and communications strategy which is simply described as branding. Like a product brand, countries seeking to brand themselves to make them attractive in order to compete in national and global markets would have their own set objectives, their target audiences, their plans and their promise, among other parameters.

Countries that have a serious focus on branding and that are keen to shape their national appeal both internally and externally have developed far beyond imagination. What they would have done is to tell a compelling story about their country using the brand. The end result is to attract social and economic development just as a brand would have attracted customers, consumers, sales and ultimately positive growth and market share.

Nation Branding: South Africa in Perspective

In Africa, if any country in its history has had to successfully build affection and transform its economy with a single-minded purpose, it is South Africa. As South Africa for many years fought against apartheid rule, key leaders of the apartheid struggle such as Nelson Mandela were arrested and incarcerated for nearly three decades. Though apartheid was broken in the mid-1990s, the country's reputation did suffer in view of all the fighting and injustices that went on at the time. They needed to push forward and create a new, vibrant and attractive South Africa, both internally and to the outside world, to tell their story of a new country while bringing back investors. In August 2002, therefore, an organization known as Brand South Africa was established to help create a positive and compelling brand image for South Africa.

What guided this new organization and what was its purpose? Brand South Africa's main objective was to market South Africa through a deliberate and consistent marketing and PR campaign. It operated on four key platforms:

- to raise awareness internationally of all that South Africa had to offer investors;
- to operate missions abroad to promote investment and export industries;
- to mobilize influential South Africans as well as members of the media abroad;
- to boost local pride and patriotism through various campaigns.

The organization looked at the many benefits of having a consolidated brand image as a marketer will do with a product brand, bearing in mind that a consistent Brand South Africa message would create strategic advantages in terms of trade and tourism for the country in an increasingly competitive marketplace. What this has succeeded in doing today is to put in place a country with an image that builds pride internally and externally, promotes investments and tourism and helps new enterprises and job creation, all with the view to developing the country. Today, nobody will deny the fact that South Africa is a giant economy in Africa with a consistent traffic flow of trade and investment.

Nation Branding: Malaysia in Perspective

In the Asia region, Malaysia, a country which is often described as a peer to Ghana in the early 1950s and at the time had the same per capita income, is today miles ahead in terms of its success stories, many of which are credited to appropriate branding advantages. When those in Malaysia decided to change their country's image and aim for a higher growth development, they said to themselves that it was never too late to do so. But perhaps what sped them on was the Asian financial crisis of 1997. They took the bull by the horns with many reforms and rolled out the *Vision 2020 Agenda* to guide their branding effort and launched the 'Malaysia Truly Asia' tourism strategy, a core principle of brand reputation.

When they tagged themselves as 'Malaysia Truly Asia', indications show that the efforts they put behind the branding started yielding good dividends (*Baxter Jolly 2012, Lessons Learned from Brand Malaysia, posted 16th July 2012*). Figures available from Tourism Malaysia (2013), a publication of the Malaysian Tourism Company, indicates that in 1998 almost eight million tourists visited Malaysia. In 2003, after the country embarked on branding and consequently active marketing campaign, the number of tourists rose to 13.3 million and by the end of 2004, the number had grown to over 15 million. What this meant in foreign exchange earnings from tourism was US$8 billion in 2004 as compared to US$6.8 billion in 2003.

Ghana and Branding

Let us look at Ghana vis-à-vis other developing countries already in this game of branding and national development. By now we know that as the economy of a country develops and grows, there is a correlation between that growth and the social and economic well-being of the population. The question is how does a country like Ghana accelerate its national development through nation branding? Developing nations such as Ghana with lower GDP levels tend to depend to some extent on the support of development partners to build their economies, but this cannot be sustainable going forward. Ghana, and for that matter every developing nation, needs to take the issue of branding and staying competitive as a must, for, after all, branding is a mind game. Whether it relates to a product or a nation, we know that a brand is a collection of perceptions. However, to the target market, the perception is a reality. If a country manages these perceptions well, a more vibrant and confident nation emerges.

How can Ghana use branding to enhance its national development? This should not be difficult. As a country, Ghana already has a name. In African history, the Ghana Empire from which Ghana took its name had an industrious people who were good at trading, powerful with large armies, and rich in gold, salt and other commodities. Ghana was the first African country south of the Sahara to win its independence from colonial rule. The role played by Dr Kwame Nkrumah, Ghana's first President, in the formation of the Organization of African Unity (OAU) in the early

1960s made Ghana an attractive nation amongst its peers. The OAU having metamorphosed into the African Union (AU) today has seen Ghana continue to play a lead role on the continent. The name Ghana therefore already has some positive notions going for it and it is time to build a strong brand around this.

Today, like many African countries, Ghana is in a much better position to brand itself and sell its attractiveness both internally and externally. Just like some other African countries, it has the advantage of rich natural resources, both tapped and untapped, which, when managed to expectation, could take the nation's development to dizzying heights. Such management also includes how we are able to package and 'sell' the potentials of the country locally and abroad, encourage trade, promote tourism and build confidence in the people both home and abroad.

However, like a product brand, Ghana as a country would not be able to attract either local or foreign interests to appreciable levels if the country does not make conscious efforts to highlight its attractiveness. The country has to right certain wrongs in order to get to this position. For now, there is political stability, the rule of law is said to be working in Ghana, and there is relative peace and a friendly environment, which is not the case for some of the country's neighbours. The country's currency, the cedi, is relatively strong and indeed, overall, there has been some positive growth for nearly three years.

Ghana certainly has travelled certain positive routes which could make the branding of the country easier. Its modest gains and impressive good governance made it the first choice of call by America's President Barak Obama when he selected Ghana as the sole country for his African visit shortly after he was sworn in as America's first black President and the 44th US President. In contemporary international relations, Ghana's Kofi Annan, the former UN Secretary General, K.Y. Amoako, the former Head of the Economic Commission for Africa (ECA), and Mohamed Ibn Chambas, the former Secretary General of the African, Caribbean and Pacific (ACP) group of states, formerly the Joint Special Representative for Darfur and Head of the African Union-United Nations Hybrid Operation in Darfur (UNAMID) and currently Head of the United Nations Office for West Africa, to name but a few, remain a source of pride. Ghana has stood out in terms of international peace keeping, with two of its nationals, Lieutenant-General E.A. Erskine and Lieutenant-General Seth Obeng, once occupying the challenging role of Force Commanders of the United Nations Interim Force in Lebanon (UNIFIL).

Perhaps the Ghanaian success story has not been adequately told. Experience has proved that where there is investor confidence, a country's development thrives. Investors, whether local or offshore, flock in ready to set up markets with job openings where they find stability and opportunities. The time to develop the tangible and intangible opportunities in Ghana is now. The country needs to deliberately market its strengths and begin to craft a different identity as if it were a product newly packaged and ready to be launched, on its way to a competitive market.

Branding a country for a competitive gain calls for radical changes. Branding Ghana to take advantage of the competitive world will therefore call for a rehabilitation of the national image. The following questions may be asked: why is branding necessary? How will the new brand help create differentiation between Ghana and its contemporaries in the developing or emerging nations? And, lastly, how will locals and the rest of the world feel about Ghana as a result of branding?

As one casts one's mind back at some of the definitions given for a brand or branding, there are clearly two key players in nation branding: the government and the people. There is therefore the need for a government that is committed to changing the image of the country for the better. Good governance with institutions that work effectively, true enforcement of rules and regulations, good policies and procedures are all within the ambits of government, while patriotism, a complete shift in attitudes which give way to love for country, will have to come from the people. Once all of these forces are in place, the promise of a country set on the path to national growth and development is sure to be realized.

Efforts to Brand Ghana

A conscious effort to brand Ghana may perhaps be said to have started in 2001 when the country took an active bold step in changing government from one political party to another through peaceful democratic means. The PNDC/NDC government had ruled the country for 19 continuous years. Through peaceful democratic means, the New Patriotic Party (NPP) was voted into power in 2000 and thus a new government was formed. All this happened without a whimper and at a time when some parts of Africa were in turmoil over electoral disputes. The government was successfully changed, but the economic environment at the time was quite difficult due to an unfavourable economic policy that the country had adopted for years. According to Ghana's *Growth and Poverty Reduction Strategy 11* (2006–9), the incoming government was faced with the grave task of finding funds to tackle its developmental agenda. It had to borrow from a number of local and international institutions. This was in addition to the already heavy debts from previous borrowing. The government applied to the international community through a facility known as the Enhanced Highly Indebted Poor Country Initiative (HIPC). The arrangement exempted the country from paying back the huge debt it owed to a number of countries and institutions abroad. The objective was to allow Ghana to use the payments due on the loans to carry out the projects and programmes that would directly reduce poverty and improve income in the country.

According to the *Growth and Poverty Reduction Strategy*, the key challenges that faced the country's development at the time included: the structure of the economy, a weak industrial base, low level of infrastructure and an over-reliance on cocoa, gold and timber for foreign exchange, among other things. Therefore, in its efforts to make the country look attractive to its locals and then to the outside world, the growth and poverty reduction strategy specifically identified some key areas in the national development policy that were going to benefit Ghana's search for growth and development. These included a robust competitive private sector, which contributed substantially to the GDP rate of the country. Many things needed to be fixed if Ghana was to stay attractive and productive. These included the following:

- Enhancing the capacity of the private sector by confronting some of the major difficulties, such as high interest rates, lack of credit, difficulties with land acquisition, cumbersome business registration, poor and erratic supply of basic utilities such as water and power, poor road networks, and complex and old-fashioned laws.
- Adequate focus on agriculture.
- Provision of quality healthcare.
- Efficient and effective information and communications technology.
- Promotion of tourism, which had the potential to become one of Ghana's main foreign exchange earners.

A focused and consistent approach to fixing all or some of the above would definitely have impacted on Ghana's brand fortunes and would have put the country in an attractive light in the eyes of both local and foreign investors.

How Would Branding Contribute to National Development? The Ghana Example

Because brands are powerful assets which provide competitive edge, countries make it a point to develop those areas that they see as their nation's potential and go ahead and prioritize them, giving them the necessary budgetary and other support to help them grow. Let us then focus on Ghana and find out how, in the attempt to brand the nation, Ghana could pick on a key area like tourism and get it transformed to bring in the growth expected in that sector and also in the national economy. Countries which have developed their tourism industry as part of their country-branding agenda have reaped huge benefits. We learn from these countries that when developed and well managed, tourism can not only bring in local and foreign attraction and revenue, but can also be a chain reaction in the growth and development of businesses in the hospitality and service industry.

To start with, tourism is a key growth target for almost every country. In Ghana currently, we know that tourism is the nation's third highest foreign exchange earner after gold and cocoa according to the *Ghana Growth and Poverty Reduction Strategy I and II*. It is projected that tourism can easily overtake all the others and become the country's main foreign exchange earner. It is feasible because Ghana already has historical, cultural and archaeological sites, many of which are of interest and are yet to be developed. Combining such sites, most of which are spread across the country, with good infrastructure and first-class hotel accommodation would transform the country's efforts to brand itself as a tourism destination and would provide a major boost to the GDP of the country (Debrah, 2003).

Fulfilling the brand's promise would mean tackling major problems, which include road networks and the fixing of communication facilities, as well as focused training for personnel in the hospitality industry. When Malaysia branded itself and tagged itself to offer the tourist a multi-cultural experience, the campaign resulted in increased tourist arrivals which translated into quantum increases annually in its tourism revenue for the nation. Ghana needs all the support it can garner from its brand ambassadors to venture out there as a global economic force, having stood out in 2011 as one of the world's fastest-growing economies that year (Press Centre, the Presidency, Republic of Ghana, 2011).

What lessons can one learn from how other countries have used nation branding to improve their economic and social development? The story of Kenya is a classic example of how nation branding can benefit a country's development.

How Kenya Positioned itself to Change its Image through Branding and its Effect on National Development: A Chat with the CEO of Brand Kenya

In a world of fierce competition, where countries that need help with their economies are scrambling for every available form of external assistance and where others are seeking to attract foreign investment, increase their exports, focus on tourism and build patriotism, for example, the name of the game is to stay attractive and maintain an enviable image. Therefore, what some countries in the developing and emerging world are doing is to re-package themselves to take advantage of the new order by going through the processes of country branding more in the spirit of a new commercial product that is yet to be launched.

With all its natural attractions for tourism, both local and international, Kenya, one of Africa's most endowed nations in terms of climate, scenery and safari parks, has ventured into the proactive and consistent selling of the country's fortunes. This was so that it could attract investment both from within and without, boost exports and make the country relevant and appealing to its own citizens, at home and in the diaspora. In 2012, the Chief Executive Officer (CEO) of the Board of Brand Kenya, Mary Kimonye, was interviewed in an effort to find out how Kenya had branded itself as a process to growth and national development. A strategist who had once served as a technical adviser at Kenya's Public Sector Reform Secretariat, Mrs Kimonye is also a former lecturer in marketing at the University of Nairobi. During the interview, she came across as someone strongly determined to lead the strategic positioning of Kenya for development and growth in the specific areas of investment, tourism and citizenship.

In the course of the discussions, the interviewer sought to understand what it meant by branding a country and how relevant it was to a nation's progress. According to Mrs Kimonye, due to the competition that countries, rich or poor, are exposed to worldwide, each country (and particularly the emerging ones) is looking to create a platform where it can attract a greater share of the world's wealth. The process of creating that differentiation is what one would perhaps refer to as branding. Premised on the assumption that countries may be treated as products, their names and other attributes define a certain image or perception upon which people then base their decision when it comes to selection – whether for a visit, to live, to work or invest in or trade with. So how was Brand Kenya conceived and how was branding going to help Kenya, a country whose international image was momentarily dented due to the political violence of 2007 which eventually brought a coalition government in Kenya into being?

Kenya's Vision 2020

It was in 2002 that Kenya seriously thought about a long-term vision that was going to drive the country's progress to becoming a middle income country by 2030. And so with the vision established, it was time to set up a board that was going to ensure that at least some of the key assumptions of Kenya's vision came to fruition. As a result, the Brand Kenya Board was created in January 2009.

To the Brand Kenya CEO, Kenya's image in a competitive world transcended safari parks and their tourism products. According to her, 'nation branding constitutes the development of a national image and identity'. She explained that the Kenya Brand is focused on positioning the country both for tourism and investment, with greater emphasis on also selling the brand to the citizens of Kenya. Therefore, in terms of branding itself, the country focused on areas that could bring about transformation in the economy such as foreign direct investment (FDI), trade, exports and tourism. They also focused on building a sense of pride and patriotism in Kenyans which, according to Mrs Kimonye, 'is the single most important asset to the Brand'. After two years into the process of branding the country, the CEO believed that the initiatives embarked on, which included a new constitution, media campaigns, youth engagement programmes and a rejuvenated economy, all helped to push up the levels of pride and patriotism internally. According to her, two clear years after the branding exercise began, there had been increases in investment and tourism. With that ticked off, the next serious focus for the country was on growing key source markets globally and engaging Kenyans in the diaspora.

Within Africa, countries such as South Africa, Botswana and Ghana served as the benchmark for Kenya as they had seriously worked on their image, while Asian countries such as Singapore and Malaysia and Western giants like the UK and the US were positive measuring sticks for Kenya. The head of Brand Kenya cited Kosovo as a country that had inspired her, having managed to change its image from a war-torn state into a young vibrant nation. Like many African countries, Kenya has great potential. As a continent, Africa has failed to develop, package and properly market its products as would be done by a business concern. Kenya may be set to redeem its image globally and highlight its appeal and pride to its nationals. From the perspective of a neutral observer, however, there is a genuine feeling that the country is on track.

Kenya's National Airline

Compared to another African country like Ghana, hotels are relatively cheap in Kenya and so is food. There is a level of professionalism in the service one experiences at hotels in Kenya compared to what one might experience in some other countries. What has impressed most about Kenya is the way its national airline has taken off and is trying to cover the world. Kenya Airways is now connecting virtually every corner of Africa – it is no wonder that the airline claims to be the pride of Africa. Many of its aircraft tend to be quite tidy and roomy too. Their overhead lockers look custom-made to carry all the excesses one tends to carry when one travels. Their services on board have dramatically improved and they also have friendly flight attendants. Their professionalism has extended to online check-ins. One thing, however, which remains to be critically examined is the airline's management of time. The airline will need to work on its time management if it wants to be taken seriously as a credible alternative on the African continent. This East African country is indeed working assiduously not only to be the pride of Africa but also the adoring star from the East.

Public Relations, Country Branding and Political Party Manifestos

One interesting area to examine when considering nation branding and development is the demeanour of political parties that seek to lead a country and their vision for the development of the countries they wish to lead. In many countries of late, politicking and interest in the conduct of governments and the governed have increasingly become active parts of the lives of citizens. Around the world and in Africa in particular, the governed are interested in accountable governments mainly because a country's development and growth depend largely on the quality of the leadership and what programmes are put forward and implemented to benefit the majority of the people, the economy and world cohesion as a whole. Reflecting therefore on political parties that put governments in place and the party manifestos or promises which generally get presented to the electorate before general elections, one is forced to look at Ghana specifically and some parts of the globe generally, and to examine the sum total of all the promises heaped on the electorate which, more often than not, give a clear agenda as to what the political parties want to achieve and, invariably, how such an agenda would help in the prosperity and development of the country and the people they want to serve.

Proactive PR in Governance

Manifestos may fail the people of a country, but there is one thing that will not fail the development agenda of a nation and its people, which is a catalyst that has lifted some countries out of a slumber and has placed them in the global limelight. This is the use of proactive public relations (PR) in governance, which most of the time encompasses nation branding. It is more about how PR can be used to strategize and plan a country's developmental agenda. A cursory look at political party manifestos reveals common threads running through them. They all invariably present the various avenues to navigate to achieve the good of a country and its people. However, one thing that many manifestos do not discuss is how they would use PR in the way a country like China has done so over the last 30 years to become a super power of the twenty-first century.

If one takes Ghana, for example, the country is now a low-middle income country. That is supposed to be a sign of positive development and sounds good in the ears of its citizens.

Whether the country measures up to it or not can be a subject of debate, depending on who wants to concur and who wants to dispute the assertion. It is known that some of the attractions of the world today were once upon a time in that low-middle income group. For example, Asian countries such as China, Singapore, Malaysia and Indonesia have now progressed considerably in the last 50 years or so since Ghana gained its independence, while Ghana is still trailing behind as far as national development is concerned.

The Rate of China's National Development Compared

China, once a Third World country like Ghana, is now a super power, one of the most powerful nations and the world's largest economy. According to He and Xie (2009) in their article 'Thirty years' development of public relations in China mainland', one of the reasons why China has got to where it is today is that for 30 years, it paid consistent attention to re-branding its country through the use of PR in its government administration. As the country's reforms began to take root, high-profile international PR firms and agencies started to feel the business attraction and opportunities in China and hence set up offices. The PR firm Hill & Knowlton was the first company to set up an office in Beijing in 1984. This was followed by Burson-Marsteller, another international PR giant, in 1985.

Five decades after independence, one would have wished that countries in Sub-Saharan Africa, who gained their independence from colonial rule, would have gone quite far in the development of their countries in view of the natural resources that are available to them on the continent. Ghana, for example, is well placed in terms of having the benefit of relative peace, stability in governance, natural and good human resources to be on a par with or close in terms of national development to many former Third World countries like China if it were to concentrate its efforts on re-branding and making good use of PR to advance its attractiveness, both in word and in deed.

However, in the last few years and with the discovery of oil, Ghana has worked hard to be able to produce enviable world records of growth; indeed, in 2011, it was recorded by the Institute of Social Statistical and Economic Research (ISSER) in the 21st edition of its flagship publication, The State of the Ghanaian Economy Report (ISSER, 2012), that Ghana's economy was one of the world's fastest-growing economies and that while the rest of the world's growth was declining, Africa and specifically Ghana was able to achieve one of the highest GDP growths in the world. As good as that may be, it is difficult to reconcile this with the fact that, to date, the country continues to have an erratic power supply. Power rationing is at its best despite all the tariffs that have been slapped on the people. Sometimes, power off means no water flowing through the taps. How in circumstances like these can a nation proudly brand itself to attract investments for the development and growth of the nation? Which investor, whether local or foreign, would want to put its resources in a country where the supply of water and electricity is irrational?

The success story of China as a super power should not surprise anyone who truly understands the power of country branding through PR, which China has used extensively in its government dealings. China's rapid development has its genesis in country branding, which meant serious reform and opening up of the country. Having re-branded itself through reforms, what followed next was the flow of foreign investment, which allowed it to be a regional centre for trade and business in the Far East. As China hit the road to craft a new direction for itself and make the country attractive to investors, it did not lose sight of a consistent image make-over starting with government ministries, departments and agencies.

As a country, Ghana has since time immemorial tried to present itself as a positive and attractive nation within and without, but there has never been any serious focus on using

PR to fix the country's image and change perceptions, particularly in relation to services and also when it comes to doing business with government departments and agencies – at least to the extent that China has done. In China, the government is said to have used PR to fix what needed to be fixed and kept up with the pace of change and development in the country. When the PR success story in China began 30 years ago, the profession was unheard of in the country. It did not mean much to it in terms of its country's development. PR was not pursued in the colleges and universities, but today the story is very different. China now has firm foundations for continuous growth because of the role PR has played in national development. When PR was first introduced to China, it started off as a copy of foreign PR but, over time, the assimilation was overwhelming. There was a gradual emergence of PR departments or personnel in institutions and companies. As the Communist Party of China embraced more and more reforms within the opening-up policy, PR came as a matter of course and it was used to turn things around during the opening-up process.

Emerging Economies and Use of PR in Branding

It definitely is not too late for any nation, particularly emerging economies like Ghana, to begin to embrace the role of PR and branding in their national development; so, for example, Ghana can make meaningful claims to being a 'Gateway to West Africa' and Nigeria can claim that it is the 'Heartbeat of Africa'. Such claims should reflect the status quo. Fortunately, a country like Ghana has professionals who can help rebrand it to reflect a nation of prospects and real achievements in national development. Some of Ghana's universities are offering communication studies and once these institutions begin to train and produce PR specialists, the country should be able to engage more PR professionals to fix some of its image problems to make it attractive and to match the promises that politicians continue to make about it. It is time for Ghana's parastatals as well ministries, departments and agencies to take a cue from countries like China and place a premium on nation branding and PR. The government has to stop using PR departments as 'fire brigades' that are only useful in times of crises and go on a proactive drive to change the country's image through the way it does things.

In China, as PR came to be understood and its role appreciated, foreign companies and other joint ventures began to establish PR departments and recruited a large number of PR practitioners. Soon, industries and hotels got hooked up using PR as a function of management, followed by the government. What perhaps might have helped in embracing PR and the role it could play in national development in the Chinese culture was a popular TV series, *PR Girls*. The series was based on examples of female PR employees. As more and more state-owned enterprises began to establish PR departments and successfully carried out a number of PR activities which promoted those enterprises, the PR function took root in the national culture.

China did accept PR and country branding as intangible assets in the management of its image both at home and abroad. This has helped the country to adjust on the international scene. With the development of global economic interpretation, PR has been adopted as a management strategy and has helped in stimulating the cross-cultural communications required to address global problems. It may not seem too obvious to the observer because the impact of PR generally is not immediately tangible. However, one should not lose sight of the fact that PR has helped to transform the fortunes of countries like China, where the government used sophisticated PR skills to resolve all kinds of social contradictions and created a harmonious socialist society.

Kenya has also used PR and nation branding to successfully help the government at one time to re-strategize when it was in deep crisis. In 2008, following the uproar created by its

2007 general election that almost threw the country into serious turmoil, PR and re-branding were effectively used by the Kenyan government to turn things around and secure the peace and calm that the government and the nation needed for continued development. The country needed to project a peaceful environment to inject confidence in its tourism industry and calm nerves back home.

Conclusions

PR and national branding may not have any specific place in any political party's manifesto when it comes to setting the agenda for a national development. However, it is not too late for governments to take time to understand how PR and branding could be used, for example, to transform the developmental agenda of a country. Ghana and indeed other African countries do not need to re-invent the wheel. Successful and advanced countries around the world have sought the need to use country branding woven around PR in their national strategizing and the development of their countries. Their success stories, without doubt, have had positive impacts on their local and external appeal. While they have an impressive impact on the outside world, back home, they succeed in touching the lives of their people, eradicating poverty and hunger, reducing unemployment by creating jobs and empowering their youth. These are the positive drops from successful national branding.

References

Baxter, J. (2012). Lessons learned from Brand Malaysia. Available at: http://webershandwick.asia/author/bjolly/.
BrandSouthAfrica.com (2013). http://brandsouthafrica.com.
China Media Research (2009).
Debrah, R.K. (2003). The Ghana tourism capacity development initiative. http://www.ghanaweb.com/GhanaHomePage/features/artikel.php?ID=37748.
Ghana's Growth & Poverty Reduction Strategy (GPRS I & II) (2006–9). Paragraphs on 'Efforts to brand Ghana' and 'How branding would contribute to national development – The Ghana example'.
He, C. and Xie, J. (2009). Thirty Years' Development of Public Relations in China Mainland. China Media Research, 5(3). Available at: http://www.gji.org.cn/images/library_resources/thirty_years_development_of_public_relations_in_china_mainland.pdf.
Institute of Statistical, Social and Economic Research (ISSER) (2012). The State of the Ghanaian Economy Report (SGER), 21st edn.
Press Centre, the Presidency, Republic of Ghana (2012). Ghana: The world's fastest growing economy in 2011, 4 January
Tourism Malaysia (2013). Nation branding – Malaysia in perspective. http://www.tourism.gov.my/en/intl.

22

Enhancing Service Delivery for National Development

Kwaku Appiah-Adu, Charles Blankson and Kwabena G. Boakye

Abstract

The purpose of this chapter is to set the scene for a broad appreciation of how efficient and effective service delivery can facilitate industrial and national development, and thereby delineate the pivotal role that services play in national economies. The topic involves many distinct elements, which, individually, are extensive enough to cover a whole book, but the essence of this chapter is to highlight the key issues inherent within the subject. In the subsequent sections, we discuss an overview of services, followed by a discussion of concepts relating to service quality. Next, services and implications for positioning are explored. Also examined are the characteristics of services. Furthermore, insights are provided into how a nation can build and sustain positioning advantage with services. As part of the discussion, recent developments in services marketing are presented and related to the context of a developing economy. To conclude, the implications of enhanced service delivery for national development are highlighted and pertinent recommendations are made for the consideration of managers and policy makers in developing economies.

Introduction: Overview of Services

Services have become an integral part of modern society. The service sector is at the heart of and is an important contributor to the gross domestic product (GDP) of many economies, both developed and developing (see Figure 22.1). The service sector, which encompasses trade, transportation, food and lodging, communications, education, government, financial services, medical services, etc., generates many millions of new jobs and fuels economic recovery (Heskett, 1987). Industries in the service sector accounted for about 70 percent of the national income of the USA in the post-Second World War era (Heskett, 1987), employing about 64 percent of the US workforce in 1965. In 2007, the service sector contributed almost 78.5 percent towards US GDP (Timimi, 2011).

Over the years, the extant literature has attempted to develop classification schemes upon which services marketing research can be conducted. The important value of these schemes is to bring parsimony and order to allow a better understanding of characteristics that differentiate

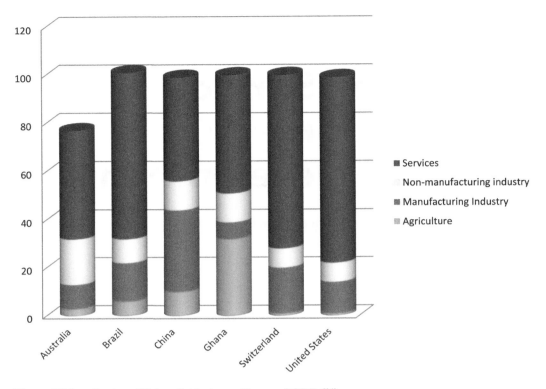

Figure 22.1   Sectoral Value-Added as a Share of GDP (%)
Sources: World Bank, Data Catalog (accessed April 17, 2011); World Factbook (accessed June 3, 2011).

services and the organizations that provide them (Cook et al., 1999; Olorunniwo et al., 2006). In fact, the overarching value of these service classifications is in their ability to facilitate and develop strategies that are meaningful and can provide useful guidelines for operations and services marketing (Cook et al., 1999).

However, service classification schemes have been criticized. For example, Snyder et al. (1982) claim that criteria and parameters used in developing these service classification schemes are ambiguous. From another perspective, the criticisms towards service classification schemes result from the many definitions of services in the literature. The Committee on Definitions of the American Marketing Association (1960: 21) defines services as:

> *Activities, benefits, or satisfactions which are offered for sale, or are provided in connection with the sale of goods. Examples are amusements, hotel service, electric service, transportation, the services of barber shops and beauty shops, repair and maintenance service, the work of credit rating bureaus. This list is merely illustrative and no attempt has been made to make it complete. The term also applies to the various activities such as credit extension, advice and help of sales people, delivery, by which the seller serves the convenience of his customers.*

According to Judd (1964), this definition was too broad and impregnated with too many examples. Judd asserts that this made the definition incomplete because it lacked precision and threw a challenge for researchers to come up with a better and more appropriate definition.

Quinn et al. (1987: 50) took up the challenge by narrowing down the definition of service as 'all economic activities whose output is not a physical product or construction, is generally consumed at the time it is produced, and provides added value in forms (such as convenience, amusement, timeliness, comfort, or health) that are essentially intangible concerns of its first purchaser'. Other researchers such as Zeithaml and Bitner (1996) define services as simply deeds, processes and performance.

From the above, there seems to be no clear-cut definition of 'service' that can embrace all the complex attributes. Instead, academic research uses typologies to address service complexities (Cook et al., 1999). In hindsight, these service typologies are primarily intended to provide manangers with strategic insights that are important for both management and the positioning of services and organizations.

In the integrated schematic representation of service typology dimensions and their respective relationships (see Figure 22.1), there are two orientations from which one can view service dimensions (Cook et al., 1999; Fitzsimmons and Fitzsimmons, 2004; Olorunniwo et al., 2006; Mackelprang et al., 2012). These two are marketing-oriented (which primarily considers the product) and operations-oriented (which mainly considers the processes involved). Within the marketing orientation dimension are product differentiation, product tangibility, type of customer and object of service. The operation-oriented dimensions include customer contact, labour intensity, customer involvement and the production process.

In his study, Schmenner (1986) used two elements to classify service businesses. These two elements, namely (i) *labour intensity* and (ii) *customer interaction and service customization*, determine which service operations managers should apply in their service businesses. Labour intensity, as defined by Schmenner (1986), is the ratio of the labour cost incurred to the value of the plant and equipment (e.g. communications, utilities, gas and sanitation services). Thus, a high labour-intensive service business involves relatively little plant and equipment, but a substantial amount of labour time, effort and cost (e.g. security and commodity brokers, insurance services and retail trade). Customer interaction and service customization, the other element of service business, is a joint measure that combines customer contact (the extent to which the customer interacts with the service process) and customization (the extent to which the service is customized for the customer). When there is high level of interaction and customization for the customer, the joint measure is considered to be high. Conversely, a low value of the joint measure reflects a low level of interaction and customization for the customer. A mixture of low interaction and high customization (or vice versa) allows the joint measure to fall in between its high and low values.

Schmenner (1986) used these two elements to develop a two-by-two service process matrix that classifies service businesses into four quadrants (see Figure 22.2), namely:

- Service factory – includes service businesses that show relatively *low labour intensity* and *low customer interaction and customization*. Examples of these service businesses include airlines, trucking, and resorts and recreations.
- Service shop – includes service businesses that show low labour intensity, but high customer interaction and customization. Examples of these businesses include hospitals, automobile repair services and restaurants.
- Mass serivce – includes service businesses that have relatively high labour intensity, but low customer interaction and customization. Examples of these businesses include retail, commercial banking and schools.
- Professional service – include service businesses that have high labour intensity and high customer interaction and customization. Examples of these businesses include accountants, lawyers and architects.

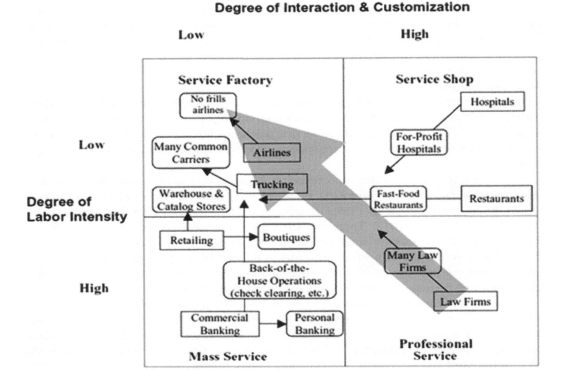

Figure 22.2   Strategic Operations Changes within the Service Process Matrix
Source: Schmenner, R.W. (1986). How can service buisnesses survive and prosper? *Sloan Management Review,*
27(3).

Obviously, each quadrant in this service process matrix has its unique and peculiar set of operations
in which it is engaged. Businesses in each quadrant also have some challenges that they must face
in order to remain competitive and maintain a committed customer base. For instance, service
businesses in the mass service quadrant must strive to make the services they provide attractive
because of the stiff marketing challenges they face. In such a situation, particular attention must be
paid to the service environment in which the service is delivered (Schmenner, 1986; Cook et al.,
1999). The next section deals with service categories and the product-service continuum.

Service Categories

The general consensus in the literature is that most products fall between the two extremes
of pure good and pure service. The latter is taken up by several authors (see, among others,
Middleton, 1983; Buttle, 1986), who have suggested two distinct areas of evaluating products
and services (i.e. service products and product service, with the former dealing specifically with
service offerings and the latter with intangible benefits). The literature shows that there are few
products which are purely intangible or totally tangible (see Hartman and Lindgren, 1993; Wolak,
1996; Wolak et al., 1998).
    Figure 22.3 highlights a number of key points:

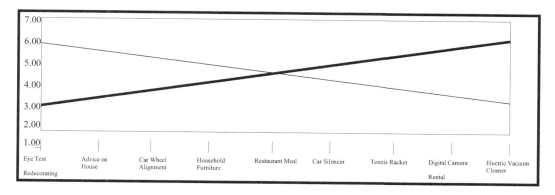

Figure 22.3   Product-Service Continuum Chart
Sources: Wolak, R. (1996). An Investigation into the Four Characteristics of Services, MA in Marketing Dissertation, Kingston University Business School, Kingston-upon-Thames, Surrey, p. 65. Wolak, R., Kalafatis, S. and Harris, P. (1998). An Investigation into Four Characteristics of Services, *Journal of Empirical Generalisations in Marketing Science*, 3, p. 32.
Note: Thin line: Average Service Rating. Thick Line: Average Product Rating.

1. Service items are shown on the left-hand side and have a low product rating and a high service rating.
2. Product items are shown on the right-hand side and have a low service rating and a high product rating.
3. Both the product and service rating lines are almost linear.
4. The restaurant meal item is positioned in the middle with an almost equal amount of product and service rating.

Service Quality

In both the quality and marketing literature, research into service quality perceptions has attracted increasingly attention among scholars. The conceptualization and measurement of service quality have been viewed differently by researchers and this intense debate shows no sign of abating. In fact, it has been touted to be a difficult and 'elusive' concept to grasp (Parasuraman et al., 1985; Smith, 1999). Though the debate is still ongoing, considerable progress on how these service quality perceptions are measured has been made (Parasuraman et al., 1994; Cronin and Taylor, 1992).

Two conceptualizations of service quality exist in the literature. The 'Nordic' viewpoint is proposed by Grönroos (1982, 1984), who categorizes service quality into two dimensions: *functional quality* (process occurring prior to, and resulting in, outcome quality); and *technical quality* (outcome of the service delivery or what is delivered to the customer during the service encounter). This is in line with the three-dimensional view of service quality (interaction, physical and corporate quality) proposed by Lehtinen and Lehtinen (1982). From the customer's perspective, Lehtinen and Lehtinen (1982) pictured quality from a higher level as being two-dimensional, that is, 'output' and the 'process'. Parasuraman et al. (1988), on the other hand, conceptualized service quality in terms of the service encounter characteristics. This 'American' perspective consists of characteristics such as reliability, responsiveness, empathy, assurance and tangibles which can be found in the classic '22-item SERVQUAL instrument'.

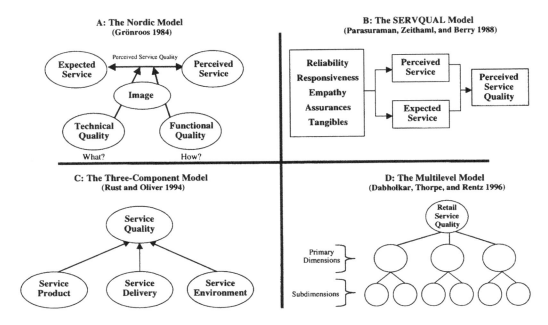

Figure 22.4   Conceptualizations Advanced in the Service Quality Literature

Other conceptualizations of service quality have been proposed. In Figure 22.4, Rust and Oliver (1994) proposed a three-component model based on the model proposed by Grönroos (1982, 1984). The components of their service quality conceptualization comprise service delivery, service product and service environment. Empirical evidences have been found to support Rust and Oliver's (1994) conceptualization in the fields of banking (McDougall and Levesque, 1994) and healthcare (McAlexander et al., 1993). Another conceptualization of service quality is that proposed by Dabholkar et al. (1996), a multi-dimensional model that has three levels: (1) overall perception of service quality by customers; (2) primary dimensions of service quality; and (3) sub-dimensions of service quality.

Owing to the lack of consensus among researchers on the conceptualization of service quality and the nature of its dimensions, Brady and Cronin Jr. (2001) proposed a new and integrated conceptualization of service quality perceptions using a hierarchical approach. In their study they concluded that service quality, as a construct, has a structure of a third-order factor model. They assert that this third-order factor model basically ties service quality perceptions to distinct and actionable dimensions. These dimensions include *outcome quality*, *interaction quality* and *environmental quality*. Here, customers evaluate and judge service quality based on three dimensions – *customer-employee interaction, the service environment* and *the outcome* – and makes a decision of positive behavioural intent or commitment towards that service. These dimensions have an impact on the positioning strategies and tactics adopted by the service organization.

Services and Implications for Positioning

In defining what a service is, Gilmore (2003) distinguishes between services as a feature of all organizations. Services are also critical in a national context, particularly in organizations that are established to promote the national interest or serve the public, and for such institutions, the perceived value of the offer is substantially determined by the service element (Appiah-Adu, 2004a).

There are service activities such as customer service, service-based activities and added-value activities to the provision of service. Consumers' expectations of service may differ depending upon whether the service is the core product or is offered as an additional element. As Coffie (2010) puts it, either way, there are key features associated with services that need to be understood and managed for greater efficiency and effectiveness. There are some unique features of services that cannot be ignored when managing services for strategic and positioning purposes (West et al., 2006). These characteristics notably include intangibility, heterogeneity, inseparability and perishability, and they have implications for positioning.

Notwithstanding the growing acceptance of several overlaps between services and physical goods, there remain scholars who continue to argue that the positioning of services is more difficult than physical goods. This is due to the features of services outlined above – intangibility, inseparability, perishability, heterogeneity and non-standardization – that render the positioning of services more difficult and challenging than physical goods (Bateson, 1995; Bitner, 1997; de Chernatony and Dall'Olmo Riley, 1997). According to Bitner (1997), services rely more on employees' actions, which tend to be stochastic in nature. Table 22.1 outlines the key features of services and their implications for marketing and positioning strategies. The debate between the interface of services and physical goods is not new. One school of thought is that the differences between service and physical goods is one of semantics and should not in practice have a great deal of effect on the positioning of services (Levitt, 1981; Middleton, 1983).

Table 22.1 Mechanisms for Sustaining Service Positioning

Competition-based mechanisms

1. Information impact, which is exploiting knowledge differences between competing firms.
2. Response lags – the time required for firms to respond to competitive initiatives.
3. Economies of scale – the ability to perform activities differently or more efficiently at larger volume.
4. Producer learning – knowledge that is accumulated through direct industry experience.
5. Channel crowding – the pre-empting of competition by gaining first entry in a distribution channel.

Customer-based mechanisms

6. Customer switching costs – place both economic and psychological barriers to brand switching.
7. Customer evaluation costs – monetary or psychological costs associated with evaluating a service offering.
8. Advertising crowding – the pre-empting of competition by being the first firm to capture a 'psychological' position in consumers' minds.

Source: Based on Fisher (1991); Blankson (1999).

Marketing and Services

In relation to the link between marketing and service delivery, it is important to identify how distinct service marketing features such as people (employees, customers), processes and product development can be used to enhance service delivery. *Service delivery refers to what actually happens when customers buy the service.* The service product defines how the service works in theory, but service delivery is how the service works in actual practice (Lovelock et al., 1999). There is an adage: *plan your work* and *work your plan.* While the service product is the result of *planning your work*, service delivery is the result of *working your plan.* For example, the service design may be that a restaurant's customer is greeted cheerfully within 60 seconds, but the actual service delivery may be hindered by a waiter joking in the backroom for five minutes with other employees. What is designed does not always occur.

A firm's employees are important in service delivery because they are the service, the organization in the customer's eyes and, above all, are the marketers. An understanding of customer satisfaction is critical and this is closely linked to employee satisfaction (Heskett et al., 1994). To deliver a highly customer-oriented service, organizations need to hire the right people, develop them to deliver service quality, provide the needed support systems and retain the best people. Consider the following example – you are in a long queue at the Post Office during the lunch hour and it is taking forever for you to be served. The Manager notices the situation and immediately gets into one of the cubicles behind the counter and starts serving. How would you feel?

Service delivery can also be enhanced through customer participation (Harrington and Akehurst, 2000). Customers have been referred to as human resources who contribute to the organization's productive capacity. Indeed, management experts have suggested that the organization's boundaries be expanded to consider the customer as part of the service system (Fitzsimmons and Fitzsimmons, 1998). Customers can contribute to their own satisfaction and the ultimate quality of the services they receive. Consider services such as healthcare and education. Research has shown that in education, active participation by students increases learning and the desired service outcome significantly (Kotler and Fox, 1995). The same is true in healthcare, where patient compliance in terms of taking prescribed medications or changing other habits can be critical to the desired service outcome (Kotler and Clarke, 1987). *Customers contribute to quality service delivery when they ask questions, take responsibility for their own satisfaction and complain when there is a service failure.* Marketing can be used to educate customers so that they know both their rights and responsibilities in order for them to cooperate with service providers so that together, high-quality service levels can be delivered by the providers to the recipients. For instance, in our national development efforts, marketing can play a key role in educating the public about pertinent issues such as paying taxes, keeping our cities clean, registration, voting, family planning, immunization, HIV/AIDS, improving literacy, upgrading the quality of life, supporting small businesses, etc. (Appiah-Adu, 1999a).

As a result of the significance of people in service delivery, three types of marketing are required in service provision (Kotler et al., 2013). *External marketing* involves the normal work done by the organization to prepare, price, distribute and promote the service to customers. *Internal marketing* describes the work done by the company to train and motivate its employees to serve customers well. *Interactive marketing* describes the employees' skill in serving the client.

Service delivery can also be enhanced through processes. Banking by automatic teller machines (ATMs) is fast becoming natural to many customers to the extent that within the next few years, bank employees will become the only people who regularly see the interiors of banks (Zeithaml and Bitner, 1996). In many developing economies, the ATM has become a way of doing business for customers, and all banks that seek to be successful will have to distribute their services (and the customer's money) through ATMs. Other potential uses of ATMs which will need to be developed over time include the use of services to settle utility and other bills. For instance, an electricity company can enter into an arrangement with a telecom company (Telco) whereby customers should be able to pay electricity bills through the Telco, a move which can improve the level of service offered in the payment of bills.

Current trends suggest that ATMs are just the first step, with home banking and online banking poised to play a key role in future banking operations (O'Brien, 1995) in developing economies. With their PCs, whether from home or their offices, online banking will allow consumers to track their accounts, apply for loans and credit cards, make transfers and pay bills electronically to anyone with a bank account number. Internet users will also be able to buy goods and services and have the costs deducted from their accounts. In fact, the only banking services that cannot be distributed electronically are withdrawing and depositing cash. The regulatory bodies in the banking and communications sectors should continue to provide the necessary infrastructure and platforms for these transactions to become a reality in Ghana.

Apart from banking, other areas where processes could be used to deliver effective service and meet customer needs are education and business-to-business communication. For instance, not all students who attain entry qualifications to universities in many developing countries are able to gain admission due to constraints on the universities' resources and facilities. Though private universities are springing up in such countries to supplement the placements offered by public universities, the needs of many of the unfortunate students are yet to be fully met. One answer to this problem is to enhance opportunities offered through distance education, as is being done in many industrialized countries where a number of tertiary institutions are using Distance Learning as a channel to provide further education. In the corporate world, video conferencing is becoming very popular in enhancing service delivery. It is believed that this form of conducting business will be the answer to escalating corporate travel costs and increasingly stressed employees. The systems have been around for years, but are only now being purchased and used by companies.

Services and National Development

Over the past few decades, many leaders of the developing world have sought to promote their countries as an attractive place in which to do business. In many developing countries, during the first three decades following independence, their economies operated under a number of controls and therefore were not liberalized enough to attract potential investors. In an effort to liberalize their economies and provide a platform for accelerated economic development, the last three decades have seen radical changes in the macro-economic policies of many of these nations. If these developing countries that are now dominated by a quest for positive strides in the private sector are to make significant strides towards achieving national development, it is imperative for their people and businesses to improve the levels of service delivery.

Services and Service Delivery

Service delivery refers to what actually happens when customers purchase a service. It is an experience we all encounter every day of our lives – when we visit a restaurant to buy food to eat, make a trip to the market to shop, pay our electricity, water or phone bills, go to a bank or an ATM to withdraw money, board a vehicle from where we live to our workplace, drive to our mechanic to have a problem with our car fixed, visit the hospital for treatment, attend school to receive tuition, get to a phone booth to make a phone call, or even pick up a phone at home or in the office to make a call.

Services lie at the very hub of economic activity in any society. In addressing the role of services in global development, three principal sectors need to be identified (Riddle, 1986): (i) extractive (mining and farming); (ii) manufacturing; and (iii) service, which is divided into five sub-groups. These are: business services (consulting, banking), trade services (retailing, maintenance and repair), infrastructure services (communications and transport), social/personal services (restaurants, healthcare) and public administration (education, government). All activity eventually leads to the consumer and this is where service delivery becomes a critical tool for enhancing national development.

Except for basic subsistence living, where individual households are self-sufficient, service activities are absolutely necessary for the economy to function and to enhance the quality of life (Fitzsimmons and Fitzsimmons, 1998). Consider, for example, the importance of a banking industry to transfer funds and a transportation industry to move foodstuffs to areas that cannot produce them. Moreover, a wide variety of social and personal services such as restaurants, lodging, cleaning and childcare have been created to move typical household functions into the economy. Public administration plays a critical role in providing a stable environment for investment and economic growth. In communities and countries where public administration services are weak or heavily skewed solely by political or idealistic concerns, essential services are inaccessible to many citizens.

Thus, it is imperative to recognize that services are not peripheral activities, but rather are integral parts of society. They are central to a functioning and healthy economy and lie at the heart of economic and national development. Services facilitate and also make possible the goods-producing activities of the extractive and manufacturing sectors. In addition to being the crucial force for change towards a global economy, services become even more important as an economy develops, and soon the vast majority of population is employed in service activities. Furthermore, at the micro-level, every organization could be considered as a service, which may or may not include a physical product (Shostack, 1977).

The management of services has unique challenges because of the distinctive characteristics of service operations. Perhaps the most important characteristic of service operations is the presence of the customer in the delivery system. Focusing on the customer and serving his or her needs has always been an important daily activity for service providers, and marketing plays a critical role in ensuring that the service is delivered to the highest levels and also to the satisfaction of customers (Kotler, 2011).

Positioning and Services

In this twenty-first century, nations (Appiah-Adu, 2004a) and businesses (Blankson, 2012) in the developing world are increasingly facing the acid test and are poised to come face to face with: (a) increasing consumer confidence, especially in urban areas; and (b) increasing consumer exposure to global influence. Ironically, it is considered that even in many developing countries that are characterized as peaceful and stable, with comparatively good governance indicators, consumer service is still not seriously embraced by many public/private organizations. This is painful to observe given 'the importance of the consumer' and the fact that customer service is pivotal for organizational positioning activities.

It is essential to note that consumer spending is the principal foundation of any market economy. In other words, customers are the purpose for the existence of organizations. For businesses, they are defined by the ability to create and keep customers (Drucker, 1998). As Mahatma Gandhi rightly put it, 'a customer is the most important visitor on our premises. He is not dependent on us; we are dependent on him. He is not an interruption in our work; he is the purpose of it. He is not an outsider in our business; he is part of it. We are not doing him a favour by serving him; he is doing us a favour by giving us an opportunity to do so' (cited in Harris, 2010: 1).

Developments in Marketing of Services

As discussed earlier in the section on the overview of services, there is an acknowledged growing importance of the service sector and its contribution to economies. In many advanced economies, services account for 60–70 percent of GDP. This trend also reflects that in emerging countries, where the service sector contributes around 50 percent or more towards GDP (World Bank Statistics, 2003, cited in West et al., 2006). The implication is that the provision of services and the associated financial gain for service organizations is set to become even more important. This suggests the likelihood of greater competition as existing providers find new ways of entrenching themselves, whilst 'new' providers entering the service aim at taking advantage of a growing sector.

Coffie (2010) writes that the 1990s saw a greater measure of de-regulation in the service sector in the UK, for example. Organizations such as British Airways and British Gas, which previously were state-protected, were allowed to compete freely in the market, resulting in the greater use of market competition measures. In Ghana, from 2001 to 2008, government policy gave much attention to the development of the private sector (Appiah-Adu, 2004b). As part of this, a private sector development ministry was set up to promote and provide loans for individuals and small businesses to flourish. The net impact in Ghana was the expansion of business activities and an increased level of competition and economic activity. The financial services sector in Ghana saw the introduction of new banks such as Zenith Bank, UBA, Guaranty Trust and Access Bank, and attempts to revive troubled airlines such as Ghana International Airlines (Coffie, 2010). It has to be noted, however, that with the development of the financial crisis in 2008 and the impact on the global economy, some governments were forced to return to regulation, particularly in the financial sector, which is regarded as having been responsible for much of the crisis. The impact of such developments continues to be felt. Still, however, organizations need to be fully aware and plan strategically in response to the services they offer.

Another factor which is already impacting on the way in which services are delivered in some industries is technology advancement. In financial services, for example, this has traditionally been focused on human interaction and, in many ways, individualized service as part of that. Banks are increasingly encouraging customers to use electronic services for activities that can be undertaken without the human touch. What is evident therefore is the movement, albeit gradually, away from the dominance of human touch to electronic automated-based service. While such developments may have some good intentions and outcomes, service organizations need to able to win customers' interest and willingness to use the technology and the convenience they offer. Gilmore (2003: 203–4) outlined that service organizations need to work to overcome some of the associated problems. The author listed the following action points:

- Service managers need to understand and develop offerings that achieve a balance between human touch and technology application.
- Consideration needs to be given to of a mix between technology and individualized service.
- They must work with technology providers to make the technology simple and easy to use.
- Ways must be found to overcome the problem of standardization and consistency in the delivery of services for greater efficiency.
- They must ensure greater efficiency of back office staff to support automated technology-based services.

In addition, service organizations both in the public and private sectors need to address not only the challenges of advancement in technology for strategic positioning advantage but also service characteristics and their implications for marketing and positioning strategies.

Conclusions

This chapter has highlighted some measures to enhance service delivery as part of the efforts to facilitate national development in developing economies. First, it is important for the government to encourage and support the development of citizens' charters. For instance, the civil service and public sector organizations such as hospitals, schools and revenue authorities, as well as utilities companies responsible for the oversight of services such as water, electricity, gas and telecommunications, should all publish their objectives, service standards and performance targets for customers to see so that they can know their rights and know how and where to lodge complaints if necessary.

It is also suggested that consumer associations and the relevant interest groups should be formed to take care of the interests and concerns of the general public in all key service areas. These associations should be able to fight on consumers' behalf, stand up against sub-standard service and challenge the status quo. Clearly defined legislation should be put in place to support the principles of high-quality service delivery. These laws should be bolstered by a host of self-regulatory professional codes which draw on the same set of basic business principles; for example, marketing professionals are to conduct their business in a *legal, decent, honest and truthful manner* (Chartered Institute of Marketing, 2001). It must be mentioned, however, that short-term, shoddy service, which slips through the system, may generate short-term gains, but in an increasingly competitive environment, this will not generate long-term sales since repeat business will not come back.

At the macro-level, government policies should be put in place to address issues relating to service delivery. For instance, in an area of national importance such as agriculture, there should be a national marketing policy and strategy for service delivery in the sector. This is definitely an issue which requires immediate attention. Moreover, acts relating to consumer protection, delivery of professional services, sale of goods, control of misleading advertisements, trade descriptions, etc. should not only be enacted but should also be marketed effectively for consumers to know that they exist so that in the process of service delivery, consumers will not be taken for a ride by service providers.

References

Appiah-Adu, K. (1999a). Marketing in a liberalised developing economy: Emerging trends and implications for strategy. *Journal of Management Studies*, 14(1), pp. 16–30.

———. (1999b). Marketing effectiveness and customer retention in the service sector. *Service Industries Journal*, 19(3), pp. 26–41.

———. (2004a). Enhancing service delivery for national development: Marketing, a critical tool. *Ghana Management Review*, 1(4), pp. 53–60.

———. (2004b). Private sector as the engine of growth. *Ghana Club 100*.

Appiah-Adu, K. and Singh, S. (1999). Marketing culture and performance in UK service firms. *Service Industries Journal*, 19(1), pp. 154–72.

Babakus, E. and Boller, G.W. (1992). An empirical assessment of the SERVQUAL scale. *Journal of Business Research*, 24(3), pp. 253–68.

Baker, M.J. (1983). *Marketing Theory and Practice*. London: Macmillan.

——. (1985). *Marketing: An Introductory Text*. London: Macmillan.

Bateson, J. (1995). *Managing Services Marketing*, 3rd edn. London: Dryden Press.

Bitner, M.J. (1997). Services marketing: Perspectives on service excellence. *Journal of Retailing*, 73(1), pp. 3–6.

Berry, L.L. and Bendapudi, N. (2003). Clueing in customers. *Harvard Business Review*, 81, pp. 100–106.

Blankson, C. (1999). Positioning and life cycle stages in the UK services industry. Unpublished PhD thesis, Kingston University, UK.

Blankson, C. (2012). Positioning Ghanaian businesses through customer service. Keynote speaker presentation at the 2nd Ghana Customer Service Conference, the British Council, Accra, Ghana, 2 October.

Blankson, C. and Crawford, J.C. (2012). Impact of positioning strategies on service firm performance. *Journal of Business Research*, 65, pp. 311–16.

Blankson, C. and Kalafatis, S.P. (1999). Issues and challenges in the positioning of service brands: A review. *Journal of Product and Brand Management*, 8(2), pp. 106–18.

Boulding, W., Kalra, A., Staelin, R. and Zeithaml, V.A. (1993). A dynamic process model of service quality: From expectations to behavioral intentions. *Journal of Marketing Research*, 30(1), pp. 7–27.

Bouman, M. and van der Wiele, T. (1992). Measuring service quality in the car service industry: Building and testing an instrument. *International Journal of Service Industry Management*, 3(4), pp. 4–16.

Brady, M.K. and Cronin Jr., J.J. (2001). Some new thoughts on conceptualising perceived service quality: A hierarchical approach. *Journal of Marketing*, 65(3), pp. 34–49.

Buttle, F. (1986). Unserviceable concepts in service marketing. *Quarterly Review of Marketing*, Spring, 8–14.

Chartered Institute of Marketing (2001). *Study Text for Diploma Examination*. London: BPP Publishers.

Coffie, S. (2010). Strategic market positioning typology for service organizations in Ghana Unpublished PhD thesis, Birkbeck College, University of London.

Committee on Definitions of the American Marketing Association (1960). *Marketing Definitions: A Glossary of Marketing Terms*. Chicago: American Marketing Association.

Cook D.P., Goh, C.-H. and Chung, C.H. (1999). Service typologies: A state of the art survey. *Production and Operations Management*, 8(3), pp. 318–38.

Cowell, D. (1989). *The Marketing of Services*. London: Heinemann.

Cronin Jr., J.J. and Taylor, S.A. (1992). Measuring service quality: A reexamination and extension. *Journal of Marketing*, 56(3), pp. 55–68.

Dabholkar, P. A., Thorpe, D.I., and Rentz, J.O. (1996). A measure of service quality for retail stores: Scale development and validation. *Journal of the Academy of Marketing Science*, 24(1), pp. 3–16.

De Chernatony, L. and Cottam, S. (2009). Interacting contributions of different departments to brand success. *Journal of Business Research*, 62, pp. 297–304.

De Chernatony, L. and Dall'Olmo Riley, F. (1997), *The Role of the Brand Revised*, 26th EMAC Conference Proceedings, 20–23 May, Warwick Business School, pp. 1614–23.

Drucker, P.F. (1998). *On the Profession of Management*. Cambridge, MA: Harvard Business Press.

Fisher, R.J. (1991). Durable differentiation strategies for services. *Journal of Services Marketing*, 5(1), pp. 19–28.

Fitzsimmons, J. and Fitzsimmons, M. (1998). *Service Management for Competitive Advantage*. New York: McGraw-Hill.

——. (2004). *Service Managment: Operations, Strategy, and Information Technology*, 4th edn. New York: Irwin McGraw-Hill.

Gagliano, K.B. and Hathcote, J. (1994). Customer expectations and perceptions of service quality in apparel retailing. *Journal of Services Marketing*, 8(1), pp. 60–69.

Gilmore, A. (2003). *Services Marketing and Management*. London: Sage.

Grönroos, C. (1982). *Strategic Management and Marketing in the Service Sector*. Helsingfors: Swedish School of Economics and Business Administration.

——. (1984). A service quality model and its marketing implications. *European Journal of Marketing*, 18(4), pp. 36–44.

Harrington, D. and Akehurst, G. (2000). An empirical study of service quality implementation. *Service Industries Journal*, 20(2), pp. 133–56.

Harris, E.K. (2010). *Customer Service: A Practical Approach*, 5th edn. Englewood Cliffs, NJ: Prentice Hall.

Hartman, D.E. and Lindgren, J.H. (1993). Consumer evaluations of goods and services – Implications for services marketing. *Journal of Services Marketing*, 7(2), pp. 4–15.

Heskett, J. (1987). Lessons in the service sector. *Harvard Business Review*, 65(2), pp. 118–26.

Heskett, J., Jones, T., Loveman, G., Sasser, W. and Schlesinger, L. (1994). Putting the service-profit chain to work. *Harvard Business Review*, March–April, pp. 71–80.

ISSER (2000). *State of the Economy Report.*

Judd, R.C. (1964). The case for redefining service. *Journal of Marketing*, 28(1), pp. 58–9.

Kinsey, J. (1988). *Marketing in Developing Countries*. London: Macmillan.

Kotler, P. (1984). *Marketing Management: Analysis, Planning and Control*. Englewood Cliffs, NJ: Prentice Hall.

———. (2000). *Marketing Management: Analysis Planning, Implementation and Control*. Upper Saddle River, NJ: Prentice Hall.

———. (2011). Reinventing marketing to manage the environmental imperative. *Journal of Marketing*, 75(4), pp. 132–5.

Kotler, P., Armstrong, G., Saunders, J. and Wong, V. (1999). *Principles of Marketing*. New York: Prentice Hall.

Kotler, P. and Clarke, R. (1987). *Marketing for Healthcare Organizations*. Englewood Cliffs, NJ: Prentice Hall.

Kotler, P. and Fox, K. (1995). *Strategic Marketing for Educational Institutions*. Englewood Cliffs, NJ: Prentice Hall.

Lehtinen, U. and Lehtinen, J.R. (1982). Service quality – A study of dimensions. Unpublished working paper, pp. 439–60.

Levitt, T. (1972). Production line approach to service. *Harvard Business Review*, 50, pp. 41–52.

———. (1981). Marketing intangible products and product intangibles. *Cornell Hotel and Restaurant Administration Quarterly*, 22(2), pp. 37–44.

Lovelock, C., Vandermerwe, S. and Lewis, B. (1999). *Services Marketing: A European Perspectiv*. London: Prentice Hall.

Mackelprang, A.W., Jayaram, J. and Xu, K. (2012). The influence of types of training on service system performance in mass service and service shop operations. *International Journal of Production and Economics*, 138(1), pp. 183–94.

McAlexander, J., Becker, B. and Kaldenberg, D. (1993). Positioning health care services: Yellow Pages advertising and dental practice performance. *Journal of Health Care Marketing*, 13(Winter), pp. 54–7.

McDougall, G.H. and Levesque, T.J. (1994). A revised view of service quality dimensions: An empirical investigation. *Journal of Professional Services Marketing*, 11(1), pp. 189–209.

Middleton, V.T.C. (1983). Product marketing – Goods and services compared. *Quarterly Review of Marketing* (Summer), pp. 1–10.

National Council for Tertiary Education Policy Report (2000). Published by the NCTE.

Nurske, R. (1971). The theory of development and the idea of balanced growth. In A. Mountjoy (ed.), *Developing the Underdeveloped Countries*. London: Macmillan, pp. 115–28.

O'Brien, T. (1995). Home banking: Will it take off this time? *Wall Street Journal*, 8 June, pp. B1 and B7.

Olorunniwo, F., Hsu, M.K. and Udo, G.J. (2006). Service quality, customer satisfaction, and behavioural intentions in the service factory. *Journal of Services Marketing*, 20(1), pp. 59–72.

Parasuraman, A., Zeithaml, V. and Berry, L. (1985). A conceptual model of service quality and its implications for future research. *Journal of Marketing*, 49(4), pp. 12–40.

Parasuraman, A., Zeithaml, V.A. and Berry, L.L. (1988). SERVQUAL: A multiple-item scale for measuring consumeer perceptions of service quality. *Journal of Retailing*, 64(1), pp. 12–40.

———. (1994). Reassessment of expectations as a comparison standard in measuring service quality: Implications for future research. *Journal of Marketing*, 58(1), pp. 201–30.

PricewaterhouseCoopers (2001). *Report on Microfinance in Ghana.*

Quinn, J.B., Baruch, J.J. and Paquette, P.C. (1987). Technology in services. *Scientific American*, 257(6), pp. 50–58.

Riddle, D. (1986). *Service-led Growth*. New York: Praeger.

Rust, R. and Oliver, R.L. (1994). Service quality: Insights and managerial implications from the frontier. In R. Rust and R.L. Oliver (eds), *Service Quality: New Directions in Theory and Practice*. Thousand Oaks. CA: Sage, pp. 1–19.

Rustow, W. (1962). *The Stages of Economic Growth*. Cambridge: Cambridge University Press.

Sasser, E. (1976). Match supply and demand in service industries. *Harvard Business Review*, 54, pp. 133–40.

Schmenner, R.W. (1986). How can service buisnesses survive and prosper? *Sloan Management Review*, 27(3), pp. 21–32.

Shostack, G. (1977). Breaking free from product marketing. *Journal of Marketing*, 41, pp. 73–80.

Smith, A.M. (1999). Some problems when adopting Churchill's paradigm for the development of service quality measures. *Journal of Business Research*, 46(2), pp. 109–20.

Snyder, C.A., Cox, J.F. and Jesse, R.R. (1982). Dependent demand approach to service organization planning and control. *Academy of Management Review*, 7(3), pp. 455–66.

Timimi, K. (2011). *Economy Watch*, 5 May. http://www.economywatch.com/world_economy/usa/different-sectors-of-economy.

University of Ghana, Legon, Basic Statistics (1995–2000).

West, D., Ford, J. and Ibrahim, E. (2006). *Strategic Marketing: Creating Competitive Advantage*. New York: Oxford University Press.

Wolak, R. (1996). An investigation into four characteristics of services. M.A. dissertation in Marketing, Kingston University Business School, UK.

Wolak, R., Kalafatis, S.P. and Harris, P. (1998). An investigation into four characteristics of services. *Journal of Empirical Generalisation*, 3, pp. 22–41.

World Bank (1986). *World Development Report*. Oxford: Oxford University Press.

World Bank Statistics (2003). www.worldbank.org

Zeithaml, V. and Bitner, M. (1996). *Services Marketing*. New York: McGraw-Hill.

Conclusion

23

Kwaku Appiah-Adu and Mahamudu Bawumia

For decades, economists, policy makers and practitioners of development have contended that national development is dependent on a myriad of factors. In this regard, several specific potential determinants of national development espoused in the pertinent literature were considered in this book classification into seven thematic areas. Findings of the analyses were highlighted and the lessons learnt were used as the bases for making recommendations on how developing countries would be able to improve efforts aimed at enhancing national development.

Our findings suggest that strong leadership coupled with a clear national vision that serves the best interests of the nation is an important ingredient to move any nation forward. Associated with the leadership factor is a governance system that allows the most support for visionary leaders and participation by the citizenry. Underlying good leadership and governance is the need to have a national development outline or document indicating the key issues that a country faces and the approaches for dealing with them that every citizen can support. The development of such documents should be conducted in a manner that ensures consensus building, ownership and commitment to implementation.

In addition, strategic thinking, described as the ability to learn from the environment while adopting a wider perspective, is established as a distinct attribute of national development. Reaching conclusions based on a holistic standpoint is critical because of the changing environment that most nations and organizations will encounter as we evolve into the twenty-first century. Managers of economies and businesses are advised to avoid a compartmentalized approach to situations and instead be strategic, and any view that is myopic in its approach is at odds with what is required in emerging developing economies given today's world, which is characterized by strong competition and rapid technological change.

A robust and comprehensive policy planning and implementation process is also found to be inextricably linked to national development programmes. Execution of the national development priorities is wholly reinforced by sound implementation systems and the ensuing policy planning practices make use of feedback from impact assessment at the macro- and micro-stages. Without the continued systematic implementation of a sound policy development and management system, developing countries will continue to grapple with development challenges that undermine the ultimate goal of attaining First World status.

A further lesson learnt is that without a well-functioning public sector, development is not possible, though describing and achieving an effective public sector that enables development is no easy task. Indeed, attempting to bypass the public sector and go 'straight to delivery' does not appear to be effective, even in the short term. Success comes from attending to the capacity of the public sector in all three dimensions: policy, implementation and efficiency. A public sector with capacity in these areas is able to understand and make decisions regarding obstacles to or opportunities for development, to deliver appropriate services and to do so in a cost-effective and sustainable way.

Regarding public financial management, there are a number of financial policies that have been shown in empirical studies to affect economic development. These policies should not be pursued in isolation, but must be part of a complete strategic approach to development. There is widespread human interest in economic development, particularly the factors that promote such development. Within the broad concept of financial management, this chapter has narrowed its focus on fiscal policies; that is, on the taxing and spending policies of governments. These policies are inextricably linked and must therefore be pursued holistically. A country's public sector is analogous to corporate overhead and must therefore be minimized, and limited to those sectors providing critical social services such as health, education and communal security. Because most developing nations are characterized by a large informal sector, financial policies that enhance the growth of the informal and SME sectors are needed to promote broad-based economic development, and such development can be achieved through a concert of financial policies orchestrated by the government.

Developing countries need to appreciate that building institutions that contribute to economic growth and national development is a critical issue that their governments continue to grapple with. For countries that have been transformed from developing to developed status, one of the pillars underpinning this has been their set of institutions. In such countries, institutions channel citizens' energies towards the development of material and human resources and improved labour productivity, the acquisition and diffusion of innovation via modern technologies, and the shifting of financial and human resources to industries that generate enhanced value. This should constitute the set of goals of all developing economies aspiring to transform their economies from a survival stage to a thriving and sustainable phase.

The analysis conducted indicates that all cultures have a potential to be positively associated with economic development and they have to discover their own methods of moving from one stage of economic development to the next. Indeed, collectivist cultures that epitomize most developing economies could strive for economic development without forgoing their cultural norms. Overall, culture can have a positive effect as a facilitator of economic development and, moreover, the negative influence of culture can be minimized by employing mechanisms that are consistent with cultural norms. Anti-cultural traditions are usually not firmly embraced or embedded, and so get misrepresented over time or are eventually discarded.

A conclusion from the study involving human capital is that it is a determinant of economic development. Efficiently harnessed human capital can facilitate competitive advantages and surplus value, which could be used to upgrade technology and diversify economic activity, facilitating national development. Improving equity and access of the population to healthcare and education will greatly enhance the quality of human capital of a nation. The development of human and intellectual capital to produce an adequate supply of knowledge and the relevant knowledge and skills required by the nation's industry is critical for national development.

Safe and sound land and property rights are fundamental to socio-economic development of nations. As land rights evolve from customary tenures through the commodification and commercialization of property rights, their value rises. They become an attractive investment venture, particularly in developing countries where investment opportunities are relatively few. Proprietary rights in land become honed and some customary tenures may mature into actual ownership. Secured property rights may serve as good investment opportunities in agriculture, forestry, residential, infrastructure, industrial and other urban land uses, offering employment and housing to many, providing social safety nets and positioning a country in an appropriate fashion to take off smoothly in its industrial development.

In relation to how to manage energy resources for national development, developing countries must seek to develop a 'dynamic technological capability' which assures the long-term development of the industry by giving nationals the complex set of skills and tools necessary to run the energy industry successfully over time and to innovate when necessary to overcome specific problems as they arise.

Developing nations cannot rely on the schemes of attracting foreign direct investment (FDI) alone, but must see it as within their ability and mandate to *choose* international companies as partners in mutually beneficial and balanced processes of development and profit making. They have an opportunity to choose partners who will move away from the traditional model and require that more of the energy business be done locally, particularly head office functions, such as business development, analysis, commercial strategy, customer relations, markets, political risk, negotiating, mergers and acquisitions, trading and knowledge management. This approach ensures access to world-class business methodologies and personnel development, technologies and processes, and local businesses, in turn, will develop and spawn local suppliers and contractors at a similar level, encouraging local businesses to develop their services to international specifications. For the international companies to enter into a process of mutual strategic adaptation, they must be assured that the government can and will implement consistent policies over time. A key strategy is for government to focus on the upgrading of local firms not only within the sector, but also as a process of innovation across the sector as a whole. Furthermore, there must be efforts to upgrade *across* sectors, actively using the innovations and systemic improvements in the energy sector to provide links and enhancements to other sectors, thus achieving the goal of economic diversification.

Regarding the contribution of mining to national development, the analysis which used Ghana as a case study revealed that benefits from the mining sector seem to be overly skewed to the central economy and thus an insufficient revenue stream from natural resource extraction is devoted to creating visible benefits such as healthcare delivery, infrastructure, and opportunities for the people in communities where mining takes place. This phenomenon often prods people to believe that the industry has not benefited the country. It is suggested that the value chain of mining is integrated into the host economy to fortify the country against the unstable behaviour of global commodity prices and also to generate more employment and income for the state. This way, the full picture of the contribution by the industry could be better appreciated.

With South Korea as a case study for science, technology and innovation (STI), it is established that if one is able to meet the existing needs of consumers with technologically driven products which are exchanged for money, this by itself could be an incentive for countries seeking dependence on STI for development to appreciate how providing innovative solutions to society can generate wealth. In order to achieve success in this pursuit, the first point is the creation of the necessary enabling environment for flourishing STI industries, the inclusion of the requisite ingredients, such as an STI personality constituting the technology visionary and an STI agent to lead the way in the development and implementation of appropriate policies. In addition, the government instituting STI processes must be the main provider of direct financial support to the pertinent institutions, must create the enabling environment needed for local industries to flourish and must become more pragmatic in creating more 'do tanks' than 'talk tanks' and 'think tanks'.

Using Ghana as a case study, ICT is found to be a critical determinant of national development. This can be measured by the increased investment in ICT infrastructure, improvement in the country's telecommunication infrastructure, the deployment of innovative technologies, increased funding of ICT-related projects, the formation of major technology-oriented organizations, the establishment of technology-oriented training institutions and universities, and the enactment of new government policies to regulate the field. These changes and investments have revolutionized the country's traditional institutions and have brought dramatic transformation to its society. Today, the impact of information technology can be keenly felt in several sectors of the country. Notwithstanding the progress made, the study suggests that more still needs to be done by the government of Ghana in terms of embarking on an aggressive human capacity building programme to address the country's human capacity shortfall in the area of ICT. On the whole, the study projects that the prospects of Africa as an ICT destination over the next half a century are optimistic.

Improved infrastructure is found to enhance a nation's competitiveness and productivity, lower the cost of doing business, facilitate trade and investment, create employment opportunities and deepen social integration though infrastructure. This has to be developed within the context of a comprehensive long-term national development plan, backed by strong leadership, local resource mobilization and a viable national construction industry. To obtain the optimum impact of infrastructure, efforts must be made to raise the bar in terms of infrastructure excellence to avoid the debilitating effects of climate change. Infrastructure also needs to be supported by a comprehensive manufacturing policy mix to reinforce the backward and forward links of investments in a developing economy. Manufacturing which is integral to economic development should be developed to obtain inexpensive construction materials for infrastructure, thereby bringing down the cost of projects. The growth pole approach to economic development and how infrastructure developed for an investment resource can be used to encourage spillovers into other sectors and unleash a virtuous spiral of growth should also be explored. Developing nations must wean themselves from financing projects with aid from development partners and focus on the long-term goal of building capacity for local resource mobilization.

On the role of the private sector in economic growth, the state and the private sector need to form partnerships in economic transformation. Indeed, African economies need more than growth if they are to transform by diversifying of their production, making their exports competitive, increasing the productivity of farms, firms and government establishments, and upgrading the technology used throughout the economy with the overarching objective of improving human well-being. To attain such an ambitious and profound transformative shift would require a high-level constructive engagement and strategic relationships between the state and the private sector. In addition, the state can promote economic transformation by providing leadership in setting a coherent vision and strategy in consultation with the private sector and other key stakeholders, and by managing the economy well and providing a business-friendly environment under conditions where there is peace and security in the country. Transparency and accountability institutions as well as civil society organizations, including labour unions, are equally important stakeholders to ensure that the unfolding close collaboration between state and business does not degenerate into corruption and crony capitalism. Similarly, cooperation between organized labour, government and business in a tripartite pursuit of industrial harmony and peace while upgrading the skills of the labour force to promote competitiveness will all contribute to the country's rapid economic transformation and the concomitant human well-being of its citizens.

Regarding the impact of capital markets on economic growth, the finding on this subject suggests that as Africa makes a bold statement to be a meaningful partner in the globalization of the financial services sector, it may actually benefit the most, as it has the furthest to go in terms of financial and regulatory reforms. Clearly, the economic renaissance in Africa will accelerate and give a big boost to capital flows into the continent. The financial services industry is expected to play a major catalytic role in driving this economic transformation as countries move towards a better financial education system and an understanding of the basic prerequisite for economic success.

Using Ghana as an example, an analysis of the effect of a developing nation's stock market on economic development has been assessed. Though Ghana's Stock Exchange has made very important strides in its 20 years of existence, much still needs to be done. The stock market as a source of funding for private sector companies remains paltry, with corporate funding being dominated by bank borrowing. The Ghana stock market has not had a major impact on economic development. This could be attributed to low levels of liquidity, which act as a deterrent to both issues and investors. Subsequently, within a given context, the study identifies some of the factors that need to be addressed to enable a stock market to play a meaningful role in national development.

On the issue of the central bank's role in reforming the financial sector, the conclusion from the experience of Ghana is that it is possible to successfully undertake wide-ranging financial sector reform within a short period of time. Furthermore, the ability of the Bank of Ghana and the government to undertake the wide-ranging reforms between 2001 and 2008 was primarily because the reform programme was domestically owned and an independent Bank of Ghana was mandated to drive it. With its newfound independence under a democratic political dispensation, the Bank of Ghana had a clear focus on the type of financial sector it desired and was willing to think outside the box to achieve this. The fact that a reform or policy had not been implemented before anywhere in the world was not a deterrent.

Marketing is established as a crucial contributor to the economic development of developing nations with *growth* potential. Indeed, marketing is considered as a significant *multiplier* of such development. Its development, above all others, facilitates economic integration and the optimal utilization of the assets and productive capacity that an economy possesses. It mobilizes latent economic energy and contributes to a principal need for the speedy development of entrepreneurs and managers.

Public relations and branding may be used to transform the developmental agenda of a country from its current position into becoming a successful economic model. Developing countries do not need to re-invent any wheel. Successful and advanced countries around the world have sought the need to use country branding woven around public relations in their national strategies and the development of their countries. In addition to the impressive impact they make externally, internally they succeed in touching the lives of their people, eradicating poverty and hunger, and reducing unemployment by creating jobs, all of which are efforts to enhance national development.

On using service delivery to enhance national development, government policies should be put in place at the macro-level in order to address the pertinent issues. For instance, acts relating to consumer protection, the delivery of professional services, the sale of goods, and services rendered by the public sector should not only be enacted but should also be marketed effectively so that consumers know that they exist and, in the process of service delivery, will not be taken for a ride by service providers.

In this book, it has been suggested that national development is a *sine qua non* for any country that wants to see enhancement in its socio-economic fabric, with an emphasis on developing economies. In this context it is contended that there are several factors that contribute to national development, either directly or indirectly through economic growth. These factors are classified into thematic areas to enable us to be able to focus our discussions, and the roles of various stakeholders, including the public and private sectors, are highlighted. It is our expectation that any nation that makes concerted efforts and ensures the appropriate levels of participation of the various stakeholders in addressing the key determinants of national development espoused in the foregoing chapters is well positioned to realize socio-economic advancement.

Index

For Product Safety Concerns and Information please contact our EU representative GPSR@taylorandfrancis.com Taylor & Francis Verlag GmbH, Kaufingerstraße 24, 80331 München, Germany

Printed and bound by CPI Group (UK) Ltd, Croydon, CR0 4YY

01/05/2025

01858349-0005